Madden MHC
1200 1ˢᵗ AVE
Harvey, il
708-531-7375

Treatment of the Borderline Personality

Patricia M. Chatham

Jason Aronson Inc.
Northvale, New Jersey
London

Library of Congress Cataloging-in-Publication Data

Chatham, Patricia M.
  Treatment of the borderline personality.

  Bibliography: p. 547
  Includes index.
  1. Borderline personality disorder.   I. Title.
[DNLM: 1. Personality Disorders—therapy. WM 190 C493t]
RC569.5.B67C48   1985   616.89   84-20425
ISBN 0-87668-754-0

Manufactured in the United States of America.

Jason Aronson Inc. offers books and cassettes. For information and catalog write to Jason Aronson Inc., 230 Livingston Street, Northvale, New Jersey 07647.

To My Three Teachers

Lillian Cartwright

Who with consummate skill and intuition taught me that things are never what they seem and who encouraged me to search beneath the surface.

Lynnette Beall

Who introduced me to object-relations theory and, with her special gift for clinical teaching, taught me how to respect theory, not only for what it says, but also for what it can do.

Donald Rinsley

Whose remarkably wide-ranging knowledge and interests are a constant and wondrous reminder that there is a world beyond psychopathology.

Contents

8. **Three Conceptual Models: Kernberg, Masterson- Rinsley, and Kohut**   **249**

Similarities and Differences among the Four Theorists
Otto Kernberg
James Masterson and Donald Rinsley
Heinz Kohut and Colleagues
Comparison and Treatment Implications of the
   Three Models

PART III. THERAPY

9. **The Initial Diagnostic Interview**   **307**

Purpose of the Interview
The Structural Interview
Using the Challenge
Using the Challenge to Evaluate Ego Functions
A Clinical Example
Review of the Structural Interview
Options for Treatment

10. **Individual Psychotherapy: Kernberg and Masterson**   **331**

Overview of Individual Psychotherapy with the
   Borderline Patient
Approaches to Individual Psychotherapy
Kernberg's Approach
Masterson's Approach
Comparison of the Two Approaches

11. **Individual Psychotherapy: The Mixed Model Approach**   **353**

Using Psychotherapy with the Borderline Patient
A Developmental Perspective
The Borderline Adult's Developmental Failure
Impact of the Developmental Perspective on
   Psychotherapy
Nonspecific Factors: A Good Working Relationship and
   the Holding Environment
Specific Factors: Sound Therapeutic Techniques

The Special Contribution of Transference and
Countertransference to Therapy
Measuring Therapeutic Success

Foreword

The flourishing interest in and the harvest of writings concerning object-relations theory reflect the continuing productivity of psychoanalytic theory and practice. The concepts of Melanie Klein, Ronald Fairbairn, Edith Jacobson, Margaret Mahler, and Otto Kernberg have provided a theory of internal representations and a developmental context that might well have warmed the heart of the late Heinz Hartmann, who envisioned a rapprochement of psychoanalysis and academic psychology. Significant to this expanding body of psychodynamic knowledge is the concept of the developmental-diagnostic spectrum or continuum, derived from classical psychoanalytic stage theory, flowering in Mahlerian phase theory, implicit in the writings of Kohut and the so-called psychologists of the self, and elaborated by Adler and myself. Of similar importance is the work of James Masterson on the internalized object relations of the borderline personality as they develop in and from the crucible of early mother-infant interaction.

Among contemporary contributors to this body of knowledge, two deserve particular consideration, namely, Margaret Mahler and Otto Kernberg. Margaret Mahler's contributions to our understanding of separation-individuation, to what she terms the psychological birth of the human infant, provide a detailed account of the chronology and phenomenology of how the individual attains selfhood. Mahler's work and that of her collaborators have advanced our understanding of human psychological development and broadened and deepened the insights of the early analysts, particularly Abraham and Freud himself, that led them to devise what can be termed pristine psychosexual stage theory. Otto Kernberg's writings offer much more than what is generally considered to be his major contribution, namely, an understanding of the personality or character disorders; of even greater significance are his related contributions to an understanding of identity formation which extend well beyond Erikson's formulations and which, in my view, constitute a testable theory of human learning. Based upon Edith Jacobson's seminal writings, Kernberg's formulations postulate a hierarchy of increasingly complex internalizations and representations that dovetail with Mahler's formulations regarding the genesis of the mother-infant symbiosis and the developing child's gradual emancipation from it. This body of developmental knowledge constitutes the most important and comprehensive current overview of human learning. Dr. Chatham's careful exposition of this work is one of this book's particular strengths.

The book is at once a succinct yet comprehensive treatise that brings together the essentials of the psychodynamic-developmental and object-relations literature and—most important for the practicing clinician—applies them clinically. Remarkable for the author's grasp of the literature, it provides a needed synthesis where none has hitherto been available. Dr. Chatham's application of theoretical concepts to the psychotherapeutic situation conveys her mastery of the subject and her sensitivity and effectiveness as a clinician. The readership of Dr. Chatham's book may be expected to be wide. It will include those who already have some grasp of psychoanalytic-psychodynamic concepts—the psychoanalytically informed reader and the mature clinician who desire an overview of current psychoanalytic research, and those who want to update their knowledge of how the findings of that research can be applied to treatment.

DONALD B. RINSLEY, M.D., F.R.S.H.
Associate Chief for Education, Psychiatry Service
Colmery-O'Neil V. A. Medical Center
Topeka, Kansas

Skillman Professor of Child Psychiatry
Menninger Foundation

Clinical Professor of Psychiatry
University of Kansas School of Medicine

Preface

Two interacting motives influenced me to write this book. The first motive was to provide the reader, as I had my students, with a roadmap to the confusing, complex, and diverse literature on the borderline patient. Views on the borderline personality disorder (BPD) had multiplied to the point where terms took on a diverse meaning, according to one's theoretical stance, and etiological issues were dominated by polemical skirmishes—all of which resulted in confusion about how to treat the borderline patient. My second motive was to provide a practical guide to psychotherapy, drawing upon the complex theoretical models in use at that time for understanding the borderline condition.

There was then, and still is, disagreement about whether the borderline is primarily a hereditoconstitutional disorder involving disregulation of the central nervous system (an affective spectrum disorder), or a defect in the sense of self and regulation of impulses due to problematic early nurturing. With few exceptions, clinicians have felt compelled to accept one approach over the other. However, an interesting shift in perspective appears to be underway. Representatives of divergent theoretical schools have been more willing to acknowledge that despite important divergence on etiological issues, there is room for a modest consensus that biogenic, psychogenic, and sociogenic factors each contribute in relevant ways to the borderline condition. None of these inputs should be minimized or disregarded.

Thus, both conceptually and practically, today's clinician is being urged to assess with each patient the possible multipathways to the borderline disorder and to design a treatment reflecting each patient's unique constellation of inputs. This multidisciplinary approach was something I had hoped to see when this book was written.

The potential of this multidisciplinary approach is being recognized by those engaged in empirical research. Looking ahead, we can expect to see research that increases our understanding of the relative contributions of biogenic, psychogenic, and sociogenic factors in the epidemiology of the borderline condition. We can anticipate continued clarification on such questions as the subtypes within the borderline spectrum, the relationship between schizotypal and borderline conditions, the prevalence of borderline symptoms among women versus men, the role of depression in borderline etiology, and, more generally, the interactional patterns of biogenic, psychogenic, and sociogenic factors. From the vantage point of clinicians, a preoccupation with one primary influence in the etiology of the condition has, as indicated above, some attendant dangers.

Although we are in a period of great flux—a time of transition, with trends in several directions—three themes can be highlighted. First, an increasing number of clinicians agree on a working definition of BPD. This has led to empirical research projects that attempt to improve diagnostic criteria (including differential diagnosis), ascertain epidemiology, develop assessment tools, and better understand psychobiology and the uses of pharmacological agents. Nothing definitive has emerged as yet, but the quality and amount of research is heartening.

A second theme revolves around the use of psychoactive medication. Although the biological factors that contribute to BPD are well known, the reader should be aware that development of appropriate psychopharmacological agents is still in its infancy. And even if patients' constitutionally based borderline disorders are successfully treated with medication (such as chronic dysphoric mood because of disregulation of the central nervous system), long-term cognitive/personality traits dealing with the self-perception of a "defect" may still develop. Thus, although the use of psychoactive medication is promising, the reader should be aware that psychotherapy probably will be needed to redress the damage and to teach alternative thinking/feeling styles.

The final theme centers on the appropriate psychotherapy for the BPD. At this book's first printing it was considered daring, if not theoretically naive, to advocate a mixed-model approach to treatment using, for example, aspects of the approaches of Kernberg, Masterson-Rinsley, and Kohut. Since then the biases against synthesis have waned, and many psychoanalytic writers now recommend a therapy involving empathic mirroring combined with limit-setting as well as ego-oriented interpretations—the key features of my mixed-model approach. Nonanalytic therapists are also addressing the therapeutic needs of borderline patients, and we are viewing the emergence of many practical therapies appropriate to the BPD in clinics and private practices.

This book has been organized from the practicing clinician's viewpoint. It begins with an overview of the three broad diagnostic approaches to the BPD and then focuses on the implementation of psychoanalytic theory in everyday clinical work.

Part I presents the main approaches to diagnosing psychoanalytic and nonanalytic borderline patients and discusses the problems of differential diagnosis and prognosis.

The contemporary psychoanalytic approaches of Kernberg, Masterson-Rinsley, and Kohut are reviewed in Part II as a key to understanding the structure, dynamics, development, and treatment of borderline patients.

Part III includes clinical treatment issues, the first diagnostic session, and examples of individual psychotherapies. I have provided comprehensive cases, brief clinical vignettes, and how-to examples of technique because applying sophisticated psychoanalytic concepts to individual patients can be a major stumbling block, not only for students but for more experienced clinicians as well. The book concludes with a review of some alternative treatment modalities that are appropriate for BPD.

Acknowledgments

It is a pleasure to record the contributions others have made to improve this book. First and foremost, I want to thank Donald Rinsley, who carefully critiqued the manuscript. Without his encouragement, I would never have thought I had a book.

Many friends offered support during the several years it took to write this book. In particular, I want to thank Nadine Payn, Ph.D., who has read every major manuscript I have written—from undergraduate term papers to dissertation, and finally this manuscript. Even more important have been her friendship, her support, and her faith in my ability to write a book such as this.

Other colleagues who provided invaluable critiques and comments of the various drafts are: David Antonuccio, Lynnette Beall, Bill Danton, Stephanie Dillon, Lawrence Hedges, and Rebecca Jankovich. They all gave far more of themselves than was asked. Each of their contributions added a unique dimension to the book.

Students who contributed their comments during lectures, clinical supervision, and readings of the manuscript include Richard Baldo, Robert Jenkins, Ingrid Moore, and Phyllis Richardson.

I am grateful to Nomi Morelli for her thoughtful criticism of the final draft and to her various associates, Emilio Amigo, Dorothy Gamble, Byron Perkins, Patricia Poos, and Sandra Sheldon, who also read part of the manuscript and offered important comments.

Although not involved with the book, James Masterson supervised me on several cases and from him I learned first hand the utility and power of the confrontive approach.

Jean Stoess typed the manuscript several times and provided valuable editorial help. In addition, Julie Anderson typed many early drafts of chapters and provided emergency proofreading, retyping, and other valuable services when deadlines were close.

To all of these people I give my heartfelt thanks for their encouragement and scholarly help.

Part I

DIAGNOSIS

CHAPTER 1

Introduction to the Borderline Concept

WHY DO WE NEED THE BORDERLINE CONCEPT?

Clinicians have realized for some time that not all patients can be diagnosed accurately by adhering to the established categories of psychosis, neurosis, and the traditional personality disorders. In clinical practice, experts predict that between 10 and 30 percent of patients exhibit a peculiar pathological condition in which normal and healthy elements intermix with psychotic, neurotic, and character disturbances, all coexisting with a considerable degree of consistency and stability. Thus, the borderline concept has become helpful in understanding such apparently intact patients who at the same time act out and behave in ways similar to those of more severely disturbed patients. This concept can be used to explain those patients who occasionally appear psychotic but cannot be diagnosed as such because their periods of psychosis remit quickly, they have better interpersonal relationships, they do not respond well to psychotropic medication, and their dysfunction is not chronically deteriorating.

The borderline concept also explains those patients who appear at first to be neurotic but then experience greater chaos and regression in intensive therapy. These patients cannot form reality-based working relationships with the clinician and instead fix on their childlike longings for the therapist and fears of abandonment or engulfment. When a patient possesses these mixed characteristics that do not fit the traditional diagnoses, the borderline concept enables the clinician to understand these patients well enough to avoid clinical faux pas that might otherwise launch destructive, chaotic reactions.

THE EARLY BORDERLINE LITERATURE

The years before the borderline diagnosis was developed were full of frustration and bewilderment for clinicians. Expecting supportive comments and/or interpretations to be helpful to their patients, clinicians instead found themselves often confronted by patients engaged in extraordinary acting out. Likewise, such patients, expecting their clinicians to help them understand their condition, found instead helpers who were often as baffled, surprised, and dismayed as they were.

Nothing is more frightening than feeling that one is at the mercy of inexplicable, chaotic, and mysterious forces. This is as true for the individual confronting perplexing impulses as for a clinician facing conflicting data. Frank (1976), noting this confusion, commented that a powerful source of mastery is the ability to name one's experiences. Naming unfamiliar, dangerous objects and people in order to master them or control their power has a long and honorable history and is a common theme in folklore and religion. For example, the queen was able to free her child from Rumpelstiltskin by guessing her tormentor's name (Rinsley and Bergmann 1983), and in the Bible, the very first task God gave Adam was to name the animals (Frank 1976, p. 85).

It is not surprising, then, that in the early 1930s, psychoanalysts who were frustrated by their inability to diagnose and help those patients who did not fit the usual categories named and began to classify their patients' confounding disorder. These patients seemed too ill for classical psychoanalysis, were neither neurotic nor clearly psychotic, and their condition could not be explained. Psychoanalysts thus named this puzzling disorder *borderline*. Stern (1938) gave the term formal status and devised the first psychodynamic diagnostic criteria for the disorder, which still describe the current thinking. For Stern, the borderline criteria included (1) a hypersensitivity to therapeutic interventions, (2) idealization and devaluation of the therapist and significant others, (3) overwhelming anxiety reactions to stress, and (4) defenses that blame external circumstances for intrapsychic problems. For many years after Stern's criteria were developed, the term *borderline* was used colloquially to designate patients who were difficult to diagnose and treat with psychoanalysis.

The psychoanalysts who followed Stern were concerned with both the problem of analyzability and the degree to which their patients resembled classical schizophrenics. Some of these writers viewed borderline patients as a kissing-cousin variant of the schizophrenias, though others did not. Consequently, the first usage of the term borderline was a "wastebasket" diagnostic entity.

From the 1930s through the 1950s, there was a proliferation of work on the borderline patient. Psychoanalytic clinicians were studying personality disorders and finding what later appeared to be subtypes of the borderline. Deutsch (1942) described a personality that she called the *as-if* personality. As-if patients seem to live normally but lack genuineness, warmth, and expression of feelings: they seem to have no sense of inner self. The as-if personality is passive and readily picks up outside signals regarding how to act or feel (e.g., engages in mimicry). Such patients appear "chameleonlike," changing their loyalties quickly and being susceptible to suggestion. Guntrip (1960, 1961, 1962) and Winnicott (1960) studied a type of schizoid "false-self" type of patient who presented an adaptive facade to the world but kept his or her true self hidden from others.

During the same time, borderline phenomena were observed from the perspective of behavioral rather than intrapsychic characteristics. Under the strong influence of Bleuler, researchers decided that Stern's borderline patient and Deutsch's as-if patient were actually subtypes of schizophrenia (Peters 1983). In 1941, Zilboorg introduced the term *ambulatory schizophrenia* for patients who did not meet the strict criteria for schizophrenia, did not need hospitalization, and could function socially. However, these patients had mild thought disorders and unstable interpersonal relationships and found it difficult to sustain stable lives.

In 1949, Hoch and Polatin identified a similar group that they described as pseudoneurotic forms of schizophrenia, also seeing this group as a subtype of schizophrenia and a trait diagnosis that was stable over time (Peters 1983). The core symptoms of pseudoneurotic schizophrenia were free-floating anxiety, multiple neurotic symptoms, and perverse sexual practices.

Throughout the 1950s, the polarity between the descriptive researchers and the psychoanalytic writers remained marked. According to Peters (1983), it was not until Knight (1953a, 1953b) that a partial synthesis between the two positions emerged. He noted that Knight combined the early therapists' descriptive data and psychostructural formulations into an ego "state" that was called *borderline* and implied that the patient could enter into and exit from this pathological condition. This entering and exiting from the condition contrasted with Kernberg's later concept of a consistent and stable personality organization. Knight felt that these borderline states lay between psychosis and neurosis, as his patients showed apparently neurotic symptoms, but also greatly impaired ego functions, and at times could not separate reality and fantasy. Knight's borderline patients might exhibit thought blocking, odd word usage, inappropriate affect, or suspiciousness (Bernstein 1982). He believed that the borderline state was a time-limited condition closely related to schizophrenia and that it reflected definite but transient weaknesses in ego function (Peters 1983).

During the 1960s a model for understanding primitive patients who were neither neurotic nor psychotic evolved from the seminal but contrasting contributions of Kernberg's work on the borderline patient and the narcissistic patient as a subtype and Kohut's work on the narcissistic personality disorder. Grinker, Werble, and Drye (1968) explored the behavioral manifestations of the borderline syndrome, using empirical research techniques and a large patient population. His research produced four subtypes.

In much the same way that Knight's paper synthesized earlier analytic and descriptive writings, Gunderson and Singer (1975) distilled the work of Kernberg, Grinker, and others into a constellation of six clinical features considered central to the borderline disorder (Peters 1983). Their synthesis not only integrates earlier work but is also valuable because it became a point of departure for more recent research.

While the psychoanalytic and descriptive writers were at work, a group of biologically oriented research psychiatrists were contributing yet another perspective. The family and genetic studies of Kety, Rosenthal, Wender, and Schulsinger (1968) showed that in the biological relatives of patients diagnosed as schizophrenic, there were an increased number of relatives who met Zilboorg's diagnosis for ambulatory schizophrenia and Hoch's and Polatin's diagnosis of pseudoneurotic schizophrenia. Concurrent with their work was that of D. Klein and his colleagues, who described a number of syndromes (hysteroid dysphoria, phobic reaction), which they believed fell within the realm of affective disorder. Klein believed that many of these syndromes overlapped with some of the borderline subtypes proposed by Grinker (Peters 1983). Is it, then, possible Peters (1983) asked that one group of patients that therapists now call borderline are genetically related to the schizophrenia disorders and that another group is a variant of affective illness? We shall later discuss the implications of this for diagnosis, treatment, and prognosis.

Attempting to incorporate the work of both Kety and Klein into their own research diagnostic criteria and later into the *Diagnostic and Statistical Manual of Mental Disorders-III* (*DSM-III*), Spitzer, Endicott, and Gibbon (1979) considered that the borderline patient belonged to either the schizotypal personality disorder or the unstable personality disorder.

As Stone (1981) reiterated, borderline is a concept that began as a name for unanalyzable patients who appeared to be somewhere between neurosis and psychosis. Their psychoticlike symptoms were compared with those of schizophrenics and found to be related, or so the term's originators presumed. Next, the concept was "teased apart from schizophrenia, and acquired the dignity of a separate nosologic entity" (p. 5). Finally, a group of researchers studying family histories and biological markers suggested that borderline might be related to several of the major disorders rather than being a distinctly separate entity after all.

Thus, by the 1980s we see various trends in the usage of the term borderline. The three primary trends alternatively characterize borderline as

(1) a distinctive diagnosis that lies between psychosis and neurosis, with its own stable and specific features; (2) a mild form of schizophrenia; or (3) a condition related to and perhaps a mild form of the major affective disorders. Historically, a fourth school of thought has viewed borderline as a disorder lying between schizophrenia and the major affective disorders (e.g., schizoaffective disorder). A more recent, fifth possibility is that the condition is a mild form of an organic brain syndrome or epilepsy (e.g., episodic dyscontrol).

Those theorists who view the borderline disorder as a distinctive diagnosis lying between psychosis and neurosis include all the major psychoanalytically oriented thinkers such as Stern (1938), Knight (1953a, 1953b), Frosch (1964), Grinker, Werble, and Drye (1968), Mahler (1971), Gunderson and Singer (1975), Kernberg (1975a), Masterson (1976), Chessick (1977), Adler (1981), Rinsley (1981b, 1982a), and Meissner (1984). Those who view the condition as a mild form of schizophrenia include Kety, Rosenthal, Wender, and Schulsinger (1968) and Spitzer, Endicott, and Gibbon (1979). Yerevanian and Akiskal (1979), Akiskal (1981), and D. Klein (1975, 1977) regard the borderline as a mild form of the major affective disorders. The fourth group, which views the borderline disorder as schizoaffective, includes Kasanin (1933) and Hoch and Polatin (1949). Finally, theorists who believe that the condition involves episodic dyscontrol include Andrulonis, Glueck, Stroebel, and Vogel (1982), and Wender, Rosenthal, and Kety (1968).

For a thorough historical perspective on the term, the interested reader can refer to the work of Capponi (1979), Mack (1975), or Stone (1980). I also recommend the excellent summaries of Perry and Klerman (1978) and Stone (1979a, 1981), who have reviewed the various diagnostic criteria across a number of diagnostic systems.

CONTEMPORARY APPROACHES TO THE BORDERLINE CONDITION

The current theoretical thinking can be understood through three contemporary approaches to diagnosing the borderline condition:

1. *Psychoanalytic*—borderline as a psychostructural level or particular psychodynamic.
2. *Biological-constitutional*—borderline as a dilute form of one of the major disorders.
3. *Eclectic-descriptive*—borderline as a specific personality disorder.

Figure 1-1 shows the contemporary diagnostic systems in the borderline realm.

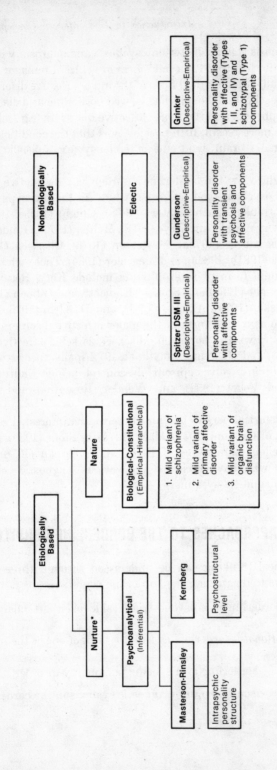

Figure 1-1 Contemporary Diagnostic Systems in the Borderline Realm.

*Theorists accept that nature can play a role

The Psychoanalytic Approach

Psychoanalytic theorists view the borderline condition as a stable, pathologic personality organization—neither neurotic nor psychotic but somewhere in between (Goldstein 1981a). They believe that the borderline personality organization lacks an integrated concept of self and that the ego structure exhibits a specific pattern of superficial ego strengths and underlying ego weaknesses. The nonadaptive use of aggression is an important borderline characteristic. These theorists regard the borderline personality as stable because it does not vacillate between neuroses and psychosis except during acute transient psychotic episodes, and the condition is pathologic because of the unintegrated self-concept, ego weaknesses, and difficulties with aggression.

Those contemporary psychoanalytic thinkers best known for their work on the borderline disorder are Adler and Buie, Kernberg, Masterson, Meissner, and Rinsley. All of them use different terms (e.g., psychodynamic, psychodynamic-developmental, psychostructural) for their diagnostic approaches, each of which has a specific meaning within their conceptual model. These theorists have established criteria for use of the term, according to a psychoanalytic frame of reference. They emphasize the psychodynamic and developmental conflicts and arrests of the borderline patient, placing less importance on symptoms, except as "red flags" that alert the clinician to the possibility of a borderline disorder.

The Single Continuum Concept

The continuum concept underlies the psychoanalytic approach to the borderline disorder. It contends that all mental disorders lie on a single continuum, with psychosis and health at opposite ends. Menninger, Mayman, and Pruyser (1963) illustrated this approach by conceptualizing mental illness as a unitary process based on a concept of homeostasis, and they ranked mental disorders according to their degree of deviation from a baseline. Kernberg further developed the continuum concept, placing the borderline disorder on the continuum between neurosis and psychosis (see Figure 1-2).

Psychosis	Borderline	Neurosis

Figure 1-2 The Borderline Condition Lies on a Continuum between Neurosis and Psychosis in Psychoanalytic Terms (Adaptational).

Implicit in this continuum is the belief that all states of psychopathology pertain to the same underlying drive determinants embedded in the id and that varying degrees of psychopathology depend on the ego's ability or inability to regulate id pressures (Meissner 1984, p. 19). Stated in another way, mental illness is a spectrum of disorders along a continuum in which symptom severity is related to a hierarchy of defenses and ego functions. Accordingly, as one moves toward psychosis, one finds a greater degree of symptom severity, along with less effective, more primitive defenses.

The continuum approach stresses the similarities as well as the differences among all disorders. This model implies that any individual can "slide" to the right or left along the continuum, depending on life circumstances and crises. The underlying processes are the same along the continuum, but as one moves to the right toward neurosis, greater ego controls are available. The continuum concept implies that all that separates psychotics from neurotics is the greater quantity of ego control in the neurotic or, put differently, the loss of some ego controls in the psychotic.

Most thinkers with an ego-analytic orientation share this belief in a continuum, even if, like Kernberg, they modify this concept.

To Kernberg, borderline refers to a specific, stable, and pathological personality organization. He does not believe that it is a state that fluctuates between neurosis and psychosis or that it is a mild form of schizophrenia. In addition, he does not believe that any group of symptoms alone is typical of the borderline.

Rather, Kernberg contends that it is the structure itself—neurotic, borderline, or psychotic—that determines the diagnosis. Thus, Kernberg (1977b) conceives of these levels as a "sequence of discontinuous, hierarchical organizations" rather than a continuum (p. 90). Each personality structure can be distinguished by its unique combination of features (e.g., object relations, defenses, degree of reality maintenance, and other ego functions), only some of which overlap from structure to structure. Once consolidated at the neurotic, borderline, or psychotic levels of organization, these stable structures act as blueprints for determining overall psychological functioning as well as specific symptoms.

Kernberg also believes that the borderline individual has certain defenses (e.g., splitting) not seen in the neurotic. Thus, in a somewhat modified sense, Kernberg does recognize both a quantitative and qualitative difference between neurosis and psychosis.

The interested reader is referred to Dickes (1974) and Meissner (1978a) for a critique of the single-continuum concept.

The Importance of Ego Development

The single-continuum concept stresses the importance of human development from birth onwards, because mental disorders are related to developmental trauma. This approach concentrates on the influence of early mother–child interaction on the achievement or nonachievement of progressive ego functions. The borderline patient is seen as having a specific group of ego defects caused during very early childhood.

Masterson (1972, 1976, 1980, 1981, 1983b) and Rinsley (1977, 1980c, 1981b, 1982a) feel that borderline conditions originate mainly from pathological mother–child interactions that occur roughly between the 16th and the 26th months of life, with Rinsley (1982a) placing it even earlier. These interactions lead to a pathological intrapsychic structure with consequent symptoms and behaviors. Kernberg (1975a, 1976a, 1980a, 1980b) accepts the notion of defective ego functions related to the above time frame, although he believes that the inherent constitutional aggression that interferes with the child's adaptation may be more important than the mother–child interaction is. Although Kohut wrote little on the borderline topic and developed his own psychoanalytic theory, he did state that the borderline condition is a near-psychotic condition, with a fragmented sense of self caused by pathological parenting. All three approaches are concerned with the *etiology*, or cause, of the disorder, in that they identify a developmental basis for the condition.

It should be added that these theorists do not discount the influence of either nature or fate on the borderline disorder. For example, an infant in a healthy family who develops a catastrophic illness at an early age may be precluded from going through the normal developmental stages. Simply because of the exigencies of fate, this child would be forced to remain dependent on the parents far beyond the appropriate developmental age and could develop a borderline intrapsychic structure despite good parenting.

The Psychoanalytic Meaning of Borderline

According to the continuum concept, borderline refers to either a psychostructural level of functioning (Kernberg) or a specific psychodynamic internalized from the mother–child interaction (Masterson, Meissner, and Rinsley), the symptoms of which are intermediate between psychosis and neurosis.

The borderline condition has specific intrapsychic structural features, with inclusion and exclusion criteria, which help distinguish it from neurosis and psychosis. On the continuum, the borderline disorder on the left is closer to psychosis, and that on the right is closer to neurosis. In Kernberg's system of structural diagnosis, one may see a variety of personality disorders (e.g., infantile, schizoid, narcissistic, antisocial) against a backdrop of a borderline personality organization. It is logical that borderline be conceptualized as a supraordinate diagnosis because both psychosis and neurosis are also conceptualized in this manner. For example, there are a variety of psychoses (e.g., schizophrenia, manic-depressive illness) as well as neuroses (e.g., compulsions, neurotic depression). This means that a sample of patients with a borderline diagnosis will be heterogeneous, exhibiting a variety of symptoms and personality subtypes. One cannot expect these patients to appear very similar on the surface, though they should be homogeneous in terms of intrapsychic structural diagnosis.

How the Diagnosis Is Made

How, then, is a borderline patient diagnosed if the structural-psychodynamic-developmental theorists do not concentrate primarily on symptoms? Instead, the diagnosis is based on a combination of clinical symptoms, inferred intrapsychic structures, and transference reactions in therapy. The material for the diagnosis comes from initial interviews and analysis of the therapist-patient relationship. Observation of the patient over an extended period is sometimes required because the diagnostic material emerges throughout the first few months of therapy. Because a considerable amount of inference is required, it is often difficult for the clinician who is not familiar with this approach to identify the proper criteria.

Although, as mentioned earlier, the symptoms appear to be heterogeneous, the clinician who has learned how to make the diagnosis psychodynamically will find that all borderline patients show a similar intrapsychic structure. This is why most psychoanalytic theorists do not feel compelled to isolate refined subtypes for the borderline personality. It is only recently that some psychodynamic-developmental theorists have acknowledged the importance of subtyping. Meissner (1984), for example, has become interested in subtyping within the borderline spectrum based on psychodynamic and descriptive criteria.

But in general, little effort has been expended in discovering and delineating numerous subvarieties, in contrast with the biological theorists' approach. Like physicists searching for "grand unification," hoping to find the single entity that governs all interactions in the cosmos, psychodynamic theorists are interested in discovering an underlying intrapsychic structure that defines and explains the various symptoms: they are synthesizers. Unfortunately for the practicing clinician, however, the psychodynamic theorists do not always agree on the precise nature of the intrapsychic structure or the developmental-psychodynamic conflict. This can confuse the clinician. Nevertheless, the sometimes confusing minor inconsistencies, varying terminology, and contrasting organization and presentation of the material may suggest greater disagreement than actually exists among psychoanalytic theorists (Goldstein 1981a).

An example of one of the major psychoanalytic approaches to the diagnosis of the borderline is shown in abbreviated form in Table 1-1.

**Table 1-1   Diagnostic Criteria of Kernberg for
Borderline Personality Organization**

Identity diffusion: contradictory aspects of self and others are poorly integrated and kept apart.

Primitive defense operations:

Splitting: the splitting of self and external objects into "all good" and "all bad"

Primitive idealization: the tendency to see external objects as totally good, creating unrealistic images

Projective identification: the tendency to continue to experience the impulse which, at the same time, is projected onto the other person, who then is both feared and experienced as someone who must be controlled

Denial: the inability to bring together emotionally contradictory areas of consciousness and to feel relevant emotions over these contradictions

Omnipotence and devaluation: the presence of ego states containing representations of a highly inflated self in relation to depreciated representations of others

Capacity to test reality is preserved.

Capacity to differentiate self from nonself

Capacity to differentiate intrapsychic from external origins of perceptions and stimuli

Capacity to evaluate one's affect, behavior, and thought content in terms of ordinary social norms

Source: Blumenthal, R., Carr, A. C., and Goldstein, E. G. (1982). DSM-III and structural diagnosis of borderline patients. *The Psychiatric Hospital, 13*(4), 143. Copyright 1982 by National Association of Private Psychiatric Hospitals. Reprinted by permission.

The Biological-Constitutional Approach

Since the 1930s, various researchers have been studying the borderline patient in terms of biological etiology. Stone (1979a, 1980, 1981) has summarized the work of this group and found that the borderline condition may be related to one or more of the major disorders in terms of clinical symptoms, family history, treatment response, and biological markers. Tests such as REM latency, monoamine oxidase activity, dexamethasone suppression, and susceptibility to motion sickness may be able to separate out borderline patients with major affective or schizophrenic disorders from those who do not have these disorders. From this, Stone and other researchers are challenging the psychoanalytic viewpoint of the single continuum and are finding an etiological heterogeneity in this clinically homogeneous entity. This in turn has led them to search for new subtypes based on distal causes.

After years of study, Stone found that some borderline cases do seem related to schizophrenia, as earlier theorists believed. A second group seems to be related to manic-depressive illness, now incorporated in the term *primary affective disorders* (Winokur, cited in Stone 1980, p. 250). A third group seems to be related to the organic brain syndromes. Finally, there is a fourth group—unrelated to any of the above—that appears to be purely experiential or psychogenic in origin, as many psychoanalytic theorists claim.

The Multiple-Continua Concept

Unlike the psychoanalysts, the biological constitutional researchers believe that homogeneous symptoms often have multiple etiologies and outcomes. Stone (1981) noted that mental illness really comprises a variety of disorders, all with differing etiologies and courses. Disorders such as schizophrenia or manic-depressive illness, which share the psychosis in common, differ in their cause, symptoms, course, and outcome. He feels that they should not be put onto a single continuum or be classified according to a hierarchy of defenses (in terms of increasing dyscontrol of ego functions) or the severity of their symptoms. Meissner (1978a), although a psychoanalyst, agrees with this position. Attempting to find a unifying structure, he has stated, may obscure the diagnostic heterogeneity, the clinical implication being that the patient may require a different or additional treatment approach if the full etiological basis for the borderline structure were taken into account.

Generally, the biological constitutional researchers recognize three major continua: one for schizophrenia, another for the primary affective disorders, and a third for the organic brain syndromes. The spectra consist of "unequivocal or 'core' cases, but then shade off into milder, less easily identifiable forms, to which the term 'borderline' may be applied" (Stone 1980, p. 492). Figure 1–3 illustrates this three-continua concept. Stone estimates that

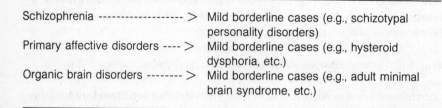

Schizophrenia ------------------ > Mild borderline cases (e.g., schizotypal personality disorders)

Primary affective disorders ---- > Mild borderline cases (e.g., hysteroid dysphoria, etc.)

Organic brain disorders -------- > Mild borderline cases (e.g., adult minimal brain syndrome, etc.)

Figure 1-3 The Borderline Condition Lies on Three Continua, Each with Its Own Etiology (Constitutional).

10 to 15 percent of all diagnosed borderline patients fit on a fourth continuum that involves psychogenic (constitutional) factors. But many of his psychoanalytic colleagues would not agree with this low percentage.

In this approach, certain inborn physiological factors are seen as predisposing an individual to become borderline. Researchers assume that a genetic factor may affect the physiological and biological mechanisms that regulate behavior, emotion, and thinking. For example, in manic-depressive illness, the "emotional thermostat may be set too low or too high" (Stone 1980, p. 3), thereby contributing to mood swings affecting the patient's adaptation, interpersonal relations, feelings toward self, and even psychostructural level. Stone (1981) noted that many diagnoses presuppose an interaction between biological vulnerability and developmental trauma or poor parenting.

Stone (1981, pp. 6-7) identified three groups of children who may develop a borderline disorder. The first group has a high degree of genetic vulnerability to serious emotional illness. Even with excellent parenting and environmental support, such children still may develop severe disorders such as schizophrenia or a more modest borderline condition. A second group of children has a less severe degree of vulnerability. Depending on their parenting and psychosocial environment, they can either become neurotic or develop rigid and contradictory views of themselves and others, ego weaknesses, and other borderline characteristics. In the third group, abysmal parenting and psychosocial environmental may swamp the developing identity of even normally endowed children, thus causing the development of a borderline structure.

Stone stresses that treatment of patients whose history shows a high degree of genetic vulnerability might be more effective in conjunction with an antidepressant, lithium, or an antipsychotic. Although they should not be given etiological primacy, the clinician still must work with these patients to resolve crucial intrapsychic conflicts and developmental arrests caused by the vulnerability as well as the parenting.

Stone also believes that the majority of patients diagnosed as borderline are etiologically tied to the affective disorders, not the schizophrenias. He reached this conclusion because so many borderline patients have relatives with affective disorders rather than schizophrenia.

The Biological-Constitutional Meaning of Borderline

In the biological-constitutional model, the term borderline refers to clinical syndromes with their own etiology, course, and outcome. Table 1-2 lists some of the common clinical syndromes, although the criteria for each syndrome are not included. Diagnostic subtyping is very important in this

Table 1-2   Subtyping According to Biological-Constitutional Theorists

Affective; MDP-Related

Unipolar Depressive-like
Hysteroid Dysphoria
Subaffective Dysthymia
Endogenomorphic
Cyclothymic
Phobic-Anxious
Abnormal Temperament
Severe Premenstrual Tension
Masked Depression
Character Spectrum Disorder
Anorexia Nervosa

Schizophrenia-Related

Schizoid Personality Disorder
Schizotypal Personality Disorder

Other

Organic Brain Dysfunction
  Adult Minimal Brain Dysfunction
  Episodic Dyscontrol
Antisocial Personality
Reactive: Affective, Non-MDP Related, 2° to severe psychogenic stress

Source: Adapted from Stone, M.H. (1981). Borderline syndromes: A consideration of subtypes and an overview. Directions for research. *Psychiatric Clinics of North America,* 4(1):13. Copyright 1981 by W. B. Saunders Co. Reprinted by permission.

model because it allows the clinician to find homogeneous subtypes that have common etiologies, treatments, and outcomes. In contrast with the synthesizing approach of the psychoanalytic theorists, the biological-constitutional researchers are nosologizers devising a hierarchy of related subdisorders for each of the major disorders, whose basis is etiological.

How the Diagnosis Is Made

The diagnosis in this approach is based on a combination of clinical symptoms (observed and reported), familial-genetic history, treatment response, and the presence of biological markers (where possible). These clinicians search for hereditary links between patients and loading for mental illness among their biological relatives (usually first, second, and third generations).

The Eclectic-Descriptive Approach

Grinker, Gunderson, and Spitzer are prominent theorists in the eclectic-descriptive group of researchers who view the borderline as a specific personality disorder. Because they differ among themselves, each has constructed his own criteria for diagnosis. Nonetheless, these theorists collectively consider the first step in the development of a diagnostic entity to be the delineation of specific abnormal behavior patterns or character traits that distinguish the borderline from other personality disorders. These researchers aim to reach a consensus regarding the disorder's clinical description, drawing on its usage in everyday clinical practice, clinical observation, review of the literature, and empirical research design.

The criteria of Grinker and his colleagues (1968) and Grinker and Werble (1977) are based on conventional clinical-phenomenological description. Grinker's findings were based on a cluster analysis study of 51 hospitalized patients. There has been controversy over both the sample size and the sample population. Gunderson's criteria utilize psychological test data and both phenomenological and psychoanalytical viewpoints. The work of Gunderson and Singer (1975) was based on an extensive review of the literature and identified six features that most theorists described as characteristic of borderline patients. The criteria of Spitzer and his associates rest primarily on a phenomenological foundation, oriented toward psychogenic rather than psychoanalytic concepts, a position reflected in the *DSM-III* (Stone 1979a). In the *DSM-III*, Identity Disturbance (Criterion 4) is phenomenologically described but is also a psychodynamic concept borrowed from Kernberg. In all three systems, the diagnosis is based on frequent abnormal behavior and traits, not etiology.

The reader who is aware that both Grinker and Gunderson are psychoanalytically oriented may wonder why they were not included with the psychoanalytic theorists. Despite their analytic orientation, their diagnostic approaches are fundamentally descriptive, based on empirical data with minimal reference to psychodynamics, thus allowing their approach to be used by clinicians who do not accept the psychoanalytic perspective. The eclectic approach also does not take a formal stand on the continuum concept.

The Eclectic-Descriptive Meaning of Borderline

Although Grinker's, Gunderson's, and Spitzer's theories do overlap, there are also differences in how each defines borderline. Spitzer is particularly known for his contribution to the *DSM-III*, the official diagnostic manual of the American Psychiatric Association. The *DSM-III* contains two diagnoses for borderline personalities. The lower-level diagnosis is the schizotypal personality disorder, which appears to be a mild form of schizophrenia and hence is etiologically related to it. The second is the borderline personality disorder, an unstable personality with many problems in the affective realm; this diagnosis is based on clinical consensus, not etiology.

Grinker's system includes four types of borderline—ranging from the psychotic border to the neurotic border—three having affective components and one appearing schizotypal. Grinker's diagnostic system is mentioned here mostly for historical interest, as it has been supplanted by the systems of Spitzer and Gunderson, although Meissner (1984) appears to have utilized Grinker's system in developing his own subtypes.

In Gunderson's diagnostic system, borderline seems to refer to an impulsive, dependent, and angry individual who can have poor reality testing in the interpersonal realm (which in Kernberg's system rules out borderline structure). Gunderson's system also includes many problems in the affective realm. Grinker's diagnostic systems are shown in Table 1–3, and Gunderson's appear in Table 1–4.

One criticism of the descriptive diagnostic approach is that diagnoses founded on descriptive symptoms (such as the *DSM-III*), though based on objective evidence, do not relate the clinical picture to the underlying dynamic psychopathologic theme (Masterson 1982). Masterson pointed out that this is much like "classifying pneumonias by symptoms, ignoring the underlying pathology. Diagnosis should be based on the most enduring and unchanging clinical evidence, i.e., the intrapsychic structure and its link to the underlying psychodynamic theme" (p. 6). Nevertheless, both the descriptive and psychodynamic approaches to diagnosis are compatible. Many of the intrapsychic structures and psychostructural criteria used by Kernberg and Masterson for diagnosis often result in the symptoms that Spitzer described in the *DSM-III*.

How the Diagnosis Is Made

The diagnosis is based on clinical interviews and the appearance or report of the central symptoms. Gunderson also uses psychological test results: the borderline patient does well on a structured test such as the WAIS and poorly on an unstructured one such as the Rorschach.

Similarities and Differences among the Diagnostic Systems

Table 1–5 shows the major differences separating the three diagnostic systems. Despite the differences, there are also similarities that confuse the distinctions. Three issues, not mentioned in the table, muddy the waters even more because they have important conceptual and treatment implications. They are the continuum notion, the degree to which depression is

Table 1-3   Diagnostic Criteria of Grinker et al. for Borderline Syndrome

Common Characteristics

Anger is main or only affect
Defect in affectional (interpersonal) relations
Absence of consistent self-identity
Depression characterizes life

Characteristics of the Four Subtypes

Type I: The Psychotic Border

Behavior inappropriate, nonadaptive
Self-identity and reality sense deficient
Negative behavior and anger expressed
Depression

Type II: The Core Borderline Syndrome

Vacillating involvement with others
Anger acted out
Depression
Self-identity not consistent

Type III: The Adaptive, Affectless, Defended, "As-if" Persons

Behavior adaptive, appropriate
Complementary relationships
Little affect; spontaneity lacking
Defenses of withdrawal and intellectualization

Type IV: The Border with the Neuroses

Anaclitic depression
Anxiety
Resemblance to neurotic, narcissistic character

Source: Adapted from Perry, J. C., and Klerman, G. L. (1978). The borderline patient: A comparative analysis of four sets of diagnostic criteria. *Archives of General Psychiatry, 35*:145. Copyright 1978 by American Medical Association. Reprinted by permission.

caused by biological factors or psychodynamic conflicts, and how strictly the patient must maintain reality testing in order to be classified as borderline rather than psychotic.

The Continuum Concept

As stated earlier, the psychoanalytic theorists hold that psychotic-borderline-neurotic conditions lie on a single continuum with an underlying pathology that defines each according to degrees of ego controls. The biological-

Table 1-4   Diagnostic Criteria of Gunderson for Borderline Personality Disorder

Lowered Achievement (diminished work capacity)

Impulsivity (especially drug abuse and promiscuity)

Manipulative Suicidal Threats (namely, wrist cutting)

Mild or Brief Psychotic Episodes (often of a paranoid quality and sometimes more sustained in duration, if provoked by abuse of psychotomimetic drugs; but severe depersonalization, or widespread delusions, in absence of drugs, contraindicates the diagnosis)

Good Socialization (mostly a superficial adaptiveness, beneath which is a disturbed identity camouflaged by rapid and shifting identifications with others)

Disturbances in Close Relationships
Tendency to be depressive in the presence of the important other, and to be enraged or suicidal should the latter threaten to leave; tendency to have psychotic reactions when alone   .
In general, a predominance of rageful affect rather than emotional warmth

---

Source: Stone, M. H. (1980). *The Borderline Syndromes: Constitution, Adaption and Personality* (p. 268). Copyright 1980 by McGraw-Hill Book Co. Reprinted by permission.
Note: Psychological tests will tend to show good performance on the structured portions of the test and poor performance (with the emergence of primitive ideation) on the unstructured portions. Except for possible temporary lapses, reality testing is preserved.

---

constitutional researchers reject this notion, asserting instead that there are three basic distinct continua and that the borderline is a mild form of several major disorders (e.g., primary affective, schizophrenia, organic brain syndromes). The eclectic-descriptive clinicians differ according to their theoretical background. Grinker and Gunderson accept the single-continuum concept. Spitzer, on the other hand, appears to follow more closely the three-continua notion of the biological group, implying that there is a mild form of schizophrenia called *schizotypal personality* and a mild form of the affective disorders called *borderline personality disorder*.

Function of Depression

A form of depressed affect has been part of the diagnosis in most of the systems covered in this chapter, except Kernberg's. Its presence has led the biological researchers to conclude that the borderline diagnosis (structural or personality) reflects a mild form of affective disorder. I consider that mild to moderate clinical depression is so pervasive in both the psychiatric and general population that it is a dangerous generalization to state that all depressions are mild forms of primary affective disorders.

Table 1-5   Similarities and Differences in
Contemporary Borderline Diagnostic Systems

Dimension	Psychoanalytic	Biological	Eclectic
Major theorists	Adler, Kernberg, Masterson, Meissner, Rinsley, etc.	Akiskal, Andrulonis, Hoch, Kasanin, D. Klein, Kety, Polatin, Stone, Wender, etc.	Grinker, Gunderson, Spitzer's DSM-III
What is meant by Borderline	Psychostructural level or psycho-dynamic conflict	Mild variant of one of the major disorders	A specific per-sonality disorder
Data on which diagnosis is based	Symptoms Inferred intrapsychic structures Transference	Clinical symptoms, familial-genetic history, treatment response, and biological marker	Combination of symptoms and behavioral observations, psychodynamics, and psychological test data
Etiology of disorder	Nurture* Nature Fate	Nature†	Unspecified
Sample composition	Homogeneous: intrapsychic structure Heterogeneous: descriptive symptoms	Heterogeneous: total sample Homogeneous: each subtype	Heterogeneous
Importance of diagnostic subtyping	Not important, except Meissner (synthesizers)	Important (nosologizers)	Somewhat important (synthesizers)
Basis on which subtyping is made	---------	Etiology	Spitzer: clinical and etiology Grinker and Gunderson: clinical
Recommended treatment	Modified psychoanalysis Confrontive psychotherapy	Chemotherapy	Unspecified

*Constitutional components can play a role, as can fate; most theorists except Kernberg consider nurture a major cause.
†Stone (1981) believes that 10 to 15% of all borderline adults are purely psychogenic in origin.

The clinical implications of this debate pertain to the use of antidepressant medication in treating the borderline patient. For many of the psychodynamic theorists such as Masterson, giving an antidepressant simply masks the problems that need to be worked out in the therapy (e.g., the developmental arrests and conflicts that induce the depression). Because Kernberg does not accept depression as one of his diagnostic criteria, he may or may not agree with Masterson. For many of the biological researchers, the use of an antidepressant is essential. To resolve this debate over the use of antidepressants, we must determine the degree to which the borderline personality disorder and the affective disorders are biologically related.

Reality Maintenance

Reality testing is the ability to differentiate oneself from others, to differentiate inside stimuli from outside ones, and to evaluate oneself according to ordinary social norms. There is much controversy within the psychoanalytic approach about whether poor reality testing is an exclusionary criterion for the borderline psychostructural diagnosis. (*Exclusionary criteria* are those whose presence rules out a particular diagnosis.) This controversy becomes important when the clinician determines the level of developmental arrest, from which the treatment approach evolves.

Kernberg and Masterson believe that transient psychosis occurs in the borderline, but they also contend that pervasively poor reality testing or even the ongoing loss of reality testing in one area is a criterion for exclusion from the borderline diagnosis. This disagreement illustrates an important difference among the diagnostic systems (e.g., those who permit some limited soft signs of thought disorder versus those who exclude such patients from the borderline diagnosis).

Soft signs of thought disorder include the milder manifestations of thought disorder such as superstitiousness, magical thinking, or unrealistic fixed ideas. Frequently such patients can acknowledge the unrealistic basis of these beliefs, although they still continue to believe that they are true. Grinker, Gunderson, Rinsley, and Spitzer (schizotypal personality) believe that limited defective reality testing (or soft signs of thought disorder) can be present and still permit a diagnosis of borderline. Table 1–6 illustrates the relative positions of these theorists.

PRACTICAL CONCLUSIONS

The diversity and lack of consensus regarding the diagnostic criteria led Perry and Klerman (1978) to conclude that (1) the borderline disorder is an illusion, (2) a valid disorder does exist but is so well explained by broad

Table 1-6   The Role of Reality Maintenance in the Various Diagnostic Systems

Must Be Maintained	Limited Defective Reality Testing Can Be Present
Kernberg	**Grinker**
Poor reality testing is an exclusion criterion. Transient psychosis permitted.	Poor reality testing is permitted in Type 1 Borderline (border with psychosis).
Masterson	**Gunderson**
Poor reality testing is an exclusion criterion. Transient psychosis permitted.	Poor reality testing in evaluating self or others permitted (pervasive delusions is an exclusion criterion). Transient psychosis permitted.
	Rinsley
	Soft signs of thought disorder permitted. Transient psychosis permitted.
	Spitzer (DSM-III)
	Soft signs of thought disorder permitted in Schizotypal Personality Disorder.

criteria that additional criteria are unnecessary, or (3) there are discernible subtypes within the borderline category, and hence researchers may be dealing with different samples among the larger borderline group. The experts will continue to disagree over the precise etiologies and diagnostic criteria for a long time to come. Unfortunately, the resulting Tower of Babel leaves many clinicians totally bewildered. Without a conceptual system to rely on, diagnosing the borderline and planning a treatment approach are difficult, and communicating with colleagues is even more trying. But any broad, stable diagnostic system, though imperfect, is better than no system at all.

This book does offer a diagnostic and treatment system, assuming that a valid disorder exists that is sufficiently explained by broad criteria—and that most borderline patients can be defined by these criteria. This book also recognizes subtypes, which may require additional diagnostic criteria with a slightly different emphasis in treatment and differing prognoses. Alternative approaches to diagnosis and treatment will also be discussed in this book because it is useful to draw on other systems when patients simply do not fit the clinician's conceptual and diagnostic model. Such an awareness opens a different window onto reality and enables the clinician to see things from a different angle. Familiarity with several systems and the ability to choose among them are, of course, great assets as long as consistency is maintained with each patient.

This leads to a second conclusion. Although researchers cannot agree on the meaning of borderline, the clinician should try to use precise terminology when describing a patient's signs and symptoms. It is essential for the clinician to know whose diagnostic system is being adopted in order to justify his or her diagnosis when challenged by someone using a different system. The clinician who uses precise terminology and relies on a specific system is better prepared to defend diagnostic differences.

Finally, in choosing a conceptual framework, the clinician is making an important commitment. I believe that it is necessary for the psychotherapist to maintain a diagnostic conceptual framework at all times. This framework underlies and emphasizes the goals of treatment and frequently the tactics for achieving them. It should be a guide in the difficult and rocky work with the borderline patient as well as a benchmark against which to measure any technical deviations or countertransference problems.

THIS BOOK'S PERSPECTIVES

Although this book focuses primarily on the psychoanalytic approach to diagnosis and treatment, it also incorporates the important contributions of the biological and eclectic groups. The seminal work of Rinsley (1981b, 1982a, 1984a, 1984b) provides a way to synthesize the psychoanalytic and biological diagnostic approaches, as well as to heal the breaches (Kohut versus Kernberg) within the psychodynamic schools. This book's perspectives thus can be categorized as follows: (1) the importance of the developmental-diagnostic continuum, (2) the borderline diagnosis as a spectrum of psychiatric disorders, (3) nature and nurture as codeterminants of the borderline disorder, and (4) the contribution of the developmental perspective to treatment.

Perspective 1: The Developmental-Diagnostic Continuum

Most theorists, from the psychoanalytic to the biological, accept that there is a spectrum of psychopathology. This perspective introduces the notion that the spectrum of psychopathology and the continuum of normal development are related (Adler 1981; Rinsley 1981a, 1982a, 1984a). Among other theorists, Rinsley (1981b) relates the severity of the psychopathology—the particular patient's position on the spectrum—to the patient's self- and object differentiation. He views borderline patients, regardless of specific symptoms, as sharing developmental psychodynamics centering on partial self-object differentiation and fixation at a certain developmental level. A particularly important contribution to this perspective is the research of Mahler, Pine, and Bergman (1975), who postulated normal childhood developmental phases. They identified the normal processes of symbiosis and the child's gradual emancipation from it through separation-individuation, providing the framework for understanding the developmental etiology, specific ego weaknesses, and the self-system pathology of the borderline adult, as well as the particular point of developmental fixation.

This book will rely on Kernberg's comprehensive structural diagnostic approach in order to establish the broad psychostructural criteria shared by most borderline patients, so that they can be placed on the developmental-diagnostic continuum that then identifies their degree of self- and object differentiation. I shall also use the diagnostic systems of other writers to complement Kernberg's approach and to explain patients not adequately covered by it.

Perspective 2: Borderline as a Spectrum of Disorders

The borderline condition might be described as a *congeries*, a Latin-based word meaning "a collection of things heaped together." In this perspective, borderline includes a congeries of other disorders that fit within the borderline phase of the continuum from psychosis to neurosis. Rinsley (1981b), in reviewing the literature and his own work, noted that the syndromes that properly can be included in the borderline part of the spectrum are primary affective disorders (if reality testing is sufficiently maintained), paranoid disorders (with reality testing), borderline personality, other personality disorders (if they also meet the criteria for borderline), and the lower-level narcissistic personality. These disorders share many developmental themes (disordered identity and interpersonal relationships) whose pathogenesis is often found in the early mother–child relationship. Rinsley (1984a, 1984b), summarizing other contributions from self psychology (e.g., Kohut and others), concluded that most of the various personality disorders lie on the borderline part of the continuum. He feels that these personality disorders represent examples of two pathologies of the self-system: the borderline and the narcissistic, with the narcissistic usually functioning at a higher level. We shall return to this concept in subsequent chapters because it points a way toward understanding the relationship between the borderline and narcissistic personality disorder and also integrates the several conflicting psychodynamic schools.

As a diagnostic and treatment approach, the borderline disorder is significant because of the breadth of patients included in this part of the spectrum or continuum. (Giovacchini [1979b] wrote that he doubts he has ever seen a neurotic in analysis and treatment.) Except for the better-functioning narcissistic patients, these borderline spectrum disorders are often referred to as the *primitive personality disorders*. At times these patients are also referred to as *severely disturbed* patients, but this rubric can also include psychotic individuals.

Perspective 3: The Borderline's Nature-Nurture Basis

Psychoanalytic developmental theory leans heavily on the vicissitudes of the mother–child relationship in order to explain the genesis of the various borderline disorders. Yet even these theorists increasingly acknowledge, for example, the role of constitutional factors or unexpected psychosocial factors.

How all these factors—genetic, biochemical, psychodynamic, and environmentally determined psychologic disturbances—influence one another is still being debated. Kernberg (1980c) recommends a flexible analysis of clinical data to give depth to what otherwise might become just a mechanistic grouping of symptoms (descriptive approach) or an overemphasis on individual psychodynamics (psychoanalytic approach). Each patient must be considered in terms of clinical syndromes and underlying psychophysiological predisposition and how they alter or interface with personality structure, which then shapes the matrix of affective and behavioral responses (Kernberg 1980c, p. 1080).

Rinsley (1981b) also agrees that the genesis of the borderline disorders is

> multifactorial, with the role of innate, constitutional and heredocongenital determinants assuming increasing importance toward the psychotic portion of the developmental-diagnostic spectrum ... and the role of dyadic-interpersonal, familial, and wider social determinants assuming increasing importance in the reverse (p. 128).

However, regardless of what the constitutional determinants and their relative proportion in any given case may be, their final pathway remains the mother–child relationship and the ensuing personality structure created (Rinsley 1981b).

Yet the biological-constitutional determinants certainly should not be ignored. Whenever possible, the clinician should diagnose the predisposing constitutional determinants in order to assist in determining the patients' level of vulnerability to stress or potential for psychotic decompensation, the type of therapy they can tolerate, their capacity for change, and their need for chemotherapy.

The sophisticated clinician must constantly be alert to the interaction among all these various factors as they vary from case to case. Because many of the spectrum disorders have similar developmental conflicts and traits, the clinician needs to keep the overall picture in mind to avoid getting lost in its complexity. Stone (1981) noted the need for both perspectives:

> There is merit to both schools of thought and clearly one must be cautious about adopting an extreme position—either as a "lumper," oblivious to possible subtypes, or as a "splitter," inattentive to the common psychodynamic, defensive and prognostic features uniting many borderline conditions (p. 19).

One must be aware of possible constitutional inputs in order to design a good treatment program and to predict the prognosis, as well as common psychodynamics in order to maintain a focus in the psychotherapy.

The Developmental Approach's Contribution to Psychotherapy

Once the infant and childhood developmental malformations are identified, the developmental approach points to the developmental tasks that must be resumed in psychotherapy. We shall review several differing psychoanalytic approaches to addressing these deficits and conflicts, including Kernberg's interpretative technique, Masterson's and Rinsley's confrontive approach, Kohut's and his colleagues' empathic-interpretative style, and Rinsley's recent eclectic approach. Nonetheless, I believe that the psychodynamic-developmental perspective yields the most relevant insight into the actual issues that arise in psychotherapy, and so that will be this book's major focus.

It may be difficult for the reader to understand the psychodynamic-developmental perspectives. First, the therapist must be able to infer from clinical data the mind's structural processes. This approach requires practice, skill, knowledge, and the ability to recognize the patient's intrapsychic processes.

Unlike the descriptive approach, the psychodynamic-developmental approach is based on psychoanalytic theory, with its many metapsychological difficulties and oblique, metaphorical language. Unfortunately, there is often no consensus on any aspect of Freudian thought. Many theorists use the same psychoanalytic terms to refer to slightly different clinical phenomena, and these terms may not always have the same relation to other terms. This confusion has occurred in part because patients report their experiences in such a dazzling array of ways, using their own terminology. Unfortunately, psychoanalysts have rarely come to grips with this situation by clarifying their terms and synchronizing their hypotheses (Schafer 1968, p. 3). I shall attempt to clarify and synthesize my hypotheses wherever possible.

A final criticism of psychoanalytic theory is its dependence on inferential processes and its lack of systematic empirical documentation. But despite their difficulties, the developmental perspectives offer a richness absent in the other approaches. I shall try to conceptualize the relationship among symptoms while at the same time offering important prognostic and therapeutic information.

TERMINOLOGY

The psychotic, borderline, and neurotic personality organizations will be referred to as *personality structures* or *structural levels* throughout this book. These personality structures should not be confused with the predominant personality character types, which will be referred to as *personality subtypes*. The following 13 personality subtypes are commonly used by psychoanalytic clinicians:

Antisocial	Narcissistic
Depressive	Obsessive (obsessive-
Explosive	compulsive)
Hypomanic	Paranoid
Hysterical	Passive-aggressive
Inadequate	Phobic
Infantile	Schizoid

The reader may note that this list of personality subtypes differs somewhat from that in the *DSM-III*. Both the *DSM-III* and Kernberg recognize the following personality subtypes: antisocial, narcissistic, paranoid, passive-aggressive, and schizoid. The *DSM-III* also lists atypical (mixed), avoidant, borderline personality disorder, compulsive, dependent, histrionic, and schizotypal.

Several other terms that appear throughout this book should be defined. *Object* is a rather cold term that is used to represent other people, although historically it has also referred to animals or significant inanimate objects. The mother is the primal object. *Object relations* refers to interpersonal relationships. The whole person, including his or her body image and psychic organization, is known as the *self*. *Representation* refers to an enduring organization of information that an individual gradually constructs from images; it can be regarded as a patterning that organizes experiences and leads to certain interpersonal actions.

The state of affairs in which adult patients believe that they and another person are one, that someone else shares their exact thoughts, that they and the other are identical, or that they and the other are physically connected is known as a *fused self-object representation* or merger. Some theorists believe that borderline individuals have underlying fantasies in which they believe this to be true, particularly in regard to themselves and their therapists. Others contend that a fused self-object representation occurs only in psychosis.

All infants undergo *separation-individuation,* a complex developmental process in which they must separate their self-representations from those of others and then achieve intrapsychic autonomy. The borderline adult, who has failed these tasks, must also undergo separation-individuation while in psychotherapy.

The use of projection as a defense mechanism, acting out, the inability to tolerate frustration and delay, and other aspects of ego weakness are some examples of the *ego capacities and functions* that will be mentioned throughout this book.

Finally, *disorders of the self* is another term that is critical to an understanding of the borderline patient. Some theorists such as Kohut consider it as a supraordinate diagnosis that includes all other psychopathological diagnoses and such defects as identity diffusion, self-fragmentation, and intense feelings of vulnerability.

CHAPTER 2

The Clinical Picture

The three clinical cases used as examples throughout this book demonstrate the similarities as well as the differences among patients with varying symptoms and severity of borderline arrest. In addition, they illustrate psychotherapies of different durations, frequency of sessions, and, to some degree, differences of technique. Two of the therapies had been completed (Mary Markham's was still in progress) when this book was written.

All three patients were proud of the progress they had made and agreed to share their therapy process in order to help others. Key identifying data concerning each patient have been disguised to ensure anonymity. However, because personal interactions and other events are presented accurately, each patient was given the option of refusing to participate in this book, and each was given the opportunity to restrict certain details of history or process, but none requested that any data be omitted.

CASE I: MARY MARKHAM

Mary Markham is a pleasant, quiet, obviously intelligent woman (IQ of about 125). She dresses in a drab, dowdy manner and is about 80 pounds overweight. Mary is in her early 30s and has never been married. She has not dated since her early 20s and has never had a sexual relationship. Although she holds an advanced degree, she has a semiskilled job and lived with her parents until a few months before starting therapy with me.

Mary was referred to me after a suicide attempt in which she almost died. She had previously made seven or eight other attempts, each time by overdosing on prescribed medication. (She has been taking anti-depressant medication since her early 20s.) Mary refused to return to her therapist of the past three years, and there appear to be many unresolved problems in that therapeutic relationship.

About a month after leaving her former therapist, Mary Markham saw an intake worker at the facility at which I am employed. During her interview, Mary reported feeling depressed but not suicidal. The intake worker suggested individual psychotherapy, which Mary accepted. Mary and I met briefly after the intake session, and we set up an appointment for the following week. Two days later, however, she again attempted suicide and almost died in the intensive care unit of her local hospital.

After recovering, Mary was transferred to the inpatient psychiatric unit of my facility, at her mother's request. The staff of the psychiatric unit soon informed me that they were worried about her because she remained so isolated. They felt that they did not understand her or her problems. She was willing to discuss her inability to get close to others when the staff requested. She showed no obvious signs of schizophrenia, and the staff considered that she met the criteria for a borderline personality with depressive episodes.

Mary had been on the ward for five days when we had our first session. She entered my office slowly, looking pale and slightly wobbly, and announced, "Well, here I am again." I asked how she was feeling. "Good enough to talk, I guess," she replied lethargically.

We sat down, and she stated, "Well, I guess you want me to talk about my suicide attempt." Her voice, almost a monotone, conveyed little emotion, and I was uncertain whether this was the blunting of affect due to schizophrenia or recovery from drug overdose. Nonetheless, I found myself growing interested in her. I responded, "Of course, that is an important topic for us to explore, but I am more interested in what you would like to talk about." I wanted to set the stage to help her differentiate between her needs and those of others. She answered that she first wanted to talk about her former therapy and therapist.

Mary stated that her first year with Mrs. Jensen, her former therapist, went well. She spent most of the time discussing her anger at her mother's "bossiness—trying to take me over." It was clear that Mrs. Jensen had tried unsuccessfully to get Mary to examine her own role in this process, as Mary sometimes seemed to invite her mother's bossiness.

Eventually, Mrs. Jensen seemed to tire of the empathic role and Mary's passivity. She began to insist that Mary become more active both in the therapy and in her life—"to date, to make friends, to diet, to confront mother." Mary felt that Mrs. Jensen was acting just like her mother, and she admitted feeling angry at her, although she never expressed her anger.

"What made it difficult for you to tell her your feelings?" I asked. "I don't know. I just couldn't," Mary replied.

Mary then began hoarding her medication. When she had saved enough to overdose, she made a mild suicide attempt. Mrs. Jensen was unaware of Mary's hoarding until notified by a physician at the emergency room of the local hospital. With the clinic psychiatrist's agreement, Mrs. Jensen herself started to dole out Mary's medication weekly. Again, Mary decided that Mrs. Jensen was acting just like her mother. She now believed that Mrs. Jensen had too much power over her and, in retaliation, acted compliant while she plotted a more serious suicide attempt.

When I gently questioned her about the meaning of *plot*, she ignored my inquiry and replied, "Mrs. Jensen said my suicide attempts were manipulative—but they *weren't*. And that just made me madder." How did she interpret the meaning of her suicide attempts? Mary was not certain but admitted thinking that she must die because she was so evil. Mary added that she then went to a private physician to get psychoactive medication. Afterward, she dropped a hint about this to Mrs. Jensen, who missed the disguised message. This was an example of Mary's well-planned "test" to see whether her therapist perceived that she was again planning suicide. When Mrs. Jensen failed the test, Mary concluded that the woman not only was stupid but also really did not care about her.

Mary made several other suicide attempts, each requiring hospitalization. After each attempt, she felt that she could make a fresh start in therapy. But Mrs. Jensen, acting increasingly distant and annoyed, imposed a variety of limits on Mary and reduced the frequency of their sessions.

The real crisis occurred when Mrs. Jensen suddenly announced that she was placing Mary in group therapy and canceling her individual sessions. Mary apparently did not protest at the time, but she abruptly terminated her treatment by not showing up for her first group session. Shortly thereafter, she began mutilating her inner thighs with razor blades. She planned another suicide attempt for several months in advance (the attempt that she made immediately after being accepted at our facility). But after four or five weeks without therapy, Mary felt compelled to return to Mrs. Jensen. She was not sure why, although she felt that her need for Mrs. Jensen indicated her own stupidity.

According to Mary, Mrs. Jensen asked little about the missed visits and stressed the importance of attending the group sessions. She did not offer individual sessions again. Mary expressed little emotion as she told me about her last few interactions with Mrs. Jensen. When tears came to her eyes, she brushed them away angrily, stating that the entire event made her feel evil and bad. I asked what else she had felt during these last few sessions, commenting that I had noticed her tears. She said she had felt totally consumed by her involvement in the situation and then added, "I felt angry." I told Mary that it seemed to me that she also felt hurt and rejected. She responded, "Yes, but then it hardly mattered at all. Mrs. Jensen wasn't important to me any longer." I hypothesized to myself that Mary may have made the suicide attempt in order to provoke rejection from Mrs. Jensen so that she could feel that she had some control over her. Mary clearly felt intense anger at what she viewed as Mrs. Jensen's "betrayal." Her attachment to her was obvious. But Mary did not recognize that she cared so deeply for Mrs. Jensen and was so dependent on her. Mary sensed only that Mrs. Jensen had not met her expectation—which had to mean that Mary was bad.

Toward the end of the session I shared my perception that their relationship had clearly been important to Mary and that she felt deeply hurt and angered by the transfer to group therapy. Rather than work with the deeper meaning of this event, I asked how in the future this process might be played out between the two of us. Mary supposed it might happen just as it had with Mrs. Jensen and another therapist before her. Then, without artifice or guile, she dangled the carrot: If I stayed in contact with what she was feeling, then maybe the entire process leading to suicide could be prevented.

I predicted that the time would probably come when she felt that I was "out of sync" with her and she would feel suicidal. How would she handle this? Mary agreed to let me know when she thought I was ignoring her feelings, and she promised to telephone me before attempting suicide. But she was not sure she could confide in me or stop the cycle if we got too far into the process—if I missed too many cues from her and she felt I did not care. "Let's work on this problem together," I suggested. Our first meeting concluded with an agreement to meet weekly while she was in the hospital.

Observations from Our First Session

The mistakes of other therapists are always more apparent than one's own. It would be easy to assume that Mary's suicidal acting out could have been prevented by Mrs. Jensen, but I was never sure, as I heard only Mary's side of the story.

Unlike most clients, Mary refused to give me permission to contact Mrs. Jensen, even to request her medical records. Apparently Mary feared that Mrs. Jensen would convince me that she was "bad" and that I would then turn on her. One now could question whether it was wise to even start therapy when Mary was so much in control of the treatment, but I did so, anyway.

Mary's parting remark continued to trouble me. If I failed her, she implied that we would switch roles. She would become the sadistic controller, and I would become the masochistic receiver in our relationship. Perhaps this would occur no matter what I did. Mary implied that—just like she and her mother—we would be stuck together like "tar babies."

My efforts to understand her subtle hints (in other words, to pass her tests) deterred her suicidal acting out for two years. Yet it still did emerge despite all my efforts. Mary became so fearful of her closeness to me and so enraged by it that she again attempted suicide, just as she did with Mrs. Jensen. More than any other patient, Mary taught me there was simply no way a clinician could prevent certain kinds of acting-out behavior directed against the therapist if the patient were compelled to manifest that behavior.

Emerging Themes from Early Sessions

Over the next few months, Mary faithfully kept her weekly appointments but appeared to have little conscious attachment to me. She was aloof and distant, often lapsing into prolonged silences. I explored her provocative statement that her suicidal process could be prevented if I stayed in contact with her feelings. In effect, Mary reported that once she became involved in a relationship, she could not bear to leave it, no matter how bad it was; it was too upsetting. On the other hand, if the other person left her, she would feel so rejected and bad about herself that she would become suicidal. Thus, Mary placed herself in an emotional "double bind"—a relationship she hated but could not leave—which at the same time imprisoned the other person if he or she cared for Mary. Because of her tendency to become embroiled in stifling relationships, Mary maintained few. She would allow herself to become involved only with her mother, her therapist, and a physician.

One of Mary's most striking aspects was her unawareness of the many contradictions between her words and her deeds. For example, she appeared stoic and calm; yet reported feeling depressed, overwhelmed, or furious. When asked if her anger at Mrs. Jensen or her parents' moving had anything to do with her recent suicide attempt, Mary replied "no" or "I don't know what I felt." She denied that she had tried to manipulate Mrs. Jensen, even though Mrs. Jensen had accused her of that. Yet in the next breath, she warned me that she would try again if I did not detect her subtle hints. She denied ever feeling lonely or needing people; yet she hunted out therapists and physicians and lived with her parents.

Much of Mary's behavior was often inexplicable at first glance. Even more frustrating was the fact that Mary could honestly give me few, if any, leads to the meaning of her behavior. It was up to me to learn to understand Mary's unconscious dynamics or personal myth. Mary was so out of touch with her own motivation that the only clue she could give me was her acting-out behavior, which always happened at home, not in the session. Mary remained very compliant and agreeable during most sessions, but her therapy always kept me on my toes, as I could never be sure what would set her off. It could be a word; it could be a look; or it could be something I did not say or something about her mood I missed.

Suicide Attempts, Self-Mutilation, Depersonalization, and Pseudoserenity

Mary sometimes alluded to her suicide attempts but always waited for me to bring up the topic. She knew that her latest venture had been almost catastrophic, and she seemed somewhat proud. In the middle of our second session, I commented, "I notice that you have never mentioned your suicide attempt." "That's right," she replied. "It seems as though it happened a million years ago." She paused briefly and started to tell me about it. She was living alone for the first time in years, feeling depressed and angry, when she decided to attempt suicide again. She denied that her problems with Mrs. Jensen or her parents' recent move out of state had played a role in her decision. Instead, she said, she began to feel strangely out of touch with the world around her. Daily routines such as paying her bills or feeding her beloved cats ceased to matter. This was highly unusual behavior for her, as she always met her obligations, even under the worst of emotional conditions. Sometimes during this period she could not feel her own body; it seemed as if it had no substance or did not even exist. She described feeling compelled to mutilate her inner thighs and arms with razor blades. (Mary always mutilated places that could be hidden by clothing.) She remarked that the pain felt good and brought her back to reality. But coming back to reality meant feeling empty and desperate.

Then Mary picked a suicide date that coincided with a planned visit from her parents. She rarely made an unplanned attempt but almost always chose a specific date, although she could not explain why. After setting the date, Mary felt strangely content, even sublimely happy, and began to look forward to it. During her period of waiting, she reported continuing to perform adequately at work.

Paradoxically, it was toward the end of her two-month waiting period that Mary decided to seek out therapy, which was when she came to my clinic. She decided, however, that she could not tell either the intake worker or me her entire story:

Therapist: Why weren't you candid with the intake worker or me about your suicide plans?

Mary: I liked you right away, and then I felt some hope. But a part of me just said, "Don't tell them." And after I left, it was as if the clinic and you didn't exist any more [object permanency failure]. Anyway, a part of me kept telling me I had to die. I just felt there would be too much of a loss of face if I didn't keep my word to myself. I had to go through with it.

Mary said that she went home from the clinic experiencing no particular feelings. She telephoned her parents, suggesting that they come a few hours later than they had originally planned. She then took all the pills she had hoarded for the occasion. Interestingly, this attempt occurred only one day later than the date she had set two months previously. Fortunately, Mary's parents had sensed something odd in her manner over the telephone. Worried because of her earlier suicide attempts, they came as soon as they could. They broke down her door, found her unconscious, and rushed her to the hospital.

Later, Mary denied any interpersonal meaning in her phone call to her parents: "I just didn't want them interfering with my suicide plans. I thought if they showed up after I died, they would look after my cats and make the funeral arrangements so the burden wouldn't fall on my landlord."

Did Mary intend to be found? She told several professionals on the psychiatry ward that she did not. Her physician reported that upon awakening in intensive care, Mary screamed, "I want to be dead! Why didn't they let me die?" This kind of behavior usually represents a serious intent to kill oneself. However, I had an odd sense about the attempt and asked spontaneously, "Did you think you would really die?" She looked thoughtful and replied, "You know, I am not sure I did. Maybe I would just go to a higher plane of existence, like moving to another room in a house. I wouldn't really be dead—I just wouldn't have all the misery any more." She reported feeling "serene" just before the attempt, but for many months she was unable to elaborate on this. Eventually she remembered entering a transcendent state of consciousness in which she felt "above" all human strife and conflicts.

Only much later in the therapy was Mary able to admit to setting suicide dates at the same time that her family planned to be home or visit, believing that if they loved her, they would stop her or else be punished by her death.

Parts of Herself and Identity Problems

Very early in therapy Mary and I identified the "Megalomaniac," which she experienced as an independent part of herself. Perfectionistic and vengeful, the Megalomaniac had a drive and motivation of its own and was not governed by the adult, rational aspect of her personality. The Megalomaniac controlled her, put her down, and told her to die when she made mistakes. It ordered her to mutilate herself, to retaliate against or trick the therapist, or to attempt suicide. The Megalomaniac planned her last suicide attempt, Mary observed.

Much later in the treatment, Mary discovered a second part of herself, which she named the "Baby." She considered it to be her "true" self, which no one had ever accepted. It was like an infant—totally dependent, demanding, needy—locked away in her mind when it was very young because its needs had never been met. The Baby operated by the infantile rules of an 8-month-old infant (crying and raging).

These parts of Mary's psyche were not multiple personalities, as she was aware of them as parts of herself. Sometimes she felt like a weak ruler trying to control her warring feudal lords. Just as the feudal lords sometimes gain temporary power over their ruler, so did Mary's parts sometimes overwhelm her, assume temporary power, and force her to do their bidding. Mary eventually joined her unruly parts in their irrational deeds.

Most of the time Mary felt that she had to be compliant and cooperative in order to merit any human contact. This, she stated, was her "false self," and submerging her real feelings was the price she had to pay for any human contact. As a result of these unintegrated parts, Mary did not feel she had a cohesive self. Often she could not differentiate between what she thought or felt and what others wanted her to think or feel. She resented the pressure this put on her and often directly or indirectly blamed the other. Later she admitted that she was not even certain she wanted to be female, as women are "as powerless as any people in the world."

Former Therapists, Hospitalization, and Medication

When Mary was in her early 20s and had just finished graduate school, she took a challenging job in a distant city. But after one month on the job, she suffered a major mental health crisis and was hospitalized for severe depression.

She had had a series of male therapists during her hospitalization. She reported having many power struggles with the therapists but doubted that they were aware of any problems because she was always quiet and cooperative. They regarded her as an ideal patient until she started to manipulate her medication.

After returning to live with her parents, Mary periodically received antidepressant medication from a variety of physicians and therapists. The medication was only partially helpful in controlling her depressive symptoms. From then on, she periodically hoarded her medication in anticipation of suicide attempts. It was at this point, after a series of temporary therapists, that Mary began to see Mrs. Jensen. Mary thought that a female therapist would be less threatening and less likely than a male therapist to fail her (as she believed that her mother had never failed her).

Hypochondriasis and Relationship to Male Physicians

Mary moved from one male physician to another in search of relief for her various physical ailments (e.g., headaches, insomnia, and lower-back pain). Although Mary seemed unaware of the process, she immediately developed romantic leanings toward her physician. Having chosen him for his warmth and empathy, she always idealized him. She spent most of her time fantasizing about him, although the fantasies were never sexual and she never let him know of her longings. But she knew in her heart that she would set up a situation in which he would "reject" her or she would "reject" him.

As she did with her therapists, Mary overdosed when a physician did not ask the right question. The physician failed her "test" and, by extension, failed her. Only much later did it become obvious to Mary that she felt compelled to force each physician to reject or fail her as she believed her father had. This act also allowed her to displace her need-fear dilemma with her overly intrusive, engulfing mother onto a male. It also set up the male to fail her and look foolish in the process, just as her father did.

Depression and Anger

Mary stated at the beginning of her therapy that depression and anger were her two major feeling states. Her depression was not that of guilt or loss but, rather, "emptiness, hopelessness, lethargy, and wanting to sleep all the time." She cried when she was depressed and generally felt evil and bad. Her depressive episodes lasted for several months and were punctuated by a few days of normal mood. She was uncertain why she had such a low opinion of herself and tried to hide these feelings from others by appearing placid and self-contained. However, she sometimes felt overwhelmed and was barely able to go to work. She thought that others would be surprised to know that she felt like a volcano inside.

Mary was afraid that she would be unable to control her anger if she ever permitted herself to acknowledge its existence. To do so, she feared, would cause her to disintegrate. She experienced this anger traumatically in the form of disorganization and fragmentation and tried to avoid experiencing that emotion. Early in her therapy she was unable to speculate about the causes of her anger. However, it appeared to be related to her perception that others were not aware of her inner feelings and needs. This recognition precipitated terrifying feelings of annihilation, as she seemed to have magic expectations regarding others meeting her needs.

Impulse Control Problems

Mary presented as a highly controlled person, and it was only months later that she mentioned her overeating and overspending. In fact, I first learned about these problems from an extensive psychosocial history done on the inpatient ward during her hospitalization at my facility. Mary had periodically gone on uncontrollable eating binges, sometimes eating several cakes at a time and then following these binges with laxative purges. She also had periods of compulsive overspending, which generated serious debts and kept her on the edge of financial disaster. Although she faithfully paid her bills, her overspending "forced" her to live with her parents so as to reduce her expenses.

Dichotomous Thinking

Mary relied primarily on dichotomous thinking when contemplating herself or others. For example, she regarded her father as all-bad—"weak, ineffectual"—with no redeeming qualities. On the other hand, Mary saw her mother as the only person who truly understood her and, therefore, as "perfect." When Mary expressed irritation at her mother's bossiness and I confronted this contradiction of how her mother could be both perfect and bossy, she replied, "Oh, that really doesn't matter because she always comes through for me."

Reactions to Dependency, Use of Distancing, Sadistic Control, and Lying

Mary stated that she did not want people in her life; her cats were enough. Yet she had sought out many therapists and continued to live with her parents. She had interesting ways of managing her incompatible needs: she denied her dependency, explaining it away with the statement that the therapist "helps me manage my depression" and her mother "helps me pay my bills." In other words, she denied the reality of the dependency and used distancing as a defense against her own unconscious desires for closeness.

Mary probably did not regard her mother or therapist as persons but, rather, as essential life-support systems who had to cater to her or else she would perish. When either failed her, she resorted to a terror tactic (e.g., suicide attempts) to bring them into line. Although such an approach often induced her therapist to give up on her, even the act of giving her up probably met Mary's need for self-punishment. If the terror-tactic approach did not work, she then moved into a revenge mode. She seemed totally unaware of her manipulation of others. She also appeared completely unaware of the contradiction between her belief that she was an honest person and her episodic lying to her therapist and physician about hoarding pills or other self-destructive activity.

Reality Testing

Early in the therapy, Mary reported that she believed that her mother and she had mutual ESP and that her mother always knew what Mary was feeling and thinking. When confronted about this belief, she responded, "Perhaps we don't exactly have ESP but it feels that way." She admitted that she knew they did not literally read each other's mind but were unusually "in tune" with each other. In addition, Mary claimed to possess magical thinking, by believing that she would not really die after committing suicide. In any case, her beliefs appeared to meet the criteria for soft signs of thought disorder and not the strict definition of loss of reality testing.

Fantasizing

Mary admitted that she often fantasized during her waking hours. She remarked that none of her former therapists had asked about that, and she had never volunteered anything. She usually imagined having a husband and children, but her fantasies always ended with her being betrayed and left alone, if not physically disabled or dead. Her fantasies often intensified when she improved behaviorally.

Family History

Mary seems to have had a love-hate relationship with all of the members of her family. She tended to dwell on the hate aspect and did not admit to her obvious dependence on her family. When I confronted her about this early in her treatment, she became distant and anxious or reported feeling "weird." I wondered whether this was a psychoticlike response to a confrontation, a matter we shall take up in later chapters.

Mother   Mary's family history showed that her hypochondriacal mother, Eleanor, dominated Mary, her father, and her younger siblings. Eleanor Markham often contemptuously put down the "ne'er-do-well" father, whose constant schemes for making the family wealthy never bore fruit. Mary remembered that very early in life she had to side against her father in order to win her mother's love.

Mary admits seeing her mother as domineering and controlling. Nevertheless, she also described her as the only person "who understands what I really need and does it." Mary felt that she and her mother resembled Siamese twins, sharing the same organ systems, although she knew this was really not so. Mary also knew they did not really have telepathic power but did feel that her mother sensed and responded to the most oblique clues to how she was feeling. On several occasions early in therapy, Mary observed that her life would end when Mrs. Markham died because they were "one"; yet she denied being dependent on her mother.

Mary described her mother as the matriarch of the family—in control, competent, a woman who sacrificed her personal happiness for her children, who kept the family intact, and who stood by her husband despite his weaknesses. Mary saw her mother in a highly idealized manner. But the psychiatric ward staff viewed Eleanor Markham differently. They saw a disturbed woman who chattered compulsively and interrupted them in mid-sentence. She rarely understood what her daughter was really feeling and even responded poorly to ordinary social clues such as indications that a meeting was about to terminate.

Mary thought that her mother had been depressed when she and her siblings were small. Perhaps as a result, Eleanor Markham pressed Mary into service as a confidante who performed many adult functions for her. Mary sided with her mother in every family battle and tried never to be a burden to her. Her mother constantly praised Mary for her independence.

Father Mary saw her father as weak, withdrawn, and incompetent, failing his children and wife in just about every way. When Eleanor Markham urged her daughter to get married, Mary refused because she feared that all men were like her father.

Siblings Mary was the middle child, and she remembered feeling intense anger toward her younger sister, whom Mary blamed for usurping her place as Mrs. Markham's favorite. Mary's older brother, Alan, engaged in delinquent behavior and temper tantrums as an adolescent but went on to become a highly responsible adult. Mary remembered thinking often that she could not act the same way as Alan did or even get angry because she would disappoint her parents just as he had—and she would be excluded from the family. She had never been close to either of her siblings.

Early Childhood Mary had a normal birth with no major childhood illnesses or separations from family. Her earliest memory was the birth of her younger sister when Mary was 3 or 4 years old. She remembered feeling angry and hurt after she lost her status of being the favorite baby. She also recalled her mother's reporting being depressed during this period and having many verbal fights with her husband. She entered kindergarten without difficulty.

Latency Mary reported doing well academically but having no close friends, just acquaintances. Her mother expected her to be at home when not in school. Mary spent most of her leisure time reading. She became quite close to her maternal grandfather, who died when she was 11, but all that she remembered of him was how kindly and loving he was to her. She had no behavior problems (eating, sleeping, bed-wetting, thumb sucking, tantrums) during this time.

Adolescence Mary reported always being a "loner." She had acquaintances in school but no close friends. At that time, she felt that her mother wanted her to have friends and to date, but she never did so. Much later in therapy, Mary revised that memory, stating that her mother was terribly overprotective and strongly indicated that the children should be home with her rather than out with other people. In fact, her mother was suspicious of other people and kept to the house; she had no close friends. She never encouraged Mary to bring friends home, so Mary read extensively and fantasized to pass the time. She continued to do well in school.

Sexual History Mary never had a sexual relationship and denied ever masturbating. She said she experienced a sexual sensation only on the rare occasion when she was reading a romantic novel and denied ever fantasizing about sex. She did become engaged after high school, but the relationship was extremely distant, almost father-daughter-like and ended when Mary felt engulfed by her fiancé.

Education and Work Experience Mary attended college and got her baccalaureate degree while living at home. Although she went away to graduate school in another state, where she received a master's degree in business, she felt as though she had never left home because she talked to her parents by phone every day. Her first mental health problem occurred after she moved to the East Coast, where her contact with her mother was less frequent and her job demanded independence. She had held only semi-skilled jobs since her mental health problems began but had been a reliable and responsible employee.

Family Mental Health Problems Mary reported a vague history of mental illness in her paternal grandmother. The only information she could provide was that her grandmother had been psychiatrically hospitalized for long periods in the state hospital for "alcoholism and temper." There were no reports of mental illness on her mother's side of the family. We can speculate that both mother and father may have character disorders.

I saw Mary for many years of intensive psychotherapy, mostly twice a week. During much of that time, she was maintained on a low dose of Mellaril.

CASE II: JOHN ELLIOTT

John Elliott is an attractive, intelligent man in his early 30s. Since facing combat in Vietnam, he has lived a hippielike existence on the West Coast. His discharge diagnosis from the service was paranoid schizophrenia.

John is extremely impulsive at times and cannot finish any projects. He has problems with authority and with anger. Since his military service in Vietnam, he has been using street drugs heavily. John has been married twice but is now single. He is obviously intelligent, with an IQ of around 130.

On the day before our first interview, John cut his wrists superficially in a suicide attempt, his second mild suicide attempt since leaving the service. Then he telephoned my clinic to request antidepressant medication. After speaking with him on the telephone, I became sufficiently

concerned about his overwhelming sense of panic to recommend hospitalization, but he refused. He did see a psychiatrist that same day for
crisis intervention, but the psychiatrist refused to give him any medication until he had been off all street drugs for at least ten days. My first
session with John came the following day.

John Elliott arrived at his appointment looking anxious and disheveled.
He was an attractive, bearded, long-haired young man dressed cleanly but
casually in the style of the 1960s. Cooperative, polite, and highly verbal, he
managed to remain coherent, although his words flowed in a torrent. He
reported that he had grown suicidally depressed over the last several weeks
but admitted that on the preceding day he had not been able to bring himself
to commit suicide.

Clearly agitated, he squirmed in his chair and twisted his fingers in
anguish. He wept frequently and once even broke into racking sobs. At
times he implored, "Can I be helped? Will this ever stop?" Instead of turning
the question back on him, I answered, "Let's work together to see what we
can do about these problems." It became increasingly clear that he was
experiencing an intense panic attack that was related in part to the following factors.

John's major love relationship had recently ended (the first since his
divorce). He felt that his girlfriend had left him for another man, thereby
recapitulating the end of his second marriage. After the breakup, he started
to feel "strange," and his environment felt "different." Sometimes he felt that
his body took on odd new shapes. As a result, he increased his marijuana
consumption to 10 to 15 joints per day because "I can at least control how
strange I feel this way." (Later the clinic had John tested for temporal lobe
dysfunction, but the results were negative.)

John also feared that his father was having him watched. He recognized
that such a suspicion was unfounded because his father lived in another
part of the country and they had not seen each other for over five years.
Nevertheless, he acutely felt that he was "being spied upon," although he
could not describe how it was being done. This feeling enraged him and
made him feel totally unable to protect himself.

In addition, he still relived his combat experiences from Vietnam and had
bitter feelings about his military service. John had been given a medical
discharge after being misdiagnosed as having paranoid schizophrenia, probably due to his heavy drug usage. He received very little mental health
care before his discharge, however, which he resented deeply. Since leaving
the service he sought psychiatric treatment several times, only to drop out
because the therapist was "insensitive" or "authoritarian."

During this session I focused on calming him down with empathic
comments and a few clarifying questions, and he felt somewhat better by the

end of the interview. He agreed to stop all drug usage for at least the next few days, but I doubted that he could do it. He again refused hospitalization, saying that he did not trust doctors after his experience in the military. But he did agree to see me briefly the next day so that I could assess him further. I concluded the session by dealing with important practical matters—discussing how he would manage until our next meeting and making sure he knew of the crisis services that were available to him. He then agreed to a "no-suicide contract."

Observations from Our First Session

The intensity of John's panic and suspiciousness could be part of a functional psychotic process, but it also could be drug related. He might be suffering from delayed stress as a result of his Vietnam experience, or he might even be having an exacerbated paranoid schizophrenic episode. I simply did not know the cause of his difficulties, nor could I assess his level of personality structure on the basis of his behavior during one session, particularly because of his heavy drug usage. What I did know was that he was able to calm down and plan rationally how he would manage until our appointment the next day. Because he was not a danger to himself or others and was not gravely disturbed, I let him leave. Because John's past and present drug-induced psychotic episodes provided confusing symptoms, it was several months before I felt I could make a clear diagnosis of borderline personality disorder.

Emerging Themes from Early Sessions

I saw John Elliott four times over the next two weeks, and his panic subsided completely within a couple of days. On the surface, his life appeared chaotic and troubled, perhaps with symptoms of schizophrenia. But once his acute panic passed, his symptoms appeared less psychotic in nature, and overall, John demonstrated the ability to maintain reality testing.

John admitted that he was trying to give up street drugs, although it was very difficult for him to stop using marijuana. I contracted with him not to smoke marijuana before a session, and we agreed that a session would not be held if he smoked beforehand. We also agreed that one goal of his treatment would be that he would stop taking street drugs altogether. Because of his conduct with me and his self-reported history, John appeared to be a person of some integrity and personal honesty. Therefore, I tended to trust his self-reports and found myself liking him. (During the next several months, we had to cancel only two sessions because he had smoked marijuana, and he notified me each time at the start of the session.) One could, of course, ask whether John lied to me about smoking before a session. But when he smoked marijuana, he was noticeably different—bemused or panicked. Thus I could tell that he was obviously honoring our contract. In addition, John refused any psychotropic medications, clearly preferring to medicate himself through street drugs.

John attached in psychotherapy quickly. He soon let me know that he found the therapy helpful, unlike his bad experiences in the military. He kept all his appointments, was always on time, and rarely made demands or emergency phone calls. He always let me know how much he had been anticipating the session, thereby showing me how important the sessions were to him. As I basked in his warmth and praise, I realized that the process of idealization had begun.

I noted that in his quiet way, John tried hard to please by being compliant and nondemanding, an issue that had to be addressed. His communication style tended to be somewhat obsessional and intellectualized, but when confronted or asked about feelings, he could give up the intellectualized posture and share his emotions.

I found that John often talked about himself as either a totally good or a totally worthless person. Upon confrontation, he was able to acknowledge, without regressing, the distortions in his "all-bad" opinion of himself and started to integrate the confrontation. He also discussed life situations in a dominance-submission motif, usually with his having to submit to someone else's dominance. He hated this and ruminated a great deal about it, often in his remote, intellectualized fashion.

We continued meeting twice a week, and over the next several months the following themes emerged.

Suspiciousness and Ideas of Reference

John soon developed a fairly trusting relationship with me. When he doubted my ability to help him, he was able to assess realistically the situation with my help. Overall, we enjoyed a good working relationship.

Throughout the first year of therapy, John experienced brief periods of unwarranted suspiciousness and ideas of reference. However, his drug usage interfered with an accurate assessment of these problems. Initially, his suspiciousness centered on his father, continuing his belief that his father was having him watched. He also believed that his father knew about and disapproved of his current unskilled job. John related real events to his paranoid suspicion (e.g., if a car drove by his house twice, he thought that the driver was a private detective hired by his father). But, as always, he sensed that this fear was unrealistic and found it embarrassing.

After several months of therapy, these brief periods of paranoid thinking decreased, and his fearfulness became more rooted in real interpersonal events. Instead of focusing his suspicion exclusively on his father, he now vaguely distrusted friends or coworkers. For example, early in his treatment he took a job as the night manager of a laundromat, a position clearly beneath his abilities. He liked a young woman coworker, although her messiness created extra work for him. Yet he was unable to assert himself and complain about her habits. Then he became suspicious of her motivation, feeling that she was trying to get him in trouble. He felt so threatened when she looked at him that he hid in the darkened office every time she came to work. He told me he was afraid that her eyes could penetrate "right through me." He felt overwhelming anger and anxiety but was unable to verbalize the reasons for his feelings. It later became apparent that John experienced tremendous anger when he felt controlled or put down. He then feared that the other person, having noticed his vulnerability and anger, would try to hurt him emotionally. John used classic projection to rid himself of these unacceptable feelings. However, between these brief episodes he reacted normally and warmly, if subassertively, to his peers and girlfriends.

Intense Anxiety and Episodic Depression

John felt particularly irritable and moody at times. When he worried too much about "coming unhinged," he also became depressed. Then he felt hopeless and helpless and occasionally even suicidal. Fortunately, he was never at much risk of suicide during his entire therapy. And overall, his initial constant state of anxiety and depression diminished as his therapy progressed. More and more, John came to see how dependent he was on others for maintaining his equilibrium and internal sense of comfort. His depression seemed more centered on helplessness, weakness, emptiness, and abandonment and being unloved and inferior, as opposed to feeling guilty or failing to meet his own standards.

The following incident demonstrates how John's anxiety manifested itself interpersonally. After being in my care for several months, he met with a local psychiatrist regarding a government compensation claim. John had such intense feelings about dealing with any authority figure that he worked himself up into a state of panic. Fearing that the psychiatrist would recommend termination of his compensation, John became diffusely anxious, even angry, before the interview and was so agitated that he burst into tears at the start of the meeting. As the concerned psychiatrist queried him about problems of trust, John had a full-blown anxiety attack accompanied by hyperventilation. He was able to remain in the room, however, and did not display any psychotic symptomatology. But when the conversation shifted to Vietnam, John lost control and hit the psychiatrist's bookcase with his fist. (This was the only time he became physically violent in the presence of a professional.) He then apologized profusely, feeling that he had made a fool of himself by being childish and that he had mistreated a fellow human being who now would not like him or help him.

Alterations in the Sense of Reality

At times John experienced intense estrangement in which physical objects around him seemed strange or menacing. At other times he felt himself to be different or unusual (depersonalization). These states, which he was unable to describe in detail, panicked him, and he used drugs to soothe himself.

Polydrug Abuse

When we began therapy, John used marijuana heavily and cocaine to a lesser extent, habits he picked up in Vietnam. Like many servicemen, he had used marijuana, cocaine, amphetamines, and LSD to regulate his mood and anesthetize himself during combat. He had never been part of the drug culture in adolescence. During his early therapy he smoked marijuana so heavily that he experienced major altered states of consciousness, but he rarely enjoyed them. John tended to rely on drugs both to regulate his mood and as a substitute for a love relationship (e.g., the drug-induced states that preoccupied him). These altered states disappeared as he reduced his marijuana consumption and learned how to relax and to soothe himself without the help of drugs.

Sexual Acting Out (Masochism) and Sexual Fantasies (Sadism)

Early in his therapy John reported that he had episodes of sexual acting out. When asked what he meant, he flushed a deep red and replied, "I go to gay hangouts and present myself to be chosen by a man." These episodes, which occurred four to five times per year, deeply embarrassed him. He had no idea what precipitated these incidents or what he was feeling at the time, aside from the fact that they began with a casual idea—"you need to drop by the gay bar." These incidences happened regardless of whether he was in a relationship with a woman or was unattached. Then within several hours, fantasies of homosexual activities dominated his thoughts until he felt compelled to find a gay bar. He usually had sex in the most anonymous way possible (e.g., in bathrooms or cars), and it almost seemed like masturbation rather than interpersonal sex. Whenever possible, he played the passive role, often with sadomasochistic partners who sometimes came close to hurting him physically. When John talked about his homosexual episodes (which he found enjoyable at the time but distasteful afterwards), he tended to obsess, spending ten minutes stating why homosexuality was natural and he was OK, followed by ten minutes about how disgusting homosexuality was and how bad a person he was for engaging in it. As he reported each stand, he seemed to forget his opinions from the opposing position. He denied having any adolescent homosexual activity but mentioned that his "macho" father worried constantly that John was effeminate and might become a homosexual.

Additionally, John volunteered that he had intense fantasies of picking up a young adolescent girl in his car and having sex with her. At this point it was not clear whether he wanted to rape her or seduce her. I confronted him, pointing out the emotional and legal consequences of such an act for both of them, and he was able to keep his fantasy under control and never act on it.

Identity Problems and Dichotomous Thinking

John seemed to see himself and others in dichotomous ways. For example, his father was "all-bad" for trying to spy on him. On the other hand, his girlfriends were "all-good" as long as the relationship gratified him, but he viewed them as "all-bad" when they left or frustrated him. He struggled to maintain a good image of them, however, and tended to see himself as the "all-bad" one.

His self-other boundaries were fluid, and he seemed unaware of projecting his own unconscious feelings onto others.

His sexual identity was confused, and it later became apparent that sometimes he was even uncertain whether he was male or female. His sexuality was played out more in terms of dependency and replay of past fantasies about his relationship to his father than in a mature, adult interest in genitality.

John had little sense of himself, his feelings, or his own values and felt desperately afraid of life because he had no cohesive self.

Labile Emotionality

John's moods could change because of the most minor stimuli, internal or external. In the beginning it was impossible to tell what set off a mood change, say, from feeling good to feeling desperate, depressed, or panicked. A key aspect of his therapy was clarifying the events that set off his reactions. At times John could have rage reactions that were diffuse and not unlike the intense reaction of an infant. His emotional lability continued even after his drug reduction. His desperation and dependency on others to help him control his moods gave a quality of entitlement to some of his demands.

Separation Anxiety and Dependency

Aside from his problems that developed in Vietnam, John's acute symptoms occurred after the breakup of a love relationship. He then experienced intense depression, often with estrangement experiences or suicidal ideation. He was happy only during a love relationship and felt as if he would fall apart when the relationship broke up.

Unrealistic and Idealized Love Relationships

John tended to idealize the women with whom he became involved, only to feel devastated when they did not live up to his expectations. Whenever he began a new relationship, he immediately fell in love. He felt that he gave himself completely to the woman and asked very little in return. But his intensity and covert demands were intimidating (which he did not seem to recognize early in the therapy), and frequently the affair ended abruptly. He then tended to blame himself totally, feeling that he would take the woman back under any circumstances because she was "perfect" and he would never find anyone like her again. However, over time he also subtly put down his former partner as "unworthy."

John was briefly married right after returning from Vietnam; he remembered little about this wife because this marriage lasted less than a month. He married for a second time some months after his first divorce, and this marriage lasted for several years. When his second wife asked for "an open relationship," he became jealous and fearful of losing her and could not assert himself by refusing her request. He eventually left her because he could not tolerate the ambivalence engendered by her wishes for other men.

Performance Anxiety

John felt acutely anxious whenever he was put on "performance demand." After Vietnam he went to college briefly, where he got low grades because he became so anxious during examinations that he almost passed out. Although he was performing well in a nonprofessional job, he lived in terror that he would "mess up" while his supervisor was watching.

Low Self-Esteem and Fear of Criticism

John felt inadequate most of the time and believed that his father was terribly disappointed in him—he knew he was not living up to his potential. He felt that his inability to maintain a long-term love relationship was because of his poor choice of women or because he was unlovable. He always overreacted to criticism and demands from authority figures and then regretted his reactions. His negative self-image tended to predominate, at least superficially.

Vietnam Experiences

His Vietnam experiences were frequently a topic early in his therapy. He described the horror of seeing "80 to 100 bodies hanging on a wire fence" after his compound was accidentally shelled by American troops. John received only minor injuries, but many of his buddies were killed. He remembered wandering among the bodies, sobbing. (A review of his official military records later confirmed this story.) Apparently John suffered a transient psychosis after the shelling. Within a month of this incident he attempted suicide by drug overdosing. Then he climbed to the top of an observation tower and started shooting randomly around the camp in the futile hope that someone would shoot him. Before he could hurt anyone, his superior officer "talked him down." John was sent back to the states for treatment and then was ordered back to Vietnam. He refused to return and eventually was given a medical discharge.

Family History

John's father was an executive in a multinational conglomerate, and his mother was a medical professional. A typical corporate family, Mr. and Mrs. Elliott and John moved around a lot, both within and outside the United States.

When John was about 1½ years old, his mother was hospitalized for 18 months after a hit-and-run accident. During that time he was raised by a maid who did not speak English, and his father occasionally cared for him.

His parents were divorced when John was about 5. He lived with his mother until he was 9, seeing his father during the summer. Then, on the pretext of visiting, Mr. Elliott kidnapped his son and took him out of state. He immediately took John to a hospital to be circumcised, which the boy found both humiliating and extremely painful. John never understood why his father insisted on circumcision.

Mr. Elliott was awarded custody of John, and they lived together thereafter. John never understood why his father did all this, although Mr. Elliott did tell him that his mother was "neglecting" him and that he needed more of a family life in order to "toughen up" and stop being a "sissy."

Mother Initially, John described his mother as a warm, kind person and tended to see her as good and perfect. He had a particularly vivid memory of his friends making fun of him when he was about 6 because she had put nail polish on his fingernails. But, he was hard pressed to describe her or to remember any interactions between them. "She let me be on my own. She always cooked and pressed my clothes but generally didn't interfere." Later in therapy he came to view his mother somewhat differently. When confronted with his idealization of her, he did acknowledge some of his negative feelings toward her, particularly because she did not rescue him from his father.

Father   Apparently John's father ran his home, as well as his corporate staff, with military precision. He subjected his son to discipline so strict that it bordered on sadism. For example, when Mr. Elliott was teaching 8-year-old John some basic metal crafting, John made a mistake. To "teach him to pay attention," Mr. Elliott angrily plunged John's hand into the fire, burning it moderately. What did John do then? "Nothing, or I would have been punished even more."

Mr. Elliott also accused John of watching television instead of doing his homework and even installed a metering device on the TV to monitor his son's viewing. He also said that he knew everything John was doing because John's friends and classmates reported to him all the time. Always accused of things he did not do, John began to distrust his own perceptions and his own reality. When I asked how his father affected him, John became extremely anxious and said through clenched teeth, "I hate him enough that I could kill him—even though I am a pacifist."

When John was about 14, his father married an 18-year-old woman by the name of Tammy. Tammy and her new stepson got along very well, and John regarded her as his friend. Worried as usual that his 14-year-old son might be homosexual, Mr. Elliott decided to let Tammy teach John about sex. After several months of "lessons" with Tammy, John caught his father observing them to make sure that his son was "doing it right" and that he was "man enough." John was then forced to watch as his father and stepmother made love. After that, with no explanation, Tammy stopped visiting her stepson's bed. And John, confused by the entire matter, felt he had lost a good friend.

Shortly thereafter, Mr. Elliott sent John to an expensive private school. John decided that he was a real misfit there; he felt too intellectual for the rugged boys and often was ridiculed. But he did well academically and made a few friends.

Mr. Elliott apparently sent mixed messages to his son. At one point, when John was about 18, he started to flirt with the wife of a friend of his father. Mr. Elliott seemed to enjoy it and enticed John into pursuing the woman. After John and the woman agreed to meet secretly, he told his father about his conquest. But much to John's surprise, his father insisted that he break the date because the entire liaison was "out of line" and improper. John, who had expected to be praised, was shocked by his father's unpredictable behavior.

Siblings   None.

Early Childhood   John reported a normal birth and no major illnesses. He remembered little of the period when his mother was recuperating from the automobile accident and he was cared for by the non-English-speaking maid and his father (when he was home). John did, however, remember an incident that occurred upon his mother's return. He was excitedly showing her his ability to throw a ball when the ball hit her. His father immediately grabbed and severely punished him. John then became fearful of hurting his mother with his exuberance.

He remembered being fearful of going to kindergarten but adjusting within several weeks. His mother and father divorced when he was 5, and his father remarried immediately; after a second divorce several years later, Mr. Elliott married for the third time when John was 14. John remembered little of his life events before age 9 or 10.

Latency   John had little contact with his mother during this time. Many of the events earlier described between father and son started during this period. John's school performance became erratic during latency; he did either very well or poorly. He had no really close friends but did have pals at school. He denied any major behavior problems during this period (e.g., bed-wetting, thumb sucking, fire setting) but in looking back felt that he was depressed and socially isolated.

Adolescence   John felt particularly alienated in high school, when his father made many accusations, spied on him, and claimed that John's school friends tattled on him. When John started doing poorly in school, he was transferred to a private school. He dated very little during this period.

Sexual History and Marriages   John's first sexual experience was with his young stepmother. As an adult, he was sexually active, mainly with females, although he periodically had impulsive and transient homosexual experiences that were fairly impersonal and started in the service. He denied having any sexual problems with women. He said that he masturbated occasionally.

John was married twice. He could not describe his first wife. His second wife was a young hippie he married after Vietnam. He reported their sexual relationship as average to good.

Education and Work Experience   John worked only briefly after high school before being drafted. After the service, he worked as a semiskilled laborer. He started college but dropped out after getting Ds and Fs.

Family Mental Health Problems   John reported knowing of no mental health problems on either his mother's or his father's side of the family. But as with Mary's family, we can speculate that both his mother and his father may have had character disorders.

I saw John twice a week for almost four years of individual psychotherapy. He eventually was able to enroll in college, get a degree, keep a job commensurate with his intelligence, and pursue an increasingly satisfying social life.

CASE III: SARAH GARDNER

Sarah Gardner is a very beautiful woman in her late 20s. I had seen her once before, about a year ago, just before her divorce. At the request of her husband, Mike, she came to see me for two sessions to discuss her feelings about the divorce. But it was clear that she had already made up her mind and was unwilling to examine her motivation for leaving him. She said simply, "He bores me. We just don't share the same interests."

Ten months after the divorce, Sarah phoned me in a panic. She said she had been feeling overwhelmed and had not been out of bed for the last two days. She did not know what was wrong, but she felt "terrible" and hated her life. I scheduled an appointment for the following day.

When I opened the door to greet Sarah, her appearance startled me. Last year she had dressed attractively but casually in jeans and a lumberjack shirt. Now she sat in my waiting room looking as if she were waiting for a high-fashion photographic session. On this warm summer day she was wearing an expensive-looking, very short hot pink playsuit that showed off her long, tanned legs. Her waist-length blonde hair was braided in a Bo Derek style, with a pastel bead at the tip of each tiny braid, and her makeup was flawless. She looked stunning.

Sarah smiled animatedly and bounced into my office, hardly the picture of depression. Dropping casually onto my couch, she announced, "Boy, am I glad to see you." She said she had been feeling empty and lost for the last month and had had long crying jags. She had been sleeping too much during the day but had resorted to drinking gin at night to get to sleep. She had no appetite and had lost ten pounds from her already slim frame.

Sarah told me that her 4-year-old daughter, Tracey, crawled into her bed at night and pleaded, "Please, Mommy, don't cry—it will be all right." She continued dramatically, "So I lie there with my arms around Tracey, with big droplets of tears falling on her—splash, splash! I know this isn't right. I am supposed to be the parent, and Tracey is supposed to be the child. I love Tracey very much, but I don't feel that I am a very good parent—and that makes me feel guilty."

She said that her crafts business was doing quite well, but only because she had several good employees who were holding down the fort while she pulled herself together. She had not been to the office regularly for at least three weeks. She paused and then added, "Jesus, I am just plain depressed. But I have a child and a business to look after. How am I ever going to get out of this funk?"

I asked her whether she knew what set off this episode of depression. She responded that she thought it might be related to her divorce. She talked vaguely about her marriage, and I remarked, "It sounds like you regret divorcing Mike." "Yes, I think that's it," she agreed. Sarah told me she now believed that she had divorced Mike too quickly and began to sob.

I asked her to refresh my memory about the marriage and divorce. Sarah said she was a senior in college, majoring in the arts, when her parents were killed by a drunk driver. She became terribly depressed and began to see a college therapist. During this period she met Mike, who was completing a graduate degree. He was solid, responsible, and quietly caretaking while she grieved over the death of her parents. As Sarah and I explored her grieving, it increasingly seemed to me that she felt lost and overwhelmed without her parents. Mike seemed entranced by her vivaciousness and obvious talent, and she by his devotion and caretaking. After some probing on my part, Sarah told me that she had stopped her therapy when she met Mike, but she did not find that very curious.

Eight months later, Sarah and Mike were married, and Tracey was born the following year. After they had completed school, Mike landed a good job as a business executive, and Sarah worked part time to save money to start her tapestry firm.

Sarah soon began to look down on Mike, who catered to her every wish, even pitching in to help with her business. Their sex life was not very good because of Mike's periodic problems with impotency (which he had experienced since adolescence) and Sarah's inability to reach orgasm. Mike always seemed vaguely depressed and passive, preferring to stay at home and watch television. Sarah began invidiously to compare him with her father, who had been a charismatic businessman who wheeled and dealed in high finance. Whenever she felt low or needy, Mike always babied her, and she felt good about him; but when she felt strong, he seemed weak and unappealing. She found herself either thinking he was wonderful and loving him passionately or despising him for being a wimp. She felt bad about herself when she found him disappointing, wondering how she could find fault with a person who was so basically "good."

Around this period she decided to leave Mike. Her business was doing well. Several good female friends were urging her to dump Mike, and she had had several brief sexual affairs. (It was at this point that she first saw me, though she did not tell me about the affairs then.)

Soon after her divorce, Sarah met a fascinating industrialist in his early 50s. He was wonderful to her and frequently advised her on managing and expanding her business. She often left Tracey with Mike and took off with her new boyfriend for three-day weekends in Mexico. But she was beginning to sense that her boyfriend preferred her to be a somewhat dependent child, for whenever she spoke her mind, he dismissed her opinion.

Then, during one trip to Mexico, he asked her to engage in group sex with several of his friends. Sarah found his request disgusting. She had already admitted to him that in some ways she was quite proper and strict about sex, which was why she never wanted to try certain exotic sexual practices. He seemed surprised at her refusal because she appeared so sophisticated and worldly. Not long afterwards, they both lost interest in the relationship and drifted apart.

Sarah gestured charmingly, tossed her head about, and crossed and uncrossed her legs in various revealing poses as she told me this story. She seemed totally unaware of the discrepancy between her physical seductiveness and her stated sexual inhibition.

After the breakup, Sarah decided that she had underestimated Mike and that perhaps she should reconsider him. But, in the meantime he had fallen in love with a woman named Connie. They were living together and were thinking about marriage. Sarah now despaired that she would ever meet a man who could meet her needs, and she was beginning to feel inadequate and worthless. Sarah could not explain to me what made her feel so bad. "Perhaps it is just that no one loves me. I can't think of anything I do that is so bad," she said. When I asked why she needed someone to love her in order to feel good about herself, she responded, "I don't know. But it's a good thing I am coming to see you. I have a feeling you can really help me."

We concluded the session by talking briefly about how I saw Sarah's problems, particularly the relationship of her depression to her need always to have a man in the picture. I noted that she did not have an ongoing relationship at the moment and seemed afraid to be alone and to test her wings. I warned her that she might reach a point in the therapy when she suddenly wanted to break off the relationship, as she did with the college therapist and with Mike. I told her that although she was free to do so, it might be important for her to understand this pattern of breaking off relationships suddenly. She agreed with this, and I had a chance later to remind her of it. Sarah informed me that within the coming year she planned to move her business to a more metropolitan area. But now money was tight, and she could afford to come only once a week, though she wanted to start working on her problems while she was still here.

Observations from Our First Session

I had two strikingly different reactions after that first interview. First, I felt very positive toward Sarah. She was delightful and enjoyable. I was intrigued that she could be so sophisticated and so adept at managing her business and yet be so much a child-woman in her relationships. Her histrionic behavior seemed more engaging than disturbing or off-putting, and she had developed many of her creative talents.

But I was concerned about how helpless and dependent she could be in the therapy. I had already noted some of her cognitive maneuvers to avoid dealing with reality (e.g., denial), and I sensed that Sarah would say "I don't know" and avoid unpleasant affect with a spectacular array of acting-out behavior outside and inside the session. Finally, although she could charm others into taking care of her, I could feel an aggressive, competitive edge to some of her maneuverings. All in all, I felt she would present quite a challenge in the therapy.

Emerging Themes from Early Sessions

Because of Sarah's dramatic overstatements, her "forgetting" certain important details and "not knowing" what she thought or felt in certain situations, much important information did not emerge until late in the therapy. The following themes, however, were revealed in the two sessions before her divorce and several of her most recent sessions with me.

Identity Problems

Closer examination revealed that Sarah was not as intact as she appeared to be. For example, she really lacked much of a sense of self, except in her work. Basically, she was uncertain about what she wanted out of life or from relationships.

When she was involved with a man, she felt beautiful. But sometimes she developed an amazingly poor body image and believed that she was "ugly, grotesque"; then she dieted and exercised to absurd degrees in order to improve herself.

Sarah described herself mainly in two stereotyped roles—"cute, adorable little girl" or a "sophisticated jet setter/international businesswoman/artist." But she did not feel that either role was her natural self. When she felt bad about herself, she regarded herself as "ugly, stupid, vaguely evil, and bad."

Even her private business held hidden terrors for Sarah: "Ever since high school, I knew I wanted to be in the arts. I could always count on that. I never doubted that part of my life. Well, now I am doing it for a living, and, frankly, I've got doubts that I will be strong enough to pull it off."

Troubled Intimate Relationships

Although Sarah did not complain much about her relationships, it was clear that they were frequently conflicted, particularly her relationships with men. In general, she used her charm and appeal to persuade others to give to her, and she gave something back until her ambivalent feelings destroyed the relationship.

She volunteered little about her boyfriends before her marriage. Her relationship with her ex-husband seemed first to be fraught with dependency, and then disappointment and some competitive feelings. Apparently she avoided dealing with the competition and disappointment by suddenly wanting to escape from the marriage. Her relationship with the industrialist was that of a child–woman with her mentor, until Sarah was shocked by his sexual requests and simply lost interest in him. I did not explore her relations with her female friends at this point.

Use of Dichotomous Thinking, Denial, Idealization, and Devaluation

Sarah relied on a variety of lower-level defenses, including splitting. For example, she regarded Mike as alternately "all-good" or "all-bad." When he was "all-bad," she used massive denial to mask his good traits, and when he was "all-good," she denied his bad traits. She related to others according to how well they would take care of her, provide status, and help her feel good about herself. She devalued those who failed her and rarely thought about them again. Both of these patterns represented primitive idealization and devaluation. She did not appear to be particularly revengeful. Sarah also used denial in acknowledging certain significant facts (e.g., affairs) that she cognitively dismissed as unimportant.

Depression and Anxiety

Sarah did not report many depressive or anxious periods but, upon inquiry, admitted that she had felt depressed or anxious for lengthy periods. We eventually established that the breakup of a love relationship usually precipitated such an episode. She said that she had hardly ever been without a boyfriend since she was 16. She remembered that between boyfriends she got restless and bored and would have to go out every night with friends, telephone her parents, or work for hours on artistic projects. When she was without a man, she felt "lost" and "empty." When talking about her handling of time alone, she said, "I'm just your basic nonliberated woman," apparently oblivious to the deeper dependency feelings beneath her self-deprecating humor.

Sensitivity to Criticism

Although Sarah had verve and style, I noted that she often seemed particularly sensitive to criticism, both real and implied. She described how devastated she felt after her industrialist lover teased her repeatedly about some minor habit. She never told him how bad he made her feel but told me now, "I felt totally worthless. When we got into the car, I would have just been happy if he had run me off the road and killed me." Fortunately, these episodes usually passed quickly, but Sarah could not explain why they occurred. I later learned that she quickly inhibited negative feelings, and if she experienced them, she made amends to the other person to get rid of them. Generally, Sarah was not comfortable being openly angry at someone.

Dependence and Independence

Sarah described several incidences when Mike helped out at her business because she felt overwhelmed by especially large orders. She mentioned in passing that he always seemed to try to take over, which made her feel inadequate. Sometimes he just did not perform as brilliantly as she wished, but she rarely criticized him. It became clear that she wanted to be taken care of, although she insisted on controlling the form of the caretaking and felt that her independence was being infringed upon if she could not control the other person.

Sexual Provocativeness and Sexual Problems

Sarah seemed unaware of her sexual attractiveness and exhibitionism. Although always fashionable, her outfits were also slightly seductive. For example, she came to one session in a peasant outfit with a blouse that dipped precariously over the bosom. Yet she viewed herself as "straight" and "always a lady" and was constantly surprised when men came on to her sexually and expected her to be a swinger.

When I asked her directly, Sarah reported never being orgasmic, although she "faked it" for her sexual partner. She admitted that she tended to view sex as "something dirty . . . yes, I know, it sounds right out of some 1940s textbook on women and sex, but that is the way I feel. Men's bodies turn me off." She preferred to be held and cuddled and had considerable ambivalence about her sexuality. During her marriage, she spent many nights in bed while Mike rubbed her shoulders or stroked her long hair.

Indirect Expression of Aggression

Upon inquiry, Sarah admitted that she had had a lot of "pouty" episodes during her marriage. Whenever she did not get her way, she resorted to teasing and sarcasm to make Mike feel guilty. She openly manipulated him into giving in to her. "Well, it's a woman's prerogative to try to get her way," she remarked charmingly.

She denied any competition with Mike over her business: "He concedes that I am the artist. Frankly, he is a flop when it comes to anything creative," she asserted. This may or may not have been true, but Sarah said it with an undercurrent of competitive pride.

Diffuse, Impressionistic Cognitive Style

Sometimes Sarah did not seem to understand what she was saying. Ten months ago she was unable to explain why she so desperately wanted to end her marriage; now she could not say why she wanted to get back into it just as urgently. And she showed little concern about her motivations.

Sarah answered "I don't know" to a lot of questions. She engaged in acts (e.g., affairs) but did not seem to relate them to her value system; she seemed to operate without establishing cause-and-effect links among her feelings, thoughts, and actions. She often did not seem to notice the implications of what she was sharing with me. When she did have unpleasant or conflicted thoughts or feelings, she cognitively shut them off or prevented them from remaining conscious.

Self-Involved and Emotional Behavior

Sarah seemed to respond dramatically and then quickly forgot many events. She had hated Mike, and now she loved him. She felt depressed, held Tracey in her arms all night long, and "splashed huge tears" onto her. Sarah was very sensitive to what others thought of her. She related life events to herself and really could not understand other peoples' needs. On the other hand, she could give to friends and employees. She provided some parenting to Tracey, being strict in some areas (e.g., manners) and indulgent and playful when she could also act like a child (e.g., climbing trees or dancing around the house together).

Impulsive Behavior

Sarah's brief affairs, precipitous divorce, and jaunts to Mexico when her business needed attention all exemplified her impulsivity. Once when Mike was out of town, she slept with one of his coworkers. She could not explain why and worried that Mike would find out about it and would feel devastated. Sarah also tended to drink too much when depressed, but alcohol was not a problem in the therapy.

Family History

Sarah was raised in a wealthy middle-class family and had one older sister. She suspected that her parents had a marriage of convenience only and did not know why they stayed together.

Mother   Sarah described her mother as a quiet, very attractive woman who stayed at home while Sarah was young. By Sarah's adolescence, religion had become an important part of her mother's life (she went to Catholic Mass daily). Her mother was active in church and community affairs and hosted a number of expensive benefits for charity.

Sarah felt her mother was somewhat withdrawn and distant from her daughters, although she was available if they sought her out. Although Sarah wanted her mother's love, she felt she rarely got it, except perhaps when she pleased her by faithfully going to Mass. Her mother also was delighted by Sarah's artistic ability, but she always punished her daughter for any "bad manners."

Father   Sarah's father was an attractive, highly charismatic man who traveled extensively on business. He fancied himself to be a ladies' man, and Sarah thought he may have had a mistress. He adored and indulged both daughters and particularly reinforced Sarah's flirtatious behavior. She vividly remembered how disappointed he once was in her when she came down to breakfast in jeans and without makeup; she never did it again. She wears jeans now only when she is feeling defiant.

Both daughters spent a lot of time with their father. The mother rarely joined in and did not interfere with their activities. The father took the girls to business conferences and expensive restaurants, and as they got older, he even took them to bars, although no one told the mother.

Siblings   Margaret, attractive and self-contained, was two years older than Sarah. The family considered her brilliant, and Sarah was jealous of her performance in school. Margaret went on to a prestigious career in the sciences and maintained little contact with Sarah.

Early Childhood   Sarah had a normal birth, no major illnesses, and no separations from her family. She was vague about her early childhood. She thought she had had some fear about going to kindergarten and some death anxiety during adolescence.

Latency   Sarah reported no behavior problems during this time. She did well in school and had two close girlfriends. She took ballet and piano lessons and had an active social life.

Adolescence   Sarah did B and C work in high school, except for the arts, in which she got As. She was popular and was elected to several other offices related to artistic endeavors. She was a cheerleader during her senior year.

Sexual History, Marriage, and Parenting   Sarah never masturbated because she considered it "weird—something a man should do for you, not something you should do to yourself." She was a great flirt but never had sex until college. She constantly had boyfriends but could not explain why the relationships ended, saying simply, "We grew apart." As mentioned earlier, she was nonorgasmic. During her therapy she did become orgasmic with one partner.

Sarah reported hating pregnancy and not really liking motherhood until recently, now that she could teach Tracey the arts and they could do more things together. She said that she loved Tracey very much but probably would not have become a parent if she had to do it all over again. She enjoyed married life but admitted to "running hot and cold" in her feelings toward her husband.

Education and Work Experience   Sarah majored in the arts and did well academically, completing a bachelor's degree. Sarah's business, which she founded with savings from her salary, became both an artistic and a financial success.

Family Mental Health History   There was no history of schizophrenia or major affective disorder on either her mother's or her father's side of the family. It was difficult to determine whether either parent had anything more than mild to moderate narcissistic problems.

I saw Sarah for ten months of supportive-confrontive psychotherapy aimed at helping her overcome depression, manage her life better (particularly in regard to men), and improve her parenting skills.

In what ways are these three patients similar? How are they different? It is important to note how accurately they saw others and themselves, as well as how they coped with interpersonal relationships, impulse control, management of anxiety, and problems of self-esteem.

Mary Markham, with her psychoticlike episodes, represents a lower-level borderline. John Elliott, particularly after he restricted his usage of street drugs, represents a more typical borderline patient, frequently seen in inpatient units and outpatient clinics. Sarah Gardner belongs at the higher level of the borderline spectrum.

The following chapters, with their emphasis on the intrapsychic structures that define the key diagnostic symptoms of the borderline personality, will show how these symptoms relate to one another and how understanding their relationships can sharpen the therapist's diagnostic skills.

CHAPTER 3

Structural Diagnosis

We shall now apply Kernberg's structural diagnosis to see whether Mary Markham, John Elliott, and Sarah Gardner indeed meet the criteria for borderline personality organization.

ASSUMPTIONS OF THIS APPROACH

The structural diagnostic approach assumes that the borderline condition is a stable personality organization that does not vacillate between neurosis and psychosis, although the patient may have transient psychotic episodes and quickly return to previous levels of functioning. In other words, the borderline disorder is not a *state* that a person enters only temporarily; rather, it is a *trait* diagnosis. The borderline individual has a stable but pathologic personality organization characterized by specific strengths and weaknesses that distinguish it from both neurosis and psychosis. It is a specific syndrome with a high degree of internal consistency and thus should not be viewed as a regression in response to internal or external stress. Hence, at least according to Kernberg, the borderline personality organization can be considered a category diagnosis with its own intrapsychic structure, descriptive symptoms, and natural history. Although advocates of the various psychoanalytic approaches (Kernberg, Masterson, Meissner, Rinsley, and others) differ among themselves on minor details or emphasis, they agree completely on these points.

Kernberg's *structural diagnosis* is the most abstract of the psychoanalytic diagnostic systems. Most of the other approaches can be considered sub-types of Kernberg's diagnostic system and differ from it more in emphasis than in form. Kernberg believes that the borderline concept is adequately defined by common criteria that apply across the borderline spectrum, making refined subtyping unnecessary.

Definition of Structure

The concept of mental structure has had a complex development in psychological and psychoanalytic theory. In these contexts, structure has three meanings. The first refers to psychological rather than physical structures (e.g., enduring ways of viewing the world, modes of thought, or strategies of processing information) that become more complex and differentiated from infancy to adulthood (Piaget and associates).

A second meaning of structure centers on the division of the psyche. In the topographic theory of the mind, Freud described the unconscious, preconscious, and conscious. Later he organized these mental processes into three structures: id, ego, and superego, theoretical constructs that categorize and cluster functions of the mind simultaneously with the child's evolving identity. Kernberg believes that the way in which these agencies of the mind evolve depends on the development of intrapsychic structures, predating, in particular, the creation of the id and superego in the child, which in his model occurs after the age of 3.

Kernberg sees three types of structures—normal-neurotic, borderline, and psychotic personality organization. Psychosocial, developmental, constitutional, genetic, and familial factors form the basis for these structures. Once formed, psychological functioning stabilizes in terms of the structure that forms the matrix from which behavioral symptoms develop. Motivation is closely linked to these hierarchical structures, which are formed from internalizations and representations of self and object. Each structure has its own characteristics and traits, which allow the individual a repertoire of responses.

To understand what is happening in an individual, Kernberg analyzes three aspects: descriptive, structural, and genetic-dynamic. Taken together, these three aspects allow the borderline individual to be comprehensively understood. Kernberg calls this *structural analysis,* and it represents a third contemporary meaning of the term *structure.* It is Kernberg's most important contribution to the diagnosis and prognosis of the borderline disorder. Kernberg's structural analysis is based not only on object-relations theory but also on psychoanalytic developmental theory which adds the concept of phases, tasks, and progression through time.

Conceptualizing Kernberg's Diagnostic Approach

If Kernberg were an architect, he would be interested in a house's overall design and framework (e.g., foundation, beams, roof). He would not be particularly concerned with the interior decoration, the subtle variations in the house that a builder might make, or the relationship of the people who would live in the house. To Kernberg, the overall structural design would define the house just as the ego structure organizes psychic experience. In contrast, other theorists are concerned with subtle variations (Meissner) or the psychodynamics of the family living in the house (Masterson and Rinsley).

Kernberg's approach to the borderline condition follows a "lumping" strategy—he provides a global but specific description that encompasses all borderline individuals, making no attempt to differentiate among subtypes. Thus, his diagnostic approach gives clinicians the overall form of the borderline personality.

Second, Kernberg believes that all patients seeking treatment can be placed in one of three categories—neurotic, borderline, or psychotic. His approach allows a variety of personality subtypes (e.g., paranoid, schizoid, infantile) to be included within the diagnosis borderline personality organization.

Finally, a variety of symptoms can be included in the structural diagnosis as long as the structural criteria are met. This means that patients with different symptoms can be diagnosed as borderline. For the clinician, Kernberg's well-defined diagnostic system, with its inclusionary and exclusionary criteria, offers a great advantage over intuition and guesswork.

SYMPTOMS OF A BORDERLINE PERSONALITY ORGANIZATION

Although psychoanalytic theorists do not organize their criteria in a statistical or symptom-oriented way, they do believe that certain symptoms can alert the clinician to the diagnosis. Kernberg lists several symptoms that suggest a borderline personality organization, particularly if they do not justify a clear-cut diagnosis of manic-depressive illness, schizophrenia, or an acute brain syndrome. (Incidentally, he recommends taking a personal history and performing a mental-status examination in order to rule out pervasive psychosis, past or present. Transient psychosis, in which the patient returns to normal functioning within several days, does not contraindicate the borderline diagnosis.)

The common presenting symptoms shown in Table 3-1 function as a "cuing device." They may appear neuroticlike, but because of their

Table 3-1 Suggestive Symptoms of the Borderline Personality: A Summary

Anxiety—diffuse, chronic, free floating.

Polysymptomatic neurosis—two or more of the following:
Multiple phobias that severely limit the patient's life-style.
Obsessive-compulsive symptoms that have become ego syntonic and have acquired a quality of overvalued thoughts and actions.
Multiple, bizarre, chronic conversion symptoms.
Dissociative reactions such as hysterical "twilight states," fugues, or amnesia.
Hypochondriasis.
Paranoid and hypochondriacal trends with any other symptomatic neurosis. This is presumptive of borderline personality organization; not every borderline displays it, but its presence verifies the diagnosis.

Polymorphous perverse sexual trends—the more chaotic and multiple or with elementary aims replacing genital aims along with unstable object relations, the more presumptive this is of borderline personality organization. For example, infantile needs replace adult needs (e.g., the desire for sexual intercourse might be motivated by a chronic need to be held rather than a need for adult sexual pleasure). In addition, the person may randomly have sex with members of either sex or with children and may also use voyeurism and even cruelty in order to enjoy sexual activity.

Classical prepsychotic personality structures—(e.g., paranoid, schizoid, hypomanic, and cyclothymic personality organizations with strong hypomanic trends). "Subpsychotic" is probably a better term than "prepsychotic," inasmuch as a majority of these disorders do not actually deteriorate into frank psychosis.

Impulse neurosis and addictions—should be ego dystonic outside the episode (period of the activity) but *ego syntonic* (pleasurable) during the episode (e.g., alcoholism, drugs, psychogenic obesity, kleptomania). *Ego dystonic* means an action that is repugnant (e.g., an adult who feels compelled to exhibit himself in public, even though he is offended by doing so).

Lower-level character disorder—infantile, narcissistic, or antisocial behavior.

Source: Adapted from Kernberg, O. F. (1977b). The structural diagnosis of borderline personality disorder. In P. Hartocollis (ed.), *Borderline Personality Disorders: The Concept, the Syndrome, the Patient* (pp. 101–103). Copyright 1977 by International Universities Press. Reprinted by permission.

intensity—the way they limit the patient's life—they suggest a more primitive personality structure. Their presence thus would alert the clinician to the need to explore the possibility of a borderline personality structure.

The reader is reminded that for Kernberg, a definitive diagnosis would depend not on descriptive symptoms but on specific ego pathology. Kernberg lists three specific and three nonspecific structural—not descriptive—ego characteristics of borderline personality organization (Table 3-2). In addition, Table 3-3 at the end of this chapter outlines how these characteristics can be used to differentiate the borderline from the neurotic and psychotic personality organizations. Interviewing techniques for eliciting these characteristics and distinguishing among the three personality organizations will be presented in Chapter 9.

SPECIFIC STRUCTURAL CHARACTERISTICS

Identity Diffusion or Impaired Ego Integration

Kernberg defines identity diffusion, a term borrowed from E. Erikson, as clinically represented by sharply contradictory and unassimilated attitudes toward important aspects of the self and significant others. Most major psychoanalysts agree that the *lack of an integrated self-concept is a core problem of all borderline personalities.* Goldstein (1981a) found other terms that could equally well describe this phenomenon, such as the lack of a stable, real self or the existence of an as-if or a false self. This criterion has two major aspects: (1) cleavages in the self-image, resulting in contradictory and problematic attitudes, feelings, and behaviors directed toward the self and life choices and (2) cleavages in the object image (others), with consequent problematic interpersonal relations (Kernberg 1977b).

The Self-Image

A poorly integrated concept of self is reflected in a subjective experience of chronic emptiness as well as contradictory self-perceptions and behavior (toward the self or others) that cannot be meaningfully integrated or explained (Kernberg 1977b). Unintegrated, contradictory perceptions and behaviors are necessary for a diagnosis, but this does not always mean that borderline adults must feel chaotic. The lack of an inner definition of a self can lead them to avoid or to join others or groups in order to achieve definition. When pressed, borderline individuals cannot determine, except superficially, what they want out of life, career, or relationships.

The Object Image

Borderline adults may have many acquaintances and seem to relate well to others, but scrutiny reveals a different picture. Because of their impoverished perceptions of others, borderline adults use people to meet their own

Table 3-2 **Summary of Structural Characteristics**

Specific Structural Characteristics: must appear in the borderline patient.

Identity diffusion or impaired ego integration
Primitive defensive operations that center around splitting
  Splitting
  Primitive idealization
  Projective identification
  Denial
  Omnipotence and devaluation
Maintenance of reality testing

Nonspecific Structural Characteristics: may or may not appear in the borderline patient.

Ego weakness
  Lack of anxiety tolerance
  Lack of impulse control
  Lack of developed channels of sublimation
Lack of superego integration
Genetic-dynamic characteristics
  Aggressivization of Oedipal conflicts
  Idealization of heterosexual or homosexual love object is exaggerated
  Complex intermingling of parental images projected onto therapist
  Genital strivings acquiring pre-Oedipal functions
  Premature Oedipalizing of pre-Oedipal issues.

Source: Adapted from Kernberg, O. F., (1977b). The structural diagnosis of borderline personality disorder. In P. Hartocollis (ed.), *Borderline Personality Disorders: The Concept, the Syndrome, the Patient* (pp. 103-117). Copyright 1977 by International Universities Press. Reprinted by permission.

needs and do not regard others as individuals in their own right. As a result, borderline persons talk about others as if they were one-dimensional "cardboard" figures who have no needs or motivations. In relationships, borderline adults may vacillate between states of indifference and intense dependency. Several terms have evolved to represent this phenomenon, including need-fulfilling relationships, as-if relationships, and part-object relationships.

Kernberg (1980b) found that identity diffusion has three effects. First, borderline individuals are unable to maintain any long-term integration of the concept of self or others. Hence, they are forced to rely on others for what is missing in the self, namely, the ability to evaluate realistically oneself and others over time.

Second, borderline adults' perceptions, especially of those to whom they are close, become increasingly distorted, chaotic, and shallow because of their inability to evaluate others realistically. Instead, borderline individuals rely on primitive cognitive and emotional states to relate to others; these states are often highly conflicted and infantile and thus make poor evaluative tools.

Finally, borderline individuals cannot feel any real empathy with others because of their inability to integrate others' good and bad traits. Successful integration would enable patients to keep a whole image of the others during periods of frustration, but borderline adults' pathological dichotomous thinking makes this impossible. Consequently, in the borderline adult's view, a small flaw can turn a former "angel" into a "devil." Thus, the defense of splitting promotes identity diffusion.

Persons with an integrated identity experience conflict over the emergence of major contradictions in their self-concept or concept of others. Healthy adults usually understand and resolve this contradiction or at least accept it (albeit painfully) until resolution is possible. But borderline individuals, who operate with dichotomous thinking as a way of avoiding the anxiety associated with experiencing contradiction, cannot tolerate ambivalence.

Why does identity diffusion occur? All psychodynamic theorists agree that it represents a developmental failure early in life. The child's inability to integrate various conflicting identifications with the parents causes the arrest in self-definition and self-assertion. As Meissner (1982–1983b) has pointed out, borderline adults' underlying fears pertain to the threat imposed by the developmental reality of surrendering childlike fantasies and dependencies. Their commitment to life, work, and love means accepting change and limitations, giving up infantile omnipotence and entitlement, and reconciling themselves to human limitations and death (p. 42). But borderline individuals are unable to make such a commitment because it means giving up their fantasy of returning to an infantile state of total relatedness and caretaking.

Kernberg reasoned that borderline individuals have achieved a developmentally sufficient differentiation of self-images from object images to permit firm ego boundaries (unlike those of the psychotic patient) but have not yet integrated good and bad aspects of the self and object (like those of the neurotic person). This lack of integration is, supposedly, due to the predominance in the young child of severe aggression, which was activated by the frustrating environment or by constitutional aspects.

Clinical Manifestations of Identity Diffusion

Kernberg (1977b) reports that identity diffusion may be detected during the interview by the following manifestations:

1. The patient reports a history of contradictory behavior or oscillations between feeling states that imply contradictory behavior. The interviewer is unable to understand the patient or to explain the behavior. It is important to remember that the patient shows contradictory but not necessarily chaotic behavior and feelings.
2. The patient describes significant others in such a way that the interviewer cannot understand them or their motivation.
3. The patient's interpersonal relationships appear shallow, chaotic, and manipulative; or across time the motivations of others are distorted.
4. The patient distorts the interviewer's motivations and is unable to empathize with efforts to make sense of the interviewer's contradictory images.

Using Identity Diffusion to Distinguish Personality Structure

Identity diffusion is one of the three essential characteristics of the borderline personality organization. It can be seen in persons with both borderline and psychotic structures, but it does not occur in the neurotic patient. Accordingly, identity integration differentiates the neurotic from the other two personality structures, though there are two exceptions to this rule. Patients with paranoid schizophrenia and manic-depressive illness may have an abnormal, pathological, but integrated identity (as shown in some chronic delusional symptoms), but they lack intact reality testing. Narcissistic personalities, who some consider to constitute a subgroup of the borderline organization, usually present an integrated but pathological grandiose self-image, rather than the lack of integration of the self-concept. However, they lack an integration of the concept of others, and this pathological self-concept obscures their underlying identity diffusion with primitive defensive operations, such as omnipotence and devaluation (Kernberg 1977b). But for all practical purposes, it is the presence or absence of identity diffusion that most clearly differentiates borderline from nonborderline conditions.

Kernberg distinguishes between neurotic and borderline adults. Neurotic patients, he says, can explain their dilemma in an integrated fashion, can often empathize with others with whom they are in conflict, and frequently feel excessive guilt. This process reflects the presence of integrated but pathological object relations. When confronted with contradictions, neurotic adults can acknowledge them cognitively. For example, neurotic adults who cannot describe someone because that person is too unpredictable may be telling the truth—there truly are some genuinely perplexing and confusing people.

Borderline patients, on the other hand, usually do not readily see contradictory elements and can rarely empathize, except superficially (e.g., closer inquiry indicates a lack of true understanding). When confronted with contradictions, borderline persons feel intense anxiety. They often try to explain away the contradictions or attack the interviewer for seeing them as bad. Finally, borderline patients will acknowledge contradictions only when they are confronted by the interviewer.

Borderline patients also lack the neurotic adult's ability to maintain relations with others by demonstrating warmth, concern, tactfulness, and dedication. In addition, borderlines, unlike neurotics, cannot maintain empathy, understanding, and involvement in a relationship once conflicts or problems arise. This is why borderline adults' relationships are shallow, chaotic, and usually heavily tinged with either idealization or aggression. Consequently, the borderline patients' interaction with the interviewer is an immediate indicator of the quality of their object relations. Even in a brief interview, the interviewer may note distortion in the form of inappropriate behavior, blaming, idealizing, projection of undesirable qualities onto the interviewer, inability to relate, or shallowness. The observation of severe distortion (e.g., delusions) indicates a serious problem and thus allows the interviewer to eliminate the neurotic or borderline level from consideration and to consider instead the psychotic level (Kernberg 1977b).

Psychotic patients, who also display the contradictions of borderline adults, usually decompensate after the contradictions are pointed out to them. As a result, they can become overwhelmed by disorganizing emotions and intense primitive fantasies, often regressing behaviorally as well. In contrast, borderline individuals may function at a more adult level after confrontation.

Example 1   A female patient reports that she made a suicide attempt last week after her boyfriend left her. Her history reveals that they were inseparable for over a year. She claims that she is quite independent, does not miss him—"it's over"—and does not know why she tried to kill herself. She is unaware of her attachment to him, her sense of loss, and its effect on her behavior.

Borderline   When confronted, the borderline patient admits being more dependent on her boyfriend than she wishes to be, that when she lets herself think about him, all she does is cry. Her version of her postconfrontation depression and her feelings for her boyfriend seem to be much more congruent with what the therapist observed from her history.

Neurotic   The neurotic patient probably would not have made a suicide attempt under these circumstances; even if she had, she would enter the session and, upon inquiry from the therapist, admit more freely her dependency and mixed feelings toward her ex-boyfriend and herself.

Psychotic   When confronted with her suicide attempt, the psychotic patient denies trying to take her life. Instead, she insists that her boyfriend never mattered to her at all and claims that she simply got to a place in her life where she thought it was time to leave her body and go on to a "higher consciousness." She then becomes agitated, tearful, and somewhat disoriented and illogical when answering subsequent questions.

Example 2   A 25-year-old man, still living with his parents, speaks glowingly of his mother: "She's wonderful, participates in community affairs, and gives unstintingly of her time to others." But midway through the interview, he says that she forgot his birthday. He also mentions that she refused to spend time with him after the breakup of his recent love relationship. He, also, seems unaware of the contradiction in how he presents her—so loving but somehow so neglectful.

Borderline   When confronted, the borderline patient admits that he has ignored his mother's forgetfulness in his haste to consider her as a "perfect mother." He concedes that some elements in their relationship hurt him but that he has been unwilling to recognize the contradictions until now, for reasons he does not understand.

Neurotic   If the young man were neurotic, he would have an integrated but pathological view of the relationship between an adult and his parents. He might say of his mother:

> Mom is a wonderful woman in many ways, but she just isn't a very caretaking type of mother. She expects me to do my own laundry and cook my own meals. I feel I am her son—and a man—and as long as I am in the house, she owes it to me to look after these basic needs. They are a woman's job. She acts hurt when I tell her so, and I end up feeling guilty and angry at her for putting me in this position.

Psychotic   The psychotic patient would either decompensate upon confrontation or cling to his opinions, despite contradictory evidence, while at the same time showing increasing cognitive disorganization, affective withdrawal, or emotional storminess.

Primitive Defensive Mechanisms Centering on Splitting

Borderline individuals tend to use primitive defenses, which make an immediate interpersonal impact on others. Not all theorists, however, agree with Kernberg's position that primitive defense mechanisms are an essential criterion of the borderline personality. Kernberg (1984) views this criterion as less elegant and less easily identified in a few sessions than is identity diffusion.

Persons with borderline or psychotic structures rely on primitive defenses of splitting, idealization, denial, projective identification, omnipotence, and devaluation (Kernberg 1975a, 1976a, 1977b). These defenses "protect the ego from conflicts by means of dissociating or actively keeping apart contradictory experiences of the self and significant others" while allowing both to remain in the person's awareness (Kernberg 1977b, p. 107), but this occurs at the cost of weakening ego functioning and adaptive effectiveness. When confronted, borderline individuals can acknowledge their dichotomous thinking but often seem surprisingly indifferent to this contradiction. Strong positive or negative affects appear to dominate cognitions and to eliminate cognitive discrimination; thus, strong contradictory and alternating affects often alert the clinician to the presence of cognitive splitting.

Psychotic adults use primitive defenses to avoid disintegration or merger. Merger here refers to the intrapsychic fusion of self- and object images, subjectively experienced as dedifferentiation experiences (e.g., a patient who cannot tell whether he had spoken and said "hello" to another patient or whether that patient had spoken to him and said "hello," delusions, and hallucinations). Thus, primitive defenses support and keep identity diffuse and unintegrated in both borderline and psychotic patients, but for different reasons.

Neurotic adults' higher-level defense mechanisms keep certain information and feelings out of consciousness. They rely on such mechanisms as repression, reaction-formation, intellectualization, and rationalization. Some neurotic and healthy people, for developmental reasons not yet understood, may use primitive defenses along with higher-level defenses. This is why primitive defenses alone cannot distinguish the borderline from the neurotic adult.

Kernberg's (1976a, 1977a) definition of primitive defenses embodies the following ideas:

1. Contradictory ego states are kept separate from one another.
2. These states are alternately activated.
3. This separation reduces or eliminates anxiety related to conflict regarding contradictory images of oneself and others.
4. Patients cognitively acknowledge the different ego states but are emotionally indifferent to their contradictory state of affairs.
5. This state of indifference emotionally protects borderline adults from potential psychosis—but at the expense of a healthy life and reality orientation.

Splitting

Splitting is the central defense mechanism that supports and maintains the other primitive defense mechanisms. The most common manifestation of splitting is the division of the self or others into "all-good" or "all-bad" representations. Splitting also may be revealed by rapid shifts from an all-good to an all-bad set of affective reactions. Affect (the feeling tone accompanying ideation) is a complex subject. Basically, disordered affect and moods promote and maintain the mechanism of splitting. For the toddler such a cognitive process is considered normal, but for the adult it is considered pathological.

Developmentally, in the borderline, the self-image is properly differentiated from the object image, but the good and bad aspects of each are not blended (as in neurosis); they are kept apart and compartmentalized, and they are alternately activated. For this reason, borderline patients are not consciously aware of their ambivalence, that is, of both aspects of the self or of others (Stone 1980).

The clinical implications of splitting, as outlined by Akhtar and Byrne (1983, pp. 1014–1015), are (1) the inability to experience ambivalence, which leads to rapid devaluation and idealization of others, rapid shifts in allegiances, and generally chaotic relationships; (2) impaired decision making (e.g., certain options are passionately pursued only to be suddenly abandoned; relationships are abruptly ended only to be renewed quixotically without proper assessment; and therapy is stated enthusiastically only to be dropped upon the first sign of frustration); (3) oscillation of self-esteem (e.g., feeling great about oneself turns to self-hatred upon some small interpersonal slight or omission); (4) ego-syntonic impulsivity usually involving pleasure at the time (e.g., shoplifting, promiscuity, or substance abuse), with little guilt afterward and only a bland denial of the emotional impact or significance of the act; (5) intensification of affects (e.g., good feelings are often experienced as euphoria or exhilaration, sometimes leading to infatuation, awe, and worship of another; and bad feelings are overwhelming, rageful, and murderous or suicidal in intensity).

We use ambivalence here and elsewhere to refer to the healthy and normal ability to be simultaneously in touch with both the virtues and shortcomings of the self and others or, put differently, to experience a blended, adaptive mix of both love and aggression toward the same object. It is not used in the sense of the schizophrenic's ambivalence, as defined by Bleuler, or in the sense of obsessional ruminative worrying.

Splitting may be manifested through various external objects, which range from people, pets, and inanimate objects (such as an article of clothing in a fetish) to internal self-images. Objects, either internal or external, can be further broken down into parts, as distinct from wholes (i.e., a woman can be generally happy about herself but feel enraged toward one part of her body). For example, in extreme cases, patients may mutilate those parts of their body that they find offensive, as if they did not belong to them.

Mary Markham's splitting (when she regarded her mother as all-bad and her father as all-good) demonstrates several ways that splitting can operate. First, she split external objects (in this case, two parents) into a good one and a bad one. Then she treated each parent as a part instead of a whole person. Finally, she forced them, both in fantasy and real life, into a disharmonious relationship with each other (e.g., playing them off against each other). But when Mary was bad and called on the Megalomaniac to make her feel good and to punish the bad Baby, she was splitting internal parts of herself into good and bad segments. These four approaches exemplify splitting and, as Pruyser (1975) pointed out, show what people do to and with the objects that populate both their inner and outer worlds.

Clinical Example   A clinical example of splitting, the separation of others into all-good and all-bad parts, may be observed in the following vignette of how a particular patient created such a split environment for himself: A young man in his 20s was in outpatient treatment in a clinic. He had a psychiatrist who prescribed medication and a psychotherapist. He seemed to adore his therapist, whom he waited impatiently to see each week, but he hated his psychiatrist. During his psychotherapy sessions he told his therapist how much better he was doing at home and at work. During one brief meeting with his psychiatrist, he admitted he was spending most of his free time sleeping and was having occasional intrusive thoughts of suicide.

Splitting thus allows adults to entertain only "pure" loving or hateful reactions to the self or others. It protects good feelings toward the self or others from being contaminated by the bad, hateful feelings, just as a whole beaker of crystal-clear water can be colored gray by just a drop of black ink. For the borderline patient, one bad encounter in a long-standing good relationship can make that person and relationship worthless and bad. For the borderline, the beaker of clear water turns black whenever there is frustration or anger at another. This results in a compromised view of the world because people and their acts rarely exist in an all-good or an all-bad form.

Rapid oscillation between all-loving or all-hating states gives borderline patients an erratic, unpredictable, and impulsive quality. On the other hand, not all borderline patients engage in chaotic behavior; some adhere rigidly to one side of the split. A rigid adherence to the other's all-good state may make those borderline adults appear gullible and naive, and borderline patients who adhere inflexibly to the other's all-bad state may appear paranoid.

Pure-state reactions, regardless of whether they are loving or hateful, tend to be intense because they are not tempered by feelings from the opposite state. As people mature, as mentioned above, they rarely find real situations that call for such "all-or-nothing" reactions. It is this realization that differentiates healthy adults from those who rely on splitting as a primitive defense mechanism.

Not all clinicians agree on usage of the term splitting, but we shall use it in this commonly accepted form throughout this book.

Primitive Idealization

Primitive idealization refers to the tendency to see some objects as totally good in order to feel protected from all the bad objects or to protect good objects from one's own aggression. Thus, primitive idealization supports defensive splitting. Persons with a borderline personality often feel safe and good when they have a relationship with an idealized object. The "halo effect" of such a relationship allows borderline adults to feel whole because they often see themselves as bad or terribly vulnerable. Mary Markham's idealization of her professional friends and her therapist are examples of this mechanism. It has been hypothesized that envy usually underlies primitive idealization.

Projective Identification

Projective identification has been used in a variety of ways across the years since its original definition by Melanie Klein. Ogden's (1979) clear definition of the term is compatible with Kernberg's clinical definition:

> Projective identification ... refer[s] to a group of fantasies and accompanying object relations having to do with the ridding of the self of unwanted aspects of the self, the depositing of those unwanted 'parts' into another person; and finally, with 'recovery' of a modified version of what was extruded (p. 357)

Ogden's article outlines the several stages in this entirely unconscious process. First, there is a wish to rid oneself of a part of the self because that part is in danger of being attacked by other parts of the self. The threatened part must be safeguarded by being held inside a protective person (p. 358). The fantasy of putting a part of oneself into another person and then controlling both that person and the ejected part represents a developmental level on which the self and the object are blurred. The projector tends to feel attached to and at one with the recipient.

Second, the projector exerts real interpersonal pressure on the recipient of the projection to behave congruent with the projective fantasy. There is often an "induction phase" in the interaction (p. 359) in which the projector tests to see whether the recipient will cooperate with the projection. Ogden has stressed that projective identification does not exist when there is no pressure exerted through interpersonal interaction such that the recipient experiences pressure to think, feel, and behave in a manner in line with the projection. Even when there is such pressure, though, the recipient is still responsible for his or her own response.

Finally, the projected feelings, after being consciously or unconsciously processed by the recipient, are enacted in some type of behavior and are reinternalized by the projector. If the recipient plays out the prescribed role, the projector will remain in the old pattern. If the recipient does not play the prescribed role and behaves in a new and better way, then the projector will reinternalize a new response and will have the opportunity to learn and grow in a healthier way. There are numerous examples in Chapter 12 of Mary, John, and Sarah projecting unacceptable thoughts and feelings onto their therapist, the therapist's responses to their projections, and the patients' responses to the therapist's reactions.

Several theories, such as attribution theory and research on the induction of affects, offer empirical data that help explain projective identification. In brief, borderline individuals often have exquisite antennae out looking for someone who will accept their projections—a person who unconsciously resonates with them (Carter and Rinsley 1977). Because most people have some conflicts in the major areas of life (Am I a good person? Can I rescue others? Am I really bad and defective?), accepting such projections is not too difficult for the average person. Therefore, when the projections resonate with internally felt conflicts, recipients often accept them willingly, at least at first.

In this situation, projectors are really having a relationship with a part of themselves. This dovetails with Winnicott's (1953) notion of the child's use of transitional objects, such as temporary imaginary friends, because they are less threatening than real relations. One might say that adults who rely heavily on projective identification are unable to have a relationship with a separate, autonomous other and instead have a relationship with a projection of part of the self (e.g., a transitional object).

Projective identification can be either negative or positive. In our culture, positive aspects of this mechanism are manifested, for example, as empathy for others, vicarious satisfaction, romantic experiences, and emotional-poetic communication in literature and the arts. A negative manifestation would be pathological disavowal of one's own unacceptable images and feelings, such as Adolf Hitler's projection of his own defects onto the Jews.

Kernberg (1977b, p. 109) outlined this common paradigm of projective identification:

1. Projection onto another of an impulse while still experiencing that impulse.
2. Fear of the person onto whom the impulse was projected.
3. Need to control the other person because of the projected impulse.

Because the projected image/feelings really belong to the self, this process weakens judgment and ultimately threatens the integrity of the patient's selfhood. In addition, it creates a dangerous external object that the patient feels compelled to control in order to avoid retaliation. For example, to simplify a complex event, once Hitler projected onto the Jews, he could not bear to have them near him. He persecuted them and then began to fear that they would retaliate or contaminate him, thus leading to his systematic extermination of them during World War II.

Finally, because the projection is really part of the patient, who now identifies with the recipient of the projection, the borderline adult needs to control the object in order to stay in contact with it and the projection (unlike pure projection, in which the projector feels alienated from the recipient). This process eventually leads to severe confusion about the attributes of self and the attributes of the object—for example, just who is feeling the hate and revenge and who is wishing harm to the other.

Other theorists have reported important variations on this theme. Grotstein (1981, p. 179) commented that patients who use projective identification often tend to idealize others. Consequently, patients project their own valuable, creative feelings at the expense of their self-esteem. Additionally, he noted that some patients identify with their own sick selves and assign their healthy parts to an idealized other for safekeeping. Grotstein also observed that both borderline adults who project negative, unwanted qualities and those who project positive qualities usually enter into difficult relationships with others. These relations are marred by manipulation, coercion, and seduction, in which the other is used as a collusive partner in conforming to the way the projector sees him or her. Eventually the recipient may feel stifled or sullied and may end the relationship.

Novick and Kelly (1970) saw projective identification as a defense mechanism in which parts of the self are externalized in order to avoid narcissistic injury. As a result of attributing devalued characteristics to the other, the patients identify the object as being unlike the self and often coerce the object into behaving like the projection.

For example, John Elliott's father, who saw himself as "macho," repeatedly quizzed John about any adolescent homosexual exploits, a practice that probably could be traced to the unconscious sexual desires that the hypermasculine father found unacceptable.

Grotstein (1981) pointed out that many borderline patients engage in yet a different type of projective identification—intrapsychic projection—or split personalities within the psyche. In this case, patients seem to use "dissociated twin selves as targets for projection" (p. 136). Sometimes the projection is so complete that they totally lose "the capacity to experience the experience" (p. 132).

Striking examples of both processes were obvious in Mary Markham: only the Baby could feel dependent; Mary never did. Mary split off some mental content (dependency) and projected it onto the Baby. She then disowned the Baby, saying that it was a separate person and that she never felt dependent. Grotstein (1981) calls this "projective *dis*identification" (p. 131).

In psychotherapy, the therapist needs to experience the projection, identify it, and contain it. Patients (like children) feel safe only when they know that the therapist (mother) remains unchanged (e.g., does not become bad, helpless, or aggressive) (Malin and Grotstein 1966). At a deeper level, patients desperately need to be reassured that they have not created a potential aggressor who will persecute them for their "badness," even though some patients consciously feel better after creating a hostile other. Therefore, if the therapist remains unchanged while acknowledging the projection (thereby neutralizing it), the patients will have a greater sense of safety and confidence in the therapeutic relationship (Grotstein 1981, p. 125).

Primitive Denial

Primitive denial is manifested by disavowing the existence of contradictory ego states; thus, denial reinforces splitting. Persons who utilize primitive denial are aware that their thoughts, feelings, and perceptions about themselves or others at one time are completely opposite to those they have had at other times, but this knowledge has no emotional relevance and cannot influence their present feelings (Kernberg 1977b, p. 110). Borderline adults may adopt a type of emotional *la belle indifference* or complete lack of concern or anxiety about an immediate conflict or danger in their lives. Patients may convey a cognitive awareness of the situation but deny its emotional importance. For example, a patient whose wrists are still bandaged after being slashed with a razor blade may act unconcerned about the attempt. In more mature denial, the emotional relevance of what has been denied has never been present in consciousness and remains repressed (Kernberg 1975a).

Omnipotence and Devaluation

Omnipotence and devaluation are linked to splitting operations that affect both self- and object representations. The self-representation is seen as all-powerful, omnipotent, extraordinary, and special, whereas others are seen as worthless, inferior, stupid, and incapable of love. Narcissistic personalities rely heavily on this primitive defense.

Members of special interest groups sometimes use this defense. The group idolizes certain politicians, believing that they can do no wrong. But when the group disagrees with one political action, they turn against the politician, even though he or she continues to support the group's cause in every other way.

Clinical Manifestations of Primitive Defense Mechanisms

Primitive defenses manifest themselves either in the content of the interview (including the history) or through interaction with the interviewer. Sometimes the defenses are not always obvious, but good interviewing techniques should help the therapist bring them to the surface. As Kernberg observed (1977b, p. 111), most patients try to act normal and well mannered during an interview. Aberrational behavior should be a signal to the therapist to explore further.

The clinician can observe *splitting* by talking to the patients about themselves and others, work, school, family, and sexual life. Are there mutually contradictory images of self or significant others? Do the patients have an unrealistic, rigid image of themselves and others? Is the patients' world populated by some all-good and some all-bad people, including the interviewer? All of these examples demonstrate splitting. Because splitting protects borderline adults from ambivalence, Kernberg believes that confrontation of splitting leads to anxiety, followed immediately by better functioning, both cognitively and affectively. Because splitting protects psychotic individuals against fragmentation, they usually decompensate upon confrontation and experience affective as well as cognitive disorganization (e.g., loosening of associations, total withdrawal, increased delusions). But some splitting is too rigid to yield to confrontation, and so patients who continue to deny the obvious split may have adopted a psychotic thought process. Of course, the therapist should be certain that the patients' beliefs are wrong.

Primitive idealization may show itself in the history as well as how patients treat the interviewer if the correct technique is employed. Does the interviewer become an omnipotent figure who will protect the patients against other bad people? Do the patients talk about others as if they were omnipotent, godlike, and all-loving? If so, primitive idealization may be at work.

Projective identification also may be assessed in other ways during the interview. For example, patients may accuse the interviewer of being seductive, when they are actually trying to induce seductiveness in the interviewer by acting coy, being ingratiating, and exhibiting parts of their body.

When aggression is constantly being projected, confrontation will help distinguish between paranoid personalities and paranoid schizophrenia. Paranoid schizophrenia can be identified because confrontation will precipitate an immediate loss of reality (Kernberg 1977b, p. 110).

Grotstein (1981) reported that persistent "confusion, disorientation, autistic detachment, claustrophobia and agoraphobia, and fantasies of controlling or being controlled by objects" are red flags indicating projective identification (pp. 123-124). He found that all the phobias represent a complex projection onto others or the environment and that they often represent instances of projective identification. Although the therapist may have little difficulty getting patients to discuss their phobias, it usually takes months or years to clarify the causes. The presence of phobias, however, should alert the interviewer to explore these areas further, and theoretically this makes sense because confusion and disorientation do represent a loss of personal boundaries. When so many thoughts and feelings have been projected out, patients feel empty because their stock of thoughts and feelings have literally been depleted. After such depletion, particularly sensitive patients may believe that they have become transparent and that others can actually see into their brain and read their evil thoughts. People who are vulnerable to this mechanism are often highly manipulative and dependent in their relationships because they feel so panicked and helpless.

The discrepancy between the life situation and how the patient talks about it will highlight *denial*. For example, the patient who recently lost her job and has just attempted suicide talks nonchalantly, as though nothing has happened. She tells the interviewer about all the gifts she wants to buy her family when they come to visit, although she has no money.

Omnipotence and devaluation are revealed in the way patients talk about themselves, talk about and interact with others, and act during the interview. A haughty and grandiose self-presentation combined with a devaluation of others (and their kindness and assistance) is often obvious in the interview.

Using Primitive Defense Mechanisms to Distinguish Personality Structure

The mechanisms discussed above are considered to be lower-level defenses and are used by either borderline or psychotic patients. Neurotic persons generally do not use them, relying instead on repression and other higher-level defenses. The presence of lower-level defense mechanisms, therefore, usually indicates either a borderline or psychotic personality organization. The therapist then must attempt to distinguish between the two by confronting the patient. Borderline adults will exhibit improved functioning when confronted; psychotic persons will regress, disintegrate, and/or experience merger with the therapist.

Maintenance of Reality Testing

Reality testing is an ego function that permits the differentiation between borderline and psychotic organization. Paraphrasing Bellak, Hurvich, and Gediman (1973), reality testing is

1. The ability to distinguish self from nonself.
2. The ability to distinguish between ideas/images (intrapsychic stimuli) and perceptions (outside stimuli).
3. The ability to assess accurately one's own actions, emotions, and thoughts vis-à-vis the cultural and scientific context in which one lives.

Frosch (1964) differentiates three types of involvement with reality: (1) the relation to reality (e.g., adaptive social behavior), (2) the feeling of reality (e.g., not experiencing alterations in reality such as depersonalization and derealization), and (3) the capacity to test reality (as described above). In borderline patients, all of these functions may be impaired, but the best preserved should be the capacity to test reality.

As Goldstein (1981a) found, borderline patients may appear to have a superficially good adaptation to reality, seeming intact and normal in work or school. But a closer examination shows a less-than-optimal adaptation, and it is often difficult for borderline individuals to maintain the adaptation consistently across time. Their sense of reality is often impaired by either transient or chronic feelings of depersonalization, derealization, or estrangement, a point with which Kernberg concurs. Finally, reality testing per se should be intact except at times of stress, drug or alcohol usage, or transference psychosis, when there can be transient loss of reality testing. Kernberg concludes that among the three types of involvement with reality, reality testing remains the most important criterion. Alterations in the subjective experience of reality and an alteration of relationship with reality, which may appear in any patient from the neurotic to the psychotic, are of diagnostic importance only in extreme forms (Kernberg 1980c, p. 1084).

Clinical Manifestations of Reality Testing

Kernberg (1977b) clinically defined reality testing as

1. "The absence of hallucinations or delusions." A *hallucination* is an apparent perception of an external object when no such object is present (e.g., hearing a voice when no one is there). A *delusion* is a false belief that is maintained despite incontrovertible evidence to the contrary. Further, the belief is not one held by other members of one's subculture (e.g., a commonly held superstition).
2. "The absence of grossly inappropriate or bizarre affect, thought content, or behavior."

3. "The capacity to empathize with and clarify other people's observations of what to them seem inappropriate or puzzling aspects of the patient's affects, behavior, or thought content within the context of ordinary social interactions" (p. 111).

Because everyone is capable of a transient loss of reality testing under stress, these brief lapses must be differentiated from those of pervasive loss of reality testing.

How patients talk about past or present "hallucinations" may be significant in determining whether they can maintain reality testing. When patients say they have had hallucinations (e.g., God talking to them) in the past, the therapist needs to ask, "What do you think about that?" If the patient responds, "Nothing much. God just isn't talking to me now," clearly there is still a loss of reality testing. On the other hand, if the patient says, "I must have been crazy to think God talked to me, and I don't think it now," reality testing probably has been regained (Kernberg 1984). Pseudohallucinations (strongly experienced transient sense perceptions for which there are no external stimuli and the patient knows this) are common in the lower-level borderline structure, but patients should be aware that the experience was only illusory, that it went on inside their heads rather than externally. They should be able to discuss their pseudohallucinations as an event they now understand to be intrapsychic in nature (not real), although they may lack insight into its causes (Frosch 1970). Therefore, in order to ascertain the degree of reality testing, the therapist should clarify any hallucinatory or delusional experiences. A continued firm belief in the hallucinations represents a marked loss of reality maintenance. The massive domination of the patients' lives by the pseudohallucinations, although the patients acknowledge that they are false, would be considered a soft sign of a thought disorder or a mild loss of reality maintenance.

As mentioned in Chapter 1, a soft sign of a thought disorder refers to a milder version of one of the formal thought disorders (e.g., delusions, hallucinations, concrete thinking, circumstantiality). It is still a form of affect-dominated (autistic) thinking, however at a more subtle level, and includes magical thinking. Certain forms of magical thinking (e.g., superstitiousness, ESP capacities) are encountered in many borderline patients. Stone (1980) noted that the mildest examples of magical thinking occur when both the element of bizarreness is absent and the person is "aware" that the belief is not true, although he or she may feel unable to break the habit of mind. For example, a woman patient had a fear of germs picked up in public places; she feared the germs would get in her eyes and make her blind. Although she knew the probability of this happening was remote, she worried about it constantly, and it affected her willingness to travel, eat out, or shop.

It is important to pursue all aberrant responses until the interviewer understands their function and can rule out misinterpretations. For example, many psychotic persons can maintain appropriate behavior during interviews. Only occasionally might aberrant responses such as rhyming, punning, malapropisms, and other speech oddities punctuate their other-wise appropriate behavior.

Finally, patients should be able to understand that their behavior perplexes others and may even cause them discomfort. Their complete inability to assume the role of others or to view the situation as others see it is considered a massive loss of reality maintenance. For example, a patient's gross inability to understand how his spouse might feel hurt or angry about his suicide attempt or how his erratic behavior affects friends and community demonstrates a lack of reality maintenance.

Using Reality Maintenance to Distinguish Personality Structure

Both neurotic and borderline individuals are able to maintain reality testing. They can differentiate self from nonself as well as thoughts and fantasies from externally based perceptions and stimuli. However, unlike neurotics, borderline adults are not easily able to evaluate themselves and others realistically and in depth. Borderline adults have transient alterations in their feelings of reality because of stress or, frequently, drug or alcohol abuse. When borderline persons have a psychotic episode, it should be brief with a quick return to the previous level of functioning. If there is not a quick return to the previous level of functioning, the borderline diagnosis should be questioned. If the psychosis occurs in the therapeutic relationship (transference psychosis), it should appear mainly during the therapy and not affect the person's life outside the therapy.

Psychotic patients, on the other hand, are almost totally unable to test reality. Consequently, reality testing is the criterion that differentiates borderline from psychotic adults.

NONSPECIFIC STRUCTURAL CHARACTERISTICS

Nonspecific structural characteristics may or may not be present in the borderline individual and are not required to make the diagnosis.

Ego Weakness

Theoretically, it is assumed that the following three areas are compromised because of the failure of both ego and superego integration, because such integration tames the "immediacy" with which needs must be met and allows the individuals to use various ongoing activities for sublimatory purposes instead of resorting to direct discharge and the need for instant gratification.

Anxiety tolerance refers to the way patients handle increased stress without developing psychological symptoms or regressing. The degree to which persons can experience strong emotions, fantasies, or images without acting on them against their best interests is known as *impulse control*. *Sublimation* refers to the degree to which patients can develop creative outlets rather than continuously pursuing only instant gratification or survival interests.

Clinical Manifestations of Ego Weakness

Patient histories often are a better source of information about ego weakness than are brief interviews (Kernberg 1977b). Histories, for example, often reveal how well patients handle anxiety-provoking situations such as marriage, illness, and job changes. The person who frequently goes on drinking or eating binges, overspends, is sexually promiscuous, or acts on impulse is said to have poor impulse control. Kernberg observed that some patients may have good impulse control in all but one area. In these cases the impulsivity may show up in oscillating, contradictory behavior, such as a patient who is sexually impulsive and promiscuous on one day and fearful of sexual expression and moralistic on the next day. The patient who easily becomes depressed or anxious in the face of any additional stressful encounters is described as having a poor tolerance for anxiety. The person who cannot find meaningful work, a hobby, or other interests to occupy time is said to have poor sublimatory channeling. Some borderline patients can find satisfaction in creative activities but cannot sustain any interest in day-to-day routine. During the interview, how patients handle a tactful confrontation and manage their anxiety provides clues to their anxiety tolerance and impulse control.

Using Ego Weaknesses to Distinguish Personality Structure

Neurotic adults have fairly good ego controls; borderline and psychotic patients usually have poor ego controls. It is important to understand that ego weakness is not diagnostically conclusive. Although it may often be present, it is not always found in all borderline individuals.

Lack of Superego Integration

The degree to which patients voluntarily adhere to ethical principles in the absence of external control indicates their superego integration (Kernberg 1977b, p. 113). This might be represented on a continuum with honesty and integrity at one end and reliance on exploitation, manipulation, or mistreatment of others at the other.

Bellak and his associates (1973), citing Brenner, list five superego functions:

1. Approval or disapproval of actions and wishes on the grounds of moral consideration.
2. Critical self-observation.
3. Self-punishment.
4. Demand for reparation or repentance of wrongdoing ("an eye for an eye").
5. Self-praise or self-love as a reward for virtuous or desirable thoughts and actions. (p. 36)

Extremes of any of these categories can lead to pathology.

Clinical Manifestations of Lack of Superego Integration

The level of superego integration can be difficult to ascertain. Usually it is best (while taking histories) to find out how patients deal with their superego functioning. It is important to determine whether they have been overly lenient or particularly harsh on themselves. Also, patients' self-reports of lying must be examined because the therapist's ability to help them is based on the assumption that accurate information is being provided. If patients withhold information, the therapist–patient relationship will be compromised, and change will probably not take place.

For purposes of diagnosis, this structural criterion is considerably less reliable than the others. Neurotic adults have well-integrated but excessively severe superegos. Borderline and psychotic patients have unintegrated superegos that are characterized by primitive, sadistic, and idealized features. Some people with borderline organization, however, also have good superego integration despite pathology in identity integration, object relations, and choice of object (Kernberg 1977b, p. 114).

Using Lack of Superego Integration to Distinguish Personality Structure

On the healthy end of the personality structure continuum are those persons who manifest ethical values in their everyday lives and respond to difficult choices with modulated, goal-directed responses. They are self-critical (within reason) of deviations from these internal values, and they are able to maintain honesty and integrity without external control and to limit their self-punishment.

Farther down the scale are neurotic persons, who experience excessive guilt or depression over daily experiences, such as turning down a date or saying no to family invitations. They berate themselves long after healthy persons would stop.

At the opposite pole of the continuum are several manifestations of pathological responses as seen in borderline and psychotic people. One example might be persons with a sadistic, primitive superego who mutilate themselves because they acted "dumb" in a social situation. Another group consistently manipulates and exploits others without regard to their fate.

Superego functions can be a difficult dimension to assess because many borderline patients have good overall superego integration, except for unexpected "holes." An example of such a hole would be a highly honest person who impulsively shoplifts on one occasion. It is important that the therapist learn about these inconsistencies and not be beguiled by the patients' apparent good functioning in this area. Despite its lack of reliability in defining borderline organization, Kernberg finds the quality of both object relations and superego to be the best prognostic criteria in long-term therapy.

Genetic-Dynamic Characteristics

Genetic-dynamic characteristics can be inferred from the patient's history and emergent themes in the therapy. *Dynamic* refers to competing, conflicting forces that prevent an idea or feeling from becoming conscious or that allow it to enter consciousness only in disguised form. *Genetic* is used here to describe how these conflicts develop from multiple origins in childhood. According to Kernberg (1977b, pp. 115–117), the following themes may be seen in persons with a borderline personality organization.

Clinical Manifestations of Genetic-Dynamic Characteristics

Aggressivization of Oedipal Conflicts

To borderline adults, the image of the Oedipal rival is terrifying and destructive, not just a competitor to be defeated. The fear of castration is exaggerated, and prohibitions against sexual relations take on a primitive, even paranoid quality.

Idealization of Heterosexual or Homosexual Love Object

Idealizations of the heterosexual or homosexual love object are positive or negative Oedipal reactions. They are exaggerated, and have marked defensive functions against primitive rage. They can surface at any time, causing rapid reversals from love to hate. Mary Markham, for example, idealized her mother while devaluing her father. But in the middle phase of her psychotherapy, she developed a brief but intense hatred of her mother.

Complex Intermingling of Parental Images Projected onto Therapist

Borderline individuals seem to select a hodgepodge of traits, behaviors, and attitudes from both parents, condense both father–mother images, and project them willy-nilly onto the therapist. In contrast, neurotic persons' transference elements are more closely related to the developments of the past and the traits or behavior of each parent.

Genital Strivings Taking on Pre-Oedipal Functions

For borderline adults, sex acquires aspects of nurturance and maternal function rather than being merely a pleasurable adult experience. The maternal longings underlying sexuality are commonly seen in promiscuity, when these adults desperately want to be held and comforted more than they desire sex. Another example of this is the impotent male who fears the vagina. Perhaps he may unconsciously associate it with a mouth showing bared teeth (oral aggression), which he associates with a withholding or attacking mother. Both are pre-Oedipal problems that influence this man's genital functioning.

Premature Oedipalizing of Pre-Oedipal Issues

In the Oedipal triangle, the son is attached to his mother and fears that his father will punish him for the attachment. The opposite situation occurs in the Elektra triangle, in which the daughter becomes attached to the father and fears that the mother will punish her. Oedipal problems center on the competition in the triad and occur prematurely for borderline individuals. For example, when a girl has to turn to her father for "mothering" because of her mother's inattention or invasiveness, the daughter's attachment feelings (pre-Oedipal problems) become sexualized because she normally experiences sexual feelings toward her father at a later time. These sexual feelings, although premature, are caused by so much closeness to the father. The daughter feels great guilt for abandoning her mother (no matter how inadequate the mother has been). Consequently, the girl is afraid to love anyone else for fear of being punished for "abandoning" her mother. These complications were apparent in Sarah Gardner's case when she turned to her father during her Oedipal (Elektra) stage.

There are several types of pre-Oedipally distorted Oedipal conflicts, and the reader is referred to Kernberg (1977b) because they have more significance for the course of treatment than for the diagnosis.

Using Genetic-Dynamic Characteristics to Distinguish Personality Structure

These themes do not occur in neurotic adults, although they can appear in either borderline or psychotic patients.

Level of Character Pathology and Borderline Personality Organization

Kernberg (1970) noted that specific character pathology can often alert the clinician to borderline pathology and can be ranked according to the level of severity, by using ego-analytic criteria. Briefly, Kernberg (1984) stated that the lower-level character disorders—paranoid, schizoid, hypomanic, antisocial, and lower-level narcissistic—are typically borderline. The intermediate-level character disorders—sadomasochistic, infantile, and better-functioning narcissistic—may be either borderline or neurotic, and the structural features must be carefully diagnosed. Typically, the obsessive-compulsive, hysterical, and depressive-masochistic personalities are neurotic. Again, although the clinician should not make the borderline diagnosis based just on the personality subtype, the subtype can often alert the clinician to the possible level of personality organization.

SUMMARY OF THE FOUR CRITERIA

Borderline refers to a group of individuals whose diagnosis lies on a continuum between neurosis and psychosis. Borderline adults have stable pathologic personality organizations that are characterized by (1) identity diffusion, (2) an ego structure consisting of reliance on primitive defenses, and (3) the maintenance of reality testing. Their personalities are stable and do not alternate between neurosis and psychosis (except for brief, transient psychotic episodes). In addition, they can have various ego weaknesses, poor superego integration, and certain characteristic psychodynamic-genetic patterns. The borderline personality organization is considered pathologic because of the unintegrated identity, primitive defenses, and various ego weaknesses. Borderline adults thus have both descriptive symptoms and structural aspects that distinguish them from neurotic and psychotic individuals. Table 3–3 reviews the structural criteria for neurotic, borderline, and psychotic personality organizations.

The first step in a structural diagnosis is to differentiate the neurotic from the borderline and psychotic patient. Patients who have identity integration (lack identity diffusion), use higher-level defenses, and are able to test reality can be identified as neurotic and may be eliminated from

**Table 3-3   Comparison of Structural Criteria for Neurotic,
Borderline, and Psychotic Personality Organizations**

Neurotic

Identity Integration

Self- and object-representations are clear, separated.
Integrated Identity: Contradictory images of self and others are integrated into in-depth representations.

Defensive Operations

Defenses (e.g., repression, reaction formation, rationalization, etc.) are higher level.
Defenses protect from intrapsychic conflict.
Interpretation improves functioning.

Reality Testing

Reality testing (e.g., self from nonself, fantasy from external events) is good.
Others can be evaluated realistically and in depth.

Borderline

Identity Integration

Self- and object representations are clearly separated.
Identity Diffusion: Contradictory images of self and others are not integrated into in-depth representations.

Defensive Operations

Defenses (e.g., splitting, projective identification, idealization, devaluation, denial, omnipotence) are mainly lower level.
Defenses protect from intrapsychic conflict.
Interpretation improves functioning.

Reality Testing

Reality testing (e.g., self from nonself, fantasy from external events) is good.
Sense of reality (e.g., depersonalization) and relationship with reality are distorted.
Self and others cannot be evaluated in depth.

Psychotic

Identity Integration

Self- and object-representations are poorly separated.
Identity Diffusion: Contradictory images of self and others are not integrated into in-depth representations.

Defensive Operations

Defenses (e.g., splitting, projective identification, idealization and devaluation, denial, omnipotence) are mainly lower level.
Defenses protect from decompensation and fragmentation and/or self-object merger.
Interpretation promotes regression.

Reality Testing

Reality testing is poor.
Sense of reality (e.g., depersonalization) and relationship with reality are distorted.
Self and others cannot be evaluated in depth.

Source: Adapted from Kernberg, O. F. (1981). Structural Interviewing, *Psychiatric Clinics of North America*, 4(1): 169-195. Copyright 1981 by W. B. Saunders Co. Reprinted by permission.

further consideration. The therapist then can apply two criteria to distinguish between the borderline and psychotic personality organizations. First, borderline patients maintain some ability to distinguish between self- and object representations, whereas psychotics' self-representations and object representations are poorly delineated, with delusional identity or self-object merger occurring. Borderline patients sometimes do change roles with the therapist, attributing to the therapist some of their own characteristics while acting like their object images and then reversing the roles; but this is not true psychotic merger (when patients think they and the therapist are one entity). Second, borderline adults maintain reality testing, whereas psychotic patients lose reality testing, both overtly and subtly.

Neither neurotic nor psychotic adults have all three specific structural characteristics. Therefore, patients who exhibit all three structural characteristics can be identified as having borderline personality organizations. For Kernberg, identity diffusion is one of the hallmarks of the borderline personality organization.

Thus we can say that borderline individuals differ from psychotics in that the borderline almost always maintains reality testing. Borderlines differ from neurotic patients because borderline adults rely more on splitting than repression. Table 3-3 shows how these characteristics help the therapist differentiate among the three personality structures.

DIAGNOSING THREE CLINICAL CASES USING STRUCTURAL DIAGNOSIS

Case I: Mary Markham

Specific Structural Characteristics

Identity Diffusion   Mary Markham manifested identity diffusion, which showed up most obviously during regressive periods and when she perceived that others were "out-of-sync" with her. There were many sharp, contradictory, and rigid cleavages in the way she saw herself and others. She oscillated between normal mood and depression without understanding the cause, thereby implying contradictory behavior. In addition, her limited interpersonal relationships appeared both intense and manipulative, although she denied the importance of the other person or even the act of manipulation.

Mary had distinct parts of herself: the Megalomaniac part "tells me to hurt myself" and the Baby part "is so needy—crying and crying." Confrontation revealed that she believed these parts did indeed belong to her (rather than being separate outside agencies or people possessing her), and the feelings they engendered overwhelmed her and made her feel helpless. She was often unable to state her own feelings, so she attributed many feelings to the Megalomaniac and the Baby instead of to her phenomenological self.

Mary's descriptions of her parents were shallow and stereotyped: her mother was "perfect and totally understanding," and her father was "weak and ineffectual."

When I confronted Mary about her obvious dependency on her mother (in order to test her reality maintenance), she denied it and became upset. "I don't like to see myself as dependent upon my mother—we're just extremely close, she's the only one who understands me." At this point, Mary became silent and, upon exploration, admitted she was angry with me for reasons she did not understand. She voluntarily returned to the topic later in the session and observed, "Maybe I really am dependent on her" and began to cry. The following week she returned to the session, saying that she could not remember what we talked about but was upset all week. Thus, her reality testing was precariously maintained.

Although Mary had a master's degree, she felt unconnected to any career plans and was working at a semiskilled job, confused and anxious about her future plans.

Self-assertion or decision making in almost any aspect of her life raised enormous conflicts, anger, and anxiety, so Mary stayed home, doing nothing and relating to few people other than her parents. She had no friends. She was afraid to reveal her real thoughts and feelings to her coworkers, although she could not explain why she felt this way.

She hated being female because "women are treated as inferior to men" and had never been able to experience or integrate sexuality into her self-concept.

Conclusion   Mary Markham did not meet the identity integration criteria for neurotic functioning. Therefore, she met the criteria for either the borderline or the psychotic level of functioning. She met the criteria for identity diffusion in several ways by manifesting sharp cleavages in the way she saw herself and others at times of crisis as well as other selected moments and a false, compliant facade at times of noncrisis, to the point of lacking any awareness of her own wishes or feelings.

Primitive Defenses   Mary relied on many primitive defenses. Using primitive denial (disavowal), she complained about her mother's bossiness but immediately claimed her mother was perfect, forgetting what she had just said. Primitive denial also was revealed when she doubted that she would really cease to exist if she died. Mary employed primitive idealization (of professionals and mother) and devaluation (of people who failed her, particularly male physicians). She relied on splitting (mother is good and father is bad) and internal splitting into twin selves, each with a specific disowned feeling or experience associated with it—Baby feels dependent; Megalomaniac feels elated, powerful, and omnipotent.

Confrontation of these defenses frequently led Mary to feel anxious or to withdraw, although cognitively she could admit the validity of the confrontation. Occasionally she regressed immediately after confrontation—feeling depersonalized or distrustful and wanting to go home and overeat or sleep (which she then did).

Conclusion   Mary Markham's level of defenses ranked her as either borderline or psychotic.

Maintenance of Reality Testing   Mary presented in the initial and subsequent interviews as oriented, lucid, and intelligent (IQ estimated to be 125). She related appropriately while hinting (in an intriguingly distant, subtle manner) to the therapist as how to relate to her. She had no past or current history of delusions or hallucinations.

Several observations were made immediately about Mary's reality testing. She believed that she and her mother had ESP. She seemed oblivious to the impact of her serious suicide attempts on her family or the therapy and neither acknowledged nor appreciated the sacrifices her family had made to look after her. Finally, she seemed unaware of the many contradictions in her feelings and behavior (e.g., stating "I am a fairly independent person" and yet continuing to live at home and be supported by her parents). How did the Megalomaniac and the Baby, both of whom she talked about as if they were separate people inhabiting her body, fit with reality? And did she really believe she would not die during her latest suicide attempt?

Early in the sessions, I made tactful confrontations to test whether these were delusional beliefs. Mary was always able to acknowledge cognitively the confrontation and its basis in reality, although at the following session she often reported feeling disrupted emotionally during the week or distrustful of me.

Conclusion   Mary's reality testing was impaired (showing soft signs of a thought disorder) but not so severely as to be categorized as psychotic. When confronted, she could acknowledge the reality of the confrontation, although it did occasionally precipitate some regressive behavior. Thus, Mary maintained her reality testing adequately enough to be seen as borderline rather than psychotic.

Nonspecific Structural Characteristics

Nonspecific Ego Weaknesses   Mary Markham had all the nonspecific ego weaknesses. She was particularly impulsive when depressed (e.g., overeating, overspending). She mutilated herself and attempted suicide. Her anxiety tolerance was low. She rarely allowed herself to reach out to others for soothing, relying instead on petting her cats or overeating. She did have some sublimatory channels—pastimes of cooking and reading.

Conclusion   Mary's nonspecific ego weaknesses were sufficiently severe that she met this criterion for borderline or psychotic personality organization.

Lack of Superego Integration   In addition to Mary's identity diffusion, I could also see spotty integration of her superego. Overall, she was moral, ethical, and honest, generally living her values except for some notable exceptions for which she felt little guilt—her suicide attempts to manipulate others and take revenge on them. Although her motivation was apparent to others, Mary herself was unaware of her revengeful behavior. She admitted deliberately lying to her therapist about hoarding pills but seemed indifferent to having done so. She allowed her parents to support her but continually got herself into debt, with no regard as to how this would affect them.

The Megalomaniac appeared to be a primitive and sadistic superego figure that punished her for making the slightest mistakes at work or for being dumb. This part also told her she should die.

Conclusion   Mary clearly did not have an integrated, tamed, or realistic superego. Her primitive, sadistic, unrealistic superego was so punitive and at times so disabling (convincing her to kill herself) that she qualified for the borderline or psychotic level of functioning in this category.

Genetic-Dynamic Characteristics   Mary Markham's history showed many of the characteristic borderline themes, as outlined by Kernberg. She idealized her mother (homosexual love object), and her limited contact with males early in adulthood was simply for caretaking. Her sexuality was undeveloped, and she denied even having sexual feelings. Competitive issues with others stirred up enormous rage, mainly at losing a significant other that she regarded as a need-gratifying object.

Summary of Her Structural Diagnosis   Mary's level of functioning was definitely not neurotic because she manifested identity diffusion. At times her reality testing appeared defective, but it was not so severe that she could be called psychotic. In my opinion, Mary did not meet the criteria for schizophrenia because she lacked flattening of affect or an obvious thought disorder such as loosening of associations or delusions. Therefore, Mary Markham met the structural criteria for a borderline personality disorder.

Case II: John Elliott

Specific Structural Characteristics

Identity Diffusion   John Elliott manifested identity diffusion, substantiated by his chaotic and contradictory behavior. Early in his treatment he stated openly, "I don't know who I am, what I want, what I even feel." Since leaving the military, he had been aimless, failing in school and working in a series of low-level jobs. He had been involved with a series of women who appeared to use him while he idealized them, and he unconsciously devalued them after they left him.

John's sexual identity was confused, and he had momentary confusions about whether he was female or male. He had two distinctive ego states—being hurt sexually (victim state) and hurting others (aggressor state, which he only fantasized).

In addition to obvious contradictory behaviors toward himself and others, which John clearly could not explain, he also presented a false, compliant self to the world in order to obtain love. Underneath this front, he was confused as to what he really felt and often was angry that he *had* to comply and appease others.

John saw himself as bad and worthless, demonstrating the hysterical defense of "all that is bad is inside and all that is good is outside" (Fairbairn 1952). This defense operated with everyone but his father, who was "very bad." Confrontation of this behavior led John to agree, "I know I am not all bad, but I *feel* that way." Upon exploration, he was able to demonstrate some empathy for others and to understand how his behavior affected them.

Conclusion   John met the identity diffusion criterion for the borderline or psychotic level of functioning.

Primitive Defenses   John relied on many primitive defenses. Initially, his chaotic state and drug usage complicated my assessment. At the start of therapy, his most prominent defense was projection—his father was having him followed and the world was dangerous (e.g., John was projecting his own aggression onto the world and then becoming afraid).

John also used idealization (mother and other women) and devaluation (father). In addition, he relied on splitting: "I am bad—they are good." Confrontation led to his cognitive acceptance that the facts did not support that he was all bad; however, he continued to feel and hence believe that he was bad.

Conclusion John Elliott's level of defenses ranked him as borderline or psychotic.

Maintenance of Reality Testing John presented himself in the initial interview in a highly regressed state. In subsequent interviews he was oriented, logical, intelligent (IQ of 130), and personable, although somewhat clinging and dependent.

A full assessment of John's reality testing was not possible until the regressive panic had passed and his drug usage was reduced. Overall, John maintained his reality testing. Upon confrontation, he was able to acknowledge reality and to function temporarily at a higher level.

How, then, do we explain John's unwarranted suspiciousness, such as his paranoid belief that his father was having him followed? And how can we interpret the momentary sensation that his body was becoming female? His initial delusional suspiciousness seemed related to drugs, and indeed it stopped after he reduced his drug usage. His later occasional suspiciousness of others' motivations or fears of meeting acquaintances on the street were always relieved upon confrontation and clarification of his fantasies and feelings. The depersonalization episodes of body changes seemed to be examples of an altered sense of reality rather than loss of reality testing per se, because upon confrontation he was able to state that he knew the experiences were not real.

Conclusion John's reality testing was intact although somewhat impaired. He maintained enough reality testing to be seen as borderline rather than psychotic.

Nonspecific Structural Characteristics

Nonspecific Ego Weaknesses John had a number of nonspecific ego weaknesses. He was impulsive in making all life decisions, from love relationships (starting to live with a woman the day after meeting her) to drugs and homosexual acting out. His anxiety tolerance was low, and he could panic or become enraged when anxious. He had no sublimatory channels.

Conclusion John's nonspecific ego weaknesses qualified him for a borderline or psychotic diagnosis.

Lack of Superego Integration   Over the months of treatment, John proved to be an ethical and honest person, but he showed some spotty superego elements. The fact that he had considered and struggled against sexual impulses directed against young girls is one example. Certain aspects of his impulsive homosexual behavior also indicated poor superego integration. In addition, he had a punitive, sadistic superego that whipped him whenever he made a mistake or felt foolish or helpless.

Conclusion   John's spotty superego was sufficiently severe and sadistic to qualify him for a borderline ranking.

Genetic-Dynamic Characteristics   John's polymorphous sexuality, projection of and conscious fear of aggression, and clinging dependency hinted at characteristics developed by Kernberg (but were not obvious until many months into the therapy).

Summary of His Structural Diagnosis   John's level of functioning was definitely not neurotic. As with Mary, certain aspects of his reality testing were suspect. Nevertheless, he met the criteria for a borderline diagnosis and, in fact, seemed to typify the borderline patient in the literature (e.g., impulsive, angry, dependent, and needy, with severe acting-out problems).

Case III: Sarah Gardner

Specific Structural Characteristics

Identity Diffusion   Sarah Gardner's identity diffusion was somewhat less obvious than Mary's and John's. In addition, Sarah presented with more social skills than either of the other two did.

But under Sarah's charming, socially adept facade was a woman who frequently answered "I don't know" to questions about her feelings. She was uncertain about what had motivated her to leave her husband or what made her want to reconcile with him, and she seemed indifferent to the contradictions of these states. Although she had some insight into and empathy for others, she used her former husband without regard to his needs and showed only superficial guilt for her behavior. She also allowed other relationships to lapse without a second thought and was not curious as to why she had done that.

Sarah had distinct ego states implying identity diffusion—"cute little girl" or "sophisticated woman," as well as a state in which she felt "ugly . . . and bad." In other words, she felt either superior or inferior. This inferior-superior motif could be seen in her behavior toward her former husband.

Sarah also had a pronounced area of strength—her arts-and-crafts talent. Most of the time her performance in this activity was consistent both artistically and in business.

Conclusion   Sarah had enough identity diffusion to meet that criterion for either the borderline or the psychotic level of organization.

Primitive Defenses   Sarah relied on primitive defenses mainly during her love relationships. She tended to idealize and then devalue her husband. When experiencing abandonment or guilt, she also tended to devalue herself. Both are examples of splitting as a mechanism of defense. She seemed to use both denial and repression in her lack of awareness about her sexual provocativeness and her own thoughts and feelings.

Conclusion   Sarah Gardner used enough primitive defenses to be diagnosed as borderline.

Maintenance of Reality Testing   Although Sarah showed some poor interpersonal judgment, her reality testing was never in question. She had no history of hallucinations, delusions, or thought disorder, and her fantasies and dreams resembled those of neurotic patients.

Conclusion   Sarah Gardner met this criterion for either a borderline or a neurotic level of functioning.

Nonspecific Structural Characteristics

Nonspecific Ego Weaknesses   Sarah revealed areas of impulsivity (e.g., leaving her huband precipitously, drinking when depressed) as well as some areas of strength. She had good impulse control in her work and was patient and thoughtful when dealing with projects, customers, and staff.

Conclusion   Sarah showed some nonspecific ego weaknesses and could meet that criterion for a borderline level of functioning.

Superego Integration   Sarah had some spotty elements in her superego integration. For example, she felt only minimal guilt about her several extramarital affairs. In addition, she could feel devastated by criticism and then deal harshly with herself as a result.

Conclusion   Sarah had enough superego problems to warrant a borderline diagnosis for this characteristic.

Genetic-Dynamic Characteristics   These were not clear from the early material.

Summary of Her Structural Diagnosis   Sarah met the criteria for a borderline level of organization, although at a higher level than either Mary Markham or John Elliott.

A FINAL LOOK AT THE CRITERIA

Because structural diagnosis is such a fundamental contribution, theorists—including Kernberg himself—have only recently begun to question certain aspects, suggest alternatives, and propose future modifications.

Before exploring the proposed modifications, it may be useful to compare Kernberg's approach with the other major psychoanalytic approaches to diagnosis. Kernberg (1984) has made a sharp distinction between his structural approach and what he calls the psychodynamic diagnostic approach of Masterson, Meissner, Rinsley, and others. Kernberg believes that the psychodynamic approach is based on diagnosing unconscious motivations that take months of psychotherapy to ascertain, is too broad in its definition, is not linked to descriptive psychiatry, and hence cannot be researched. His approach, he reports, is based on enduring structures of the personality, is more defined, is less broad and less inclusive, is better linked to descriptive psychiatry, and thus is easier to diagnose in several meetings with patients.

But a closer examination shows that Masterson and Rinsley also consider their approaches to be structural—that certain interactions between the mother and child are internalized and become a pervasive psychodynamic that is structured in enduring patterns in the personality. It appears that the differences among these approaches are less sharp than Kernberg claims. It is true, nevertheless, that the psychodynamic approach may include a broader population of patients because many so-called neurotic patients may show the dynamics (because all humans have to struggle with the same developmental problems) and, if the dynamics were found, could be called borderline.

In regard to modifications to the structural approach, Meissner (1978a, 1978b, 1982-1983b) and Rinsley (1981b, 1982a) have independently reflected that many of the borderline adult's defective ego functions seem to operate on a continuum, subject to various degrees of severity, rather than as discrete categories. Kernberg, on the other hand, seems to regard these ego functions as either present or absent, functional or impaired. For example, he treats maintenance of reality testing as either present or absent, and at first glance this seems to make sense. Many clinicians do indeed treat it as a discriminator of the presence or absence of psychosis.

But scrutiny reveals a more subtle situation. Reality testing may be intact in certain areas of an individual's life and impaired in others; or the individual may have a "soft" impairment, not quite meeting the criteria for a loss of reality testing but not merely neurotic, either. An example of such a situation is Mary Markham's belief that she and her mother had some form of telepathic communication, even though she knew logically that this could not be so. The use of these more subtle indicators would probably result in the placement of fewer individuals with soft impairments into the psychotic level of organization. And in many ways, such subtle indicators might facilitate finer distinctions within the impairments.

Related to this first modification is the position of such theorists as Horner, Rinsley, and Searles, who reason that the borderline adults' dilemma has as its point of origin the symbiotic phase, although the developmental fixation becomes apparent only in a later developmental phase (e.g., the rapprochement subphase). If this position were correct, then one would expect to see some modest loss of reality testing (or soft signs of thought disorder) and greater confusion between self-images and object images (particularly in the interpersonal areas such as "who has done what to whom" and "who is responsible for the patient's feelings"). For Kernberg and Masterson, this state of affairs should in most cases occur in psychosis because the borderline individuals' dilemma comes from a higher stage of development than symbiosis does. For the above theorists, more leeway is possible.

Second, both Kernberg and Meissner (1982–1983b) reported that splitting is not necessarily only a borderline defense, because it also can be seen in neurotics. Additionally, borderline individuals regularly use neurotic defenses, and only in a regressive crisis may the clinician see the full flowering of all the primitive defenses (Knight 1953a). In other words, in acute borderline *states*, the clinician can get a full picture of the primitive defenses; otherwise, it may take extended evaluation and long-term psychoanalytic work for these mechanisms to be revealed. This may explain why so many clinicians have a difficult time identifying splitting in the initial interview.

Meissner (1984) also believes that in many borderline individuals, splitting shows up in more subtle ways, less as seeing the self and others as all-good or all-bad than as the sequential activation of ego states that the clinician infers are contradictory (e.g., the victim and aggressor states described by Meissner). In borderline adults these states usually alternate, both accessible in consciousness, with patients often having a more favored state. The clinician also may require some time in order to observe the splitting inherent in contradictory ego states (e.g., patient feels helpless in a session and charges that the therapist is being "mean." Two sessions later, the patient imperiously acts as if the therapist is stupid.)

Finally, Meissner (1982–1983b) found that the type of identity diffusion explained by Kernberg (sharp cleavages) was only one of several possible resolutions available to the borderline individual. Meissner believes that these cleavages may pertain more to the lower-level than to the higher-level borderline adult. In other words, not all borderline patients enter treatment admitting or even seeming as though they have contradictory views of themselves or others. Many have reached some type of compromise within their identity diffusion, by superficially imitating the values and attitudes of others (as-if personality), by developing a compliant false persona that hides their true feelings and fantasies (false self), or by withdrawing from all relationships (schizoid). Only through extended psychotherapy will the identity diffusion underlying these compromises be revealed.

Kernberg (1977b) himself has observed that the reliability of structural diagnosis and interviewing has yet to be refined. He suggested that this approach be given operational criteria so that clinicians using it on similar patients can derive similar diagnoses. To this end, he has identified several diagnostic problems that need to be addressed.

The first problem is how the clinician, using the criteria during the interview, can discriminate among chronic schizophrenic patients in remission who have sealed over, or manic-depressive illness in remission, and a borderline personality organization. This is an important issue for Kernberg, because he sees borderline as a stable category diagnosis. Although the above diagnosis might meet the criteria at certain points in remission, they do not represent the "true" borderline because they may be "borderline" only when not in the acute phases of their illness in which they are psychotic. Another problem Kernberg found (again using the criteria and interview process) is the difficulty of distinguishing between the borderline personality organization during periods of psychotic regression and the patient who is chronically psychotic. A third problem is the accurate assessment of the impact of antipsychotic and antidepressant medication on the patient's interview behavior (e.g., if medicated, will the patient still reveal the structural criteria?). Resolution of these problems will contribute to the development of a reliable and valid diagnostic basis for the borderline personality organization.

CHAPTER 4

Differential Diagnosis

The reader may wonder why the *DSM-III* method is included in a book that stresses structural diagnosis. There are several reasons for this. First, the *DSM-III* is the official diagnostic manual of the American Psychiatric Association. It is used in most mental health facilities across the country, and most clinicians are required to know it. Second, it is the diagnostic code required by most insurance companies for the reimbursement of psychotherapy and hospitalization expenses. Finally, the *DSM-III* is frequently quoted in professional literature, and most researchers on the borderline phenomena compare their own criteria against it. Thus, the student needs to know how to use the *DSM-III*, be able to compare and contrast it with other diagnostic systems, and understand its strengths and weaknesses.

The *DSM-III* operates on a multiaxial system, which requires that every case be assessed on each of five axes. Axis I pertains to clinical syndromes (e.g., substance abuse disorders, affective disorders, schizophrenic disorders); Axis II to personality disorders; Axis III to physical disorders; Axis IV to the severity of psychosocial stressors; and Axis V to the highest level of adaptive functioning during the past year. According to the *DSM-III*, a patient can have multiple diagnoses. The authors of the *DSM-III* hope that within Axis II each personality disorder is sufficiently well defined and distinctive that a patient would not have multiple personality disorder diagnoses, an issue to which we shall return later.

The *DSM-III* method is very different from Kernberg's, which defines borderline as an enduring structural level of organization, assumed to have continuity and sameness, that underlies the multifaceted clinical symptoms that change over time. The *DSM-III*'s criteria for the borderline diagnosis, on the other hand, are based on symptoms and empirical evidence. Unlike

Kernberg's procedure, the *DSM-III* attempts to avoid a commitment to any particular theory of human development or etiology; it does not try to explain either the cause of the symptoms or their relationships. Some items can be observed or reported by the patient, although the therapist may require experience with the patient across time in order to identify other items. Again, this contrasts with Kernberg's criteria, which must be inferred from observation and thus are often difficult for some clinicians to learn.

The reader should be aware of the status of empirical research into the borderline phenomenon, because it is the basis of much of the *DSM-III*. By 1980, over 20 major empirical research projects were studying borderline phenomena. These projects have helped discriminate between borderline and nonborderline patients, generating diagnostic criteria, developing various diagnostic instruments, and comparing the major diagnostic schemes.

DSM-III: BORDERLINE AND SCHIZOTYPAL PERSONALITY DISORDERS

Borderline and schizotypal personality disorders are the two diagnostic categories that cover the spectrum of behaviors considered borderline by many clinicians. Both diagnoses are included in the *DSM-III*. These diagnoses are based on the work of Spitzer and his colleagues (1979) at the New York State Psychiatric Institute. They drew up a list of items that they believed could accurately distinguish among patients diagnosed as borderline and those with other disorders. According to Stone (1980), the researchers used several sources for their items, including the work of Gunderson and Kolb (1978), Grinker and Werble (1977), Gunderson and Singer (1975), Kernberg (1975a), and Wender and his associates (1968). Then Spitzer and his colleagues (1979) devised two lists—a 17-item list that included items deemed unstable and a 9-item list that included items more characteristic of the borderline concept as developed by Kernberg, and Gunderson and Singer.

Spitzer and his colleagues (1979) asked 4,000 randomly selected members of the American Psychiatric Association to judge the two lists' discriminating ability. The 808 usable responses indicated that the 17-item list would accurately discriminate borderline from nonborderline patients 88 percent of the time, whereas the 9-item list would do so in 80.9 percent of the cases (Gunderson 1982).

Spitzer and his colleagues (1979) then identified two main usages of the term borderline as noted by Stone (1980): (1) a "constellation of relatively enduring personality features of instability and vulnerability which have important treatment and outcome correlates"; and (2) a "set of psychopatho-logical characteristics which are usually stable over time and are assumed to be genetically related to a spectrum of disorders that includes chronic schizophrenia" (p. 289). The conclusions that Spitzer and his colleagues drew from the two lists are considered controversial by many researchers. Nevertheless, these two usages were subsequently incorporated into the *DSM-III* as borderline personality disorder and schizotypal personality disorder, respectively. The inclusion of both lists accommodates the affec-tively colored borderline personality as well as the borderline patient with more schizoidlike symptoms, as defined by Wender and his associates (1968). By selecting two diagnoses, the authors of the *DSM-III* acknowl-edged that some borderline patients may have traits closer to the psychotic (e.g. schizophrenic) border and that others fall into the affective realm.

Stone (1983) noted the following differences between schizotypal and affectively unstable borderline individuals that prove helpful in making the diagnosis and in conducting treatment:

1. *Cognitive distortions.* Schizotypal patients' inability to distinguish among and rely on emotions leads them to overstress the cognitive in their efforts to cope with uncertainty. These patients, especially when paranoid mecha-nisms (e.g., projection, projective identification) are predominant, cannot stand randomness. There must be a reason for every unpleasantness, and they try to reduce every problem of daily life to a differential equation; but there are always so many variables that they become swamped with pos-sibilities and often find it easier to eschew any human relationships. Schizo-typal patients have concrete, rigid suppositions based not on their feelings or on what others do but, rather, on their own self-depreciated self-image; these rigid thoughts govern their reactions. Therefore, "reason" more than emotion goes "haywire" with them (p. 381). For the affectively ill borderline (*DSM-III* diagnosis), "emotions" more than reason go "haywire"; under the sway of strong emotions, this borderline patient will ignore facts and reality in order to maintain these feelings.

2. *Defense patterns.* There is little difference between the two groups, but schizotypal adults appear to rely more on projective identification than do affectively ill borderline patients.

3. *Behavior patterns.* Affectively ill borderline adults seem more impulsive, suicidal, erratic, and demanding in the transference, whereas schizotypal adults appear more withdrawn and impoverished.

Table 4–1 presents the *DSM-III* criteria for both diagnoses. Given the empirical source of these criteria, it is not surprising that the *DSM-III*'s borderline criteria and Gunderson's criteria (see Table 1–4) appear to be closely related.

Table 4-1(a)   DSM-III Criteria for Schizotypal Personality Disorders

Schizotypal Personality Disorder[1]

At least 4 of the following are required.

1. Magical thinking, e.g., superstitiousness, clairvoyance, telepathy, "6th sense," "others can feel my feelings" (in children and adolescents, bizarre fantasies or preoccupations)
2. Ideas of reference
3. Social isolation, e.g., no close friends or confidants, social contacts limited to essential everyday tasks
4. Recurrent illusions, sensing the presence of a face or person not actually present (e.g., "I felt as if my dead mother were in the room with me"), depersonalization, or derealization not associated with panic attacks
5. Odd speech (without loosening of associations or incoherence), e.g., speech that is digressive, vague, overelaborate, circumstantial, metaphorical
6. Inadequate rapport in face-to-face interaction due to constricted or inappropriate affect, e.g., aloof, cold
7. Suspiciousness or paranoid ideation
8. Undue social anxiety or hypersensitivity to real or imagined criticism

Does not meet the criteria for Schizophrenia.

Source: [1]American Psychiatric Association (1980). *DSM-III* (pp. 312–313). Copyright 1980 by American Psychiatric Association. Reprinted by permission.

Applying the DSM-III Criteria to Mary Markham

The DSM-III Borderline Personality Disorder

Most of Mary Markham's symptoms were reported in the first few sessions with me or were gathered by the staff during Mary's initial hospitalization. Other symptoms (e.g., loneliness and emptiness) emerged only as she established a trusting relationship with me. Then Mary began to verbalize inner experiences that she had not noticed before.

Mary's symptoms are grouped below according to the *DSM-III* descriptive criteria. Patients must meet five of the eight criteria in order to be diagnosed as borderline personality disorder:

1. *Impulsivity.* Mary binge-ate with periodic laxative purges, overspent to the point of financial jeopardy, and mutilated herself with razor blades.
2. *Intense interpersonal relationships.* Mary idealized and subsequently de-

Table 4-1(b)   DSM-III Criteria for Borderline Personality Disorders

Borderline Personality Disorder[2]

At least 5 of the following are required.

1. Impulsivity or unpredictability in at least two areas that are potentially self-damaging, e.g., spending, sex, gambling, substance use, shoplifting, over-eating, physically self-damaging acts

2. A pattern of unstable and intense interpersonal relationships, e.g., marked shifts of attitude, idealization, devaluation, manipulation (consistently using others for one's own ends)

3. Inappropriate, intense anger or lack of control of anger, e.g., frequent displays of temper, constant anger

4. Identity disturbance manifested by uncertainty about several issues relating to identity, such as self-image, gender identity, long-term goals or career choice, friendship patterns, values, and loyalties, e.g., "Who am I," "I feel like I am my sister when I am good"

5. Affective instability: marked shifts from normal mood to depression, irritability, or anxiety, usually lasting a few hours and only rarely more than a few days, with a return to normal mood

6. Intolerance of being alone, e.g., frantic efforts to avoid being alone, depressed when alone

7. Physically self-damaging acts, e.g., suicidal gestures, self-mutilation, recurrent accidents, or physical fights

8. Chronic feelings of emptiness or boredom

If under 18, does not meet criteria for Identity Disorder.

Source: [2]American Psychiatric Association (1980). *DSM-III* (pp. 322–323). Copyright 1980 by American Psychiatric Association. Reprinted by permission.

valued male physicians, was attached to her mother while simultaneously "putting her down" for her "bossiness." She found her father to be totally defective with no good qualities, and she attached to her therapist with feelings of vengefulness whenever her therapist failed her.

3. *Inappropriate, intense anger.* Mary felt that the great anger she experienced was one of her major emotions and had great difficulty in expressing it verbally.

4. *Identity disturbance.* Mary believed that she could never show her "true self" and thus had to be publicly compliant, cooperative, and obedient, even when she did not feel that way (false self). She had parts of herself that were not integrated (the Megalomaniac and the Baby) and believed she had no executive self that managed these unruly parts. She disliked

being female and considered it an inferior gender. Finally, she was uncertain about her direction in life, including career, friendships, and dating.

5. *Affective instability.* Mary mainly felt depressed and lethargic, but this state could be suddenly and unexpectedly punctuated by a normal mood. Occasionally (when the Megalomaniac was in control), she felt highly energetic, even good about herself.
6. *Problems of being alone.* Mary denied this criterion.
7. *Self-damaging acts.* Mary took multiple overdoses of medication, made two major life-threatening suicide attempts, and mutilated herself with razor blades.
8. *Chronic feelings of emptiness or boredom.* Mary felt emptiness (from feeling depressed, and at times guilty and bad about self) and boredom (from having a limited life with few outside interests).

Mary clearly met six of the *DSM-III's* criteria for the borderline personality disorder. She met Criterion 3 (anger) only partially because she rarely expressed her anger verbally, and she denied experiencing any problems of being alone (Criterion 6). Several of these criteria require further explanation.

Inappropriate, Intense Anger   Mary admitted experiencing considerable anger, although she could not ascertain its cause. Rather than express her anger, however, she avoided the precipitating person or situation. Consequently, as a result of turning the anger against herself, she had fantasies of something bad happening to her, usually an accident or disaster. She appeared unaware that her suicide attempts were a way of expressing anger at a significant other. Early in the therapy, in fact, she denied this possibility. Thus, Mary admitted that she had angry feelings but denied being aware of ever expressing them verbally or behaviorally. However, her suicide attempts were inappropriate expressions of anger and hence are listed here as a problem.

Identity Disturbances   Mary's identity disturbances were fairly obvious: multiple selves that were named; loss of body boundaries; ambivalent relationships with everyone in her life; and a lack of friends, life goals, and sexual feelings. Many borderline patients, however, do not have such graphic symptoms of identity disturbance.

Affective Instability   Mary did not have the classic profile described by affective instability. Rather, she had a stable, pervasive sense of depression that was briefly interrupted by several days of good mood or even hypomania. However, her mood was dependent on external stimuli and occasional internal stimuli (e.g., fantasies or dreams). Her moods frequently, but not always, could be somewhat improved by others' caretaking (e.g., spending time with her, soothing her, or building her up emotionally). But because she was extremely afraid that the caretaker might intrude upon her, she usually avoided others.

Problems of Being Alone   Mary denied having problems of being alone at the beginning of therapy, explaining that she relied on reading, fantasizing, and her cats for stimulation. She disagreed that she was heavily dependent on the presence of her parents to sustain her, just as she denied the role of therapy in providing companionship and assuaging her loneliness. It was years into the therapy before she could admit that being alone was a major problem.

Although the *DSM-III* borderline personality disorder diagnosis allowed many of Mary Markham's symptoms to be recorded, it did not categorize such symptoms as her beliefs that she and her mother were telepathically linked or her episodic depersonalization and pseudoserenity (with their transient psychotic qualities). In order to categorize these symptoms, we must turn to the other half of the *DSM-III* borderline diagnosis, the schizotypal personality disorder.

The DSM-III Schizotypal Personality Disorder

The symptoms of the schizotypal personality disorder tap experiences that are more related to soft signs of a thought disorder (e.g., impaired abstract capacity and poor self-object differentiation) than do those of the borderline personality disorder. It is in the schizotypal category that some of Mary's other symptoms can now be presented.

In order for the schizotypal personality disorder to be diagnosed, patients must meet at least four of the following eight criteria and *not* meet the criteria for schizophrenia:

1. *Magical thinking.* Mary believed that she and mother had telepathic communication on some nonverbal level and that she would die when mother died.
2. *Ideas of reference.* Not obviously applicable.
3. *Social isolation.* Mary had no friends, associated little with coworkers, did not date, and often talked little with parents, who lived with her.
4. *Recurrent illusions, depersonalization, or derealization not associated with panic.* Mary had episodes of depersonalization and derealization that did not appear related to the panic preceding her suicide attempts.
5. *Odd speech.* Not applicable.

6. *Inadequate rapport.* Not applicable.
7. *Suspiciousness or paranoid ideation* (related to item 2). When feeling criticized, abandoned, or narcissistically injured, Mary was suspicious of everyone near her and inappropriately co-opted everyone into her suspiciousness.
8. *Undue social anxiety or hypersensitivity to criticism.* Mary originally avoided this problem because of her long isolation, although she admitted early that it was a problem. She was extremely sensitive to the most subtle criticism, which caused her to fragment and to feel evil, bad, and rageful at the other person.

Mary Markham clearly met Criteria 1, 3, 4, 7, and 8 for schizotypal personality disorder, but it is unclear whether she met Criterion 2. She clearly did not meet Criteria 5 and 6. Because Mary met five of the eight criteria and did not meet the criteria for schizophrenia, she could be diagnosed as having a schizotypal personality disorder.

It is not unusual for some borderline adults to meet the criteria for both borderline and schizotypal diagnoses (Axis II), a nosological problem for the *DSM-III* that has been noted in the literature and has not been clarified to date.

We shall not take John Elliott or Sarah Gardner through this process, though a perusal of their symptoms shows that John met the *DSM-III* criteria for both diagnoses and Sarah met the criteria for a borderline personality disorder.

Problems with the DSM-III

The *DSM-III*'s criteria for the borderline personality disorder present several problems. First, as mentioned above, there is evidence that some patients simultaneously fulfill the criteria for both the borderline personality disorder and other personality disorders, which means that the diagnostic criteria for the personality disorders are not independent enough to prevent overlapping on Axis II. The schizotypal personality disorder is the most blatant example of this overlap, but duplication can also occur with narcissistic (Kernberg et al. 1981, Rinsley 1984a), antisocial (Akiskal 1981), histrionic personality disorders (Kroll et al. 1981), and others.

The second problem pertains to two factors that many researchers have found to be discriminating criteria for the borderline adult—poor work or school achievement, and brief psychotic experiences (Gunderson 1982). Some researchers, including Gunderson, have called for a revision in the *DSM-III* definition to include these criteria.

A third difficulty is that many persons who meet the criteria for the borderline personality disorder also display affective disorders. This is not a problem in the *DSM-III* diagnostic system because the two disorders lie on different axes, though it does have conceptual and treatment implications. For example, various empirical studies have shown that depression is a highly characteristic but not very discriminating aspect of borderline patient's symptom cluster (Gunderson 1982). Some professionals (Stone 1979a) believe that affective dysregulation (rapid mood changing) is responsible for borderline adults' character pathology, whereas others believe it is often secondary to the personality pathology (Masterson 1976). Clearly, each position leads to a somewhat different treatment approach. Although a positive response to antidepressant medication lends some credence to the possibility of a constitutional basis, it alone cannot resolve the debate, because patients with clearly brief reactive depressions can respond positively to these medications. Even though this debate cannot be resolved at the present time, the reader should note that many borderline patients now also meet the criteria for an affective disorder.

Fourth, one area of conceptual difficulty is the question of whether the borderline is a discrete personality disorder or a mid-level personality organization that encompasses a variety of more specific personality character types. Kernberg's concept of the borderline, as explained earlier, is a broad, mid-range form of psychotherapy that differs from the psychotic and the neurotic personality structures. According to his concept, there may be areas of similarity of treatment, given the range of patients, and there may also be major treatment differences. Kernberg's view contrasts with the concept of borderline personality as a discrete form of personality disorder with unique treatment issues and problems, as shown in the studies of Grinker, Gunderson, and Spitzer.

Finally, the *DSM-III*, as opposed to other diagnostic systems, can be appealing because it offers a rational basis for diagnosing the borderline personality disorder. Its criteria are descriptive and may be readily determined during the initial intake and in subsequent evaluation sessions. The *DSM-III* borderline personality disorder does not, however, have an evaluation of reliability, except for the general reliability given all personality disorder categories on Axis II (Spitzer et al. 1979). We might say that what the *DSM-III* gains in its interdisciplinary origins, it loses by not having a theoretical explanation for the symptoms.

Comparing the DSM-III with Kernberg's Criteria

Kernberg considers the *DSM-III* borderline personality disorder as similar to a subtype of borderline personality organization that he calls the *infantile personality*. Thus, he believes that the *DSM-III* borderline disorder pertains only to a subsection of the borderline spectrum. Kernberg does acknowledge the *DSM-III*'s contributions, but he believes its emphasis on symptoms, exclusion of intrapsychic structures, and lack of an organizing theoretical position are serious deficiencies in the *DSM-III* diagnostic system. See Table 4–2 for a comparison of the *DSM-III*'s and Kernberg's criteria for the borderline personality disorder.

There is no reason, however, to believe that the *DSM-III*'s criteria and Kernberg's criteria are incompatible. In fact, recent research (Blumenthal et al. 1982) shows that a majority of patients diagnosed as borderline according to the *DSM-III* are also diagnosed as borderline according to Kernberg's criteria, thus showing considerable congruence between the two systems. For example, in order to be diagnosed as borderline by the *DSM-III*, patients would almost have to have the identity diffusion, primitive defenses, and ego weaknesses of Kernberg's diagnosis.

Comparison of the various diagnostic systems is still a science in its infancy. Overall, research comparing the criteria of Kernberg, the *DSM-III*, and Gunderson has yielded confusing data. Although there seems to be considerable overlap among the three systems, Stone (1980) thus far is the only theorist willing to take a stand on the domain of patients covered by each system. According to the *DSM-III*'s criteria, including both borderline and schizotypal diagnoses, the range of patients called borderline is broad because it includes those with psychoticlike features. This contrasts with Kernberg's approach, which permits only transient psychotic experiences. Accordingly, Stone (1980) believes that the *DSM-III* diagnosis covers the largest population with heterogeneous symptoms, that Kernberg's structural diagnosis applies to a smaller population with heterogeneous symptoms, and that Gunderson's borderline personality covers the smallest population.

Clarkin, Widiger, Frances, Hurt, and Gilmore (1983) found that "identity disturbance" and "unstable intense relationships" appear to diagnose the *DSM-III* borderline personality with high probability, lending credence to Kernberg's structural approach with its heavy emphasis on identity diffusion. They also found 93 possible ways to select five or more of the eight features, irrespective of order, which allows considerable heterogeneity in how patients present.

MAKING THE DIFFERENTIAL DIAGNOSIS

The purpose of a differential diagnosis is to rule out other plausible diagnoses. The *DSM-III*, which has a specified set of criteria for each of the major personality diagnoses and the multiaxial approach, is an excellent resource for this task. Under the borderline-as-level-of-functioning approach (Kernberg), the most significant differential diagnostic problem is separating borderline from psychosis and neurosis. For example, in this approach, patients can meet the criteria for a borderline level of organization and also have an affective disorder or be a paranoid personality or a compulsive personality, among other possibilities. Of course, borderline adults with a paranoid personality give a slightly different twist to the therapeutic encounter than do borderline adults with, say, an infantile personality. Diagnostically, however, there are no contradictions inherent in having a borderline personality organization with a paranoid personality subtype.

On the other hand, the clinician who believes that the borderline is a specific personality disorder or syndrome must then distinguish, for example, among the borderline, hysterical, and antisocial personalities.

It is not always easy to distinguish among the borderline and certain other diagnoses, regardless of the approach used. The clinician may be required to make a judgment early in the diagnostic process when there is limited information. Sometimes the discrimination is subtle, as between a lower-level borderline and a higher-functioning psychotic adult, when there exist some transitional disorders in a gray area that are hard to define.

Distinguishing the Borderline Personality Disorder

Following the spectrum concept, we shall start with those disorders that are lower on the continuum and end with the psychoneurotic disorders. Diagnosing borderline personality disorders requires time and experience, usually under expert supervision in order to refine the necessary clinical skills. The reader can review the vignettes in Stone (1980, pp. 351–490) for practice in differential diagnosis. When going through this section, the reader may find it helpful to compare the *DSM-III*'s criteria for borderline and schizotypal disorders with the criteria for the differential diagnoses being considered.

The reader needs to know that from the psychoanalytic point of view, some of the following diagnosis can overlap with borderline personality organization. But some cannot. When there may be an overlap, it will be noted in the section on the particular diagnosis.

Lower-Level versus Higher-Level Borderline Personalities

The continuum from lower-level to higher-level borderline functioning covers much ground. Lower-level borderline adults may look psychotic at first, and higher-level borderline patients may look healthy. Lower-level borderline adults appear to regress periodically into psychotic decompensation, but higher-level borderlines do not. Higher-level borderline individuals frequently resemble neurotic adults. In accordance with the concept of the developmental-diagnostic continuum, Rinsley (1984a, 1984b), Adler (1981), and Bursten (1978) consider the narcissistic personality to represent a

**Table 4-2   Comparison of DSM-III and Kernberg's Criteria for
Borderline Personality Disorder**

DSM-III Criteria for Borderline Personality Disorder[1]

At least 5 of the following are required.

1. Impulsivity or unpredictability in at least two areas that are potentially self-damaging, e.g., spending, sex, gambling, substance use, shoplifting, overeating, physically self-damaging acts

2. A pattern of unstable and intense interpersonal relationships, e.g., marked shifts of attitude, idealization, devaluation, manipulation (consistently using others for one's own ends)

3. Inappropriate, intense anger or lack of control of anger, e.g., frequent displays of temper, constant anger

4. Identity disturbance manifested by uncertainty about several issues relating to identity, such as self-image, gender identity, long-term goals or career choice, friendship patterns, values, and loyalties, e.g., "Who am I," "I feel like I am my sister when I am good"

5. Affective instability: marked shifts from normal mood to depression, irritability, or anxiety, usually lasting a few hours and only rarely more than a few days, with a return to normal mood

6. Intolerance of being alone, e.g., frantic efforts to avoid being alone, depressed when alone

7. Physically self-damaging acts, e.g., suicidal gestures, self-mutilation, recurrent accidents, or physical fights

8. Chronic feelings of emptiness or boredom

If under 18, does not meet criteria for Identity Disorder.

Source: [2]American Psychiatric Association (1980). *DSM-III* (pp. 322–323). Copyright 1980 by American Psychiatric Association. Reprinted by permission.

higher-level borderline personality. Kernberg (1984, in press) believes the narcissistic personality can be either borderline or neurotic but usually is borderline.

How can we distinguish, then, between lower- and higher-level borderline patients? Although higher-level borderline patients appear to be normal, they usually believe that their life is "phony" or unreal and relate to others as need-satisfying objects rather than as whole persons. These patients may function acceptably in most areas of life except for major difficulties with intimacy. Many of the patients described by Masterson (1981) are higher-level borderline.

Lower-level borderline adults are prone to temporary psychotic attacks under separation stress, with feelings of depersonalization, unreality, and

Table 4-2
(Continued)

Kernberg's Differentiation of Borderline Personality Structure[2]

All 3 of these criteria are required.

1. Identity diffusion: contradictory aspects of self and others are poorly integrated and kept apart
2. Primitive defense operations:
   a. Splitting: the splitting of self and external objects into "all good" and "all bad"
   b. Primitive idealization: the tendency to see external objects as totally good, creating unrealistic images
   c. Projective identification: the tendency to continue to experience the impulse which, at the same time, is projected onto the other person, who then is both feared and experienced as someone who must be controlled
   d. Denial: the inability to bring together emotionally contradictory areas of consciousness and to feel relevant emotions over these contradictions
   e. Omnipotence and devaluation: the presence of ego states containing representations of a highly inflated self in relation to depreciated representations of others
3. Capacity to test reality is preserved
   a. Capacity to differentiate self from nonself
   b. Capacity to differentiate intrapsychic from external origins of perceptions and stimuli
   c. Capacity to evaluate one's affect, behavior, and thought content in terms of ordinary social norms

---

Source: [1]Blumenthal, R., Carr, A. C., and Goldstein, E. G. (1982). DSM III and structural diagnosis of borderline patients. *The Psychiatric Hospital, 13*(4): 143. Copyright 1982 by National Association of Private Psychiatric Hospitals. Reprinted by permission.

paranoid projection. Their lives may have been greatly impaired by their borderline symptoms, and they may have soft signs of a thought disorder. But they do not meet the criteria for schizophrenia and return to their previous levels of functioning after brief psychotic episodes.

Kernberg (1970) has stated that one must look not only at the level of personality organization but also at the quality of the pathological traits or superego functioning. For example, a patient with a neurotic personality organization and masochistic personality subtype may seek out such harmful love relations that his or her personal life is more self-destructive than is that of a patient with a higher-level borderline personality organization. One cannot assume that a higher structural level automatically ensures good functioning. In actuality, this patient is not functioning on the level that one would expect.

Generally, however, the prognosis is better for upper-level than for lower-level borderline patients, simply because of the upper-level patients' greater ego strength and ability to tolerate frustration (as shown by their ability to function in life).

Schizophrenia

The starting point for distinguishing borderling from schizophrenic is the DSM-III's criteria. Kernberg's structural criteria for psychosis (identity diffusion, use of primitive defenses, and loss of reality testing) should also be considered. Do patients meet the DSM-III's criteria for schizophrenia? Are they currently psychotic? Both a full history and an analysis of current behavior are important in making a diagnosis. The clinician may also want to search for major mental illness in the patients' biological relatives. As mentioned earlier, patients diagnosed as having a borderline personality disorder tend to have more relatives with affective disorders than do those diagnosed as schizophrenic (Stone 1980, 1981). The pattern is reversed for patients having a schizotypal personality disorder.

If patients do not meet the criteria for schizophrenia, then other diagnoses should be considered, including schizotypal and borderline personality disorders in the *DSM-III* or Kernberg's structural diagnosis for borderline personality organization. Kernberg believes that psychotics decompensate when confronted and that borderlines do better when confronted. Thus, confrontation helps clarify the diagnosis.

Several other characteristics can help differentiate borderline from schizophrenic adults. For example, borderline adults always depend on and may manipulate others, and they are rarely comfortable alone. By comparison, schizophrenic patients often are loners and socially isolated.

Borderline patients are clearly aware that they are physically separate from others, but schizophrenic adults may have difficulty distinguishing between themselves and others, including between fantasy and reality.

Borderline adults are clearly aware of social conventions, unlike schizophrenic patients, who may talk to themselves in public or engage in peculiar social behavior.

The brief, transient psychoses of lower-level borderline patients contrast with schizophrenic patients' flattening or blunting of affect, obvious thought disorder, possible hallucinations, grossly delusional thinking, and episodes of severe, pervasive depersonalization and derealization. Schizophrenic adults probably will have a history of reduced capacity to maintain reality on a job, in relationships, or in social activities, particularly from their mid-20s onward. Schizophrenic patients may share some psychodynamics with borderline adults, but the intrapsychic functioning of schizophrenics is so fragmented that the therapist must adopt a different approach from that required for the borderline patient. Kernberg (1984) has clearly stated that when patients are psychotic, it is impossible to determine their underlying personality subtypes.

Although delusions are the hallmark of psychosis, and overvalued ideas that respond to confrontation are characteristic of the borderline thought disorder, the continuum of thought disturbance often complicates categorical diagnoses (Stone 1980). Given these numerous possibilities, determining the extent of the patient's unusual thinking may require considerable time.

A diagnosis usually can be made on the basis of the patients' treatment experience and response to antipsychotic medication. A favorable response to antipsychotic medication typically indicates a psychotic disorder. Middle- to higher-level borderline patients rarely respond well to antipsychotic medication. Usually, only over time do the responses to medication and treatment and the patients' behavior and clinical material allow the clinician to distinguish low-level borderline patients from schizophrenic patients in remission. The patient's history is also an important source of information. Finally, borderline adults generally have a better prognosis than do schizophrenic patients.

Major Affective Disorders

The primary affective disorders include Bipolar I and II, major depression, and cyclothymic, dysthymic, and atypical affective disorders. Borderline patients can regularly have an affective disorder, particularly the garden variety of depression. Some believe that the affective disorder causes borderline symptoms; others think that the affective problems are secondary to personality pathology; and still others believe that the two are separate disorders.

The claim that affective disorders cause borderline symptomatology is strengthened by the fact that a number of symptoms of the borderline in the *DSM-III*'s or Gunderson's diagnostic system (e.g., impulsivity, mood changes, depression when alone) can be explained by dysregulation of the patients' "psychobiological thermostat" (a term standing for a complex process that scientists do not understand well at this time) (Stone 1983, p. 387). When these patients' "emotional thermostat" is set either too high or too low, they experience impaired frustration tolerance, irritability, and impulsivity. When their thermostat is set too high, they act out, and when it is set too low, their feelings of pessimism, listlessness, and thoughts of suicide may be heightened.

When borderline patients (diagnosed either structurally or descriptively) have an affective disorder, it is impossible to determine which disorder is the primary causal agent. But that is not a problem in the *DSM-III* because the two disorders are on different axes; hence, patients can have both. Conceptually, the relationship between the two disorders is now at the stage at which distinguishing borderline structure from schizophrenia was in 1970.

The chief consideration when using Kernberg's approach is the degree to which affectively disordered individuals maintain their reality testing, except for transient loss. If overall they maintain their reality testing and meet the criteria for the borderline personality organization, a simultaneous diagnosis of borderline and major affective disorder will be possible. In structural diagnosis, a certain number of better-functioning primary affective disorders can meet the criteria for the borderline personality organization. Kernberg (1984) considers most persons with schizoaffective and manic-depressive illnesses to be psychotic.

When there is overlap, the chief treatment issue then becomes the advisability of medication. The use of lithium or even ECT when appropriate is rarely questioned. Instead, the debate centers on the use of antidepressants. The fundamental question in the debate is whether medication controls a genetically based disorder or merely masks the underlying psychodynamic problems causing the depression, as a steriod can mask inflammatory diseases. This question cannot be answered at present.

The reader who is interested in those affective disorders regarded as clinically borderline should review Table 1–2, as well as the work of D. Klein (1967, 1973, 1975, 1977), who has worked extensively in this area; his *hysteroid dysphoria* is a particularly well described disorder.

Paranoid Disorders

Many of the same issues pertaining to the affective disorders also apply to the paranoid disorders. For example, if patients with a paranoid disorder maintain reality testing and meet the structural criteria for a borderline personality organization, then both diagnoses will be possible. Kernberg (1984) has said that one of the hardest differential diagnostic problems is distinguishing between the paranoid personality and paranoid schizophrenia. In the *DSM-III* the clinician is forced to choose a primary personality disorder or to make a mixed personality diagnosis.

More Primitive Character Disorders

Generally, Kernberg considers the antisocial, narcissistic (most cases), paranoid, schizoid, schizotypal, and hypomanic personalities (hypomanic personality being a psychoanalytic, not a *DSM-III*, diagnosis) to be at a borderline level of functioning, as does Rinsley. The schizoid, schizotypal, and paranoid personalities are often far less unstable, impulsive, and prone to acting out than is the *DSM-III*-defined borderline personality. This does not mean that individuals with these personalities are better off than are the *DSM-III* borderline adults. Severe ego defects usually lead schizoid, schizotypal and paranoid patients to live marginal, unsociable, and lonely existences. Ego defects in these patients simply affect their behavior differently from the way ego defects affect the more unstable, histrionic borderline adults.

Antisocial Personality

Most psychodynamic theorists see the antisocial personality as a subvariety of either the borderline (Kernberg) or the narcissistic personality organizations (Bursten), depending on the intrapsychic structures and propensity to regression. Kernberg (1984) has noted that because many narcissistic patients engage in antisocial acts, it becomes crucial to distinguish between the antisocial personality proper and other disorders in which there is antisocial behavior. It is useful to distinguish behaviorally between the typical borderline adult and an antisocial personality even functioning at a borderline level, because research has shown that the antisocial borderline or narcissistic patient does much more poorly in individual psychotherapy.

In addition, borderline adults are rarely as ruthless toward societal norms and conventions as are antisocial personalities. Antisocial personalities appear to have absolutely no guilt (at least consciously), social tact, or concern for others and are unable to tolerate any anxiety without instant gratification. Many theorists recommend that the clinician review the subculture to which the patients belong. For example, a certain behavior might be explained by the fact that these patients are just following the rules of their subgroup. Kernberg (1975a) and others point out that even healthy persons who belong to a deviant subgroup will maintain some ties away from the group and probably will adhere to fairness and honesty somewhere else in their life.

Masterson (1982) reported that antisocial patients either ignore or respond angrily to confrontation, unlike borderline adults, who usually will acknowledge the accuracy of the confrontation. This may be a clue that these antisocial persons are more narcissistic than borderline.

Narcissistic Personality

Even experienced clinicians find it difficult to distinguish between the borderline and the narcissistic personality disorders. Part of this difficulty is because all individuals have narcissistic traits and because all forms of personality disorders, including borderline, contain narcissistic elements that influence pathology.

Adler (1980) and Rinsley (1977, 1981b) postulated the existence of a continuum of personality disorders based on developmental determinants. On this continuum, the borderline personality is characterized by a relatively greater degree of psychopathology, and the narcissistic by less psychopathology. In this schema, the borderline personality is marked by "fragmented, unstable self and selfobjects" and the narcissistic personality by "stable, cohesive self and selfobjects" (Ornstein 1974). As Rinsley (1977, 1981b, 1984b) has noted, the borderline personality is considered to be developmentally closer to the major psychoses, and the narcissistic personality closer to the psychoneuroses. In this newer approach, the concepts of higher-level borderline and narcissistic personality are interchangeable.

Masterson (1981) and Kernberg (1975a) believe that the narcissistic personality may operate at the borderline level but also may be neurotic. In Kernberg's approach, one must determine the structural level of personality organization in order to reach a decision.

As if this were not confusing enough, Bursten (1982) has complicated matters further. In the *DSM-III*, he found several types of patients with a firm sense of self and intense narcissistic focus, all meeting the criteria as subtypes for narcissistic personality. These subtypes are (1) narcissistic personality disorder, (2) paranoid personality disorder, (3) antisocial personality disorder, and (4) dependent personality disorder. Bursten now prefers this classification system to his earlier work (Bursten 1973) on narcissistic subtypes based on psychodynamics. These approaches clearly need to be refined, as there are inherent contradictions in these newer positions. For example, the paranoid personality is usually considered a lower-level disorder, so how can it be narcissistic if narcissistic is seen by some experts as a neurotic personality organization?

Descriptive Criteria   Akhtar and Thomson (1982) have listed clinical features of the narcissistic personality disorder (see Table 4–3). Although it is similar to the *DSM-III*, their listing is somewhat more comprehensive because it includes both covert and overt clinical features. The reader may want to compare Table 4–3 against the *DSM-III*'s Borderline Personality Disorder and Narcissistic Personality Disorder.

Generally, it is safe to say that borderline personality patients have a poorer self-image than do narcissistic personality patients and that borderline adults rarely have the contemptuous, haughty, or cool self-presentation of the narcissistic personality patients. Behavior typical of borderline adults, such as transient psychotic episodes, poor impulse control, and self-mutilation, would be unusual in narcissistic patients unless they were functioning at the borderline level. Finally, borderline patients' work-social adjustment is poorer than that of narcissistic patients, who often are able to function effectively at work and are less conflicted in regard to achievement.

Table 4-3   Clinical Features of the Narcissistic Personality Disorder

Features	Overt	Covert
Self-concept	Inflated self-regard; haughty grandiosity; fantasies of wealth, power, beauty, brilliance; sense of entitlement; illusory invulnerability	Inordinate hypersensitivity; feelings of inferiority, worthlessness, fragility; continuous search for strength and glory
Interpersonal relations	Lack depth and involve much contempt for and devaluation of others; occasional withdrawal into "splendid isolation"	Chronic idealization and intense envy of others; enormous hunger for acclaim.
Social adaptation	Social success; sublimation in the service of exhibitionism (pseudosublimation); intense ambition	Chronic boredom, uncertainty, dissatisfaction with professional and social identity.
Ethics, standards, and ideals	Apparent zeal and enthusiasm about moral, sociopolitical, and aesthetic matters	Lack of any genuine commitment; corruptible conscience.
Love and sexuality	Seductiveness; promiscuity; lack of sexual inhibitions; frequent infatuations	Inability to remain in love; treating the love object as extension of self rather than as separate, unique individual; perverse fantasies; occasionally, sexual deviations.
Cognitive style	Egocentric perception of reality; articulate and rhetorical; circumstantial and occasionally vague, as if talking to self; evasive but logically consistent in arguments; easily becomes devil's advocate	Inattention toward objective aspects of events, resulting at times in subtle gaps in memory; "soft" learning difficulties; autocentric use of language; fluctuations between being overabstract and overconcrete; tendency to change meanings of reality when self-esteem is threatened.

Source: Akhtar, S., and Thomson, J. A., Jr. (1982). Overview: Narcissistic personality disorder. *American Journal of Psychiatry, 139*(1):20. Copyright 1982 by American Psychiatric Association. Reprinted by permission.

In summary, in order to be diagnosed as having a narcissistic personality disorder, patients should meet the *DSM-III* criteria. Some theorists (Masterson 1981, 1983a) believe that the patient's response to confrontation is a diagnostic indicator. True narcissistic personalities manifest anger or haughty behavior upon confrontation, but borderline patients tend to hear the confrontation and to work with it; their behavior improves under confrontation.

Psychoanalytic Criteria   Kernberg (1982a) has stated that he sees the narcissistic personality functioning with a specific character constellation, namely, the grandiose self, which reflects a particular pathology of internalized object relationships as well as distortions of ego and superego structures. Kernberg (1975a) has identified the key qualities as grandiosity, envy, devaluation, and lack of empathy and commitment. A variety of superego pathology ranges from mild inability to experience depression, a propensity toward shame (not guilt), and the absence of an internal value system, to more malignant pathology involving antisocial acts, paranoid trends, aggression, and self-destructiveness. Kernberg adds that in atypical narcissistic cases, many surface inhibitions and feelings of inferiority hide the underlying grandiosity. Most narcissistic personalities are borderline, but a few are neurotic.

Kohut (1971, 1977) disagreed with this description, viewing the narcissistic patient as functioning at a much higher level than the borderline does. The narcissistic patient is defined less by descriptive symptoms or behavior than by a certain self-pathology (e.g., temporary loss of self-cohesion under conditions lacking proper mirroring or idealizing).

Rinsley (1984a, 1984b), synthesizing some of Kohut's work with his own, regards the narcissistic personality as a higher-level borderline personality disorder on a developmental-diagnostic continuum between the borderline and the neurotic. He views narcissistic personalities less as haughty, arrogant, and envy laden than as patients with a specific self-pathology. Rinsley believes that the separation process (disengagement and distancing from mother) of narcissistic personalities was arrested, although the individuation process (development of intrapsychic autonomy) apparently did occur, resulting in pathologically pseudoadults with an immature, unseparated character structure. This is in contrast with the borderline personalities, whose overall separation-individuation was arrested.

Rinsley also identified the following differences between the borderline and narcissistic personality disorders. First, individuals with a borderline personality disorder labor to maintain their fragile sense of intactness. On the other hand, adults with a narcissistic personality disorder, who have a cohesive but vulnerable sense of self, guard against its fragmentation by bolstering their self-esteem and unconsciously reuniting with a nourishing parent. Second, borderline personality disorder patients suffer from impaired object permanency (inability to summon the image of another) and impaired evocative memory. In contrast, narcissistic personality disorder patients enjoy object permanency but suffer from impaired object constancy (inability to summon up the gratifying image); their evocative memory is intact, but the evoked images are ungratifying or anxiety provoking (Rinsley 1982a, in press).

Rinsley (1984b) noted several pieces of clinical evidence supporting the position that the narcissistic personality disorder is higher on the developmental continuum than the borderline is. For example, Adler (1981) found that successfully treated borderline personalities regularly function as well as narcissistic personalities do. Conversely, narcissistic personalities who regress behave the way typical borderline personalities do. He concluded that both personalities share many themes (e.g., abandonment, loss of inner controls, unintegrated good-bad self- and good-bad object images, impairment of self- and sexual identity, eruptive rage, depression, and symptomatic behavior of unrequited symbiotic needs). Borderline adults blatantly exhibit these themes, but narcissistic personalities keep them under control except during stress and ongoing psychotherapy.

Meissner (1979, p. 199) recommended the following rule of thumb for separating narcissistic from borderline disorders. Patients who present with chronic difficulties in fragmentation of the self and regressive tendencies should be categorized as borderline rather than narcissistic personalities. Evidence of traditional narcissistic pathology, such as the grandiose self, the ideal self and ideal others, and the formation of idealizing or mirroring transferences (Kohut 1971) should not automatically lead to the diagnosis of a narcissistic personality. The existence of such pathology simply alerts the therapist that narcissistic pathology can exist throughout the developmental continuum.

Mary Markham is a good example of a patient with many narcissistic issues. Under the above definition, however, she would not be thought of as a narcissistic personality, even though at times she felt powerful and omnipotent (the Megalomaniac part), felt the need to be totally "perfect" or else felt worthless, and formed merger and idealizing transferences in therapy. Mary, however, was too prone to depersonalization, transient psychosis, and extreme regressive tendencies to be categorized as a narcissistic personality.

In summary, narcissistic patients should have a sufficiently cohesive self-image so that major regressive episodes do not occur. Second, narcissistic patients should not oscillate rapidly from bad to good self-images, as do borderline adults. Third, narcissistic patients usually experience shame, not guilt, which signals the loss of narcissistic equilibrium, but borderline adults may experience intense anxiety related to problems of separation or survival. Thus, patients who have severe separation or survival anxieties related to their inner fear of fragmentation or dissolution of the self should be placed within the borderline range, even if their transferences have a markedly narcissistic quality (Meissner 1979).

Psychoneuroses

Although it is not much in vogue, the term *psychoneurosis* is used here because it is still used in psychoanalytic literature to represent a higher level of functioning than the borderline.

In the *DSM-III*, neurosis includes such conditions as anxiety, depersonalization, dysthmic disorder, hypochondriasis, conversion disorder, and dissociative disorder. In the psychoanalytic literature on character neurosis, references have been made to the hysterical, obsessive-compulsive, depressive-masochistic, and better-functioning narcissistic personalities as being neurotic. Kernberg has been quite clear regarding his criteria for the neurotic level of functioning (integrated identity, higher-level defenses, and maintenance of reality testing). We should also point out that just because they are neurotic does not mean that these patients do not suffer—they may suffer a great deal, and their therapy may be long and arduous.

Borderline and neurotic individuals differ in a number of ways. Unlike borderline patients, neurotic adults rarely experience brief psychotic episodes, and their work achievement records are better than those of borderline patients. Although typically intolerant of being alone, borderline patients' close relationships are unstable and characterized by dependency that alternates between devaluation and exploitation. Borderline patients are unable to understand themselves or others in depth. Neurotic adults, on the other hand, have a far greater capacity for empathy, genuine concern, sacrifice of immediate gratification in the service of love for another, altruism, and management of interpersonal conflict.

Until a therapeutic alliance has been formed, borderline patients rarely use between sessions what they learned in therapy. Neurotic patients, on the other hand, observe their behavior and dreams and derive new insight into themselves between sessions as well as during therapy. We might say that neurotic patients are allies in the therapy, whereas borderline patients often act like adversaries (Masterson 1983a).

Obsessional or histrionic features can occasionally be observed in borderline adults, though the same factors that pertain overall to psychoneurosis also apply to the traditional definition of obsessional and hysterical personalities (e.g., they function in love and work at a much higher level than do borderline adults). The chief problem here is differentiating obsessive-compulsive from schizoid and narcissistic personalities, because all three can present as intellectual, cold and distant. Nonetheless, true obsessive-compulsive patients function at a higher level than do schizoid patients.

Hysterical individuals often are more mature and are better able to show empathy, to compete, and to maintain stable, in-depth relationships than can borderline adults with an infantile personality.

Substance Abuse

Because many persons with a borderline personality also suffer from alcoholism, drug addiction, and various eating disorders, the therapist must determine whether they meet the criteria for both conditions. Because these two conditions can overlap, this is not an either-or diagnostic problem for either the psychodynamic or the *DSM-III* approaches.

An important diagnostic problem here is that alcohol and drug abusers often need a prolonged period of being "dry" before a personality dimension can be assessed. This is because the effects of alcohol, for example, can mimic many borderline characteristics. Informal estimates of the time required before a character pathology can be ascertained have varied from three months to one year. At that point many treatment providers feel that alcoholics, in particular, usually meet the criteria for the narcissistic personality disorder. By now, the reader will know that because many experts consider the narcissistic personality to have a borderline level of personality organization, that makes many alcoholics borderline.

Sexual Deviation

Sexual deviation includes, among other things, homosexuality if ego syntonic (no longer a deviation in *DSM-III*), polymorphous perverse activity, and sexual activity with children. Once again, the individual needs to meet the criteria for both conditions, and the clinician must be familiar with the literature on the specific deviation, because the prognosis varies among these deviations, regardless of the borderline diagnosis.

Gender-Identity Problems

Kernberg (1984) discovered that borderline patients often at the same time have gender-identity problems. His opinion is that many transsexuals are borderline, whereas transvestites may be either borderline or neurotic. Rinsley (D. B. Rinsley, personal communication, May 21, 1984) considers both to be borderline or narcissistic personalities.

Multiple Personalities

Multiple personalities are considered to be a broad spectrum of disorders. Kernberg (1984) stated that they can be neurotic, borderline, or psychotic, and Brende and Rinsley (1981) regard them as, at best, borderline. The neurotic cases usually have the Dr. Jekyll/Mr. Hyde syndrome, with one personality totally repressed and unknown to the other personality (Kernberg 1984). In the borderline cases, which are the most common multiple personalities, all parts are aware of the others. There is a splitting of affect, and each part carries a certain image linked to a specific affect. In psychotic cases, there is a delusional belief that several people live in the patient's body.

Minimal Brain Dysfunction

Some patients who have been diagnosed as having a borderline personality structure have a history of minimal brain dysfunction in childhood (Murray 1979). Andrulonis and his associates (1982), in a study of 106 patients, found three distinct subgroups: history of no organicity; history of trauma, encephalitis, or epilepsy; and history of attentional deficit disorder/learning disabilities. Some have found anticonvulsants or stimulants to be useful in treating the latter two subgroups. It is important to remember that even with a history of organic features, how the family manages the child with organic impairment will determine whether or not the child develops a personality pathology.

Special Diagnostic Tools

Psychological Testing

In 1975, Gunderson and Singer published psychological test results that they concluded were characteristic of the borderline patient. (See also Knight 1953a, 1953b, who originally described this test pattern, and Singer 1977.) Typically, borderline patients performed well on the structured portions of the test battery (such as the WAIS or the Bender Visual Motor Gestalt Test) and poorly on the unstructured portions (such as the Rorschach test). The Rorschach responses of borderline adults often indicate a weakening of ego boundaries. Borderline adults also may give bizarre and highly idiosyncratic responses, some confabulation, and many "minus"-forms (F-). Whether or not this type of response is confined to the borderline personality disorder is controversial. Some theorists find that high-functioning schizophrenic patients also exhibit this duality of response.

Kwawer (1979) reported that the Rorschach test was particularly useful in pinpointing difficulties with the developing selfhood. He identified four modes of object relatedness reflecting the early developmental processes of growing selfhood through differentiation from a primary mothering figure (pp. 521–522): (1) *narcissistic mirroring*, reflecting a degree of self-absorption in which others exist solely to mirror the self ("these are two men mirroring each other, two little mimes"); (2) *symbiotic merging*, with its theme of attachment, merger, fusion, reunion, and the denial of separateness ("two women, like Siamese twins attached to each other"); (3) *separation and division*, showing unconscious conflict and ambivalence regarding separation and reunion ("it's an animal going from one divided into two"); and (4) *metamorphosis and transformation*, indicating enmeshment or involvement in the early stages of the organism's development from biological to interpersonal, such as with one-celled organisms, fetuses, or embryos ("it's a woman metamorphosing into an animal"). He also rated boundary disturbance themes.

Dreams as Diagnostic Clues

Although the analysis of dreams is not a major diagnostic tool, it can be useful when working with a borderline adult. The neurotic adult's dream, no matter what bizarre or violent elements it may contain, will generally preserve a measure of disguise even when depicting primitive, incestuous, incorporative, or sadistic themes. The dreams of borderline and psychotic adults, on the other hand, have more elements of literal incest, dismemberment, or death. Generally, the more disturbed the personality is, the more gory, primitive, and literal will be the dream (Stone 1980, pp. 310–316).

Interview Instruments

Several instruments that are currently being created, mainly for research projects studying borderline phenomena, should become available to the general clinician within the next few years. One such instrument, Gunderson's Diagnostic Interview with Borderlines (DIB), is an example of a semistructured interview. Kernberg's structural interview procedure elucidates the patient's psychostructural organization and leads directly to a structural diagnosis, prognosis, and treatment. The therapist should be aware that none of the instruments presently available is particularly easy to use without formal training.

ORGANIZING THE DIAGNOSTIC DATA WITH STONE'S DIAGNOSTIC CUBE

Stone (1980) has developed a three-dimensional diagram or "diagnosis cube" (see Figure 4-1) that allows the clinician to assess each case with respect to

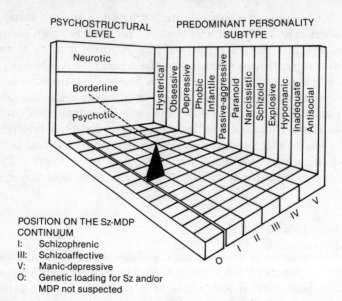

Figure 4-1 The Diagnosis Cube: Illustrative Example. (From Stone, M. H., *The Borderline Syndromes: Constitution, Adaptation and Personality*, p. 36. Copyright 1980 by McGraw-Hill, Inc. Reprinted with permission.)

the individual's psychostructural level, personality subtype, and constitutional type. This cube is being introduced here to remind the reader that diagnosis cannot be based just on the psychostructural level but also must take into account the other dimensions portrayed in the cube, a position with which Kernberg agrees (Kernberg 1980c). It is particularly helpful when used in conjunction with Kernberg's approach to diagnosis. Stone's three-dimensional diagnosis uses the following elements to complement Kernberg's structural approach:

1. *Level of Personality Organization*: Wall A is divided into Kernberg's tripartite personality organization structure—neurotic, borderline, and psychotic. The height of the pointer on Wall A defines the patient's current level of adaptation or level of personality organization. It is assumed that the higher the pointer is on Wall A, the better will be the overall ego functioning.

2. *Personality Style*: Wall B is divided into the 13 personality disorders used in traditional or psychoanalytic nomenclature.

3. *Constitutional Contribution*: The floor of Stone's cube is divided into tracks that represent constitutional or biological contributions to the development of the personality organization. These tracks are arbitrary

divisions of a continuum ranging from "pure" schizophrenia on Track 1 to schizoaffective on Tracks II through IV (with fewer schizophrenic symptoms and increasing affective symptoms as one moves closer to Track V), to the "pure" affective disorders (unipolar depression, bipolar I and II, and so on). An additional track, 0, has been added for those patients in whom no predisposition to any form of classical psychosis is discernible.

Stone's cube enables the clinician to derive a diagnosis by considering all three frames of reference simultaneously. The patient can be represented by a single marker that is then viewed three-dimensionally. For example, a patient with a paranoid personality, currently functioning at a borderline level and perhaps showing some soft schizophreniclike symptoms, or a past history of schizophrenic symptoms, is represented by the marker in Figure 4-1. The marker, which has been placed on the schizophrenia track at its intersection with the paranoid personality compartment, extends to the height of the borderline on Wall A.

Although Stone's cube is a useful heuristic device, particularly in formulating diagnoses, there are conceptual problems with the cube. First, the dimensions illustrated by the cube are not orthogonal (e.g., each dimension is separate and distinct from one another). For example, according to Kernberg, most hysterical, obsessive-compulsive, and depressive personality types would be assigned to a higher psychostructural level, narcissistic and infantile to the intermediate level, and antisocial to the lower borderline level. The implication is that there is a good deal of correlation between the psychostructural and personality type dimensions. The constitutional dimension also seems highly correlated with the personality types. A patient with a hypomanic personality is much more likely to be seen as belonging to the manic-depressive (Type V) or perhaps the schizoaffective (Type IV) constitutional types than to the schizophrenic type (Type I). Similarly, a schizoid personality is more likely to be diagnosed as a constitutional Type I (schizophrenic). Highly correlated dimensions add complexity to the diagnoses, but little information. Although the overlap between psychostructural level and personality subtype is perhaps excusable, the overlap between constitutional and personality subtypes is less so, especially when one considers the difficulty of making constitutional diagnoses in the first place. The usefulness of this third dimension is questionable. Even so, all three dimensions of Stone's cubic will be retained and applied to Mary Markham, John Elliott, and Sarah Gardner: the first two dimensions because of their heuristic value, the third as a reminder of the genetic contribution to psychostructural organization (W. G. Danton, personal communication, September 9, 1983).

USING STONE'S CUBE: THREE CLINICAL CASES

Mary Markham

Level of Personality Organization

Mary met the structural criteria for a borderline personality, at the lower end of the continuum.

Personality Subtype

Mary seemed to show features of several personality subtypes: narcissistic, passive-dependent, paranoid, and schizoid. The narcissistic and passive-dependent elements included her feelings of omnipotence and vengefulness along with her simultaneous self-perception as bad and worthless. Also narcissistic was her inability to involve herself with others except superficially, and even then only to the degree that they met her needs without demanding anything in return and without intruding on her. She manifested this behavior in her quiet dependence on parents, therapist, and physicians, making few verbal demands. Instead, she usually gave subtle clues about her needs and waited for them to be met. If her needs were satisfied, she remained nondemanding and unobtrusive. She could be suspicious and tended to project her aggression onto others.

But schizoid features overshadowed both Mary's narcissistic and passive-dependent traits ("schizoid features" have been fully discussed by Guntrip [1969]). Schizoid personalities have a constricted and undeveloped emotional life, are emotionally distant from others, and are preoccupied with inner thoughts and fantasies. Underlying their social distancing is an inferred need-fear dilemma in which the need for others (even wishes for engulfment) is countered by a great fear of others, and a consequent fear of engulfment. Schizoid individuals minimize these fears by withdrawing from others (see also Guntrip 1962).

Thus, Mary seemed to fit the psychoanalytic personality diagnosis of schizoid personality. In *DSM-III* terms she met the schizotypal and borderline personality disorder criteria.

Constitutional Contributions

Aside from the "alcoholism and temper" that led to the long-term psychiatric hospitalization of Mary's paternal grandmother, little is known about her grandmother's diagnosis or any other history of mental illness in Mary's family.

Mary reported that her own prolonged periods of depression (during which she overate, cried, and felt helpless, hopeless, or lethargic) were punctuated by normal moods and an occasional day of elation. Given some of her schizotypal features, depersonalization and derealization experiences, and continued rigid perception that her therapist and she were linked in some way and the therapist was responsible for her (fused self-object image), Mary might well have a dilute form of schizoaffective or manic-depressive illness.

A possible confirmation of this impression is the fact that although Mary had had long trials of lithium and antidepressant medication (tricyclic and MAO inhibitors), she did best on a low dose of Mellaril, an antipsychotic medication with limited antidepressant qualities. Interestingly, psychological testing showed good performance on structured portions and acceptable performance on unstructured portions of the test battery (borderline patients usually do poorly on the unstructured portions). Mary's multidimensional diagnosis is shown in Figure 4–2.

John Elliott

Level of Personality Organization

John also was diagnosed as meeting the criteria for a borderline personality organization at the psychotic end of the continuum. In many ways, John resembled the affectively ill borderline described by Stone (1983), though his soft signs of a thought disorder also qualified him for the lower end of the borderline continuum. John appeared to meet Grinker's Type II (the "core borderline syndrome").

Personality Style

John showed signs of several personality disorders: closet narcissistic (put himself down with hidden grandiose referents), obsessional (intellectualized and distanced by obsessional thinking), paranoid (was suspicious of others' motivations and intentions), masochistic (put self in abusive situations and subjected self to others), and infantile (was histrionic, labile, dependent).

The infantile personality diagnosis fit John best. Kernberg (1975a) defined the infantile personality as being similar to the hysterical personality but functioning at a lower level. Infantile personalities present warmly with a clinging dependency. They have a more obvious lack of impulse control and lability of mood than hysterical personalities do. In addition, infantile personalities are more regressive and childlike regarding involvement in relationships, even though they can have good superficial adaptive social

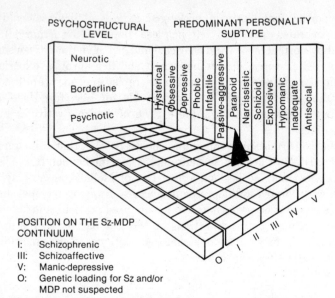

Figure 4-2 The Diagnosis Cube: Mary Markham. (Adapted from Stone, M.H., *The Borderline Syndromes: Constitution, Adaptation and Personality*, p. 35. Copyright 1980 by McGraw-Hill, Inc. Reprinted with permission.)

skills. They are more helpless, demanding, and primitively narcissistic than hysterical personalities are. Other qualities of infantile personalities also distinguish them from the hysterical category. For example, the sexuality of infantile personalities has a more primitive, polymorphous-perverse quality, and their masochism is of a lower level, less motivated by guilt. Also, infantile personalities are rarely competitive with men and women, shifting instead between positive and negative feelings on one hand and submission and oppositionalism on the other.

John seemed to meet the criteria for an infantile personality with obsessional, depressive-masochistic, and paranoid features. According to the *DSM-III*, he met the criteria for the borderline personality and partly met the criteria for schizotypal personality disorder. His history of reliance on street drugs to regulate his moods hinted at a possible affective disorder as well.

Constitutional Contributions

Many of John's problems could be attributed to a dilute form of one of the major affective disorders or even schizophrenia, though there was no known history of major mental illness in John's family. In addition, John's prolonged early-childhood separation from his mother and physical abuse by his father during John's latency and adolescence (nothing is known about possible abuse during infancy) could account for his depressive and vulnerable character structure. His depressions usually centered on abandonment themes, and his soft thought disorder related to times of fragmentation and attempts at repair. John received no medication during his therapy, and his symptoms remitted in a long-term psychodynamically oriented therapy; thus it is unclear whether there were any constitutional elements in the clinical picture, based on history or treatment response.

John's multidimensional diagnosis can be seen in Figure 4–3. It should be noted that if a full *DSM-III* axial diagnosis were done on John, his substance abuse would be coded on Axis I.

Sarah Gardner

Level of Personality Organization

Sarah Gardner met the criteria for a borderline personality organization, higher-level, or narcissistic personality. She appeared to be on the border with the neuroses.

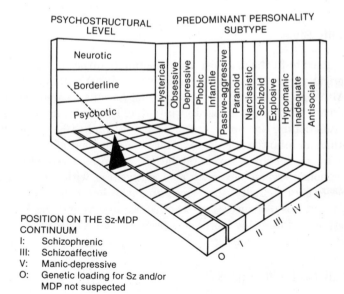

Figure 4-3 The Diagnosis Cube: John Elliott (Adapted from Stone, M. H., *The Borderline Syndromes: Constitution, Adaptation and Personality*, p. 35. Copyright 1980 by McGraw-Hill, Inc. Reprinted with permission.)

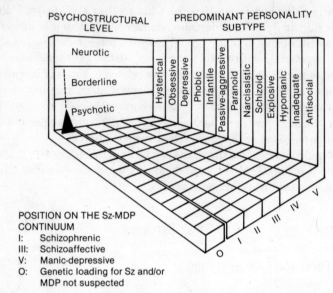

Figure 4-4 The Diagnosis Cube: Sarah Gardner. (Adapted from Stone, M. H., *The Borderline Syndromes: Constitution, Adaptation and Personality*, p. 35. Copyright 1980 by McGraw-Hill, Inc. Reprinted with permission.)

Personality Style

Sarah seemed to fit the diagnosis for either an infantile (Kernberg 1975a) or a hysterical personality (Blacker and Tupin 1977) with narcissistic features. Although some experts would say that Sarah appeared to be childlike and therefore could be diagnosed as infantile, I believe that Sarah's overall higher functioning and intrapsychic structure ranked her as a hysterical rather than an infantile personality. Her ability to maintain some depth and stability in relationships, sexual inhibition with pseudosexuality instead of polymorphous-perverse sexuality, competitiveness with men and women, and selective immaturity all seemed to make her more hysterical than infantile. But it is really a toss-up whether Sarah was hysterical or infantile. Kernberg would probably label her infantile because he reserves hysterical for neurotic-level functioning.

Constitutional Contributions

Sarah's periods of depression (e.g., when she felt blue or guilty, lost her appetite, and had difficulty sleeping) seemed to be associated with separations from significant others and with criticism. Although some of her symptoms (e.g., feeling terrible about herself after receiving criticism) were consistent with D. Klein's hysteroid dysphoria criteria, her symptoms were so mild that a diagnosis of hysteroid dysphoria did not seem warranted. (And after psychotherapeutic treatment, Sarah was able to bring her episodic depressions under control.) Therefore, she was seen as having no constitutional elements. No psychological testing was performed on Sarah, and she received no medication. See Figure 4-4 for Sarah's diagnosis.

In conclusion, a differential diagnosis between a borderline personality disorder and other disorders can be made early in treatment, although a good history and some visits with the patient may be necessary to be certain.

CHAPTER 5

Prognosis

REFINING THE DIAGNOSIS

The therapist has made a diagnosis of borderline using both Kernberg's structural diagnosis and the *DSM-III*. Both agree. The next step is choosing the treatment approach most likely to help the patient get better. Personality styles, character traits, ego weaknesses, superego pathology, and object-relations pathology whose prognosis is poor for psychodynamically oriented individual psychotherapy will be emphasized. Before selecting and starting the treatment, the clinician must complete the following steps:

1. Distinguish the patient's personality subtype as well as any prominent character traits that may influence the therapy's success. For example, let us say an individual has been diagnosed as having a borderline personality organization and an infantile personality subtype with paranoid traits. As Kernberg (1975a, p. 113) has noted, such a complete diagnosis gives immediate, relevant information for both the prognosis and the treatment of the patient. The fact that the patient has a borderline level of organization tells us immediately about the psychotherapeutic strategy, and the personality subtype gives us information about the prognosis. The subtype also offers additional information about the individual's defenses, object relations, degree of superego development, and characteristic ways of behaving, all of which will influence the therapy.
2. Identify any major affective components and any traces of schizophrenic symptomatology in either the patient's history or present behavior. This information will help the clinician determine the need for medication and/or anticipate psychotic regression.

3. Compare this three-dimensional diagnosis (e.g., level of function, personality subtype, and constitutional components) with Stone's Cube (Figure 4–1) and then Figure 5–1, in which such a complete diagnosis can be related to success or failure in psychoanalytically oriented psychotherapy.
4. Select the appropriate treatment, based on Figure 5–1 and the prognostic information in this chapter.

Figure 5–1 is another view of Stone's Cube that includes a specially delineated area. This three-dimensional area represents a territory within which Stone and Kernberg consider *intensive* or *expressive* psychotherapy (psychoanalytically oriented psychotherapy) to be useful. It includes the borderline region plus the lower end of the neurotic level (where certain severe phobias might be represented) and the highest part of the psychotic level. This territory also includes most of the "healthier" character types, but it begins to collapse near the narcissistic and schizoid characters (the less-responsive groups). The area vanishes altogether in the region of the non-responsive hypomanic and antisocial characters.

Figure 5–2 shows the prognosis only for characteriological types. This second figure is included to emphasize the importance of personality types

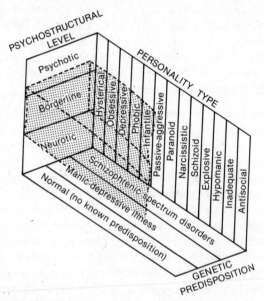

Figure 5-1 The Diagnosis Cube: Region of Optimal Response to Analytically Oriented Psychotherapy. (From Stone, M. H., *The Borderline Syndromes: Constitution, Adaptation and Personality*, p. 37. Copyright 1980 by McGraw-Hill, Inc. Reprinted by permission.)

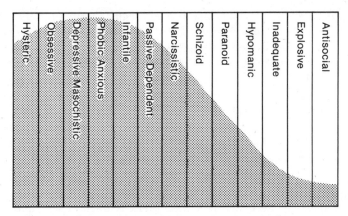

Figure 5-2 Prognosis for Characterological Types. (From Stone, M. H., (1979b). Psychodiagnosis and psychoanalytic psychotherapy. *Journal of the American Academy of Psychoanalysis,* 7(1):90. Copyright 1979 by Wiley and Sons. Reprinted by permission.)

in making a differential diagnosis and shows clearly that a few select patients on the right do benefit from psychoanalytic psychotherapy.

Overall, the prognosis for persons with a borderline personality organization is relatively good (with the exceptions noted in this chapter), although the change may take many years of intensive psychotherapy. Several types of borderline patients, however, do poorly in intensive psychoanalytically oriented psychotherapy, according to Stone and Kernberg, particularly antisocial or narcissistic patients operating at the borderline level. Kohut, however, would not have agreed that the narcissistic personality is a poor treatment risk; in fact, he would have seen the narcissistic personality as being a better treatment risk than the borderline, a position with which Rinsley has concurred (D. B. Rinsley, personal communication, May 21, 1984).

As shown in Figures 5-1 and 5-2, several other personality types also do poorly in the primary type of psychotherapy described here. Therefore, differential diagnoses should be made carefully. In some cases, the clinician might try intensive psychotherapy for one year before shifting to an alternative form of treatment or abandoning treatment altogether.

There are few data on how borderline patients do without treatment. Werble (1970) reported that a five-year follow-up of Grinker's sample of untreated borderlines showed little change in the clinical picture; there was the same dysfunctional behavior with no decompensation into schizophrenia. Beyond this one study, we simply do not know what happens to the untreated patient. But, the accumulated wisdom of many experienced clinicians in regard to how borderline adults fare in a variety of psychodynamic approaches and other treatment modalities can be utilized.

Several kinds of individual psychoanalytically oriented psychotherapies will be considered in this chapter. Each has its own techniques and goals, and none is necessarily better than the others. Briefly, *psychoanalysis* refers to a treatment approach that takes place three to five times a week, using an analytic couch, free association, and strict rules governing the therapist's behavior, with the goal of fully resolving the transference neurosis. *Intensive* or *expressive* psychotherapy uses psychoanalytic theory to understand the patient, meets one to three times per week, does not use the analytic couch, and has strict rules for the therapist's behavior, with the addition of parameters or modification of psychoanalytic technique in order to achieve far-reaching character change. *Supportive* psychotherapy can use psychoanalytic theory to understand the patient but employs only a few of the techniques of psychoanalysis, meets once a week or less, and is much less strict about the therapist's behavior, with the goal of helping the patients adapt better. Which individual treatment is appropriate depends largely on the patient's personality subtype, the severity of the traits, object relations, and superego pathologies.

FORECASTING PROGNOSIS

The review of the more important prognostic indicators for psychoanalytic psychotherapy—henceforth to be referred to as *intensive psychotherapy*—relies heavily on Kernberg's schema and findings (1975a) and other experts as noted.

Personality Subtype

The common character pathologies and their special problems can be divided into two broad categories. The following personality disorders can do well in either psychoanalysis or intensive psychotherapy because they are higher on the diagnostic developmental continuum and thus have more ego strength.

Hysterical, Infantile, and Obsessive-Compulsive Personalities

Hysterical and obsessive-compulsive individuals tend to do well in (i.e., appropriately use and benefit from) psychoanalysis. Infantile personalities do well in expressive or intensive psychotherapy but are not recommended for psychoanalysis (Kernberg 1975a). The major consideration here is to evaluate these patients' ability for introspection and their motivation for change—two facets of prognosis that will be discussed at the end of this chapter.

Depressive-Masochistic Character Pathologies

Depressive-masochistic individuals are generally neurotic (Kernberg 1975a). They believe that they do not deserve to enjoy life and that they have to pay for it with frustration. Thus they have superego distortion, and their sense of being mistreated leads to depression.

Their prognosis varies according to the extent that these symptoms or character traits interfere with the patients' psychotherapy. For example, masochistic patients may have so much unconscious guilt or may be so dedicated to using suffering as a form of revenge on those they envy or depend on that the therapist cannot intervene in the process.

Depressive-masochistic personalities functioning on the borderline level have a relatively good prognosis with several qualifications (Kernberg 1975a, p. 120). The depressive-masochists have the best prognosis for intensive work, but the more sadistic elements they have in their personality, the worse the prognosis is. The more generalized self-destructiveness they present, in which the main intention seems to be self-harm (chronic suicide acts or self-mutilation), the worse the prognosis is. The implication here is that the more primitive the forms of self-directed aggression are and the more diffuse the aggression is, in the sense of poor differentiation of self from nonself, the less favorable is the prognosis. The reason is that these patients react to anxiety by trying to commit suicide or mutilating themselves. In turn, therapy increases anxiety and thus the patients may not survive the therapeutic experience. In other words, they may kill themselves before they resolve their conflicts.

Masochistic elements can appear in many disorders other than the depressive-masochistic personality. Kernberg (1977a) has ranked the masochistic elements according to their severity: the least severe level is moral masochism, in which unconscious guilt interferes with the patients' allowing anything good to happen to them. An intermediate level of severity alternates between sadism and masochism, often with sexual deviation, including an inability to achieve sexual satisfaction outside a specific type of act (e.g., fetish) or except in fantasy. The most severe level includes self-destructiveness (e.g., refusal to accept the therapist's help because of envy of the therapist), self-mutilation (e.g., self-mutilation as a triumph over life), or a rare condition in which hate and love are condensed, and the patients believe that only someone who kills one loves one totally.

Long-term hospitalization may be required for patients with severe self-destructiveness, such as chronic self-mutilators. Mary Markham is a good example .of such a patient, although she made substantial progress over long-term therapy, with one hospitalization of intermediate length.

Narcissistic Personalities

Narcissistic personalities tend to function at a higher level than do narcissistic patients at a borderline level. They often come into psychotherapy in their middle years, at the start of the aging process when they have to begin to deal with the loss of beauty or limitless possibilities. They tend to do best when they are suffering. Kernberg (1975a) feels that psychoanalysis is most effective for these patients because only it fully treats the highly defended character structure; otherwise, such patients tend to remain distant and aloof in therapy. He believes that narcissistic personality patients should be restricted to short-term crisis treatment when psychoanalysis is not an option. Others, such as Masterson (1981), Rinsley (1984a), and adherents to the Kohut approach, may well disagree that only psychoanalysis can help the narcissistic personality and frequently use a modified psychoanalytic approach and report success with it.

The following narcissistic characteristics must be closely examined because they are bad prognostic signs in an intensive psychotherapeutic approach. Kernberg (1984) refers to them as *malignant narcissism*. They are (1) antisocial features, (2) ego-syntonic aggression or self-destructiveness, and (3) paranoid trends.

The following five groups with borderline personality organization are questionable candidates for intensive psychotherapy, and accordingly, they must be scrutinized before being assigned a treatment modality. The reasons for their poor performance vary (Kernberg 1975a, pp. 112–152).

Addictive Personalities

The prognosis for addictive personalities depends on several things. Many with a borderline personality also suffer from alcoholism, drug addiction, overeating, or compulsive gambling. How much impulse control patients have over this symptom is prognostically important, as is the availability of environmental structure (e.g., day hospital if needed). To control their addictions, many patients need the support of self-help groups such as Alcoholics Anonymous or Narcotics Anonymous. The patient's willingness to obtain the needed adjunctive help is prognostically significant. John Elliott is an example of a patient who was able to use his therapy and keep his addiction from disrupting his treatment, even without environmental support. However, many addicted patients require extra support. Again, the prognosis for narcissistic or antisocial personalities with addictive problems is poor. The chances of success for substance-abuse patients depends on their underlying character pathology, as well as on their ability to forgo using the substance as a way to avoid dealing with their feelings while in therapy.

Narcissistic Personalities Functioning at the Borderline Level

Narcissistic personalities with borderline personality organization tend to do poorly in intensive or expressive psychotherapy until after a long course of supportive psychotherapy (Kernberg 1975a, p. 114). More recently, Kernberg (1984) recommended expressive psychotherapy for this group. The decision as to which of these latter treatments is appropriate depends on the patients' ability to introspect, their motivation, and any secondary gain from their problems (e.g., receipt of compensation).

Antisocial Personalities

Antisocial patients tend to do poorly in intensive psychotherapy, according to Kernberg (1975a) and Masterson (1981). Kernberg believes that this diagnosis should be made mainly from the patients' history and how they relate to the interviewer or therapist across time. He feels that the best treatment is probably a facility that combines the characteristics of a high-security prison and a psychiatric hospital. Lion (1972, 1978), Lion and Leaff (1973), Vaillant (1975), Vaillant and Perry (1980), and Adler and L. N. Shapiro (1969, 1973) all have found that gains with antisocial personalities are possible if the treatment starts while the patients are institutionalized, though few others take this position. (See Yochelson and Samenow (1976) for a discussion of treating the criminal personality.)

Paranoid, Schizoid, and Hypomanic Personalities (the Classic Subpsychotic Personality Structures)

Paranoid, schizoid, and hypomanic personalities have variable prognoses and often do poorly in intensive psychotherapy. In order for paranoid patients to do well, their treatment must be structured so that their need for omnipotent control (e.g., withholding secrets from or attempting to control the therapist) does not distort the therapy. Otherwise, such behavior can stall the treatment (Kernberg 1975a).

The prognosis for schizoid patients is even more guarded. Their coldness, contempt, and withdrawal from the therapeutic interaction also may stall the therapy. Because of these problems, Kernberg (1975a) believes that the therapist's personality (e.g., warmth, emotional wealth, and capacity for empathy) may be the key to helping schizoid patients do well.

Hypomanic patients, whose defensive operations are related to those of the narcissistic personalities, have an even poorer prognosis than the narcissists do. Kernberg contends that this is true because hypomanic personalities have difficulty experiencing depression and hence flee into stimulation rather than working through in the therapy whenever they start to feel depressed. Their prognosis is somewhat better if they can tolerate depression without severe decompensation (e.g., psychotic breaks or massive acting out).

Impulse-Ridden Character Disorders
(Including Multiple Sexual Perversions, Heterosexual or Homosexual Promiscuity, and Polymorphous-Perverse Sexual Trends)

The prognosis for patients with impulse-ridden character disorders varies (Kernberg 1975a, p. 117), but as a general rule of thumb, the more unstable and chaotic they are, the better the prognosis will be, and the more stable the sexual deviation is, the worse the prognosis will be.

The quality of object relations is the major prognostic sign. The prognosis improves for those patients who are able to maintain nonexploitive object relationships even with the impulse-ridden behavior. Patients who have unstable or massively inadequate object relations have a poor prognosis. For example, adults who live in isolation for many years and who engage solely in masturbatory activity with perverse fantasies have a guarded prognosis because they lack any sustained object relationships.

Persons with chaotic or impulse-ridden character disorders do fairly well in expressive psychotherapy unless they have an underlying narcissistic personality with a stable sexual deviation, in which case the prognosis is poor. This is because patients with an underlying narcissistic personality have difficulty tolerating the psychoanalytic approach and often do poorly in any treatment modality. In other words, if the perverse fantasies and actions are chaotic and multiple, the object relations connected with these sexual interactions are also unstable, and if the patients have a borderline personality organization, the better the prognosis is (Kernberg 1975a). John Elliott is an example of such a case.

Patients who have no sexual desire at all, even to the point of not having sexual fantasies and not masturbating, regardless of diagnosis (unless the inhibition of sexual desire is caused by repression in the hysterical or depressive-masochistic personality) have a very poor prognosis for intensive work (Kernberg 1984).

Type of Character Traits

Kernberg (1975a) reported that certain pathological character traits are also potential negative prognostic indicators. His discussion, which is complex and rooted in psychoanalytic metapsychology, has been reduced to four themes that can be seen as severe cases of various ego or superego distortions.

The following criteria should be considered when assessing these character traits.

The Willingness to Accept Contradictory Ego and Superego Distortions

The willingness to accept contradictory ego and superego distortions is a negative prognostic sign for intensive therapy and should be monitored continually. Two examples of this trait were cited by Kernberg (1975a, p. 124): highly honest adults who accept their own episodic lying behavior and persons who sadistically tease others while believing themselves to be constantly "victimized."

In the first example, obsessive, overscrupulous patients can be dishonest under certain circumstances without experiencing conflict. Often during the first interview they will alert the clinician to their mendacity by citing an example of their own behavior. Beginning therapists sometimes mistakenly assume that because patients honestly and openly admit their previous lying, they will not lie to the therapist. But, such patients almost always do lie to the therapist. These lies may range from misrepresentations of their financial situation to denials that they have resumed an activity or relationship that they previously claimed to have stopped.

Kernberg's second example pertains to patients with a serious masochistic personality element who act with covert sadism. These patients rationalize personal failure as the result of fate or another's aggression, and at the same time they exhibit sadistic behavior with a teasing quality. They tend not to be disturbed when confronted with the contradiction between their teasing behavior and their tendency to complain about being mistreated by others.

Self-Destructiveness as an Ego Ideal

In the case of self-destructiveness as an ego ideal, the prognosis varies according to the behavior's severity. Patients who exhibit relentless masochistic, self-defeating behavior and who mutilate themselves or repeatedly attempt suicide are included in this category (Kernberg 1975a, Chessick 1977).

Briefly, a scrutiny of the patient's history and perhaps many therapy sessions will be necessary to distinguish between the self-destructive *effects* of certain behaviors and self-destructiveness as a major *intention* (Kernberg 1975a, p. 125). For example, patients who lose jobs or disrupt their studies whenever they are threatened with confrontation regarding their shortcomings may rationalize such disruptions as self-destructive. On the surface, they are right, but their underlying intention may be to protect a primitive grandiose self-concept, not to destroy all that is good in their life (Kernberg 1975a, p. 125). These patients have a better prognosis than do patients who need to destroy their therapy in order to triumph over the therapist.

Kernberg (1975a, p. 125) reports that only in regard to patients who chronically mutilate themselves can one say with certainty that the self-mutilation is a serious negative prognostic sign, which alerts the clinician to the strong possibility of a negative therapeutic reaction. The *negative therapeutic reaction* in this case refers to the patients' strong need to destroy the helpful aspects of the therapy in order to triumph over those they envy (many narcissistic patients) or to inflict suffering on those to whom they are too close (many borderline or schizophrenic patients). Mary Markham is an example of this type of problem, although her need to destroy help was limited to times of disappointment and not generalized to all help. Therefore, even within this group there is a range of severity.

Loss of Reality Testing When Expressing a Trait

Uncontrollable, intense rage is an example of patients' losing touch with reality and engaging in highly destructive behavior without regard for its later consequences. The prognosis is poor. This behavior occurs whenever these patients feel slighted, even for reasons they do not understand. The therapist may well feel intimidated by such explosiveness, particularly if it frequently leads to physical action. Enraged patients may require more supportive or behavioral treatment before intensive treatment can be instituted (Kernberg 1975a).

Degree and Quality of Ego Weakness

Although all borderline patients have the following ego weaknesses, their severity determines the prognosis (Kernberg 1975a).

Predominance of Primitive Defense Operations

Clearly, the more higher-level defensive operations that the patient uses, the better the prognosis will be. Patients with severe splitting and primitive denial are often difficult to work with except in long, intensive psychotherapies.

Tendency toward Primary Process Thinking and Weakened Reality Testing

The prognosis becomes more negative as patients engage more in primary process thinking or have frequent and severe losses of reality testing. In such cases, the therapy is conducted more like that for psychotic patients. Instead of using major confrontations, the therapy will provide a holding environment for the patients, helping them differentiate their reality from that of the therapist and providing sensitive understanding of their primary process world.

Lack of Impulse Control

Lack of impulse control is prognostically very serious, and most borderline patients have some selective problems with impulse control. Patients with a *generalized* lack of impulse control point up the potentiality for acting in (during) and acting out (outside) the treatment hours. Acting in (within the treatment) may include eroticizing the relationship with the therapist or reacting to interpretations with chronic rage. Kernberg (1975a) has said that "some patients obtain much more gratification of their pathological instinctual needs in the transference than would ever be possible in extra-therapeutic interactions" (p. 130). At times, these patients will thwart the change process simply to maintain the therapeutic relationship in order to receive unhealthy gratification. Acting out (outside the treatment) may also be a major problem, particularly in cases of substance abuse, impulsive behavior involving criminal activity, or other behavior that jeopardizes the patient's job and family.

The lack of generalized impulse control tends to shift the treatment from an interpretative to a supportive approach. Patients whose impulse control is so poor that the therapist must constantly intervene in their daily problems may require hospitalization or at least day hospitalization concomitant with the psychotherapy (Kernberg 1975a).

Inability to Tolerate Anxiety

For patients unable to tolerate anxiety, the prognosis is poor, because experiencing more anxiety than usual (as often happens in therapy) may induce further symptom formation. Some patients have intense panic reactions to almost any additional stress in their life. In addition, the same problems arising from a lack of impulse control pertain to the lack of anxiety tolerance (Kernberg 1975a).

Lack of Sublimatory Channels

The lack of sublimatory channels is an important indicator but difficult to evaluate. Nonetheless, the more ways the patients have found to enjoy work and life, the better will be their ability to sustain interest in the therapy. The clinician must carefully evaluate both the general quality of the patients' activities and their effect. Do the patients generally enjoy and find some personal worth in the activity, or are they doing it only for prestige and money? The significance of this degree of interest is related to the patients' potential for an authentic dedication to something that transcends their self-interest. This, of course, is relevant to how well the patients will be able to participate in an intensive psychotherapy and forgo immediate gratification for a long-term gain (Kernberg 1975a).

Degree and Quality of Superego Pathology

The degree to which patients adhere to issues of conscience and social norms is also prognostically significant. The more awareness the patient has of values other than those of immediate satisfaction, the better the prognosis is (Kernberg 1975a). And the more the patient is able to experience guilt or anxiety over hurtful behavior, the better the prognosis will be. Again, a history of lying or episodic and frequent criminal activity bodes ill for the patients' ability to be honest verbally or to direct their feelings and thoughts to verbal discussion within the psychotherapy without serious acting out later.

But because some antisocial behavior in its broadest sense is often seen in persons with a borderline personality, how the behavior reflects on the superego structure is as important as the behavior itself. In particular, the following dimensions (when they appear) have important negative prognostic implications and should be assessed: (1) no personal values; (2) no awareness of value systems in other people; (3) no awareness of the interpersonal implications of not having such value systems and the impact of this deficiency on others; (4) the predominance of generalized ruthlessness toward others, in contrast with the aggressive, impulsive, tumultuous behavior of ordinary borderline patients; (5) contradictions between stated ethical values and behavior and the toleration of these contradictions without guilt or concern; and (6) no "signal guilt" by which adults self-correct inappropriate behavior after receiving some clue that they are acting unethically or are violating personal or commonly held societal values (Kernberg 1975a, pp. 141–143).

Degree and Quality of Object Relations

An analysis of the patient's present or past relationships with significant others can also provide important prognostic information. Although border-line individuals tend to have highly disturbed interpersonal relationships, the following are negative prognostic indications: (1) a history of few if any meaningful relationships (e.g., complete social isolation); (2) a history of ruthless manipulation of relationships; (3) an inability to maintain relation-ships, regardless of how neurotic; (4) in the case of narcissistic individuals, good surface adaptation with an internal world of envious, contemptuous relationships with others; and (5) in the case of dependent persons, a view of dependency as submission to a hostile, damaging person, manifested by chronic self-destructive behavior and an unwillingness to escape from such relationships.

Positive prognostic signs include the ability to discriminate realistically among different people with whom the same kind of neurotic conflict may be expressed. Another positive sign is the ability to tolerate, at least to some extent, both loving and hateful feelings toward the same person. Finally, a pathological dependency on the same person over time is probably more promising prognostically than is social isolation from all people (Kernberg 1975a, pp. 144–146).

Motivation, Ability to Introspect, and Secondary Gain

For a long-term, intensive psychotherapy, the patient needs to have motiva-tion, time, and introspection, and his or her symptoms must not be too urgent (Kernberg 1984). In determining motivation, the patients' expecta-tions and ability to introspect are important. The least motivated are those who expect the therapist "magically" to cure them. They will almost always become frustrated with the treatment when this does not happen imme-diately. They are unable to see the problem as belonging to them and hence will probably blame others when they do not get better. The best motivated and most introspective are those patients who want to learn about them-selves, seek new life options, and want the therapist to help them achieve this (Kernberg 1984). Between these two poles are several gradations, including those patients who do not expect magic but who believe that if they do what the therapist wants, they will get better, and a higher group of patients who do not know what is wrong and simply want the therapist to diagnose it so that they can follow the therapist's directions and get better.

Another poor prognostic sign for intensive psychotherapy occurs when patients receive various secondary gains from being "ill" (e.g., they receive financial compensation; their family looks after them), and so these patients stand to lose from getting better. This state of affairs requires scrutiny.

Frequency of Early Separation Experiences

Masterson (1976) considers too many early childhood separations to be a bad prognostic sign for a therapy designed to work intensively through abandonment depression. This is because the patients will probably be too vulnerable to cope with the intensity of the abandonment depression that must be worked out. Supportive psychotherapy then becomes the treatment of choice.

Poor prognostic signs for psychotherapy in general are severe corruption of the superego, severe social isolation, and exploitive or manipulative relationships. In addition, a number of other indicators are poor prognostic signs for an intensive psychotherapy, although supportive psychotherapy may remain an option. Anxiety and suffering by patients regarding their symptoms are good prognostic signs because these characteristics will assist in getting them into and staying in therapy. In the long run of therapy, however, the other prognostic signs listed in this chapter will be more important prognostically than will anxiety over the symptoms.

The therapist acquires valuable information by evaluating patients on the basis of each of these prognostic indicators. Such an assessment identifies the characteristics that need to be addressed early in the therapy, either by confrontation or environmental intervention. It also identifies characteristics that may destroy the therapy. Because one person can treat only a few difficult borderline patients at a time, a prognostic forecast helps the therapist choose which patients to accept for treatment. Finally, this information offers a rational basis on which to select the treatment modality, ranging from psychoanalysis to supportive psychotherapy.

Part II

THEORY

CHAPTER 6

Psychoanalytic
Developmental Theory

The developmental approach is based on the belief that infants must pass certain psychological milestones in order to achieve a healthy identity. The failure to pass these watershed marks, hence deviation in certain specific ways, is seen as the causal agent of adult borderline psychopathology.

The object-relations approach, in focusing on the early developmental experiences that underlie the emerging psychic structure, fills a void in psychoanalytic theory. Object-relations theory, of course, draws on the developmental approach for the concepts of fixation and developmental deviations or arrest. But the developmental approach adds an important dimension—progression through time—that allows for the emergence of certain deficits in a phase-specific sequence of developmental vicissitudes (Meissner 1984, p. 49).

In essence, the developmental approach emphasizes experiential over constitutional factors (Meissner 1984). Because the quality of the infant's object-relations experience is critical to the developmental approach, there is a significant overlap between developmental perspectives and specific object-relations theories. For this reason, the developmental approach provides a unifying theory within which the multiple perspectives discussed in this book can be organized.

The notion of failed developmental tasks and the role of the parents (particularly the mother) in this failure is crucial to understanding borderline pathology. Although the mother's role in the infants' earliest development is emphasized, children do exist from birth in a family unit, and in some indefinable way, the family's emotional atmosphere influences infant development.

The literature is filled with warnings about the dangers of directly extrapolating from studies of preverbal infant behavior to adult behavior. Nonetheless, these conceptual efforts to relate child and adult phenomena, although inferential and speculative, do create new and useful pespectives for the diagnosis and treatment of borderline adults.

THE IMPACT OF PSYCHOLOGICAL DEVELOPMENT ON THE BORDERLINE PERSONALITY

According to the developmental approach, optimal developmental experiences in early childhood are necessary for the evolution of a healthy personality. I have outlined below a scenario that might result from an unhealthy nurturing situation:

> Under certain circumstances children may learn very early what they are not allowed to feel, lest they run the risk of losing their mother's love or making her insecure. These children soon learn the art of not consciously experiencing feelings such as jealousy, anger, vulnerability, and anxiety. After all, they cannot truly have such an experience without someone to support them and help explain to them the meaning of their feelings. But the feelings remain, festering inside, diverting the children farther and farther from their potential normal development. They gradually come to feel somehow different from others, alien, a species apart. Approaching adulthood, they feel increasingly lost, amorphous or fragmented into parts that war among themselves. As adults, they come to therapy—lost or angry, implicitly demanding that they be given what they never got originally, refusing to accept that they can never go back and get the caretaking that they missed as children. Little by little, these patients unconsciously reenact their forgotten experiences, and the therapist begins the process of helping them truly grow up.

How the borderline adult acquires such a damaged sense of self is explained by developmental theory.

CONCEPTUAL ISSUES OF DEVELOPMENTAL STAGES

The reader should keep in mind the following conceptual issues when reviewing this chapter:

1. Developmental stages are continuous rather than discrete, with each stage building on the material from the preceding stage (Mahler and Kaplan 1977). Although theorists might like to pinpoint the exact stage at which fixations or arrests occurred, all stages contribute to the total

personality problem. These stages are not sharply delineated chronologically, nor is their developmental content always the same (Rinsley 1981b).

2. In epigenetic terms, developmental difficulties may be highlighted in one phase, but these difficulties have their precursors and sequelae that are also affected by and influence other phases of the developmental process (Meissner 1984).

3. Subphase inadequacy in children can be subsumed in the long haul of development; problems in one developmental subphase will not automatically lead to adult pathology (Mahler and Kaplan 1977).

4. Adult pathology or diagnosis does not replicate early developmental arrests in a one-to-one relationship. Rather, adult pathology is reflected in the distorted, telescoped, and condensed symptoms that appear clinically in fluctuating states of exacerbation and remission (Blanck and Blanck 1979).

5. Borderline adults may act like children at times, but the problems of adults are by no means identical with those of small children.

6. Development of the borderline personality disorder cannot be attributed exclusively to defective child-rearing practices. Constitutional factors, as well as fate, also can contribute to the condition.

Stages of Development

Breger (1974) has summarized the main features of the general developmental model, as explicated in the work of Freud, E. Erikson, Loevinger, Piaget, the object-relations theorists, and Mahler:

1. There is an invariable order of the stages of development.
2. No stage can be skipped.
3. Each stage is more complex than the preceding one; it represents a transformation of what existed before in a new form.
4. Each stage is based on the preceding one and prepares for the succeeding one (p. 9).

According to Breger (1974), the developmental model assumes "an inner logic, a built-in plan that gives direction to the sequence of development" (p. 9). Thus, the human being can be understood only in a developmental context. Each stage of thinking, ego functioning, defense, or identity represents a more complex, differentiated, and integrated transformation of thought and personality than that preceding it (p. 8). In this sense, the development of the human mind is "analogous to the development of an embryo or the evolution of animal species—the thought of the infant is as different from that of an adult as the germ cell is from the developed fetus, or as a human being is from a monkey" (pp. 8–9). In other words, the personality structure of one stage becomes transformed into something related to but different from that of the former stage. And each developmental stage—in a "layering" process—builds on the achievements, no matter how limited, of the earlier stages.

What, then, are the important constituents of personality that are transformed from stage to stage? Loevinger (1976) considers the development of the sense of personal identity to be derived from cognitive structures related to the self and to others. It takes place within the context of early relations with a primary caretaker and is essential to overall personality development. Therefore, knowledge of the normal development of such cognitions and their pathological variants should yield important information about the personality structure of persons with all forms of psychopathology. The findings of Mahler and Kernberg confirm this assumption.

When introduced to this theory, clinicians are often tempted to scrutinize their patients for pristine remnants of self- and object images from particular developmental stages in order to identify and modify these images so that personality growth can be resumed. But deficits cannot be so easily assigned to a particular developmental stage.

Why is this so? A pathological outcome in any individual results because of developmental deficiencies and conflicts occurring at several levels (Meissner 1984, p. 360). Earlier developmental phases set the stage for pathologic outcome at later stages, and later phases can modify the pathologic processes of earlier phases. Therefore, an adult can have a layering of developmental defects, with a pattern of pathologic expression reflecting conflicts and defects at many developmental levels. For this reason, the human psyche has been compared to a core sample of sedimentary rock, in which each layer shows evidence of earlier events.

In theory this is a good analogy except that unfortunately, the human psyche rarely can be analyzed as quickly or precisely as can a geologic core.

It may be well into the therapy, when the presenting symptomatic conflict (which may have occurred at a more superficial layer) has been worked through, that the underlying more serious structural deficits based on earlier developments may be revealed. An example would be a medical student who sought treatment because of uncertainty about which medical specialty to choose (a charged issue because his father, a physician, wanted him to enter internal medicine, and he did not—a conflict that appeared to have both Oedipal and competitive ramifications). It was only later in the therapy that problems of identity diffusion and separation-individuation were revealed. Thus it may be only at the end of therapy that the therapist can see all the layers and their relationships with one another.

An analogy that provides a way to look at the human psyche is drawn from the unity of parts and wholes in Indian art. Each small figure, leaf, building, animal, or symbol in some way duplicates or recapitulates the overall design, shape, and color, as well as the theme, of the picture. The parts recapitulate the whole. Pribram, the noted neuropsychologist, has extended that analogy to humans, noting that each piece of their behavior recapitulates their whole personality structure. Commenting on the same phenomenon, Blasi (1976) noted that "every bit of behavior in some way reflects the whole person" (p. 183).

How can we extrapolate this concept to the psychotherapy situation? It would seem that each patient's complaint, painful encounter with others, reported fantasy or dream, or behavior toward the therapist can be seen as a miniature of the patient's psyche. When enough of these miniatures have been collected, along with the patient's association to them and the therapist's responses to the associations, the therapist can begin to understand these bits of behavior and relate them to the structure of the patient's whole personality. Now the therapist can speculate about the range of childhood fixations and arrests that led to the present personality distortions. This deciphering process is what takes so much time in the therapy.

When deciphering patients' behavior, the therapist should not spend too much time looking for the specific state during which the personality arrests or conflicts arose, because all kinds of development (intellectual, psychosexual, personality) in children occur simultaneously, influencing one another, and the forces involved may never be fully known. There is a tremendous number of developmental tasks for the child in the first 36 months of life. It is like cramming 30 years of work into 36 months, and many things can go wrong. Another reason the therapist should avoid hunting for the "right stage" is that borderline adults regularly reveal distortions that arose from more than one stage. These distortions, after all, are influenced by the previous stage. Early developmental pathologic problems are played out again in the Oedipal period, with perhaps a subsequent distorting of this process, and yet again during the second individuation process that occurs in adolescence.

Contribution of Parenting

Although the quality of parenting does indeed influence the development of borderline personalities, it is important not to "vilify" the parents and hold them responsible for all of their child's problems. This is because constitutional inputs as well as fate play significant roles in overall personality development. For example, some children are unusually active, aggressive, demanding, and sensitive from birth (for reasons that vary from biological-genetic programming to infant diseases). Their unceasing requirements for care tax the parents unbelievably, and few parents can cope with such demanding offspring. These children may then develop psychological or personality problems, and as adults they may put all the blame on their parents.

This does not mean, of course, that all parents are successful. Some may fail in one or more of the differing roles that confront parents across time. For example, Mahler and her colleagues (1975) found that the responses of the optimal mother for one phase of infant development may well not be those of the optimal mother for another phase. As children traverse the various phases, their needs change, including the behavior they need from their mother. One mother may be well prepared to soothe and nurture infants but less able to tolerate toddlers' needs for autonomy. On the other hand, another mother may dislike infants but may enjoy caring for toddlers. Some parents may be unable to modify their behavior in response to their infants' and toddlers' needs, and this behavioral inflexibility may contribute to the children's changes across developmental phases. (The role of the father as well as the mother will be discussed in detail throughout this chapter. The mother is being emphasized in this discussion because she usually has a closer relationship with the infant than does the father.)

Mitchell (1981) has suggested a way to view parental responsibility for early childhood development:

All caretakers, by virtue of their humanity, inevitably fail their children, each in their own particular way. Thus, internal object relations, concerning both "bad" and "good" objects are generated out of both the intensity of infantile passions as well as parental character pathology. An approach to both the child and the parent based on *accountability without blame* is necessary, making possible a more balanced view of the origins of neurosis in the interaction between the parents' difficulties in living and the child's infantile needs, immature understanding of the nature of reality, and primitive loyalties. (p. 396)

Reliability of the Patient's History

Patients rarely supply a completely reliable developmental history early in treatment. The experiences that patients supply are usually permeated with elements of fantasy, wish, desire, and defense. Frequently this results in a distorted and less than accurate history, especially for the early phase of treatment (Meissner 1984).

After a lengthy therapy, patients may view their history quite differently from the way they recounted it earlier. A parent they originally viewed as evil and demonic might now be seen as a well-meaning person who had natural limitations as a human being. At this point, the therapist may note two possibilities—that the patient described the source object fairly accurately in the first place or that the object is in fact strikingly different and only subtly resembles the patient's fantasied object. For example, Mary Markham viewed her mother as extraordinarily competent, but this view was not shared by the inpatient staff who met her. Early in therapy, John Elliott saw his father as sadistic and cruel—almost satanic. But after reconciling with his father four years later, John saw him as a likable but limited man who was rigid but caring.

Although clinically the patient's history is important in determining the origins, types, degree, and progression of the psychopathology, his or her behavior toward the therapist over time often reveals the developmental fixation or arrest far more clearly than a history ever will (see the cases in Chapter 12). Why is this so? Some of the most important developmental events take place during the infant's preverbal period. Therefore, often only through therapist-patient replications of the original mother-child dyadic relationship can the therapist grasp the essential quality of what the patient wants to convey, because the patient often has no words for the experience.

Childlike Behavior

Adult pathology should not be equated with normal childhood behavior, although adults who regress may sometimes act like children. But the two behaviors are not identical. Adults' rage because of some narcissistic injury, for example, may resemble toddlers' tantrums. But adults' aggression is colored by multiple distortions in regard to hurt feelings, revenge, retribution, and fear of retaliation. Adults may prolong the rage by engaging in litigious behavior, or they may feel suicidal or plot to harm the other. This pathology differs markedly from the behavior of children, who are intensely angry for only a few minutes before regaining their composure. Serious errors can occur in therapy if a therapist treats adult patients like children or infants.

MAHLER'S THEORY OF DEVELOPMENT AND THE EMERGENCE OF BORDERLINE PATHOLOGY

The infant's development of a sense of self is the core of Mahler's theory. She believes that after biological birth and an extrauterine period of normal autism, babies experience a second "psychological" birth. It is during this rebirth that the self is distinguished from the other and the foundation for identity is laid. Mahler has identified a universal sequence of developmental phases and tasks of this rebirth process and pinpoints where the borderline psychopathology emerges in this sequence. Her findings are based on studies of disturbed and normal children who were tracked from infancy through latency and adolescence (Mahler 1968, Mahler and her associates 1975).

Greenberg and Mitchell (1983) have noted that it is the task of the psychoanalytic developmental theorist to chart the infant's path from chaos to structure (p. 270). As with all map-making attempts, certain choices must be made at the start. Infants' motor changes, or their ability to conceptualize or to relate to others, can be charted, but not all such developments can be tracked simultaneously; no one map can contain all the relevant information. Accordingly, a theorist must decide which elements should be emphasized.

Mahler found the organizing principle of the Freud-Abraham map of libidinal stages too limiting—it simply omitted too much important information. In addition, she did not agree that the hallmark of successful development was "the establishment of genital primacy following the resolution of the Oedipus complex" (Greenberg and Mitchell 1983, p. 272). Instead, she believed that the achievement of a solid personal identity, within a world of predictable and realistically perceived others, was the hallmark of successful development.

The organizing principle of Mahler's map, then, is the relationships between the self and its objects, backed up by concepts from drive theory (Greenberg and Mitchell 1983, p. 272). These relationships occur within a sequence of developmental phases, moving from a symbiotic experience between the mother and infant to a gradual sense of autonomy.

As Greenberg and Mitchell (1983) observed, the Mahler child, unlike the Freud child,

> is less a creature struggling with conflictual drive demands than one who must continually reconcile his longing for independent, autonomous existence with an equally powerful urge to surrender and reimmerse himself in the enveloping fusion from which he has come. (pp. 272-273)

Mahler's methods also differed from the earlier psychoanalytic child theorists who regarded the study of children as an objective science that did not consider the observer's empathic understanding, feelings, and intuitions as useful scientific tools. It is true that Mahler began her research by studying children's overt, age-related interactional behavior, as did these psychoanalytic child theorists. But Mahler also noted the changes of both the children's and their mothers' experiences, including an empathic understanding of their inner states during these interactions. Thus, the observer functions empathically as well as objectively in Mahler's observational model. This is not unlike what the clinician does (e.g., observing and inferring), a fact noted by Mahler herself on many occasions (Fourcher 1979).

Mahler considers her theory of normal child development and developmental disturbances to be a contribution to object-relations theory. Both theories are important to understanding borderline personalities, and we could easily have begun this discussion with either one. It seemed useful, however, to start with the theory that specifically deals with the mother–child adaptation, the multiple defects that can be created within this adaptation, and this theory's contribution to understanding the borderline patient. Object-relations theory will be discussed in the following chapter, particularly in regard to the early developmental experiences that create the core of the child's emerging psychic structure, inner-world experience, and identity, as well as this theory's contribution to understanding the borderline personality. The reader will see that the developmental perspective has a significant degree of overlap with object-relations theory.

Definition of Terms

The terms *object representation, ego states,* and *introjects,* as used by the experts quoted in this chapter and Chapter 7, refer to very similar phenomena.

Self-image refers to an experience of the self at a particular time. It may be the experience of one's body or inner mental state. Self-image is constructed from sensations, emotions, and thoughts and may be conscious or unconscious, realistic or unrealistic. In a parallel fashion, *object images* may be viewed as the more transient perceptions of others gained directly or indirectly. *Representation* refers to a conglomerate of either self- or object images that is constructed over time, with a slow rate of change; it usually signifies a term with purely cognitive and memory components. Thus, images are more transient than are representations. *Internalization* is a process by which object attributes become internal percepts and come to shape the self-image and thereby create a sense of identity.

The term *configuration* is used by Kernberg to refer to the earliest existence of an object image and a self-image that are linked by an affective coloration (either pleasure or pain). At a certain developmental point, Kernberg refers to this configuration as an *ego state.* In psychoanalytic parlance, configurations coalesce by means of similar affective valences; all of the good images attract one another, as do all the bad images. Such groupings are called the *good internal object* or the *bad internal object,* respectively. Various theorists use the term *introject* for these groupings.

Aggressive and *libidinal* drives are used in their ordinary psychoanalytic sense to mean biological constituents that produce some demand on the mind for work. Drives can never be seen directly but are known by their derivatives (drives filtered through experience). Affects are considered the major drive derivatives. In his theory, Kernberg appears more concerned conceptually with the aggressive drive than the libidinal, and he defines the former in its narrow meaning (e.g., the aggressive ragefulness of the infant) rather than the broader meaning of all active, goal-seeking behavior or exuberant discharges.

Fixation generally implies pathology caused by retaining excessive amounts of libidinal or aggressive energy in one or more of the infantile structures. Along with the concept of fixation is the notion of *conflict*, in which various psychic structures or energies are pitted against one another (e.g., love/hate, libido/aggression, drive/defense, id/ego). Kernberg accepts the fixation-conflict notion of borderline pathology.

Arrest refers to failures to attain adequate self and object constancy because of deficiencies in early care, as a consequence of the parents' psychopathology. Arrest does not mean that development was completely stopped, but the patients' intrapsychic structure is so uneven and incomplete that the patients are vulnerable to regressive dissolution (Stolorow and Lachmann 1980, p. 5). Kohut and the self psychologists accept the arrest notion of borderline pathology.

MAHLER'S PHASES OF DEVELOPMENT

According to Mahler, children pass through three major phases of development between birth and 3 years of age. The ages listed below are approximate, as different theorists propose slightly different schedules, and Mahler herself is somewhat vague about precise time periods. Mahler believes that borderline personalities do not complete the rapprochement

Table 6-1   Summary of Mahler's Phases of Development

1. Phase of Normal Autism (birth to 4 weeks).
2. Phase of Symbiosis (2 to 5 months)
3. Phase of Separation-Individuation
   a. Differentiation Subphase (5 to 10 months)
   b. Practicing Subphase (10 to 16 months)
   c. Rapprochement Subphase (16 to 25 months)
   d. On-the-Way-to-Object Constancy (25 months to 3 years). Originally considered a subphase of separation-individuation, this developmental milestone is now viewed by some as a phase in its own right.

Table 6-2   Subphase Tasks

Stage 1	Normal Autism
Process A	*Attachment*
Stage II	Normal Symbiosis
Process B	*Separation-Individuation*
Stage III	Identity, object constancy, and healthy self-esteem

Source: Horner, A., *Object Relations and the Developing Ego in Therapy*, p. 26.
Copyright 1979 by Jason Aronson. Reprinted by permission.

subphase tasks, because of a predominance of congenital aggression or
severe family pathology.

Although latency and adolescence are important developmental periods,
Mahler has emphasized that these periods essentially recapitulate the structures that were laid down during the first three years of life. For the
borderline adult, it usually contaminates the Oedipal situation with excessive aggression. Experiences of latency and adolescence either repair earlier
damage or further weaken the defective structures.

Horner's summary (1975, 1979), as shown in Table 6-2, illustrates the
crucial developmental stages and the key process that must be achieved
before the child moves to the next stages. Thus, attachment to the mother and
then separation from her, with a concomitant sense of personal self, are the
predictors of future healthy adults. Borderline adults have partly failed in all
three of these processes.

Only those developmental benchmarks that are seen as necessary for the
evolution of the spectrum of adult borderline pathology will be considered in
this chapter. Accordingly, the impact of childhood illnesses, congenital
limitations, or extreme deprivation on the unfolding developmental process
will not be included. Nor will all ego functions be traced across the phases. I
have relied heavily on the schema and the analysis by Edward and her colleagues (1981) of Mahler's phases and their relation to borderline pathology.

Normal Autism Phase (Birth to 4 Weeks)

Description of Phase

Immediately after birth, normal infants spend most of their time sleeping,
awakening to be fed in response to hunger pangs. They appear to have only
the briefest moments of alertness and activity. They are unaware of inside or
outside or of the mother, and self and object are not differentiated. Their
world appears to be objectless. (The phrase "appears to be" conveys the

essential view of object-relations theory that the infant seeks objects from the very beginning. It is understood that the infant lacks organized object images at this early time.) It is assumed that the infants' needs are met from an inner omnipotent orbit.

Optimal Mother–Child Adaptation   The infants' task during this phase is to achieve physiological homeostasis. As in all the other developmental stages, achievement of this benchmark requires interaction with the mother. Although protected against external stimuli, infants do not have protection against excessive internal stimuli such as hunger pangs. The mother's task, then, is to see that the infants are fed in a timely way and that they are comfortable. The outlook for both the psychological and the physiological development of infants who thus achieve a state of well-being is favorable because even at this very early age memory traces are starting to be laid down (Edward et al. 1981).

Mahler and her colleagues (1975) have said that experiences in this phase are mediated by what she calls *coenesthetic reception*. This means that the infants' sensing and experiencing are primarily visceral (of the inside of the body) and are centered in the autonomic nervous system. For example, if infants feel pain in one place in the body, they are likely to sense that their entire body is in pain. Infants experience and familiarize themselves with their mother through coenesthetic receptivity (e.g., responding to her temperature, skin, and rhythm) before experiencing her as a need-satisfying person. They are starting in a rudimentary way to explore the object and to have a "feel" for it. And at the same time their responses to various internal sensations trigger the development of a sense of "inside," a body-self, and eventually will be a point of reference around which a sense of identity will form (Mahler 1968; Edward et al 1981).

Status of Self- and Object Representations   Infants have been described as being in a state of *primitive hallucinatory disorientation* during this phase. Because they are not aware of a mothering agent, except in a reflexive sense, infants are assumed to experience themselves dimly as the agent of their own satisfaction and tension-reduction (referred to in the psychoanalytic literature as magic-hallucination). Autism has also been referred to as the period of absolute primary narcissism. In terms of representational theory, this phase is called the *undifferentiated matrix*.

Some child researchers believe that infants have a greater sense of external objects than Mahler reported. These researchers claim that infants are born with a rudimentary sense of awareness and the ability to differentiate themselves from others (e.g., knowing to nurse from a nipple rather than a pencil). However, these newer findings do not really alter the basic tasks of the mother–infant adaptation that must occur during this phase.

Arrests and Fixations

The clearest phase-related pathology is early infantile autism, in which children remain fixed at this earliest stage of life and make no movement toward attachment. Such children do not exhibit attachment-seeking behavior as reaching-out gestures, a smiling response, or an anticipatory posture at nursing. Mahler believes that early infantile autism is caused by severe constitutional deficits in the child.

Implications for Adult Borderline Patients This stage is usually not implicated in borderline pathology. But it should be noted that many borderline patients long for a state of blissful coenesthetic receptivity with another. Also, when borderline adults lose an important other through separation or death, they will frequently describe the experience as one of losing an arm or a leg or having their insides ripped out. Although all persons have such experiences, they are more intensely experienced by the more severely disturbed patients (Edward et al. 1981).

Normal Symbiotic Phase (2 to 5 months)

Description of Phase

When the stimulus barrier drops around the age of 3 to 4 weeks, infants begin to show increased sensitivity to external stimuli (e.g., how they are held or fed, the surrounding noise level). They begin to fuss, cry, and thrash about. Now the mother must shield them from excessive external stimuli. As far as the infants are concerned, a fused mother–infant membrane replaces the inborn stimulus barrier (Edward et al. 1981).

A State of Psychological Fusion Infants are now vaguely aware that someone "out there" satisfies their needs, and they also realize that they cannot satisfy these needs without assistance. But at the same time they perceive the mother as coesthetically a part of themselves, the other part of the symbiotic orbit. From the infants' perspective, there is no essential differentiation between mother and infant. The term *symbiosis* describes this inferred state of undifferentiation or psychic fusion between the mother and child. In this context, symbiosis does not refer to the biological state in which the host usually benefits from a relationship with another organism, nor does it refer to the infants' clinging behavior. Instead, it pertains to the infantile experience of a common membrane with the mother, a sense of "dual unity," and the belief that mother and child experience each other's moods (Hedges 1983).

Optimal Mother–Child Adaptation   The infants' major task during this phase is to have an optimal symbiotic experience with minimal frustration. A successful symbiosis enables infants to attach solidly to and bond with their mother (Bowlby 1969). Mahler has said that positive *mutual cuing* between infants and mothers (called *communicative matching* by Masterson and Rinsley) is a prerequisite for successful bonding. Both infants and mothers have important roles in this process.

Infants must let the mother know they have needs by stimulating her attention and guiding her (e.g., quieting down when the mother does the right thing, crying until she responds correctly). The infants' contribution to the cuing arises from their perceptual ability (e.g., the capacity to receive and seek nurturance and to link together patterns of experience) and stimulus sensitivity (e.g., sensitivity to touch and visual response) (E. R. Shapiro 1978, p. 1310). The mother's contribution to the mutual cuing is accepting her own infantile impulses by accepting and responding to such impulses in her infant. To meet the infant's need for empathic nurturing and soothing, the mother undergoes a regression that reawakens positive fantasies of her own childhood (E. R. Shapiro 1978). This experience develops the maternal capacity to provide the proper holding environment. It has been noted that many mothers empathically imagine their infant's mood (e.g., "My baby frets when I am gone too long") and regulate their own behavior (e.g., "I really can't be gone that long") to accommodate that imagined mood and their own empathic response to it. Winnicott (1963) said that for the symbiotic phase to proceed normally, infants need a "good-enough mother" to function as an ego while their rudimentary ego develops. Good-enough mothers may not be perfectly empathic, but they are empathic enough to satisfy the infants' needs during this phase.

The mother's tasks are central to the infant's formation of a good attachment and preponderance of pleasurable experiences. The mother has two interrelated tasks, to *nurture* and to *soothe*. In nurturing, the mother feeds, rocks, pats, cradles, and maintains eye contact with her infant, all of which contribute to a sense of oneness and draws the infant's attention to her. These nurturing functions are carried out with enjoyment and pleasure, which are conveyed to the infant and promote a sense of comfort, safety, and union with the mother. Balint (paraphrased by Main 1957) noted the infant's need for the mother to love her nurturing duties:

> The infant requires his mother not only to be constant and to manage the world and his own body for him in automatic anticipation of his wishes, but also to enjoy it and to find her greatest joy in doing so, to experience pain when he is unhappy, to be at one with him in feeling, and to have no other wishes (p. 143).

Mothers also protect their infants against excessive stress, not allowing them to cry for hours, refusing to feed them upon demand, or keeping them waiting in wet diapers. An overload of such stress may tax the infant's resources, leading to what Mahler has called *affectomotor storm-rage reactions* in which affect and movement become overwhelming. Affectomotor storm reactions are a forerunner of anxiety and are akin to panic reactions in adults (Edward et al. 1981).

Thus, the mother's job is to soothe the infant appropriately and in a good-enough way to maintain the infant's homeostasis. Her failure to do so may have serious implications for the infant's ability to attach properly or to develop healthy neurophysiological patterning for dealing with anxiety (Mahler 1968). Many theorists consider mutual cuing between the mother and infant to be the foundation for projective identification in the adult.

Developmental Achievements   Although attachment to the mother is considered the primary accomplishment of this phase, other important achievements are also made during this time. If mothers properly soothe and nurture, their infants will come to have confidence in the mothers' consistency, reliability, and sensitivity to their needs. These infants will develop a basic trust that their needs will be met and assistance will be available when necessary. During subsequent phases, this basic trust helps them control their disruptive impulses toward immediate tension discharge, and eventually it contributes to their development of frustration tolerance and anticipatory thought. When infants learn that their mothers can satisfy their needs, they tend to long for their mothers whenever they have needs to be gratified (Edward et al. 1981, p. 10). This realization transforms infants from purely biological organisms to psychological creatures with the human need for relatedness.

Smiling Response   Early in symbiosis, infants make an unspecified, smiling response toward any human face. Spitz (1965) considers this response to be the first step toward the need-gratifying object relationship and truly the beginning of infant social awareness and activity. Around the middle of symbiosis, infants begin to smile specifically at their own mother. That smile attests to a special milestone in the infants' progression toward the capacity for human relatedness because it marks the start of their ability to invest in, and eventually care about, one special person (Edward et al. 1981).

Narcissism   The vague awareness of an outside source of gratification moves the infants from absolute primary narcissism, a period of hallucinatory omnipotence, to secondary narcissism and conditional hallucinatory omnipotence because the mother is now a contributing source of gratification. During symbiosis, infants assume that the mothers' unconditional love will never end and is centered inside them. Optimally, this secondary narcissism based on the mother–infant unit persists long enough to become integrated into the infant's evolving mind. This positive state of oneness carries with it the experimental feeling of grandeur and power, a reservoir of good feelings that allows the infants to weather the demands of the later phases.

Mahler has contended that both infants and adults must have a healthy narcissism made up of appropriate self-love, pride, regard, and bodily love (Edward et al. 1981). Healthy narcissism is the bedrock of a healthy sense of self and self-esteem. Jacobson (1964) and Kernberg (1976a) both observed that the later creation in the mind of an ego ideal (created from the images of the idealized self and an idealized other) is a mechanism that forever retains the oneness of the mother–infant symbiosis.

Status of Self- and Object Representations and Drive Differentiation
According to Mahler, the experiential precursors of self- and object images are laid down during symbiosis, and the libidinal and aggressive drives also begin to differentiate at this time. These developments are assisted by the maturation of the ego's various functions, especially the memory. As a result, infants begin to categorize experience as "good" (pleasurable) or "bad" (painful or unpleasurable). Gradually these affective experiences come to be associated with scattered part-aspects of self and object (mother). The bad, frustrating experiences become associated with the bad self-object and the good, satisfying experiences with the good self-object, which Masterson and Rinsley (1975) have called *split-object-relations units.* According to Mahler, libido and aggression are differentiated in relation to such good or bad scattered images. Thus a predominance of bad, hostile, frustrating, and anxious experiences threatens drive differentiation and tilts it toward the side of aggression (Edward et al. 1981). Because the infants are protected initially from bad stimuli by the capacity to eject such stimuli (as with bad food), too much frustration fosters excessive expelling maneuvers, which leads to a reliance on projection (Edward et al. 1981, p. 9). This will be elaborated in detail in Chapter 7.

In summary, if attachment takes place during symbiosis with minimal disruption, infants will develop a rudimentary body image and ego (with predominantly positive experiences). They will identify with the good self-object and will continue to experience the hallucinatory wish fulfillment noted in the autistic phase, but now they perceive mother as part of the unit that is contributing to their satisfaction. Infants will perceive a frustrating experience as "not me; out there" and will experience the outside at such times as being frightening and disturbing. This ejection of badness is the start of an identification of "me." Later, the ejection process forms the basis of the defense mechanism known as *projection*, in which unpleasant or unacceptable experiences must be externalized, usually onto the primary caretaker.

Arrests and Fixations

During symbiosis, several mother–child misalignments may affect the infant's maturational abilities and contribute to pathological outcomes. An optimal symbiosis is essential to all subsequent development because it offers the experience of confident expectation, sound secondary narcissism, and the safe anchorage that facilitates the child's transition to the other-than-mother-world. As Edward and her associates (1981) have noted, although severe early failures lead to psychosis, less serious deprivation or the prolonging of symbiosis beyond its phase-specific point can also distort later development.

Psychoses Childhood psychosis, or symbiotic psychosis, is linked to this phase, although it frequently does not become apparent until the age of 3 to 5. The clinical picture with these children varies and shall not be detailed here. As with childhood autism, Mahler (1968) has reported that innate constitutional factors ordinarily cause this childhood psychosis. She also considers that a disturbance in the mother–child relationship may contribute to this disorder (e.g., the infantilizing mother who prevents the infant from experiencing any small dosages of separation).

Less-Than-Optimal Symbiosis If the symbiosis has been frustrating and unfulfilling, several processes may be noted. First, infants with a deficient symbiosis long for the gratification they have missed, and this may be carried over to other subphases, when it may distort the infants' development. Second, Rinsley (1982a) has noted that if there has been excessive frustration, infants may remain at the level of wish fulfillment. Such infants conjure up perfectly gratifying mothers who magically meet their needs whenever they gesture or wish for gratification. This fantasy protects against the harsh reality of unresponsive or frustrating mothers and perpetuates the sense of infantile megalomania, entitlement, and specialness. If perpetuated, of course, this perfect-mother fantasy will have profound implications for the older toddlers' sense of reality testing (because they continue to operate at the level of the perceptually fused self-object image). (Some mothers insist on maintaining a parasitic symbiosis with their infants, which may also contribute to these symptoms. Clinically it may be difficult to determine whether the mother frustrated the symbiotic needs or parasitically indulged them.) (Edward et al. 1981).

Negative Identity   In addition, infants who actively experience excessive frustration and sense their mothers' negative attitude toward them tend to develop predominantly negative memory traces. These children cannot identify with the positive self-object experience, perhaps because it occurred so infrequently. If this negative self-object experience is not modified by later parenting, it will evolve into the growing child's predominant self-percept. This percept will then distort new life experiences as they are assimilated, thereby consolidating the early negative memory traces. The negative conglomerate will begin to emerge in the form of the diffuse identity or negative identity captured in the work of E. Erikson. As Rinsley (1982a) has observed, this will affect the infant's progression through subsequent stages, paving the way for the development of a sense of *basic fault* (Balint 1968). Basic fault is a fundamental feeling of badness, wrongness, emptiness, and worthlessness, regardless of adult reality successes. This negative sense of self will have serious consequences for the total personality.

False-Self Attachment and Defensive Detachment   Horner (1979) has classified the pathology of attachment in children into four broad areas: (1) failure to make initial attachment; (2) disruption of early attachment; (3) unintegrated, multiple attachments; and (4) attachment through the false self (p. 48). Each can contribute to borderline pathology. John Elliott represents a patient with a disruption of early attachments and multiple unintegrated attachment (occurring around the age of 2), but as far as can be determined, his earlier experiences were normal. Thus, the disruptions during rapprochement, although serious, were perhaps less disorganizing than if they had occurred in symbiosis.

One of these attachment problems is of particular interest in the formation of borderline personality disorder. It is attachment through the *false self.* The establishment of the false self represents an effort to build a sense of self by taking on attributes that please the mothering figure instead of attributes of the infant's own emerging spontaneous self. Winnicott (1965) found that attachment through the false self developed when mothers were unresponsive to or openly ignored the infants' needs. It can also happen when parasitically oriented mothers give the infants what meets their own maternal needs rather than what the infants really require for their growth (e.g., excessively holding and restricting movement because the mother needs skin contact). In response, infants may prematurely inhibit their dependency needs or other spontaneous behavior because these threaten the mother who is so desperately needed. Instead, the infants give what they think the mothers want—their *false self.* Their identity then consolidates around these fraudulent defensive reactions. Rinsley (1980c, 1982a) has discussed this subject in detail in terms of his concept of *depersonification (appersonation).* The mother, throughout this process, is relatively immune to the infant's feedback, and the infant develops a self-image based on the mother's projections and responds accordingly. What emerges is the infant's pseudoidentity based on and developing in relationship with the mother's own pseudoidentity (Rinsley 1980c).

Both Guntrip (1960) and Winnicott (1965) observed that the false self may be revealed later when the infants are adult patients in treatment and complain of feeling that they do not really exist, despite having what appears to be a normal life with job, friends, marriage, and children. Such patients feel empty and nonauthentic. Or it may show up in a more extreme form.

Mary Markham manifested an extreme false-self pathology. The following example oversimplifies her complex dynamics, but it illustrates the intensity of the dynamic surrounding the false self. Early in life Mary perceived that she had to act as her mother wanted her to act and believe as her mother believed (i.e., that her father was bad), or else her mother would abandon her. Consequently, Mary obeyed her mother in order to win love and care. Mary still continued to be what others wanted her to be, even though she deeply resented the process: she was an as-if person (Deutsch 1942).

For example, Mary's boss wanted to change her work schedule, and he asked how she felt about the change. Mary suspected that the new schedule might be better for her but had trouble making a decision because she was inexperienced in determining her own needs. Mary agreed to the schedule change but continued to worry that it was not in her best interest. She started to blame the boss for making her change the schedule (i.e., some loss of reality testing). Next, she felt intense anger at having her autonomy taken away (e.g., Mary became terrified that the boss would punish her for feeling angry toward him, an example of projection). Nevertheless, she refused to assert herself and ask to have the original schedule reinstated, because of her fear of rejection and abandonment and its resultant fragmentation potential.

In this kind of situation, Mary usually felt so overwhelmed by her tumultuous feelings that she retreated into the Megalomaniac part of herself, which helped her feel detached from her problems. Under the Megalomaniac's influence, Mary felt that she had only to give some indirect telepathic clue and others would immediately satisfy her unspoken needs (hallucinatory wish fulfillment). She now felt superior to the person that she was originally trying to please (in this case, her boss). But her detachment, however, led to psychotic isolation and emptiness, which frightened her into abandoning the detachment—thus restarting the cycle.

The false-self attachment, it should be remembered, is a way of maintaining some relationship with the mothering figure. In Mary's case there also appears to have been a parasitic symbiosis between Mary and her mother. In psychotherapy Mary came to realize that her symbiosis with her mother had several false aspects: (1) instead of meeting Mary's real spontaneous needs, her mother had been responding to her own concept of what Mary needed, particularly as that concept agreed with the mother's personal needs; (2) the mother would abandon Mary if she ever deviated from the established formula (e.g., she left to go live with other siblings whenever Mary got better); (3) Mary worried that if she violated the symbiosis, her genuinely fragile mother would be harmed and killed. Mary had her own particular way of staying attached to her mother through her false self, while privately feeling defensively detached.

Winnicott (1960, pp. 142–143) described the continuum of false-self pathology, beginning with its most serious form:

1. The false self is all that exists; patients feel there is no true, authentic self.
2. The false self protects and defends the true self, which is known only to the patients. (In these cases, "known" usually means "dimly perceived"; in many cases, however, there is no conscious awareness of the true self.) Patients are terrified that the therapist will learn of the dimly perceived true self and will obliterate it.
3. The false self searches out conditions in which the true self can come into its own and be shown. Patients are aware of this fraudulent process but believe it is necessary in order to obtain love. The true self may not be shown if the false self is overly rewarded by the therapist (e.g., if the patients' high level of surface functioning is rewarded).
4. The false self is built on identifications that do not fully represent the children's unique personality (e.g., a young man who denies his artistic talent and instead follows the career his father chose for him).
5. The false self is represented by adaptive social behavior, and the true self is intact.

A phenomenologically experienced true self that has been kept hidden (not reality tested across time) may have psychoticlike aspects that are not based on reality. Therefore, therapy is not simply the process of releasing this true self. Therapy really has two tasks, to release the true self and to help it develop.

Defensive Detachment   Unlike the other attachment pathologies, defensive detachment does not arise from the lack of optimal symbiosis (Horner 1979). Instead, it occurs because of premature differentiation out of symbiosis, usually because of a parasitic, intrusive mother. Defensive detachment protects the boundaries of the self from invasion by the other and enables individuals to be their real, initiating self rather than the passive false self. The toddlers' "no!" that typifies the "terrible twos" is an example of defensive detachment. Spitz (1957) viewed this response as the children's effort toward self-differentiation that becomes caricatured in oppositionalistic adults.

Adults use defensive detachment to keep their distance from the other. Much like infants, adults come to know their self by defining it in opposition to the object (Horner 1979, p. 85). Adults who have prematurely detached as children will usually use oppositional behavior in therapy (e.g., refuse to talk to or to accept the therapist's ideas). Such adults can do this safely only if the therapist is mature enough to tolerate their aggressiveness without becoming enraged, hostile, punitive, and hence rejecting.

Implications for Adult Borderline Patients   The foundation of lower-level borderline pathology is laid down in this phase. Many lower-level borderline patients experience transient psychosis, in which they regress to the fused self-object level of representation, analogous but not identical with this phase of infancy. However, when the patients are not psychotic, their symbiotic ideation and longings may be masked by pseudoadult behavior, which can temporarily hide their developmental fixation.

Separation-Individuation Phase

According to Mahler (1971), intrapsychic separation encompasses differentiation, distancing, boundary structuring, and disengagement from the mother, whereas individuation is the achievement of endopsychic autonomy and a sense of self (p. 407; also Rinsley 1984a). Separation and individuation run on two related but not totally parallel tracks. If symbiosis has been successful, the separation-individuation phase will overlap symbiosis when the infant is 4 or 5 months old.

Mahler and her associates originally divided the separation-individuation period into four subphases, during which the fixations central to the borderline psychopathology first become apparent. Here, for the first time, the conflict between the push for autonomy and the "wish to reunite" (symbiotically re-fuse) becomes apparent.

Differentiation Subphase (5 to 10 months)

Description of Subphase

Hatching   Differentiation, the first of the subphases of separation-individuation, begins at about 5 months with a process that Mahler and her associates (1975) call *hatching*.

> The hatched infant has left the vague twilight state of symbiosis and has become more permanently alert and perceptive to the stimuli of his environment, rather than to his own bodily sensations, or sensations emanating within the symbiotic orbit only. (p. 290)

It is this process that Mahler and her associates (1975) have compared to a second psychological birth. These infants, who only a month or two ago tended to mold themselves to their mother's body, now seek more active, self-determined positions. In addition, they are now beginning to differentiate their body from their mother's, through manual, tactile, and visual exploration. They like to play peek-a-boo games and are fascinated with their mother's eyeglasses or hanging pendant.

Breaking Away Somewhat later during differentiation, infants begin to respond to and search out stimuli coming from beyond the mother–child symbiotic orbit. Mahler and her colleagues (1975) found that maturational processes such as locomotion enable normal infants to begin to break away from their mother in a physical sense, making their first tentative moves away from their passive lap-babyhood by playing at her feet. Thus they are beginning to distance from mother while still holding onto her.

Transitional Objects During this period infants also become attached to a *transitional object* (Winnicott 1953) such as a soft, pliable toy or blanket that they cuddle to their body as a substitute for their contact with their mother, because she can no longer provide the full measure of symbiosis that served to calm or soothe at an earlier stage. Because these infants have total control over a transitional object, as they did not with their mother, they are beginning to deal with holding on and letting go. The transitional object takes on some of their mother's soothing qualities, and it is also an extension of the self at the same time it functions as an object. Eventually the mother's tension-reducing effects that were invested in the blanket or teddy bear undergo transmuting internalization and are preserved as part of the child's ability to calm down.

Optimal Mother–Child Adaptation Mothers function as a frame of reference or point of orientation for the individuating infants. Once again, the relationship between the mother and infant is crucial. The mother must continue to provide the mutual cuing started in symbiosis while allowing the infant to explore her and the world, within safe limits. Loss of their mother through temporary separations still evokes in these infants a distressing sense of disorganization and dissolution of the self (because the self is still part of the object). But they smile upon the mother's return, thereby demonstrating the development of *recognition memory*, the ability for perception to revive a memory trace.

Developmental Achievements Although attachment continues during this subphase, the infants are now starting to compare their mother with others, to check back to her, and to explore the areas near her, in other words, to separate tentatively and gradually. Identity formation is fostered as the mother responds to and selectively reinforces a variety of needs, tension, and pleasure (Edward et al. 1981). But at the same time, recognition that mother is not always there exactly when she is wanted elicits separation anxiety. Her loving ministrations, however, alleviate this anxiety and continue to build normal narcissism. Infants are now emerging "as the unique child of his or her own mother" (Lichtenstein, as paraphrased by Edward et al. 1981, p. 17).

The Father's Role When infants are about 8 months old, the father starts to play the role of a desymbiosizing force to help them leave the totality of the mother–child unit. He is another person to whom the child can relate, and he provides nutrients and stimulation as the infants try to pull out of the mother's orbit. By now, they have begun to live a bit less in their body (coenesthetic receptivity) and a bit more in their environment on their bodily surface (epicritic receptivity).

Stranger Anxiety Between 6 and 8 months, infants develop *stranger anxiety.* Mahler reported that infants react to strangers with curiosity rather than anxiety if the symbiosis was healthy, but if the symbiosis was unsatisfactory, they demonstrate more anxiety. Both Kernberg (1975a) and Rinsley (1982a) found that if too much frustration during symbiosis threatened the infants' loving perceptually fused self-object image, they will now exhibit prolonged defensive splitting and project the negative self-object image onto the stranger. This is an example of how the changes in one developmental phase affect the achievements of subsequent stages.

Status of Self- and Object Representation The *fused self-object* representation continues during this period, although differentiation of body image from that of the mother begins during this subphase. Infants acquire the capacity to discriminate between the self and object, and late in this subphase they will be able to distinguish between their mother and others. Such a capacity provides an exciting experience of this "different" person and pulls the infant out of the symbiotic orbit with the mother. Horner (1979), Kernberg (1975a), and others believe that although physical differentiation occurs during this phase, full psychological differentiation (self-image from object image within the realms of both pleasurable and unpleasurable experience) does not take place until the end of the rapprochement subphase.

Arrests and Fixations

Premature Differentiation Premature differentiation, which upsets the developmental progression, heightens the awareness of object loss and fosters separation anxiety. Causes of premature differentiation include (1) precipitous recognition of the separation of the self from the mother; (2) failure in mother–child communicative cuing, a too-early interruption of the feeling of symbiotic unity; (3) unpredictable maternal attachment and care; (4) the child's or mother's need to escape from a parasitic symbiosis; and (5) development of an unusually and defensively precocious ego despite favorable maternal behavior (Edward et al, 1981, p. 49).

Infants who differentiate prematurely must find some way to compensate for their disorganizing fears in order to achieve equilibrium (Spitz 1965). Accordingly, they may accelerate their ego development, and as in the case of false-self attachment, they may develop a false self or an as-if self in pseudoadaptation to the mother and the world, or they may begin to take over their own mothering (Edward et al. 1981, p. 50). Although sustaining at the time, these responses tend to distort later development.

Although the false-self attachment was mentioned earlier as a way of maintaining a tie to a vitally needed mother, the detached true self also represents a premature severing of the maternal tie before the mothering functions can be internalized (E. R. Shapiro 1978). Thus, such a process represents both an attachment (the pseudoself validates the mother) and a distancing (the true self remains detached and unformed). In defensive detachment, the child actively distances from the mother through oppositional behavior.

In adult borderline patients, the dissolution of the self associated with object loss is analogous to the disturbance of primitive self-feeling in the differentiation subphase. Using Kohut's framework, such dissolution helps explain the patients' severe reactions to failures of empathy by the therapist. Such failures, in effect, deprive patients of the therapeutic function, which is analogous to the maternal function and has the same organizing importance (Horner 1979).

Accelerated Ego Development   Adults do not necessarily require human object relatedness in order to develop creative skills. The sense of a self without an object can evolve from nonhuman stimuli, such as the crib, rattle, and playing with toes and fingers. If this state is rewarding, it can stimulate intellectual endeavors and skill-based activities. Bright, creative children who are ignored by their mother (e.g., who have no or little object relatedness with her) may go on to become highly educated professionals, but their creative endeavors alone cannot guarantee a happy life. On the other hand, however, these autonomous functions can be compromised if they become enmeshed in the various attachment conflicts or the grandiose self of the following practicing subphase (Horner 1979).

Mothering the Self   As Mahler has noted, children who turn to the self as a narcissistic resource may give up on the world of objects, thereby reducing the opportunity for healthy identification. Unfortunately, many parents consider this compensatory effort as highly desirable and reinforce it (e.g., inappropriately or too often telling toddlers what a grown-up little boy or girl they are, expecting too much of these children). Mothering the self may lead to narcissistic traits that are difficult to change in psychotherapy (Edward et al 1981).

Fear of Normal Aggression   Fear of normal aggression is another problem that may first emerge in this subphase. It originates from a negative maternal reaction to infants' healthily aggressive, goal-seeking behavior. Some mothers find the infants' constant explorations too disruptive, or they may want to cling to the symbiotic orbit. Either way, the infant may come to believe that self-assertion leads to the mother's becoming angry and the baby's becoming frustrated. Self-assertion, then, becomes fused in the infant's mind with the mother's anger and the infant's rage. A show of infantile anger can lead to rejection by the mother, with its resulting fragmentation of the infant's fragile sense of self.

Internalization of Negative Introject   Rinsley (1982a) observed that very young infants "spit out" the bad food associated with aggressive affect-charges. As the infants are able to build up images of themselves and others and to recognize some of the differences between this self and others, the situation becomes more complicated. This is because their cognitive apparatus is better developed. Now, bad self-object experiences come to be associated with the infants' anger over the suppression of self-assertive behavior. These experiences are dangerous to assimilate because of the intensity of their hateful tone (mothers' and infants'). Consequently, bad self-object experiences remain as unassimilated introjects—felt presences in the nature of foreign bodies neither outside the self nor inside it. Giovacchini (1979b) stated that introjects play a major role in persons with character disorder, their social relationships in general, and the therapeutic transference in particular.

Implications for Adult Borderline Patients   Schizoid patients and some patients with primary affective disorders are fixated at this phase. The schizoid person has emerged from symbiosis, yet still longs for and fears it at the same time. The self- and object representations are still partially fused, and these patients are constantly threatened by the possibility of their refusion. These patients thus may use distancing or hypomanic defenses to protect them from a refusion. They also may have a harsh and punitive primitive conscience that contains the fusion of the hating other vis-à-vis the bad angry self, which may be expressed as self-hatred (Horner 1979). Thus, they may experience a pervasive depression. Mary Markham is a case in point: she experienced the Megalomaniac, which partly represented her punitive conscience, and also was a malevolent maternal introject that punished her when she was angry or assertive with others. In addition, the true- and false-self attachment issues from earlier phases are further elaborated in this phase.

Practicing Subphase (10 to 16 months)

Description of Subphase

Mahler believes that there are two distinct periods of the practicing subphase—early practicing and the practicing subphase proper. Each one, like the preceding phases, is influenced by the developmental contribution of new physiological capabilities. Favorable negotiation of this subphase depends on what has gone before, because the behaviors of this period merge into the behaviors from the differentiation subphase.

Early Practicing   The early practicing subphase starts around the end of the differentiation phase, when infants begin to crawl, climb, paddle, and make other motions. Infants are now beginning to explore the world more fully, while at the same time still usually holding onto their mother, who is regarded as a kind of home base that provides, from time to time, emotional refueling and safety. Mother and her refueling function now take precedence over any other objects in the environment. Nonetheless, the infants are now starting to take interest in the objects that the mother brings (e.g., blankets, bottle), which may lead to choosing a transitional object at this time. The infants' developing ability to move away physically from the mother assists in their tentative cognitive ability to differentiate their mother's body from their own.

Later Practicing   With the onset of the practicing subphase proper, toddlers achieve upright locomotion and start to walk—a big step toward eventual individuation. This mastery of independent movement allows the children to explore new frontiers of reality: there is more to see, touch, learn, and explore. With their horizons widened, toddlers seem to be at the height of elation during the practicing subphase. Even the knocks, bumps, and falls that are so common during this period do not seem to interfere with their sense of elation (Edward et al. 1981). Toddlers are exhilarated by what they see, and they take pleasure in their own body and in new functions. In addition, they are now starting to relate to adults other than their mother. Although they seem to ignore their mother during their gradually lengthening explorations, these toddlers still return to her periodically for brief contact that rapidly restores their energy and momentum.

Optimal Mother–Child Adaptation   Despite the practicing toddlers' seeming obliviousness to their mother, her partnering remains crucial. Opportunities for refueling—checking back to her for support and reassurance—are essential. As yet, however, the toddlers do not really appreciate her as a separate person.

The start of this subphase requires certain specific responses from the mother. She ordinarily reacts to the toddlers' new accomplishments with delight and admiration. She must be able to let go and even "mirror admiration" at their increasing capacity to operate at a distance from her. She must also mirror admiration at the toddlers' entrance into an exciting new world. But at the same time, for safety's sake, the mother must be able to keep the children in mind even when they are out of sight (thus testing her own object constancy) (Edward et al 1981). Support of the infants' appropriate autonomy enhances self-esteem and increases their healthy love of self.

Closer observation shows that toddlers seem to need the presence of their mother to produce and maintain their mood of elation. Healthy toddlers experience a state of "low keyedness" when their mother is absent, but they do not become anxious. This is interpreted to mean that they are now strong enough to long for the missed mother without panicking or experiencing organismic distress. It appears that the pleasure in exploration counteracts any lowering of mood because of the mother's absence (Edward et al 1981).

Omnipotence, the Mood of Elation and Separation   Toddlers are now at the peak of believing in their own magic omnipotence, which is still derived from their sense of sharing in the mother's magic powers (Mahler et al. 1975, p. 20). Mahler has speculated that this exhilaration may result from the infants' increasing abilities as well as their escape from the symbiotic embeddedness with their mother. This deduction is based on the observation that toddlers' first steps are almost always taken away from the mother. Mahler infers that this points to a tendency toward separation.

The Father's Role   Mahler has said that the father's role is most important during the practicing subphase because the infants' feelings about themselves now depend on subphase-adequate responses from both parents (Mahler and McDevitt 1982). Just as the mother represents a home base for refueling, the father represents the space outside the symbiotic orbit with the mother. His role, then, is symbolic as well as behavioral. He is not a second mother; he is a person who introduces toddlers to the world in a variety of ways.

Developmental Achievements   Toddlers develop several capacities in the practicing subphase, including the rudimentary ability to soothe themselves and to appreciate the mother's functions, including her ability to relieve anxiety (Tolpin 1971). The capacity to self-soothe is achieved in two steps, according to Tolpin (1971). First, because the mother cannot and should not continue to provide as much soothing and nurturing as she did during symbiosis, the infants continue to choose an object (e.g., a blanket or teddy bear) that has the feel of their mother and invest it with tension-reducing and soothing attributes connected with symbiosis. This transitional object is given up when the children can provide the soothing for themselves without the need for an external substitute (a skill that will not be consolidated until the rapprochement subphase).

In addition, children at this stage increasingly appreciate various maternal activities, including the mother's function as a reliever of anxiety (Tolpin 1971). They recognize the relationship between the signal of anxiety and its relief (Edward et al. 1981). Each action the mother takes to relieve distress adds to the infant's perception that the start of distress precipitates maternal activities that bring relief. Eventually the infants will be able to internalize this connection and thus start to provide their own relief (again, a skill that will not be consolidated until the advancement of evocative memory in the following subphase).

During the practicing subphase, male children start to notice and find pleasure in their penis, particularly because they can now stand up and see it clearly in the upright position. The female child will react to anatomical differences later, during the rapprochement subphase.

Status of Self- and Object Representations Kernberg (1976a) has suggested that children begin to differentiate between positive images of the self and positive images of the mother during this period. Differentiation between self- and object images of negative experience occurs later. This differentiation of images (within both the good experience and later the bad experience) is still tentative and vulnerable to refusion at times of stress.

Not all experts, however, agree on this timetable. Piaget and Inhelder (1969) and Pulaski (1971) differ from Mahler and Kernberg in one important respect. Piaget and Inhelder found that children under 2 years of age do not have the capacity for symbolic representations. Piaget reported that before age 1½, cognitive development is characterized by the coordination of action in the absence of representation (sensorimotor period) and that thinking is concrete and animalistic. Mahler, however, has said that representational thought starts in the first year of life. The burden of research proof in this debate currently rests with Mahler. Nevertheless, even though these theorists disagree over the timetable, they do agree that this separation of images must take place.

Arrests and Fixations

Excessive Aggression or Passivity Edward and her two colleagues (1981) found two styles of maternal interaction likely to cause problems for toddlers.

First, the mother who has difficulty relinquishing the good feelings she experienced during symbiosis may prolong it by interfering with normal maturation (e.g., by excessively holding the children or restricting them). In response, the toddlers' impetus for exploration may wane, leading instead to a defensive, almost frantic effort to be free of their mother. This frustration at excessive bodily control may stimulate a surplus of aggression, which can have three manifestations: (1) deflection of the normal aggression of the practicing subphase into temper tantrums, passive-aggressive behavior, excessive negativism, and misdirection away from exploration and other separation-individuation activities; (2) for adults, difficulties in feeling ownership of their own body (e.g., expecting others to make things happen to their body—stop them from smoking, cure their physical ills, make them lose weight); and (3) a flight into defensive detachment, perhaps already started in symbiosis.

On the other hand, if the heretofore-doting mother prematurely withdraws her availability, refueling, mirroring, or mocking the toddlers' childish efforts, they may panic or become excessively preoccupied with securing her partnership. Infants who are preoccupied with concern over their mother's availability may only briefly engage in the critical practicing activities. Thus, they may be deprived of the narcissistically enhancing experiences that are necessary for the promotion of a positive sense of self (Edward et al. 1981).

The Pathologic Grandiose Self   Toddlers experience a peak of narcissism during the practicing subphase, when they omnipotently believe in their own newly emerging functions (e.g., absorb the power of the object into their own self-image). This is a significant change from the infants' belief in the omnipotence of the dual unit that occurred during symbiosis. Now they feel grandiose and omnipotent.

But for infants who experienced defective partnering and excessive frustration during symbiosis (e.g., false self alongside a core psychotic true self), practicing offers a pathological way to cope defensively with less than optimal practicing interaction between mother and infant. The formation of a grandiose self-structure can emerge to protect against the mother's intrusive, impinging behavior or her inability to be emotionally available (Horner 1979, p. 102). As Horner discovered, under such circumstances the grandiose self enters a developmental cul-de-sac and does not undergo the necessary modulation across time.

Implications for Adult Borderline Patients   This phase continues the elaboration of problems from earlier phases. Horner (1979) has stated that the infant's omnipotence in this phase is analogous to the adult's grandiose self seen in narcissistic personality disorders. Clinically, the grandiose self protects a person against the disorganizing dangers of object loss, shame, or humiliation. Sometimes memory and perception may be absorbed into this pathologic self, which then prevents the development of a healthy, reality-based self-esteem. Mary Markham is a case in point. Her Megalomaniac part told her that she would not really die if she committed suicide. It also told her to forget what was discussed in psychotherapy because it was shameful. The grandiosity of this phase can frequently be seen in patients with primary affective disorders.

The grandiose self is not always as obvious in therapy. Modest, self-effacing people ("closet narcissists") often have a hidden, secret grandiose self; it is the hidden referent against which they denigrate their real achievements. Persistent problems of shame and loss of self-esteem in otherwise competent and able patients often alert the therapist to the existence of a hidden grandiose self.

Rapprochement Subphase (16 to 25 months)

Description of Subphase

If conditions are favorable at this subphase, toddlers may overcome minor problems that arose during earlier developmental subphases. On the other hand, earlier deficits may be compounded, or new problems may emerge because of difficulties during this subphase.

Deflation of Omnipotence   During the early part of this phase, toddlers become more aware of separateness from mother as their perceptual and cognitive faculties grow. This enhanced sense of separateness does not develop without cost, however. The mother, who now is recognized as separate, takes on a new significance. Children who were independent and able to function at a distance from their mother in the practicing subphase now are constantly concerned about her whereabouts. Greenberg and Mitchell (1983) observed that toddlers come to realize that contrary to their former narcissistic sense of omnipotence, they really are "a very small person in a very big world" (p. 277). Their sense of magic wish fulfillment disappears, and instead they experience a sense of heightened vulnerability.

Two new processes emerge: (1) the infants' ideal sense of self becomes attenuated, and (2) a kind of separation anxiety reappears. Toddlers again wish for their mother to participate in all their activities. They woo her into sharing activities by bringing her toys and constantly trying to get her attention. Separation fears (e.g., fear of losing the object) are temporarily warded off when the toddlers succeed in convincing their mother to share in their activities. But this behavior is often confusing to mothers who just a month ago had such independent children.

If the *grandiose self* is the derivative of the practicing period, then the *idealized object* is a derivative of this period as the toddler starts to feel vulnerable again and desperately needs the mother (Horner 1979).

Rapprochement Crisis   The loss of the ideal self and the recognition that the world does not revolve around them lead toddlers to experience what Mahler has termed the *rapprochement crisis* (18 to 24 months). The wooing behaviors are quickly replaced by coercive types of behavior aimed at re-establishing the mother–infant duality of symbiosis. This is frequently a very difficult time for both mother and child. The mother's behavior is critical to resolution of the rapprochement crisis and its impact on many of the toddlers' later personality traits.

Optimal Mother–Child Adaptation   The mother needs to be particularly resourceful during rapprochement in order to deal with the toddlers' contradictory messages. She must be unobtrusively available to share in activities, but she also must be able to let go at a moment's notice, even giving a little push in the direction of individuation and autonomy (Edward et al. 1981).

Rapprochement puts a particular strain on the mother and her partnering efforts. During the rapprochement crisis, toddlers often have temper tantrums, are indecisive, try to coerce their mother into certain behavior, and appear to feel alone and shy. Whininess, nightmares, and vivid, fearsome nocturnal hallucinations may make their appearance, adding further to the toddlers' efforts to coerce intimacy with their parents, especially, of course, their mother. The conflict of this subphase arises from the toddlers' contradictory needs for help and their fear of engulfment. They need and want help from an outside source, but because of the individuation drive and ongoing consolidation of separateness, they do not want too much close body contact with their mother, whereas at other times (especially at night), they attempt to coerce it. Nor do toddlers want to acknowledge that they need help, because that would be damaging to their sense of omnipotence. They are frequently motivated by a fear of reengulfment by the mother that they often view as dangerous and threatening. Although the mother is still viewed as omnipotent, toddlers feel separate enough from her so they no longer share in her omnipotence (Meissner 1984). This conflict leads to stormy scenes in which the child is intensely needy and clinging to mother while at the same time battling with her and saying "no." Demands for attention often alternate dramatically with fighting, which is confusing and unnerving to the mother.

Mahler has inferred that the wish for reunion and fear of engulfment are conveyed in toddlers' "shadowing" of their mother, watching her every move, and then "darting away" with the hope of being chased and swooped up in her arms. This behavioral manifestation of wanting to push away and hold onto their mother at the same time is called *ambitendency* and represents in motor behavior the toddlers' contradictory feelings. Ambitendency will evolve into the emotional and cognitive capacity for ambivalence.

Edward and her colleagues (1981) found that toddlers gradually realize that their parents are separate people with interests of their own. In addition, these children begin to undergo the painful process of modifying their delusions of grandeur. At that time, they experience anger and frustration from the realization of their helplessness and powerlessness vis-à-vis their parents. The mother's "no" is now seen for what it is—evidence of her superior power. One interpretation of the frequent use of "No!!" during this part of rapprochement is that the children are identifying with the aggressor; another, as Spitz (1957) pointed out, holds that the "No!!" response represents that first manifestation of the toddlers' use of *judgment* (hence, further evidence of separation-individuation).

Thus, the mother's continued nurturing, her availability, and her active willingness to let go but not abandon the toddlers are prerequisites for the successful completion of the critical subphase of rapprochement.

Developmental Achievements   Other capacities also develop during the pivotal rapprochement subphase, including language, memory, and reality testing. Both mother and toddler rely more on verbal communication now, and gestural communication, with its implication of the magic wish fulfillment, is gradually abandoned.

During this period toddlers use a variety of coping mechanisms to deal with their mother's absence. They now have object permanence (e.g., knowing that their mother still exists even though she is out of the room), but they still miss her when she is not nearby. Toddlers may cling to their mother and then react with depression and be unable to play when she leaves. There may be a burst of motor activity that dissipates into inactivity. Other adults in the room may be sought for soothing, and transitional objects may still be utilized.

Improved memory expands the soothing and nurturing capabilities. Adler and Buie (1979a) found that infants with only recognition memory cannot evoke a soothing memory and thus are likely to cry helplessly when their mother is gone. But children who can retain the memory of a concrete object after it has disappeared (object permanence) and can evoke the image of the mother in her absence (evocative memory) now have an additional self-soothing resource. Rinsley (1982a) has also observed the importance of evocative memory in helping toddlers remember the good object. He emphasizes that evocative recall represents the achievement of stable mental representations, having superseded the infants' reliance on magical hallucination and, later, simple recognition memory (p. 66). These repositories of good, positive images of self and mother further stimulate the use of evocative memory, because what is recalled is positive and soothing. Toddlers who have a predominance of negative (aggressive) internal images will continue to rely on projection, as noted earlier, with the constant possibility of creating an external world of persecutors. Evocative memory appears to start around the end of the first year, approximately around the time that the child gives up transitional objects, but it is not consolidated with the next phase.

Horner (1979) reported that one of the most important aspects of this final phase of separation of the symbiotic self-object unit is the assimilation of maternal functions of soothing and calming into the developing self-image:

> In terms of process this is analogous to the pathological assimilation of the power of the object into a grandiose self-structure during the previous practicing period. However, what is assimilated now is based upon reality experiences with a good-enough mother rather than upon illusions of omnipotence. (p. 123)

E. R. Shapiro (1978) also commented on the importance of this process to the modulation of aggression:

> Toward the end of rapprochement, the child's cognitive apparatus sufficiently matures so that he can notice that the same mother both gratifies and frustrates. Winnicott ... suggested that if the mother can "contain" the child's aggression (by nonanxious, firm limit setting) while continuing to provide love and understanding, she will demonstrate to him that she is not created or changed by his impulses and that she is separate from him and not a creation of his projections. Such a response ... helps the child to tolerate his anger and put it in perspective by allowing him to recognize that it cannot destroy his loving mother (by turning her into a bad, angry or anxious mother). In addition, the mother's response will help strengthen the child's conviction in the strength of his good self-image and that of his mother and will decrease the child's fear of his own aggressive tendencies. (p. 1312).

Gender Identity and the Father's Role   As toddlers become aware of anatomical differences between the sexes, concepts of individual gender identity contribute to and interact with the individuation process. Female toddlers discover sexual differences during rapprochement. Often they feel angry and disappointed in their mother for not giving them a penis. This in turn fosters ambivalence toward their mother, on whom they are still so dependent (Edward et al. 1981).

The father now plays a vital role in the toddlers' life. Toddlers struggle with the love-hate reaction toward their mother, but their father's image is less contaminated. But some children are so enmeshed in symbiosis they hardly notice their father, whereas others turn exclusively to him in order to evade the regressive pull of symbiosis. Some of the latter in fact press the father into use as a substitute symbiotic mother, with dire results in terms of later self- and gender identity. Edward and her colleagues (1981) commented that this transfer of attention to the father for libidinal supplies because of the mother's unavailability or intrusiveness interferes with seeing the father as separate from the mother, thus precluding the child from developing triadic relationships. As mentioned, it may also complicate the father's role in establishing gender identity and resolving the Oedipus complex.

Resolving the Rapprochement Crisis   At around 21 months, the rapprochement crisis fades, and toddlers are now more comfortable with some distance from their mother. Various factors have helped this resolution: (1) the mother's successful balancing of the children's need for both dependency and autonomy; (2) the acquisition of language, which enables the toddlers, by naming objects, to let the world know their needs; (3) identification with a good-enough mother and father; and (4) the use of play activities for mastery and expression of wishes and fantasies through symbolic play (Edward et al. 1981, p. 28).

Status of Self- and Object Representations   Splitting is considered to be at its height during rapprochement. However, within both the good and the bad experience, the self- and object images are continuing to pull farther away. Kernberg (1976a) has said that children develop firm boundaries between the experience of self and mother during this period, though the *split-object-relations unit* still prevails during this period.

With the successful negotiation of rapprochement, toddlers develop two important capacities, (1) the ability to experience ambivalence and (2) object constancy (the ability to summon up gratifying images even in the face of frustration). Ambivalent images of mother are more stable in the face of frustration and provide an inner sense of comfort. Toddlers become less demanding and more sharing (e.g., give gifts).

Arrests and Fixations

Implicated in the creation of both borderline and narcissistic disorders, rapprochement is an important time for the toddler because it is necessary for the formation of a healthy sense of identity. A number of interlocking events during this time may lead to borderline pathology, including (1) discrepancies between the individuation track and the separation track because of precocious motor behavior or parenting patterns (e.g., Rinsley

[1984a, 1984b] believes that narcissistic personalities have separated but not individuated and that the borderline has done neither); (2) the distorting influence of excessive symbiotic longings on the rapprochement subphase achievements; (3) the premature deflation of the toddlers' omnipotence by the parent or prolongation of the omnipotence by parental support; (4) difficulties modulating the aggression associated with struggles of this subphase (Edward et al. 1981, p. 58).

Longing to Return to Symbiosis   Toddlers who enter rapprochement still longing for symbiotic relatedness with mother will find that the approach-avoidance scenario of this subphase only intensifies these longings for closeness. Such children manipulate their mother and cling to her. The merger, however, is now no longer totally acceptable—the children desire but at the same time fear and dread merger. Ambitendency may be excessive during this period. It may become crystallized into the borderline dilemma noted by Masterson and Rinsley, that individuated behavior leads to depression, with a consequent retreat to dependence or acting out.

A Clinical Example of Ambitendency   The therapist often encounters borderline patients who are gravely entangled in ambitendency. If the therapist supports the patients' realistic functioning in the world, they will claim the therapist does not understand them (i.e., the therapist is ignoring their frightened, enraged, true self). Then if the therapist remains silent so that the patients can explore this "true" self, they will charge that they have been abandoned (e.g., the therapist is not helping by telling them how to think or what to do). This leads to intolerable depression for the patients, some of whom then state that they will have to commit suicide. But when threatened with hospitalization to avert a suicide attempt, they accuse the therapist of trying to control them and keep them from acting autonomously. Finally, when confronted on these points, the patients claim that it is the therapist who is confused, angry, and crazy.

Weathering this kind of relationship is critical to the therapeutic alliance, and techniques for managing such a situation will be discussed in subsequent chapters. We should emphasize here that the therapist must not engulf patients (out of concern) or reject them (out of anger). The ability to walk this narrow line is the hallmark of the good therapist.

Premature Abandonment of Child   Toddlers' conflicting demands during rapprochement often produce conflictual processes for the mother regarding her own unresolved dependency or abandonment issues. Mahler and her associates described two kinds of empathic failure (as paraphased by E. R. Shapiro 1978):

One group of mothers who had difficulties in tolerating their own dependency responded with hurt and anger to their child's clinging by saying in effect, "A minute ago you didn't want me, now I don't want you." Presumably, this response would evoke anxiety in the child about his wishes for nurturance. A second group of mothers with conflicts about autonomy responded to the child's autonomous moves with, "You think you can manage on your own, well go ahead." This response threatens the child with abandonment and inhibits his freedom to explore because of the reactive fantasy: "If I grow up, I'll be all alone." (pp. 1311–1312)

These examples of empathic failure represent a mother who actually needs the toddler to be dependent on her for the sake of her own well-being instead of acceding to the child's need for autonomy. The mother may not see it this way because she may feel that she is pushing the child toward independence; however, this occurs only after the child has upset her by not meeting her needs for dependency. Thus, her "encouragement" of autonomy really has a defensive quality, which the toddler is capable of sensing: "If I don't do what Mommy wants, I will lose her love and support and be unloved."

Deflation of Omnipotence Edward and her colleagues (1981) found several ominous processes occur when omnipotence is deflated prematurely through abrupt abandonment by the mother. First, both the infantile and the parental omnipotence that underpin the toddlers' self-esteem and well-being are shattered, leaving the children vulnerable and enraged. Second, as the toddlers experience this vulnerability and rage, they see the mother as bad. The splitting of representations so common to this subphase will be prolonged, and the mother will be crystallized into a bad introject. But when trying to eject this bad introject, the toddlers may tend to identify or confuse it with the self-object representations, because their sense of self is still closely tied to their sense of the object (e.g., the mother). This may lead to the aggression's being turned against the self as well as the object and to a proclivity to depressive affect in regard to their inability to feel realistically good about the self. In borderline adults, such dependency will often be a conflictual experience, causing both rage and longings.

Excessive Gratification of Omnipotence Such parents usually ignore their children's own needs and instead overvalue in their children those behaviors and skills that they themselves need for self-esteem. Mary Markham's parasitic mother rewarded Mary for being smart, compliant, and totally devoted to her. Mary was thus led to believe that she was special and a cut above children her own age.

Intensification of Aggression Interaction in which omnipotence is prematurely deflated, especially when infants are in the anal phase, usually increases temper tantrums, rage reactions, manipulation, and passive aggressive behavior. Then, the mother's withdrawal of support for autonomous behavior has profound affects on the toddlers' ability to deal with spiraling feelings of aggression mixed with dependency feelings, which extends their reliance on splitting and projection.

Gender Identity   A sense of maleness or femaleness is another important process that occurs during rapprochement. Borderline adults have gender-identity problems as well as a diffuse sense of self and others, which may imply that the two disorders are related. For example, John Elliott's diffuse identity as well as his polymorphous-perverse sexual behavior and sexual object choice can be partially attributed to the fact that he resorted to a substitute caretaker and his father for maternal care during his mother's lengthy hospitalization when John was 2 years old. Therefore John confronted and confused all types of identifications.

Problems with sexual identity are just one aspect of the issues confronting borderline adults. These patients may have problems establishing and consolidating many types of identifications (including sexual) into a cohesive, stable identity. Hedges (1983) observed that borderline adults' search for identity shows up in various social and cultural stereotypes, such as

"housewifery," the drug subculture, Alcoholics Anonymous, mystical religious cults, teenage conformity or rebellion norms, television or science-fiction addictions, corporation "ethics," or adoption of a "gay lifestyle." (p. 127)

Common to all of these may be a wish for a symbiotic merger experience with a partner, group, or larger culture (see also Brende and Rinsley 1979).

Vicissitudes with Transitional Objects   Borderline patients do not experience the normal integration of the mother's soothing function based on real experiences with a good-enough mother. The children's transitional objects are contaminated with a higher degree of anxiety, particularly separation anxiety, and their transmuting functions are impeded, providing little more than temporary comfort. Children do not learn how to use such objects for optimal growth. Transitional phenomena may not develop or may be subverted into the formation of a fetish or even autistic object. One psychotic woman patient remembered as a child having a favorite doll that later became an alter ego who taunted her.

Implications for Adult Borderline Patients   Both borderline and narcissistic disorders are believed to have their origins or to appear symptomatically during the rapprochement subphase. The phenomenology of rapprochement, with its conflict between the drive for autonomy and the wish to return to the enmeshment of symbiosis, and the toddlers' oscillations between helplessness and omnipotence evoke images familiar to therapists who work with borderline patients.

Various disturbed behaviors are manifested in the rapprochement-fixated toddler: manipulation, idealization, envy, excessive splitting, and fear of self-assertion. As Rinsley (1984a) pointed out,

> regarding the narcissistic personality, Kernberg ... advances the view that after self-representations and object representations have become differentiated ... a trauma-based, regressive representational refusion sets in. In effect, he claims that the narcissistic personality does not evolve on the basis of primary developmental arrest. According to that view, the pathogenetic experiences ... would have had to occur no earlier than very late during or following the rapprochement subphase. (p. 4)

Rinsley (1984a) continues that Masterson "postulates that the developmental arrest in such cases must occur before completion of the work of the rapprochement subphase ..." (p. 4). Rinsley himself holds that insofar as a consideration of subphase-related chronology (timing) is relevant to the origin of personality disorders, then the narcissistic personality does not originate until late in the rapprochement subphase and that its endopsychic (intrapsychic) structure represents a more advanced variety of the borderline's structure.

On-the-Way-to-Object Constancy (25 months to 3 years)

Mahler and her colleagues (1975) have contended that the main tasks of the on-the-way-to-object constancy phase are the achievement of a distinct individuality and the attainment of some degree of object constancy. During this period, children attain a sense of self and a sense of the other as a positive, internalized presence. This permits adequate functioning in the absence of the other person and implies the achievement of intrapsychic separateness. Unlike the preceding three subphases, on-the-way-to-object constancy is open-ended because the achievements of this subphase are a lifelong task. The achievement of libidinal object constancy starts around the second year and is usually consolidated by the end of the third year.

Status of Self- and Object Representations and Drives

The slow establishment of object constancy requires several psychic developments. First, the object's good and bad images must be unified into one whole mental representation. This, in turn, fosters fusion of the libidinal and aggressive drives, tempers these drives, and allows an array of affects to emerge. The self's good and bad images also must be unified into one whole mental representation, which also fosters a more modulated affective response to the self.

Libidinal object constancy presupposes but is not identical with Piaget's meaning for object permanence. *Object permanence* simply refers to the idea that things continue to exist in the child's mind even when they are not present. *Object constancy* is a far more affectively charged event, and it occurs some time after object permanence has been achieved. Object constancy refers to this unification of the object's good and bad representations and the supposed fusion of the aggressive and libidinal drives with which these representations are cathected. A most important by-product of this is the development of evocative memory, that is, the capacity to summon up a soothing inner image of the mother and, then later, of others. The result of this fusion is known as *whole-self- and object relations.*

Developmental Achievements Toddlers who achieve whole-self- and object relations can accept both their own loving and hating responses to the image of their mother and others who are both gratifying and frustrating (E. R. Shapiro 1978, p. 1308). The implication is that such children can continue to have an investment in the parent even when the parent frustrates them. Children who have had good subphase experiences will sense that their mother is available and dependable, even when she is physically absent, frustrating them, or they are angry with her. This internal sense comes from the gradual buildup of predominantly stable and loving images of mother that are now integrated into whole-object relations.

During this subphase, children develop a number of other ego strengths, including impulse control and affect modulation. Their newly developed object constancy now enables them to evoke the loving image of their mother to soothe them in times of distress. Consequently, children are now more sharing, trusting, giving, and confident. They also feel free to assert themselves spontaneously without fear of abandonment.

Kernberg (1976a, p. 73) pointed out that children can now fantasize about past good internalized object relations, an ability that gives them a basic trust in themselves and their world. This basic trust derives from the accumulation of positive memory traces of a reliable, gratifying mother caring for a loved and gratified self.

The consolidation of conscience or superego will not be completed until age 7 or 8. The conscience or superego, however, begins to develop in this subphase as children develop the rudimentary capacity to feel guilt and depression regarding past extreme hatred.

Implications for Adult Borderline Patients Adult borderline patients are left with a particularly sadistic and often omnipotent superego. They lack evocative memory, have not achieved whole-object relations with all its benefits, and still rely on splitting.

Latency and Adolescence

There are relatively few descriptions of borderline phenomena in the latency period. Several theorists see adolescence as a period of recapitulating the dynamic themes of separation-individuation. Many theorists believe that borderline children pass unnoticed through adolescence because they still live under an umbrella of dependency from childhood that obscures their lack of confidence, lack of assertiveness, and poor object relations (Masterson 1983a).

CLINICAL IMPLICATIONS OF DEVELOPMENTAL DEFECTS

The experiences of early childhood development contribute heavily to the creation of borderline difficulties. But as Meissner (1984) explained, it would be too simplistic to say that the borderline personality emerged exclusively from any single phase of this process, such as the rapprochement subphase. Instead, the borderline condition seems to reflect a combination of difficulties, arising with varying emphasis and intensity from all the phases of the developmental process. The more severe levels of borderline psychopathology certainly reflect the residues of conflicts from infantile symbiosis.

The mother's role is particularly important in the earliest phases of development. During the attachment and then separation and individuation phases, her role parallels the changes that are occurring within the child. The mother must first be able to devote herself to her child and then slowly put aside her maternal preoccupation (Winnicott); she must be able to move in an orchestrated fashion with the needs of her offspring. How she carries out this role is an important determinant of her child's character formation, perhaps even as significant as the child's drives and their fluctuation (Greenberg and Mitchell 1983, p. 281). The way in which the mother performs her role is shaped not only by her own personality and its pathology but also in part by the emotional complexities of her family life, the quality of her relationship with her husband, the role of any other children, and the wider social milieu in which the family lives (Meissner 1984). These many interacting sources often cause much strain and stress on the mother, which can also affect the quality of maternal caretaking.

In the current enthusiasm for discovering the earliest roots of developmental difficulty, located in the preverbal periods, clinicians frequently forget that one of the most important results of the distortion of the separation-individuation experience occurs in the Oedipal configuration, in which the distorted pre-Oedipal object relations contaminate the Oedipal experience. These new deficits then can reemerge during the second individuation process that occurs during adolescence, impeding the resolution of this phase. The outcome is that more advanced Oedipal problems can take on pre-Oedipal meanings, as in the example in Chapter 3 in which the impotent man came to view the vagina as a mouth with teeth (oral-aggressive issues). More often, the multiple distortions lead to the contamination of adult problems of competency, mastery, competition, anger, love, and hate, with a series of distortions that reflects a multitude of developmental phases dating from symbiosis. This is seen in the borderline adult who cannot function adequately in the world of adult expectations and relationship matrices.

Horner (1979) has pointed out that this situation gives rise not so much to the classical Oedipal configuration involving rivalry, competition, and fear of punishment as to a masochistic relationship involving the good object image projected onto one parent and the bad object image projected onto the other. There may result a masochistic relationship with a bad, persecuting object and an idealized rescuing object. Although there may be sexualization, these problems are not of a truly Oedipal nature and reflect instead narcissistic investments from the pre-Oedipal period.

Horner (1979), Meissner (1984), and Rinsley (1982a) basically accept the multiple interacting developmental phase approach. They do see the lower-level borderline with psychotic features (Grinker's Type I) as reflecting more serious and earlier damage, probably from symbiosis, and elaborated by later developmental phases. The higher-level borderline (Grinker's Type IV) may well have had the most difficulties during the rapprochement crisis. Even in such a case, the mother having problems letting her child be autonomous in rapprochement may also have had difficulty with childish attempts at self-feeding during earlier phases.

Kernberg (1978a) and Masterson (1976) consider the rapprochement subphase to be the point of origin for the majority of borderline cases, although the conflicts of this subphase then become confounded by the Oedipal complex and later adolescent struggles. Kernberg (1978a) stated that he believes the borderline adults' problem is "not between autonomy or merger, or between true and false self, but between non-integrated and integrated self, non-integrated and integrated object relations" (p. 88). In accordance with this view and except for transient psychotic episodes, borderline adults should show no perceptual fusion of images—and hence require no special help with self-other differentiation—and should be able to tolerate the frustration of interpretive psychotherapy.

Kohut, as expressed in Kohut and Wolf (1978), agreed that the borderline patient, unlike the narcissistic patient, has not achieved a cohesive self, and thus the borderline personality is seriously threatened by disintegration. He considered borderline pathology to be similar to that of the psychotic, except that the borderline uses elaborate defenses against the psychosis. Kohut suggested that when the child required acceptance and mirroring of its healthy, aggressive, goal-seeking independence (around age 2), the parent, because of personal incompleteness and fragmentation fears, insisted instead on maintaining an archaic merger. This would seem to place the borderline as a prerapprochement phase problem in Kohut's system (Rinsley 1984a).

Common Developmental Defects of Borderline Adults

No developmental theory of borderline psychopathology explains all the difficulties of borderline adults. Accordingly, the reader must be prepared to assimilate clinical and theoretical data from various theorists to explain certain aspects of borderline patients.

Meissner (1978b) has summarized eight different characteristics of borderline personality organization that have been identified by the various experts, each of whom may stress different characteristics. These characteristics are (1) instinctual defects, (2) defensive defects, (3) defects in other areas of ego functioning or integration, (4) developmental defects, (5) narcissistic defects, (6) defects in object relations, (7) organization and pathology of the false self, and (8) forms of identity diffusion.

Each of these defects represents a normal developmental process that has become arrested. Each has its own developmental line (A. Freud), progressing from a simpler, more primitive form to a more complex and modulated form (e.g., the ability to control feelings of discomfort until relief arrives rather than immediately screaming and crying.) The defect of the borderline tends to represent middle-level arrests, as it were, that is, arrests not as primitive as those of the psychotic but also not as advanced as the more mature neurotic form.

We shall now briefly review each of these defects, remembering Rinsley's (1981b) cautionary note that regardless of the patients' unique mix of pathogenic determinants (genetic, organic, familial), their final common pathway for expression is, for better or worse, the mother–child relationship and the ensuing personality structure that emerges from that relationship.

Instinctual Defects

Instinctual defects include either excessive aggression or the failure to achieve psychosexual phase-dominance. Many borderline adults have both of these defects.

Aggression Instinctual defects are most heavily stressed by Kernberg (1975a), who stated that excessive aggression and the resultant splitting mechanism prevent the achievement of object constancy. This may be due to the inherent strength of the drive, the inability of the ego to deal with the

drive, or excessive frustration of the mother–child relationship that intensifies the drive (Edward et al. 1981). The consequences for adults are usually the
inability to tolerate frustration without rage, combined with the inability to
self-soothe, to quiet affectomotor storms, and to use evocative memory for
self-comforting.

Because of the childhood defense mechanism of expelling painful stimuli,
borderline adults rely on various projective mechanisms to rid themselves of
painful thoughts and feelings. Such adults probably have never integrated
their good and bad self-images, and good and bad object images. This lack of
integration leaves these patients vulnerable to the exigencies of the moment.
They have no way to modulate this aggression because they have not
achieved the cognitive prerequisites for doing so, and the structuralization of
their inner world now preserves the aggression in a pervasive ego state (see
Chapter 7). Although they may defend against the aggression, they are also
vulnerable to either its eruption or subtle infiltration (e.g., as in the
depressive-masochistic individual). Some theorists (Rochlin 1973) believe
that the destructive and unneutralized aggression is mobilized to protect the
patients' injured narcissism.

Psychosexual Phase Dominance   Successful completion of the Oedipal
negotiation produces the general urge toward pleasure that is then directed
at a whole, unified object, thus promoting further consolidation of both self-
and object representations. This marks an important shift from part objects
to whole objects. In terms of psychic structure, it is the Oedipal negotiation
that leads to the formation of the mature superego, the special structure of
self-regulation, and the maintenance of self-esteem. External regulation
becomes transformed into internal control. Earlier dependence on the love of
the object gives way to a capacity to provide for oneself some measure of the
love and approval once afforded by the object (Edward et al. 1981, p. 82).

In the case of borderline adults, the failure to achieve psychosexual
phase-dominance is related not only to the impact of defective drives but
also to the inability to integrate various early identifications into a cohesive
sense of self. Both the borderlines' gender identity and sexual object choice
are diffuse, chaotic, and polymorphous-perverse. Sexuality is often used as a
means to acquire nurturing and soothing rather than sexual pleasure.

Finally, another source of sexual confusion for children may be that their
parents eroticize or sexualize their caretaking; this may well complicate the
achievement of psychosexual phase-dominance, Oedipal negotiation, and,
ultimately, superego development.

Distorted Affects   Affect (the feeling tone of an experience) is considered
to be instinctually related (e.g., a drive derivative). Hence, it is placed under
the instinctual defect section, although others might well place it under
developmental defects because of the ways in which certain moods (e.g.,

pervasive depression or anger) can arise from an unhealthy parent–child adaptation.

Hartocollis (1980a) reasons that it is not any particular affect that determines pathology but, rather, the ideation and affect that accompany it. He commented that a chief dimension of affective disturbance is that it implies inappropriate affects, inappropriate to the circumstances that elicit them objectively. Yet, in the subjective reality of the person experiencing such affects, there is nothing inappropriate about them. These patients can describe feelings quite differently from what they seem to others. They report feeling depressed while acting cheerful, acting angry while reporting no feelings at all, and changing their feelings quickly without explanation or even conscious recognition. Thus, both inappropriateness and contradictoriness appear to be pathognomonic of borderline and narcissistic conditions.

He found common distorted affects experienced by both borderline and narcissistic patients are (1) a sense of injustice (narcissistic) and alienation (borderline), (2) a pervasive sense of boredom, (3) anger and its variants, (4) depersonalization, and (5) a sense of emptiness.

Although the full range of disturbed affects, their developmental roots, relationship to specific defenses, and developmental fixation points will not be elaborated here, it is important to remember that affective states frequently defend against other affective states. In addition, the same affect can be associated with different defenses and have ideations associated with them that represent differing developmental phases. For example, boredom can be a defense against inhibited rage, the fear that one's rage can destroy the good internal object, or the behavioral equivalent of narcissistic greediness. To give another example, depersonalization is a perceptual-affective state that can be employed defensively to protect against the awareness of destructive intent or internal danger to the self (Hartocollis 1980a, p. 142).

Meissner (1978b) discovered that the instinctual theory provides a good basis for understanding the role of aggression, the sense of vulnerability and typical overwhelming traumatic anxiety, oral themes, polymorphous-perverse sexual behavior, the tendency toward volatility, and frequently seen hypomanic behavior patterns (p. 592). Because this theory does not explain many other borderline features, such as the coexisting sense of entitlement and feelings of worthlessness, we shall turn to other models to explain these phenomena.

Defensive Defects

Defenses range from the developmentally primitive to the more advanced. Kernberg (1975a) reported that borderline adults rely on primitive defenses such as splitting long beyond its phase-appropriate time and also use other primitive defenses (e.g., primitive denial, projection, projective identification, idealization and devaluation) that inhibit the achievement of object constancy (see Chapter 3). Splitting is maintained, in Kernberg's model, to defend against anxiety related to the instinctual impulses now embedded in the internal object-relations units.

Kernberg has made a good case for the importance of defensive splitting in the borderline adult, though many question the concept. Is splitting even a defense? Does anxiety upon confrontation of splitting of representations logically prove that it is a defense? Is splitting really a form of denial? Does splitting distinguish between borderline and neurotic adults, as both use the defense? Is splitting anything more than a descriptive division in the mental apparatus, and not necessarily a defense (Pruyser 1975)?

Stolorow and Lachmann (1978) take the position that splitting may be either a division in the psychic apparatus or a defense. They believe that each defense (defense-conflict manifestation) can be viewed as existing on a developmental line. During earlier develpomental phases, denial, splitting, and projective identification function more according to the brain's lack of integrative ability than as a defense.

Stolorow and Lachmann believe that the clinician must decide whether a patient has a deficit in the cognitive apparatus or whether the inability to meld images represents a defense against some unbearable conflict. They use the following rule of thumb to distinguish between an arrest and a defensive use of splitting: if a patient persistently and rigidly sees one person as good and another as bad across time, this probably represents a defensive use of splitting; but if a patient rapidly oscillates between projecting good and then bad images on another person, this probably represents an arrest or lack of integrative ability of the psyche.

The use of denial has also received considerable attention from other theorists (Modell 1961, Masterson and Rinsley 1975) who have studied the role of denial in borderline adults, particularly in relation to separation anxiety. The denial of separation creates the illusion that the object is somehow part of the self and, therefore, cannot be lost. This creates a condition in which individuation cannot be acknowledged because separation becomes equivalent to loss, threat of destruction, or annihilation. Borderline adults differ from the psychotic in that psychotic denial is more severe and leads to delusions and hallucinations.

Although this difference in opinion between the Kernbergians and the Kohutians has implications for the clinician's approach to these problems, they are deeply embedded in metapsychological differences.

Defects in Other Areas of Ego Functioning or Integration

The many possible ego defects that plague borderline adults were outlined in Chapter 3. As Meissner (1984) found, the focus on ego defects to explain the borderline syndrome in terms of ego weakness has not been successful. Not only do the specific ego defects not explain all manifestations of the borderline pathology, they also need to be explained themselves, either developmentally or from an object-relations perspective.

For borderline adults, all the ego functions associated with the achievement of object constancy will have been only partially developed or will have been distorted (e.g., anxiety tolerance, signal anxiety, delay of gratification, impulse control, reliance on primary process thinking, lack of developed sublimatory channels, and weakened reality testing). Because these patients operate from perceptually fused self-object representations and preoperational thinking, they are prone to rely on magical thinking, assuming that somehow others will intuit or divine their needs without having to be told. Accordingly, these patients will feel rage when this does not occur (Rinsley 1982a). Magical thinking also involves entitlement, another ego defect typical of borderline adults (Rinsley 1982a).

Healthy children are able to make the transition from magical wish fulfillment to the capacity to delay gratification through the mechanism of anticipatory fantasy. But borderline adults continue to operate to some degree in the realm of magical entitlement and thus lack the skills for the delay of gratification, reality testing, and realistic evaluation. In the more extreme borderline cases, such as those of schizotypal adults, magical entitlement blends into various forms of soft thought disorder (e.g., telepathy, clairvoyance, superstitiousness). Among psychotic individuals, this process appears even more regressively in frank delusions, both nihilistic and persecutory, as well as in illusory, hallucinatory, and somatic delusional experiences (Rinsley 1982a, p. 168).

Developmental Defects

Mahler has made the most consistent attempt to specify developmental defects, relating developmental failure to the separation-individuation process. According to Mahler, the failure of separation-individuation "tends to produce a relatively unassimilated bad introject around which the child's inner experience is organized. Specifically, it is the upsurge of aggression in the rapprochement phase of the separation-individuation process that provides the conditions for the organization of the borderline intrapsychic economy." (Meissner 1984, p. 50).

The original Masterson-Rinsley (1975) conceptualization of the borderline adult can be considered representative of the developmental defect perspective. In their original formulation, Masterson and Rinsley stated that the issues of reemersion in symbiosis versus autonomy were at the core of the borderline dilemma. They also saw that mothers of borderline adults withdrew libidinal supplies during this period and rewarded regressive behavior. This abandonment threat prevents the toddlers from moving forward, and they alternate between coercive clinging and angry demands.

Such behavior is analogous to Masterson's and Rinsley's description of the adult borderlines' core conflict: the drive toward individuated behavior causes abandonment depression.

As Meissner (1984) observed, splitting, according to Masterson and Rinsley, pertains to the failure of developmental integration resulting from the perceived threat of the withdrawal of maternal availability, which requires that the image of mother be split into good and bad parts, with a fantasy of being loved by a good mother and projecting the frustrating aspects onto other people (p. 51). This definition differs from Kernberg's, who sees intense aggression as causing the splitting. Meissner (1984) also points out that like Kleinian clinicians, Kernberg ignores the etiologic role of the mother–child interaction and hence pays little or no attention to environmental determinants.

Meissner (1984) found that an inadequate symbiosis may leave infants longing for closeness. During the practicing subphase, they have a developmental option to maintain the grandiose self as a protection against abandonment fears that were stimulated by the differentiation subphase. During rapprochement, the power of the idealized object outweighs that of the grandiose self, and toddlers oscillate between the grandiose self and the idealized object. Mary Markham's Megalomaniac is an example of the grandiose self protecting against low self-esteem and feelings of abandonment and rejection.

Narcissistic Defects

Problems of pathological narcissism have often been viewed as narcissistic entitlement, which in this case refers to the patients' belief that they have a right to life on their own terms (Meissner 1984). A fixation at narcissistic levels can reflect either excessive gratification or deprivation. Either the patients' wishes were never satisfied, and they feel the world should make it up to them, or because the wishes were always granted in infancy, the patients assume that they always will be granted in the future (p. 53).

Narcissistic entitlement is central to borderline pathology because borderline adults see themselves as persons with special rights and privileges. Meissner (1984) stated that any frustration of these (entitled) needs and desires can undermine and shatter their self-esteem. Such patients are often equally afraid to assert themselves for fear of suffering humiliation, emptiness, or worthlessness. It appears as they metaphorically alternate between the grandiose self of the practicing subphase and the vulnerable, degraded self vis-à-vis the idealized object of the rapprochement subphase.

Narcissism has its own developmental line that moves from absolute primary narcissism (stated metaphorically as "I am the center of my own satisfaction, omnipotence, and self-sufficiency") to primary narcissism ("a vague force out there is supplying some needs") to secondary narcissism ("we are meeting my needs") to, finally, a mature ability to love the self and to recognize and value the love and sustenance given by others.

This narcissistic defect is so pervasive in borderline adults that Rinsley (1981a) believes that it, along with the interrelated problem of incomplete self-object differentiation, diagnoses the borderline condition. But as Buie and Adler (1972) have commented, there is more than one form of entitlement. When the mother's emotional unresponsiveness and withdrawal threaten the infant's psychic survival, these children feel completely dependent on others to supply survival nutrients, much as infants need the mother's total devotion (Meissner 1978b). The adults' experience is analogous to the symbiotic or differentiation-subphase child who feels when the mother's presence is lost. Borderline adults often experience intense survival entitlement related to any abandonment. A frequent cause of the borderline patient's rage is the inherent threat of destruction or annihilation caused by such abandonment.

As Meissner (1984, p. 55) observed, the shift to a narcissistic basis introduces a new theoretical paradigm in which pathology is shifted from a concern with structural integrity, or ego/superego functioning, to the stabilization of the self as the significant principle of intrapsychic integration as seen in the work of Kohut.

Object-Relations Defects

Borderline individuals display a range of capacities for object relatedness. In addition, at any given moment the quality of object relatedness depends on the amount of internal or external stress. Just as rapprochement toddlers have some limited capacity for empathy and can realize that their mother has needs of her own, higher-functioning borderline adults seem capable of some degree of genuine relatedness under normal circumstances.

Core or lower-level borderline adults, however, operating under the perceptually fused self-object image of symbiosis, tend to relate to others solely as need-gratifying objects: a good person is one who gratifies and a bad person is one who frustrates. Borderline adults often use other adults as transitional objects, much as a child will use a teddy bear or blanket, and for the same reasons (Modell 1963). This outlook gives the chaotic, shallow, and contradictory quality to object relations, as noted by Kernberg. Under times of stress, borderline adults who rely heavily on splitting and who lose evocative memory may become extremely coercive and demanding of others for caretaking. In addition, borderline individuals may use the defenses of regression to the grandiose self-structure or merger with the idealized other to protect against disorganization from the object's real or imagined loss. Mary Markham used both of these defenses, alternating between narcissistic superiority and intense longings for merger.

Forms of Identity Diffusion and Organization and Pathology of False Self

Kernberg considers identity diffusion to be the hallmark of borderline adults, caused by the inability to fuse self- and object representations into whole-object relations and to achieve object constancy. Again, the false self is a way of attaching to a mothering figure who is unresponsive to the infant's unique needs.

In summary, the reverberations from early childhood are captured in Rinsley's (1982a) description of the psychodynamics of borderline adults:

> The borderline adult experiences relationships in terms of whether they "provide" and "gratify" or whether they "withhold" and "deny." His ideation is characterized by "soft" or "hard" thought disorder, which is governed by the ever-present pull toward either-or, black-and-white, autistic-preoperational thinking. He feels that he is "bad," that something is vaguely or indefinably wrong with him, that he does not really know who or even what he is. His grandiosity leads him into positions that reflect a pervasive sense of entitlement; via a repertoire of quasi-communicative metaphors and magic-gestural actions, he believes he can command the hostile, ungratifying environment to provide for his needs. His combination of egoism and readily frustrated dependency leads him into a seemingly endless array of short-lived and/or unstable relationships; he passes from one person to the next as if changing tires on his automobile. His sexual relations are usually characterized by deviation as to aim (e.g., sadomasochism) and as to object (i.e., anomalous sexual object "choice") and are fundamentally polymorphous-perverse. His personality generally reflects a proneness to addiction, which may involve drug abuse or may mean relating to others much as if they represented pharmacologic agents capable of easing tension, providing "highs," and the like. (pp. 157–158)

Table 6–3 summarizes the stages, role of infant and caretaker, caretaker and infant pathology, status of the self-object representation, and diagnosis related to each phase.

Again, the therapist should not be too literal in trying to determine the patient's exact fixation point. Events are rarely that simple in the psyche of the real person. Each behavior has received contributions, healthy and unhealthy, from all of the developmental phases. Each behavior has many meanings and is tied to many therapeutic themes, and it is this diversity that gives psychotherapy its richness and complexity.

Table 6-3 Developmental Phases, Tasks, Defects, and Adult Diagnosis

Phase	Infant's Role	Caretaker's Role	Status of Self-Object
Normal autism (birth to 4 weeks)	Homostatic equilibrium	Total management of infant's needs	Undifferentiated matrix
Symbiosis (4 weeks to 5 months)	Attachment to the caretaker	"good enough mother" Satisfy needs Buffer and modify incoming stimuli Act as auxiliary ego	Fused self-object representation
Separation-Individuation			
Differentiation (5 to 10 months)	Physical differentiation from mother	Consistent frame of reference for infant	Start of differentiation of body image from that of mother
Practicing (10 to 16 months)	Exploration with temporary ability to ignore mother (height of omnipotence)	Tolerate, enjoy, and set appropriate limits on infant's exploration	Split self-object representations Positive self-image differentiates from object image first
Rapprochement (16 to 25 months)	Consolidation of autonomy; acceptance of separateness from mother (height of dependence and reliance on idealized caretaker)	Respond without anxiety to infant's conflicting needs for both dependence and autonomy	Continuation of above
On-the-way-to-object-constancy (25 months to 3 years)	Consolidation of previous stages Achievement of object constancy	Continuation of above	Whole self (and object) representations

Table 6-3 (*Continued*)

Forms of Caretaker Pathology	Infant's Pathologic Response	Diagnosis Related to Arrest
Serious failure of caretaking (perhaps inadequacy of organism)	No anticipatory position at nursing No reaching out No smiling response	Infantile autism
Persistent unresponsiveness to needs Start of parasitic symbiosis	Failure of optimal attachment (e.g., false self) Defensive detachment	Symbiotic psychosis Schizophrenia Schizoaffective syndromes Psychopath Borderline personality (original point of difficulty according to some)
Increased resistance to child's move toward autonomy	Premature differentiation and chronic anger Anxiety over differentiation Proclivity to depression	Schizoid personality Some primary affective disorders
Inhibiting exploration or abandoning child Failing to mirror pleasure at new skills or deflating at will	Formation of pathologic grandiose self (to protect self) Excessive aggression Failure to explore	Narcissistic personality (original point of difficulty according to some) Some primary affective disorders
Withdrawal of libidinal supplies for autonomy Reward for regressive behavior Excessive overvaluing of child, with disregard for child's authentic needs Reward for premature independence	Inhibition of self-assertion (abandonment fears). Heightened anxiety Excessive splitting Excessive aggression Proclivity to depression Belief in magic solutions	Borderline personality (original point of difficulty according to Kernberg and Masterson) Narcissistic personality (Kernberg and Rinsley place between rapprochement and object constancy)

Minor aspects of the above	Continued dependence on object to provide sense of well-being
	   Ambivalence toward caretaker
	   Anxiety and depression regarding fear of loss of love of object
		Preneurotic character

A BRIEF NOTE ABOUT THE FAMILIES OF BORDERLINE ADULTS

Masterson and Rinsley (1975) found evidence that the parents of borderline preadults and adults tend to be borderline themselves. Both, however, have since modified that position. Masterson later said that the mother may be borderline, or she may have simply been libidinally unavailable for the infant's individuation needs. Rinsley (D. B. Rinsley, personal communication, October 26, 1983) explained that their earlier inference was based on extensive experience with inpatient or residential cases drawn from more severely disturbed families, admittedly a skewed sample.

Rinsley has emphasized that the mother's adult diagnosis is not the important issue. Rather, he stresses that the important issue is the maternal mode of interaction with the child, which may be conducive to the development of borderline disorder, irrespective of whether the mother is clinically psychotic, borderline, suffering from affective disorder, or even "neurotic" when she later comes to professional attention. Rinsley's current view is supported by Singer (1977), E. R. Shapiro, Zinner, R. Shapiro, and Berkowitz (1975), who found the parents of borderline patients to be neurotic, normal, or highly variable in their pathology.

E. R. Shapiro (1978) attempted to explain these earlier disagreements over maternal or parental diagnosis by pointing out that family members' primitive developmental problems become activated in response to the problems of certain offspring. Singer and Wynne (1965), in studying families with a schizophrenic member, commented on the discrepancy between the severity of the disturbance when family members interact and the relatively mild disturbance that each family member shows in relation to the therapist. In other words, the family as a whole elicits more pathological behavior when interacting among themselves than they do when they are alone with the therapist or reporting their interactions outside the family.

In earlier research, Zinner and R. Shapiro (1972) elaborated on the family's pressures on growing children to incorporate them into the family system as a collusive participant responding to the family members' (primarily the parents') unmet needs. Zinner and Shapiro delineated the following important dynamics:

The common threads are: (1) that the subject perceives the object *as if* the object contained elements of the subject's personality, (2) that the subject can evoke behaviours or feelings in the objects that conform with the subject's perceptions, (3) that the subject can experience vicariously the activity and feelings of the object, (4) that participants in close relationships are often in collusion with one another to sustain mutual projections, i.e., to support one another's defensive operations and to provide experiences through which the other can participate vicariously. (p. 525)

Mary Markham's and John Elliott's interactions with their parents illustrate the above dynamics.

More recently, Mandelbaum (1980) catalogued the characteristics frequently found in the families of borderline or narcissistic patients. This combination of characteristics appears sufficiently cohesive to provide a clear picture of such a family and is congruent with findings from other researchers. These characteristics are

1. Marital relationships are troubled and volatile, and the children are often the target for parent projections, thereby protecting the parents from their disappointment in each other.
2. Parents disagree over parental discipline and compete with each other, with one parent being seen as adequate and the other as inadequate.
3. Both parents are enmeshed with their families of origin, even though contact may be infrequent or geographical distances great.
4. There are frequent family traumas (e.g., early death of parent, divorce, alcoholism).
5. The parents do not keep clear boundaries in their roles, and there are many accusations between them.
6. The parents and children have poor family boundaries, with the parents at times acting as children and the children taking on the role of parent. The parents invade the children's privacy, and there may be incestuous interactions.
7. There is usually a family history of several generations of severe difficulties in interpersonal relationships, failures to achieve separation and individuation, marital conflicts, and tensions.

In addition, Rinsley (1980c, 1982a) listed the specific patterns of projection by parents onto their children (ranging from the most pathological to the more subtle).

CHAPTER 7

Object-Relations Theory

Object-relations theory fills an important gap in the developmental perspective by articulating how the early child–caretaker relationship lies at the root of the child's emerging identity and psychic structure (Meissner 1978b). This theory explains how object relations become internalized and provide the structural components out of which the adult personality and its pathology are created, expressed, and perpetuated (Meissner 1984).

TWO CONNOTATIONS OF THE TERM

Within psychoanalytic theory, Greenberg and Mitchell (1983) found that the term *object relations* has been used to describe both real people in the external world and the images of these people that are established internally. Because of this dual meaning, object relations has been a useful concept in describing the interchange between "outside" events and "inside" fantasies, beliefs, and evaluations regarding these events that occur in all work between the patient and therapist (p. 14). More frequently than not, the work of psychotherapy is exploring what appears to be serious to moderate discrepancies between a real event and the patient's reaction, belief, and feelings regarding it.

As explained in Chapter 6, the early child–caretaker relationship shapes the initial development of images of oneself and others. These images become enduring representations, which in turn shape adult interpersonal relations and then generate new input that leads to revisions in the schemata of the self and others in a never-ending process.

The Interpersonal Component

In more contemporary definitions, *object* refers to another real person, and *object relationships* refers to peoples' relationships with others. Psychotherapists are particularly interested in object relationships because everyday clinical work is concerned with patients' relationships with others.

Patients usually come to psychotherapy worried about their inability to form loving relationships with others, to sustain relationships, or to be less angry or less dependent within relationships. They also worry about why others treat them badly, why they do not like themselves, or why they lack self-confidence. Even when patients talk about phenomena that do not obviously relate to other people—symptoms, dreams, fantasies, or values—the therapist can often infer the contribution of others (Greenberg and Mitchell 1983). This may range from the early influences of parents to pressures from significant others or even fantasies about what others think or want. Finally, the psychotherapeutic situation itself is a relationship, for patients are always telling their story to another person.

All types of psychotherapies generally accept that the quality of the therapeutic relationship (e.g., the therapist's acceptance and empathy) is important in helping patients understand their problems, grow, and change. Conversely, a less-than-optimal therapist-patient relationship may impede therapeutic progress. It is not surprising that over the past 50 years of psychoanalytic theorizing, there has been an increasing emphasis on understanding the individual's relations with others, ranging from the early mother–father–child relationship to that of the adult with spouse, social groups, and therapist.

What Is a Healthy Relationship?

Bellak and his colleagues (1973) have identified two major contributions to healthy object relations, "the ability to form friendly and loving relationships with others with a minimum of inappropriate hostility" and "the ability to sustain relationships over a period of time with little mutual exchange of hostility" (p. 142). Disturbances in object relations result in emotional coldness and detachment, helplessness and clinging dependency on others, the inability to fall or stay in love, self-centeredness, and perversion—all typical relationship problems of borderline adults. Hence, a theory of object relations that can explain how the borderline condition arose as well as suggest how to modify the fixation or arrest and resume growth in therapy is relevant to the study of borderline psychopathology.

The Cognitive Component

Although object relations at this point sounds remarkably like a theory of interpersonal relationships, the contemporary meaning of the term is far more encompassing. A second aspect of this theory is that much of what constitutes "personality" is found in peoples' current inner set of models that organize information about the self and others, as well as the relationship roles between the self and others (M. Horowitz 1975, 1979). E. R. Shapiro (1978) underscored this unbroken circle between intrapsychic structures and interpersonal relationships by observing that the cardinal feature of object-relations theory is that "one can understand the relationships between people through an examination of the internal images they have of one another" (p. 1309).

The buildup of dyadic and subsequent triadic cognitions (maps of oneself and others as they have been perceived and colored by the infant's desires, fantasies, and defenses) and the relationship of these internal objects to one another are referred to as *internalized object relations,* to distinguish them from external object relations, or *interpersonal relationships.*

These inner models or templates have been given various names in the literature, including images, representations, introjects, internal objects, and the representational world. Not only are these terms used in different ways by different theorists, but the function of each term within the personality is a matter of debate. The more cognitively oriented psychoanalytic theorists regard models as a loose, anticipatory image of what can be expected from real people in the world or from the self (Greenberg and Mitchell 1983). This image may be realistic or unrealistic, conscious or unconscious. For the more classical theorists, the critical process is how object images become internalized, connected to an emerging self-image, and end up influencing how people experience themselves. And among the classical theorists, inner objects can be conceptualized as internalized aspects (albeit distorted) of real others and can function as critical and condemning internal saboteurs (used in a more general sense than as used as Fairbairn [1952]) or as a source of comfort that can be invoked in times of loneliness or stress (Greenberg and Mitchell 1983, p. 11). All of these usages are interesting and important, and frequently one different usage will permit better insight into patients' problems than another usage will.

Despite the differences in usage of object and object relations, there is some agreement that these templates constitute a memory trace of a person and of relationships with significant people from early childhood onward. In addition, Greenberg and Mitchell (1983) found that important exchanges are internalized and somehow come to shape subsequent attitudes, perceptions, feelings, and behavior. All people carry such templates around in their heads for use in dealing with other people or in evaluating the self.

The Inner Image Is Not Identical with the External Object

Patients' accounts of how other people behave do not always agree with the report of an impartial observer. Why is this so? Sigmund Freud first noticed this phenomenon in the clinical case of Anna O. Anna O mistakenly believed that she was pregnant and that Josef Breuer, her physician, was acting like a lover. Freud's analysis of this dynamic led to the first understanding of transference, making it impossible for therapists ever again to assume with any certainty that the people about whom patients are talking correspond in any one-to-one way with the real person (Greenberg and Mitchell 1983, p. 10). Rather, the person being discussed is at best only a partial or amended version of the other. This is because within the mind is an internal representation of the other that is colored by unresolved infantile wishes, fantasies, drives, defenses, loves, and hates. Thus, this internal other is not a totally accurate representation of the external other. In the case of severely disturbed patients, the discrepancy between the inside image and the external person may be great, for reasons that will be examined later in this chapter. Regardless of the degree of accuracy, these internal representations of others and how they shape feelings and beliefs about the self and others can and do influence feelings as well as behavior, as it did with Anna O's unrealistic reaction to Breuer.

An Introject Is a Special Type of Object Representation

In recent years the term *introject* has increasingly become an important explanatory concept in psychoanalytic theorizing. It is used by a number of important psychoanalytic theorists (e.g., Adler and Buie, Giovacchini, Horner, Meissner), although Kernberg prefers to avoid using the term, substituting instead *internal object*. Thus, although commonly used in the literature, introject can be employed in a broad or narrow way and is seen as a controversial construct by some theorists (Jacobson 1964).

As used here, the term *introject* refers to an image or representation of another person or part of another person that the individual experiences with varying degrees of vividness.

It may be experienced within oneself, like a photograph within the mind. The patient will almost always realize that it is not real but may respond to it psychologically as if it were. It may also be experienced as outside oneself, as in the case of a pseudohallucination that seems real. The introject may be experienced as a vague, unformed percept or in exceptional visual detail. What particularly defines an introject is its perceptualized relationship with and striving, as it were, to become a part of a corresponding self-representation. An introject therefore comes to combine the characteristics of an object image and a self-image, and when the combination has been achieved, we call it an *identification* (M. Horowitz 1975, Volkan 1976, p. 76).

M. Horowitz (1975) gives an example of such an introject. A woman found her arousal during intercourse reduced by a "sense" or seeming visualization of her mother's face scowling at her. As Horowitz explained, the mother image was an unclear fusion of an object representation with the self-representation. He used the term *fusion* because the antierotic attitude not only represented the mother's feelings but also were aspects of the patient's own attitudes learned from her mother but now externalized onto the mother image. The patient had some belief that sex was bad, as learned from her mother, but she did not completely identify with this belief. Hence, it was externalized, "sequestered" in the representation of the mother, which was briefly perceived as a "scowling face" (p. 8 - 8).

Thus, the concept of introjection and introjects is complex because these terms also include projective processes that endow the original object image with qualities derived from the self, which then in turn modify the self (Buie and Adler 1982–1983, p. 55). These qualities influence the self, and the self is in a dynamic relationship with them. Introjects, then, appear to be the product of an intermediate phase of development. They are not raw representations or introjected identification, and they have not progressed from object representation to identification. We might say that they represent transitional phenomena, which in some persons are perpetuated and become structuralized into the personality. Buie and Adler (1982–1983) conceptualize that introjects can occur when the toddler has achieved evocative memory and can now internalize the functions of the parents. At that time, introjects come to exist and have functions, motivations, and dynamics within the personality.

Not all theorists consider introjects to be percepts. Meissner (1982), for example, uses it in a broader sense, treating the structuring of the patients' inner world of introjects as equivalent to the internalized object relations derived from developmental experiences (p. 362). Usually, such internalized object relations are not experienced as felt presences.

As Kernberg (1976a) has pointed out, patients take for granted their contradictory beliefs and behaviors and are usually not aware of their primitive object-relations units (self- and object images and affective coloration). Meissner (1984) found that borderline patients begin psychotherapy with their introjects more or less undifferentiated from their subjective sense of self. Even though the introjects have not been assimilated, they do not always stand out in bold relief. It is as though the figure (the introjects) and the ground (the self) have merged and all that patients can identify is a sense of chaos, emptiness, anguish, or confusion. Months of sifting through the patients' empty or contradictory experiences may be necessary before the pathological introjects will emerge clearly. Meissner still believes that the term or concept *introject* is warranted under such circumstances.

Buie and Adler (1982–1983) accept Meissner's use of the term introject. They conceptualize treatment as an effort to help patients form a new, healthy type of introject to "fill a hole" in their psychic structure. These theorists believe that borderline patients not only have pathological introjects but also lack the healthy adult identification that would allow them to perform certain functions for themselves. Accordingly, Buie and Adler want patients to form a "holding introject." To do this, the therapist must behave in such a consistent and supportive manner that the patients can use the therapist's "presence" to soothe themselves when they are away from the session. In order for a healthy developmental progression to take place, such an introject must eventually be selectively assimilated and become part of the patients' self-system—a function they can perform themselves.

Although patients may talk about introjects as though they actually exist and may discuss their relationship with the introject or the relationships among introjects (e.g., Mary Markham's Megalomaniac and the Baby), the clinician should be careful not to infer the physical reality of such objects. They are not entities or *homunculi* within the mind. Although interpersonal relationships can be observed, the clinician must infer internalized object relations or introjects on the basis of the patients' material or in view of their subjective sense of such a phenomenon as an introject.

Adaptative or Healthy Templates

Representations that have slowly built up and evolved through interactions with parents, siblings, teachers, and other significant people become a permanent part of the adult psychic structure. In healthy people, these representations of self and others are flexible and are continually reprogrammed to fit new reality data. These representations correspond accurately to the perceptions of others, as confirmed by feedback received from others across time (E. R. Shapiro 1978). Although flexible, such representations are strong enough that unrealistic criticism or adversity do not destroy positive images of the self or others, nor do they undermine self-confidence or individuality. Instinctual life, both sexuality and realistic expressions of anger, can take place without damaging the self- or object representation.

In contrast, the representations of borderline adults tend to be rigid, unresponsive to new data, limited in number, shallow, and usually stereotyped rather than multifaceted (E. R. Shapiro 1978). Because their representations are still at the split-object-relations level, it is not surprising that they are limited, contradictory, polarized, and a poor tool for reality testing, particularly in the charged arena of interpersonal relationships. Borderline adults have both unhealthy templates and in many cases lack appropriate templates (e.g., holding and self-soothing capacities).

The Unbroken Thread—From Childhood to Adulthood

Now we can bring together the two meanings of object relations. Childhood interpersonal relations create enduring cognitions of self and others, which in turn direct and regulate adult interpersonal relationships. The way in which adults perceive the external world is guided by constructs already established within the mind by early child–caretaker interactions and modified by later developmental sequences and experiences.

Because interpersonal relationships and internalized object relations are not always identical, there are many ways in which life can go awry. For example, when patients' external behavior does not make sense, the therapist should determine whether internalized object relations can explain the incongruent social behavior. On the other hand, sometimes patients will report in therapy that although they get along fine in the social environment, something inside them prevents them from enjoying this success. This situation may indicate internalized object relations that are incongruent with successful social behavior. The following simplified clinical examples illustrate the relationship between internalized object relations and interpersonal relationships and show some of the ways in which patients' interpersonal actions can confuse or prevent the therapist from perceiving the internalized object relations.

Example 1

A competent and intellectual man is in marital counseling with his wife, an underassertive and timid woman. He requested the therapy to work on her problems in "speaking her mind." During the counseling, she finally objects to her husband's limited contribution to the upkeep of the house and yard and timidly suggests that she is unhappy about this. She says that she wants them to look at this problem together and consider the options. The husband becomes furious and accuses his wife of being hostile and giving him ultimatums. She then emotionally withdraws in the session and becomes quiet. The husband's unexpected reaction seems incongruent because he has often claimed to want his wife to be more assertive.

Exploration reveals that the husband feels he is responsible for everything that happens in the marriage and to the family. Thus, he believes that if his wife is unhappy, it is because he has failed her, which in turn means that he is bad. Because of this internal model, he now feels guilty for failing her. At the same time, because the ejection of bad feelings is still a prominent defense for him, he also feels angry at his wife for having caused the guilt and tells her that she is to blame. His internal model of himself and others is "unhappy wife = bad husband." This, of course, represents some perceptual fusion of self-object images in his mind. He now feels compelled to rid himself of the painful, bad images by attacking his wife and accusing her of being the bad one. It is as though he experienced his wife as telling him he was a "bad aggressor," an image he found to be intolerable, and now needs to see her as the aggressor and himself as the victim.

Example 2

Agreeable interpersonal behavior often masks strikingly discrepant internalized object relations and externalized object relations from both the patient and the therapist. For example, Mary Markham usually maintained a compliant, agreeable, nondemanding facade. She asked for very little, and the therapy proceeded smoothly. Unpredictably, however, she had sudden depressions or rageful episodes that she dutifully reported in therapy but never understood. Mary did not know what triggered this behavior or even what her inner fantasies were at the time.

Only after lengthy exploration did the therapy uncover Mary's fantasies about how she and others should behave. For example, Mary perceived both her mother and her therapist as devoted slaves who were supposed to cater to her every need. In addition, she erroneously inferred that the therapist deeply loved her (just as a mother cares for her infant) and that the therapist was aware of this primal connection, approved of it, and wanted to continue the relationship forever. Then, whenever the therapist "failed" her by not behaving as expected (e.g., rescheduled a session), Mary experienced either intense depression or suicidal-homicidal rage. Before one of these episodes, Mary had a self-image of power because she felt connected to (and controlling of) an idealized and perfect other. Not surprisingly, she experienced happiness and pleasure with this self-object image. But when the fantasy was disrupted, she experienced intensely negative feelings as well as helplessness and rage. The therapist would never have guessed Mary's internal model if exploration had not revealed it so clearly.

It usually takes some time for the socially compliant veneer to wear thin, as with Mary, and for the internalized object relations to intrude into the social behavior. Then, however, important therapeutic work can begin.

Example 3

At other times Mary reported being praised by others for successfully performing at work, and her coworkers frequently asked her for advice. But she never believed their compliments. Why? Mary had an internal representation of herself as unsuccessful—a failure, an inadequate person. She found the praise from others somehow "unreal" and less persuasive than the representation of herself that she carried around in her head. Thus she accepted her internal image of herself and not what others told her. No amount of convincing by the therapist could persuade her to give up this inadequate self-image, despite repeated episodes of successful behavior at work.

One of the tasks of an object relations–based psychotherapy is to work with these inflexible and unhealthy internalized object relations in order to modify them. This must be done over a long time and in a sensitive manner.

Stierlin (1970) reported that inner objects can go awry in two different ways, preventing the individual from experiencing an enduring relationship in which one can learn from experience and correct oneself. Such inner objects may be too rigid, as in the case of Mary Markham, or the object images can be too loose and changeable, as in the case of an as-if personality.

According to Greenberg and Mitchell (1983, p. 14), objects have the following meaning and dynamics:

1. Objects are both a description of real people in the external world and images that are established internally; the internal image may not correspond directly to the real person.
2. Objects (external and internal) influence the development of self-images and, later, enduring self-representations; somehow the way the object is perceived becomes intertwined with, shapes, and colors the emerging self-representation.
3. Internal objects [e.g., called introjects by some theorists] exhibit a wide range of characteristics [e.g., active, static, helpful, harmful, soothing]; inner objects have all the variability that persons have with real objects in their environment.
4. Patients often experience their inner objects as having all the reality of external relationships and believe that they have relationships with their internal objects [e.g., Mary Markham, the Megalomaniac, and the Baby, and as a less extreme example, Sarah Gardner's struggles with her "swinger" and her "helpless little girl" selves in which the object has been more assimilated into the self but is still conflicted].
5. Despite their tenacity and slow rate of change, objects can be modified [e.g., cease to exist, split in two, be reduced in intensity]. Patients report

experiencing these changes. This psychoanalytic concept of the intrapsychic operations that can be performed on objects is significant because changing internal objects and helping patients create some new positive objects will be a goal of therapy.

Using Greenberg's and Mitchell's analysis as a background, one can see that relationships with real people can create a sense of tension between one's self and one's introjects (representations). For example, consider a woman who is the daughter of an abusive, alcoholic father. When she meets a man who treats her well, she may experience unconscious conflictual feelings about being close to a man quite different from her father. Ilan (1977) notes three alternatives she can use to restore her sense of inner balance: (1) she can close herself off from this new emotional experience (e.g., retreat from relationships with men); (2) she can choose men who have qualities similar to her inner dominating introjects (e.g., she can choose men who are alcoholic and abusive); or (3) she can project onto the external object characteristics of the dominant introject and in this way experience new objects as reinforcing entities (e.g., she can choose a nice man and try to persuade him to act like her father via projective identification).

All three of these alternatives, although unhealthy, will restore a sense of balance to an inner world in which introjects are either too rigid or too loose and changeable. A healthier way to restore this woman's sense of inner balance would be for her to select a man who would not be cruel to her and to learn how to be comfortable with her choice, not letting herself be driven to repeat the old destructive pattern.

A BRIEF HISTORY OF THE THEORY

The concept of object relations began as an inherent part of Freud's drive theory. Greenberg and Mitchell (1983) stated that Freud believed that the object was either a libidinal object or an aggressive object; he used the term *object* to refer to both a thing (not necessarily a human) and a target. Freud's object was a *thing* that was the target of a drive. Thus, in Freud's original use of the term, the concept of object was intermixed with that of drive. Furthermore, the object was the means or instrumentality by means of which the aim of the drive (i.e., the reduction of the drive's intensity) was achieved. At first, Freud believed that object relations were secondary to drives, that they were simply the outcome of drive activity.

From the later work of Freud onward, psychoanalysis has become increasingly interested in ego development as well as drive theory. Freud's final conception of the ego, in fact, created a new field of psychoanalytic endeavor concerned more directly with object relations and the purely ego aspects of object relations (G. Klein 1976).

The British object relations school (M. Klein 1935, 1940, 1946; Fairbairn 1952, 1963; Guntrip 1961, 1969; Winnicott 1965; and Bowlby 1969) developed shortly after Freud introduced object-relations theory in 1923. The American culturalist school, represented by Sullivan (1953), also participated in the evolving theory of object relations, although it did not embrace the concept of drive theory. Further contributions came from contemporary theorists of ego psychology such as Hartmann (1939, 1950); Hartmann, Kris, and Loewenstein (1946); E. Erikson (1950, 1956); Jacobson (1954, 1964); Sandler (1960a, 1960b, 1976); Sandler, Holder, and Meers (1963); Sandler, Holder, Kawenoka, Kennedy, and Neurath (1969); Sandler and Rosenblatt (1962); Anna Freud (1936, 1965); Mahler (1968); Mahler, Pine, and Bergmann (1975); Modell (1968); Kernberg (1976a); and Rinsley (1982a). All focused on only one ego function—object relations—and began to view it as the core of identity. Each theorist also decided whether or not to retain drive theory as part of his or her conception of object relations. (See Greenberg and Mitchell [1983] for a review and critique of the various object-relations theorists and their positions on drive theory.)

Despite these valuable contributions to the field, it is still too early to proclaim the existence of a unified object-relations theory that is accepted by the majority of the psychoanalytic community. In addition, object-relations theory is being challenged by a new theory—Kohut's self theory.

The challenge of Kohut's self theory, however, really resurrects a schism that has existed in psychoanalytic theory since Freud and his earlier students. The debate centers on whether psychotic, borderline, and narcissistic pathology arises from a surplus of constitutional (drive-derived) aggression in the infant (e.g., Kernberg) or arrested ego development caused by the empathic failure of the parenting figure (e.g., Kohut). This disagreement has led to differing conceptualizations of severely disturbed adults and competing therapeutic techniques (see Chapter 8). Despite some of the contradictory positions generated during this recent healthy renaissance in theory building, many clinicians continue to find psychoanalytic object-relations concepts a valuable frame of reference for understanding both the clinical characteristics of severely disturbed individuals and appropriate treatment approaches.

The tenets of object-relations theory can be brought closer to the clinical data than can those of classical psychoanalytic metapsychology. This allows the clinician to apply the theoretical concepts to such questions as how patients see themselves; how they see others (including their unconscious fantasies about themselves, others, and relationship roles); and how this view explains their love, career, friendship, and identity difficulties.

CONTEMPORARY OBJECT-RELATIONS THEORY: KERNBERG

Over the past decade, Kernberg has introduced object-relations theory to the therapeutic community and is the only American to call his work an object-relations theory (Greenberg and Mitchell 1983). Kernberg has synthesized the work of many, but particularly that of M. Klein, Fairbairn, Jacobson, and Mahler, into a sophisticated and comprehensive system.

Kernberg does not, however, see his work as a general theory of the mind, replacing Freudian drive theory. Rather, Kernberg (1976a) limits his usage of the term object-relations theory to the following: (1) the buildup of the dyadic self- and object images as reflections of the original mother–child relationship and (2) the later development of these images into dyadic, triangular, and multiple internal and external interpersonal relationships. To Kernberg (1976a), it is theoretically important that these internalizations are *bipolar* and that each dyadic unit of self- and object image is established within a particular affective context (pleasure or pain) (p. 57). Kernberg's emphasis on the sequential buildup of representations while not examining in any detail the child–caretaker relationship led Meissner (1984) to refer to Kernberg as an object-representation theorist instead of an object-relations theorist. Nevertheless, Kernberg does give at least theoretical credence to the influence of the early caretakers on the developing quality of internalized object relations.

How the Clinical Material Shaped the Theory

Kernberg constructed this theory from the clinical material provided by his patients, enriched by the findings of the Menninger Foundation Psychotherapy Research Project, in which he participated (Kernberg et al. 1972). In accordance with the scientific method, of course, the theory is revised as new clinical data are revealed.

The impetus for such theorizing comes from the very nature of psychoanalytic inquiry, which presupposes that something is missing in the patients' experiences of themselves. The assumption is that some important dimension of meaning is absent from the patients' accounts (whether or not they are aware of this absence) and that the therapist's job is to offer reasons for these missing meanings (Greenberg and Mitchell 1983, p. 15).

Thus, Kernberg began to analyze the behavior of his severely disturbed patients. He observed their often chaotic and vacillating transference reactions—seeming to find him bad and hateful one session and then good and wonderful the next. He also noted similar vacillations in the patients' opinions of themselves. When confronted with these contradictory states of mind, however, they could acknowledge the accuracy of Kernberg's recounting of their behavior but seemed unbothered by these inconsistencies (Greenberg and Mitchell 1983, p. 15).

Along with the process of splitting, Kernberg observed a number of other primitive defenses now considered so common to borderline adults, including projective identification, denial, idealization, and devaluation. The ease with which primitive ego states and defenses were produced in the transference and in the patients' life suggested to Kernberg that the primitive childhood psychic structure continued to exist within the psychic apparatus (Kernberg 1976a, p. 24).

Kernberg still needed a concept to explain the persistence of such primitive intrapsychic structures. Mahler had already described the cognitive structure of the rapprochement-subphase toddler (e.g., the use of splitting to keep good images of mother separated from bad images). But how could such mechanisms exist in the adult? Kernberg concluded that the readiness with which such primitive transferences emerged in the therapy suggested that the early configurations on which they were based continued to exist. He described these early configurations or ego states as *nonmetabolized*.

The metabolization of early object relations refers to the same phenomenon that Kohut called *transmuting internalization*, that Jacobson called *depersonification*, and that Hartmann called *internalization* (Greenberg and Mitchell 1983). Although using different terms, each is saying that early relations with the environment give rise to enduring psychological structures that reflect those interactions. In normal development, early relationships "lose their specific early qualities and become assimilated into a smoothly functioning psychological structure"; in other words, they are metabolized (Greenberg and Mitchell 1983, p. 329).

Greenberg and Mitchell (1983) observed that

> in this sense, the process is very much like the digestion and use of food (Bion used "digestion" to describe the same phenomenon), and the concept of metabolization suggests that "We are what we eat" or, more specifically, "We are what we experience." (p. 329)

Continuing this thought, Greenberg and Mitchell (1983) noted that unlike physicochemical metabolism, the psychological process is reversible. In the prolonged psychoanalysis of neurotic patients, the superego's demands and prohibitions that these patients initially consider as their own can finally be experienced by them as parental attitudes that arose in specific childhood interactions with their parents. It was such experiences in psychoanalysis that led theorists to develop the concept of metabolization. But with the severely disturbed patients, there never appeared to be any metabolization, and hence these early structures were formed very quickly (Greenberg and Mitchell 1983, pp. 329–330). Their formation is usually traced in the transference reactions and contributes to a chaotic and contradictory picture in both therapy and the patients' lives.

Drawing on the developmental theories of Jacobson and Mahler, Kernberg continued the psychoanalytic practice of conceptualizing the difficulties of adults, by searching for a fixation point in infancy that would explain the pathology. He concluded that his patients had been fixated at an early stage of development when the ego was unable to integrate different kinds of experiences, especially intensely pleasurable with intensely painful ones. The ego is dominated by affect at this stage, and experiences are organized by whether they are pleasurable or unpleasurable, "good" or "bad." The lack of integrative ability keeps these experiences apart.

Then Kernberg (1976a) noticed some additional clarifying clinical data. When he confronted his patients with their contradictory statements and behavior, they would become anxious. He inferred that this anxiety suggested the presence of intense conflict, not merely the ego's inability to contain different kinds of experiences (Greenberg and Mitchell 1983). He was convinced that what was originally ego weakness could be used defensively by the adult, and he termed this process *splitting*. As both Mahler and Kernberg discovered, the defensive splitting of cognitions according to affective valences is common in toddlers in the rapprochement subphase but is pathological in adults. Thus Kernberg placed the fixation of the borderline adult in the rapprochement subphase.

Kernberg then had to explain the content of these early experiences—the experiences that were first unintegrated and then defensively split, the experiences that should have been metabolized into a smoothly functioning psychic structure but were not (Greenberg and Mitchell 1983).

The Theory Proper

As the reader might expect after reading about Mahler's and Kernberg's work, Kernberg believes that the experiences that optimally would be metabolized into the psychic structure are primarily shaped by the mother–child interaction and involve a specific relationship configuration (Kernberg 1976a, p. 26). The following passage summarizes Kernberg's (1980b) current position on what this configuration comprises:

> The stages of development of internalized object relations—that is, the stages of infantile autism, symbiosis, separation-individuation, and of object constancy—reflect the earliest structures of the psychic apparatus. Discrete units of self-representation, object representation and an affect disposition linking them are the basic substructures of these early developmental stages, and will gradually evolve into more complex substructures (such as real-self and ideal-self, and real-object and ideal-object representations).

This process—which, roughly speaking, covers the first three years of life—includes the earliest substructures of the psychic apparatus that will gradually differentiate and eventually become integrated into ego, superego, and id.

In this context, Jacobson's, Mahler's, and my own conceptions have in common the assumption that the earliest internalization processes have dyadic features, that is, a self-object polarity, even when self- and object representations are not yet differentiated. By the same token, all future developmental steps also imply dyadic internalizations, that is, internalization not only of an object as an object representation, but of an interaction of the self with the object, which is why I consider units of self- and object representations (and the affect dispositions linking them) the basic building blocks on which further developments of internalized object and self-representations, and later on, the overall tripartite structure (ego, superego, and id) rest. (p. 17)

Kernberg regards these early configurations as an internalization system that forms the basic material or building blocks that constitute experience, then psychic structure, and eventual ego identity. They constitute a progressive sequence in the process of internalized object relations and are crucial to both ego and superego development.

Before we examine how object relations are internalized and create psychic structure, we need to explain several terms. *Internalization* is a way of copying another and includes a series of processes such as mimicry, general imitation, and modeling in addition to incorporation, introjection, and identification. These last three forms of learning—incorporation, introjection, and identification—have been of most interest to psychoanalytic theorists and have been collectively called, also, *internalization.* These terms refer to taking upon or into the self more wholistic attributes from the object. They are considered to be motivated in part by stress and to be involved in what is called the conflicted sphere of ego functioning, the central focus of psychodynamics (M. Horowitz 1975). Thus learning and building are taking place, but these processes may also have a defensive use.

Phase 1: Internalization

Kernberg recognizes three kinds of internalization systems: introjection, identification, and ego identity. Each reflects the normal state of affairs at a particular developmental level.

\. *Introjection* is the most primitive and earliest form of internalization. It represents "the least organized, least differentiated self- and object images in the context of the most violent, least modulated" feeling tone (Greenberg and Mitchell 1983, p. 331). During this phase, infants are introjecting into their self-representations global aspects of the mother's functioning, ways of being, and ways of relating. Infants have two unions with their mother. They experience an undifferentiated union or "good me" with a gratifying mother and an unpleasant nonunion or "bad me" with an ungratifying mother. Splitting is a result of the infant's inability to integrate complex experiences. At first the "bad me" is an uncanny, dangerous environmental experience, and later it will be ejected and disowned through the process of projection. Introjection continues as a mode of internalization through Mahler's symbiotic phase and part of the differentiation subphase. During this period, configurations with similar valences start to cluster together and are called *ego states*. Kernberg calls the good ego states the *good internal object* and the bad ego states the *bad internal object*. During this period, infants engage in both introjection and projection, the latter a defensive process that protects the good ego state.

Identification, the next level of internalization, occurs when toddlers are able to appreciate the role played by the parents and themselves in significant interactions. The components of identification are (1) an image of the object in a specific role, (2) an image of the self in perhaps a complementary role, and (3) an affective response that is modified in intensity (Greenberg and Mitchell 1983). Identification begins during Mahler's differentiation subphase and continues into the rapprochement subphase. It is easier to determine role identification in patients than it is to determine introjection. An example of identification is the father who takes interest and delight in teaching his son how to ride a tricycle. The son may then internalize (1) an object image of a helpful and loving father, (2) a child who is "good" despite his inexperience, and (3) the affect of pleasure untainted by any shame about being helpless or ignorant in regard to tricycle riding. When grown, this child may take delight in helping others without berating them for their inexperience.

Ego identity, the most mature level of internalization, refers to the organization of all the introjections and identifications under the guiding principle of the ego's synthetic function (Kernberg 1976). He stated that the components of ego identity are (1) a consistent view of the object world, (2) a consolidated sense of the self as an ongoing organization, and (3) a mutual recognition of this consistency by the child and the child's environment (p. 32). Children have achieved object constancy and can experience ambivalence, which reduces the intense affects and leads to a greater affective range. Children are now able to provide in themselves the functions that were formerly provided by the object; hence, object relations are now starting to be metabolized or depersonified. These children now have a self. Kernberg (1982d) has begun to refer to the self as the sum total of the self-representations connected with the sum total of object representations (p. 900). The self is no longer just a representation—it is on a par with the id, ego, and superego (Greenberg and Mitchell 1983).

Phase 2: The Tripartite Structure

Kernberg (1976a) suggests that ego as a structure comes into being with the first use of introjection for defensive purposes. The consolidation of the ego enables patients to feel repression and the higher-level defensive operations organized around it that characterize the defensive style of normal or neurotic people. The emergence of repression in turn reflects the formation of a dynamic unconscious composed of rejected self-object-affect configurations (e.g., bad, sadistic internalization units that are unacceptable to the newly strengthened ego). The final stage in structure formation is the establishment and consolidation of the superego. The superego has various layers: (1) the precipitates of early, hostile (sadistic) object images that reflect the children's projective process; (2) an ego ideal that includes the fused ideal-self-image and ideal-object image (preserving those aspects of symbiosis); and (3) the integration of realistic parental images, including their values, prohibitions, and demands. Until this final layer is formed and consolidated, it is the ego ideal that tames the sadistic, fused self-object images (Volkan 1982). In children who have few good self-object remnants and lack a formed ego ideal, such taming cannot take place. Thus, the immature ego remains the victim of sadistic assaults by the hostile self-object images, leading to feelings of badness and emptiness and, in some, to pathological perfectionism. Another perspective is that without the mediating force of internalized realistic parental images, the unrealistic ego ideal may dominate, encouraging self-indulgent behavior based on magical expectations.

How the Self Is Shaped

As M. Horowitz (1975) has explained, the child mixes self- and object attributes not only by taking on object qualities (internalization) but also by extruding facets of the self (externalization). Projection is a specific kind of externalization in which ideas or feelings that would be threatening if consciously felt as part of the self are experienced instead as coming from another person (M. Horowitz 1975, p. 8 - 9). Rinsley (1982a) has reaffirmed the view that the precursor of this process in earliest life is related to the spitting out of unpleasant food. To infants, those unpleasant foods that were spit out become attached to the aggressive affect charges that also must be ejected. Later, the aggressive instinct will become separated from the food and will itself be externalized, and there will be no further necessity for food or any other tangible item to serve as its vehicle (Rinsley 1982a, p. 13). What is good is identified as "me" and kept inside, and what is bad and frustrating is projected onto the surrounding environment, frequently the mother.

Infants who massively project their bad, frustrating objects onto the surrounding environment thereby come to experience a predominance of bad objects outside in the world. Thus they create a welter of what Melanie Klein called *external persecutors* and thereby a hostile, even terrifying environment. At the same time, this massive projection of bad internal objects threatens to carry along with it the infant's good internal objects, and the result is a potentially terrifying state of inner emptiness or impoverishment. Thus the already-disturbed infant and child, later to become the psychotic adult, attempts frantically to "get back" the "lost" good objects while equally frantically attempting to ward off the projected bad (persecutory) objects. Much of the psychotic adult's symptomatology can be traced to these occurrences. Among borderline patients, this pathologically persistent introjection-projection and splitting occur to a lesser extent, but even in them, the feelings of inner emptiness are easily seen, as is the profound mistrust of others derived from the persistent use of projection (Rinsley 1982a, Ilan 1977). The following example illustrates the dilemmas arising from this early stage of development, in regard to the continued reliance on introjection-projection in an adult.

Clinical Example A young man returns to college after a series of brief admissions to inpatient units for transient psychotic episodes and depression. Because he is warm and charming, he soon befriends two of the best students at the college, and they invite him to join their study group. He does so, and they study together for a few months. He gets excellent grades and appears to be an asset to the study group. One day he learns that the other two have recently been meeting for study sessions without him. He does not know why and is too embarrassed to ask.

The young man becomes extremely upset, decompensates, and is rehospitalized. With his therapist, he explores the meaning of this situation. He begins to realize that he had assumed that some specialness was conferred on him by being in a study group with these top students. This inferred sense of specialness had infused him with power; it allowed him to study comfortably and get good grades because of the others' omnipotence. When they excluded him, he felt no subjective anger at them, only desperation and a belief that he was bad. Then he began to believe that the brick classroom building of the college harbored "evil harpies" that would kill him and rip him to shreds if he entered the building. Once he decided the building was dangerous, he had to drop out of college.

Reviewing this material, we can see introjection-projection and splitting at work. Initially, this patient introjected what he perceived as his friends' omnipotence and idealized them. When they excluded him, he protected them against his rage at them by using splitting (seeing them as good and himself as bad) and then projected his rage onto the building (the building was bad and evil). Then he reintrojected his projected rage, which he experienced as the building hating him and subjecting him to extreme danger. Finally he panicked, fearing that he was in extreme personal peril for his bad behavior in not being liked by his friends (as well as his unconscious rage and hatred) and that the building would kill him if he entered it. This is an example of the mechanism of introjection-projection and splitting at work in a psychotic individual. Such introjective-projective relatedness can be seen in projective identification, idealization, projection, and a variety of other mechanisms.

Toddlers in the practicing subphase can use these mechanisms in a more sophisticated form. There is greater differentiation of the self- and object representations, and thus there is some separation of self and other in the area of frustrating, anxiety-producing, or hostile interactions. Under these new circumstances, infants first perceive their own hostility as naturally justified because of what they experience as hostile behavior from a bad mother (Kernberg 1976a, p. 66). Internalization and externalization are still easy to accomplish. That is, bad attributes (the most common projection) can be conceptually assigned to the other person rather than the self (M. Horowitz 1975). Eventually, in order to protect mother's good image, the child may be willing to take the blame.

For example, a toddler cries angrily at his mother because she has frustrated him by not feeding him as soon as he became hungry. Believing that she made his stomach hurt, he decides that she is bad and is responsible for his discomfort. How the mother handles this projection is critical. If she is prone to feeling guilt, she may readily accept responsibility for the toddler's unhappiness. He may learn through her direction to blame her when things do not go well. If the mother gets angry, on the other hand, and slaps him for crying and thrashing about, he may well internalize this new experience as "bad baby for being hungry and angry." In time he may even come to believe that good mothers hit bad children and that such feelings as anger are bad to experience and must be disowned.

Children may come to have two different introjection-projection patterns, depending on the parenting pattern and their response to it. M. Horowitz (1975) reported that in the first, rage is projected onto the object (and, of course, the object representation). The object is represented as a persecutor not only because of the deprivations it inflicts but also because the persecutor (the projected bad object) will perceive the self as a dangerous object and will proceed to attack and destroy it. These toddlers believe they will be destroyed because of their feelings of anger (aggression). Fearing of an enraged object is called the *paranoid position* (M. Klein). Destructive cycles of introjection-projection-reintrojection may be instituted, creating distorted intrapsychic structures and chaotic and painful feeling states. In the second pattern, rage is aroused by frustration, and the object can be seen as bad; the badness attributed to the object is then internalized (because self and object are still partially fused), and this establishes a bad self-representation that is reinforced by seeing the self as harboring unduly aggressive impulses. These toddlers believe they will be rejected because of their feelings of anger (aggression). This situation of self-depreciation has been called the *depressive position* (M. Klein). (M. Horowitz 1975).

In summary, M. Horowitz (1975) noted that children learn to perceive the traits of their parents and then identify such patterns in themselves as they have been internalized. This ability permits more differentiated perceptions of the parents and then of the self. As a result, almost everything found in the self is also found in the significant other. Hence, children learn the characteristics associated with both the self and the other—the passive receiver and the active doer. This has been referred to as the *dialectic of learning*. Because a common defense is turning a passive role into an active one, children who have been abused (passive position) may become adults who use excessive punishment (active position).

The implications of the dialectic of learning for psychotherapy can be seen in Weiss's and Sampson's (1982) approach, the "control-mastery" theory. In this model, patients are seen as motivated to solve their problems, not just to gratify forbidden impulses (id model). They are inspired to make the pathological unconscious beliefs (or introjects) conscious. They wish to enlist the therapist to help them solve their problems by creating a relationship with the therapist in which they will feel unconsciously safe; the purpose of this relationship is to invoke unconscious goals without the fear that they will be traumatized as they were in childhood.

These patients "test" the therapist to disconfirm the pathological ideas in two ways: (1) through the traditional transference paradigm in which the patients provoke the therapist to act like the parent, and (2) through turning "passive into active," acting toward the therapist as the parent acted toward them.

If the therapist passes the test to disconfirm the patients' pathological fears (e.g., that separation is harmful to the parent), the patients should show more boldness and involvement in pursuing in real life previously feared goals. In the second paradigm, the patients treat the therapist as they were treated and hope the therapist will not be traumatized as they were. When the therapist demonstrates the capacity that the patients hope to acquire (e.g., the ability to tolerate separation with trauma), the patients feel safe, although they may immediately show a negative reaction to the very same behavior that unconsciously makes them feel safe. For example, a patient who immediately has a negative reaction to a therapist's interpretation may come to the next session and say, "Now that I've thought about it, you were right," or they may show improved functioning in their life without acknowledging the rightness of the interpretation.

Weiss and Sampson believe that the turning "passive-into-active" paradigm, which is more difficult to manage, is used by severely disturbed patients and that higher-level patients tend to use the transference paradigm (personal communication, L. Beall, September 5, 1983).

Adults in psychotherapy are often surprised to find how much they act like their parents, even engaging in behaviors that they did not like in their parents. The power of the other person seems to be a powerful motivator for internalization, particularly in identification (Horowitz 1975). Feared as well as loved persons are common sources for learned patterns of behavior. Theorists differ among themselves as to whether identification with the good object is simply a normal developmental process containing a small amount of defensiveness (Schafer 1968) or whether the internalization of objects serves only a defensive purpose (Fairbairn 1952). In this latter position, the good object simply promotes good ego development and, in becoming material for a healthy self, disappears into the structure of the self while the unsatisfying object is internalized—and frequently maintained as an introject—in order to master it (Stierlin 1970). We do know that most borderline adults have engaged in introjective-projective mechanisms with parents who have been distorting mirrors. Consequently, these borderline individuals have built up pathological self- and object representations with all types of fears concerning their "hidden" aggressive, narcissistic, or sexual fantasies. Psychotherapy often becomes the means by which such errors in learning can be identified (Horowitz 1975). Patients can be helped to reveal their introjections and to engage in improved learning with their therapist as a new object. Such patients will eventually relate to the therapist through some form of introjection-projection and splitting, before new learning can take place.

Hedges (1983) has said that some patients may unexpectedly start talking about a new situation as if the therapist were already familiar with all the details. This illustrates the patients' assumption that the therapist is being treated as part of the self. Other patients may assume that the therapist feels what they feel, that they must be what the therapist wants them to be, or that the therapist is like them. Some patients may try to induce in the therapist what they are feeling. Depending on how the therapist handles this process, the patients may reintroject their feelings as indeed bad, or they may feel soothed, understood, and contained.

The Role of Drives and Affects

Affects (the feeling tones of an experience) are crucial ingredients in the development of internalized object relations. Kernberg (1976a) explains that affects

AFFECTS represent inborn dispositions to a subjective experience in the dimension of pleasure and unpleasure. . . . Differentiation of affect occurs in the context of the differentiation of internalized object relations; . . . affect and cognition at first evolve jointly, only to differentiate much later. . . . Pleasurable and painful affects are the major organizers of the series of "good" and "bad" internalized object relations. . . . (p. 104)

Kernberg considers that early affect states form the basis for future development. The early undifferentiated, physiologically determined pleasurable affects evolve into specific pleasure experiences on the basis of four elements: oral satiation, excitement of the erotogenic zones, gratification of exploratory behavior, and interpersonal experiences (Kernberg 1976a, p. 63). A parallel process is believed to underlie the evolution of unpleasure (Greenberg and Mitchell 1983, p. 337).

At an unspecified point in the developmental progression, representations that have been organized according to affective coloration (pleasure versus unpleasure) now become invested, respectively, with libidinal and aggressive drives, and drives become important organizing forces in the psyche. Before that, however, relationships and their feeling tone precede and actualize drives (Kernberg 1976a, p. 64). Kernberg's sequence is in sharp opposition to both Freud's and Hartmann's positions, which hold that object relations result from drives and neither precede nor actualize them.

The integration of internalization systems with opposite affect valences promotes *drive neutralization* (reduces the intensity of earlier unmodulated affects such as hate and love through their integration). Kernberg sees drive neutralization as providing the important energy source for repression. Thus, the developmental relationship between splitting and repression is reflected in their metapsychological relationships: splitting keeps apart opposite valence introjections, which prevents neutralization and thereby deprives repression of the continuously flowing energy source that it requires. This leads to a weakened ego that falls back on more primitive splitting defenses. In other words, as good representations and bad representations eventually integrate, the drives become modulated and neutralized (Greenberg and Mitchell 1983).

Figure 7-1 is a schemata of Kernberg's theory of the transformation of representations and affects into drives and the tripartite structure and then into ego identity (or self). This schemata represents Kernberg's position that his theory in its broadest sense is an application of systems thinking that maintains ties to Freudian drive theory.

Kernberg (1976a, p. 86) has clearly stated that he is not proposing a neurophysiological model of the mind or a linear model of body-mind equivalence. Rather, he proposes that neurophysiologically based functions constitute physiological units or "building blocks" that are integrated into a

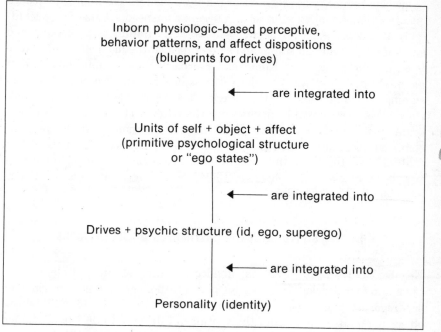

Figure 7-1   Schemata of Kernberg's Theory

system of purely psychological structures (i.e., the primitive units of self + object + affect). These units, in turn, constitute the building blocks for the hierarchy of other purely psychological structures such as the tripartite structure and drives. The tripartite structure and drives, in turn, are integrated into ego identity. Kernberg thus remains a drive theorist who very indirectly grants the importance of early relationships to the formation of internal psychic structures (id, ego, superego). As the reader can see, object-relations theory as developed by Kernberg attempts to tie together drive, affect, perception, and cognition within the context of the evolving tripartite structure.

Do we really need a drive theory to explain aggression in the child? Clinically, Mitchell (1981) has pointed a way to conceptualizing the child's early ragefulness without necessarily positing a drive. M. Klein and Kernberg posit infantile greed and envy in the child because of a surplus of inherent aggression. But there is another way that children's behavior can be conceptualized. As Mitchell (1981) suggests, the preceding formulation of inherent infantile greed and envy can be used without positing inherent aggression within the child. After all, the infant's helplessness and inability to mediate rationally between his or her needs and the environment create a quality of emotional storminess and urgency for need satisfaction. Accordingly, this deprivation predictably causes rage, hatefulness, greediness, and envy of what the child wants and cannot have at the moment. At the same time, the formulation by Kohut and Fairbairn that the internalization of parental difficulties leads to character pathology can be used without assigning unilateral blame to the parent. This is possible because the child's storminess creates real difficulties for the parent. Thus, the child's representational world arises both from infantile passions and the parents' character pathology. Each patient has a different blend from these two sources. The therapist thus might apply the therapeutic techniques of Kernberg, Masterson, Kohut, or others, depending on the particular circumstances (Mitchell 1981).

Kernberg's Five Stages of Internalized Object Relations

Kernberg (1976a, pp. 56–83) has divided the internalization of object relations into four developmental stages plus a fifth stage in which the ego and superego are consolidated. His identification of patterns of internalized object relations complements the writings of Jacobson (1964) and Mahler and her associates (1975).

Stage I: Normal Autism or Primary Undifferentiated Stage (First Month of Life)

Normal, primary, undifferentiated self-object representations are built up during this stage. When the infants' relationship with their mother is unsatisfactory, a psychosis or an affectionless character may result, leading to an antisocial personality structure.

Stage 2: Normal Symbiosis or Stage of the Primary, Undifferentiated Self-Object Representations (2 to 8 Months)

This stage overlaps Mahler's symbiotic phase and differentiation subphase. During this period, good self-object and bad self-object representations are fused. The first part of this stage is dominated by the mechanism of introjection, and the latter half is dominated by identification. Again, infants are at the height of their reliance on introjection-projection and splitting.

Fixation of internalized object relations at this level is likely to impair the subsequent ability to test reality and to be aware of ego boundaries (e.g., differentiating the origin of experience according to whether it arises from inner fantasy, memory, or a perception of external reality). Such patients have difficulty in differentiating self from nonself, and the human from the nonhuman. Fixation at this stage also results in symbiotic psychosis and adult schizophrenia. Rinsley (1981b) traces the origin of affective disorders to the period of 6 to 12+ months, in accordance with classical stage theory (late orality), and the origin of paranoid disorders to the next (anal) stage. He points out that Kernberg's chronology omits any serious consideration of these major syndromes (D. B. Rinsley, personal communication, May 21, 1984).

Stage 3: Differentiation of Self- from Object Representations (8 to 36 Months)

Kernberg believes that fixation at this stage, which overlaps Mahler's practicing and rapprochement subphases, causes borderline personality development. Identification remains the chief internalization mode. Self- and object images are starting to pull away from each other, first in the good configuration or ego state and then in the bad. It is assumed that this occurs first in the good configuration because the negative introjection has been disowned as "not me," has been projected, and must be reclaimed before differentiation can take place. Even though good and bad self-object representations are still separated by splitting, ego boundaries do stabilize because self-images are pulling away from object images and, therefore, self becomes differentiated from nonself. Thus, there can be a projection of self-attributes onto external objects; however, the self is still closely enough associated with the object image that the self-image can still be contaminated.

Blanck and Blanck (1979), who have also studied the progression of self- and object images through Mahler's phases, contend that in the practicing subphase, positive feelings are more associated with the self-representations ("I am great"). In the rapprochement subphase, the situation reverses, and the good feelings are once again more strongly associated with the positive self-object representation ("mother is good"): infants feel vulnerable and once again need an omnipotent other to protect them. Integrated conceptualizations of other people are not possible at this stage because good and bad configurations referring to the same object remain separated. Consequently, such children remain at the part-object relationship level. Because superego integration is not achieved until Stage 4, a fantastic "ideal-self" representation without any relationship to reality may produce difficulties (Volkan 1976, p. 46).

Stage 4: Integration of Self-Representations and Object Representations and Development of Higher-Level Intrapsychic Object Relations-Derived Structures (3 to 5 Years)

Ego identity is now achieved, with the consolidation of the good and bad self-images into a self-system and consolidation of the good and bad object images into a whole-object representation.

During the first three stages, intense bliss versus rage dominates and shapes cognitions, and images are segregated according to these affect valences. By this stage, the situation is reversed. Cognition now dominates and shapes affect. With the creation of a whole image of the self and object, there are now options for more diverse affective responses than just pleasure or pain (e.g., anxiety, hostility). Kernberg's theory has been called an *affect differentiation theory* because of this process. Other representations of an ideal self and an ideal object are also developing, and reflect in fantasy the wishful state of the self longing for a return to the closeness of the object of symbiosis (Kernberg 1976a, p. 68) and help in superego formation.

An early superego also forms during this period. Repression replaces splitting as the central defense mechanism, and some of the bad rejected self-object images have been relegated to the newly created unconscious (id). Displacement, condensation, and other primary process operations connect these negative introjections. Reality testing is now consolidated.

By the time toddlers reach Stage 4 (object constancy), they can cognitively relate to events with a greater repertoire of responses. For example, when they are hungry and dinner is late, they can respond by thinking: "Mother is bad, but I am OK"; or "Mother is bad and neglectful, and I must be bad"; or "Mother is busy but good, and I am OK"; or "Mother is good, but I must be bad." This stage offers several more cognitive options than merely the symbiotic-level response, "Mother is bad, and I must be bad," with the strong need to eject and externalize this negative feeling. Negative feelings toward the self are now possible.

Figure 7-2 shows the developmental progression of internalized object relations. The basic developmental tasks are the differentiation between self and others (this is partially accomplished by borderline personalities but not by psychotic adults) and the ability to integrate and interrelate positively felt or loving and negatively felt or aggressive images of self and others, which leads to the capacity for both empathy and ambivalence.

Stage 5: Consolidation of Superego and Ego Integration (5 to 7 Years)

Ego identity continues to evolve in Stage 5, but superego functioning is probably not consolidated until the end.

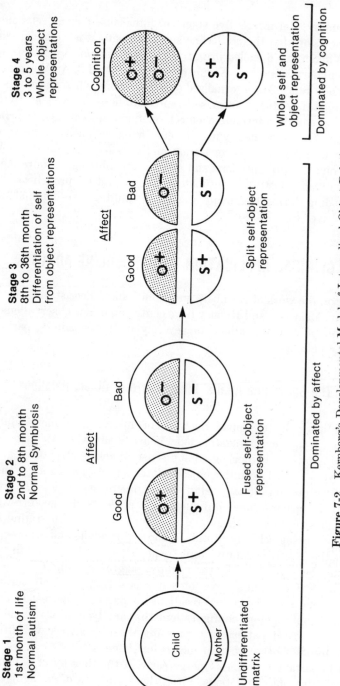

Figure 7-2 Kernberg's Developmental Model of Internalized Object Relations

In summary, Kernberg's five stages of internalized object relations lead to the conclusion that the borderline spectrum patient is a clinical example of what Volkan (1976) called *primitive internalized object relations,* which has particular references to Kernberg's Stages 2 and 3. As Volkan (1976) noted, even at Stage 3 of internalized object relations when object representations are differentiated from self-representations as well as from one another, the adult's internalized object relations are considered *primitive* when they are associated with (1) continued reliance on introjective-projective mechanisms, (2) separation of the "all-good" and the "all-bad" self- and object representations and reliance on splitting, (3) unrefined and ineffective reality testing in intimate relations, and (4) proneness to emotional flooding during treatment because of unintegrated libidinal and aggressive drives (pp. 57–58).

CLINICAL APPLICATION TO BORDERLINE ADULTS

Building on the work of Kernberg and Kohut, such theorists as Adler, Buie, Masterson, Meissner, and Rinsley have contributed new observations to the application of object relations to severely disturbed adults, particularly borderline patients.

The Borderline Adults' Inner World of Object Relations

Although it is risky to compare the world of children with that of adults, it is useful to use the developmental model heuristically when viewing severely disturbed adults. A borderline adult's sense of self is structured around a core of two polarized primitive object-relations units, analogous to the split-self-object representational level of the rapprochement toddler (Kernberg's Stage 3). In general, one configuration represents the good, rewarding, pleasurable self-object unit, and the other represents the frustrating, hostile, anxiety-provoking self-object unit. In borderline adults and rapprochement toddlers, the positive primitive unit frequently defends against the anxiety that would be engendered by the negative, aggressive unit.

The borderline adult's sense of self arises from not only the infant's dynamics but also his or her reactions to parental figures. It exists in oscillating, contradictory configurations that are dynamically related to one another. The exact pattern of expressing these polarities will differ, and various theorists have different names for them.

Two important processes emerge early in the therapy of patients who have primitive object relations. First, these patients often fight strongly against changes in their introjects, creating a variety of rigid barriers to keep the therapist from intervening (Meissner 1982). And if this process were not perplexing enough, these patients then organize their view of the world to confirm and sustain their current configurations. They engage in projective maneuvers to prove the accuracy of these configurations, even at the cost of happiness, good relationships, and success. Why is this so?

To understand the answer, the functions of introjects must also be understood (Meissner 1982–1983a). Introjects seem (1) always to exist in polarized form, (2) always to be linked together dynamically, (3) never to occur alone even if one is not obviously present, and (4) to function within a reciprocal relationship within the psyche (p. 92).

The reason that introjects always exist in polarized form, Meissner (1982–1983a) found, is that they represent a fixated structure from an early developmental level. The young child's central nervous system deals only with extreme dichotomy—good-bad, pleasant-unpleasant. Even if one does not accept drive theory, important dimensions of early childhood include the aggressive, the libidinal, and the narcissistic. Thus, we would expect the polarities to have the content of these dimensions, and, in fact, some combination of these dimensions occurs in most theorists' systems (e.g., Kernberg's libidinal versus aggressive split-units, Masterson-Rinsley's withdrawing versus rewarding split-part-units, and Meissner's victim versus aggressor and inferior versus superior introjects).

Why, then, are introjects linked together dynamically, and why do they function reciprocally within the psyche? The reason differs according to the theorist. For Kernberg, as a drive theorist, they represent instinctual impulse and defense against impulse played out in object-relations units. For other theorists, such as Masterson, Meissner, and Rinsley, impulse and defense are of secondary importance, and they are linked because they are derived from a specific relationship between child and caretaker and, eventually, family. Keeping these polarities maintains the original relationship intact in the psyche, thus avoiding separation, loss, or narcissistic injury. These introjects have come to be experienced as the core of the person's identity and thus must be maintained at all costs.

All theorists have noted that the inactive or repressed introject is often the one projected onto the other person, such as the therapist. For example, patients may be actively experiencing themselves as frightened of a harsh and critical therapist, as small and frightened and the therapist as big, powerful, and cruel. Such patients are usually unaware that sometimes they themselves act critically or harshly toward others. Even when one introject is repressed for a substantial period of time, as with depressed persons (in whom the controlling, perfectionistic introject may not be obvious), it will emerge with sufficient work in therapy (Meissner 1982–1983a).

Meissner (1982, 1982–1983a, 1982–1983b) has listed four reasons that patients struggle to maintain their introjects even when they are limiting and self-destructive. First, it is a way of preserving the introjects' narcissistic functions, which provide the core around which their sense of self is organized. Second, it preserves the infantile dependence on and attachment to the parental introjects (even though the parents may no longer be around); thus, these patients do not have to experience the abandonment, loss, or loneliness that would accompany giving up these introjects. Third, it is a fantasied way of having the acceptance, love, and closeness to the parents (as introjects) that often were not present in reality, serving as a sort of defensive repossession of the object that cannot be achieved in reality (Meissner 1982). Fourth, maintaining both the introjects and splitting serves as an important defense against the rage, disappointment, disillusionment, and loneliness that would be felt if the patients ever had to give up their infantile introjects for more mature identification. To avoid the pain involved in integrating introjects, patients maintain this system at great cost to their own growth, self-worth, individuality, and the quality of their interpersonal relationships. The reader who is interested in the motivational power of introjects should review Meissner (1982, 1982–1983a, 1984) and Searles (1951).

A simplified clinical example may be helpful. John Elliott saw himself primarily as a helpless victim in life and tended to see others, particularly authority figures, as powerful and sadistic. This appears to be both an introjection of his mother's helpless role as well as how John experienced himself as treated by his father. However, our theory leads us to infer that John had also learned a more aggressive posture, because this was the only form of caretaking that he knew from his father. He protected his therapist from this aggressiveness by initially idealizing her. In the therapy, John reached points at which the aggressive primitive introject did emerge. The first was a session in which he treated the therapist in a highly hostile, critical, and belittling way, and the second was when he reported a series of fantasies about having violent sexual intercourse with a woman against her will. John had made an identification with both the victim and the aggressor and had introjected both the depressed and devalued aspects of his mother (as well as his own role) and the parallel elements of grandiosity, paranoid suspiciousness, and specialness of his father (Meissner 1982, p. 374). He spent a great deal of time setting himself up interpersonally in order to be victimized, and he felt particularly special as a victimized Vietnam veteran. It was some time into the therapy before the more aggressive primitive object-relations unit emerged and could be treated.

The Experts' Position on Object Relations and Borderline Adults

The following theorists, except Kohut, follow an object-relations theory for their conception of borderline adults.

Adler and Buie believe that a major problem of borderline adults is their organization of pathological internalized object relations. They tend to agree with Meissner's conceptualization of the specific polarities. But Adler and Buie believe that an even greater problem with borderline adults is their failure to develop a "holding introject," or the tendency toward emotional flooding and affectomotor storms. Accordingly, these theorists emphasize therapeutic techniques for developing a holding introject. The reader is referred to Adler and Buie (1979a, 1979b) and Buie and Adler (1982–1983) for a review of their theory and therapeutic approach, which will be reviewed briefly in Chapter 11.

Kernberg, of course, believes that the pathological organization of internalized object relations (Stage 3) is the major problem with the borderline adult. He argues that two primitive split-object-relations units exist—one is libidinally derived, and the other is aggressively derived—and he does not organize them according to theme or content. One unit may defend against the emergence of the other unit. As with the rapprochement toddler, the libidinal unit usually defends against the emergence of the aggressive unit.

Kohut did not formally espouse an object-relations framework, although a rudimentary developmental model is implied in his theory. He believed that infants must have had an optimal fused self-object experience in order to have a cohesive sense of self as adults. He saw borderline patients as either never having achieved a good fused self-object experience or having achieved it but then regressing to a state of fragmented self-object. He viewed aggression, acting out, and many other disturbed behaviors as by-products of a nonempathic situation between the patient and the therapist or family. Kohut put little emphasis on polarized introjects and their dynamic relationship with one another; rather, he concentrated on how a cohesive self-object could be built up. The approach of Kohut's colleagues to working with fragmented self-objects will be reviewed in Chapter 8.

Masterson and Rinsley also emphasize pathological internalized object relations as the borderline's central pathology. Unlike Kernberg, they believe that there is a typical content for each of the polarized split-object-relations units that is based on repetitive pathological maternal behavior regarding the toddlers' rapprochement-crisis behavior. The two polarized states are the *rewarding* split-object-relations unit and the *withdrawing* split-object-relations unit. Masterson and Rinsley also see a dynamic relationship between these two units, with frustration of the rewarding unit activating the withdrawing unit in the adult. Their definition of these split-units will be discussed in Chapter 8.

Meissner also agrees that the primary dilemma of borderline adults is the pathological organization of introjections, which he calls *introjects.* He sees introjects as motivated by attempts to retain internal possession of the object to protect against fears of abandonment and annihilation as well as more advanced attempts to retain, control, and preserve some form of relationship with a loved, yearned for, feared, and hated object.

Meissner explains these introjective configurations as having a structure that reflects the dynamic change of the infant's relationship with the caretaker. He found the following polarities: (1) the victim-aggressor introjects (derived from the aggressive dimension); (2) the superior-inferior introjects (derived from the narcissistic dimension); and (3) the erotic introjects, which reflect broader aspects of demands for physical closeness, fears of object loss, dependence, and assaultive antagonism (derived from the libidinal dimension). To comprehend borderline pathology, it is necessary to understand how the polarities work, especially the aggressive and narcissistic.

If we consider one of Meissner's introject polarities, we can see how the polarities function. For example, the narcissistic push toward being special and entitled accepts no compromise (Meissner 1982–1983a, pp. 92–93). One *must* be first and best; anything less is worthless inferiority. When reality inevitably interferes with the narcissistic demand, patients will feel defeated and thus are forced to retreat to the inferior narcissistic position in which they feel worthless and shamed. This position, however, is intolerable and forces the compensating move to the superior narcissistic position of superiority and high expectation.

Meissner's approach to the treatment of introjects is psychoanalytic, with some modification of technique to deal with the patients' needs for soothing and good-enough holding.

THE DEVELOPMENTAL-DIAGNOSTIC SPECTRUM: RINSLEY

Figure 7-3 reproduces Rinsley's (1981b, 1982a) schema of the developmental-diagnostic spectrum for object relations. Rinsley's schema is a utilitarian but elegant method for positioning the borderline spectrum on the developmental-diagnostic continuum. It allows the reader to compare and contrast the descriptive diagnosis against the key concepts of various developmental systems, ranging from classical stage theory (Section A) through Kohut's self theory (Section F), by a vertical examination of these dimensions. This schema shows why some of the descriptive diagnoses share symptoms, dynamics, and object relations across a number of systems. Rinsley (1982a) described borderline symptomatology as follows:

> Viewed from a phenomenological or descriptive standpoint, borderline symptomatology may be seen to fall midway, as it were, between psychosis on the one hand and psychoneurosis on the other. Viewed from a developmental standpoint, borderline psychopathology is conceived as ensuing from a specific

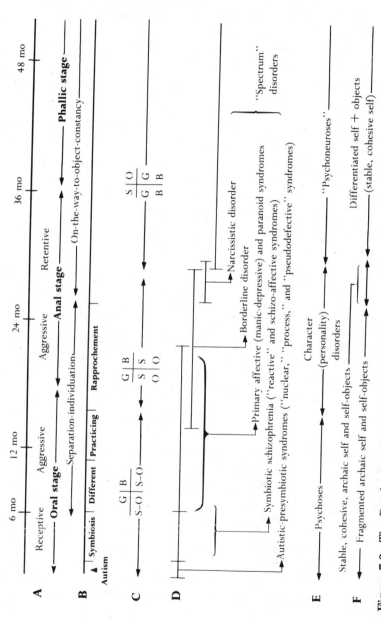

Figure 7-3 The Developmental-Diagnostic Spectrum of the Major Groups of Psychopathological Syndromes. (From Rinsley, D. B., *Borderline and Other Self Disorders: A Developmental and Object-Relations Perspective*, p. 180. Copyright 1982 by Jason Aronson. Reprinted with permission.)

developmental arrest or fixation between the extremes of pervasive failure of self-object differentiation (psychosis) on the one hand and its essential achievement (neurosis) on the other.... The recognition of an object-relations basis for the diagnosis *borderline* thus contributes significantly to the resolution of a number of problems long associated with the nosology and clinical understanding of borderline psychopathology. (p. 106)

Rinsley's schema should be read both horizontally and vertically. Section A presents the classical psychosexual stages, and Section B depicts Mahler's phases on the same time line. Section C diagrams the evolution of object relations, based on contributions from a number of object-relations theorists and described by Kernberg (see Figure 7-2 for another view of children's object relations). Section D is a continuum of the major groups of psychopathological syndromes, arranged according to the known chronology of developmental arrest or fixation based on historical and current psychoanalytic data (Rinsley 1982a, p. 179). The psychoanalytic continuum concept appears in Section E. Finally, Section F displays Kohut's contributions to self disorders.

Although Kohut's view is not anchored to a chronological continuum per se, he used the concept of progressive self-object differentiation. Impairment of the latter merges within the self-disordered patient's self-object transference. The psychoneuroses are characterized by the attainment of self-object differentiation and a stable, cohesive self, which corresponds to Kernberg's Stage 4. The psychosis and borderline personality disorders are marked by the fragmented, archaic self and self-objects (Kernberg's Stages 2 and 3). They are termed *archaic* because in regressed states, they are produced in vivid and often terrifying reanimated form as primitive ego and superego forerunners. They are termed *fragmented* because they comprise part-objects that "pass in and out," as it were, in accordance with the mechanism of splitting in any of its forms. Finally, the narcissistic personality disorder is characterized by self-objects less prone to fragmentation and hence is seen as a higher-level borderline.

Returning to Section D, Rinsley notes that classical stage theory views the affective disorders as arising during the late oral, early anal period, in conformity with the findings of Abraham (Section A). Corresponding and relating to the chronology of classical stage theory, Mahlerian phase theory suggests that the developmental arrest underlying primary affective disorders probably occurs during the differentiation, practicing, and early rapprochement subphases of separation-individuation. The contiguity of borderline and primary affective disorders therefore accounts for the depressive characteristics of borderline patients at the lower end of the continuum. Thus, borderline is noted by Rinsley to be closer to the primary affective disorders than to the schizophrenic disorders (Rinsley 1981b, p. 126). Rinsley also mentions that the developmental contiguity of primary affective and paranoid disorders likewise accounts for the frequency of persecutory ideation among both manic patients and those with major depression. Finally, Rinsley points out the clinical observation that many individuals with schizotypal, borderline, paranoid, narcissistic, and histrionic personality disorders (*DSM-III*) are considered particularly vulnerable to the development of what the *DSM-III* terms a brief reactive psychosis under conditions of stress (Rinsley 1981a, p. 127).

Rinsley then concludes that a variety of disorders, including both the higher-functioning affective and paranoid disorders and many of the personality disorders listed in the *DSM-III*, may be viewed as constituting a subspectrum of descriptively distinguishable conditions that share a developmental etiology and basically similar internal object relations, as well as certain classical stage features and features from Kohut's model. Hence, they can be subsumed under the borderline rubric (Rinsley 1982a, pp. 184–185). In review, the reader can look at Section D, locate the borderline disorder, and then check it against each of the other sections, A through F, thus placing the disorder in these other conceptual models. The borderline disorder, although it encompasses a wide range of disorders, is itself part of a supraordinate disorder called *spectrum disorders* or *disorders of the self*. Rinsley's (1982a) diagnostic criteria for the full range of spectrum disorders will be examined in Chapter 11. Rinsley fully accepts that multietiologies contribute to the borderline conditions and that biological inputs should not be ignored.

A BRIEF CRITIQUE

Despite the efforts of Kernberg and others to explain children's cognitive development in terms of internalized object relations, the science of the mind's structuralization is still in its infancy. Before using object-relations theory indiscriminately, the reader should be aware of a number of criticisms of it.

Source of Information about Intrapsychic Tasks of Childhood

Infants cannot, of course, describe their inner worlds, as they cannot talk or answer questions about what they feel or think. For this reason, psychoanalysts have relied on three sources of information about childhood: the analysis of adults, the analysis of children, and the observation of children. But none of these sources really conveys what small children think and feel. Because of this gap in information, many infancy researchers confine themselves to infants' behavior, biology, and physiology and avoid making assumptions about their subjective experiences (Peterfreund 1978, p. 430).

Psychoanalysts, Peterfreund (1975) noted, are interested in the world of subjective experiences. Thus, psychoanalytic theorists make rough estimates of what is going on inside infants' heads. To do this, theorists use terms and statements drawn from adult psychology: *absence of boundaries, egocentric, symbiosis,* and *omnipotent.* He reviewed the use of these terms and showed that in each case the term implies an adult norm. For example, individuals are egocentric when they act differently (e.g., more selfish) from other adults. Is this adult norm applicable to a child when all children behave in a certain way because of their limited cognitive apparatuses? Peterfreund thinks it is not.

He noted that adults may be termed narcissistic when they behave in a self-centered manner, wrapped up in themselves and incapable of responding to the needs of others. When used to describe adults, it brings to mind the standard of a nonnarcissistic adult who does not behave self-centeredly and can respond to others. One can also use the word to describe subjective inner feelings, again comparing it with a norm.

Turning to infancy, what does narcissistic mean? As Peterfreund (1978) observed:

> By *adult standards* an infant may behave as though he is self centered . . . but that is the way *all* normal infants are. . . . The characterization of infants as 'narcissistic' represents a confusing adultomorphizing of infancy. (p. 436)

Accordingly, a major problem of this theory is a tendency to assume inappropriately that adult pathology necessarily has a one-to-one relationship with a similar pathology in childhood. This is called *adultomorphic theorizing about infancy.*

Peterfreund added that a key ingredient in psychoanalytic developmental theory is the need to have a "mind" that is "separate from body." This mind is the "ego," an inner mind, and thus must have a development separate from the body. The separation of the mind from the body is accomplished by having the "psychological birth" follow "biological birth" by several months so that an ego can be formed that directs and controls biological and psychological development. The mind separate from the body recreates the proverbial chicken-egg problem—which one creates the other? Peterfreund does not accept this psychoanalytic developmental position, believing instead that the mind and body evolve together and are closely linked.

Misinterpretation of Infants' Experiences and Actions

Bemporad (1980) and Robbins (1980) expressed concern with another tendency to misunderstand what happens in infancy. For example, Melanie Klein assumed young patients were describing introjects when they may have been using animalistic, concrete thinking to describe internal and external events (Bemporad 1980, p. 70). It is then assumed that adults often have such introjects outside their awareness, without, in addition, explaining how introjects grow and are modified across time. This is called *infantomorphic misconceptions of adult pathology* (Robbins 1980, p. 489).

Bemporad (1980), summarizing Laing, suggested that a way out of this dilemma is to abandon the notion of inner objects and to talk about how internal representations develop across time as psychic representations of an external being and how internalization really requires a "set of rules of conduct, a certain structuring of experience, a mode of relating" (p. 71). In other words, we should abandon the notion of "internal objects" that exists timelessly inside persons and motivates them. But Bemporad's approach does not adequately explain the adult patient who talks about "inner presences" or how such experiences developmentally arise.

Stierlin (1970) has taken a position similar to Bemporad's, stating that inner objects (introjects) are really object representations. He prefers to see these inner objects as having functions comparable to, but not identical with, ego functions (p. 321). They are inner referents that are best described as object representations, representing external objects within the psyche in a manner that emphasizes the inner representations' congruence with the external object; they presuppose memory and the ability to symbolize; and they resemble engrams in that they allow a new percept to be tied to a familiar image. Second, they function as a guide for interpersonal relationships, both present and future, and they provide an inner anticipatory set (healthy or unhealthy) that narrows the possible selection of outer objects. Third, inner objects contribute to people's relative autonomy and allow them to fall back on themselves by relating to some part within themselves.

The Problem of Introjection

Although Kernberg has avoided the Kleinian problem of determining how introjects are modified after the first year of life, he is still wrestling with the process of introjection. Kernberg (1976a, p. 29) stated that introjection is the most primitive process, consisting of a cluster of memory traces of an object's image, an image of the self in interaction with the object, and the affective valence (coloring of the self-object relationship).

It is difficult to describe what sort of phenomenological experiences Kernberg had in mind when he talked of introjection (Bemporad 1980, p. 66). He never quite theorized how the child experiences the introjection. Is it a holistic impression of the parent-self now inside the child? That would seem to make it an introject. Although Kernberg accounted for the maturation of these introjects (unlike Klein), he did not explain how the child can form images of the object before the stage of self- and object differentiation, which does not occur until some months later. How can something that cannot be differentiated or perceived be taken into the mind?

Bemporad (1980) has suggested that Kernberg (and Mahler also fits this description) postulated a stage of primitive processes in order to locate a fixation point by which he explained adult, not childhood, behavior. Kernberg found splitting and the fusion of self- and object images in borderline adults and therefore postulated an early stage of development that is revived, via regression, in such patients. By doing so, Kernberg continued a long tradition of using fixation and regression to account for adult symptomatology (p. 67).

Oversimplification of Kernberg's Model

According to Grotstein (1982), all the stages exist from birth in some degree and then gradually form hierarchical layers:

> Traumatic insults and empathic failures can be registered by the infant's sensitive psyche from the very beginning and then held in check until "coded" by a later, sophisticated, verbal capacity which then re-presents these traumata to the psyche. (p. 13)

Bemporad (1980) and Robbins (1980) believe that new theoretical efforts must be made to better separate normal infant development from pathological development and pathological adult functioning. Robbins concluded:

> Theories must broaden their initial base to include . . . newer data about perceptions and cognition and other complex neurobiological substrates. The theories must be more attentive to development as a multichanneled and phasic process. . . . This should lead to theories which are more complex, both with regard to number of variables as well as organizational principles; for theories based on a single model or a few variables do not more than provide a window into limited aspects of development and pathology. (p. 490)

As elegant as Kernberg's theory is, some consider it too simple, given the child's complexity.

When Expected Capacities Exceed the Child's Developmental Abilities

Kernberg postulates sophisticated, intellectual, and emotional capacities beyond that of a 3-month-old child and ascribes cognitive processes to the child well before the timelines developed by Piaget. Rinsley (1982a, p. 64, footnote) has objected to Kernberg's timetable, as have other experts (Chessick 1977).

Splitting

Splitting is a normal activity up through the rapprochement subphase. After that, Kernberg has claimed that it ceases and is replaced by repression. Adults who continue to use splitting thus have a severe character disorder or a psychosis if reality maintenance is impaired. Many clinicians, however, including Chessick (1982a) and Kernberg himself, have noted that neurotic patients may manifest massive splitting. This could be explained in a more complex multichanneled model. But Kernberg's model, in which splitting is a linear process that goes "away" at a certain point, does not adequately explain how, then, the neurotic patient can engage in splitting.

When Developmental Stages Are Not Retraced

Finally, Peterfreund (1978) pointed out that when persons undergo regression, they may *not* necessarily retrace earlier developmental stages:

> When a complex machine breaks down it rarely retraces the processes by which it was formed, and one must be very careful in drawing inferences about the construction of the machine from observation of its products of breakdown. Likewise, when complex biological systems break down they do not necessarily retrace the steps by which they developed, and one must be cautious about viewing the products of a breakdown as representing steps in normal development. For example, many child psychotics do not initially manifest obvious, gross disorder, and the 'breakdown' phenomena observed do not necessarily represent any stage of normal development, as some psychoanalytic theoreticians seem to imply. (p. 439)

Object-relations theory, the developmental schema of mental structuralization, is currently being used by many psychoanalysts. Nonetheless, it has many inherent problems, including determining how outside experiences become internalized, how they evolve and change over time, and how they influence the adult. Kernberg has addressed some—but not all—of these problems. In any case, this theory is currently the psychoanalysts' best educated guess at what goes on inside a child's head. This theory can be expected to change during the next few years as new information from the biological sciences is introduced. Until further information clarifies the psychoanalytic metapsychology, however, clinicians can continue to work with a lower-level theory that is based on the clinical situation and focuses on dilemmas, conflicts, and wishes, without necessarily relating the adult's problems back to a hypothesized childhood stage in a simple, one-to-one fashion.

CHAPTER 8

Three Conceptual Models
Kernberg, Masterson-Rinsley,
and Kohut

Greenberg and Mitchell (1983) remind clinicians that no therapy is free of values or theory. The ways in which therapists view their patients and describe their struggles, the diagnostic categories into which they place patients, and the treatment techniques that the therapist selects are contingent upon the clinician's prior conscious or unconscious assumptions concerning the constituents of human experience (p. 383). These assumptions, in turn, are inevitably based on some kind of theoretical model. Thus, it is helpful to know the theoretical models on which senior clinicians build their treatment approaches.

This chapter reviews the theories of Kernberg, Masterson and Rinsley, and Kohut in order to help the reader with the difficult problem of conceptualizing clinical data from the perspective of these four theorists, the ones who have written the most extensively. In addition, they have developed comprehensive treatment approaches.

None of this important work was done in a vacuum. Theory building around ego psychology blossomed in the 1930s and 1940s and then became almost dormant. Thus, in the 1960s, Kernberg's emerging object-relations theory and its application to the borderline personality generated considerable discussion by other experts. Masterson and Rinsley were two who used Kernberg's theory as a launching pad for their own work, which gradually took shape as a theory and approach to treatment related to but yet distinctive from Kernberg's.

Another exciting surge of theoretical activity occurred during the 1970s. During this period, Kohut was writing on the narcissistic personality, which he considered as higher functioning than the borderline. His work implied that therapists would be able to understand this difficult patient, whose vulnerability to slights and violent outbursts had confused analysts and led to failure in psychoanalysis (Greene 1984). Kohut concluded that his approach, which he called *self psychology*, was a new theory, in some ways quite different from classical psychoanalysis in both theory and practice. Gradually, self psychology was extended to all psychopathology. Adler and Buie, and Rinsley are among those who have extended Kohut's work into the area of the borderline patient. Thus, the field of psychoanalysis is in a period of great flux, reexamining its fundamental premises and creating new concepts and theories. Although it is premature at this time to make a synthesis of classical psychoanalysis and self psychology, the cross-fertilization between the two theories is healthy for the field.

SIMILARITIES AND DIFFERENCES AMONG THE FOUR THEORISTS

Kernberg, Masterson, Rinsley, and Kohut all have some notion of a developmental progression. They agree that faulty parent–child relationships can lead to either fixation or arrest at the self-object representational level, which in turn creates either a borderline or narcissistic personality disorder. In addition, each theorist has constructed a treatment approach based on techniques borrowed from classical psychoanalysis. They all believe in the concept of the unconscious, endorsing the idea that most of the motives that move people are outside normal awareness. Each contends that the most effective way to work through arrests or conflicts is by using collaborative inquiry that defines the psychoanalytic situation. Finally, each theorist believes that the faulty self-structures (object-relations units) will emerge in the therapeutic relationship. Focusing heavily on the transference is the way to repair the arrest or modify the fixation. As a group, these theorists seem to be more similar to one another than any one of them would be to, say, a behaviorist or a rational emotive therapist. But the similarities end here. Their positions on various metapsychology issues (e.g., conflict versus arrest, the role of aggression), their strategies, and their tactics in psychotherapy are strikingly different.

Definitions

Before proceeding, a number of terms must be defined. A *therapeutic alliance* is a whole-object relationship in which the patient and therapist work together to help the patient grow and to work through conflicts. A successful alliance is predicated on the capacities of both the patient and therapist to continue to recognize each other as separate, whole objects with both negative and positive attributes. Because borderline adults cannot maintain whole-object relations, a therapeutic alliance cannot be established with such patients until late in the therapy (Adler 1979). But patients with primitive personality disorders can form a narcissistic alliance in which the therapist's bodily presence, interest, and rapport are sufficient for the patient to attach; these patients substitute the therapist's presence for their own defective coping or defensive mechanisms (Paolino 1981, p. 110).

Transference refers to the projection of feelings, thoughts, and wishes onto the therapist (or another person), who represents an object from the patients' past. Patients may also project superego, ideal-self, or id aspects onto the therapist. The ability to maintain whole-object relationships is essential to a therapeutically usable transference, because patients must be able to view the therapist as a separate person in order to recognize the transference when it is interpreted. Thus, borderline patients, with their difficulties in maintaining whole-object relationships, are considered to have a primitive form of transference because they treat therapists as part-objects, need-satisfying objects, or transitional objects.

Transference acting out refers to behavior occurring during the course of treatment in the form of enactment rather than a verbalization of feelings and fantasies arising in the transference. Acting out can occur within or outside therapeutic sessions. Acting out within therapeutic or analytic hours has also been called *acting in*. An example of acting out within a session would be patients who demand that the therapist hold them as a parent would cuddle an infant. Transference itself is a reenactment and can be considered an instance of acting out.

Interpretation refers to the therapist's formulation of the meaning or significance of patients' verbal or nonverbal productions, including unconscious meanings and motivations. Linking the patients' current behavior or material in therapy to the past is called *genetic-dynamic interpretation.*

A *selfobject* is Kohut's term for supportive others such as parents who, from the infant's perspective, have yet to be differentiated from the self.

In reviewing Kernberg's, Masterson's and Rinsley's, and Kohut's theory and treatment, we shall examine five components as they pertain to the borderline disorder: (1) the etiology of the disorder; (2) the makeup of the intrapsychic structure; (3) the diagnostic criteria used, including comparisons with the narcissistic personality disorder; (4) the clinical manifestations; and (5) the treatment approach.

Kernberg still does not fully differentiate the borderline disorder from the more recently described narcissistic personality disorder; he considers borderline to be the overarching diagnosis for a number of personality subtypes that include the narcissistic subtype. Kohut and, more recently, Rinsley have made such a distinction, however; they see the borderline as lower level, more to the left on the diagnostic continuum, and the narcissistic as higher level, more to the right on the continuum. (See Rinsley's schema,

Figure 7-3, for the relative positions of the borderline and narcissistic personalities on the developmental-diagnostic continuum.)

OTTO KERNBERG

Kernberg (1973, 1975a, 1975b, 1976a, 1976b, 1977a, 1977b, 1978a, 1978b, 1979, 1980a, 1980b, 1980c, 1981, 1982a, 1982b, 1982c, 1982d, 1982e, 1982f, in press) presents a thorough, systematic, and comprehensive overview of borderline patients. Kernberg's structural diagnosis and object-relations theory was so comprehensively discussed earlier that we shall, after reviewing the etiology and diagnosis, examine his treatment techniques.

Etiology

Kernberg (1976a) has stated that the major cause of developmental failure in borderline personalities is a predominance of negative introjections during early childhood (up to age 3 or 4). This occurs because of severe aggression, a chronic inability to deal with the frustration that precludes the integration of loving and aggressive images of self and others. In turn, this results in the inability to achieve object constancy and achieve the capacity for ambivalence, with an array of affects.

As explained earlier, Kernberg believes that borderline pathology arises from the failure to complete the tasks of rapprochement, including neutralizing the aggression of that phase. The one exception to this rule is the lower-level schizoid borderline patient, whose conflicts seem to arise during the differentiation subphase. Lower-level schizoid patients require more help with boundary differentiation (self-object) and more of a holding environment than do ordinary borderline patients (Kernberg 1980a).

Kernberg (1984) believes that the following three pathways, or any combination of the three, can lead to development of a borderline personality organization: (1) pathology of the separation-individuation process (for any reason); (2) genetic predisposition to manic-depressive illness, schizophrenia, or minimal brain dysfunction; and (3) severe family pathology that can induce excessive frustration and aggression in the infant.

Intrapsychic Structure of Borderline Adults

According to Kernberg, the inner world of borderline patients is populated by unmetabolized, unassimilated, dissociated primitive object relations units (self + object + affective coloration representing a particular drive derivative). As explained in Chapter 6, Kernberg considers the defensive splitting of introjections into opposite components to be the major cause of the structural and descriptive symptoms. Eventually this results in two perpetual, polarized, contradictory, and oscillating ego states in the adult—the bad part ego state and the good part ego state (Kernberg's Stage 3). Both ego states are conscious and need only some appropriate stimuli to put them into effect.

In some higher-functioning borderline patients, these polarized ego states appear only under stress; in others, they operate all the time. The therapeutic relationship usually becomes so important that these primitive, fantastic, and unrealistic ego states are projected onto the therapist as the internal object relations are reenacted in the transference relationship (Kernberg 1980b). Thus, all character defenses really reflect the activation of a defensive self- and object constellation directed against an opposite, dreaded, and repressed self- and object constellation. One constellation is usually under the power of intense love, and the other is under the power of extreme hatred. As noted before, this is an important deviation from the classical Freudian drive theory, which states that drives and the defenses against them are primary and that object relations, whether internalized or external and interpersonal, are in effect mere derivatives. In Kernberg's model, clinically repressed impulses and the defenses against them are expressed through mutually opposed internalized object relations, each under the impact of a determined drive derivative (clinically, a certain affect). In other words, one primitive unit defends against the emergence of a second primitive unit (Kernberg 1980b, p. 155).

Except for the neurotic-level narcissistic personality, Kernberg generally sees the narcissistic personality as a subtype of the borderline personality organization. Diagnostically, he views such patients as having a grandiose self (fused real self + ideal self + ideal object) that appears integrated (unlike the borderline), although their object relations are usually not. Beneath the grandiose self, the usual two split-object-relations units as seen in the borderline will be revealed in a lengthy therapy.

This example from Kernberg (1981) demonstrates how two typical ego states interrelate and how they may show up in treatment toward the therapist: A patient may have a chronically submissive self-image that is operating under the influence of a self-unit submitting to a powerful parental (object) image. But this self-unit may be defending the patient against a second unit comprising a violently rebellious self-image relating angrily to a sadistic and castrating parental (object) image. This rebellious self may be repressed or obscured totally until some interaction in psychotherapy reveals its presence. Kernberg admits that these entities are often layered upon one another and usually are at least partially hidden at the start of psychotherapy.

How can borderline patients be so indifferent to the contradictions inherent in what they are reporting or how they are acting during therapy? According to Kernberg they rely on splitting. To acknowledge these ego states would cause enormous, often paranoid anxiety, because of the intense aggressive feelings associated with the bad ego state. Therefore, splitting precludes experiencing both intense states simultaneously (e.g., blissful submissiveness and rageful rebellion).

Borderline adults experience (at least unconsciously) their envy and aggression as potentially destructive to themselves and to the others on whom they so desperately depend. These patients fear both their own self-hatred for harboring such emotions and others' retaliation upon learning that they harbor such feelings. Splitting and other defenses protect borderline adults from experiencing these contradictions in themselves and in their dependent and manipulative relationships with others. Thus, splitting protects the ego against unbearable conflicts between love and hatred, dependence and independence, and inferiority and superiority, but this occurs at the cost of the ego's integration. And, of course, such defenses break down frequently, exposing borderline patients to overwhelming affect and anxieties, often of a paranoid sort.

Diagnostic Criteria

Kernberg's diagnostic model presents three structural criteria for distinguishing borderline from neurotic and psychotic patients: identity diffusion, use of primitive defenses, and maintenance of reality testing. Kernberg has pointed out that descriptive characteristics alone can be misleading because many symptoms seen in borderline adults (e.g., depression, anxiety, impulsivity, anger) may also be seen in neurotic patients. Kernberg believes it is structure—not symptoms—that determines the diagnosis of borderline personality organization.

Structural criteria reflect the patients' current intrapsychic structures and internalized object relations, which can become apparent to the therapist either during a structural interview and/or from the primitive transference paradigms that emerge during the course of psychotherapy. Kernberg considers confrontation to be an important diagnostic tool, and the patients' functioning should improve under confrontation.

Clinical Manifestations

Borderline patients enter treatment with various descriptive symptoms and complaints, for their structural defects have frequently invaded many areas of their functioning. They may feel empty or appear too dependent on others to provide the missing continuity in their sense of self (identity diffusion syndrome). They may oscillate between considering friends or spouse as good or bad. They lack empathy with or insight into others' motivations, considering people as parts rather than wholes, as need-gratifying objects instead of individuals in their own right (lack of object constancy). They may have overly lenient or overly punitive superego functioning. Because of their reliance on splitting, these patients may be highly impulsive or too emotionally restricted, too aggressive or too passive. In addition, they may be unable to tolerate stress, to delay gratification, or to find meaningful sub-limatory activity such as hobbies, recreation, or career. Or they may manifest any of the other presumptive symptoms detailed in Chapter 3.

All of these problems may simply appear to be ego weaknesses. In the following paragraph, Kernberg (1976b) attempts to base object-relations phenomena on the classical drive-defense model:

> I think that much of what appears as "ego weakness," in the sense of a defect of these patients, turns out, under psychoanalytically based exploration, to reflect conflictually determined issues; for example, what first appears as inability to establish object relations or unavailability of drive derivatives or lack of affective response or simply lack of impulse control eventually reflects active defenses against very intense and primitive object relations in the transference. (p. 797)

The reason that Kernberg stresses transference as the vehicle for revealing these primitive object relations is that the therapeutic relationship usually becomes such a significant relationship that the patient's early object-relations units will emerge.

Kernberg does not label the content of these paradigms or give names to them (as do Meissner, Masterson, and Rinsley), preferring instead to study each patient's own blend of Oedipal and pre-Oedipal issues. Because he believes that primitive unresolved aggression (envy and rage) has hindered the integration of self- and object representations, he considers that working through the negative transference paradigm (as well as the positive) is crucial in resolving and neutralizing the power of the aggressive drive. He points out that patients defend against the emergence of the negative transference in various ways (e.g., idealizing the therapist, which defends against envy); however, the techniques that patients use to ward off the frightening aggressive images or feelings (e.g., projective identification) have weakened their ego structure.

Usually, such patients start to distrust and fear the therapist, whom they experience as bad or attacking. Because of their need to maintain empathy with that projected aggression, however, they desperately try to control the therapist. Naturally, the therapist frequently feels aggressive in return. It is as if patients push that aggressive part of themselves onto the therapist through various interpersonal maneuvers intended to induce hostility and aggression in the therapist.

Borderline patients characteristically alternate rapidly between moments of projecting the object representation while identifying with the corresponding self-representation (negative unit). For example, patients may project a primitive, sadistic mother image onto the therapist while experiencing themselves as the frightened, attacked, desperate small child. Moments (or sessions) later, they may experience themselves as the stern, prohibitive, moralistic, and sadistic primitive mother and view the therapist as the guilty, defensive, frightened, but rebellious little child (Kernberg 1982c, p. 474). At this point, the therapist must be careful to avoid acting like the sadistic object or the guilty child because the patients will sense such behavior and will assume that it confirms their original object relationship and basic sense of helplessness in the face of their own terrifying aggression.

Kernberg believes the therapist must experience the projections, process them internally, and explain them to the patients at the appropriate moment. This helps the patients work through and integrate unacceptable aggressive images. Anything less than this interpretation of the aggression is superficial (e.g., making supporting remarks).

A Clinical Example

The following account of my experience with Mary Markham illustrates Kernberg's version of the oscillation between transference paradigms:

> During her first 1½ years in psychotherapy, Mary Markham kept her distance. She constantly mentioned how much she distrusted me, and yet she seemed comfortable most of the time in therapy. Although she had a history of suicide attempts with a previous therapist, she made no attempts during this period.
>
> Mary experienced some dependency on me after 2½ years, and at the same time she began to have consciously hostile feelings toward me. If I seemed supportive and empathic, she felt hateful. She reported that I was failing her; she didn't know why, but I was. Exploration led nowhere.
>
> She made a mild suicide attempt. She had become furious during the session before the attempt when she dropped an oblique hint about her suicidal feelings—and I did not come to her house to save her. In subsequent sessions, we explored her contradictory wishes to be left alone and yet be taken care of, and she felt better.
>
> Then without warning she suddenly made a major suicide attempt, and I hospitalized her. While on the ward she decided to leave, against

medical advice. She became furious because a staff member followed her to the ground floor to talk about her "elopement"; she viewed that as an intrusion.

After her discharge from this hospitalization, Mary informed me that she was starting to hoard pills again and nothing I could do in therapy would help. But she said she could not stop therapy because she could not give me up. To have to give me up, she felt, would lead to another suicide attempt, though she would probably make another attempt if she stayed in treatment.

At this point I realized that a transference paradigm was being played out. Mary had forged an internal alliance with a sadistic part of herself, the Megalomaniac. Now the Megalomaniac was torturing me as well as Mary's weaker part. Under the Megalomaniac's influence, Mary was strong—almost Nazi-like—in the revenge she would take on me and on herself. Death would be the final defeat of my pathetic efforts to help her, and in death she would defeat her weak, despoiled self.

Interestingly, Mary had reversed an earlier transference paradigm in which I was critical and she was suspicious (hiding her dependency needs). Now she became tyrannical and I became the weak victim who deserved to be tortured. She took on the mother's role, and I took on the patient's helpless-self role.

This clinical example illuminates two important processes. First, as do many borderline patients, Mary had identified with her mother's harsh, superegolike attitude and saw her mother as controlling and dominating her in every way. As Mary grew up, she adopted her mother's domineering attitude. In this example, she treated me, her therapist, as she perceived her mother treating her. Thus, in behaving like her mother, Mary showed a submission of her ego to her mother image internalized in her superego (Kernberg 1976a, pp. 79–81). As Kernberg notes, the internalized object relations are frequently expressed not so much in the relationship between the patient and the therapist as in the intrapsychic relationship between the patient's ego and superego, with the therapist simply the screen onto which this intrapsychic relationship between ego and superego can be projected.

Kernberg (1980b) also has suggested that the borderline patient may, during periods of intensity in the therapy, change roles with the therapist—rapidly shifting from projecting an object image to projecting a self-image onto the therapist, as Mary did. As chaotic as this role exchange can be, however, it usually never reaches psychotic proportions of fusion or merger. The fluid ability to change from self to object in a given role dyad was discussed as a mode of learning in childhood. At other times, however, such rapid role exchange with the therapist can confuse patients about what is "inside" and "outside" of the self, and such rapid oscillation can lead to a breakdown of ego boundaries and a loss of reality testing. A loss of reality testing in the transference can interfere with the patients' ability to distinguish fantasy from reality, past from present, and projected transference objects from the real therapist. Transference psychosis can occur when patients experience the therapist and their projection, say, of the mother, as the same person (Kernberg 1982c, p. 474).

Kernberg believes that these primitive transferences should be the major focus of the therapy, but he is aware that it may take some time for them to emerge in a meaningful way. Why, if these ego states are dissociated but in consciousness, would they take time to emerge in the treatment? Kernberg (1976b) explains:

> What complicates the picture further is that, not only is there a rapid escalation or change of transference dispositions ... [projecting the self and then the object images in rapid succession, which gives an overall chaotic picture of the transference developments], but the very nature of primitive defensive operations . . . all bring about a general deterioration or destruction of human experience in the hours, so that even the dissociated primitive internalized object relations are at first unavailable and may need to be reactivated or reconstructed by means of the interpretation of these primitive defenses (pp. 811–812).

In other words, in the early phases of therapy, the therapist must focus on emptiness, meaninglessness, and control issues. The distorted self- and object representations may appear after a period of interpreting the defenses that keep them obscured. These interpretations pertain to the defenses or ego states in the here and now, not in the then and there.

Kernberg does not make dynamic-genetic interpretations because he finds the borderline patients' history so unreliable. He believes such interpretations may lead to regression by confusing the patients about whether or not the therapist is indeed the figure from their past. Kernberg (1975b, pp. 15–21) offers the following three-step strategy for unearthing and interpreting primitive object-relations units and setting the stage for their integration across many sessions. The patient, not the therapist, performs this integration; the therapist provides the condition for change but not the change itself. The therapist interprets the primitive transference paradigm in three consecutive steps: (1) sifting through bits of material (including nonverbal) to find relevant transference references; (2) identifying the self- and object images as well as the affect linking them, and interpreting them to the patient; and (3) relating this primitive self-object-relations unit to other contradictory, defensively dissociated units until the patients' world of objects can be consolidated.

Step 1

The therapist highlights the chaotically conveyed, seemingly fragmented aspects of the patient's intrapsychic conflicts in order to begin to understand the patient's primitive internalized object-relations units or structures. At first, the patients usually present material in such a chaotic, irrelevant-sounding fashion as to make identification of these units difficult or impossible. By means of personal responses and intellectual understanding, the therapist becomes immersed in the patient's communicated material so as to begin to synthesize it into a comprehensive picture of the patient's internalized object-relations. At the proper time, the therapist presents these pictures to the patient in the form of explanations, confrontations, and clarifications of the patient's thoughts, feelings, and behavior inferred to result from the operation of one or another of the object-relations units. This work may require many months.

The following example from Kernberg's (1975b) article demonstrates how meaninglessness can be transformed into a significant human interaction that illuminates one of the primitive units:

> Kernberg's patient, a businessman in psychoanalytic treatment, presented associations that were aimless, lacking depth, and giving no real clues as to his intrapsychic conflict or even a deepening understanding of his personal life. After months of such an empty interaction, the usually conservative patient arrived at the office wearing a faddish outfit. He immediately caught Kernberg's surprised look and speculated that Kernberg was criticizing his attire. The patient then commented on a brief disgusting impression of a spider crawling on the couch. He then smiled and talked intellectually and ironically about analysts' interest in such things.
>
> Kernberg commented on the patient's reaction of disgust and ironic smile, and the patient ignored this attempt to highlight one of his fleeting feelings. Then using his full observation of the process, Kernberg commented that he wondered if the patient had difficulty pursuing the spider theme because of the disgust it elicited and because it contradicted his perception of himself as cool, elegant, and secure. Kernberg continued the interpretation by speculating that the fantasy of the spider reflected the man's fear that disgusting thoughts or feelings might come out in the session and that the patient suspected that behind his cool facade there might be such disgusting things to explore. The patient then opened up and started to talk about himself, his fantasies, his envy of Kernberg, his own emotional reaction to the image, etc. Kernberg elaborated his interpretation by relating the fears to dependency and homosexual concerns. (pp. 16–17)

Kernberg believed that this patient's Oedipal and pre-Oedipal themes were condensed. Clinicians, however, usually should not make such elaborations on the basic interpretation unless they thoroughly understand psychoanalytic clinical theory and feel that the interpretation fits the particular patient.

The following example by Kernberg (1976b, pp. 805-810, and 1979, pp. 279-284) demonstrates how chaos can obscure the primitive units:

The patient arrived looking bedraggled and distraught. It was raining heavily, and she was drenched because she had not brought an umbrella. She ignored her pitiful presentation as she talked about a fight with her boyfriend, worries about school, and the fact that the money for therapy had not yet arrived from her parents. Her verbalizations were punctuated by forced gaiety alternating with distrustful stares. At one point she became significantly confused about the details of her story, which worried Kernberg and led him to believe she might be drinking again.

Kernberg felt that the predominant human relationship enacted at that moment was of a frightened little girl who wanted a powerful parental figure to take over and protect her. At the same time, he thought she would hate that figure because the taking over was precipitated by extreme circumstances of the patient's suffering and not out of natural love and concern for her. In addition, she was afraid of a retaliatory attack from that needed and yet resented parental figure because she projected her own angry demands onto it. He then deduced that she intended to escape from that dreaded relationship by drinking herself into oblivion; this would create a situation of chaos in which she would be rescued without having to acknowledge or relate to her rescuer as an enemy to fight off.

During the first few minutes, Kernberg inferred from the patient's verbal and nonverbal expressions of helplessness and distrust that she was expressing contradictory wishes. After absorbing the situation, he said she wanted him to know that she was still in control of her life while dramatically conveying that things were falling apart. He then commented that whatever he might do under these circumstances would be disastrous. If he explored whether she could really handle her immediate life situation (e.g., asked about her drinking), she would interpret that as an attack and perhaps as a cross-examination. If he listened without raising any question, she would consider him as callous and indifferent. In either case, she would be disappointed by his reaction. At this point, the patient opened up and started to talk about her feelings and worries vis-à-vis her life and therapy.

Kernberg then observed that she was concerned whether he really cared about her or if he were just interested in being paid. Also, he said he wondered whether or not she felt the only way she could get help was by presenting herself as a helpless human wreck. If that was so, any help from him would seem like that of an irritated parent who had no choice but to take care of an unwanted child. She started to cry and talk about her feelings of despair and worthlessness.

Now he felt the situation had become more coherent and permitted full exploration of the transference and life situation. As the patient discussed matters such as love, feelings of rejection, and anger, she appeared to be more normal, and some of the bizarreness disappeared.

Kernberg perceived the patient's chaos and her attempts to deal with it, and he noted his own reaction, which was a blend of concern and annoyance at her unwillingness to look after herself. Thus he used his observations, his knowledge of the patient, and his own reactions to formulate his interpretation. But before using his own reactions, Kernberg checked for any inappropriate countertransference.

Step 2

The therapist must evaluate the predominant object relation in the transference in terms of the self-image, the object image, and the affect involved. It is also necessary to ascertain whether the self- or object image is being projected onto the therapist. These aspects need to be interpreted and clarified in the transference, which may take weeks to accomplish.

The following example illustrates this step:

A young man had been in therapy with me for some time and felt the therapy was helping him. The patient felt that his mother had dominated him and belittled him during his childhood. In addition, she was vehemently against psychotherapy.

His mother was visiting him and continued her tirade against his therapy. She pointed out a well-publicized murder case and what a fool the therapist in the case had been. The patient attended his next session and commented in a superior tone that most psychotherapists were fools and charlatans, as shown in this recent case. I experienced a variety of feelings, mainly anger, but also some warmth, which surprised me. This could be seen as my way of identifying with the object image while experiencing the projected self-image. I interpreted that the patient had just identified with his mother and her attitudes and was projecting his self-image onto me (the young man was his sadistic mother, and I was the devalued self). At other times in the therapy, the patient had seen me as the cruel, humiliating mother image who had him under his thumb. Now the patient was feeling superior and free of the help I had given in the earlier sessions, but he was still ultimately submitting to his mother and the grandiosity in himself by rejecting my help. Kernberg (1982e) has noted that an example like this illustrates both oscillating object relations and the ego's submission to a maternal superego identification.

This interpretation of the part-object, part-self, and affect of superiority played out in the transference proved helpful to the patient, who started to explore actively this heretofore dissociated ego state that was linked with his aggressive feelings and based on his identification with the aggressive mother image. Thus, the purpose of this step is to determine whether the part-self- or part-object image is being projected, to note when the reversals take place, and to interpret the reversal to the patient.

Stage 3

The part-object relation activated in the transference has to be integrated with other part-object relations activated across sessions; the various good and bad self-images and the good and bad object images must be brought together through interpretation. This step may be done in one session and may need to be repeated during many sessions because patients generally play out transference paradigms repetitively over many months or years.

Using the previous example of the young man: the patient's part-units of himself as both the superior, sadistic, belittling self and the victimized child-self need to be linked together and explored. The same is true for the good and bad object images. This process will help the patient reach a more integrated and realistic view of himself, his mother, and his therapist. The therapist must be prepared to repeat the interpretations many times, modifying the wording to match the nuance of the material presented each time.

While following these steps, the therapist must monitor how the patients are receiving the interpretation. The therapist must be prepared to interpret the patients' reaction, particularly if the interpretation is distorted magically or aggressively (e.g., if they perceive that the therapist can read their mind—"the therapist and I are one"—or that the therapist is accusing them of being bad). Determining how the patient receives and uses the interpretation is an important aspect of the interpretive process.

Summary

Kernberg believes that major structural change in the borderline adult's personality is facilitated by resolving primitive ego states as they become manifested in the transference, by means of diagnosis, interpretation, and working through. Most patients, he states, express their major psychopathology with a limited repertoire of primitive internalized object relations.

This direct interpretation of the split-units causes patients to get in touch with forbidden sexual and aggressive fantasies played out in split-relational units, reduces the intensity of the fantasies, and facilitates integration of the split-relational units. The strategic aim then is to transform these primitive dissociated ego states into higher-level transference reactions (Kernberg

1979). This helps patients reach whole-object relations (central to an integrated identity), develop the overall tripartite structure, and actualize the capacity to work, to play, and to love.

The Treatment Approach

Although Kernberg has written extensively about treatment, this chapter will examine just a few aspects of his approach.

Kernberg believes that only a very select group of better-functioning borderline patients can benefit from psychoanalysis. For most borderline adults he instead recommends either *expressive psychotherapy* or *supportive psychotherapy,* in view of the borderline patient's ego weakness, instinctual conflicts, and proneness to act out and to transference psychosis.

Expressive psychotherapy maintains technical neutrality (siding with neither the id nor the superego), introduces parameters in the treatment to control acting out, and emphasizes clarification over interpretation in the early phases and the interpretation of unconscious meanings in the here and now over the there and then. *Parameters* is a term used by Eissler (1953, 1958) to describe departures from the strict application of the rule of free association and the rule of abstinence as observed by some classical psychoanalysts. (See also Rinsley 1982a, pp. 217–236.) The primitive object-relations units are interpreted mainly as they enter the transference relationship. Transference is the major vehicle of interpretation, but it is always balanced against the patient's resistances, immediate reality of the patient's life, and the long-range treatment goals (Kernberg 1982f, p. 183).

Supportive psychotherapy, the second form of therapy, is used for patients who lack the time, motivation, or introspective ability for expressive psychotherapy. Supportive psychotherapy, which relies mainly on suggestion and environmental intervention, does not use interpretation and only occasionally employs clarification. Both expressive and supportive psychotherapy will be discussed in detail in Chapter 10.

For the narcissistic personality operating at the borderline level, Kernberg (1975) recommends a similar therapy (psychoanalysis for the higher-functioning narcissist). Several technical considerations must be integrated into the expressive form of psychotherapy so as to adapt it specifically to the narcissistic personality: (1) systematic analysis of the grandiose self as it presents in the transference, (2) analysis of attempts to exercise omnipotent control over the therapist, and (3) analysis of attempts to discount and spoil, because of envious feelings, what the therapist gives.

Although Kernberg stresses the technical aspects of the therapy, he also acknowledges the importance of aspects of the nonspecific relationship. For example, he believes that the therapist provides auxiliary cognitive ego functions for borderline adults by settling limits and clarifying reality. In addition, the therapist's ability to withstand the patients' aggressive behaviors and fantasies, instead of falling apart or retaliating, and the ability to remain concerned and emotionally available implicitly reassure borderline patients that their aggression is not lethal and can be resolved (Kernberg 1979, p. 294). But he does not believe that these auxiliary functions should extend to gratifying the patients' demands for caretaking or a direct expression of love (e.g., taking an endless number of phone calls outside the session, having a social relationship with the patients).

In addition, Kernberg (1975a) has found that the therapist's personality is a crucial prognostic variable in treatment. He believes that good therapists for borderline patients will have a capacity for true object relations, control of their own hostility, and clear moral values. These therapists also will have worked through their own narcissism.

Countertransference is an important therapeutic tool for understanding the patient's primitive object relations and is why appropriate therapists for borderline adults must have the capacity for observing, controlling, and privately reviewing their own countertransference. They can use the countertransference to understand what is being projected (self- or object images) during the session rather than enacting the primitive object-relations units with the patient.

JAMES MASTERSON AND DONALD RINSLEY

Masterson (1976, 1978, 1981, 1982, 1983b), Masterson and Rinsley (1975), and Rinsley (1968, 1977, 1978, 1980a, 1980b, 1980c, 1981a, 1981b, 1982a, 1982b, 1984a, 1984b, in press) have jointly developed another complete model for understanding the life struggle of borderline adults, which Masterson refers to as "one long rapprochement crisis." In this model, Masterson and Rinsley relate findings from child observation to explain adult pathology. Although they acknowledge the problems of extrapolating from normal child development to adult pathology, and vice versa, they both believe that when these observations reinforce each other, they can be used in theoretical assumptions about adults.

The early collaborative contributions of Masterson and Rinsley evolved from their parallel work with children and adolescents and their families. Drawing heavily on classical psychoanalytic drive metapsychology, on Kernberg's, and particularly on Mahler's work, Masterson and Rinsley formulated their original concept of the split-object-relations unit (SORU) of the borderline personality. Through extensive writing and teaching, Masterson has elaborated its basic concepts in respect to clinical application. Rinsley, on the other hand, has recently reexamined and further developed its representational and object-relations underpinnings. As did Kernberg, Rinsley has concluded that the earlier concept of the SORU did not do full justice to the complexity of the range of personality disorders that are encountered in clinical practice. Rinsley now believes that the SORU serves instead as a starting point for an expanded understanding of the pathogenesis and internalized object relations of the borderline and related personality disorders (D. B. Rinsley, personal communication, October 26, 1983).

The original Masterson-Rinsley formulations were predominantly oriented toward the drive-defense view. More recently, Masterson (1983a) stated that he considers himself a "deficit" rather than a drive-defense theorist. Rinsley's later writings have increasingly diverged from those of Masterson. Rinsley also incorporates ego defect concepts, drawing heavily on the writings of Winnicott and Fairbairn as well as the concept of the selfobject as set forth by Kohut and his associates (D. B. Rinsley, personal communication, October 26, 1983). But Rinsley and Masterson continue to hold that in the early phases of therapy, the role of confrontation of the split-units is crucial to their respective therapeutic techniques.

Etiology

Masterson and Rinsley view Mahler's rapprochement subphase, with its twin issues of engulfment versus abandonment, as the chrysalis from which borderline adults emerge. They pinpoint the failure of the extended separation-individuation phase as the cause of the borderline patient's pathology. But as noted earlier, Rinsley has revised his position on this and now holds that the rapprochement subphase is where the fixation becomes apparent, with the point of origin in the symbiotic phase. As Horner (1975, quoted in 1976) stated, borderline adults are confronted by a dilemma:

> The engulfment of symbiosis if he moves towards the object or the experience of loss and abandonment if he moves away. In such instances, we often find a mother who withdraws love at the child's first move to define himself as separate from her. (p. 479)

Masterson (1982) and Rinsley (1981b) have stated that three common pathways converge during this subphase—nature, nurture, and fate: the exact mix must be determined clinically for each patient. *Nature* includes brain damage or hereditary loading for major mental and physical disease syndromes, which complicates separation-individuation because the parent has to do more caretaking for a longer time, thereby prolonging the symbiosis. *Nurture* includes the mother's lack of support for individuation efforts. This lack of support may be caused by the mother's own borderline tendencies that expose her to intense anxiety if she tolerates any separation, even from her child. It also may stem from unavailability or fatigue, which prevents the working mother from dealing with her child. *Fate* refers to factors during the first year of life, such as a child's prolonged separation from parents because of hospitalization or a parent's death.

Masterson and Rinsley emphasize that infants have a natural drive toward ever-greater differentiation and take pleasure in mastering new functions. These infants' healthy development depends on whether the mother appropriately rewards them for separation-individuation while allowing them to exhibit some continued dependency. Rinsley (1977), quoting Masterson and Rinsley (1975), has explained what occurs if the mother behaves otherwise:

> *The borderline child has a mother with whom there is a unique and uninterrupted interaction with a specific relational focus, i.e., reward for regression, withdrawal for separation-individuation* ... the unique "push-pull" quality of this sort of mother–infant interaction becomes powerfully introjected and forms the basis for the progressive development of the borderline syndrome. (p. 56)

Masterson (1982) has elaborated on this phenomenon:

> The crisis occurs during the rapprochement subphase ... the maternal cueing and communicative matching to these essential characteristics of individuation fail to develop.... The child needs these supplies to grow; if he grows, they are withdrawn. This initiates an abandonment depression ... and the need to defend against it produces the developmental arrest. (pp. 6–7)

This, then, becomes the core psychodynamic of borderline adults. Under self-initiated or societal pressure for individuation, borderline patients become depressed. They often do almost anything to control this depression, including behaving in ways that give relief at the moment but are self-defeating or self-destructive in the long run. All other defects and structural problems—splitting, ego weakness, chaotic or distorted interpersonal relationships, lack of object constancy—flow from this developmental arrest.

Intrapsychic Structure of Borderline Adults

Masterson and Rinsley believe that borderline adults have a "personal myth" that has been internalized from interaction with the mother. This myth is made up of two distinct ego states, each of which has an object image, a self-image, and a linking affect. Thus far, their theory sounds remarkably like Kernberg's, though there is one notable difference: Masterson and Rinsley assign a specific content to each of these ego states.

The first ego state is derived from one principal theme of interaction with the mother—her support for clinging, regressive behavior. The object image is of a mother who offers approval for regressive behavior; the self-image is of a good child who may also be special and entitled; and the affect is pleasurable, of being fed and cared for. Masterson and Rinsley have commented that the rewarding part-unit is invested predominantly with libidinal energy.

The second ego state is derived from the other principal theme of interaction—withdrawing support for the child's efforts toward separation-individuation. In this case, the object image is of a mother who becomes angry, critical, and rejecting in the face of assertive behavior; the self-image is of an inadequate, bad, flawed, indentured slave; and the affect is abandonment depression (a "semantic umbrella" to cover a number of affects). This unit is predominantly invested with aggressive energy. Thus, Masterson's and Rinsley's theory is drive related.

Because whole-object relationships have not been achieved, Masterson and Rinsley (like Kernberg) consider each of these images to be a part-image, which remains unintegrated because of the intensity of aggression surrounding the withdrawing unit. They also remain separate because of the abandonment depression that will be activated when the patients finally acknowledge the conflict between their individuation needs and their mother's promotion of regression, which is now internalized as their own wish. After all, it is natural for children as well as adults to avoid such painful feelings at any cost. Splitting therefore continues to predominate, and it keeps separate the rewarding and withdrawing split-object-relations units (Masterson 1982). Both units remain preconscious or conscious but do not seem to influence each other. The term *preconscious* refers to mental contents that are not conscious but may be called into consciousness by an act of will. Masterson and Rinsley generated the following concepts to explain the persistence of these split-units and their impact on behavior.

The Split Ego

In rewarding regression and punishing development, the mother is really rewarding the key defense mechanism of denial of the reality of separation, "which in turn allows the persistence of the wish for reunion (clinging), which later emerges as a defense against abandonment depression" (Masterson 1982, p. 9). Consequently, part of the ego fails to be transformed from reliance on the *pleasure principle* (a mechanism that reduces psychic tension in the most pleasurable way possible, regardless of reality) to reliance on the *reality principle* (which modifies the pleasure principle and brings it into accord with societal norms). Accepting the reality principle would mean accepting the reality of separation—thus activating abandonment depression. "The ego structure is split into a pathological (pleasure) ego and a reality ego, the former pursuing relief from the feeling of abandonment and the latter following the reality principle" (Masterson 1982, p. 9). In adolescence, the gap widens between the patients' feelings, fantasies, and behavior and the reality of their functioning, because of the lack of integration between the pleasure and reality mechanisms.

Pathological Alliances

Alliances develop in childhood between the pathological pleasure ego and either the withdrawing or rewarding units. These alliances promote good feelings and defend against abandonment depression. Both alliances become the borderline adult's principal defenses against "the painful affective state associated with the withdrawing part-unit, i.e., either externalize it or defend against it with the rewarding unit" (Masterson 1982, p. 12). However, as Masterson notes, both units are pathological.

The rewarding-unit pathologic ego alliance can be seen clinically in dramatic or subtle clinging and compliant behavior. Borderline patients project the part-object representation of the rewarding unit onto people in the environment and then expect to receive their approval and support. This promotes the acting out of reunion fantasies and relieves abandonment depression. The withdrawing unit remains internalized and is defended against by this alliance (Masterson 1982, p. 11).

The withdrawing-unit pathologic ego alliance is manifested in projecting the negative, critical attitudes of the part-object of the withdrawing unit onto someone in the environment. For some patients, chronic negativism toward others is a style of relating. An example would be a man who felt that all women were demanding, insensitive fortune hunters and thus felt justified at being angry at all of them, avoiding them and remaining distant while secretly having fantasies of the perfect caretaking woman. The rewarding unit remains internalized and is expressed with fantasies, perhaps of being loved, cared for, and looked after (Masterson 1982, p. 11).

Henceforth, the withdrawing part-object-relations unit (which Masterson calls the WORU) and the rewarding part-object-relations unit (the RORU) will be referred to by their initials. In order to reduce the difficulty in pronunciation, Rinsley refers to these two acronyms as the rewarding and withdrawing SORUs.

Patients usually have a favorite unit from which they operate most often, though most borderline adults typically vacillate between the RORU and WORU, depending on what is happening at the moment. Any individuation move usually will activate some form of depression that will be defended against in some idiosyncratic way. Both the RORU and the WORU can be experienced as vague, amorphous sensations or as sharply etched alter egos. (The powerfully raw instinctual energies of the RORU and WORU correspond to Kernberg's unmetabolized good and bad inner objects.) The task of therapy is to neutralize the energies associated with the split-units and permit their assimilation into whole-object relations. Table 8-1 categorizes the elements of these split-units.

Narcissistic Pathology

The concept of narcissism is also essential to understanding this model of borderline adults. Masterson appears to use the term *narcissism* not in a formal diagnostic sense but in a developmental-dynamic manner. Masterson (1982) defined the narcissistic psychopathology of the borderline as "1) Poor self-image; 2) Difficulty identifying and articulating in the environment individuative thoughts, wishes and feelings and difficulties in autonomously

Table 8-1   Summary of the Borderline's Split Object-Relations Unit

Withdrawing or Aggressive Part-Unit		
Part-object-representation	*Affect*	*Part-self-representation*
A maternal part-object which is attacking, critical, hostile, angry, withdrawing supplies and approval in the face of assertiveness or other efforts toward separation-individuation	Chronic anger, frustration, feeling thwarted, which cover profound underlying abandonment	A part-self-representation of being inadequate, bad, helpless, guilty, ugly, empty, etc.

Rewarding or Libidinal Part-Unit		
Part-object-representation	*Affect*	*Part-self-representation*
A maternal part-object which offers approval, support, and supplies for regressive and clinging behavior	Feeling good, being fed, gratification of the wish for reunion	A part-self-representation of being the good, passive compliant child

Source: Rinsley, D. B. (1982). *Borderline and Other Self Disorders: A Developmental and Object-Relations Perspective* (p. 39). Copyright 1982 by Jason Aronson. Reprinted by permission.

regulating self-esteem; 3) Difficulty with self-assertion" (p. 12). Some borderline patients have a narcissistic defense (e.g., haughtiness, self-centeredness, ragefulness) that protects the borderline structure from being revealed. For example, Mary Markham could be considered a lower-level borderline whose narcissistic issues (e.g., omnipotence and control) protected her from intense dependency longings. Much time and effort is usually required in the therapy to work through the narcissistic defense before the borderline issues can be treated.

Rinsley's (1982a) concept of entitlement and its behavioral equivalents are also aspects of narcissistic pathology in borderline adults (see Chapters 6 and 7).

Diagnostic Criteria

Masterson (1983a) believes that the following six criteria confirm the diagnosis of a borderline personality:

1. Presence of ego defects (poor reality testing, impulse control, ego boundaries, frustration tolerance).
2. Presence of primitive ego defense mechanisms (e.g., splitting, avoidance, denial, projective identification).
3. Appearance of the split-object-relations units (RORU and WORU).
4. Appearance of the borderline triad (individuation → depression → defense), which is tested out in the initial interview by means of confrontation.
5. Presence of a specific type of narcissistic pathology (e.g., poor self-image, problems with self-assertion).
6. Presence of certain symptoms related to lower-level structures (e.g., paranoid projections, separation psychosis, feelings of depersonalization and unreality) or upper-level structure (e.g., primarily problems with intimacy and sometimes anxiety attacks, phobias, obsessive-compulsive or hysterical symptoms).

For diagnostic purposes, Masterson considers the appearance of the RORU and WORU pathognomonic of the borderline personality, as they appear in both the history and the therapeutic interaction.

Masterson agrees with Kernberg on a number of diagnostic issues. First, transient psychosis will be present only in the lower-level borderline, and then only in specific ways (separation psychosis). Thus, the borderline disorder arises from failure to complete the rapprochement subphase. Second, confrontation should improve functioning, even if only temporarily. Finally, distancing and schizoid defenses are common to lower-level borderline patients, and clinging defenses are more common to the higher-level borderline.

Rinsley (1982a) has constructed his own diagnostic criteria for the range of self disorders (see Chapter 11), which are compatible with both Masterson's and Kernberg's diagnostic systems.

Both Masterson and Rinsley see the *narcissistic personality disorder* as a higher-functioning personality disorder than the borderline, making a greater distinction between the two disorders than does Kernberg. Like Kernberg, Masterson believes that the narcissistic personality usually presents differently from the borderline (e.g., the narcissistic personality presents as haughty, arrogant, and self-centered). Masterson (1981) defines the narcissistic disorder intrapsychically as having two split-object-relations units, although the second unit often remains hidden until later in the therapy. The more obvious part is made up of a fused self-object unit that is omnipotent and special, containing supplies and power. When experiencing the grandiose self, patients expect their specialness to be mirrored by the therapist. When projecting the idealized object, they expect the therapist to be omnipotent and also to share and participate in the "narcissistic glow" (p. 15). The second unit is called the empty or aggressive unit, which contains an object representation that is harsh, punitive, and attacking and a self-representation that is being humiliated, attacked, and empty. Both are linked by the affect of abandonment depression.

Masterson, unlike Kernberg, believes that the therapist must initially be empathetic with any slights incurred in the therapy (in the fashion of Kohut's therapy) until the patients can accept a more confrontive approach. I assume that therapeutically Rinsley uses a psychoanalytically oriented approach that is similar to the mixed model or eclectic approach discussed in Chapter 11.

Clinical Manifestations

Borderline adults often arrive in psychotherapy with several broad-based complaints: (1) acute symptoms from a recent separation, (2) chronic difficulty with intimacy (probably related to fears of engulfment or abandonment), or (3) feelings of not getting enough out of life (related to separation-individuation fears). Sometimes these complaints are spelled out clearly, but at other times they are vague. The personal history may reveal possible borderline problems. Has a separation stressor (going to college, getting a job, and leaving home) led to depression, poor functioning, or impulsivity? Does the patient feel best when in a relationship that encourages dependency or distancing? Does the patient become severely depressed after losing such a relationship or become anxious if people get too close? These complaints indicate that under an individuation pressure, the patient becomes depressed—the key psychodynamic of the borderline.

While the history is being collected, patients often report a variety of intense, kaleidoscopic feelings. Masterson (1976) and Rinsley (1977) have grouped these feelings into six categories under the rubric of *abandonment depression*. Patients eventually report all six, but in a different blend. It is not until the middle phase of the psychotherapy that the full flavor of the abandonment depression will be experienced by the patients and seen by the therapist. Masterson (1976, pp. 38–42) has defined these six components of abandonment depression, calling them the "Six Horsemen of the Apocalypse."

1. *Depression* is the feeling that springs from the loss or threat of the loss of a part of the self or of vital emotional supplies. The depression initially may not be very strong and may be felt as numbness or boredom. Eventually, as the defenses against this feeling are interpreted, patients slide into the bottom of their depression and feel suicidal despair about their ability ever to get what they need to exist.
2. *Rage* at first may be mild and directed toward people and events currently in the patients' life. But eventually the rage increases and is directed specifically at the mother and the therapist for refusing to give what is needed to maintain fantasies of symbiosis.
3. *Fear* is the feeling of being helpless, being abandoned, having supplies cut off, or being killed. Feelings of panic may obscure the depression and rage. There may be two psychosomatic accompaniments of this fear (e.g., asthma and peptic ulcer). The degree to which the mother used abandonment as a disciplinary technique appears related to the appearance of fear in the clinical picture.
4. *Guilt* is the introjection of the mother's attitude toward the patients. The patients feel guilty about the self-assertive part of themselves, about individuating and leaving their mother without a role or job in life.
5. *Passivity and helplessness* cause overwhelming paralysis because any self-assertive behavior means abandonment.
6. *Emptiness* is the introjection of the mother's attitude toward the patients, leaving them devoid of positive introjects with which to nurture themselves during separation stresses.

Masterson (1982) has stated that infants experience the mother's withdrawal as a loss of a part of self. In psychotherapy, patients express this withdrawal as a loss of supplies that are necessary to their survival. These abandonment-feeling states are so intense and overwhelming that borderline patients will do almost anything to avoid them. But avoiding them, of course, is impossible. Therefore, the therapist is always dealing with some combination of abandonment feelings and the defenses against them. According to Masterson (1983a), there are at least four ways to deal with abandonment depression: you can stuff it (obesity); you can starve it (anorexia nervosa); you can project it (paranoia); or you can drown it (alcoholism).

Acting Out

Acting out—putting feelings into behavior rather than remembering, experiencing, and expressing them—is a major component of the psychodynamics of borderline adults. Masterson (1983a) reaffirmed Freud's view that acting out is a form of discharge through behavior that makes remembering in therapy unnecessary. In other words, because the past is replayed every day in the patients' life, they do not feel a need to remember and consequently to discuss their behavior in the therapy. Patients frequently do not want to remember the feelings they are acting out because they fear that intense abandonment feelings will be aroused.

Masterson and Rinsley stress that the compulsion to act out rather than remember needs to be controlled through the therapist's confrontation, which will lead to memories and working through in the therapy. But before that happens, a particular repetitive sequence of events will be seen in the therapy (Masterson 1981, Masterson and Rinsley 1975). Patients begin their therapy feeling that the behavior engendered by the alliance between their rewarding part-unit and infantile pleasure ego makes them feel good, and they are unaware of the ultimate cost of this alliance. Through the therapist's interventions, these patients begin to realize that the self-destructive alliance is undesirable, and so their behavior seems to come under control. But this control triggers abandonment fears, and soon the WORU is activated as a resistance to these abandonment feelings, followed by the RORU as a regressive move against the bad feelings. Rinsley (1977) summarized this sequence between patient and therapist:

> There now ensues a sequential process, involving resistance, reality clarification, working through of the feelings of abandonment (withdrawing part unit), further resistance (rewarding part unit) and further reality clarification, which leads in turn to further working through. (p. 61)

Masterson (1981) in turn developed a formula to capture this sequence: separation-individuation leads to depression, which leads to defense.

The Overall Strategy of Therapy

In intensive psychoanalytic therapy, the therapist's first task is to engage the patients' reality ego so that it can become allied with the therapist's healthy ego. Then the patients' encapsulated rage and depression can be worked through; the self- and object images can be split from their part-unit; and the good and bad self- and object images can become integrated. Repression will replace splitting, and the patients can mourn their lost images, which is the final work of separating from the mother and necessary for the development of a healthy adult personality (see Masterson 1976, p. 65). Masterson believes there are several conceptual problems for the psychoanalytically oriented therapist trying to plan a treatment regimen. Because borderline patients cannot experience a true therapeutic alliance or transference reaction to the therapist, they relate in therapy by acting out. Hence, the first task of therapy, regardless of the modality, is to help the patients turn transference acting out into a therapeutic alliance. But the therapist cannot count on either the therapeutic alliance or the transference to contain borderline adults in the way it contains neurotic patients.

Use of Confrontation

Confrontation becomes the first-choice technique to make the pathologic ego/split-object-relation unit alliance ego dystonic. Because acting out makes patients feel good (while denying the reality impact on their life), the therapist's job is to confront the denial. A tentative therapeutic alliance will result from a circular process including resistance → reality confrontation → working through of abandonment (activation of the WORU) → further resistance (activation of the RORU) → reality confrontation. In such an alliance, patients accept their destructive process and work with the therapist as an ally. During this process, the therapist should always perform as though the patients will act in their own best interest (assume the highest level of functioning). Any deviations from acting in their best interests as adults simply become grist for the mill.

Why does confrontation work? Masterson (1983a) hypothesized that the patients' observing ego must be silenced before they act out. By confronting them, the therapist reactivates the observing ego. The reactivated observing ego helps patients test reality against the regressive pull of their pleasure ego. Once again, the therapist just keeps "stuffing" the RORU and WORU back in the patients' heads through confrontation. As acting out is brought under control, patients start to remember feelings and thoughts from session to session (until then, acting out discharged impulses through behavior, and so there was no need to remember). Before confrontation, the patients were living out their past each day like an instant replay.

Several clinical examples may help illustrate this sequence:

Example 1   During her first session, a woman patient often waited for her female therapist to ask questions and to tell her what to do or explain what things meant. The patient was trying to institute the RORU by having the therapist take charge of her psychotherapy. When the psychotherapist confronted her on this ploy, the patient became mildly annoyed and then reported feeling desperate (by which she meant panicked). She felt that she did not have the capacity to think out meanings and solutions. At this point the patient was experiencing abandonment depression (mainly panic and helplessness): the WORU had emerged, although she could not clearly express its elements. After a few minutes, the patient felt better and observed with some pleasure that maybe she could grow up and solve problems as other adults do.

The next day, however, her resistance to this tenuous sense of control emerged, and she telephoned the therapist in panic. The therapist took the call as part of building a therapeutic alliance but once again confronted her by pointing out that the patient was checking to see whether the therapist would take care of her (RORU). The therapist explained that if she had provided such caretaking immediately, the patient would have felt much better—but at the expense of her eventual growth. The therapist then asked the patient to wait to discuss the feelings at the next session. The patient hung up the phone angrily but reported feeling better at the next session.

And so went the cycle of attempts at individuation → depression → defense. At no time was this patient able to describe much about her inner workings. The therapist had to infer a great deal by watching typical moves and countermoves in psychotherapy and draw conclusions from them.

Example 2   A male inpatient considered finally cutting loose from his dependence on his mother. He talked enthusiastically about his decision with his therapist on Tuesday. During his Wednesday appointment, he felt empty, bored, and vaguely depressed but did not know why. He was having a strong urge to go out and drink. Again: A separation-individuation thought → abandonment depression → defense (e.g., drinking).

Unconscious Collusion with the Patient

There are many ways for the psychotherapist to collude unconsciously with the patients' pathologic split-ego states and transference acting out. The following examples show common collusions:

Example 1   A borderline woman who had been in therapy with a male therapist for four months was feeling better, but little had changed in her troubled personal and job life. Her therapist talked whenever the patient ran out of topics, giving advice and sharing similar personal experiences. The patient was always appreciative and grateful. But now she called the therapist at home at night and on weekends and became angry when he tentatively and erratically tried to set limits. The psychotherapist felt overwhelmed, and the patient felt betrayed and abandoned.

Example 2   A borderline man was testy with his treatment and his female therapist since he began psychotherapy three months ago. Some of his anger was justified because the therapist had changed his appointments several times without explanation (which may have activated the WORU). The therapist had absorbed the patient's anger while trying to explore its origins, although she had gotten nowhere. She now felt overwhelmed and angry at his abusive behavior, and the patient seemed unwilling to move on to any other process.

What went wrong in these two situations? In the first example, the therapist promised more than he could deliver, initially evoking the RORU and then stimulating the emergence of the WORU. The therapist, who probably felt that he was just being a nice person doing supportive therapy, was clearly unaware of this problem. He probably would deny that first he rewarded the patient for clinging and then tried to set limits on her, thereby activating the WORU. But to the extent that the patient was not doing for herself and the therapist was doing for her, the old RORU pattern was being replayed. The subtleties of the therapist's theoretical position would be lost on the patient. In fact, if the therapist explored his own motivations, he might well agree that he was "rescuing" the patient because of his own psychic needs.

In the second example, the psychotherapist colluded with the WORU. The therapist accepted all the anger the patient wanted to direct at his mother for abandoning him or not meeting all of his needs. In doing so, the therapist might have been unconsciously accepting the accusation that she had failed the patient by not giving enough. The therapist might deserve some anger because of her erratic scheduling but did not deserve complete condemnation. The therapist bought into the patient's pathologic process by allowing him to "dump" on her and act out (not work out) his anger. This process could drag on forever unless controlled, as some patients will express anger endlessly for not getting enough from their parents (Masterson 1983a). Once again, the psychotherapist must look at her own process.

The therapist must remember that both the rewarding and withdrawing part-units are oscillating states for the adult borderline and will be alternately projected onto the therapist. The patient is also committed to maintaining the RORU as a link to the parent and a mechanism to ward off abandonment depression at all costs.

Two Common Defensive Patterns

All patients have characteristic styles of defending against abandonment feelings. Masterson (1981, pp. 134–135) has conceptualized two common patterns that illustrate this phenomenon of projecting either self- or object representations from either the WORU or RORU onto the therapist, a phenomenon also noted by Kernberg. Masterson recognizes one pattern of internalized defense that involves an alliance between the rewarding part-unit and the pathologic ego.

Pattern 1—Internalized Defense

Withdrawing: The part-unit is internalized, experienced as abandonment-depression, and defended against by acting out and projection of the RORU onto the environment.

Rewarding: The part-unit representation is externalized onto others. The patients project part-object representation onto therapist or person in the environment.

Therapy: The patients are compliant and good and expect the therapist to reward such behavior. They bring nothing into the treatment that will disrupt the symbiotic fantasized relationship with the therapist and thus activate depression.

Masterson also recognizes two types of externalized defenses, involving an alliance between the withdrawing part-unit and the pathologic ego.

Pattern 2—Externalized Defense

Pattern A:

Withdrawing: The part-object representation is externalized by projection and acting out onto the therapist or person in the environment.

Rewarding: The part-unit is internalized and is expressed only through hidden fantasies.

Therapy: Patients have "distancing" transference and see the therapist as critical and hostile. They feel distancing is justified because of their projection. Patients use silence, intellectualization, and paranoidlike attitudes toward the therapist's motivation to keep himself or herself at bay. The patients will deny all thoughts, feelings, or life situations that interfere with this defense.

Pattern B:

Withdrawing: The part-self-representation is externalized onto therapist, and the patients play out a part-object representation. The abandonment depression is externalized onto therapist.

Rewarding: Masterson is not clear on this point, but one can assume the rewarding part-unit remains internalized and is expressed only through hidden fantasies.

Therapy: Patients see the therapist as bad, evil, or helpless and they respond by feeling critical and rejecting toward the therapist. In other words, the patients play the role of mother and treat the therapist as the self as child.

The example of Mary Markham in the Kernberg section of this chapter represents switching from Pattern 2-A to Pattern 2-B over the course of a year.

Masterson has commented that with Pattern 1, the therapist usually starts by confronting the discrepancy between how wonderful therapy is and how terrible life is. Usually the therapist concentrates the confrontation on events outside therapy. In Pattern 2 with the distancing patient, the therapist usually comments on events inside the therapy. This, of course, must be done carefully, or the patient may withdraw from treatment. Masterson (1981) has reported that the patients' need to be taken care of is often articulated in a fantasy that remains hidden. Although hidden, this fantasy is the fuel that drives the RORU/pathologic ego alliance. From an instinctual point of view, it is an oral craving. From an object-relations point of view, it is a gratification of the wish for reunion expressed by clinging to the object. From a descriptive point of view, it is a demand for unconditional love or a desire to be taken care of. But, if the therapist meets these needs, the patients will never have to acknowledge consciously that the needs exist. They will thus be able either to obtain love or to relieve their frustration at not having their needs met, without acknowledging what they are really doing or the cost to themselves (Masterson 1981, p. 168).

Clinical Clues and Countertransference Reactions

The therapist can choose, of course, whether or not to accept or to confront the WORU and RORU projections. Often, however, therapists do not recognize either the patients' destructive behavior and transference acting out or their own countertransference behavior.

Masterson has stated that a major impediment to growth in the therapy is the therapist's resonating with the RORU or the WORU, thus enacting the role projected by the patients. Therefore, Masterson stresses that learning to identify and control one's identification with the patients' projections is crucial to a successful psychotherapy.

The following list adapted from Masterson (1983a) shows some of the common clinical responses that can alert the therapist to unproductive collusion with the split-units.

The Patients' Behavior (alerts the therapist to RORU and WORU):

Inside the Session:

1. Waiting for the therapist to ask questions, do the talking, or give advice.
2. Showing a variety of clinging behaviors (e.g., excessively complimenting

therapist, trying to seduce therapist, bringing gifts, telephoning frequently, wanting to know details of therapist's life, bringing referrals of friends and family).

3. Manifesting prolonged hostility, anger, or depression over any limit setting by therapist.

4. Trying to control therapist's verbalization by threatening violence or suicide.

Outside the Session:

5. Acting dependent on others, allowing others to manipulate or treat them badly in order to maintain the relationship.

6. Manifesting inability to self-start or self-activate in normal life (e.g., cannot negotiate needed services).

7. Engaging in acting-out behavior after any individuation move or thought (e.g., drinking to abuse, eating too much, starving self, driving too fast, shoplifting, exhibiting various dangerous behaviors, mutilating self or experiencing abandonment feelings).

8. Denying reality by ignoring bad behavior of others because patients need them too much.

9. Engaging in impulsive, self-destructive behavior even when patients know it can harm them, lead to loss of job or relationship, and lower self-esteem.

The therapist's most common error is to resonate with the RORU by *rescuing* patients or *trying to provide them with a better childhood experience* than the parent did. This shows up in the following typical behaviors:

The Therapist's Behavior (resonating with RORU):

1. Not making patients pay bill on time, not stopping sessions on time, not charging for extra time given to patients, not charging for failed appointment, giving extra time when patients arrive late.

2. Accepting too many phone calls from patients.

3. Giving too much advice and sharing personal information with patients.

4. Allowing patients to change appointment because of their elective needs (e.g., chance to play tennis with a friend).

5. Not confronting patients because they are "feeling so bad" or because they have outside stressor. This, of course, does not pertain if there is a catastrophic happening.

6. Trying to "explain away" why limits are being set (e.g., "I have a family that needs my attention, and that's why I can't talk").

7. Often touching patients in order to comfort them or holding them for reparenting purposes.

8. Excusing acting-out behavior (e.g., "anyone gets drunk once in a while").
9. Not confronting failed or late appointments (letting them pass without comment).
10. Taking "responsibility" for patients' growth; feeling that only you, the therapist, can keep them safe and can stop the acting out (which justifies all kinds of "extra" contacts and interventions) and thus can accept the patients' projection of an omnipotent mother.
11. Not confronting defenses against working in treatment (e.g., silences, accusations, acting out).

Some therapists resonate with the WORU and exhibit the following behaviors:

12. Blanking out and being unable to say anything in the session.
13. Becoming furious with patients, being mean to them, making inappropriate or sarcastic remarks, or terminating them from therapy.

Masterson acknowledges that primitive object relations activated in the transference can combine pre-Oedipal and Oedipal meanings as well as more advanced types of transferences. But overall, he believes that focusing on the RORU and WORU will lead to improvement in the patients' functioning.

Some Common Clinical Questions

Clinicians often are initially excited and then disheartened by their inability to find immediately the RORU and WORU in the clinical material. Second, they often become confused when the WORU, in particular, becomes activated at moments that seem incongruent with their therapeutic behavior.

There are several reasons that the RORU and WORU may be difficult to identify. First, there is a great range in the ways and intensity in which split-units may be expressed. Therefore, affect, both subtle and strong, may be the first clue. Masterson (1982) has commented that the WORU, for example, may be expressed as homicidal rage by the delinquent adolescent or as just a whisper of withdrawal shown as mild guilt in the anorexia nervosa patient. Patients are often unable to identify self- and object images early in the treatment because they take their pathologic situation so for granted. This is why affect is such an important indicator of the RORU or WORU.

Second, although abandonment feelings may bring patients into psychotherapy, they may feel better after undertaking the therapy. After all, they now have a therapist who in fantasy will meet all their needs. These patients may also settle in, fantasize, and be relatively calm, and the split-units may be hidden for a long period. In general, some time and exploration are required before the RORU and WORU can be fully identified, and some working through in the therapy will be necessary before the full impact of the abandonment depression can be revealed.

Third, if the inexperienced therapist initially falls into either the RORU or WORU, and this meets the patients' needs, the patients may settle in and be compliant; and then the units will be played out rather than observed and dealt with. In other words, mutual acting out will replace working through.

Fourth, clinicians often do not understand why the WORU emerges when it does. For example, a patient announces a positive move, and the therapist enthusiastically supports this self-initiated act (e.g., to get a better job, stand up for self). Some patients then may accuse the therapist of forcing them to do something they do not want to do, of not liking them, or of being callous and indifferent. In this case, the WORU is being activated, even though the patient presented the self-initiated act. The therapist believes that the patient is behaving in a healthy way and makes some brief supportive remark. But the patient experiences the old dilemma with the mother, believing that loss of love will follow an individuated act. In this period of losing good reality testing, such patients no longer remember that it was their idea to individuate. Many believe it was the therapist's idea and conclude that the therapist is trying to take away the good regressive feelings and punish them for doing what their mother wanted (e.g., regressing and feeling good about it). The therapist must remember that the patients' reality testing is lessened at times of individuation moves, particularly in regard to issues of "who is doing what to whom" and when there is still a strong internal regressive pull to maintain the old familiar RORU relationship.

In addition, some patients activate the WORU when the therapist has been neutral or even playing into the RORU. Why is this? The patients may be getting the taste of some caretaking—and now they want more. What the therapist is giving is not enough! Also, some patients feel perfectly justified in dumping all their anger about past parental deficits onto the therapist, regardless of what the therapist is doing. The patient is figuratively coming home and kicking the dog after a bad day (Masterson 1983a).

Finally, some patients become angry when the therapist engages in RORU behavior because they understand that at some level the therapist is colluding with an unhealthy part within them. In each case, the therapist needs to recall the sequence of events in the therapy, examine any personal countertransference behavior, and clarify the patients' reaction. Out of this examination the therapist can usually reach some understanding of the precipitants and sequence.

The following summary will help the therapist identify the separation-individuation conflicts (Masterson 1983a):

1. Abandonment feelings expressed or denied, but obvious from the behavior.
2. Signs of resistance to truly experiencing the feelings, as shown by activation of regressive, infantile, acting-out behavior; and projection of critical, withdrawing behavior onto the therapist.

The Treatment Approach

Like Kernberg, Masterson recommends several types of psychotherapy: intensive psychoanalytic psychotherapy, confrontive psychotherapy, and counseling. The approach selected depends on the patients' motivation, level of functioning, and ability to come for several visits per week. Masterson has recently begun to advocate confrontation as the major technique in the early phase (from 12 to 18 months) of both intensive psychoanalytic psychotherapy and confrontive psychotherapy. He feels that at that point patients may be ready to transfer into a reconstructive or psychoanalytically oriented psychotherapy, in which dynamic-genetic reconstruction and working through are emphasized.

Masterson, Rinsley, and Kernberg have commented that their confrontive approach would not be appropriate for psychotic patients, who might well regress under the pressure of confrontation; nor do they recommend it for the neurotic, who usually does not need such confrontation. It is an approach designed specifically for the problems of borderline adults.

Rinsley (D. B. Rinsley, personal communication, October 10, 1983), who considers himself an object-relations eclectic, uses confrontation less extensively than does Masterson. Although Rinsley also applies confrontation in the early phases of psychotherapy of borderline and narcissistic adults in order to strengthen the therapeutic alliance, he frequently also uses Kleinian interpretative techniques early in the therapy. His use of interpretation depends on the patients' capacity to "withstand" such interpretative work, as well as their need for a good holding environment and for the therapist to function as a selfobject.

What rationale do Masterson and Rinsley offer for the use of confrontation as a major technique? As Masterson (1981) has explained,

> psychotherapy, through its requirement that the patient assume responsibility for the initiation, identification and reporting of his feeling states—in other words, he must assume responsibility for the emotional state of the self and its expression, or if not, examine why not—rekindles the separation-individuation process and immediately brings the patient in the interview up against all the difficulties which have created this defect in the structure of the self in the first place—his need to defend against the abandonment depression that separation-individuation induces. The psychotherapy becomes itself an ex-

periment in individuation. In the therapeutic crucible, when the patient activates his usual defenses, such as avoidance or transference acting-out, these are dealt with by the therapist by confrontation and/or other techniques which refocus and provide a framework for the patient to work through his abandonment depression or reexperience the disappointment, anger and depression that helped to produce the defect in the first place. (p. 231)

Masterson believes that ego defects and reality perceptions will become internalized by bringing them to the patients' view through confrontation and that elaborate interpretations will simply be ignored or used as rationalizations by borderline patients.

Elaborating on Masterson's comments, Rinsley (D. B. Rinsley, personal communication, October 10, 1983) noted that confrontation is a way to tell patients they are doing self-injurious things to themselves via symptomatic behavior and acting out. The therapist expresses concern about the patients and indicates his or her desire that they stop engaging in such acts. This, in effect, represents an effort to help patients control themselves, akin to a parent's disciplined efforts at controlling a child's inappropriate behavior so that the child can be socialized. However disturbed patients may be, they cannot fail on some perceptive level to "hear" the therapist's concern and, as a result, begin to develop trust in the therapy and the therapist.

As does Kernberg, Masterson and Rinsley consider that the projection of the RORU and WORU offers important therapeutic information about borderline patients. Masterson believes, however, that the therapist's most difficult task is to confront (not interpret) the RORU and WORU in the treatment and to resist the temptation to overidentify or resonate with the projections.

HEINZ KOHUT AND COLLEAGUES

Kohut (1971, 1975, 1977; Kohut and Wolf, 1978) developed a comprehensive and far-reaching theory of the pathogenesis and treatment of primitive types of patients, particularly the narcissistic personality disorder. Kohut's writings have gained wide exposure and acceptance over the past decade, both within and outside the psychoanalytic community. In 1971, with the publication of his first book, *The Analysis of the Self*, Kohut positioned himself squarely within the traditional drive and structure model of classical psychoanalysis. In this book, he focused on issues of technique with a group of severely disturbed patients whom other analysts had considered unanalyzable. He classified these patients as "narcissistic personality disorders," which he considered to be a diagnostic entity with a particular developmental etiology.

Patton and Sullivan (1980) have pointed out, however, that Kohut's book deviated slightly from the classical position, because of his contention that the self is not only a content of the ego or a representation but also the organizing center of the personality, an active agent. They noted that this deviation created enormous logical problems for Kohut's adherence to the traditional psychoanalytic theory of drive and structure. His approach, especially to treatment, as set forth in his second major work, *The Restoration of the Self* (1977), has deviated to such an extent from classical concepts that many consider that it can no longer be considered psychoanalytic. Again, self psychology has been extended to constitute a theory encompassing all forms of psychopathology.

We should define *self*. Although Kohut (1977) stated that the self is ultimately unknowable in its essence, it can be defined as the core of the personality (Kohut and Wolf 1978). The self has three major constituents, referred to by Kohut as *poles*: (1) one pole that contains the strivings for assertive ambitions, success, and power (called the *grandiose-exhibitionistic self*); (2) one, opposed to it, that harbors the basic idealized goals, values, and ideals (called the *idealized parental imago*); and (3) an intermediate area of basic talents and skills that are activated by the tension-arch that establishes itself between the two poles (p. 414). Although Kohut avoided calling the self a structure, he has indeed used the term as the equivalent of a person's total psychic structure.

This new theory has several parts: (1) a central concept of the "nuclear self"; (2) the development of the nuclear self from an infantile state to its transformation in adulthood into a firm, cohesive structure; (3) the genesis of disorders of the self; and (4) psychotherapeutic implications. As this new theory was put to work, several implications were soon identified. (1) There is basically only one disorder in psychic life—a disorder of self-organization —and all other psychopathology is secondary to failures of the self. (2) Intrapsychic conflict develops only at the Oedipal period. (3) Neurotic disorders (Oedipally organized disorders) involve intrapsychic conflict. (4) Severe disorders of the self (as in borderline and narcissistic patients) predate the Oedipal level and therefore reflect arrests or deficits rather than conflict. (5) The task of treatment is to generate missing self-structures rather than to resolve intrapsychic conflict. (6) Narcissistic patients will form one of two typical selfobject transferences (mirroring or idealizing) in the therapy, according to unmet developmental needs. (7) The therapist's role is to be empathic and introspective and to provide a reparative selfobject relationship. In fact, the central impact of the psychology of the self on the conduct of psychoanalysis pertains to the analyst's empathic-introspective stand, which allows him or her to be responsive to the patient's *total self,* and not prematurely to the self's breakdown products, such as defenses, drives, aggression, conflicts, and compromises (see Ornstein 1982 for a summary of self psychology).

Etiology

As mentioned earlier, Kohut did not focus on the problems of borderline adults, whom he considered to be basically akin to schizophrenics. He believed that borderline adults either had a cohesive self that fragmented later in life or had never formed a cohesive self. He did not believe that his therapeutic approach was appropriate for them because he thought that they required supportive or custodial therapy. Instead, he focused on narcissistic disorders, which he considered to be at a higher level.

We will examine Kohut's self psychology in regard to borderline adults, for two reasons. First, the many theorists who have reviewed Kohut's case material, including Masterson (1981), believe that many of Kohut's narcissistic patients meet the criteria for a borderline disorder in several diagnostic systems. This is because borderline patients have an enfeebled self (e.g., disorder of the self), although not of psychotic proportions, and many of them form idealizing or mirroring transferences, as do the narcissistic patients. Although it is useful to differentiate between the two disorders, not enough work has been done in this area to support a clear-cut distinction. Theorists such as Adler and Rinsley are currently working on developmental-diagnostic criteria to distinguish between the two groups, but for the time being, some diagnostic overlap appears inevitable.

Basic to Kohut's assumptions about the development and etiology of disorders of the self is his belief that children must be born into an empathic, responsive human environment in order to flourish. He believed that "relatedness with others is as essential for his psychological survival as oxygen is for his physical survival" (Greenberg and Mitchell 1983, p. 353). He explained that the infants' weak, tentative self begins to form when their potentialities and the parents' expectations converge. Because of the infantile need for relatedness with others, their budding self requires the parents' support to provide continuity, stability, and cohesion. It was these supportive others for whom Kohut coined the term *selfobjects*. From the infant's perspective, selfobjects are not yet differentiated from the self; yet they are objectively separate persons who serve functions that will later be performed by the infants' own psychic structure (Greenberg and Mitchell 1983). The infants' expected control over selfobjects is closer to the control that adults expect to have over their own body and mind than to the control that they expect to have over others (Kohut and Wolf 1978, p. 414).

The helpless infant experiences the feeling states of the selfobjects through tone of voice, touch, and other subtle means. Kohut stated that the relations between the infants and the selfobjects formed the basic constituents of psychic development and structure. Hence, Kohut held that relations created psychic structure.

Greenberg and Mitchell (1983) noted that Kohut believed that infants seek two fundamental relationships with early selfobjects. First, they need to display their evolving capabilities and to be admired. Kohut regarded this as the infants' healthy sense of grandiosity. This concept is similar to Mahler's grandiose self of the practicing subphase. Second, infants need to form an idealized image of the father, and to feel a sense of merging with this idealized selfobject. These twin poles make their debut in the middle of the second year of life. Greenberg and Mitchell (1983) explained:

> In the course of optimal development two relational configurations emerge sequentially: grandiose, exhibitionistic self images become connected to "mirroring" selfobjects ("I am perfect and you admire me"); toned-down images of the self become fused with idealized selfobjects ("You are perfect, and I am part of you"). (p. 354)

Continuing, they pointed out that under optimal conditions, the microtransformations of self- and object images from the primitive to the more complex are brought about by the parents' inevitable failure to mirror properly or to permit the idealizing merger. If these minute changes occur in the context of "good-enough mothering" (Winnicott's term), a slow, incremental internalizing of the selfobject will take place. Kohut termed this process *transmuting internalization,* which gives rise to the development of the psychological structure known as the self. Greene (1984) discovered that "this process is analogous to the body's intake of foreign protein, which is then metabolized so that the resultant amino acids can be used to build the structure of one's own body" (p. 41).

This permanent psychic structure consists of the two poles from the early relationships described above. Either pole can form the core of a healthy and cohesive self. Thus, personality may be derived from the mirroring selfobject, usually the mother. Such a personality would be organized around a grandiose, exhibitionistic trend and be expressed as healthy ambition or assertiveness. On the other hand, the idealizing selfobject, usually the father, is the dominant force, and such a personality would be expressed as healthy, strongly held ideas and values (Greenberg and Mitchell 1983).

The nature of a personality is determined by the content of both poles of the self and their relation to each other. If there is a disturbance at one pole, the adequate development of the other can compensate. But failure to develop at least one of them leads to narcissistic psychopathology, which is characterized by a defective sense of self and an inability to maintain a steady level of self-esteem. In accordance with Kohut's theory, the self of borderline adults is fragmented, and neither pole functions.

Unlike Mahler, Kernberg, and Masterson, Kohut believed that selfobjects never fully differentiate. Instead, they simply develop from infantile to more mature forms by transmuting internalization. Thus, he dismissed the need for phases of development (symbiosis and separation-individuation) and for the separation of the self and object in the developmental sequence.

One of Kohut's colleagues (Wolf 1980) extended Anna Freud's concept of developmental lines to selfobjects, detailing the developmental lines of self-object relations from birth to adult life. His analysis recognized the need for an "antagonist" selfobject at certain points in the process of differentiation, a selfobject to whom children can say "no" and be self-assertive without retaliation (Spitz's "no" response). Wolf added that although adults never give up the need for selfobjects (particularly in the form of spouses, children, friends, and their love and admiration), many depersonalized forms of self-objects take the place of specific people in adult life (e.g., good causes, community and civic projects, and altruism and ideals).

According to Kohut, the parents' character pathology undermines the healthy development of the infants' self. In the face of parental failure to respond empathically to the emerging self, the children's search for self-objects breaks down. These children are forced to make do with whatever meager empathy they can find. Such chronic failures of maternal empathy have several unfortunate consequences. They cause an impediment in the child's expression of archaic narcissism with optimal mirroring by the parent, or there can be impediments in the idealization of the parents. Chronic failures of maternal empathy lead to the child's inability to limit expectations of maternal perfection as well as failure of transmuting internalization. Instead, there is the continuing psychic expectation and wish for absolute perfection in the selfobject and the continued quest for mirroring (Bernstein 1982). Bernstein also reported a blockage of narcissist (self-love) maturation results, affecting later areas of self-esteem and self-worth or ambitions and creativity. Under such conditions of poor mirroring, Kohut (1977) explained, the selfobjects split off and endure, rather than being slowly established and then dissolved through transmuting internalization. In other words, one or more of the narcissistic selfobject configurations may become defensively isolated from the other parts of the personality, thus forming a psychic cul-de-sac.

Intrapsychic Structure of Borderline Adults

According to Kohut and Wolf (1978), the basic pathology of all the major disorders lies not in conflicts concerning libidinal or aggressive impulses but in a weakened or defective self (pp. 415–416). The existence of a cohesive self means the patient has attained stable psychic structures, stable and realistic relationships with others, and a realistic and modulated self-esteem, even under stress (Bernstein 1982). A weakened, enfeebled, or fragmented self in its milder forms shows up in symptoms of easily experienced disappointments, lowered self-esteem, and boredom or helplessness, to more extreme symptoms such as serious and protracted experiences of psychotic regression, depersonalization and derealization, delusions, and hallucinations. The narcissistic personality is seen as having shorter or more transient episodes of enfeeblement or fragmentation and as regaining cohesion quickly with empathic comments from the therapist.

M. Tolpin (1982) has stated that a large portion of the spectrum of self disorders includes borderline patients. Self psychology has not, however, delineated a concept of the intrapsychic structure of borderline adults. Several theorists have described the borderline adult's intrapsychic structure. Stolorow and Lachmann (1980) reported that borderline patients have not attained a cohesive self and may not be able to form either idealizing or mirroring transferences. These patients appear to have a precarious self-organization that is prone to massive shattering and collapse and does not necessarily remit under the therapist's empathic responses. M. Tolpin (1982) stated that whatever defense and pathological reorganization there is in this disorder covers over but does not repair the enfeebled self.

P. Tolpin (1980) found that there are really two types of borderline structures. He termed the first a *true* borderline disturbance in which there is a state of permanent or protracted breakdown, enfeeblement, or serious distortion. Its essential psychotic organization is controlled and concealed by a complex set of defensive structures, the best known of which are the schizoid and paranoid personalities, who protect against psychosis by distancing from others. The second borderline structure is a self that is generally cohesive, although its contents and its mode of organization are eccentric, fluid, brittle, and generally less successfully put together than in the healthier narcissistic personality disorder. This group does not have the hidden psychotic elements of the true borderline adults and thus may respond to an intensive psychotherapy. No examples or diagnostic labels were given to this second group of borderline patients.

Diagnostic Criteria

The entire diagnostic approach of self psychology is strikingly different from Kernberg's structural diagnosis or that of descriptive psychiatry. Kohut's approach to diagnosis is not based on manifest behavior but on the basic organization of the self as demonstrated by the transferences (or the defenses against it) that arise in the course of a long-term treatment (P. Tolpin 1980, pp. 301–302). P. Tolpin (1980) indicates that self therapists do use the patient's history and psychiatric diagnosis to make initial decisions about the patient's condition but that really only a trial basis in therapy can confirm the diagnosis. In other words, no amount of history taking or cataloguing of complaints will definitely establish the presence of any of the disorders of the self. The diagnosis can be established only by how the patient attempts to use the therapist to elevate self-esteem or provide or restore cohesion to the self.

Kohut did catalogue some common syndromes and character typologies. In addition to the psychotic and borderline cases, he found *narcissistic behavior disorders* showing perverse, delinquent, or addictive behaviors, as well as *narcissistic personality disorders* showing hypochondriasis, depression, hypersensitivity to slights, and lack of zest. Unlike patients with narcissistic behavior disorders, those with narcissistic personality disorders are usually concerned not about how they act but rather about how they feel. Kohut believed that both of these disorders do well in intensive analytically oriented psychotherapy or psychoanalysis.

Both of these narcissistic disorders have major difficulties in maintaining self-esteem. Although on the surface, Bernstein (1982) noted, they may resemble neurotics, such patients show signs, on the one hand, of haughty grandiosity, coldness, and contempt and, on the other hand, shyness, sensitivity, and feelings of inferiority. They may even alternate between these behaviors. When entering treatment, they do not establish classical transference neuroses but, rather, form one of the mirroring or idealizing transferences representing the revival of their unmet narcissistic childhood needs. This will confirm the diagnosis.

Beyond these two types of disorders, Kohut and Wolf (1978) formed a group of syndromes that reflect whether "over" or "under" stimulation took place at either the grandiose or idealizing poles during early developmental phases. These syndromes are the understimulated self, the fragmenting self, the overstimulated self, and the overburdened self. Kohut and Wolf also developed the mirror-hungry personality, the ideal-hungry personality, the alter-ego personality, the merger-hungry personality, and the contact-shunning personality.

Kohut considered only these last two personality disorders to be inherently pathological, whereas the others were variants of the normal personality. These last two types are pathological because of the *extent* of the pathology. Mary Markham could be considered a merger-hungry personality whose need for merger with a selfobject dominated the clinical picture. Because she experienced others as her own self, she was sensitive to separations and expected, without question, the continuous presence of the selfobject. The external behavior of the contact-shunning personality is just the opposite. Such patients avoid social contact and become isolated, not out of disinterest but because the need for a selfobject is so intense that they fear that the yearned-for, all-embracing union will destroy the remnants of the nuclear self. Many symptoms such as rage attacks, impulsivity, substance abuse, and intense shame all are considered by-products of the loss of self-cohesion and are not considered by themselves to be diagnostic; they just point the way to the loss of self-cohesion.

Clinical Manifestations

Self-disordered patients enter therapy with a plethora of complaints and symptoms. If the defect occurs in the area of the grandiose self, patients may believe they are special and are entitled to be treated as such. They may or may not be aware of this attitude. These attitudes can be manifested in several forms, ranging from a vain to a pseudohumble demeanor. Clinically, the therapist can expect patients with a defect in the grandiose self to feel a painful sense of shame and worthlessness when their fragile self-esteem is injured. Such patients respond frequently with rage, arrogance, withdrawal into isolation, or hypochondriacal complaints. If the defect is in the area of the idealized, parental imago, these patients are likely to be extremely vulnerable to separations from others and to react with greater than normal enfeeblement and depression to such separations. Clinically, they may report feeling helpless, depressed, fatigued, and without zest.

Clinically, these defects at the mirroring or idealizing poles can show up in a number of additional ways. First, persons with a narcissistic personality can develop defenses of denial, disavowal, shame, and disgust, which help them deal with and defend against their narcissistic vulnerability. Second, they may show outward behavior of grandiosity, arrogance, coldness, or extreme self-sufficiency or, on the other hand, show withdrawal from relationships, shyness, decreased self-esteem, and hypochondriasis. They may also alternate between both types of behavior. Third, in order to maintain their internal equilibrium, they may engage in various behaviors, such as defensive sexuality, drug and alcohol usage, or various types of exhibitionism or idealization (Bernstein 1982). Fourth, higher-level narcissistic patients usually deny the perceived self-defect (e.g., vulnerability, flaw, sense of emptiness). Such patients may project it onto others, viewing them as incompetent and themselves as the "greatest," or they may deny it by means of masochistic, injustice-collecting self-aggrandizement (Rinsley 1982, p. 232). In other words, they will block out certain selective aspects of reality that would bring them face to face with their vulnerabilities and anxieties. Finally, persons with narcissistic personality disorders usually have object relations in which they try to have others fill the void of their unmet needs to be admired (mirrored) or to admire someone else (idealize).

Whether or not the patients develop one of the two selfobject transferences discussed earlier is critical. There are basically three variations of the *mirror* selfobject transference. Each reflects the activation of the unmet needs for mirroring grandiosity (and represent the reactivation of the primitive grandiose self). These three variations lie on "a continuum from the most archaic *merger transference,* to the intermediate *alter-ego* or *twinship transference,* to the most mature or *'mirror transference in the narrower sense'"* (Bernstein 1982, p. 97). These self object transferences seem to lie on a continuum from symbiosis to separation (Adler, as cited in Bernstein 1982).

Merger Transference

The therapist is seen as an extension of the patients' omnipotence, grandiosity, and exhibitionism, and the patients demand total oneness with the selfobject. An example of a merger transference expressed by a patient in therapy is: "I sometimes feel as though we are almost one person; you somehow know my every need. When I come into therapy after the first few minutes I feel like I come alive; I don't even know how it happens, it just does. I feel if anything ever happened to you, I would die."

Alter-Ego or Twinship Transference

The therapist is seen as being exactly like the self; although experienced as a separate person, the therapist is regarded as the bearer of "the patients' own repressed perfection" (Bernstein 1982, p. 97). An example of a twinship transference is: "Sometimes I feel like we are Siamese twins. I am really intellectual and perceptive, and a mark above the average person, and I see you as more broadly educated than the typical therapist, with a broader exposure to literature, politics, and social revolutionary movements. I bet that you even like the same type of fantasy and sci-fi movies that I do because most creative people like such things."

Mirror Transference (Narrow Sense)

Here the therapist is seen as a separate person who is supposed to confirm or echo the patients' greatness, admire them, and silently approve of their exhibitionistic productions. An example of a mirror transference reported by a patient is: "I finally asserted myself with my husband as we agreed I would do. All the way to the therapy session I imagined how pleased and proud you would be of me. I have to admit that sometimes I really think I am your favorite patient—just the look on your face seems to show that you are more interested when you greet me than when you greet the patient after me."

In the *idealizing* selfobject transference, the idealized parental imago is mobilized. The patients need the therapist as "a powerful, perfect, idealized person with whom the patient can merge and, through such a union, complete a part of himself previously experienced as deficient" (Bernstein 1982, p. 99). An example of an idealizing transference is: "Sometimes when I go to parties I tell people you are my therapist. They tell me how competent you are, and I feel really special to be your patient. It lifts my entire mood for the night when I see you in therapy."

These selfobject transferences should emerge in the therapy, though they may be defended against by a variety of maneuvers that require long and careful exploration (Bernstein 1982). The systematic analysis of such resistances eventually leads to their full development and working through.

When the therapist (as well as the outside environment) fails to provide the proper selfobject relatedness, the patients' inner cohesiveness weakens. They may exhibit any number of symptoms (e.g., they may be listless, hypochondriacal, and angry and may abuse substances); they may feel "out-of-sync" with the therapist and generally feel "not right." These symptoms often indicate that the therapist has failed to be a proper selfobject and needs to reevaluate the therapeutic role.

The Role of Anxiety

Bernstein (1982) found that with neurotic patients, anxiety functions as a signal related to a specific danger or conflict. With narcissistic patients, anxiety signals an awareness of imminent disintegration or fragmentation in self-cohesiveness. Intense anxiety alerts the therapist to this fragmentation, which usually leads to all the symptoms discussed earlier. He noted that with narcissistic personalities, fragmentation of the self may result from transient empathic failures by the therapist or others, frustration over important events in their lives or separation from important others. Such a sense of fragmentation may be transient, and the selfobject transference may be reinstated by the appropriate empathic responses by the therapist (just as in optimal mothering, transient poor mutual cuing can be corrected and can restore the infant's homeostasis). With the borderline personality, intense anxiety is often related to separations from significant others and loss of evocative memory of the good object. The therapist's empathic response may or may not restore the patient's equilibrium.

Linking Self-Esteem (Narcissism) and Interpersonal Relationships

Kohut reported the existence of separate parallel early developmental lines for narcissism (self-love) and object love. Individuals who have not achieved a healthy cohesive self have difficulty with mutuality and often enter relationships under the burden of emotional pain and decreased self-esteem. They attempt to use their relationships with others to satisfy their inadequate childhood needs and functions, which are felt to be unfulfilled. When another person does satisfy a missing function, that person—who is then known as a selfobject—is considered to be a part of the patient's self, and the patient experiences a temporary decrease in pain and a temporary increase in self-esteem because of this completion of the self. Such relationships become precarious, however, because others often resent the degree of selfobject functioning they must provide while their own needs go unmet. Thus, in psychotherapy, the working through of the various selfobject transferences should, at least indirectly, offer an option to the patients for a more mature relationship with others, although Kohut did not claim that this occurred.

The Treatment Approach

The therapeutic goal of self psychology in treating personality disorders (including the more cohesive borderline patients) is the rehabilitation of the defective or weakened self. This is accomplished through a psychoanalytic approach that stresses the recognition and empathic interpretation of the various selfobject transference failures in the therapy (Greene 1984). Thus, the therapeutic situation is defined not as a neutral observer interpreting conflicting ego states, as with Kernberg, but as an interpersonal field in which the therapist's participation is crucial. Therefore, it is important that the therapist allow patients to dwell in and consolidate the relationship with the therapist (Greenberg and Mitchell 1983).

Structural growth, in an optimal childhood or in the therapeutic situation, occurs by means of transmuting internalization (Bernstein 1982). In therapy, this process continues the work blocked during development. But for any progress to occur, the patients must develop one of the selfobject transferences, and the therapist must respond empathically to the patients' mirroring and idealizing needs. Inevitably, Bernstein (1982) remarked, the therapist has minor empathic failures, which may lead to transient self-fragmentation. In such a situation, the therapist must analyze his or her own behavior and empathically acknowledge the failure to understand or respond properly. Such interpretations restore the selfobject transference and consolidate the patient's cohesiveness so that treatment can continue. It is expected that the patient's ego functioning will improve with such interpretative understanding. In short, the cure occurs by "filling in the defects" in the self-structure by means of working through the selfobject transference and transmuting internalization (p. 102).

Adler (1981) has commented on the sense of inner incompleteness that temporarily disappears in the therapy of the narcissistic personality when the therapist performs a needed function that the patient cannot at that time. Rinsley (1982a) noted that when this occurs, the patient feels good, and when it does not, the patient feels bad. At this latter moment the patient may feel tension and turmoil or may have feelings of abandonment. Then the patient may lash out at the therapist in anger or "indulge in self-defeating and self-injurious behavior in a magical attempt to 'punish' the therapist and to force him to banish the 'bad' feelings" (Rinsley 1982a, p. 233).

The role of empathy in Kohut's model is so basic to the entire therapeutic approach that it requires closer definition. Usually, the term *empathy* means the momentary identification with another in order to experience vicariously that person's feelings, thoughts, attitudes, and fantasies. Most forms of therapy rely to some degree on the therapist's empathy with the patient, though Kohut (1975) offered a different interpretation of the term:

> I will first summarize my opinions about the importance of empathy in human life in general. I have compressed my views into three propositions: (1) Empathy, the recognition of the self in the other, is an indispensable tool of observation, without which vast areas of human life, including man's behavior in the social field, remain unintelligible. (2) Empathy, the expansion of the self to include the other, constitutes a powerful psychological bond between individuals which—more perhaps than even love, the expression and sublimation of the sexual drive—counteracts man's destructiveness against his fellows. And (3), empathy, the accepting, confirming, and understanding human echo evoked by the self, is a psychological nutriment without which human life as we know it and cherish it could not be sustained. (p. 355)

As Greene (1984) has pointed out, this last definition is operative in the much-used phrase by self psychologists, *empathic interpretation*. Greene also noted that this definition seems to conflict with other comments by Goldberg (1978) that there is no greater gratification in the interpretations in self therapy than in any other analysis. Goldberg (1978) has even said that the therapist does not actively soothe but rather interprets the patients' yearnings to be soothed and does not actively mirror but rather interprets the need for confirming responses (pp. 447–448). Kohut's definition of empathy, however, would lead one to view empathy as an "act of empathy" rather than a momentary identification and, hence, an introspective awareness of the other followed by an interpretation of the patient's longings and yearnings.

In an increasing number of case reports, self therapists openly acknowledge that they consider empathic interpretation as partly providing the patients with an appropriate response to their unmet development needs, not an interpretation of their need for such a response (Hedges 1983, Buie and Adler 1982–1983).

The following clinical examples may be helpful to the reader in understanding the process of making an empathic interpretation in this model.

Example 1

This example from Hedges (1983) refers to a therapy between a male therapist and a female patient:

> A week's vacation with Mother brought on a month's regression during which she turned to me for selfobject functions which had been stimulated but unmet by Mother. She expressed increased needs for confirmation of her experience, as well as for archaic forms of mirroring. The form of my empathic contact with her regressed briefly also during this month. For example, more than usual, I enjoyed looking at her. "Do you enjoy looking at me?" she asked. "Yes," I replied. My enjoyment of her was accompanied by a great sadness for her mother. I said, "What a shame for anyone to miss out on this experience." With that, the regression ended. (p. 97)

In reviewing the self psychology approach, Bernstein (1982) explained that the therapist must realize that the patients' needs to idealize or be mirrored should not be treated as the result of impaired reality sense. Rather, because the needs are phase-appropriate responses related to early blocked normal development (as in the above case, mirroring of the grandiose self), the therapist must show that the patients' desires, as revived in the transference, were appropriate in childhood, rather than dismissing these desires as simply being unrealistic now. These patients will then be able to express grandiose and idealizing fantasies because their desires have not been questioned. Their fantasies will eventually modify and mature the grandiosity (integrate the grandiose self) and produce a more realistic psychic structure. Confronting such grandiose needs only stifles their expression. Requesting the patients to form a more mature working alliance, which is experienced as abandonment, may also lead to transient fragmentation of the cohesive self (Bernstein 1982, p. 101).

In the above example, the therapist chose to provide the mirroring and not necessarily to interpret the need for such mirroring, a point the therapist himself made in summing up the case. This reflects a general move by a number of self psychologists to provide direct gratification.

Example 2

This clinical example (Goldberg 1978) shows that fragmentation in patients or distortion in their feeling states can often by traced back to some unempathic response from the therapist. It is drawn from the fifth year of analysis with a 39-year-old woman who gave birth to twins when her analyst was on vacation overseas.

> Despite her clear awareness that I could have had no way of knowing precisely when she would deliver, she was convinced that I would, of course, call her when she did deliver, particularly since she was going to have twins.

Somehow I would know, and would attempt to reach her by phone from overseas during my absence. . . . Despite the verbalized conscious recognition of the improbability of such an eventuation . . . it developed that my not having called her on or near the day of her delivery had been a terrible blow to her. I had been too concerned with myself to be concerned with her. . . . The inherent, realistic difficulties and the transference irrationalities of all this notwithstanding, I believe that *in principle* the patient was correct. Her psychological make-up was such that a special effort at this time was probably in order. (p. 340–341)

Here, the analyst felt that some special contact with the patient should have been supplied in order to meet her needs. Consistent with Greene's (1984) observation, this therapist felt that in this approach the "least possible frustration" rather than the "optimal frustration" of traditional psychoanalysis should be put on the patient (p. 52).

Example 3

The following example from Hedges (1983) shows how a therapist rectified an empathic failure via interpretation. The patient was a professional man in his 30s who had been in a lengthy therapy with a male therapist.

The next narcissistic injury was afforded Lou during the second session of the following week. It seems refinancing a large loan for his business was necessary in just two weeks [and he could no longer afford twice weekly therapy]. . . . Unempathically (in retrospect), I reaffirmed my stress on the importance of our time together . . . I offered to cut my fee in half for a month or so. . . . Lou was surprised and pleased. . . . The subsequent tension [loss of cohesion of the self] was manifest in insomnia . . . fantasies of establishing a new (more controlling) relationship with his family. . . . The tension was relieved in the following session when it became clear to both of us that I had once again insulted him with my interest and my good intentioned, but ill-timed willingness to do for him what he felt unable to do for himself. Tears again expressed his relief at the restored empathy as I showed that I understood the insult which I had provided in offering to cut the fee temporarily. (pp. 91–92)

The proper empathic interpretation restored this patient's equilibrium, and he was able to recoup and feel more cohesive.

There are few case reports using the self psychology approach with borderline patients, though the reader is referred to Hedges's book (1983) for several case reports of borderline children and adults. Hedges (1983) has suggested that the distinguishing feature of the borderline personality organization is the demand for some type of merger experience. Accordingly, in Kohut's approach, the need for a merger object is the borderline adults' most pressing demand:

It appears that *the subjective experience of merging personalities* must be accomplished in the therapeutic replication of symbiotic and/or postsymbiotic areas of arrest before the separation-individuation process can move on to the rapprochement crisis. (p. 131)

Merger here refers to two minds merging into a single, mutual cuing (Hedges 1983, p. 158). According to Hedges, therapeutic contact with the borderline patient takes a considerable amount of time and mutual accommodation before a sense of psychological merger can be achieved. The therapist can then come to understand the replication interactions (idiosyncratic early self-object relationship between mother and child) in the here and now and how they pertain to the there and then, and only then can differentiating activity take place. Hedges thinks that the patient needs the actual symbiotic experience itself in order to get better (see Searles 1976).

Blanck and Blanck (1979) regard the therapist as the catalyst of reorganization and have suggested that patients be allowed to maintain the fantasy of symbiotic merger until they are ready to give it up, with a little urging from the therapist (p. 242).

Chessick (1977) has alluded to an even simpler process, by observing that the more fragmented borderline patient seems to need the unification of a fragmented psyche that is brought about by the continued reliability of a consistent object and setting. It is enough to have an uninterrupted relationship. Thus, as Chessick notes, it makes little difference what the therapist interprets, for "the consistency, stability and reasonableness of the relationship to the patient" is now more important than the material being discussed (p. 85). Technically, this means that therapists may engage in some behaviors that resemble reparenting (e.g., allowing the patients special access through extratherapy phone contact or sending them postcards when on vacation). An example of a catalytic act might be explaining rather than interpreting the patients' subphase inadequacies. In this approach, therapists work in very small steps, slowly taking patients through a developmental experience until they are ready to advance to the next higher step. Rinsley's (1980c) years-long intensive work with seriously disturbed adolescents reflects this approach, combining reparenting techniques with technical analytic methodology.

Hedges (1983) found:

The "parenting" which helps a young child differentiate and consolidate basic ego and self functions in the second 18 months of life is strikingly similar to the process which a borderline undergoes during the course of analytic therapy. Many frankly call the therapy process "reparenting." . . . In any event, those familiar with watching the rapprochement of young toddlers continue to liken that period to therapeutic work with borderlines. (p. 130)

Hedges adds that it is not what clinicians do in the therapy but how they listen and respond that is critical to the therapy of borderline adults. Some theorists call this a replication approach.

Additional Aspects of Kohut's Approach

First, narcissistic rage and many other symptoms are seen as disintegration by-products of the loss of self-cohesion and not as primary symptoms often considered to be caused by the therapist's lack of empathic response. The narcissistic vulnerability underlying the rage is what is addressed by the therapist.

Second, Kohut (1977) felt strongly that part of the treatment was helping patients understand that narcissism and the need for selfobjects throughout life were neither pathological nor shameful. He believed that people should not deny their ambitions, wishes to dominate, wishes to shine, and their yearnings to merge into an omnipotent other. Such wishes may need to be modified but should not disappear. Kohut contended that all humans need selfobject relationships throughout life because the self can live only in a matrix of selfobjects, and it is neither immature nor contemptible to search for and elicit their empathic support.

Finally, Adler (1980), a theorist who increasingly uses Kohut's formulations, found that patients experience occasional disappointments with their therapist because of expectable failures in the therapist's understanding of the patient. The patient comes to realize that the object of his or her need-fulfilling desires is imperfect and withdraws part of the investment in the external object into the self, thereby strengthening the internal structures (Bernstein 1982). But if the therapist frustrates the patients beyond what they can tolerate, as shown by frequent fragmentation or rage episodes, then these difficulties will probably be caused by the therapist's countertransference problem or inexperience or because the therapist is operating from a different theoretical framework. Adler concluded that the good-enough therapist does not fail the patients excessively.

COMPARISON AND TREATMENT IMPLICATIONS OF THE THREE MODELS

Whether or not psychotherapists like it, they eventually find it necessary to accept a certain philosophical position, usually one that is consistent with their own predilections. This choice then affects and limits their clinical practice. As an example, this section will examine the ways that the similarities and differences of the approaches of Kernberg, Masterson-Rinsley, and Kohut may affect treatment.

With Kernberg and Masterson at one pole and Kohut at the other, the theories just discussed are sufficiently different that clinicians cannot adopt them all without grossly distorting the goals and tactics of each. The most serious current problem in psychoanalytic psychotherapy is the conflict between Kernberg's object-relations theory and Kohut's psychology of the self. The original Masterson-Rinsley tactical deviation from Kernberg will be discussed later.

Kernberg's Approach

Therapists who follow Kernberg's object-relations theory in working with borderline patients will focus on splitting. Such therapists will seek out manifestations of the split-ego states (both idealizing and aggressive) being projected onto them. These split-ego states will then be actively interpreted to the patients to help neutralize the primitive conflicting drives that maintain splitting and to help the patients form whole-object relations of the mature adult. Clinicians who use Kernberg's approach will rely as much as possible on interpretation and clarification and will use confrontation only in special circumstances. They will be empathic and concerned but in no way will make supportive remarks or use supportive gestures because such acts nurture the pathology rather than work it through. While maintaining professional devotion to the therapeutic task, these therapists also will maintain distance from the patients and their behavior, except for certain necessary treatment parameters that must be instituted because of the patient's self-destructive acting out.

In summary, clinicians using Kernberg's approach will operate under the following assumptions:

1. The etiology of severe personality disorders lies in early drive conflicts, as represented in conflicting object-relations units (*conflict theory*).
2. Aggression in the form of rage and envy is the primary cause of the structure of severe personality disorders.
3. The narcissistic patient is a subtype of the borderline.
4. Narcissism and object relations are closely related.
5. Narcissistic transferences are defensive and pathological (masking split-off paranoid and devaluing object relations). They must emerge in the therapy and be modified via interpretation.
6. Although the influence of the family is not ignored, patients are responsible and accountable for their own behavior.
7. The achievement of object constancy and the reduction of primitive defenses and resistances are the goal of therapy.

8. Abstinence (technical neutrality) and optimal frustration are essential to the therapeutic setting.
9. The therapeutic techniques used are clarification, confrontation, and interpretation of resistances, defenses, and primitive transferences.
10. The basic anxiety is castration or paranoid anxiety, or fears that forbidden drive derivatives will erupt into consciousness.

Kohut's Approach

Therapists who follow self theory will view splitting, rage, and all of the patients' behavior as signs of a lack of cohesion in the self because of a developmental arrest. These therapists will use themselves as a selfobject to mend the patients' fragmented self through empathic understanding, mirroring, and at times even minor types of reparenting.

In comparison with Kernberg's approach, Kohut's model assumes that the early mother–child exchange must be reenacted, not merely verbalized in the therapeutic relationship, and that the therapist must decide how the patients' expectation will be received. Thus, in Kohut's approach, it is considered acceptable for therapists to act as a selfobject until the patients reach a more mature level of development. This is because Kohut believed that the patients' development is only arrested—not completely stopped, but vulnerable to regressive dissolution because of early structural defects. Instead of being a conflict, their rage and other behavior are simply a byproduct caused by the lack of a cohesive self. Such patients operate in a sensorimotor or concrete mode and need direct help in progressing, just as a crawling toddler needs help in learning to walk.

Kohut's approach then revolves around the therapist's behaving as a good selfobject and demonstrating an empathic understanding of the function of rage. In addition, the holding environment and good-enough mothering are conceptually and experientially important, and the therapists' warmth, sensitivity, and empathic understanding are essential to the therapy. Confrontation will seldom be used in this approach.

In summary, clinicians using the self psychology approach will operate under the following assumptions:

1. The etiology of severe personality disorders lies in the child's unmet needs for mirroring and idealizing (*deficit and arrest theory*).
2. Aggression is a disintegration product or a reaction to the fragmentation of the self caused by the failure of empathic mirroring.
3. The narcissistic patient's inner world of selfobjects is cohesive, whereas the borderline's is not.

4. Narcissism and object relations are separate and have different developmental pathways.
5. Narcissistic transferences are not defensive (although they may be unhealthy); they reflect unmet needs and are essential to this type of therapy; and they must emerge so they can mature.
6. The parents and the therapist are responsible for the patients' behavior—the patients are not responsible because their needs have not been met.
7. The achievement of a functioning self in the area of ambitions, skills, and ideals is the goal of therapy.
8. Minimal frustration and acceptance of selfobject relatedness are essential to the therapeutic setting.
9. The therapeutic techniques are introspective and empathic interpretation of any mirroring failures by the therapist.
10. The basic anxiety is fragmentation anxiety or fear that there will be an intrusion of archaic structures into the mature self.

There are, of course, other techniques within contemporary psychoanalysis, such as the ego psychology approach of Blanck and Blanck (1974, 1979), which addresses the strengthening of ego functioning through clarification and a benevolent atmosphere. This approach is still a viable model for treatment of borderline adults and will be discussed in Chapter 11.

The debate between Kernberg and Kohut highlights two approaches to working with very difficult patients. Kernberg's approach claims that borderline adults must give up their infantile structures, confront their developmental trauma, and grow. Kohut's approach, on the other hand, teaches that borderline patients must be healed, must be lovingly helped to grow beyond their arrested development, and in many ways must be reparented.

Borderline adults should not be described as having deficits, Kernberg contended, because when a developmental process is stopped, a new pathological structure is created to fill the void. That new structure is more than just a deficit because it takes on a life of its own, and thus, Kernberg (1982e) feels, *deficit* is a good term only for organic brain damage.

Grotstein (1982) has called conflict theory a *weaning theory* and self theory a *bonding theory*. He views self psychology not as an ego psychology but, rather, as a symbiotic theory, a theory of psychology of selfobjects. Masterson (1981) has objected to Kohut's elimination of any differentiation of the self- from the object images, feeling that the exclusion of object relations can produce patients whose narcissistic defect is repaired but whose relationships continue on a narcissistic level. He further stated that expressing so much "love" for patients will make it more difficult for them to express their hatred. Robbins (1982) has noted that self psychology is discontinuous from the body of knowledge that precedes it and thus recommends trying to incorporate some of Kohut's ideas into the existing framework of psychoanalytic theorizing about infancy, object relations, and later stages of life.

It should be clear by now that each theorist has a fundamentally different belief concerning the basic nature of humanity. In addition, one might ask whether these theorists are even talking about the same population of patients. Is it possible that these differing approaches developed because of different patient populations? Kohut, after all, originally devised his theory for narcissistic personality disorders. This is a difficult question to answer because there has never been a systematic review of cases between the two theorists. It is likely, however, as noted earlier, that some of Kohut's published cases would meet Kernberg's, Masterson's, or Rinsley's criteria for borderline personality organization. It seems more likely that each theorist is dealing with the same clinical data, at least in part, but viewing them through a different lens. What they see and conclude are thus very different. Certainly the debate between these two approaches cannot be resolved at this time, and any attempt at synthesis would be premature.

Overall, the theoretical positions of Masterson-Rinsley and Kernberg are similar. Masterson and Rinsley are more interested than Kernberg is in the internalization of the actual process between mother and child and the myth that arises from that internalization. Kernberg focuses on structure, being interested in separation-individuation to the degree that it explains defects in structure, but not interested in the content of the mother–child process.

The greatest differences between the two approaches revolve around tactics in psychotherapy, not goals. Masterson stresses direct confrontation of the split-units as they are manifested in the patients' life and in therapy. In response, Kernberg (1978b) stated that he found the RORU and WORU to be overly simplified representations of the patients' internal object relations. He also found Masterson's style of confrontation to be almost "super-egoish" in its impact (pp. 153–154). Masterson (1981) retorted that an object-relations theory or therapy without the core individuation perspective would be aimless and unfocused. In addition, Masterson argued that his approach helps patients more rapidly gain control over acting out and that a more sophisticated psychotherapy can follow a confrontational approach. In addition, a confrontational psychotherapy can be taught to therapists who are not psychoanalytically trained. Because the majority of therapists in this country are not analytically trained, Masterson's approach can be both effective and practical, as it stays close to the clinical data. Clinicians can more easily learn and become effective using a technique that closely follows the clinical data.

Certainly it is more feasible to combine Kernberg's and Masterson-Rinsley's approaches, because both rely on either confrontation or interpre-

Table 8-2 Comparison of Kernberg, Masterson–Rinsley, and Kohut

Theorist	Major Theoretical Stance	Implicated Development Stage in Borderline Pathology	Status of the Self- and Object Images	Primary Etiology*	Major Technique
Kernberg	Object relations theory; less attention to developmental stages as phases	Rapprochement subphase of separation-individuation	Split contradictory ego states—libidinal vs. aggressive	Constitutional aggression in child and/or severe family pathology	Interpretation of contradictory ego states with structuring of patient's life, as needed
Masterson and Rinsley	Object relations theory and Mahler's developmental phase concept	Rapprochement subphase of separation-individuation (Masterson) Same with residual from symbiosis (Rinsley)	Specific intra-psychic structures: RORU vs. WORU	Family pathology—specific kind of mothering	Confrontation of split units (Masterson) Same, with in-depth interpretation as tolerated by patient (Rinsley)
Kohut	New dual theory: self psychology	Pre-Oedipal period	Defective self-objects	Family pathology—poor mirroring by mother	Empathic interpretation of wounds and defects

*All these experts recognize the mutual influence of genetic, psychophysiologic, familial, and developmental factors on personality development.

tation weaning behavior in the here and now, than it is to combine Kohut's and Kernberg's approaches, because both their strategies and tactics are so different.

The following example illustrates these three approaches. Given the same patient, these are the ways that each would interpret or confront the process:

> *Kernberg*: I believe that a part of you wants me to step in and give you advice and to treat you as a helpless child, and yet if I do so, you will see me as a dominating parent trying to take over your life and run it for you.

> *Masterson-Rinsley*: I am astonished that you see yourself as so helpless in this matter and I as somehow so powerful and all-knowing. I wonder why you don't stand up for yourself!

> *Kohut*: When I didn't respond to your request for advice on managing your husband's angry outburst toward you, you became angry because you feel so desperate and scared, and you experienced me as not caring and not understanding how difficult it is for you to stand up to him, how much you need him to care for you.

There are no easy answers to this debate. The controversy in the psychotherapy of difficult patients can only be healthy, leading to yet new clinical insights into how to stimulate the resumption of ego development, regardless of whether the clinician believes it stopped because of a defect in structure, a conflict, or a developmental arrest. Time will undoubtedly resolve many of these issues.

I use a synthesis of Kernberg and Masterson-Rinsley, with a respectful gratitude for Kohut's contribution to the understanding of selfobjects, the holding function of the therapist, and his focus on empathically understanding and accepting the patient's inner world in all its nuances.

Table 8-2 summarizes the four theorists' similarities and differences on several dimensions.

Part III

THERAPY

CHAPTER 9

The Initial Diagnostic Interview

This chapter is designed to help the reader elicit clinical data for making a psychodynamically based diagnosis of split-ego states as well as the other ego weaknesses. It relies heavily on the structural interview approach created by Kernberg and his colleagues.

PURPOSE OF THE INTERVIEW

The purpose of a diagnostic interview is to learn something about each patient and to decide whether treatment is indicated. There are many ways to conduct such an interview, but those elements common to most diagnostic interviews include:

1. identifying the presenting problems
2. exploring the background of those problems
3. assessing the mental status/cognitive functioning
4. beginning to understand the patients as persons
5. reaching a working formulation of the patients' problems and making a preliminary diagnosis.

Most clinicians have been well trained to do such an interview.

For the clinician interested in determining the patients' level of personality organization (neurotic-borderline-psychotic), a special emphasis is required in the diagnostic interview. The interviewer must explore three target areas—identity diffusion, maintenance of reality testing, and pathological character traits—and use certain specific techniques for clarifying each of these areas.

THE STRUCTURAL INTERVIEW

The *structural interview* is so named because it has been designed to determine the patients' psychostructural organization. As Kernberg (1981) explained, the structural interview focuses sharply on "the relation between the interaction of patient and diagnostician, the patient's interpersonal functioning in general, and the history of the present illness" (p. 169). In a structural interview, the therapist follows the patient's lead instead of a prescribed set of questions, as in a questionnaire. The structural technique enables the therapist to elicit information and assess the patient's interactions during the interview. This information enables the therapist to measure the patient's degree of or lack of integrated identity, reality maintenance, and higher-level of defensive operations. Having evaluated these structural criteria, the interviewer then should be able to diagnose the patient's level of personality organization.

Features of the Structural Interview

The structural interview combines the following features (Kernberg 1981, p. 170):

1. Aspects of a mental status examination.
2. A psychoanalytic interview emphasizing the patient–interviewer interaction.
3. Clarification, confrontation, and interpretation of manifestations of identity diffusion, primitive defensive operations, and reality distortions as shown in the here and now of the interview.

Kernberg (1977b) has pointed out that the confrontation and interpretation of conflictual areas of the personality do subject patients to some stress during the interview. Although the technique is not intended to be a traditional "stress" interview, the interviewer is trying to create a situation in which the patients' pathology will show (Kernberg 1977b, p. 96). Therefore, in a tactful, nonjudgmental fashion, the interviewer attempts to acknowledge the patients' emotional reality while testing the depths of their problems and their ability to acknowledge these problems. This approach rests heavily on the patients' ability to recognize and acknowledge conflicts upon confrontation. This conscious acknowledgment is a key component in the diagnosis of a borderline personality organization.

The structural interview uses a search pattern that "cycles" through each of the following criteria. First, the interviewer evaluates the presenting symptoms, then the pathological character traits (e.g., masochism, narcissism, lying), then identity diffusion, and finally, sensorium, intelligence, and reality orientation. The therapist clarifies, confronts, and interprets each target area. If the patients show psychotic processes or organic impairment at any point during this cycling process, however, the interviewer immediately switches to a more traditional interview in order to avoid triggering dysfunctional behavior. The exact cycling approach is highly dependent on what emerges in the interview.

Guidelines for Administering the Structural Interview

Kernberg (1981) devised the following guidelines for administering the structural interview:

1. The interview requires approximately 1½ hours. Kernberg recommends two 45-minute segments separated by a small break.
2. The psychosocial history allows the interviewer to see the repetition of current problems as played out in the past. Therefore, a brief psychosocial history should be taken at the *end* of the structural interview. It is taken last because personal histories from borderline and psychotic persons are notoriously unreliable, being highly colored by primitive fantasies. Thus, asking for a psychosocial history at the beginning of the session allows borderline patients to hide their anxieties and defensive operations.
3. A brief history of antisocial acts also should be obtained. This information has prognostic importance because people with such a history do not do well in individual psychotherapy.
4. The closer patients are to the psychotic end of the spectrum, the more the interview format should resemble a traditional mental status and history-taking technique. Because borderline adults probably have been in the mental health environment before, they should be used to conventional interview methods. Thus, they expect a conventional approach, which allows them to deal with the safer historical material from outside the session. It also avoids stirring up highly threatening material.
5. The interviewer must (a) see the world through the patients' eyes, and (b) observe the process between himself or herself and the patients and note personal subjective reactions that are stirred up by the patients' material. *Material* is used here to describe what patients say, their body language, and the unconscious meanings that the interviewer ascribes to the patients' comments.
6. Finally, the interviewer mentally builds up a model of the patients' self-images and interpersonal relations. At the same time, it is necessary to determine what is realistic in the patient's thoughts, feelings, and behavior and tactfully to confront unrealistic aspects in order to assess the patients' reality testing.

Every interview is different, and no general rules apply to all situations. Therefore, the therapist should be creative, use intuition and common sense, and be familiar with psychodynamics. Above all, the therapist must be prepared for all kinds of unexpected contingencies.

Although this book is not intended to teach the reader all of the techniques, it does present the basic ideas of structural interviewing as summarized in Kernberg (1977b, 1981). It is intended as a broad overview rather than a schematic or computer program on the subject. Most instruction in structural interview techniques must take place under the supervision of clinicians familiar with the approach. In addition, this book concentrates on techniques for distinguishing the borderline from the psychotic or neurotic personality organization.

Interview Techniques

Kernberg (1981) suggested that three techniques—clarification, confrontation, and interpretation—be used in a cycling approach in the structural interview.

Clarification refers to the nonchallenging exploration of all elements that remain unclear to the patients, the interviewer, or both. Clarification is completed when the patients cannot explicate any further and remain puzzled or when the patients and interviewer reach a common view of the material.

Confrontation is the tactful pointing out of areas, either cognitive or affective, that seem contradictory or incongruent. A common example of a contradiction occurs when patients deny being sad but have tears in their eyes. An example of contradiction between an occurrence in the past and material in the here and now is "You say you love your mother, but you tried to strangle her last week." During confrontation, the patients' attention is drawn to material that they have previously presented but contradicts the material now being discussed. The interviewer raises the possibility of significance between this contradictory behavior and the patients' current level of functioning. This starts the process of reality testing. If patients are able to reflect more deeply because of this confrontation, the interviewer may suggest that there is a connection between their contradictory behavior and their overall personality difficulties.

During *interpretation,* the therapist links data gained during the interview with what he or she has hypothesized to be the patients' underlying anxieties or conflicts. Then the therapist explores the origins of the split-ego states, defensive transient abandonment of reality testing, and maintenance of primitive defense operations. Interpretation introduces new elements, such as underlying unconscious motives and defenses that can explain the patients' contradictory behavior.

At times the interviewer may wish to make a *transference interpretation,* that is, to comment that the patients are reacting to the interviewer in a certain way because of unconscious reenactment in the present of past disturbed relations with significant others (Kernberg 1977b, pp. 94–96, 1981, p. 170). For example, a male patient who is forever asking for advice may be idealizing the interviewer as a result of being infantalized by his parents. He may also react with childlike suspicion, accusing the therapist of preventing him from having his own apartment or from having a girlfriend.

Kernberg (1977b) provided the following example of the interview process: The therapist confronts a patient by pointing out that he is acting suspicious of the therapist and then exploring the patient's awareness of his own suspiciousness. The therapist interprets by suggesting that the patient is suspicious because he is attributing to the interviewer something "bad" that he is trying to eliminate in himself. And the therapist makes a transference interpretation by explaining that the patient is now struggling with an internal enemy that has the characteristics of suspiciousness because he once experienced a similar interaction with his parents (pp. 95–96).

Tasks of the Structural Interview

Kernberg (1981) stated that there are a number of ways to orchestrate the interview; in fact, the material that comes from the patients may dictate the interview's final format. Kernberg personally recommends the approach developed in this section. The tasks facing the interviewer are

1. Obtain information about the patients' symptoms. Assess reality testing by means of clarification, confrontation, and interpretation.
2. Elicit information on pathological character traits. Assess reality testing by means of clarification, confrontation, and interpretation.
3. Assess patients' identity diffusion, particularly in the here and now of the interview. Assess reality testing by means of clarification, confrontation, and interpretation.
4. Evaluate sensorium and memory.

The cycling pattern and content of the interview may vary according to whether the patients have a neurotic, borderline, or psychotic personality structure.

Well-put-together neurotic patients may give a great deal of information through their symptoms, including origin, onset, and development. Borderline or psychotic patients, however, may have problems in responding. The challenge facing the interviewer thus is to clarify the exact nature of the patients' difficulties in answering. Making this determination is so important that the bulk of this chapter will be devoted to investigating patients' ego functions.

How is this done? The interviewer clarifies, confronts, and interprets in order to identify the patients' difficulties in answering the questions. If the interviewer determines that the patients' difficulties are psychotic or organic, he or she then immediately switches from the structural interview to a more traditional format. When exiting from the structural interview to a more traditional approach, the therapist may want to share with the patients his or her perceptions of unusual affect or other disturbing elements uncovered in the interview. If the problems seem large, the therapist should move directly to studying hallucinations or delusions by means of the traditional mental status examination.

Because Kernberg and his associates have not published a user's manual for conducting the structural interview (e.g., directions about how to cycle) or rating scales for each of the key characteristics, I have pieced together some helpful hints from several sources.

USING THE CHALLENGE

As the interviewer reviews the symptoms, sense of self, relationships, and other observations with the patients, he or she should at each phase be able to determine the patients' ability to maintain reality testing (the major way to distinguish the borderline from the psychotic person).

Goldstein (1981a) has evaluated ego functions in neurotic, borderline, and schizophrenic patients. He believes, as does Kernberg, that borderline patients (1) lack an integrated *self*-concept, (2) have particular ego weaknesses, and (3) have a nonadaptive use of aggression. Goldstein's review of ego weaknesses is shown in Table 9-1, and the reader may find this review of ego functions useful.

Several parts of Table 9-1 require explanation. *Adaptation to reality* refers to the ability to maintain normal behavior, with adequate achievement in work or school. Reality testing has been defined earlier. *Sense of reality* refers to transient or enduring feelings of unreality (e.g., derealization, depersonalization). Autonomous functions include perception, language, and thinking as well as other functions that comprise the conflict-free ego sphere. Synthetic functions refer to the ability of the various ego functions to fit together and maintain a good overall level of functioning. This is clearly impaired in the borderline individual (see also Goldstein 1981b).

Table 9-1   Comparisons of Ego Functions in
Neurotic, Borderline, and Schizophrenic Patients

Ego function	Neurotic	Borderline	Schizophrenic
Relation to reality			
Adaptation to reality	Intact	Superficially intact	Can be superficially intact, but more often grossly deficient
Reality testing	Intact	Intact, except under severe stress	Often deficient
Sense of reality	Usually intact	Deficient	Deficient
Impulse control	Intact	Poor impulse control, low frustration tolerance	Poor impulse control, low frustration tolerance
Object relations	Mature, show depth, whole-object	Superficially intact, but tend to be part object and need fulfilling	Lack depth, tend to be part object and need fulfilling
Thought processes	Secondary process	Secondary process, but can regress to primary process in unstructured situations	Proclivity to primary process
Defenses	More mature, center around repression	Proclivity to use more primitive defenses: splitting, denial, projection, etc.	In addition to borderline defenses, often use even more primitive defenses, such as fusion, dedifferentiation, fragmentation delusions, hallucinations, etc.
Autonomous functions	Intact	Intact	Intact
Synthetic function	Intact	Impaired	Impaired

Source: Goldstein, W. N. (1981a). The borderline personality. *Psychiatric Annals, 11*(8):24. Copyright 1981 by Charles B. Slack, Inc. Reprinted by permission.

When used in the structural interview format, confrontation, clarification, and interpretation take on the quality of a "challenge" to the patients' usual defenses and distortions. Although not much has been written about the qualities or dimensions of the challenge, the following statements are based on Kernberg's articles. The challenge must

1. Occur in the arena of the patients' important structural conflicts. It must not occur in nonconflicted areas (e.g., many schizophrenic patients, if asked whether it is raining when it is sunny outside, will be able to give a reality-based answer, though this gives little useful information for a structural diagnosis).
2. Be appropriately stated, neither too persistent nor so intense that it disorganizes the patients (e.g., any patient can be "broken" or lose some reality testing through interrogation methods).
3. Be followed by clarification so that the patients have an opportunity to correct themselves if they have misunderstood the challenge.
4. Be used at each juncture in the interview so that the patients' reality maintenance is constantly retested.
5. Be stopped immediately if the patients show psychotic or organic symptoms.

The following examples of Kernberg's use of the challenge are found in Stone (1980, pp. 299–304). Although they were not necessarily conducted by Stone himself, they show the basic approach of challenging the beliefs of a neurotic, a borderline, and a psychotic patient.

Stone has offered a helpful hint to interviewers using this approach. Neurotic persons, he stated, respond appropriately to fairly mild confrontation. Borderline adults may require very strong confrontation, several times, to acknowledge the conflicts. Psychotic adults do not acknowledge the confrontation, and their behavior worsens, which may be manifested by regression, increased chaotic thinking or affect, or extremely rigid denial of reality.

Example 1: Confrontation in a Patient with Psychotic Structure

Interviewer: Are you convinced that reversing the order of how you eat your breakfast "caused" your grandfather's death?

Patient: Yes. The Force told me something terrible would happen if I made one false move.

Interviewer: This is like saying, in effect, your thoughts could cause someone to die!

Patient: Yes.

Interviewer: You see yourself as such a powerful person?

Patient: But they're not *my* thoughts! Those are the thoughts put in my head by this Force.

Interviewer: Might it not have been you were annoyed about your grandfather, though? After all, you told me earlier, you had to sleep on a couch in the living room because your parents gave him your room when he came back from the hospital. And he coughed all night and kept you up . . . that could make you angry, couldn't it?

Patient: No! Never!

Interviewer: No? You could have had no fleeting fantasy of his dying . . . ?

Patient: No! I'm convinced.

Example 2: A More Subtle Example of Psychotic Structure

Consultant: What led to your coming here?

Patient: Well, I don't know really. I mean, I made this suicide attempt which I'd been thinking about making for a couple of weeks . . . a month or so, maybe . . . but then, I made an attempt last year and they didn't put me in, so I don't know why they did this time.

Consultant: What did the attempt consist of? . . . I mean, this last one.

Patient: I tried to hang myself. . . . But the cord broke.

Consultant: Oh? (*Pause*)

Patient: (*Smiling cryptically and looking away from the consultant*)

Consultant: How would you size up this attempt? How serious does it seem to you?

Patient: Well, ya' know . . . I was planning this for a long time. I really thought I would die. I didn't see any point in going on. . . . But then, the cord broke, and I didn't die, and . . . (*smiling cryptically again*) here I am!

Consultant: You say this as though it were not too serious a matter. Yet it seems that only a chance thing saved you: the cord snapping unexpectedly. For me there's a big contrast between your saying, in effect, that it wasn't anything much, and your description of an extremely serious suicide attempt. You were even expressing some surprise that "they" saw fit to hospitalize you.

Patient: But last year they just let me stay at home. My parents brought me to my therapist . . . I had taken a few sleeping pills . . . and he saw that I was OK, so he said I could go home . . .

Consultant: Your comment suggests to me two things: first, you regard the hanging attempt as no different from taking a few pills, and second, you believe the therapist last year was acting appropriately in not getting too worked up over a suicide attempt. Is that how you see things?

Patient: Well, I don't know. (*Pause*) I'm OK now. I'm not thinking of suicide now. So I don't know why I'm being asked to remain in the hospital. I'm not thinking of it actively. . . .

Consultant: Suicide is still in the back of your mind?

Patient: Oh, sure. I can't see living beyond the age of . . . (*pause*) So someday I probably will . . . kill myself.

Consultant: Wouldn't that state of mind, if your relatives had any awareness of it, make them want to pursue a conservative course, and have you here for safety's sake?

Patient: Well, last year, ya' know . . . nobody put me in the hospital then, and . . .

Consultant: (*Interrupting*) You know, I'm not really sure I'm getting through to you. I keep asking you to tell me what *your* impression is about the apparent contradiction between these suicidal feelings you speak of, and how you react in the face of them . . . and you always switch to something else.

Patient: Well, I just think you're trying to make something out of nothing. . . .

This patient, who did not exhibit a formal thought disorder or any productive signs of psychosis (recently), showed nonetheless a bland unconcern for the gravity of her suicide attempts. Fairly strong confrontation did not break through her denial. Her structure was thus considered psychotic. Clinically, she was thought to have a schizoaffective disorder.

Example 3: Confrontation with a Borderline Patient

Consultant: What led to your hospitalization?

Patient: I made a suicide attempt. There was a string of them, over the past few months.

Consultant: I see. And what seemed to prompt them?

Patient: I was having this intense relationship with a man. It was too intense, I guess. Anyhow, after a year or so of being together, he told me he didn't want to see me anymore.

Consultant: Uh huh.

Patient: I told him, "I want to die!" I felt worthless. I took an overdose of pills. Three separate times. This last time it was aspirin and some phenobarb.

Consultant: "Some"? Did you take a lot, or. . . .

Patient: No, only a few. I didn't really want to die. I just couldn't go on, though. I wanted him to feel really bad.

Consultant: You were feeling vengeful, in other words?

Patient: Yes, I felt angry; I couldn't see how else I could make him understand how I felt or what he did to me. I had become so withdrawn after we broke up. The whole world seemed unreal to me. . . .

Consultant: How do you mean, "unreal"?

Patient: I was scared; I felt like an automaton. Just going through the motion of things. I was panicky much of the time. And I felt terribly depressed, though I couldn't say exactly why, at the time. I felt people could see through me, somehow, and just sense what I was feeling, like they could read my mind. . . .

Consultant: Did you feel they could do that literally?

Patient: No, never that far! It was more a question of my hoping, actually, that my friends, especially, could know how I was hurting without my having to repeat the whole story. Without having to say how hurt and angry I was.

Consultant: But what was behind your doing such dramatic things to make your feelings known to your boyfriend or your other friends . . . ?

Patient: I don't know exactly. But all my life I feel I don't know who I am. I idolized this one, I looked up to that one, I worshiped my boyfriend. . . . If one of them let me down, I felt crushed. Like I was no one without *them*. I was so busy being Mr. L.'s daughter and Timothy's sister, and so forth. . . . When they go away, I feel there's no "me" anymore . . . no reason to go on.

Consultant: How does that strike you now, as you relate all this to me?

Patient: I know it doesn't hold up. I mean, I know there's a "me," even though I get so lonely I can't bear to go on. Even when my boyfriend left me, there was still a "me" that was left behind—but it's a "me" I can't stand . . . so empty feeling . . . and helpless. . . . I sometimes invent people in my mind, who think I'm fine, talented, and so forth . . . but I know that's only fantasy.

Despite her feeling of helplessness, this patient had functioned quite well at her work for several years. Reality testing was intact, as exemplified by her being able to say that the notion people could "read her mind" was only a fantasy, as was the conjuring up of admirers in her mind's eye. At the same time her sense of identity was very undeveloped. She saw herself and also others as alternately all excellent or all worthless. Her tolerance for stress was low as was her impulse control. Other primitive defenses, denial, projection, and so on, were not present. Psychological testing showed good functioning on both the structured and unstructured portions. Clinically, she exhibited the syndrome of hysteroid dysphoria, manifested the features of Gunderson's borderline personality disorder, and had many of the features of Grinker's healthiest type of borderline patient—the anaclitic-depressed type.

Example 4: Confrontation with a Neurotic Patient

Patient: My mother warned me that I'd need a woman to cater to me as far as my asthma was concerned, as a matter of health . . . of safeguarding my health. And I went and told my fiancée the same words my mother told me: what my "needs" were, how I'd have to be "catered to" as if to say, "or else!" I handed her an ultimatum. For no reason! I should have realized she's such a terrific and considerate person, she'd fuss . . . if she had to . . . without my saying anything. Without my yelling about it. I got mad at my mother, but, of course, it was my fault. I didn't *have* to repeat everything she said right back to my fiancée.

Therapist: Mmmm. . . .

Patient: I notice also that my mother, who's ordinarily very tuned in where other people are concerned . . . , has little interest in my fiancée as a person . . . never asks her about what she's been doing, what her opinions are, etcetera. My mother only talks about her own interests in front of my fiancée. It's weird: I mean, here I am in my twenties, still repeating stuff my mother says like I was a kid. I wound up being very unthoughtful toward Nicole, which I don't want to be. It took some pretty long conversations to patch her feelings, because she was pretty miffed, which I don't blame her. (*Pause*) Why do you think my mother acts so different around Nicole?

Therapist: (*Pause*) You ask that with a very puzzled expression. . . .

Patient: Yeah, well. . . .

Therapist: . . . is it really beyond your imagining how your mo——?

Patient: (*Interrupting*) Ah, you think she might be jealous of my fiancée . . . the whole "triangle" business!

Therapist: Never mind what I think! What do *you* think? You're the one who's relaying the facts to me. If you have the facts at your disposal, I have a hunch you can spell out their meaning pretty well.

Patient: Well . . . put it this way: I like to think of my mother as being above that sort of reaction somehow. Like, I'd be the first husband, maybe, without a mother-in-law daughter-in-law problem. (*Pause*) Then, too, I kinda hoped I'd be completely mature enough so I wouldn't get caught up in crossfires of loyalty and all that sort of thing. I guess I'd have to say we're all of us "mere mortals" . . . a lot more so than I thought.

Therapist: You say that as though it's a bit of a comedown!

Patient: Well, I try to live my life according to certain ideals; I always hope the people around me try to lead exemplary lives, too. . . .

Therapist: But I think the difficulty you have is this: you equate the "good life" with *leading* an exemplary life; for most of us, *trying* to lead an exemplary life is the good life. You allow yourself no room for failure.

Patient: Yeah . . . I see your point. I guess I'm trying to walk too narrow a tightrope.

Therapist: Mmmmm.

This extract was chosen to illustrate the candor, psychological-mindedness, and flexibility of a well-functioning person with neurotic structure. Integration in the sense of identity was well established; the mechanisms of defense were restricted to those associated with higher levels of personality development. Repression, rationalization, intellectualization, and isolation of affect were the main defenses utilized by this man, whose more noticeable characterological traits were along obsessive lines.

Note how little confrontational pressure was needed to elicit from this man the awareness of the . . . [conflicts] that were surfacing between himself, his mother and his fiancée.

USING THE CHALLENGE TO EVALUATE EGO FUNCTIONS

The structural interview will be presented sequentially and simply, following Kernberg's (1981) recommendations.

The Initial Phase

Information about Symptoms

The typical initial questions to ask patients are what problems brought them to treatment and what they expect to receive from the therapy. Even if the patients have spoken with others before this session (e.g., intake staff), the interviewer should ask them to tell their story in their own words. Thus, the interview starts at the beginning of the cycle, presenting symptoms and conflicts.

As the patients begin talking, the interviewer should note any psychotic material or manifestations or distortions in sensorium, memory, or intelligence. The interviewer may ask for specific information about the symptoms, their onset, and their development. In the well-put-together patients, this relating of symptoms may give considerable information about all the other target areas as well. If the patients are unable to answer, the interviewer must ascertain why.

A Brief Review of Reality Testing

Reality testing is the most important dimension that distinguishes between borderline and psychotic personality organization, and therefore, it must be explored fully as the therapist cycles around the cardinal symptoms and structures. Reality testing has three components: (1) the absence of hallucinations or delusions; (2) the absence of bizarre thoughts, feelings, or behavior; and (3) the ability to empathize with others' reactions to one's own behavior. The extreme situation would be represented by pervasive delusions. The borderline patient can have alterations in the sense of reality (e.g., depersonalization).

Stone (1980, pp. 304–310) believes there is a continuum for reality testing; Kernberg, on the other hand, treats it as a category. Stone prefers to rate reality testing from good through subtly impaired (as in the process of "double awareness" in which patients know, for example, that an illusion is in their head but cannot stop dwelling on it).

The Challenge in Assessing Reality Testing   Patients may respond to the interviewer's initial question in one of four ways: (1) they may answer in an excessively concrete, vague, confused, or evasive manner; (2) they may answer in ways that have only minimal or no apparent relation to the inquiry; (3) they may answer appropriately but get lost in details; or (4) they may answer appropriately and be able to expand on the initial question in a way that gives good evidence of reality testing. The first three stages of responses should be studied and clarified (challenged tactfully). If the patients are concrete or evasive, it will be useful to clarify tactfully the discrepancy between the question and the response. This can be done by inquiring whether the patients feel they have responded fully to what they thought they were asked, whether the question was unclear, or whether it was overwhelming. If they admit difficulty in understanding the question, it should be reworded and repeated. If they still have difficulty in understanding, this problem should be explored further. This process allows the interviewer to distinguish among confusion due to anxiety, psychotic confusion or misinterpretation, cognitive deficits, stubbornness, or alteration of sensorium.

Clarification is also necessary if the patients respond in ways that have little or no relation to the initial question. Examples of such responses may involve paranoid evasiveness, obsessive perfectionism in clarifying every statement by the interviewer, or a masochistic reaction (e.g., the patient breaks immediately into tears). The clarification of each of these usually reveals any loss of reality testing, psychotic or organic symptoms, and premature transference development characteristic of patients with a severe character pathology (Kernberg 1981, p. 176).

If the patients respond appropriately to this first question but get lost in details when attempting to expand the answer, once again the interviewer should be mentally exploring the following: In regard to neurotic symptoms, are the patients getting lost in details because of obsessive tendencies? Are they vague and cautious in expressing paranoid tendencies? In regard to the loss of reality testing and psychotic symptoms, are they evasive because of underlying paranoid delusions or other psychotic interpretations of the interview? In regard to organic problems, do they get lost in details because of problems in cognitive functioning, chronic or acute? Again, tactful clarification, exploration with the patients of their difficulty in responding (confrontation), and tentative study of the reasons for the difficulty in communication (interpretation) may focus attention on one or another of the major anchoring symptoms and may provide early cues to the patients' structural problems (Kernberg 1981).

Hints for Assessing Reality Testing Reality testing is measured both subtly and overtly. A loss of reality testing is indicated if the patients acknowledge delusions or current hallucinations. Bizarre actions and strange thoughts or odd feelings that they cannot coherently explain also represent a loss of reality testing. Finally, more subtly, the patients' inability to empathize with the interviewer's puzzlement over these oddities indicates a loss of reality testing.

If any doubt about reality orientation remains at this point, the interviewer should proceed with the mental status examination, asking specifically about delusions and hallucinations and noting any bizarre or unusual affect, thought content, or behavior. The manner in which the patients handle exploration of the interviewer's puzzlement over unusual affect, for example, further determines reality testing by measuring their ability to empathize with those aspects of their behavior that perplex others. Aside from the obvious questions one might ask about directly reported delusions or hallucinations, it is sometimes possible to elicit information about reality testing as the patients discuss their symptoms. The following sample questions are taken from Bellak and his associates (1973):

1. Do people often misunderstand what you are trying to tell them?
2. Have you ever been convinced of the reality of something even though everyone around you disagreed? Has this been about things you saw? Heard? Thought? (p. 425)

If the patients show a demonstrable loss of reality testing, the interviewer should end the structural interview. But if the patients show no loss of reality testing in response to the initial inquiry and if full information has been gained about the symptoms (e.g., date of appearance, development, and relationship to other symptoms), the focus of the interview may shift to the evaluation of pathological character traits.

Evaluating Pathological Character Traits

Once the patients are able to discuss their symptoms and answer additional questions regarding the symptoms' onset, length, and other characteristics and if they show no distortions in sensorium or loss of reality testing, the interviewer now can explore any pathological character traits. This is done by asking open-ended questions. The therapist states, for example, that he or she has heard about the patients' symptoms or difficulties and would now like to hear more about them. In effect, the therapist asks the patients to describe themselves and their personality and to include everything they think the interviewer needs to know. Kernberg (1981, p. 177) has said that this represents a yet deeper level of inquiry that requires the patients to reflect on themselves, their life, and their relationships with significant others. It also measures their ability to describe others in a meaningful and integrated way.

Some psychotic persons who have been able to "keep it together" to this point will not be able to self-reflect without revealing underlying psychotic processes. In contrast, well-put-together neurotics will be able to reflect spontaneously on their life and relationships. If the patients are unable to do this, the interviewer may have to ask more specific questions (e.g., about important relationships, job, family, sex, personal interests). If the problem continues, the interviewer should point out that the patients seem to have difficulties talking about themselves. The therapist should then investigate to what degree these difficulties reflect the patients' apprehensions about being interviewed and fears about the diagnostic situation.

Some patients simply may be unable to talk about themselves. If so, the interviewer once again needs to examine the nature of the problem. At this point, he or she may acknowledge that the patients seem to have difficulty in talking meaningfully about themselves and others and that it will be necessary to investigate the problem. For borderline patients, labeling this problem may reveal their primitive defenses for the first time. In effect, the therapist begins retesting for reality orientation. One can assist the patients by asking more specific questions, such as suggesting that they describe their relationships with people who are important to them, school, work, sex, leisure time, or hobbies. This may activate, particularly in borderline or psychotic patients, primitive defensive operations and interpersonal features of those defenses that are manifested in subtle patient–interviewer interactions. At this point, the interviewer can share what seems to be most unusual in the patients' affect, thinking, or behavior. The therapist can ask whether the patients can see why the interviewer regards these behaviors or aspects of the patients' presentation as strange. This exploration once again assesses reality testing, especially of the patients' capacity to empathize with the interviewer's perception of them in a broader sense.

Using the Challenge   As the interviewer determines how the patients see themselves and their life, a sense of strain or lack of freedom in dealing with the patients may emerge. Although there is no loss of reality testing, the interviewer may begin to notice some borderline symptoms. Kernberg (1981) has given this example:

For example, the interviewer may say: "As I asked you to tell me more about yourself, you first seemed puzzled, and then began talking about the way your husband treats you. A little later, when I asked you whether you had any problem relating to your husband under such circumstances, and why you were mentioning this particular example, you responded by telling me about other aspects of your husband's behavior. So, it is as if, when I asked you to talk about yourself, you seemed to be obliged to talk about how you are treated by your husband. That is puzzling to me; can you see that I have difficulties with this attitude of yours?" (p. 179)

According to Kernberg, the patient may respond in several ways. First, she may acknowledge her behavior and report that she feels overwhelmed by her husband. She may admit that she became so preoccupied that she did not examine how she felt about herself (thereby maintaining reality testing). Second, she may reiterate that her husband is treating her badly and then may ask whether the interviewer is accusing her of being at fault (thereby raising questions about her reality testing in this situation). The interviewer then clarifies the reason for asking the question, and the patient's response once again allows an assessment of reality testing. At this point the interviewer is engaging in the cycle of clarification, confrontation, and interpretation and is using the challenge to establish the degree of reality maintenance.

Kernberg (1981) has strongly stressed that it is useless to examine the next dimension, identity diffusion, if the issue of reality testing has not been resolved, because borderline organization is distinguished from psychotic organization on the basis of reality testing (p. 180).

The Middle Phase

Thus far, our emphasis has been on reality testing. Now we shall turn to the structural characteristic of identity diffusion, which distinguishes the borderline from the neurotic individual. This phase overlaps with the first phase for many patients if there is no question of a loss of reality testing. During this second phase, the therapist first uses the data gathered about the patients and others in their life. Second, the interviewer starts to reflect on the here and now of the interview situation. It is also here that the withdrawing and rewarding split-units of the Masterson and Rinsley approach may show up and be confronted.

Evaluating Identity Diffusion

As was explained earlier, identity diffusion has two facets: (1) self- and object representations are sharply differentiated (not fused or delusional); (2) contradictory self- and object representations are poorly integrated (the patients feel all-bad at one time and all-good at another time); and (3) there is a shallow, limited, manipulative quality to interpersonal relationships. Borderline patients have shallow, constricted, and/or contradictory perceptions of themselves and others. They cannot describe cohesively their or others' internal or external experiences, and they cannot feel defined or separate enough to put themselves in another's place and test out what the other is feeling (lack of empathy). If they describe another person as angry and the interviewer asks for more detail, they will reply that the other person is "an angry person" and often have little else to offer. It is quite difficult to elicit any speculations about the other person's motivations, and those few such speculations that are offered are usually shallow or stereotyped.

Kernberg (1981, p. 184) stated that it is useful at this point to ask for information related to identity diffusion and primitive defenses as manifested in the patients' current life and relationship with significant others. Only after this has been completed does Kernberg favor returning to the patient–interviewer interaction and commenting on manifestations during the interview.

But Kernberg (1981) does recommend one exception to this approach. When the question of reality testing has not been clarified, it can be helpful to use the interactions in the here and now to clarify the presence or absence of reality testing, as was shown in the example in the discussion of the woman's perception of the way her husband treated her (p. 186). To do this, the interviewer can ask the patients to describe other significant people in their life or to describe in detail one major current relationship. It is important to remember that narcissistic-borderline patients may show their pathology only by the shallow and unintegrated way that they describe others.

Kernberg (1981) likes to begin this phase in this manner:

> "I would now like to ask you to tell me something about the people who are most important in your present life. Could you tell me something about them in such a way that, again, given our limited time here, I might form a real, live impression of them?" (p. 182)

With borderline patients, such questions inevitably activate primitive defenses in the here-and-now interaction, highlighting the contradictory self- and object representations and inadequate object relations. Further clarification and confrontation of some of the inappropriate behavior and interactions (which are often reported by borderline patients in a matter-of-fact way) afford the therapist another opportunity to examine reality testing.

If the therapist must probe deeper, he or she might ask the following questions:

1. How would you describe yourself as a person?
2. How would you describe your strengths and weaknesses?

3. How do you get along with other people?
4. How close do you like to get to others?

As the patients describe themselves and their view of significant others, the therapist will be making the following observations. Relations that are pervasively exploitative, masochistic-sadistic, shallow, or highly dependent or are marred by idealization-devaluation reveal poor object relations. Identity diffusion is represented by marked contradictions in the view of oneself or others (all-good or all-bad). Psychosis is in evidence if the discrepancy reaches delusional proportions ("I am so evil, I must die") or there is evidence of merged self-object images ("I was walking down the street, and I thought a girl said 'hello' to me, but then I got confused; I think I was saying 'hello' to her").

Primitive Defenses   Primitive defenses centering on splitting are manifested by all-good and all-bad dichotomous thinking, primitive denial, idealization, and projective identification. Primitive denial can be detected if the patients immediately forget confrontations or interpretations or if they insist on clinging to a belief that the evidence refutes (e.g., "I am a bad person" in the face of accomplishments and good friendships). Projective identification should be suspected when the patients project one of their own characteristics onto the therapist.

As explained earlier, persons with either psychosis or borderline personality organizations use primitive defenses. The therapist can distinguish between the two by the way each responds to confrontation. Psychotics regress because confrontation of their defenses removes the protection from disintegration and/or self-object merger. Borderline patients, on the other hand, improve under confrontation.

Observing and experiencing the patients' primitive defenses may be more helpful to the therapist than asking questions, which are difficult to frame for such a purpose. Nonetheless, some helpful examples are

1. Have you frequently found yourself changing your opinion about people? Do you now disapprove of or dislike people whom you once admired?
2. When you don't like people, how do you tend to act toward them? How do you treat them if you like them a lot?

Using the Challenge in the Middle Phase   Challenging in this phase continues in regard to events in the patients' social life, particularly if the patients describe socially inappropriate behavior in a matter-of-fact way. When that is completed, the major focus needs to be on the here and now of the therapeutic interactions. If the interviewer has sufficiently explored earlier facets of the patients' behavior, by now the patients will be fairly well revealing their primitive defenses and lack of integration of contradictory self- and object representations.

Kernberg (1981) has recommended the following question when the interviewer decides to return to the manifestations of primitive defenses and pathological object relations in the therapeutic interaction:

"What you have told me about your life makes me think of something I have observed here, in this hour, and that reminds me of these difficulties you mentioned. Could it be that (such and such behavior here) is a reflection, in your relation with me, of what you have said troubles you with other people?" (p. 184)

In other words, identity diffusion and primitive defensive operations are gathered first in the relatively neutral area of the patients' life, and only then is all of this information linked with the emotional implications of these characterological manifestations in the hour.

Kernberg (1981) offered the following example of confronting and interpreting projective identification in the here and now of the interview:

"I notice that you have been talking in a very cautious and fearful way with me, as if you were afraid of some danger connected with me. I also notice that you have been frowning at some of my questions. . . . Could it be that you are afraid that I might think badly of you or attack you in some way, because you, in turn, are afraid of some similar tendencies in yourself, such as, of feeling critical or angry toward me?" (pp. 188–189)

Obviously, such an interpretation requires knowledge of object-relations concepts and some experience in making interpretations. For some interviewers, that would seem to be a fairly advanced interpretation to make at this stage of the therapeutic relationship. Nonetheless, it is an option open to the interviewer if the material warrants it. Here, the interviewer is developing a hypothesis about the nature of the primitive object relation and its defensive function.

The interviewer then notes how the patients behaviorally handle this interpretation. Do they acknowledge the interpretation, decompensate, or ignore it? If the patients decompensate or ignore the interpretation, the therapist then tactfully investigates further in order to measure reality testing once again. Again, borderline patients should improve under confrontation and interpretation.

Students often ask whether borderline patients might not show identity diffusion or primitive defenses in the history, the current problems being discussed, or the here-and-now interaction. It is possible that a very schizoid or paranoid patient will be evasive or will provide little information. However, typical borderline patients will give enough information to enable the therapist to make a diagnosis within several sessions. With borderline patients, neurotic symptoms tend to merge with grave difficulties in living, thus revealing their serious personality difficulties. Neurotic patients, of course, will not show such discrepancies, as their defenses rarely manifest themselves in the interaction this early and can be inferred only from the material.

As Kernberg (1981) reported:

> The more the immediate interaction between patient and diagnostician becomes transformed, altered, and distorted by such primitive defensive processes, the more their predominance can be diagnosed, and, therefore, an important structural criterion for the diagnosis of borderline personality organization confirmed. (p. 183)

In typical borderline individuals, neurotic symptoms tend to be expressed in diffuse, generalized, chaotic difficulties in living. It usually is not easy to obtain a comprehensive view of the patients' life when they lack identity integration. This difficulty, in itself, is often a good diagnostic indicator, particularly if psychosis or organic impairment has been ruled out.

Challenging the patients' processes must cease at any time they show loss of reality. The goal should then be to establish enough empathy with the patients that they feel supported and trusting, thus forming an alliance that enables the therapist to learn more about them (Kernberg 1981, p. 187).

Evaluating Sensorium and Memory

The evaluation of sensorium and memory will not be discussed in detail because it is assumed that the reader is familiar with the techniques required in the traditional mental status examination. It is at this point that Kernberg recommends a thorough history taking in order to compare current problems with their past manifestations. He also stresses the importance of ascertaining antisocial acts such as stealing and shoplifting. Because the antisocial personality does poorly in individual psychotherapy, it is prognostically important to isolate this dimension.

Terminating the Interview

The interviewer should allow enough time at the end of the session to reduce any anxieties released during the interview, to answer questions, and to discuss what will happen next. Kernberg (1981), based on a verbal communication with R. Michels, has suggested asking, "What do you think I should have asked you and have not yet asked?" (p. 192). This question, which may elicit new information and open other doors, is partially designed to determine the patients' motivation for continuing the diagnostic process or accepting treatment.

A CLINICAL EXAMPLE

A young woman comes to an outpatient clinic requesting treatment. Since ending a love relationship three months ago, she has felt "lost, lonely, and without any life goals." These are her presenting symptoms.

The interviewer asks her to explain the terms "lost, lonely . . . life goals." This is the start of clarification. She tries to explain what she means, but after a few minutes her meaning is still fuzzy, and she cannot explain any further. The interviewer then tries to ascertain her difficulty in answering the initial question. The patient responds that she lost her boyfriend because she is such an inadequate person, whereas he is "everything I am not— well liked by everyone, loving, wonderful, just about a perfect guy."

In the next breath she casually alludes to her current financial difficulties. The interviewer has a hunch that these events are somehow connected and asks for clarification. It turns out that the boyfriend departed suddenly with the couple's rent money and is currently living with one of the patient's female friends. Her tone is angry and condemning, but when the therapist points that out—"You sound angry"—the patient denies feeling negative and answers, "No, I love him. I'm not upset with him at all."

Now the interviewer feels ready to confront the contradiction between the patient's verbal and nonverbal behavior, pointing out that although she describes how perfect her boyfriend is, she also gives examples of behavior that would lead most people to consider him callous and insensitive. The interviewer asks her if she would like to reconsider her statement that her boyfriend is perfect and that she is not angry at him.

How she responds at this point will be highly diagnostic. If she can tentatively acknowledge that she has been systematically ignoring her boyfriend's negative qualities and her own anger, she would be exhibiting improved functioning as a result of confrontation. But because she storms from the room, exclaiming that the interviewer is trying to destroy her love for her boyfriend, this indicates that the confrontation has exacerbated the situation. It probably also represents a severe state of splitting, so severe that a denial of negative feelings must be total. It also represents a loss of reality testing (as well as low impulse control) because the interviewer was only pointing out the contradictions as stated by the patient, not trying to induce negative affects. Finally, her stormy reaction indicates, at least temporarily, her inability to form an integrated view of her boyfriend. At this point the therapist still does not have enough information to make a diagnosis, but certain potential problematic structures have been identified.

Within a few minutes the young woman spontaneously returns to the interview room. The interviewer tactfully confronts her behavior and examines how she understood the original statement. The therapist may point out to her that she says one thing at one moment and gives contradictory data at another, not seeming to be aware of the contradiction. Additionally, the interviewer may, after disclaiming any desire to impugn the boyfriend's character, emphasize interest in how the patient sees her boyfriend, her own feelings, and what this reveals about herself. The interviewer now is also puzzled at her reaction and asks her to look at her own cognitive process. How she responds at this point, once again, will show her degree of reality testing. An ability to acknowledge the contradiction and say something about it will show reality testing. The interviewer, then, can continue exploring the patient's pathological character traits. If she accuses the therapist of saying that she seeks out bad men with whom to become involved or of trying to destroy her love for her boyfriend, then it will be necessary to continue to clarify the issues of reality testing.

This is an example of how the interviewer might orchestrate a cycling approach. The patient started the interview with her presenting symptoms. She demonstrated some pathological character traits through the way she talked about herself and her boyfriend (primitive defense of denial, masochism). Then she manifested both splitting ("I'm bad, and my boyfriend's perfect") and identity diffusion (lack of integration of good and bad images for herself and her boyfriend, as well as a shallow interpersonal relationship). Because the patient's reality testing is still in doubt, the interviewer needs further data, including information gleaned from the traditional mental status examination of delusions and hallucinations. If the patient appears psychotic, then the interviewer will stay with the traditional format. But if at each juncture she can demonstrate reality testing, then the interviewer can begin recycling through the target areas as they were shown in the interview interaction.

A sensitive use of the structural interview is almost an art form, and the therapist must rely on experience to know when to ask questions, when to move on to another approach, and when to support the patient.

REVIEW OF THE STRUCTURAL INTERVIEW

In the initial phase of the interview there is a heavy emphasis on distinguishing the borderline from the psychotic patient. Evaluation of reality testing is crucial here. Once it has been determined that reality testing has been preserved, the middle phase of the interview is devoted to ascertaining whether identity diffusion exists; this distinguishes the borderline from the neurotic patient.

Throughout the entire interview, the maintenance of reality testing must be ascertained. It is usually preferable to ask first about the patient's life and relations with others—thus "searching for confirmation of indications of identity diffusion in the patient's information about himself and his social life"—and only later to return to these manifestations in the interactions with the interviewer (Kernberg 1981, p. 184). Verification of reality testing, however, always takes precedence over exploration of identity diffusion outside the diagnostic situation. Here, the confrontation of interview difficulties in the here and now is paramount. At the end of the interview, the interviewer conducts the mental status examination and collects a psychosocial history. Finally, the interviewer discusses with the patient the treatment options.

OPTIONS FOR TREATMENT

The clinician who has conducted a structural interview is now ready to review the treatment options. Several factors predominate at this juncture:

1. Are the patients in a serious crisis, or is their life chaotic enough to merit hospitalization? If not, then the following questions should be addressed.
2. What do the patients want in the way of treament? How motivated are they for intensive psychotherapy? What are their finances, and how stable is their life situation?
3. What does the interviewer believe is the optimal treatment, given the patients' history, strengths and weaknesses, and prognostic signs based on character pathology (see Chapter 5)?
4. What type of treatment is available at the facility or in the community for these patients, given their circumstances?
5. How interested is the interviewing clinician in working with these patients? In what capacity? Long-term or short-term?

Numerous experts agree that the treatment of choice for borderline adults is outpatient analytically oriented psychotherapy, a minimum of two times per week and lasting from several years to many years with the same therapist. But for various reasons, it is not always possible to give patients such an intensive individual psychotherapy. Accordingly, although our emphasis is on individual psychotherapy, all the major treatment modalities will be discussed to show how they can be used in a clinic or private practice.

CHAPTER 10

Individual Psychotherapy
Kernberg and Masterson

Most experts agree that individual psychotherapy is the treatment of choice for borderline patients. Borderline adults, who are still caught in a dyadic world, require a dyadic therapy to allow the original difficulties to emerge and be resolved. Of the wide variety of treatment approaches available, those developed by Kernberg and Masterson have been effective with many patients. Kernberg's expressive and supportive psychotherapies and Masterson's confrontive and reconstructive approaches will be reviewed in this chapter.

OVERVIEW OF INDIVIDUAL PSYCHOTHERAPY WITH THE BORDERLINE PATIENT

By the 1970s, there were two different points of view concerning treatment. The debate centered on the effectiveness of intensive psychotherapy with borderline adults. Knight (1953a, 1953b) felt that intensive therapy was contraindicated and instead recommended a supportive approach stressing immediate reality concerns, adaptation, and limit setting. Friedman (1969) and Zetzel (1971) agreed with Knight, pointing out that there is too much psychotic potential because of the severe developmental deficits for these patients ever to be able to tolerate the regression inherent in transference work. They explained that borderline patients had a difficult enough time even maintaining a therapeutic alliance, let alone withstanding the transference work. Friedman (1969) even recommended that hospitalization be kept to short-term crisis intervention because of the regressive potential in a hospital setting for borderline patients.

Numerous others, however, have used intensive psychotherapy aimed at personality restructuring. For years, such theorists as Boyer and Giovacchini (1967), Giovacchini (1979b), Rosenfeld (1978) and Searles (1965, 1978) have been performing and formally recommending unmodified psychoanalysis.

Still others, such as Kernberg (1975a), Masterson (1976), and Rinsley (1982a), recommended a psychoanalytically oriented approach focusing on confrontation and clarification of the pathological character traits and defenses, in the belief that this method would help the patients develop more mature, adaptive defenses and manage their life more effectively than would supportive psychotherapy. These theorists saw supportive psychotherapy as gratifying the patients' excessive dependency needs, thus fostering regression. More recently, both Kernberg and Masterson refined their points of view, stating that aspects of their approaches could be modified in order to use a supportive psychotherapy with the more regressed or less motivated patient.

APPROACHES TO INDIVIDUAL PSYCHOTHERAPY

Kernberg (1982b, 1982c, 1984) has stated that all forms of individual psychotherapy can be defined according to three dimensions: (1) the degree to which the therapist is technically neutral (maintaining equidistance among id, superego, acting ego, and external reality—neither giving advice or support nor being moralistic, hence acting like the patients' observing ego); (2) the extent to which transference is interpreted; and (3) the degree to which clarification and interpretation techniques are used (rather than suggestion and environmental intervention).

In *psychoanalysis,* the analyst is consistently technically neutral. Psychoanalysis requires the development of a full regressive transference neurosis, which must be resolved primarily by genetic-dynamic interpretation alone. The material that patients bring into the therapy regarding people, events, and conflicts in their life is treated as one would treat the day residue in dream work. In other words, the psychoanalyst views this real-life material as stimuli-giving information about the patients' intrapsychic conflicts, not as "real events" to be resolved, as a therapist might in other forms of psychotherapy. Additionally, the analytic couch and free association are used. Only a very few high-functioning borderline patients are appropriate for psychoanalysis.

Psychoanalytically oriented psychotherapy is known by a variety of names, including *expressive* (Kernberg), *reconstructive* (Masterson), *intensive* (Chessick), and *insight oriented.* Many of those who use this approach attempt to be technically but not strictly neutral, as would be required in psychoanalysis. Transference remains a central focal point of this method, which relies on interpretation as a major tool but also uses other techniques. This approach has the far-reaching goal of effecting enduring character change without a commitment to fully resolving the transference neurosis.

In *confrontive psychotherapy,* an approach created by Masterson, technical neutrality is maintained, and transference is emphasized to the degree that it highlights the split-object relations units. Confrontation, not interpretation, is the major technique. The goal of confrontive psychotherapy is to control acting out and to increase adaptative coping mechanisms. This approach prepares the patient for a reconstructive psychotherapy.

Psychoanalytically informed supportive psychotherapy does not use technical neutrality, transference, or interpretation. However, Kernberg's definition of this approach, which will be discussed in this chapter, is still more strictly defined in terms of technique than is usual in a custodial type of supportive psychotherapy.

Finally, *crisis intervention or brief counseling* also does not use technical neutrality, transference, or interpretation. In this modality, the therapist may offer direct support. Clarification, recommendations, confrontation, direct suggestions, and environmental intervention are major techniques. During crisis intervention, the therapist avoids transference in order to deal with real, immediate life events. The goals of this therapy are to help the patients feel better, function better, and experience new emotions. This form of psychotherapy can be quite useful for borderline patients. The only cautionary note is that the therapist should be wary of attempting to shift from this modality into an intensive approach. The very techniques that help the patients feel better (e.g., giving advice) in the present may interfere with the same therapist's ability to disengage from that role in the patients' eyes and move into a more exploratory one. Although giving advice helps the patients in the present, it may interfere with their eventual individuation and development of personal self-assertion if used on a long-term basis.

The above psychotherapies have different goals and techniques, but no one method is better than any other. Accordingly, the clinician and patient must decide on the desired goals, and then the clinician must select a treatment modality to achieve those goals.

KERNBERG'S APPROACH

Expressive Psychotherapy

Kernberg (1975a, 1979) has said that expressive psychotherapy is generally the treatment of choice for borderline patients, except for the poor prognostic exceptions noted in Chapter 4. Kernberg (1982f) summarized the definition of expressive psychotherapy as used with the borderline patient:

It has a predominance of clarification over interpretation in the early stages of the treatment; and throughout the major part of the treatment, it has a predominance of interpretation of unconscious meanings in the "here and now" over genetic tracing of these unconscious meanings into the past. Transference is interpreted in expressive psychotherapy (as in psychoanalysis), but transference interpretations are partial and codetermined by three factors: the predominant transference resistances, the patient's immediate external reality, and the particular long-range treatment goals. In expressive psychotherapy one tries to maintain technical neutrality but is continually challenged by the severity of acting out and the need to structure the patient's life outside the treatment setting. It becomes necessary to reinstate this technical neutrality repeatedly by means of interpretation. (p. 183)

The goal of this therapy is integration of the split-object-relations units, with transformation into mature transference paradigms, resulting in the capacity to work, love, and play.

Candidates for Expressive Psychotherapy

In theory, expressive psychotherapy is appropriate for most borderline patients, if they have the time, motivation, and money to invest in it. In addition, these patients must be able to maintain some tenuous personality organization in the face of transference phenomena, particularly negative transference and withheld gratification. Patients who require hospitalization or day treatment in order to maintain themselves and their lives while attending this type of psychotherapy are acceptable as long as the structuring is done by someone other than the therapist, thus this kind of therapy requires a team approach. Candidates for expressive psychotherapy should have no severely negative prognostic signs that contraindicate expressive psychotherapy (see Chapter 5).

Kernberg (1984), responding to questions from the audience at a conference, said that he is selective about prescribing expressive psychotherapy because he prefers to reserve this type of therapy for patients with a high motivation and some capacity for insight.

Treatment Arrangements

Expressive psychotherapy requires a minimum of two sessions per week, preferably three or more. It involves face-to-face sessions with the therapist in order to prevent regression. This modality may last for many years.

Ground Rules of the Treatment

Kernberg (1975a) has reported that it is the lack of structure in the treatment rather than the frequency of appointments that may trigger regression in the psychoanalytic psychotherapy. Structure includes systematic interpretation of primitive defenses, firm adherence to technical neutrality, and control of acting out within the hours, combined with structuring of the patients' life outside the hours, if necessary.

Lack of structure encourages the acting out of pathological needs in the transference, to the extent that the transference neurosis replaces ordinary life. When this happens, Kernberg (1975a) said, "The patient obtains gratification of pathological, primitive needs in the treatment hours beyond what he could expect in any other life circumstance" (p. 186). Kernberg believes that many borderline adults require help in maintaining their lives outside therapy. Therefore, he recommends that early in the process, the clinician analyze the degree to which external structure is necessary to protect the patients (and others) from disruptive acting out.

Kernberg often has other professionals perform tasks that many clinicians do themselves. For example, he may assign a social worker to monitor the patients' functioning outside therapy (e.g., living situation, compliance with medication regimen, maintenance of sobriety, attendance and participation in treatment programs such as day treatment, day hospital). Kernberg feels that such caretaking functions should not be done by the therapist because they add too great a parameter to the therapy, making the interpretation of transference distortions impossible because the therapist is indeed acting like a parent.

Other parameters also may be added even as a condition for starting or continuing the psychotherapy (e.g., an anorexic patient agreeing to maintain a certain weight, a borderline adult agreeing to discuss all suicidal feelings in the treatment, a patient stopping attempts to control the therapist's life by numerous late-night telephone calls or spying behavior). Eventually these conditions or parameters need to be explored and interpreted to the patients. If the patients violate any of the conditions of therapy, this is first interpreted, and if the behavior continues, it is then confronted. It is often necessary to reinstate technical neutrality repeatedly by means of interpretation. But if interpretation and structuring of daily life outside therapy cannot contain the patients, then the therapy may need to be transformed into a supportive treatment.

Principles and Techniques

Kernberg (1975a, 1982c, 1982f) has summarized the basics of this approach:

Maintenance of Technical Neutrality   The patients' projections would be difficult to distinguish from the therapist's real behavior without the maintenance of technical neutrality, because the therapist brings so much of himself or herself to the therapeutic process.

Kernberg (1976b) noted that in treating borderline patients, neutrality constitutes "an 'ideal' but ever transitory situation, which is threatened continuously from various sources" (p. 822). The acting out and constantly chaotic personal life of borderline patients often induce in the therapist an urge to act instead of interpret. Thus, the patients' prodding the therapist to act in a certain way in order to gratify their transference fantasies yields important information. Once the therapist understands this information and has his or her own countertransference under control, the patients' primitive demands for dependent, sexual, or aggressive interaction with the therapist must be constantly interpreted.

For this reason, suggestion and manipulation are contraindicated. Kernberg has observed that often reality-oriented, supportive comments given in a crisis are a countertransference need. The best way to strengthen the observing ego is to focus on the distortions of the patients' perceptions of the therapist's interpretations. The ego, says Kernberg, is strengthened by coming to terms with the trauma, not by gratifying in the here and now what was denied in the there and then (1976b, p. 819). But the patients' potential for severe acting out may require the structuralization of their life (e.g., hospitalization). These requirements are considered parameters of treatment that deviate from technical neutrality and must be interpreted again and again. The reinstatement of technical neutrality also represents a quantitative difference from psychoanalysis.

Clarification   In the early phases of the therapy, clarification predominates over interpretation. Clarification refers to the process of encouraging patients to elaborate what is in their mind in order to determine what their conversation really means. Clarification continues until the material is understood or there is agreement that no further meaning can be extracted at that time.

Confrontation   Confrontation is the process of tactfully and subtly pointing out the internal contradictions of the patients' material after it has been clarified.

Interpretation   After the early phase of therapy, interpretation becomes the basic technical tool. In contrast with psychoanalysis, which relies on genetic reconstruction in the there and then, this approach uses the transference process in the here and now mainly to avoid regressive episodes in which the patients confuse the therapist with parental figures. Kernberg (1984) has identified the premature interpretation of the transference as the single most important cause of transference psychosis. Clarification by the patients of any errors in the therapist's interpretation takes precedence over further interpretations, an approach that is also quantitatively different from psychoanalysis.

Transference Analysis Kernberg (1975a) has found that the therapist does not respond in normal social ways to the patients' transference, using instead a specific set of therapeutic behaviors. The following therapeutic tactics must be used from session to session:

1. Negative transference should be explored in the here and now (no genetic interpretations).
2. Moderate aspects of idealization of the therapist can be left alone (e.g., patients compliment the therapist about being smart) in order to foster a therapeutic alliance. Extreme idealization must be dealt with because Kernberg believes it represents one-half of a split-off paranoid projection.
3. Systematic interpretation of primitive defenses, even when they are not demonstrating transference, is crucial.
4. Blocking of acting out within and outside the session is important. When outside the session, this should be done by a team member other than the therapist.
5. The therapist must clarify the patients' perceptions before interpreting severe regression in the transference. The therapist and patients must maintain a "common boundary of reality" (Kernberg 1984).
6. Magical use of the therapist's interpretation must, in turn, be interpreted (e.g., "the fact that you are talking with me means you love me" or "the fact that I am silent means I don't like you") (Kernberg 1984).
7. Destructive sexual acting out must be disentangled from sexual exploration, particularly with adolescents (Kernberg 1984).

These analyses must be performed empathically and intuitively because the patients, who until now have kept apart their dissociated states, face enormous anxiety when they start to experience the parts simultaneously.

Kernberg (1982c, 1982f, 1984) has suggested several practical hints for these tactical moves. First, the following occurrences in the therapy take precedence over any other work that is under way: (1) if there is a danger to the patients and others from the patients' behavior; (2) if the therapist believes the patients are lying either through commission or omission (e.g., the therapist might say, "I am sensing that you are lying to me . . . whose problem do you think it is, mine or yours?"); (3) when the patients cannot develop a dependent relationship in the therapy and hence are participating only superficially; and (4) when there is paranoid regression in the transference. Only after these problems have been resolved can the broadest therapeutic work continue.

When there is paranoid regression in the transference (e.g., suspiciousness, persecutory accusations), Kernberg (1984, in press) has suggested introducing the patients to the notion of "incompatible realities," which means that the therapist and the patient see a situation differently; if they cannot resolve these differences, perhaps they need to decide whether they can continue despite their incompatible views.

Kernberg (1984) has emphasized that the therapist's countertransference should not be shared with the patients. When patients pick up on a therapist's reaction or countertransference reaction, the therapist should discuss it with them, without giving anything away or validating anything that the patients have not observed, because this violates technical neutrality (e.g., the therapist might ask, "What does it mean to you that I look bored?" or, if appropriate, can say, "Yes, I do have something personal on my mind. You have noticed that, but I believe I can still be helpful to you in this session.") It is then necessary to control one's own affect and analyze one's own fantasies to understand the situation.

Kernberg believes that extended patient silences in the treatment are not useful. When silences occur, the first step is to stimulate the patients to talk by asking, "What's on your mind?" If they do not speak or say much, the next step is to interpret what the therapist thinks the silence means and then to observe the patients' reaction to the interpretation.

When the therapist feels lost with the material, the steps to follow are (1) determine whether or not the patients are talking openly; if not, the therapist should stimulate them to do so; (2) if the patients are talking openly but the therapist does not understand the material, the therapist should then examine the transference and work with it to see whether that is the cause of the confusion; (3) if examination of the transference yields nothing, then the therapist should examine the possibility of his or her own countertransference (Kernberg 1984).

Finally, Kernberg has said that therapy terminates when the treatment goals are reached or a stalemate forces the therapist to establish limits. If a therapist establishes a limit by threatening to stop treatment (e.g., "If you make one more suicide attempt, the therapy will stop") and the patient transverses that limit, the therapist must follow through and enforce the limit to prevent his or her word from becoming suspect.

Kernberg has acknowledged several other important corrective and "good-enough mothering" aspects of this approach that reach the very heart of the human relationship between the patient and the therapist. He believes that for some borderline adults, the real relationship in the therapy may give a "corrective" experience. This is not achieved by directiveness or suggestions by the therapist, however. It occurs because the normal gratifying nature of such a positive human relationship transcends anything that the patients have previously experienced.

Another vital therapeutic aspect that Kernberg has identified is that the therapist's ability to absorb and transform chaos and then reflect it back to the patients in interpretation offers additional cognitive functioning for these adults during a period when they cannot do it for themselves.

As noted in Chapter 8, Kernberg believes that most, if not all, borderline adults have condensed Oedipal and pre-Oedipal issues. Here, he is taking the approach that as a person moves through the developmental stages, each layer of experiences is overlaid and influenced by the next layer. His interpretations reflect this theoretical stance.

In summary, technical neutrality, abstinence in the transference, preservation of the freedom to interpret the transference (rather than to gratify it), and the introspective and private review by therapists of their countertransference reactions are linked together in Kernberg's approach to the borderline adult (Kernberg 1976b, p. 823). In addition, clarification and confrontation are crucial in the early phases of treatment because they cause pathological traits to become ego dystonic (Kernberg 1984).

Supportive Psychotherapy

Although Kernberg continues to believe that an expressive approach in three-to-four-times-weekly psychotherapy is the treatment of choice for borderline patients, he recognizes that various impediments make such an approach unfeasible for many patients (e.g., lack of money, lack of motivation, and lack of public agencies that provide such services at a reasonable cost). Accordingly, he has outlined a less intensive approach, which he calls *supportive psychotherapy* (Kernberg 1982f).

Historically, supportive psychotherapy has been seen as (1) occurring infrequently, once a week or less; (2) mainly custodial; and (3) for the seriously regressed patient. Insight has not been a goal of this type of therapy, and unconscious conflicts and concerns were not touched. Kernberg (1982c), however, has objected to all three of these definitional characteristics, arguing that the goals of supportive psychotherapy should be broader and richer: (1) to help the patients control the consequences of their pathologic defenses by nonanalytic means and (2) to foster a better adaptation to reality by helping patients understand the consequences of these defenses in their daily life (p. 483).

Through this process, obviously negative transference may be highlighted, reduced by examining the reality of the treatment situation and used to pinpoint similar problems in patients' interpersonal relationships (Kernberg 1982f, p. 189). An example would be a male patient who accused the therapist of trying to boss him around (when the therapist was not doing so). This could be investigated from the perspective of exactly what the therapist said, the patient's reaction, and any similarities to situations in the patient's life with family, friends, or work. Although the transference is not directly interpreted, it can be dealt with indirectly through clarification and confrontation (as in the example above). In addition, the therapist can educate such patients and help them transfer that learning to situations outside the session.

The techniques of supportive psychotherapy, according to Kernberg, are suggestion, environmental intervention, clarification, and at times *abreactment* (bringing repressed material to the surface with accompanying emotional expression). Supportive psychotherapy does not use interpretation. The therapist may directly express support through cognitive means (e.g., suggestion, persuasion, advice, and information) as well as affective means (e.g., praise). All of these techniques, in effect, eliminate technical neutrality. Finally, the therapist does not work with transference, although he or she remains alert to it, monitoring its development and considering transference resistances.

Candidates for Supportive Psychotherapy

Patients suited to supportive psychotherapy include those with chronic characterologic aggression and self-destructive acts, those who lack the time, motivation, or insight for more intensive psychotherapy, and those requiring considerable structuring of their lives. Other issues that may tilt the balance toward a supportive rather than an expressive mode are (1) if the patients' problems provide a moderate degree of secondary gain; (2) if the patients present severe antisocial behavior; (3) if the patients' life is so disorganized that major environmental intervention is required; (4) if the patients have severe social isolation with a history of chronic absence of actual object relations; or (5) if severe, nonspecific manifestations of ego weakness are present. However, Kernberg feels that wherever possible, the patients should receive a course of expressive psychotherapy for some unspecified period to see whether they can manage a more intensive approach. Exceptionally severe issues, though, may contraindicate even supportive psychotherapy. Examples include chronic lying (with or without an antisocial personality structure), a history of negative therapeutic reactions with violent aggressive behavior toward others or self-destructive acts during psychotherapy (with a skilled therapist), and relentless, masochistic acting out. Hospitalization may be required to assess fully the tenacity of these behaviors. The presence of any of these problems raises serious questions about whether any kind of psychotherapy should be initiated on an outpatient basis (Kernberg 1982c).

Treatment Arrangements

The frequency of sessions can be adjusted from several per week to one every other week. The sessions are face to face, and it is important that the therapist keep track of what happens between the sessions and actively connect the contents of one session to another. Supportive psychotherapy can continue indefinitely.

Ground Rules of the Treatment

Kernberg (1982c, 1982f) recommends that the therapist and the patients need to agree on one problem area that needs to be addressed, clearly defining goals and objectives early in the treatment. Thus, the therapist makes sure that both he or she and the patients are involved in the psychotherapy. Both should agree on what areas of life the patients are responsible for (day hospital, medication, conditions for hospitalization). It is preferable to set goals aimed at improving the patients' functioning and autonomy, shifting into more custodial forms of supportive psychotherapy only when these goals cannot be met.

In supportive therapy, Kernberg continued, the therapist is more active in eliciting information about what has happened between the sessions than with patients in expressive psychotherapy. The therapist should not try to mimic the analytic technique by letting the patients do all the structuring of the session; this just contributes to transference acting out. In this approach, the patients are expected to talk about significant developments between sessions, and the therapist should scan the material to ascertain its relevance and to determine whether the patients are working on the treatment goals. The therapist constantly wonders, "Is what the patient is talking about relevant? Related to the problem we are exploring? Relevant to our common treatment goals? Related to what we examined last session? Does it include important new areas for exploration?" Vagueness is always confronted, as is avoidance of working on meaningful material. In this way, splitting (e.g., what happens in the patient's life versus what is happening in therapy) is confronted.

Principles and Techniques

Kernberg (1982f) summarized the supportive approach in this way: "The basic technique of supportive psychotherapy consists of exploring the patient's primitive defenses in the here and now" (p. 189). He discussed the following ways that this might be accomplished.

Primitive Defenses The patients' primitive defenses are studied in the here and now in order to help them achieve control over the effect of the defenses by nonanalytic means and foster better adaptation to reality by becoming aware of the disorganizing effects of those defenses. For example, tactfully pointing out patients' repetitive and unhealthy interactions with others is part of this process. Pointing out others' repetitive and destructive behavior toward the patients, which the patients tolerate while still com-

plaining about the others' bad behavior (e.g., John Elliott) is another therapeutic element. Systematic attention to this process often helps the patients
bring destructive interactions under control. The fact that patients often act
the same way with the therapist as they do with others helps the therapist
understand the process.

Transference Work (Negative)   The patients' negative transference may
then emerge, and it can be highlighted and reduced by consistent examination of the treatment's reality aspects. For example, John Elliott went
through a period of being suspicious of therapy and his therapist (myself).
Constant clarification of the reality of the therapist's behavior (e.g., she was
not going to terminate his therapy or psychologically hurt him, e.g., make
fun of him) helped bring his negative projections under control. This led to
the clarification of related problems in his life.

Sometimes, the outside life may be clarified first, and at other times, the
therapeutic relationship will be examined first. It is important to examine
the therapeutic relationship first when the existence of negative transference may disrupt the treatment. Transference is not traced back to its
unconscious origins, as in expressive psychotherapy; rather, it is dealt with
in a reality-oriented way. Thus, manifest negative transference is treated,
and unconscious, negative transference is noted and left for future work.

Transference Work (Positive)   The therapist should refrain from using
advisory, supportive statements and environmental manipulation if they
would exploit unanalyzed primitive positive transference situations (e.g.,
play into the patients' excessive idealization). The therapist accepts moderately intense positive transference but is cautious about intense idealization
because of the concomitant devaluation that is usually active in other parts
of the patients' life. The therapist makes certain that advice, environmental
intervention, medication, or adjunctive therapies are given on a rational
basis.

Role of Advice Giving   The therapist does not necessarily give patients
advice on how to handle their lives, particularly when they are capable of
doing so but are avoiding the responsibility. Rather, the therapist helps the
patients understand how certain autonomic ways of functioning are detrimental (e.g., idealization and then devaluation of former idols or unwillingness to look after oneself realistically). In such cases, the therapist does not
say, "Go assert yourself with your boss." Instead, the therapist asks in effect,
"Have you noticed that when you don't speak up for yourself at work, your
boss presumes that you have agreed to work overtime? What does your
reticence mean?" This examination of all-or-nothing behavior may help the
patients distinguish reality better.

Role of Reality Testing   The therapist clarifies any and all denial in the patients' neglect of serious responsibilities at work or in home life, together with the magical assumption that what is denied cannot have any effect.

Dealing with Acting Out   The therapist recognizes that a common type of transference acting out is one in which patients present themselves as the helpless victim of mistreatment or frustration by others—all the patients' symptoms are caused by another. The therapist acknowledges the patients' unmet needs but also explores the patients' own contribution to their frustration and difficulties. The therapist studies these patterns directly in terms of reality and not as they relate back to the therapist. In addition, helping patients understand other people and their motivation may increase understanding of themselves.

Role of Reality and Instinctual Needs   The therapist is mindful of both the needs of external reality and the patients' instinctual needs and must be partial to both adaptation and impulse expression. When these conflict, the therapist must examine the conflict with the patients (e.g., some patients' urgent, aggressive need to tell off the boss even when that could cause them to lose their job and their only source of income). Kernberg (1982c, 1982f) also has provided examples in which he was partisan to instinctual needs (e.g., sexual).

Insight Not Essential   The therapist does not discourage patients from deepening their self-knowledge, and insight is always a welcome by-product of this approach. But the therapist understands that what appears as insight into the patients' past may reflect a rationalization for continuing certain pathological behavior.

Misconceptions about Supportive Psychotherapy

Kernberg has identified the following misconceptions about this form of psychotherapy: (1) it is easy; (2) primitive ego defenses should be left untouched because working with them produces more regression; (3) the transference should not be focused on because it is not interpreted; (4) negative transference should be ignored in order to maintain a friendly atmosphere; and (5) highly disturbed patients cannot participate in psychotherapy, and therefore, therapy is something that is done *to* them rather than *with* them. Kernberg believes that these attitudes lead to therapeutic stalemates and should be avoided.

In summary, supportive psychotherapy is a treatment available to some borderline patients, which relies on techniques other than interpretation. Kernberg (1982c, 1982f) has taken the stand that supportive and expressive elements should not be mixed, although he acknowledges that this is a controversial position with which many analytic clinicians would not agree. He contends that in mixing the two modalities, the clinician dilutes the assets of each (e.g., in trying to be expressive, the clinician does not give enough support, but in being supportive, the clinician loses technical neutrality and contaminates the transference, which then cannot be accurately interpreted).

MASTERSON'S APPROACH

Confrontive and Reconstructive Psychotherapy

Masterson (1976), who formerly called his approach a supportive psychotherapy, now exclusively refers to it as confrontive psychotherapy. Although Rinsley played an early role in the development of this approach to treatment, he has since gone on to advocate a more mixed psychoanalytic approach using confrontive psychotherapy for the early phase of the therapy (see Chapter 8).

Masterson believes that confrontive psychotherapy is the treatment of choice in (1) the early phases of any psychotherapy with borderline patients, (2) when psychotherapy is provided only once a week, or (3) when the therapy is limited as to time. Masterson (1981, 1983a) has stressed the use of confrontation for once-a-week patients, arguing that the therapist does not have enough input to do more.

The overall goal of confrontive treatment is to help the patients gain control over acting out and to find appropriate sublimations for the abandonment depression (e.g., jogging). Only a subsequent reconstructive therapy, however, can work through abandonment depression.

Under the best of circumstances, after a course of confrontive psychotherapy lasting 1 year to 18 months, a reconstructive or psychoanalytically oriented psychotherapy is an "expansion and outgrowth" of confrontive psychotherapy (Masterson 1976, p. 93). The aim of this latter therapy is to work through the abandonment depression associated with the original separation-individuation phase, leading to the achievement of whole object relations, with full personal growth for the patients in the areas of work, love, and creativity. Masterson believes that the same therapist can be involved with patients who transfer from a supportive/confrontive approach to a psychoanalytically oriented one, because technical neutrality should be maintained in the confrontive approach.

Candidates for Confrontive Psychotherapy

Masterson feels that this approach can be used for all mid-range to higher-level borderline patients. Lower-level borderline patients can be given a trial period, lasting up to one year, with this approach. However, if these patients cannot tolerate confrontation without frequent regressions, the therapist should then switch to a more supportive or counseling-oriented psychotherapy. Masterson (1981) also stated that many narcissistic patients need a modification of the confrontive technique, particularly in the early phases of treatment.

Treatment Arrangements

The treatment sessions can vary from once to several times per week, and the treatment may last from several to many years. Confrontive psychotherapy is usually conducted face to face between the therapist and the patient.

Ground Rules of the Treatment

The patients are expected to take responsibility for managing their life outside the sessions. Only at times of severe regression does the therapist intervene with external structuring (e.g., hospitalization, medication).

Masterson believes that such patients are unable to use interpretation (for all the psychodynamic reasons stated in Chapter 8), except for a few here-and-now interpretations of transference reactions, and so he relies mainly on confrontation and clarifications. But he does think that technical neutrality must be maintained—the therapist must maintain an objective stance and not engage in any more guidance and direction than would a psychoanalytic psychotherapist.

Masterson has stated clearly that confrontation does not mean head-to-head or aggressive interactions. Confrontations can be statements given firmly but supportively or questions that imply an answer. Masterson (1983a) has said that he does not worry about some minimal indirect "directiveness," particularly if it stirs up anxiety and depression—then the therapy is progressive and not regressive in the sense that the patients are struggling with the core borderline dilemma. There is a "net gain" even with the slight directiveness. Patients must always perceive the therapist as an ally helping them get better. At no time is the confrontation meant to be harsh or aggressive; instead, it must be made from the position of being on the patients' side and with gentleness, tact, and firmness.

Confrontive psychotherapy can be used by psychotherapists who are not fully committed to a psychoanalytic approach and, thus, may be the method that can best be used by the greatest number of professionals.

Principles and Techniques

Masterson (1976, 1981) has summarized his basic approach and techniques as three phases of psychotherapy. They are presented below sequentially for the sake of simplicity; however, the reader should be aware that these phases can overlap, with leaps forward followed by regressions.

Phase 1. Testing (Resistance)   Testing is the initial phase with which all borderline patients start, and it extends from months to years. Masterson has noted that borderline patients, by definition, enter therapy with a great deal of resistance. The repetition compulsion (the blind impulse to repeat earlier experiences) is not to master conflict, as with the neurotic, but rather to avoid separation anxiety and abandonment depression (Masterson 1981, p. 136). Borderline patients do not want to give up the only strategy they have for controlling these painful affects; thus, they deny the destructive aspects of their acting out. Convincing the patients of the destructiveness of their acting out is the hardest task the therapist faces. Complicating this task is the fact that borderline patients do not have the capacity to experience a therapeutic alliance because they lack whole-object relations, and so they relate in therapy by acting out. To avoid the pain of the abandonment depression, these patients act out in the transference (e.g., alternately activating and projecting the WORU or the RORU onto the therapist). Masterson (1976) has observed that acting out is probably the most prominent resistance to treatment (p. 102).

Thus, the first task of therapy is to help the patients transfer their acting out to a therapeutic alliance; however, the therapist cannot count on either the therapeutic alliance or the transference to contain borderline patients in the way that neurotic patients can be contained. Because borderline adults are not about to give up, without a good substitute, the gratification they derive from the pathological ego alliance, these patients must test the therapist and therapy to make certain both are effective and reliable. The testing phase is much like therapeutic work with an adolescent (Masterson 1976, p. 100). Table 10-1, an example of a testing and resistance sequence, demonstrates various patient statements, the type of projection they represent, and what the therapist might do with them.

Different therapists operating in this model would, of course, make different remarks, though all of the confrontations should address the above process. The therapist could intervene at the end of the sequence by remarking,

Table 10-1 The Testing-Resistance Sequence

Patient's Statement	Type of Projection	Therapist's Confrontation
I stopped cutting school this past week . . . took my finals on time . . . and stopped calling home every day for reassurance.	Control over RORU. *Reworking*	No need to say anything because patient has confronted himself.
I was feeling really good about my behavior. Then out of the blue, I felt depressed. I needed a treat, so I took my rent money and bought myself a new stereo . . . and now I am too broke to pay my rent.	Resistance to the control. RORU activated. *Withholding*	Wait for sequence to finish.
I wasn't going to tell you. I was afraid you'd kick me out of therapy . . . and I couldn't live without therapy and you . . . you're the only person I can talk with comfortably.	Projection of WORU onto therapist with wish for symbiosis.	Wait for sequence to finish.
I was going to take the stereo back and get my money, but then I just fell apart. Why bother? I am never going to get well.	RORU activated.	Wait for sequence to finish.
Then I got furious at you. I wouldn't be going through all of this misery if it weren't for your comments about my destructive behavior. In the old days I would have just enjoyed my stereo. Now because of you I can't even do that anymore. SILENCE.	WORU activated as a defense.	Now therapist can comment (see text).

"I wonder why you get so angry at me when I am just doing my job as your therapist."

This is what Masterson meant by "stuffing" the WORU back in the patients' head. In other words, the therapist refuses to accept the projected anger, thereby making the patient feel the abandonment depression that had been hidden under the acting out. The therapist who decided to intervene at the second statement might ask,

"Why would you put your apartment and finances in jeopardy by spending money on a stereo?"

Or if the therapy proceeded further, the therapist might observe,

"Whenever you start to get control over yourself and your life, you get scared that if you continue to assert yourself, you will be left all alone. To fight off that feeling, you do impulsive things to make yourself feel better. But in the long run it's always against your best interests."

The therapist might wait to see how this interpretation is internalized. But if the therapist is still young and acting out is still a major issue, simple confrontation probably is better.

It is important to note that in these configurations Masterson is eliciting the expression of feelings. Masterson (1983a) has stated that affect is the bridge between the present and the past. Therefore, therapists want to reach affect, not facts.

If and when patients get their acting out under control, then the therapist can offer a supportive comment:

"It is clear that when you put your mind to it you can really control yourself."

Masterson (1981) noted a paradox in this approach. If the therapist initiates (confronts) and the patients begin to respond (separate and individuate), they feel more depressed. But, as the resistances are resolved, the patients' painful emotions will be worked through and these patients will start to flourish. During periods of severe crisis, the use of drugs or environmental structure is warranted (p. 180). A temporary regression, however, is not grounds for ceasing the confrontation.

Masterson (1976) has emphasized that confrontation can be abused in the therapy (p. 101). Therefore, therapists must watch their own countertransference reactions to make certain that the confrontation is in the patients' best interest and is not used because the therapist is angry or feels narcissistically wounded. Masterson believes that the therapist must understand and control the countertransference. Accepting the RORU and

WORU and colluding with the projections are a prime cause of stalemates in the treatment.

A review of Masterson's various writings shows that his interventions in any given session are limited and focused and that his confrontations are often subtle, sophisticated, and elegant.

Phase 2. Working Through (Introject Work)   Many patients stop therapy at the end of Phase 1, particularly if their acting out is under control and their lives are better (e.g., they have often found healthy outlets for their abandonment depression). To enter Phase 2, the patients usually need to be seen more than one time a week.

By now the patients have controlled the destructive defenses, have become depressed, and use therapy and the therapist to work through the depression. This is the start of reconstructive psychotherapy, and it uses all the techniques of and shares the goals of psychoanalytically oriented psychotherapy. For example, when patients slip and start acting out, the therapist returns to confronting the transference acting out. The therapist must be prepared to switch immediately from working through to confrontation, though when the patients are working productively, the therapist shifts from working on day-to-day problems to dreams, fantasies, memories, and free association. The therapist then encourages investigation of the origins of anger and depression in the patient's conflict with his or her parents. Interpretation is used more in this phase.

Communicative matching must take place during Phase 2. At such times, the therapist approves the patient's further individuation, by discussing the patient's new-found interests (e.g., hobbies, career) (Masterson 1976, p. 103). Masterson found that it is almost as though the patients require some empathic mutual cuing (Mahler) response from the therapist in order to continue the individuation process.

But as the patients start to experience their newly individuated self, they again feel hostility toward their parents for thwarting them as children. With the therapist's help, these patients frequently discover that they have such intense, vengeful fantasies that they are even willing to stop their own growth or maintain symptoms to "punish" the parents. Masterson (1981) has termed this the *talionic impulse* (an eye for an eye, a tooth for a tooth), and speaks of the need to examine and work through this impulse (see also Rinsley 1980a). In other words, the patients must decide to give up revenge in order to get better (pp. 182–193).

During this phase, as abandonment affects are discharged and worked through, the following contribute to the patients' further growth (Masterson 1981, pp. 223–232):

1. The therapist's consistent reliability.
2. The dyadic character of the therapeutic relationship, which reinforces the

patients' symbiotic longings and projections and also increases their receptivity to new introjection and understanding.

3. The therapist's activities, such as

    a. listening, often the first time that patients have ever been listened to.

    b. confrontation, which does for the patients what they cannot do for themselves, until they eventually identify with the therapist and can perform this function unaided.

    c. interpretation, which broadens understanding.

    d. communicative matching, which provides a shared experience with the patients' new individuality, compensates for the defect left by the mother's withdrawal, and fuels their individuation.

Masterson (1981) cautioned that a major therapeutic error in this phase is mistaking transference acting out for working through (pp. 167–188). The reader is referred to his work for examples (e.g., allowing patients to express ongoing rage at the therapist because they are "working through" their anger at their parents).

Phase 3. Termination (Separation)   Patients can, of course, terminate successfully or unsuccessfully. A successful termination of Phase 3 includes working through the abandonment depression and enlarging the patients' capacities in all arenas.

COMPARISON OF THE TWO APPROACHES

After reviewing both Masterson's and Kernberg's approaches to therapy, one can well wonder how different these two approaches really are. On paper, the differences are there. Masterson believes that the impetus for individuation and the resulting abandonment depression are the core features of the borderline personality. Only a psychotherapy with this theme as its focus deals with the true borderline issue. Kernberg, on the other hand, believes that the splitting of representations is the core issue. Masterson relies on confrontation, inviting his patients to explore and supply the meaning of their behavior and thus, in his opinion, not feeding them with interpretative answers. Kernberg uses interpretations and does not necessarily consider them a form of emotional feeding, although he is alert to any magical usage of his interpretations. But when speaking on their therapies, presenting audiovisual tapes, and discussing case material, Masterson and Kernberg seem to share much. Both confront their patients in regard to acting out; both make interpretations only in the here and now; both stress technical neutrality; and both have a "weaning" approach to therapy. It is as important to consider the similarities in their approaches as to remember the differences. Table 10-2 (on following page) lists the broad inclusion and exclusion criteria for each of the therapies discussed in this chapter.

If one used Kernberg's definition, it would seem that most psychodynamically oriented clinicians in the United States are probably using some variation of a combined expressive-supportive psychotherapy. Kernberg's belief that one cannot mix expressive and supportive elements in the same psychotherapy is thus neither practically nor theoretically accepted by all clinicians. The adherents of Kohut increasingly disagree, as do certain object-relations theorists, such as Chessick and Rinsley.

Table 10-2 Appropriate Psychotherapies, According to Patient Characteristics*

Psychoanalysis (Kernberg)	Expressive (Kernberg)	Reconstructive (Masterson)	Confrontive (Masterson)	Supportive (Kernberg)
Neurotic Personality Organization (e.g., obsessive-compulsive, hysterical, better functioning narcissist, depressive-masochistic, and a few infantile personalities)	Borderline Personality Organization (e.g., infantile, schizoid, paranoid, sado-masochistic, narcissistic at borderline level)	Neurotic patients	Borderline Personality	All patients not qualifying for psychoanalysis or expressive therapy
	and	Borderline patients after acting out is under control	Middle to upper-level do best (lower-level may decompensate)	Patients requiring considerable social structuring of their lives
and	Some motivation	Has ego strength to work through underlying abandonment depression		
Highly motivated	Moderate introspection	Has time and motivation	**Contraindictions:**	**Contraindications:**
Highly introspective	No extreme antisocial behavior		Antisocial is poor candidate	Antisocial personality
Symptoms are not too urgent	Can control self-destructive behavior on their own	**Contraindications:**	Narcissistic patients may require empathic interpretation of narcissistic injuries prior to confrontational therapy	Those patients with enormous secondary gain
Has time and money	No secondary gain from illness	Has too many early separation experiences		Severe difficulty with verbal communication (e.g., mentally retarded)
		Lacks time, motivation, and money	Some lower-level borderline patients	
Contraindications:	**Contraindications:**		Psychotic patients	Severe acting out that cannot be controlled at all
All other patients	All the severe character traits, superego, and object-relations pathologies listed in Chapter 4			

*Information in this table is taken from Kernberg (1984) and Masterson (1983a).

CHAPTER 11

Individual Psychotherapy
The Mixed Model Approach

Every clinician at some point secretly yearns for a book that explains exactly what to do at confusing or desperate moments. Freud (1913) beautifully captured this wish (and explained why it is thwarted) when he compared psychoanalysis to a chess game (p. 123). He said that a beginning chess player could learn something definitive only about the opening gambits and the final moves; the rest of the game was beyond cataloguing because of the infinite number of possible moves. Thus, the majority of chess combinations could be learned only by watching and learning from the games diligently fought by the masters. The rules that can be laid down for psychoanalysis are subject to similar limitations, Freud noted.

Because the scope of psychoanalytically oriented psychotherapy is so much broader than that of psychoanalysis, it is even more difficult to elaborate precise, concise, or consistent rules about what to do in therapy. This is why the beginning student is often told specifically how to start and end the therapy but is given only general guidelines for how to conduct most of it (e.g., a few do's and don'ts).

There have been empirical attempts to study the process of psychotherapy in order to understand how process contributes to change. Findings from the Psychotherapy Research Project of the Menninger Foundation (Kernberg et al. 1972) and other psychoanalytic research projects provide some empirical information on good technique for severely disturbed patients, and they substantiate aspects of the material in this chapter. But because empirical studies of psychotherapy are difficult to design and carry out, their utility to the practicing clinician is limited. Luborsky and Spence (1971), in commenting on the paucity of such studies, reported an unsettling truth about psychotherapy and change:

Psychoanalysts, like other psychotherapists, literally *do not know* how they achieve their results, although they have searched longer and deeper than others, and possess a unique store of clinical wisdom. They have learned their craft from a long line of practitioners schooled in a master-apprentice relationship; the rules are taught more by example than by explanation. Much work must be done in a naturalistic way . . . to understand what makes a good therapist good. (p. 432)

Without empirically documented procedures, the psychotherapist frequently must turn to the conceptual formulations and advice of experienced clinicians. Thus, where there are no adequate research studies on the proposed principles of this chapter, the clinical experience of many senior therapists provides the basis for my recommendations. As Weiner (1975) observed, "cumulative clinical wisdom must be given its just due, lest uncertainty produce a paralysis of action" (p. x). What have we learned from the cumulative clinical wisdom of such senior therapists? Gitelson (1951) described the process by which patients get better, although he admitted that he could not identify exactly how the "cure" took place:

One of the as yet unsolved problems of psychoanalysis [psychoanalytically oriented psychotherapy] is concerned with the essential nature of psychoanalytic cure. It is not insight; it is not the recall of infantile memories; it is not catharsis or abreaction; it is not the relationship to the analyst [psychotherapist]. Still, it is all of these in some synthesis which it has not yet been possible to formulate explicitly. Somehow, in a successful analysis [psychoanalytically oriented psychotherapy] the patient matures as a total personality. Somehow, a developmental process which has been halted or sidetracked, resumes its course. It is as though the person, reexperiencing his past and the transference, finds in the new conditions a second chance and "redevelops" while he is reliving. (p. 285)

From our review of senior clinicians who specialize in severely disturbed patients, we have learned that a variety of psychodynamic approaches seem to work well in competent and sensitive hands. Kernberg appears to get excellent results by relying on persistent and strongly worded interpretations (with supportive interventions provided by a team member). Masterson has reported equally good results with firmly stated and persistent confrontations. Adler and Buie, Hedges, and Stolorow and Lachmann have had excellent results that emphasize the holding qualities of the therapist and the self-object relationship that must be formed. There are several explanations for the success of these differing approaches. One is the clinicians' confidence in their theoretical approach, combined with a dedicated and concerned attitude toward the patients. A second explanation is that there may be a significant overlap between the differing theories and technical approaches (e.g., being supportive of the patients, trying to make sense out of their inner chaos).

The reader may already be using the approach of Kernberg, Masterson-Rinsley, or Kohut but may also want to try other techniques in response to the unique problems presented by each patient. Thus, this chapter will offer, first, a distillation of attitudes and techniques from a number of experts, along with their rationale for the technique. Second, where there is some agreement on treatment issues, an amalgam will be provided so that the reader will know where the experts agree. I have used a synthetic approach in my work and have seen such an approach used by a number of experts. This multimodal approach stresses both the healing force of the relationship and the technique. Although it is always easier to follow a strict, delineated path than to make on-the-spot judgments, I have found that such a mixed approach justifies any uncertainty.

Chessick (1977), in summarizing this uncertainty, has recommended an open-minded and flexible approach:

> I would suggest that we try to stay as close as possible to the practical situation through the scrutinizing of clinical material—begin with the clinical material and try to see which of these various theoretical formulations fit the given clinical phenomena. This means that the intelligent reader will have to juggle in his head these conflicting theories and be prepared to try to fit the theories to the clinical phenomena the way one fits scattered pieces together in a jigsaw-puzzle opening. You scan and try out several pieces, one at a time, to see which piece fits. (p. 77)

What are these theories that we must fit into the puzzle of the patient's reports? They range from the conflict-oriented approach of Kernberg through the arrest and deficit approach of Kohut. Between these two poles are many theorists, some who are closer in spirit to Kernberg (e.g., Masterson, Meissner), some in the middle who draw the best from both theorists (e.g., Rinsley), and others who are closer to Kohut (e.g., Adler, Hedges, Stolorow).

My approach lies midway between the structural and developmental models. Grotstein (1982) has described such a mid-course path:

> The borderline patient needs more personal involvement with the therapist on the one hand and also, on the other hand, needs the intactness of the boundaries of the therapist–patient relationship, a phenomenon designated as *the therapeutic frame* by R. J. Langs. . . . There is a paradox [here] in which the borderline patient needs [both] humanness and detachment. (p. 29)

In the mixed approach, the therapist must tolerate the patients' demands for bonding while at the same time maintaining enough distance to be able to use a technique that sets the stage for the patients' optimum weaning. The reader should be aware of two broad assumptions of the mixed model approach: (1) that supportive and interpretative techniques can be mixed, as long as the therapist avoids taking over and doing the patients' work for them and instead carefully explores why they cannot do the work for themselves; and (2) that the developmental perspective is a central organizing concept and the specific technique is determined by the patients' developmental level and problems.

USING PSYCHOTHERAPY WITH THE BORDERLINE PATIENT

Kernberg (1975a) and Masterson (1976, 1981) have outlined the practical aspects of psychotherapy with the borderline adult. Both agree that a minimum of two hours a week is indispensable for intensive work, and neither feels that so many sessions are in themselves regressive. Both point out that when a borderline patient is seen once a week or less, it is hard to avoid focusing on external reality, which interferes with the interpretive work. In this situation, the therapist works mainly in a confrontive-supportive manner. An exception would be the higher-functioning patient, who may do good in-depth work in one hour per week. (Clinicians who see most of their patients on a once-weekly basis might want to refer to the sections on supportive and confrontive psychotherapies in Chapter 10.)

The therapist should see the patients face to face. The therapist will be far more active in this approach than in psychoanalysis and must encourage the patients to share their concerns but not engage in free associations. Instead of permitting prolonged silences, the therapist should comment on them and at times may inquire about certain subjects such as the patients' drinking or other known problems occurring outside the therapy.

Assessing the Need for External Structure

Kernberg (1975a) says that deciding whether the patients need external structuralization of their life is one of the initial crucial points that must be addressed early in the therapy. He has listed the following six behaviors that require intervention:

1. Acting out (both in and out of sessions).
2. Attempts to control the therapist's life by telephoning at night at home or spying on him or her.
3. Suicide attempts or persistent self-mutilation.

4. The use of street drugs or alcohol for purposes of self-medication.
5. Persistent illegal antisocial behavior.
6. Not taking care of physical problems such as anorexia nervosa, diabetes, or other life-threatening illnesses.

I shall add a seventh behavior that needs early assessment: the patients' history of and compliance with prescribed medication. Borderline patients often abuse dosage instructions indiscriminately when they feel agitated or out of control. They accumulate their favorite drugs from a variety of physicians—"just in case I'll ever need it"—and then ingest various combinations and amounts believing that "more is better." Because of such abuse, accidental overdoses occur as frequently as do deliberate suicide attempts. Medication is further discussed in Chapter 13.

Generally, each of these behaviors should be dealt with by confrontation, clarification, and, when possible, interpretation. If the patients cannot handle their impulses in words rather than actions, then confrontation, limit setting, and structuring of their life should be used (Boyer and Giovacchini 1967, Rinsley 1982a). Of course, a life-threatening matter such as a potential suicide attempt should be discussed immediately with a patient having a history of such problems.

Sometimes patients may require an intermediate-care living situation, day treatment, or disability insurance coverage. I recommend that whenever possible, a person other than the therapist make the arrangements for special care, discouraging the patients from perceiving the therapist as a maternal caretaker. In clinics it is useful to have a staff person make these arrangements. A similar approach can be used in private practice, although it is often more difficult to implement. Such massive intervention in the patients' life later in the therapy will need to be studied regarding its meaning to the patients and should be interpreted to them. Attending to these issues early in the process, however, often prevents later acting out.

Establishing Policies of the Psychotherapy

Patients should be treated as adults who will assume responsibility for themselves (Masterson 1981, p. 152). Therefore, from the very beginning of treatment, it is necessary for the therapist to explain the policies governing the conduct of treatment (including the time, place, and length of interview; fees; and attendance). It is important that patients understand and agree to these policies. Well-constructed policies free the therapist from having to decide how to handle certain issues each time they arise.

Appointments

Patients should not be allowed to change their interview times indiscriminately. In addition, a specific policy should be laid down with regard to vacations, canceled appointments, and the like. The patients should never think that they do not have to keep their appointments or that chronic lateness will pass without comment and exploration.

Patients receiving care from the public sector should realize that the right to treatment is theirs but that the conditions of treatment rest with the therapist. In clinics that charge no fee, certain issues of entitlement arise—"The system owes me; I should be seen no matter what I do"—and are often difficult to work out in the therapy. Limits must be set on the number of failed appointments, and the patients must be confronted and even terminated if they persist in missing appointments.

Fees

Basically, patients should be charged a regular fee and should pay their bill on time. They should be held responsible for appointments and should be charged accordingly if they are late. On the other hand, the therapist who is late should subtract the cost of the missed time from the bill. Appointments canceled by the patients at the last minute should be billed to them.

Availability of Therapist

Borderline patients should understand that the therapist is available by telephone; just knowing that the therapist can be reached in an emergency minimizes the patients' anxiety and reduces their impulse to call. The clinician may have to take telephone calls around the clock at the beginning of therapy, but they should be limited to office hours as soon as possible. (Frequent phone calls may be an unexpressed plea for more frequent visits.)

Use of Drugs or Alcohol

Most therapists, including myself, agree that patients should not be seen on the same day that they use either street drugs or alcohol, and this should be emphasized.

Therapist's Contact with Significant Others

Finally, the therapist should make it clear that he or she does not want to give psychotherapy to the patient's spouse, relatives, or friends. This is because the essence of the treatment is a dyadic relationship, and the therapy will become unnecessarily complicated if the patients become jealous and envious of any rivals. Significant others should be referred to other therapists so that the patients will not need to worry about rivalry and/or issues of confidentiality.

History of Previous Multiple Suicide or Self-Mutilation Attempts

With patients who have histories of such behavior, it is useful to get ground rules, at or near the beginning of treatment, regarding these behaviors. This may be a therapist–patient agreement on hospitalization, for example, at periods of intense suicidal ideation or self-mutilation episodes. Some therapists have advocated taking a fairly tough stand from the beginning of the treatment, expecting repetitively suicidal patients to talk about such feelings but not to act on them. If patients do make a suicide attempt, the therapist should warn them that he or she will see that they get the emergency care they need—and then terminate the psychotherapy. Not all therapists would take such a stand, but it is important that each therapist have some consistent method for dealing with such patients.

Other Special Problems Early in the Therapy

Previous Therapies

Whenever patients have been in therapy before, the therapist should find out how the previous therapy progressed and the reasons for its termination, so as to prevent similar problems.

Separations

The therapist should also examine the patients' history of reactions to separations. The more narcissistic patients may claim that they do not care about the therapist's absences, whereas borderline patients may report an acute panic reaction. The therapist must be sensitive to these reactions and must explore them. It is necessary to interpret the patients' fear of physical separation as well as the fear that their internal image of the therapist will be destroyed because of the rage engendered by the separation. I have found certain hypnotic techniques for imagining the therapist's face and presence to be helpful to some patients while the therapist goes on vacation. Rinsley (1982a) recommends using this technique at other times as well. But it occasionally may be necessary to arrange for the patients to see another therapist until the regular therapist returns.

Silences

The therapist should comment when patients start sessions with a prolonged silence. Silence may reveal a negative transference, an intense fear of the therapy process, or a devaluation of all human help. Prolonged silences during a session should be commented on (e.g., "What are you thinking about right now?"). If these silences continue, the therapist should make a calculated guess as to the reason and offer it to the patient in the form of an interpretative hypothesis (Kernberg 1984).

Withholding Information or Lying

If withheld information or lying is discovered or suspected, the therapist should confront the patient or investigate the reasons. Such behavior may represent the belief that the therapist is incompetent, a fool, or dishonest and allows deceit in the therapy. Or it may be an attempt to get the therapist to take over and demonstrate caring by talking for the patients. If these attempts to control the session or the lying become pervasive, it is probably better to terminate the patient than to "treat him under impossible conditions" (Kernberg 1975a, p. 206).

Using Diaries, Journals, and Drawings

Patients who have a particularly hard time verbalizing their feelings or fantasies may communicate best with the therapist by spontaneously referring to a diary or other creative artifacts. This is acceptable as long as it does not take the place of working on important everyday happenings. In summary, Masterson (1976, 1981) emphasizes that the improper management of these issues produces leaks in the therapeutic frame and that if these deficits are not promptly addressed, they may promote regressive transference acting out, which could stall the therapy.

Getting Started in the Therapy

The following two concepts are necessary for the therapist to understand when preparing to begin: how to use all of the diagnostic and prognostic information to predict the patients' first moves and how to use the patients' affect as well as the clinician's own affect to understand the patients.

Predicting the First Moves

After the therapist has collected the history, conducted the first diagnostic interview, reviewed the prognosis, and selected a treatment, he or she should now understand the patients well enough to be able to predict some of their initial maneuvers—how they will act out, what they will demand, how they will act toward the therapist, and what type of transference will occur. The ability to predict the first moves has several benefits. The therapist will be less taken aback when patients inevitably play out their dynamics in the session. Also, the therapist can do some advanced planning.

The Role of Affect in Treatment

Identifying the patients' affects is an essential aspect of any psychotherapy, but particularly so in treating the borderline patient. Patients need to experience and repossess their disowned feelings before any structural change can occur. Usually, the affect and the ideation accompanying the affect require detoxifying by the therapist's acceptance, clarification, and interpretation so that the patients believe it is safe to own their feelings. Behavior motivated by primitive ego states requires reality testing. When these steps are taken, structural change in the form of integration of good-bad self- and object representations can occur. Affects frequently are the clues to the exact nature of the patients' conflicts, defenses, and intrapsychic structure. Many affects are identified with a particular defense mechanism and developmental level (e.g., disgust-anal period and frequently narcissistic pathology) (Hartocollis 1980a). Some affects (e.g., anger) can be a defense against other feelings (e.g., helplessness, vulnerability), and full exploration of the conscious experience often reveals deeper, more basic affects and the ideation that accompanies them. Affects are often the bridge that leads from the present material to the past. Finally, the therapist's affective response to the patient is often a clue to the psychodynamics present at that moment. Therefore, understanding the affects and the techniques for exploring them is basic to conducting psychotherapy with the borderline patient. In beginning therapy, the clinician may simply want to tag feelings (help the patient put a name on the feeling) or, in the case of emotional flooding, to soothe the patient before tagging the feeling while studying the precipitant. Eventually the therapist will want to understand the affect, the ideation, and the behavior accompanying the affect.

A DEVELOPMENTAL PERSPECTIVE

A thorough analysis of the patient from a developmental perspective is a three-step process. As Glenn (1979) has explained,

> In order to fully understand someone, it is necessary to assess his present status, recognize the influence of his past development on his present state,

and evaluate the influence of these on his future states. We must ascertain where the subject stands in his journey from birth to death. (p. 21)

Shane (1977) illustrates the dynamic aspects of the process:

> The developmental *orientation* ... implies an ongoing process, not only with a past, but also with a present and a future. ... The use of the developmental approach implies that the analytic patient ... is considered to be still in the process of ongoing development as opposed to merely being in possession of a past that influences his present conscious and unconscious life. (pp. 7–8)

The borderline disorder is one of several spectrum disorders that share developmental, psychodynamic, and symptomatic features representing a failure to complete separation-individuation. This failure leaves each spectrum-disordered patient symbiotic to some degree (Rinsley 1982a, p. 174). (See Figure 7-3 for a review of the relationship among the classical psychosexual stages, phases of separation-individuation, object relations, and major diagnostic categories.)

When dealing with borderline adults or any other spectrum-disordered individual, the therapist follows all three of the steps outlined by Glenn. First, the therapist assesses the patients' present symptoms and psychodynamics (at the same time determining how the patients relate to him or her). Second, the therapist decides how the patients must have progressed through each of the psychological developmental stages—where they were and are arrested, what parenting patterns must have been operative, and how the arrest explains the core symptomatology. Finally, the therapist evaluates the developmental processes in which the patients must engage (with the therapist's help) in order to resume growing and to achieve their potential.

Five Developmental Perspectives

Hedges (1983, pp. 106–117) has constructed five developmental points of view that can be reviewed for assessment. Each perspective offers a vantage point on the patients' developmental history and current intrapsychic and interpersonal issues. Each reveals a different facet of functioning and tells us where patients are on the developmental continuum. All five must be used in order to understand the adult borderline or any other patient, although at any time one particular perspective may illuminate the patients more clearly. The five perspectives are

1. The centrality of *human symbiosis* in development, with progression out of symbiosis through separation-individuation being a critical task (Mah-

ler is a major contributor to this perspective). How deeply mired in symbiosis are the patients? Do they think that they and significant others are identical or share the same thoughts and feelings? Do they feel as though others belong to them and exist only to meet their needs? Do they feel that they must comply completely with others' expectations in order to be loved, giving up their own ideas and feelings in order to please and keep significant others? Do they report longing for merger, or do they defensively mask this longing with oppositionalism?

2. The *differentiation of affects* through integration of the good and bad self and object representations, which then gives rise to a spectrum of affects, not just love and hate (Kernberg, a major contributor, is compatible with Mahler). Where are these patients in self-object differentiation? Are their self-objects fused, split, or whole? To help answer these questions, the therapist should determine how wide a spectrum of affect these patients have and how well they are able to modulate their affect.

3. *Private world development,* which includes both conscious and unconscious fantasies as well as intrapsychic structures produced by the progression from introjection to identification to identity. It often can be diagnosed by the way the patients adopt others' traits partially or completely (E. Erikson, Kernberg, Meissner, and Schafer are major contributors). How much do these patients rely on primitive forms of learning such as incorporation and introjection? How solid is their sense of identity? Do they accept their good and bad aspects? How many identifications have they consolidated? Do they have multiple unintegrated identifications? Do the patients mimic others indiscriminately, or are they selective in choosing new identifications to incorporate into their own?

4. *Mother–child adaptation,* or how each adapts to the other through mutual cuing and other processes, such as projective and false-self identification, and how the original mother–child adaptation is maintained in the adults' intrapsychic and interpersonal style (Fairbairn, Mahler, Masterson, Rinsley, and Winnicott are major contributors). Given the patients' behavior during the psychotherapy session, what type of mother–child patterning occurred? What modalities were negatively or positively reinforced by the parents? How much was regressive behavior rewarded and autonomous behavior punished?

5. The *organizing processes of ego and self,* which rely on the notion of *average expectable* developmental progression (Hartmann), fluctuation, and the stabilization of various ego functions (Anna Freud, Blanck and Blanck, and Bellak and his colleagues are major contributors). What is the status of the various ego functions? How do they fluctuate, and under what pressures do they regress? When and under what conditions do they stabilize?

All borderline adults are not alike. After all, each parent idiosyncratically reinforced or punished different ego functions. For example, one mother might not tolerate her child's moving about too much, while another might punish her child for talking or expressing feelings (Hedges 1983). Thus, each borderline adult develops an individual psychological profile and unique ways of coping, no matter how distorted their ego functioning is. Some adults also develop unique strengths (e.g., intellectual, musical, or artistic skills) that compensate for some of their weaknesses.

THE BORDERLINE ADULT'S DEVELOPMENTAL FAILURES

Borderline adults' most basic developmental failure is that they do not feel they have a "self" (e.g., they feel empty, lost, overwhelmed, or unreal). Stated more technically, they have not achieved object constancy, operating instead in split-object-relation part-units. This leads to several interrelated consequences, such as identity diffusion, poor interpersonal relationships, and a reliance on primitive defenses, all of which have serious behavioral and emotional consequences. In other words, borderline adults have a pathological system of introjects that are maintained at great cost to the self (see Chapters 6, 8, and 9).

Common Psychodynamics of the Borderline Patient

The reverberations of early infantile experiences are expressed in the history and presenting symptomatology of all spectrum disorders, including the borderline. Borderline adults present with several symptoms ranging from the psychotic to the neurotic, all of which have profound implications for treatment. The following list of psychodynamic symptoms closely paraphrases Rinsley (1982a, pp. 175–179); findings from other theorists are noted when they appear.

Persistent Splitting

Borderline patients relate to the world and others according to the pleasure principle—"I can have anything I want whenever I want it, without negative consequences." They regard themselves and others as all-bad or all-good and probably have a favorite style, either "I am good, they are bad" (paranoid) or "I am bad, they are good" (hysterical). Others are regarded as all-good when they provide, gratify, or accept or all-bad when they withhold, deprive, and reject. Meissner (1979) commented that splitting in borderline patients is shown by their being plagued by both aggressor-victim and superior-inferior introjects.

Impaired Self-Object Differentiation

In addition to the dichotomous cognitive style, borderline patients experience varying degrees of incomplete self-object differentiation. They have a permeable external ego boundary that leads to depersonalization and estrangement and a permeable internal ego boundary at which unconscious content has ready access to consciousness (failure of repression). They deal with both their inner and outer worlds through a group of primitive defenses, including magic hallucination. As a result, they are vulnerable to a variety of primitive anxieties, according to their phase of developmental fixation (Mahler and Gosliner 1955). The types of primitive anxieties most often discussed in the literature are paranoid (M. Klein, Kernberg), separation (Masterson, Rinsley), and fragmentation (Kohut). All of this leads patients to appropriate others to provide continuity in the sense of self, and it also lends a quality of entitlement and narcissism to all of their relationships and their transference reactions.

Buie and Adler (1982–1983) commented on the impaired self-object differentiation from another angle, namely, the role that incorporation and fusion continue to play in the life of borderline patients (e.g., modes of intimacy by which patients can experience a feeling, such as soothing, as though psychologically mingling with a related quality, such as holding, of another person) (p. 62). They also noted that borderline adults constantly seek such forms of intimacy because of their own dearth of holding introjects, and yet they are in a state of need-fear dilemma concerning such intimacy. Because patients see these modes of soothing as potentially threatening, they may seek to stay distant from others, to regulate their holding needs by dividing them among a number of people, or to oscillate back and forth between closeness and distance among several people. There are threats in several aspects of this mode of relating: (1) incorporation and fusion involve oral-level impulses; (2) the greater the need is for soothing, the greater will be the mobilization of oral impulses; (3) at a fantasy level the incorporation of the object is equivalent to eating or cannibalistically destroying the object; and (4) the simultaneous wish to be eaten or absorbed by the self-object concomitant with psychological fusion involves the fantasy of literal destruction of the self (Buie and Adler 1982–1983, p. 63). The more intense the need is, the more intense will be the impulses, wishes, and fantasies. Either in regressive crisis or as the work of therapy progresses, patients will find these impulses emerging into consciousness, which will be accompanied by great anxiety, guilt, and rage, often to the point of annihilation anxiety.

Inchoate Sexuality

Borderline patients suffer from a failure to attain genital primacy. Because they are unable to integrate multiple identifications and achieve whole-object relations, they still relate to others and their bodies as part-objects to satisfy predominantly oral needs. Their sexual behavior may be either polymorphous-perverse (e.g., John Elliott), or it may appear healthy while serving the need to appropriate and exploit the partner as a part-object (e.g., Sarah Gardner).

Depressive Dysphoria

Borderline adults usually experience some depression, which they express either affectively or through acting out. Their part-object relations fixate them at the depressive position, and they are unable to work through losses or separation. This contributes to short-lived, vacillating, and superficial relationships.

In addition, borderline adults have a sense of a basic fault (Balint 1968), which refers to the impairment of primary and secondary narcissism, based on early mother–child bonding. The patients feel that they are somehow flawed, defective, or fundamentally bad. That sense arises from the persistence of the splitting (the SORUs) and a particular pathogenic mother–infant interaction (reward for regression, punishment for individuation) noted by Rinsley and Masterson. The acute feeling that "I am bad" may be due to an unconscious sense of guilt reflecting a persistent sadistic superego attack on the self (Kernberg 1975a). It may also occur when the self-representation is perceived in the "all-bad" mode, causing intense self-derogation (Rinsley 1982a).

Labile Emotionality

Borderline patients often have rapidly fluctuating and contrasting emotional responses, frequently including overt and passive aggression. They are constantly anxious and complain about feeling "totally confused" or "lost." Rinsley (1982a) stated that this continual inner tension may be traced to

> the persistent "affecto-motor storms" of the young infant, which were never adequately put to rest through the ministrations of a "good enough mother" . . . leading to a condition of chronic autonomic-vegetative hyperirritability. (p. 177)

Rinsley believes this tension engenders a chronic state of overalert watchfulness, with an uncanny ability to sense the attitudes and motives of others, including those of the therapist toward the patient. This "early warning system" gives a distinctly paranoid flavor to borderline adults.

Object Inconstancy

Object inconstancy refers to the "inability to summon up stable, reliable inner (mental) images or representations of significant others" (Rinsley 1982a, p. 178) and represents the patients' failure to develop beyond recognition to evocative memory. Between sessions these patients often cannot remember what the therapist looks like; thus they cannot soothe themselves by recalling the therapist's face.

When a friend, spouse, or therapist does not provide the needed holding function, patients view this as a threat to their entitlement to survive (Buie and Adler 1982–1983, p. 60). This sets off an intense rage reaction that, depending on the intensity, can affect memory functions for holding and soothing. Buie and Adler (1982–1983) describe two types of rages. The first is called *recognition memory rage,* in which the patients lose their evocative memory of the good holding introject but still can use support given through interpersonal means or transitional objects. This rage is directed at the self-object that is seen as depriving. The second type of rage is *diffuse primitive rage,* in which even the recognition memory is lost. The external person is then no longer recognizable as a potential source of holding, and the use of transitional objects is no longer possible. This form of rage is characterized by an unchanneled, generalized discharge of hate and aggression. Separation anxiety now becomes annihilation panic.

An additional aspect of object inconstancy is the inability to have fantasies. Patients with a "fantasy deficiency" (alexithymia) are unable to use fantasy to delay drive discharges, to plan, and to set realistic goals. These patients often have few dreams and cannot use them to work through unconscious conflict and integrate it with here-and-now experiences.

Impaired Abstract Ability

The borderline patients' thinking remains developmentally arrested at the concrete operational level, in contrast with psychotic adults, who remain at the sensorimotor or preoperational levels. Borderline patients have soft signs of a thought disorder, representing various degrees of impaired "abstract attitude" (concretism). These patients often operate concretely (as well as magically), believing that they are entitled to have their needs met through subtle and indirect metaphoric communication without having to ask for anything. The more severe the symptoms are, the more the therapist must provide holding functions.

In summary, Kernberg and Rinsley believe that the treatment approach to borderline disorders is similar, except for modifying the technique when there is severe acting out, regressive tendencies, and a need for medication and/or hospitalization. Rinsley finds the SORU to be of primary value during the first phases of the treatment, when its exposure and confrontation are essential to strengthening the early therapeutic relationship. The SORU's usefulness diminishes as the treatment proceeds into the deeper analytic exploration of complex issues related to the transference.

The Impaired Functions

Blanck and Blanck (1979) created Figure 11-1, which shows 14 major developmental tasks that patients with a borderline personality (and other spectrum disorders) have not successfully traversed. The fulcrum of development shows the progression of each function from autism through object constancy. The typical borderline adult hovers around the middle of this fulcrum, although some lower-level borderline adults are much closer to the left.

Living in the body versus living in the mind (structure) refers to the child who lives in the immediacy of the interaction of the parent–child experience, with the self- and object images remaining merged. What the parent feels, the child senses and experiences as belonging to the self. This occurs less frequently as structuralization takes place, and the child is able to sort out what belongs to him or her from what belongs to others, in terms of both body boundary and emotions (Blanck and Blanck 1979, p. 73). Interpersonal interaction versus intersystemic and intrasystemic operations means that during autism and continuing through symbiosis, self-object negotiations are largely interpersonal in nature. With structuralization, however, this diminishes. Distance or independence from the object is attained by means of internalization, and children rely less on interpersonal reactions to tell them whether they are good or bad. Although selective identification precludes object loss, the structured psyche now negotiates among its three agencies (id, ego, and superego) as well as within each of them (p. 74). Mahler calls the "toward and away from" movements *ambitendency,* which are the precursors of *ambivalence,* both loving and hating the same person or the self. Ambivalence (a cognitive state) then supersedes ambitendency (a motor behavior).

Blanck and Blanck also observe that adult borderline patients continue to live more in the experiential realm than in structure. They come to the therapy searching for an experience that will allow them to replicate the primary object experience, which Blanck and Blanck distinguish from true transference. We might also say that the patients are trying to get the therapist to collude on fulfilling an infantile-subphase need, an act that is

AUTISM SYMBIOSIS	SEPARATION-INDIVIDUATION			
Differentiation	Practicing	Rapprochement	On the way to object constancy
A. Living in the body		▲	Living in the mind (structure)
B. Interpersonal interaction		▲	Intersystemic and intrasystemic operations
C. Primary process thought		▲	Secondary process thought
D. Undifferentiated self-object		▲	Differentiated self with gender identity
E. Direct impulse discharge		▲	Ego as mediator
F. Fear of annihilation....of loss of object....of loss of love		▲ ...of castration	Superego
G. Organismic distress.......use of external soothing......use of self soothing		▲	Signal anxiety
H. Defensive capacity not organized		▲	Capacity for defense and resistance
I. Simple affects "for" and "against"....affect differentiation		▲	Full affective repertory
J. Ambitendency		▲	Ambivalence
K. Split self and object images		▲ (fusion)	Whole self and object representations
L. Need gratification	object love	▲	Self and object constancy
M. Search for primary object experience (replication)		▲	Capacity for transference
N. Dyadic relationship....expanded object world		▲	Oedipal object relationships

Figure 11-1 The Fulcrum of Development (From Blanck, R., and Blanck, G., *Ego Psychology II: Psychoanalytic Developmental Psychology*, p. 72. Copyright 1979 by Columbia University Press. Reprinted by permission.)

unhealthy, given the patients' adult status (pp. 81–82), though this latter point is not Blanck's and Blanck's position.

Blanck and Blanck (1979, p. 24) have emphasized that whatever mother–child relations have influenced intrapsychic development, the adult's organization is more varied and complex than the child's was at the original subphase. We can never be exactly sure how subphase inadequacy influences adult pathology, though the patients' behavior with the therapist provides the best clue to understanding what happened in the various subphases.

Hedges (1983) has pointed out that psychoanalytic developmental psychology (of which object-relations theory can be considered a component) when applied to borderline conditions focuses on the status of the self-object and the status of various ego functions (p. 106).

When assessing the status of various ego functions, the task is (Hedges 1983)

> defining what functions and integrations have or have not developed, the conditions under which they *are and are not available*, and the *relationships* of the developed and undeveloped functions to each other . . . and [finally] in understanding the many convoluted and/or distorted coping or adjustment attempts which . . . obscure or compensate for atypical development. (p. 106)

Unfortunately, there are more data on the relationship among ego functions in children than in adults, although there is some material on adults. For example, Rinsley (1982a, pp. 100–104) has attempted to trace the impact of the persistence of the SORU on a variety of ego functions.

IMPACT OF THE DEVELOPMENTAL PERSPECTIVE ON PSYCHOTHERAPY

The resumption of normal development is the overriding goal of psychotherapy using a developmental perspective (Loewald 1960). This involves, as Wolff (1971), drawing on insights from Winnicott, observed,

> helping the patient to resolve and overcome hold-ups in his personal development and consequent out-of-date patterns of reacting and behaving . . . allowing them in reality to re-experience in treatment those early phases of the mother–child relationship in which disturbances of development had occurred, owing to some failure in the facilitating environment. (p. 122)

In general, the developmental hold-ups accepted by the clinicians using the mixed-model approach are that (1) many borderline patients have developmental problems dating back to the symbiotic phase, and so they need some help with self-other differentiation as well as development of other ego functions; (2) their core problem seems to be their pathological organization of introjections, and so clarification and interpretation of these introjections are vital; and (3) borderline patients seem to be prone to emotional flooding, affectomotor storms, and a general inability to self-soothe (lack of a holding introject) and therefore require help both in learning to calm the self as well as in learning to label feelings (e.g., "This is what it feels like to be anxious or angry").

What general strategies or tactics does the clinician use? Gedo and Goldberg (1973) were among the first to devise a series of therapeutic approaches based on the patient's developmental level. For symbiotic patients who fear annihilation through overstimulation, Gedo and Goldberg recommend pacification through soothing interpretations, hospitalization, and medication. For rapprochement-fixated patients, the technique is unification, which reduces separation anxiety by helping the patients keep themselves together through the reliable and consistently available therapist, who becomes a transitional object repairing the patients' sense of a basic fault. Gedo and Goldberg consider this basically nonanalytic approach as the treatment of choice for the borderline patient. For more developmentally advanced patients, techniques of optimal disillusionment assist with weaning through confrontation with reality via interpretations. Accordingly, the patient's developmental level determines the approach and techniques to be used.

Stolorow and Lachmann (1980), following in the tradition of Gedo and Goldberg, also stated that the patient's developmental level determines the technique to be used. They feel that borderline patients must establish a primitive, symbioticlike selfobject relationship with the therapist in order to repair what was denied in infancy because of parental psychopathology. The relationship with the therapist is crucial; its soothing qualities must be protected against rupture; and interpretations of the relationship's psychodynamic meaning must be kept to a minimum. With lower-level borderline patients, the therapist might even have to provide reality testing and other discriminative functions so that they can develop a model for how these functions can be carried out by themselves.

Unfortunately, few patients fit neatly into the Gedo-Goldberg or the Stolorow-Lachmann schema. Many borderline patients present a mixed picture, periodically having strengths in some areas and weaknesses in others. Consequently, the treatment should be a special mix of pacification, unification, and optimal disillusionment via interpretation. Patients who manifest intense traumatic or panic states require pacification. Borderline patients always require unification in the form of a silent operating ambience in the treatment—a consistent, accepting, and empathic ambiance that allows them in time to reveal their cold, unloving, and archaic introjects, or SORUs. Eventually, between the benign atmosphere of the therapy and the therapist's clarifications and interpretations, these patients will begin to substitute new warm, loving, and reasonable introjections through identification with the psychotherapist's calm, compassionate, and sincere presence (which includes setting limits on self-destructive or other destructive behavior). This, then, is a modified psychoanalytic approach with generally more support, empathy, and soothing than Kernberg and Masterson advocate but with also more distance via interpretation, limit setting, and direct work with anger and rage than Kohut and his colleagues have recommended.

Buie and Adler (1982–1983) have a definitive treatment plan for dealing with what they consider the borderline's primary problem: lack of holding and sustaining introjects. They identified the following three phases in the development of holding introjects.

In Phase I, the primary aim of treatment is to establish and maintain a relationship with the patients so that they can acquire a solid evocative memory of the therapist as a sustaining object from which adequate holding introjects can be formed. Patients, however, find many impediments to using the therapist as a holding introject, each of which must be worked through by clarification, confrontation, and interpretation.

The first impediment is that holding is never adequate to assuage the feelings of aloneness, and so patients feel enraged and want to harm the offending therapist. Because reality and fantasy become confused in their mind, borderline adults fear they will or already have killed the therapist. In addition, they fear they will lose the therapist, who, they believe, will turn from good to bad in reaction to their hostile rejecting, assaultive, and destructive feelings. (At the start of therapy, these patients may not even be aware of their fantasies but feel instead rage, panic, or primitive guilt.) In addition, these patients project so much hostility onto the therapist when they are angry, they can no longer view the therapist as a good person or a good holding object. The therapist who is so endowed with holding nutriments and so needed by borderline adults is, at the same time, deeply envied by the needy patients, an envy containing hateful destructive impulses. The patients also harbor a primitive, guilt-related belief that they are undeserving of the therapist's help because of their wickedness, an outcome of their sense of basic fault.

During this first phase, patients will undoubtedly lose evocative recall of the therapist because of their extreme rage and feelings of aloneness and annihilation. The therapist may have to be available to them during crises (e.g., allow extra visits, make phone calls, send them post cards while on vacation) in order to be seen as reliable and sustaining. During the session, the therapist may need to confront, clarify, and remind the patient of reality (e.g., the therapist's continued caring, the therapist's not resembling the patient's projected hostile introjects). The therapist even may need to protect the patients from suicidal thoughts by means of environmental structuring.

Buie and Adler (1982–1983) believe that work with splitting of the type discussed by Kernberg must wait until the patients have formed stable holding introjects. Only then can the effort to bring together the hated and loving sides of the split be therapeutic, particularly after distorting projections that have intensified the negative side of the split have been corrected.

In Phase II, the unrealistic and childlike idealization of the holding therapist will be continually confronted by reality until the holding introject breaks down. At this point, patients feel disappointment, sadness, and anger at the therapist. It is necessary to work through each episode of disappointment and the feelings associated with it. Buie and Adler consider this work to be in the Kohut manner because it involves optimal disillusionment in the area of idealization. The narcissistic sector of borderline psychopathology must be addressed in this phase because narcissistic grandiosity and idealization can substitute for holding, soothing, and giving a sense of security through partaking of perfection. Other issues of narcissistic worth should wait until the later phases of treatment.

Once the inappropriately harsh elements have been modified, the process of superego development can be resumed in Phase III. Patients must begin developing their internal resources in order to maintain personal security and self-esteem. This development includes (1) self-holding capacities, (2) self-love and object-love capabilities, (3) trust and security in their own competence, and (4) proud enjoyment of competence (p. 81). Buie and Adler noted that the capacities to esteem the self can be developed only when the patients have adequate experience of being esteemed by significant others. This is done initially by introjection of the therapist's respectful attitude and is often referred to as the *analytic introject*. The therapist may directly or indirectly show the patients that they are esteemed (e.g., express excitement over a patient's success). But this introjection will be unstable until the patients identify with the therapist's function and attitudes, making these attributes part of themselves. Buie and Adler accept that many of these functions are outside the realm of traditional psychoanalysis and are effected through nonverbal means—facial expression, body posture, tone of voice, and a particular attitude of striving to understand the patients' inner world rather than trying to change it.

Hedges (1983) found that the distinguishing feature of borderline patients is their insistence on a dyadic style of relatedness, in which they hold to idiosyncratic mind–body boundaries (p. 158). This dyadic form is based on the early mother–child relationship style. Hedges observed that "through these developmental idiosyncrasies, the person persistently intrudes or provokes intrusions of various sorts" (p. 158). It is the therapist's job to allow this merger replication to emerge in the therapeutic relationship until it is fully understood, which may take months, and then to convey his or her understanding of their mode of relatedness to the patients. With the therapist's empathic understanding and acceptance, the patients may try new options and establish new integration, leading to a more differentiated mode of self-other relatedness. As Hedges (1983) noted, only after the reenactment of symbiotic relatedness has taken place should the therapist gradually begin to assert personal ego and self-boundaries to confront, block, or stifle the model of relatedness being lived out by the patients (p. 174). Merger can be understood only when it exists, and separation-individuation can take place only from a merged state (p. 158).

The following example from Hedges's (1983) work with a child illustrates symbiotic relatedness succeeded by the therapist's differentiating behavior:

> One child regularly pushed me into buying candy with caramel and peanuts whenever his life was disrupted at home or at school [which Hedges apparently did as part of coming to understand the replication scenario]. He blamed his mother for his having to wear braces and found that forbidden candies and nuts were an effective way of standing *against* mother. In time we found a variety of other snacks which were approved by his orthodontist, but anger and regression were regularly signaled by his wish for a Reggie bar! [Hedges asserted his personal boundaries as part of assisting differentiation.] (p. 177)

Hedges believes the therapist must first accept the symbiotic replication without confrontation or inquiry before helping the patients to differentiate, by accepting the therapist's personal boundaries.

Meissner (1982) has developed a therapeutic approach for paranoid patients that also seems applicable to borderline individuals. He regards the transference-countertransference reactions in the therapy as an important source of information about the patients' introjects. Upon receiving the projection and feeling seduced into enacting it, the therapist can stop, observe, and learn what is happening with the patients' object relations. Unlike Hedges, Meissner does not believe that the therapist should participate in the replication demand as part of understanding it. Meissner (1982) laid out a logical progression of what must be accomplished in the therapy of a severely disturbed person, noting that these steps often overlap and that they represent a schema, not a definitive step-by-step approach in the therapy.

Step 1 is the establishment of the therapeutic alliance. This is done by (1) attentively listening to the patients' verbalization, (2) empathizing with what the patients feel and experience, with an eye to certain technical procedures (e.g., defining the therapeutic situation, the therapist's role, and the patients' role), (3) noticing any distortions of the therapist's role or meaning of interpretations (e.g., interpreting comments as criticism), and (4) maintaining strict confidentiality. In this early phase (which may last for a lengthy period), all interpretations and confrontations must be balanced against the therapeutic alliance. Too much analysis of resistance may undermine the patients' fragile self-esteem and autonomy.

Step 2 is defining the projective system. The therapist elicits as much explicit, concrete detail as possible on each incident reported, as well as parallel accounts of similar reactions at other times (e.g., a patient continually reports being interpersonally abused by others). The therapist attends to the patients' emotional reactions and perceptions of the events but does not refute or confront at this point. Premature interpretation may simply stun or hurt the patients, making them feel alienated from themselves and their own sense of reality. The therapist will begin to note incidences of all-or-nothing affective responses as signs of the introjective system at work. At the same time, the therapist monitors the therapeutic relationship because it will become the primary vehicle for working with the introjections.

In Step 3 the therapist starts to test the accuracy of some of the unrealistic aspects of the introjects. Instead of confronting or challenging, this is done by a process of detailed accounting. For example, the patients are asked to describe how they know that no one at work likes them. Usually they will give details that the therapist does not find particularly convincing. The therapist tags the feeling quality rather than the specific content of the statement by saying, "That seems to be how you feel" (Meissner 1982, p. 365). The intention is to distinguish between feelings and their connection with fantasies and reality. The second technique is to define specific areas in which the patients' knowledge is lacking; for example, paraphrasing Meissner, "You feel like they don't like you, but you have no hard evidence." Meissner clearly said that this does not represent a conflict-focused approach but, rather, is concerned with the pattern of introjections that underlie and give rise to intrapsychic conflicts.

Step 4 is the clarification of introjects. As one side of the dichotomous introject is clarified (e.g., victim-introject), the therapist often finds that the opposite side (e.g., aggressor-introject) emerges. A patient who feels victimized by a coworker one week may act haughty and sadistic toward the therapist several weeks later; therefore this polar opposite introject should be studied. With repeated clarifications of both polarities, the patient will gradually understand that such elements relate to a fantasy that reflects the introjects' organization. Patients who have accepted the fantasy as their real self no longer know what their real self is like. But they now have the option of keeping the introjects or changing them.

In Step 5, exploration of the derivation of the introjects begins by retracing the patients' childhood experiences to key figures. These patients come to see that the introjects represent their ambivalent relationships with significant others (recreated within themselves in an enduring pattern). Now the patients can see the nature of the fantasy and evaluate it against real-life experiences. The therapist and patients may agree that the introject is strikingly accurate or that it has only a vague resemblance to the real parent–child interaction.

Step 6 is examining the motivation for retaining the introjects (e.g., infantile narcissism: "I am special because I sacrifice myself to others, as my mother did"; denial of loss and abandonment: "I will keep my mother and father with me forever and will never be abandoned because I will maintain the same relationship style with others that I have with my parents").

Steps 7, 8, 9, and 10 are the mourning of the infantile attachments, the emergence of real dependence on the therapist, the working through of this dependency, and, finally, termination.

As do all the theorists in this section, Meissner believes that many borderline patients require a good self-object experience with the therapist before they can modify their introjects through exploration, confrontation, and interpretation. He also stresses that protective limits and structure must be provided for more disturbed patients, as part of allowing them to experience the therapist as caring enough not to allow them to be self- or otherwise destructive.

How can these techniques and attitudes be enacted within the therapy? What is the right balance between holding and investigation, symbiosis and differentiation, and soothing and confronting? In what order should they be used? Only the evolving body of clinical lore will answer those questions, although each of the experts has his or her own answers. It is clear, however, that a good working relationship (nonspecific factors) and a sound therapeutic technique (specific factors) are complementary agents of change in the effective psychotherapy of the borderline adult. As Weiner (1975) has observed,

> inept technical procedures limit or negate the benefits that might otherwise derive from an open and trusting patient–therapist relationship, while the most polished technical skills are of little avail in the absence of a treatment climate that nourishes receptivity to them. (p. xi)

Thus, two fundamental styles of relating to patients can be corrective. The first involves a holding environment for the patients in a clinical situation. The second, which will be discussed in the next section, involves listening to the patients' verbal communication and deciphering its meaning in terms of object-relations conflict, particularly as it manifests itself in the transference in the psychotherapy situation.

NONSPECIFIC FACTORS: A GOOD WORKING RELATIONSHIP AND THE HOLDING ENVIRONMENT

Nonspecific factors refer to the therapist's personality, relationship with the patients, the patients' personality, and the treatment ambience. A favorable fit of these variables often makes the difference between success and failure in the treatment. It is from the mixture of all these elements that borderline adults, with their longings for and fears of symbiosis, will eventually develop an almost animal faith in the therapist that will allow the psychotherapy to proceed during the early difficult phases.

The Therapist's Personality and Role

Strupp (1982) underscored the importance of the therapist's personality:

> Psychotherapy (or any of its variants) is not a treatment modality or a set of technical procedures that can be defined precisely or administered in an impersonal manner. By contrast, *all techniques function within the total context of a human relationship* and they can be no better than that relationship. (pp. 411–412)

Wolberg (1967) has listed a number of positive and negative characteristics of the therapist that lead to positive or negative prognostic signs in any therapy. These characteristics listed in Table 11-1 are particularly important to the psychotherapy of patients with severe character disorders, such as a borderline personality.

Kernberg (1975a) has agreed that the therapist's personality is an essential prognostic element in the treatment outcome. He reported that the treatment of borderline cases requires a secure and skilled therapist, with a firm but nonhostile attitude toward the patient's unavoidable acting out. In addition, the therapist must have a clear personal sense of moral values but must not inflict a moralistic attitude on others. The ability to overcome countertransference aggression and to sublimate it with concern for the patients is also important.

The Roles of Concern and Hope

The importance of the therapist's concern for the patients was described by Saul (cited in Chessick 1977):

> For the unsustained, the analyst must provide the experience which the patient lacked in childhood: that of having an interested, sympathetic, under-

Table 11-1 Prognostic Signs in the Therapist

Positive

1. The therapist is capable of understanding the dynamics of the patient's illness.
2. The therapist is sufficiently sensitive to perceive what is happening in the treatment process
3. The therapist is aware of his own feelings and is capable of remaining objective irrespective of the attitudes and behavior manifested by the patient.
4. The therapist is flexible in his approach to the patient.
5. The therapist has a capacity for empathy with the patient.
6. The therapist tends to treat the patient in a respectful and cooperative manner.
7. The therapist is capable of being firm on occasion.
8. The therapist is capable of establishing a working relationship with the patient.
9. The therapist is well-adjusted and is gaining satisfactions for his own basic needs.
10. The therapist is capable of tolerating the expression of varied impulses in the patient.
11. The therapist has no neurotic attitudes toward money.
12. The therapist is able to tolerate the vicissitudes inevitable to therapy.
13. The therapist feels secure within himself.
14. The therapist is capable of giving the patient support in accordance with the patient's needs without overprotecting or overdomineering the patient.

standing person always available in his life. Without such an attitude, technically correct interpretations may be interpreted by the patient as disapproval. Accurate interpretations also require an attitude of human understanding, of being on the patient's side, of having confidence in him. . . . The analyst's confidence is partly internalized and can move even the "hollow" ones in the direction of a sense of sustainment, of identity, a good self-image, and self-acceptance. (pp. 160–161)

An important basic attitude is the therapist's capacity to experience concern on behalf of the patients and to hope that the fight against destructive tendencies may be successful. The therapist must also recognize that such

Table 11-1 *(Continued)*

Negative

1. The therapist is confused about the existing dynamics.
2. The therapist is insensitive to what is going on within the patient and within himself.
3. The therapist is incapable of maintaining satisfactory objectivity.
4. The therapist is rigid in his approach to the patient.
5. The therapist lacks empathy with the patient.
6. The therapist is domineering, pompous, and authoritarian.
7. The therapist is too passive and submissive.
8. The therapist is detached.
9. The therapist tends to utilize the patient for the vicarious gratification of his own repressed or suppressed impulses; such as, sexuality, the expression of hostility, and the gaining of prestige.
10. The therapist is incapable of tolerating such impulses in the patient as sexuality, hostility, or assertiveness.
11. The therapist's insecurity reflects itself in anxiety about fees and payments.
12. The therapist is unable to tolerate blows to his self-esteem by the patient's acting-out tendencies, by manifestations of resistance and transference, and by the inevitable failures and frustrations in treatment.
13. The therapist has a neurotic need to be liked, a compulsive tendency toward perfectionism, inordinate hostility, poor creativity, no sense of humor, an inability to take criticism, low personal integrity, a diminished respect for people, a failure to acknowledge self-limitations, a low energy level or poor physical health.
14. The therapist rejects the patient, or refuses to, or is unable to extend to the patient measured support.

Source: Wolberg, L. R. (1967). *The Technique of Psychotherapy* (2nd ed.), pp. 496–497. Copyright 1967 by Grune & Stratton. Reprinted by permission.

battles are not always won and must walk a fine line between holding on and letting go at the appropriate moments. Many believe that this attitude helps therapists neutralize and overcome their own natural aggressive response to their patients' behaviors. For example, Kernberg (1975a) found that concern in this context involves awareness of the serious nature of destructive and self-destructive impulses in the patient, the potential development of such impulses in the analyst, and the awareness by the analyst of the limitations necessarily inherent in his therapeutic efforts with his patient. Concern also involves the authentic wish and a need to help the patient in spite of his transitory "badness." (p. 63)

Kernberg (1975a, p. 64) also stated that in concrete terms, concern implies several actions by the therapist: (1) ongoing self-criticism, (2) unwillingness to accept impossible situations in a passive way, and (3) the continuous search for new ways of handling a prolonged crisis. Concern means active involvement (as opposed to narcissistic withdrawal) and a willingness to review cases with colleagues or consultants (as contrasted with secrecy about one's work when consultation appears warranted).

The Therapist's Narcissism

Kernberg (1975a, p. 149) and Chessick (1977) both have stressed the necessity to overcome narcissism. Kernberg noted that the therapist's narcissistic problems are the major unfavorable prognostic element in the long-term treatment of patients with a borderline personality organization. He pointed out that the narcissistic psychotherapist has a low capacity for sustaining interpersonal relationships under frustrating conditions. This is particularly troublesome because a high tolerance for frustration is necessary in order to sustain a relationship with such patients, who fear that their hostility will eventually lead to rejection by others.

The Therapist's Own Borderline Problems

Masterson (1981) noted that many psychotherapists themselves have unresolved separation-individuation problems but that these problems need not influence the psychotherapy as long as the therapist is aware of them and keeps them well under control. The therapist's own problems with "rescuing," "overdirectedness," or "angry withdrawal" often are the countertransference problems that inhibit the progress of therapy. Helping patients resolve their separation-individuation problems is far more beneficial than any transient "caretaking," which helps the patients feel better but not improve.

The Patient's Role

The patients' willingness to come to the therapy and to participate at least minimally are important prerequisites for success. Theorists are less concerned about whether or not borderline patients are motivated to change than whether they can tolerate the frustration of the work of therapy. Chessick (1977, p. 152) found that the following dynamics of patients may shape a negative prognostic course:

1. *Acting out*—they immediately quit the treatment or find a third party to meet their intense cravings for holding and body contact.
2. *Need for revenge against authority figures*—they actively or passively stall the treatment or allow their life situation to fail so that they cannot come to therapy.
3. *Projecting destructive introjects onto the therapist*—with fear and hatred of the therapist as a consequence of frustrating their omnipotence expectations, this may lead to an immediate breakup of the therapy.
4. *An autistic retreat into sadistic sexual fantasies or similar experiences.*
5. *Self-fragmentation*—this may be accompanied by hallucinations and delusions, thus temporarily halting the therapy.

Kernberg (1975a, p. 150) listed the following transactional variables that help determine the success (or their absence may herald the failure) of the therapy: (1) the extent to which certain destructive behavior patterns become ego dystonic; (2) the extent to which the capacities for self-awareness, introspection, and concern for others develop under the treatment's influence; (3) the extent to which the patients can develop an authentic reliance on the therapist despite the inevitable frustrations; and (4) the extent to which the patient's negative therapeutic reaction can be resolved. In other words, the degree to which the patients can come to count on the therapist, despite all of the inevitable frustrations of the process, and the therapist's willingness to continue in the process largely determine the outcome of the therapy.

The Treatment's Ambience

Many theorists consider the ambience or nonverbal aspects of the treatment to be what determines the success or failure of the therapy with the borderline adult. Chessick (1977) observed that the patients must continually experience the presence of the therapist:

> Each therapy session must "count." . . . Each session must represent an encounter between the psychic field of the therapist—which in its maturity, extends trust, confidence and hope—and the need-fear dilemma of the patient, who has fallen away from authentic living and being with another person. (p. 160)

Continuing this thought, Chessick himself (1977) observed:

> It is this calm, nonanxious and patient stance that provides the basic ambience of the treatment. Any disruption of it interrupts the subliminal soothing that is always going on in a well-conducted treatment of a borderline patient. . . . The ambient subliminal soothing the therapist provides—in his habits . . . in his deep inner attitude towards his patients, . . . [this soothing] provides the basic motor that permits the psychotherapy of the borderline patient to go forward. (p. 194)

This emotional atmosphere or ambience is conveyed in a multitude of ways—the interested look, the tactful tone of voice, the consistency and honesty in transactions.

Searles (1978) emphasized that when working with severely disturbed patients, the ambience of the sessions, day after day, year after year, is far more important than any interpretation. It is particularly important for borderline adults because they are often dealing with feelings rooted in a preverbal stage of development. Only with time and persistent clarification are they able to describe such primitive experiences. Therefore, it is important for the therapist to be there and to try to understand the experience as the patients slowly and painfully unravel the bits and pieces of their personal myth.

The Holding Environment

Many clinicians refer to the ambience as the good-enough holding environment of psychotherapy. Because this term has implications for how the therapist should act (ranging from being empathic to total reparenting), it is necessary to define the term. Winnicott (1965) introduced the term *holding environment* as a metaphor for certain aspects of the therapeutic situation and process that parallel the mother–child interaction. He believed it was the therapist's task to provide conditions that were safe enough to allow the patients to regress and then begin to resume their interrupted development. Wolff (1971) called this the *being with* function, as contrasted with the *doing to* function of therapy (e.g., making transference interpretations, explaining, or confronting). Winnicott (1963) stated the following about one of the major holding tasks in therapy:

> The analyst [psychotherapist] is holding the patient, and this often takes the form of conveying in words at the appropriate moment something that shows the analyst [psychotherapist] knows and understands the deepest anxiety that is being experienced, or that is waiting to be experienced. (p. 240)

Thus, as Modell (1976) observed, the holding environment offers a helpful illusion of safety and protection derived from the bond of affective communication that exists between the therapist and patient.

The holding environment suggests not only protection from external dangers but also protection from the dangers within (affectomotor storms). It implies a restraint, a capacity to hold the child having a temper tantrum so that his or her aggressive impulses do not destroy either the child or the caretaker. The holding environment provides, in Sandler's (1960a) terms, a background of safety for the patient.

At the beginning of therapy, patients frequently test the therapist's capacity to survive aggressive onslaughts. The therapist must show an empathic understanding of these floods of feeling, by both firmly holding and limiting the patients' response to those expressions that are safe within the therapeutic relationship. In other words, the therapist must provide a protective structure for the patient who is out of control (e.g., hospitalization). By doing so, the therapist establishes strong and firm boundaries—something from which the patient can differentiate (Hedges 1983, p. 125).

Ways to Facilitate the Holding Environment

Chessick (1979, pp. 536–537) outlined ten strategies that the therapist can use to achieve a good-enough holding for new patients and also to help forge the therapeutic alliance:

1. Consistently and frequently be at the service of the patients, at a mutually convenient time.
2. Be there reliably and usually on time.
3. Stay awake and be preoccupied only with the patients, for a limited period of time.
4. Express love by taking a positive interest in the patients and "hate in the strict start and finish of the sessions and in the matter of fees."
5. Sincerely attempt to get into touch with the patients' processes, to understand their material and where the patients are, and to communicate this understanding by interpretation.
6. Stress a calm approach to objective observation and scientific study.
7. Work in a room that is quiet (but neither dead quiet nor subject to sudden distracting sounds), with neither a variable light nor one shining in the patients' face.
8. Avoid moral judgments or mentioning one's personal life or ideas.
9. In general, avoid temper tantrums and compulsively falling in love, and be neither hostile and retaliatory nor exploitative toward the patients.
10. Maintain a consistent, clear distinction between fact and fantasy in

order not to be hurt or offended by the patients' aggressive dreams or fantasies, and avoid talionic reactions, ensuring that both therapist and patient consistently survive their interactions.

In other publications Chessick stressed that the therapist should not have unrealistic expectations about change and must be comfortable with the therapy's lengthy process. He has concluded that all this adds up to the therapist's behaving like a healthy adult and showing respect for and dedication to the profession and the patient.

Other theorists also have introduced practical strategies for facilitating the holding environment. Rinsley (1982a, p. 228) pointed out that the patient often experiences significant relief, accompanied by reinforcement of the positive transference, when the therapist empathizes with the patient's affectomotor turmoil over the simultaneous desperate need for and fear of closeness. This often greatly calms the patient. Blanck and Blanck (1979) recommended selectively and deliberately using the word *we*, as in "we need to understand what this means," in certain contexts as a way of providing a good holding environment and enhancing symbiotic relatedness. Kernberg (1984) found that an accurate interpretation can also have a good holding function. The therapist reassures the patient by calmly containing and interpreting the feelings that the patient fears most. Mark (1980) and others have warned that clinicians often believe that through a good holding environment and warm, positive relationships, the patient will learn to trust and thereby will be healed. Mark commented that Winnicott's concept of the holding environment and good-enough mothering are often misinterpreted by therapists to mean providing constant warmth and nurturance for all patients rather than an empathic accepting response within reasonable limits.

Forging the Therapeutic Alliance

The therapeutic alliance is a major part of any meaningful therapy because it provides the realistic basis on which the therapeutic work can proceed (Meissner 1982). Thus, the first task confronting the therapist who is working with borderline patients is creating a therapeutic alliance. Yet this alliance is what borderline patients often cannot form because of their lack of whole-object relationships, stormy reactions, and fears that yet another relationship may fail. Their massive and untempered feelings of love and adoration may quickly turn to hate and acting out.

Before examining how a therapeutic alliance can be forged under these difficult circumstances, we need to understand the term better. A review of the literature by Gutheil and Havens (1979) indicates that the term can mean either a rational therapeutic alliance or an irrational therapeutic alliance. A rational therapeutic alliance has many components.

Paolino (1981, p. 103) stated that a therapeutic alliance between patients and the therapist is characterized by the following conditions:

1. Patients identify with the real person of the therapist and accept the therapist's views of themselves and their resistances.
2. Patients and the therapist agree to study the patients' behavior and intrapsychic functioning in order to understand it deterministically.
3. Patients and the therapist agree that the basic treatment modality is verbal and not behavioral interaction during treatment.
4. Patients and the therapist have the same definition of mental health and personal growth.
5. Between patients and the therapist there is a healthy relationship and rapport that is non-neurotic, desexualized, and deaggressivized and that functions despite impulses from the transference, real relationship, narcissistic alliance, and the symptoms themselves.
6. Although patients and the therapist accept the patients as they are, growth is expected.
7. Patients and the therapist are confident, hopeful, and enthusiastic about the treatment and value the role of free association, the profound importance of the unconscious, and the goal of maximal awareness of bodily feelings.
8. Patients are willing to transfer to the therapist total responsibility for their coping and defensive devices.

Overall, the rational alliance includes a bond between the therapist and the patient that is based on the patient's reality orientation, and need for psychic health, which are relatively uninfluenced by the irrationality and unreasonableness of the neurosis and transference neurosis (Paolino 1981, p. 102). In contrast, the irrational therapeutic alliance is founded on the patient's neurotic view of himself or herself as helpless and their belief that the therapist can unilaterally, magically cure him or her.

Paolino (1981) noted that both alliances involve ego splits plus an object relationship with the therapist. In the rational alliance, the patients ally the healthy side of their ego with the therapist, whereas in the irrational alliance, they ally the unhealthy side with the therapist. Both alliances can be used for symptom relief and to develop a therapeutic relationship, although they have different implications and courses. At times the therapist may allow the irrational alliance to persist in order to engage the patients in treatment and start the slow process of generating a rational alliance.

When borderline adults form a therapeutic alliance, it is usually of the irrational sort. How, then, is the irrational therapeutic alliance maintained and eventually transformed into a rational therapeutic alliance?

Masterson recommends that the therapist confront the WORU and RORU from the first moment in the therapy. (The therapist using a mixed model approach moves a little more slowly.) Masterson also recommends early confrontation of the patients' destructive behavior. This paves the way for the patients to develop insight into their destructive behavior and to align with the therapist's healthy ego.

Other theorists say the first step is optimizing the positive transference. The therapist must optimize the positive transference by showing respect, concern, and a calm attitude and providing appropriate soothing during the patients' affectomotor storms. This is accomplished by a long period of "being there" for the patients and demonstrating a high capacity for empathy and frustration under conditions of little positive change (Chessick 1977, p. 140). Similar to a good-enough mother, the therapist must patiently understand and accept these expressions of confusing affect and must learn to anticipate sudden swings (Hedges 1983, p. 125). The rational alliance is stabilized to the degree that the patients can both develop meaningful trust in the therapist and sustain a sense of autonomy within the therapeutic relationship.

The therapist's contribution to this development of trust and autonomy is not totally clear, but it is generally linked to the following actions: (1) responding empathically to the idiosyncratic needs, anxieties, and inner tensions felt by the patients; (2) responding to the patients according to their individuality rather than the therapist's needs or preexisting therapeutic stereotype; (3) stating at the beginning of the treatment and again at various critical junctures both the therapist's and patients' roles; (4) maintaining strict confidentiality (no easy matter in this age of insurance forms and other documentation); (5) being certain that one's verbal and nonverbal behavior is consistent (e.g., if setting a limit verbally, being certain to do so in action) (Meissner 1982, pp. 357–361).

Rinsley (1982a) found that the therapist must be remarkably sensitive to changes in the patients' anxiety level in order to modify the therapeutic technique "at the drop of a hat." On the one hand, depending on the patients' needs, the therapist must set limits, provide a protective environment, or even stop all interpretations. At the same time, patients must be expected to work productively at a deeper level when they are capable of doing so.

It is beyond the scope of this book to review the differences among the transference, therapeutic alliance, narcissistic alliance, and real relationship between patient and therapist.

Reparenting—A Difficult Decision

The good-enough holding approach should not be interpreted as a justification for giving the patients all aspects of a better parenting experience than they received as a child. (Alexander and French [1946] have referred to this as a *corrective emotional experience* in which the therapist role-plays what the patient needs.) This is because, as Glenn (1979) observed, borderline adults are no longer children:

> Even childlike adults have different personality structures from children. A gratification later in life does not make up for a deprivation in childhood. (Analysis of the effects of the deprivation can be therapeutically effective, however.). (pp. 33–34)

I believe, however, that understanding the impact of the patients' deprivation (not feeling loved for themselves) and conveying this understanding to the patients can help as much as any direct action can.

Some theorists' positions on reparenting have been generally misunderstood. Blanck and Blanck, for example, stated clearly that they are not suggesting reparenting for the patients. Rather, they are suggesting an approach designed to catalyze the patients' organizing process of the ego. They evaluate the patients' behavior according to its subphase meaning and offer therapeutic behavior that will allow the patients to remain stable while at the same time explaining to them this subphase inadequacy.

Blanck and Blanck (1979, pp. 156–157) have discussed the use of transitional objects when the therapist cannot meet with the patients. For example, when they went on vacation, they gave one severely disturbed woman their phone number on a piece of paper so that she could have it as a transitional object. The woman never telephoned them, but she felt secure just having the number. Blanck and Blanck seldom use postcards with neurotic patients but have found them to be invaluable with borderline patients. In one case, their innocuously worded postcard would arrive at the patient's home just as she was reaching a place of despair and depression; it buoyed her up, thus reestablishing the object image.

Buie and Adler (1982–1983) and Blanck and Blanck (1979, p. 156) have said that in this way the therapist establishes continuity of self- and object images and begins to enter into the formally "closed shop" of the narcissistic unit as a consistent, reliable, dependable catalyst for development. When a patient started arriving late for her sessions with one of the Blancks, they did not regard it as traditional resistance. Instead, they saw it as a stepping away, a triumph for the therapeutic relationship because the patient had become confident enough to venture into behavior that resembled a belated practicing subphase. Hedges (1983) has agreed with the Blancks' view, though pointing out that at times important therapist-differentiating activities *must* take place (e.g., the therapist's refusal to allow the patient to engage in self-destructive behavior) even when the patient is imposing self-object merger.

As many theorists have noted, the danger in attempting directly to reparent the patients is that massive countertransference acting out may be the result. Patients can become increasingly seduced by the primary gratifications involved in reparenting, such as being touched, being held, and receiving free therapy or unlimited access to the therapist. Although this kind of gratification may temporarily soothe the patients, it inevitably leads to a fixation. Although reparenting is gratifying for the patients, it almost always involves unresolved parent transference issues for the therapist and rarely leads to lasting change (Chessick 1977).

A profound hatred of the therapist may result when patients intuitively recognize that he or she is receiving some kind of nontherapeutic gratification (e.g., competing with the patients' parents or giving to the patients in order to be loved). Even more important, these patients express rage when they realize that they can have no possible future relationship with the therapist outside the therapy, and they then conclude that eventually they will lose or be rejected by the therapist (Chessick 1977, p. 136).

How Much Reparenting Should Be Offered?

How much reparenting should be offered is a question debated by many of the followers of Kohut and Kernberg and usually has several different parts:

1. How much direct caretaking, physical affection, love, protection, and favors should the therapist give to the patients?
2. How much should the patients be "held" emotionally until they elect to change, versus how much must they be pushed out of symbiotic relatedness?
3. To what degree should therapists be "real" people and share their private life or their own reactions to and feelings toward the patients (negative or positive) during the sessions?

Decisions regarding these three issues may be particularly difficult for clinicians who do not have a backlog of experience to help them determine the best course of action.

Students and clinicians must remember that the spirit of psychoanalytic psychotherapy is not one of active intervention except in crises or life-threatening situations. The emphasis should be on understanding the patients and empathically conveying the therapist's understanding of the patients' moment-to-moment feelings and thoughts.

On the issue of reparenting, I consider the patients to be adults in a professional relationship. Because of the severity of their problems, some modification of technique is required, with an emphasis on the holding environment. The therapist should pay particular attention to the patients' affectomotor storms, their need for techniques preliminary to interpretation, and their need for an occasional structured environment. But these should not be confused with or mistaken for reparenting. After all, how is it possible to examine some of the patient's distorted transference reactions if the therapist is acting like the patient's parent?

I also discourage indiscriminate sharing of one's emotional reactions with the patients, because borderline individuals often either feel a need to be like the therapist or else fear the therapist's anger (e.g., "If my therapist is angry with me, I must be bad and worthless"). Sharing personal feelings usually scares the patients or reinforces the "false-self" process. Finally, I believe that the therapist must provide some help differentiating out of symbiosis (e.g., by pointing out splitting when it occurs or by confronting the SORU's destructive impact on the patients' life).

How Certain Forms of Reparenting May Boomerang

Example 1 A male psychiatry resident lent several books on assertion training to one of his highly responsible and ethical male borderline patients. Several weeks later, the resident took off some scheduled time. When he returned, the patient failed to appear for his first postvacation visit and did not respond to phone calls or letters. The resident was understandably angry at the loss of his books. The patient was hospitalized several months later for severe depression. He then told the resident how angry he was at being abandoned (even though he knew well in advance about the resident's vacation). The patient admitted being so angry that he decided to punish the resident by not returning his books. Then he felt so guilty about keeping them that he could not come back to therapy. The resident was shocked at the intensity of the patient's feelings and was surprised that the books (and all the associated feelings) had precipitated the patient's decision to stop therapy.

Example 2 A female psychology intern was working with a lower-level borderline woman. In a moment of crisis in the patient's life, the intern put her arm around the woman. Over the next week, the patient regressed massively and hardly left her bed. Exploration of the regression revealed that the patient felt that this human gesture was a private indication from the therapist that she would totally take care of the patient, that the patient was truly special, and that sexual contact might now take place. The patient both yearned for and feared the sexual contact. This was the first inkling that the intern had of the patient's polymorphous sexuality and fusion of sexuality and nurturance. It took months of tumultuous interactions before therapy calmed down again.

Example 3 A female psychiatric resident working with a very dependent, male borderline adult allowed the patient to call her at home when he felt overwhelmed. Soon he started calling every day, often several times per day in an intense panic. This went on for months before the desperate resident discussed it in supervision. The matter became totally out of control when the patient reported sitting outside the resident's house for hours on end in order to soothe himself. After supervision, the resident confronted this behavior and offered to hospitalize the patient, which he declined. She also told him that she would no longer accept home telephone calls but would see him more often than once a week. The patient then began to control his behavior. He told the therapist that he had felt as though he were going crazy as he longed more and more for her presence. He also felt intense anger at her for allowing this to happen to him. A number of sessions were required to work through this issue.

Example 4   I have occasionally allowed particularly responsible borderline patients to delay paying their bills or have lowered their fees because of their financial difficulties. In all cases but one, the patients became reluctant to make payments on their growing bill. When I reduced the fees, the patients clearly spent the difference on items such as clothing or furniture. Exploration revealed that they all felt anger at having to pay for what they felt should be free (e.g., the therapist's love and concern). They also felt that the therapist should see that they got "goodies" in life and should not be deprived.

These policy deviations often play into the borderline adults' psychodynamic issues, even activating them, though this does not mean the therapist should never touch the hand of a distraught patient or should never reduce fees. Certainly, all therapists can relate similar examples in which such behavior seemed to help the patient. But exceptions should not be allowed without some minimal exploration of their impact, and the therapist should never be surprised when patients act out or use an exception as part of their borderline process.

SPECIFIC FACTORS: SOUND THERAPEUTIC TECHNIQUES

Several theorists recommend the following techniques or combination of techniques for facilitating change and promoting progress:

1. Listening skills
2. Clarification and explanation (educative) skills
3. Structure, limit-setting skills, and confrontation
4. Interpretation skills

The expert dosage, timing, and blend of these techniques cannot be learned from a book, and the case material in Chapter 12 is designed to offer only a background in this area. Only by participating under supervision in ongoing cases can one learn to combine the techniques.

Listening Skills

Psychotherapists from Freud onward have taken a special interest in how to listen to patients. Learning to listen carefully to the patients' material and to use various levels of listening skills takes many years of training.

Purposes of Listening

Following Greenson (1967, p. 100), the therapist is expected to listen with evenly suspended and evenly hovering free-floating attention, with three aims in mind:

1. To translate the patients' material into its unconscious antecedents.
2. To synthesize the unconscious elements into meaningful insights.
3. To communicate these insights to the patients.

Empathy with Patients' Private, Inner-World Experiences

For example, a patient feels furious when a friend does not invite her to an annual New Year's party. The therapist listens empathically, trying to understand what this means to the patient. The goal here is not to solve the problem or give advice but rather to understand the experience both cognitively and affectively, literally and symbolically.

Wolff (see Basch 1983, p. 113) has summarized what the therapist should consider in order to reach empathic understanding:

1. Their own spontaneously occurring mental states, of which there are three types: (a) one's own mental state evoked by the patients' similar mental state, (b) one's own mental state in reaction against one evoked by the patients' mental state, and (c) the absence of the mental state expected to be evoked by the patients' mental state.
2. Deliberately constructed thought experience: the construction in one's own mind of the patients' postulated emotional position, followed by the introspection of one's own mental state resulting from this thought experience.

Using the above example, the therapist can review his or her own reactions to the patient's story of being omitted from the guest list. The therapist may have a variety of reactions, such as feeling anger and hurt on her behalf, feeling she is overreacting without having all the facts, or feeling annoyed or worried that she is so angry. The therapist then reviews all of his or her feelings to see how they help him or her understand the patient's reactions. What else might the patient be feeling? What meaning is she finding in the incident?

Empathy and understanding are an inherent part of any good therapy and that therapeutic empathy must go beyond that of the mother–infant relationship. The therapist tries to empathize not only with the patient's subjective experiences but also with the intolerable aspects that are projected and disowned. Kernberg (1980b) believes that both Winnicott's concept of holding and Bion's concept of containing have relevance. *Holding* refers not to taking care of the patient but rather to the therapist's ability to contain emotionally the patient's severe aggression while remaining emotionally available to him or her. *Containing* refers to the same phenomenon but at the cognitive level, at which the therapist understands the patient's intolerable aspects and returns them to the patient via interpretation so that they can be assimilated. Adler and Buie probably would agree with this statement but have stated that interpretation must come later in the process than Kernberg suggests.

Levels of Listening

The therapist listens on at least three levels:

1. The manifest content of the patients' material (what is readily observable).
2. The latent level of the material (its underlying meaning).
3. The therapist's own transference and resistance reactions to the patients or their material.

Suppose that a therapist is delayed for a session and does not reduce the fee. A male patient arrives late at the next session, explaining that he was delayed by a long-distance phone call (manifest content). Perhaps he was in fact unavoidably detained, and there is no other reason for being late. Nevertheless, the latent content (symbiotic meaning) of his lateness could well be anger and an unconscious wish to pay back the therapist in kind. If this is so, careful exploration will usually turn up some evidence supporting this hypothesis. In addition, the patient may drop clues regarding how he sees the therapist, by commenting about other people: "He never gets his life together" or "He is dishonest." These are often indirect comments on the therapist's personality and inappropriate changes in the therapeutic frame.

When using the developmental approach, the therapist should review both the manifest and the latent content according to Hedges's (1983) five perspectives. Patients should be observed as they shift up and down the developmental ladder from day to day. The therapist may refer to Blanck's and Blanck's 14 developmental tasks and determine the patients' position on each dimension. Selecting the appropriate therapeutic techniques depends greatly on where the therapist places the patients on the developmental continuum at any given moment. Do they need holding or weaning?

The therapist should also scan the material and his or her own reactions to it in order to discover personal countertransferences, inappropriate interventions, or inappropriate changes in the treatment. It is important, too, to monitor one's own personality, pathology, or inappropriate change in the therapeutic framework (e.g., often starting the therapy late). Both Langs (1976, 1978, 1978–1979, 1980, 1981) and Searles (1960, 1965, 1979) stress that the relationship of the patient and therapist is a bipersonal field and is mutually influential and that the pathology of both the therapist and the patient remains active within this frame.

Searles has said that patients often obliquely address the therapist's pathology in order to "heal" the therapist so that the therapy can continue appropriately. In other words, patients can become a "container" for the therapist's pathology as often as the therapist becomes a "container" for the patients' pathology (Bion 1957). Projective identification operates in both directions. Therefore, therapists must be particularly sensitive to the patients' productions, monitoring their own feelings and reactions and noting how these feelings and reactions affect the patients in the session. Often patients will test endlessly to see whether or not the therapist is really listening and is able to tolerate the onslaught of aggression that will emerge in the therapy. It is the task of the therapist, of course, to contain and calmly process the patients' material so that they can come to believe the therapist is in fact different from their parents.

Deciding what material the patients will constructively use and when to give it to them is an important aspect of the listening perspective. Beginners frequently err by giving an insight to a patient as soon as they recognize it. Many theorists oppose this, suggesting instead that the therapist's interpretation should remain "a silent one" (Spotnitz 1969), held inside but guiding some of the therapist's action until the patients are truly ready to receive it.

Reviewing Appropriate Conceptual Models

I recommend scanning the patients' behavior and verbalizations with the developmental perspective in mind, particularly Hedges's (1983) five perspectives, in order to select specific techniques.

Peterfreund (1975) has pointed out that psychoanalytic psychotherapy offers a number of models to help the clinician understand the patients. These models are as follows:

1. A general working model of people and things in our culture and times, normal expectable cognitive and emotional relationships.
2. A working model of the analyst himself, his own history, character traits, typical reaction patterns, etc.
3. A working model of experiences in infantile and childhood development; fantasied elaboration of these; and primitive ideation.
4. A working model of the analytic process.
5. A working model representing previous learning and experience.
6. A working model of the specific patient being analyzed.
7. A working model, actually a metamodel, based on clinical theories.
8. A working model, actually a group of metamodels, including informational, hormonal, chemical, genetic models, etc. (Peterfreund 1975, pp. 78–79)

There is always the possibility that these models can be inappropriately applied. Improper use of a model may mislead the clinician into continuously seeing data that support his or her own theoretical viewpoint, and sharing this theory may affect the patients' spontaneous verbalizations. But the dangers presented by the inappropriate use of models are far outweighed by the problems that confront the clinician who works without a conceptual framework, for then the therapy may become aimless and meaningless.

Clarifications

Clarifications are statements intended to emphasize some aspect of the patients' manifest material. Here one simply invites further attention to the patients' material, thereby implying its possible importance. Clarifications may also mean recapitulating a patients' remarks, sometimes in different words but without attempting to draw any inferences. Although a clarification does not present the patients with any possibilities not already in their conscious awareness, it may initiate a sequence of interventions that lead to new material. Masterson (1976), Kernberg (1982c, 1982f), and Chessick (1982b) have reported that clarifications probably dominate the early therapy with borderline adults.

Chessick (1982b) observed that in addition to allowing the "self-cohering effect of the holding environment to take over," the therapist should be devoted to the "identification of basic conflicts and a minute study of the day-to-day production and disappearance of rages," along with the patients' discovery that their rages do not incur retaliation or abandonment by the therapist (p. 419).

Clarification dovetails with one of the aims of listening—to understand phenomenologically the patients' inner thoughts, feelings, experiences, and fantasies—with the aim of linking them to developmentally relevant inter-pretations. Clarification should be continued until both the patient and the therapist understand what the patient is saying *or* the therapist is ready to admit an inability to understand the material.

A long period of working at this primitive level of explaining the conflict may be necessary before any interpretations will make sense to the patients (Chessick 1977, p. 150). For example, a therapist often points out contra-dictory ego states, helping the patients recognize their splitting long before attempting to interpret it. For example, "I notice that last week you felt your husband was the perfect man for you and that this week you seem to believe he is completely wrong for you." The therapist may work at such a level for a number of months in therapy.

Clarification also is often an important tool in resolving conflicts between the therapist and patient and may be an adjunctive technique after using confrontation, for example, in dealing with self-destructive behavior. Gun-derson (1981) and Frosch (1983) made this point. No matter what the therapist does initially in regard to, say, suicidal self-destructiveness (rang-ing from giving all of the responsibility to the patients to taking over and structuring their life), it is even more important that the therapist clarify the following: (1) the interactional elements of the self-destructiveness, (2) why the therapist responded in such a manner, and (3) the patients' re-sponse to and fantasies about the therapist's response. If the patients' reaction to the therapist's intervention is not studied and clarified, the therapist may very well unintentionally reinforce a pathological interaction that is often a repetition of what has taken place with the patients and their families. This is often the most crucial task in the early phase of therapy because it starts the process of reducing distortions.

In practice, therapists often rely too heavily on questions to clarify the patients' material. An alternative way to raise an issue is a statement such as "Although you've been talking about divorce, I notice that you haven't said how you feel about it." Questions should never be used with machine-gun rapidity or be too intrusive. Sample questions for clarification are "I wonder if you could tell me more about that?" or "What are you feeling right now?" Picking up on the last few words of what the patients have said and repeating it to them with a rising inflection—"You said you got mad at your mother?"—is another possibility.

Explanations (Educative Techniques)

Explanations have been recommended by a number of authors (Blanck and Blanck 1979, Hedges 1983, Masterson 1976), and Kernberg (1982c, 1982f) recently demonstrated how to use explanation in supportive psychoanalytic psychotherapy.

Blanck and Blanck found that at times, explanation precedes interpretation because some patients must be helped to understand the connection between some of their symptoms and the subphase inadequacy that caused them. The Blancks have developed several approaches for this purpose. They use a variety of techniques ranging from sensitively playing the devil's advocate to tactfully but gently moving the patients through a series of Socratic questions interspersed with brief statements of what must have happened to them as children and what they must be struggling with now. Blanck and Blanck worked with patients along their 14 dimensions (see Figure 11-1) and devised a way of clarifying the subphase inadequacies with the patients and moving them along the fulcrum of development. The Blancks use clarification, exploration, and explanation in this process. An example of their approach (1979, pp. 229-230, 249-251) is given in the following therapist–patient dialogue.

A 40-year-old divorced businessman is in treatment for almost a year. The therapist has had a brief vacation in February, and now the patient wishes to have an Easter vacation to spend with his young daughter who lives year-round with her mother. He asks whether he will have to pay for the missed sessions, although he has been in treatment with therapists three times before and knows the usual arrangements.

Therapist: You must have a reason for asking.

Patient: Well, I thought when you went away you didn't pay me, so why should I have to pay you when I go away? (Failure to differentiate blurs logic.)

Therapist: Does that feel the same to you?

Patient: Sure.

Therapist: (Stretching the capacity for reality testing.) You see no difference in our situations?

Patient: Yeah, I guess there are some. It still feels unfair, though. I'll be paying for all that time. (It succeeds.)

Therapist: What will I be doing with the time?

Patient: I never thought about that. (Therapist hasn't existed when not seen.)

Therapist: Can you imagine now? (Stretches object retention.)

Patient: You'll probably see someone else. (Objects are interchangeable to therapist as they are to patient because of the faulty differentiation.)

Therapist: Would you want me to do that?

Patient: No, I'd rather pay and know that the time is saved for me.

Therapist: You know, you have the right to telephone in that time if you'd like.

The following dialogue pertains to leading the patient out of the immediacy of the primary dyadic interaction and the repair of splitting.

Patient: I look awful today.

Therapist: Then you are feeling bad about yourself.

Patient: My mother called me this morning and I just could not stand it. I'm in my middle forties and she's still telling me what to do every day. So I yelled at her and told her to leave me alone.

Therapist: And so you are now feeling so bad for having done that.

Patient: It's so confusing. She's a big pain in the neck and there is nothing to like about her behavior, yet it still makes me feel so bad, to be mean to her.

Therapist: Ah! Now you're getting close to what it is. You have trouble in understanding that you can dislike just that aspect of her behavior. When you yell at her and then feel bad, it's because instead of disliking this or that aspect, you dislike and want to discard all of her.

Patient: I see that. But why does she call me every day?

Therapist: Perhaps you both encourage that.

Patient: You mean she needs to do it?

Therapist: I mean that you need it too, and so you participate in it.

Patient: But I told you it makes me mad.

Therapist: That's because part of you wants to get out of it. But we have to deal with the part of you that still needs a mother.

Patient: Great! At my age I still need a mother. I suppose you're right. How do I get out of that? It feels so difficult.

Therapist: It feels that way because we haven't yet found what it is you need her for.

Patient: Maybe I like to have her tell me what to do but the adult in me can't stand it.

Therapist: That is one possibility. But I rather think that you don't feel comfortable about her need.

Patient: Oh. I get it. I'd push her away for good and then I'd have to be on my own.

Therapist: But I think you have additional worries—not that that one is so small.

Patient: Yes. What would become of her?

Therapist: So you have to remain a child so that your mother won't lose her "job" as mother. Otherwise she'd be unemployed.

Patient: She needs me, so I need her. We're in a vicious cycle.

Therapist: Now that you see that you may find a place where you can break into it without feeling that it will destroy her.

Patient: We'd be separate persons then.

Therapist: Might that feel good?

Patient: It feels terrific already. But can I do it?

Therapist: I believe now that gradually you will, as you see that it doesn't harm either of you.

Patient: But sometimes she is so good to me. I don't want to lose her. It makes me feel good, too—just as it makes me feel bad to yell at her when she encroaches too much.

Therapist: You experience her as sometimes good and sometimes bad. That's what makes you feel bad about yourself. You'd like to think of her as perfect so that you'll never get angry with her.

Patient: That's exactly what happens. One day we have a pleasant conversation. Sometimes in the same conversation I end up hating her.

Therapist: Because you are looking for a perfect mother and she disappoints you.

Patient: Everyone does. No one is perfect. But I can see that I want that.

A pattern running through all this dialogue shows a technique of dealing with organizational malformations whenever possible, not with behavioral consequences. In the first example, the therapist refuses the invitation to do battle. It is important for the therapist using the Blanck and Blanck model to see beyond interpersonal provocation to the developmental malformations, in this case to poor self-object differentiation, poor object constancy, and the problems of entitlement. These malformations must then be worked with therapeutically.

Masterson (1976, pp. 103–104) has named his particular form of educative explanation *communicative matching,* which is an effort to explain by discussing, from the patients' own knowledge, the general and universal aspects of the new interest or feeling presented. For example, as one of his very paranoid patients started to make hesitant moves toward women, Masterson felt it was necessary not only to deal with the patient's fear of rejection but also to discuss many of the universal problems that exist between the sexes. As patients start to develop a small sense of self and to individuate, Masterson supports the individuation by talking about the patients' new interests. Generally, Masterson recommends communicative matching after the patients have attained some control over the rewarding and withdrawing SORUs and are in a therapeutic alliance with the therapist. However, he warned that the therapist must be careful not to do this too often and must be empathic and attuned to the patients' newly emerging self. Communicative matching must be done in response to the need of the patients, not to the narcissism of the therapist.

Rinsley (1982a) at times also judiciously uses educative techniques, especially in reference to object inconstancy and fantasy deficit. In regard to object constancy, Rinsley works with imagery training both to show the patients that the therapist understands their problem and to teach them how to summon up an image. Rinsley directs the patients to close their eyes and picture him "inside" and then to open their eyes and actually see him again. Next, he tells the patients to make the image "go away" by closing their eyes and then to look at him again. He remarked that one of the advantages of this method is that it is playful and clearly regressive (p. 229).

Rinsley (1982a, pp. 230–232) also uses educative explanations for patients who have a fantasy deficit. Why is this even a problem? Fantasies and dreams are ways to plan and set realistic goals and to work through unconscious conflict and integrate it with material closer to consciousness. These deficits in borderline patients are, of course, related to impaired object constancy and object permanency and also mean persistence of the transitional object and mode of experience (Modell 1968). Working this through and helping the patients learn to experience and report their fantasies, particularly as elaborated in the transference, is essential.

The following example shows how Rinsley (1982a, p. 231) might work with such a situation. In many ways, it resembles the work done by Blanck and Blanck.

Therapist: I know it's hard to tell me what you think about or daydream or even fantasize. . . .

Patient: Yup . . . I'm afraid to.

Therapist: Why is that?

Patient: Well, because if I tell you about those things you'll have them and I won't have them any more.

Therapist: Uh, uh . . . if you tell me, you'll have them and I'll have them . . . we'll both have them.

Patient: Yipe! I never thought of that!

Self-disordered patients often have great fears about sharing their inner world. Rinsley (1982a) has listed several ways that borderline patients view fantasies: (1) any fantasy per se is dangerous to oneself and others, most notably the therapist; (2) having fantasies implies that one is crazy; (3) fantasies are secrets that the therapist will steal or otherwise take away (the so-called primal exchange); (4) fantasies must be acted on and out; and (5) sexual and masturbatory fantasies, particularly in relation to the therapist, are especially fearsome and dangerous (p. 231).

Several theorists, including Masterson (1976, 1981), would probably rely on confrontation in some instances in which others such as Blanck and Blanck (1979) would rely on clarification and explanation (education). Often a combination of these three techniques is useful. Sometimes confrontation simply becomes too much for patients, and so slipping into the Blanck and Blanck approach is a useful alternative because it enables the therapist to continue working with the material.

Structure and Limit Setting

The importance of establishing and maintaining enough structure in the psychotherapy of borderline patients has been stressed by many clinicians. Meissner (1982–1983a) observed that at times of increased regressive strain, the therapist needs to increase the degree of structure in the therapeutic interaction and focus on the current reality and the patterns of current behavior. Kernberg and others have found that such patients may require hospitalization, day treatment, medication, or social services support.

Meissner (1982–1983a) noted that some of the most difficult aspects of therapy with borderline patients—particularly those in the more primitive range—is balancing the therapist's degree of activity and passivity, deciding on the appropriate level of structure, and choosing between regression and ego support. Meissner discovered that the failure to maintain adequate structure can lead to excessive regression, acting out, and a predominance of many unhealthy transference-countertransference interactions. On the other hand, maintaining a rigid structure can interfere with the development of transference. Thus, the therapist is constantly confronted with a therapeutic dilemma—the need to maintain structure as an essential ingredient in the therapeutic situation and the need to approach the borders of regression as a means of activating the potential for therapeutic change. Each therapist must learn how to titrate these two ingredients to the patient's best advantage.

Meissner (1982–1983a) and many others consider setting limits as a way of establishing and maintaining structure, particularly during an acute regressive crisis or acting-out behavior. The failure to set such limits may stall the therapy. Let us consider patients who are threatening suicide, self-mutilation, or other destructive behaviors. The more primitive the patients are, the less they may respond to verbal interpretations; they may instead need a new experience in which the therapist sets the limit ("I will hospitalize you if . . .") The therapist's actual setting of effective limits can give patients the protective and caring intervention that was lacking in the early developmental interaction with their mother. Only after the limit is set is it possible to study and interpret some of the meanings of the patients' behavior. With higher-level patients, limit setting is needed often.

Confrontations

In the psychotherapy of borderline patients, confrontation often is important, and with regressed patients, it often is essential. Confrontations refer to all those interventions from the mild to the heroic that call attention to some aspect of the patients' behavior. Confrontations are used both to foster the patients' growth and to protect the therapist's autonomy. The use of confrontation with borderline patients, nonetheless, is one of the more controversial areas in the literature.

If such theorists as Hedges (1983) are correct when they say that borderline patients need a symbiotic replication experience, then confrontation will simply disrupt the necessary symbiotic equilibrium. In such a situation, replication would not flower, be revealed, and given up naturally through the therapist's empathic understanding, exploration of options, and maintenance of personal boundaries in the face of demands for continued replication experiences. Other experts (Kernberg and Masterson), however, take a different position.

Adler and Buie (1972) and Buie and Adler (1972) were early advocates of the judicious use of confrontation with borderline patients who were engaging in clearly self-destructive behavior. On the other hand, they recommended that the therapist guard against the following actions in order to avoid undermining trust: (1) unduly upsetting patients who are already under serious stress in their lives, (2) breaking down needed defenses, (3) overstimulating the patients' wishes for closeness, (4) overstimulating the patients' rages, and (5) confronting narcissistic entitlement (until late in the therapy).

According to Rinsley (1982a), the therapist must confront the rewarding SORU in a particularly sensitive way. Otherwise, the patients who are receiving good feelings from the rewarding SORU may feel condemned for feeling good and think the therapist is saying that they are bad and is trying to humiliate or deprive them. This reaction may rupture the therapeutic alliance. Rinsley (1982a) stressed that disapproval of a deleterious symptomatic act should be conveyed or communicated in the context of both the acceptance of the patient as a whole and the need that underlies the particular act or behavior. In other words, neither the patients nor their needs are rejected.

Of all the theorists working with borderline adults, Masterson (1976, 1981) has most emphasized the use of confrontation (see Chapter 8). He (1976) explained:

> Confrontation, the principal therapeutic technique of this [the early] phase, throws a monkey wrench in the patient's defense system by introducing conflict where there previously had been none. . . . When the therapist points out the harm the patient can no longer act out without recognizing the harm. Therefore conflict and tension are created. . . . He has to recognize the cost of "feeling good." . . . It is important to keep in mind that confrontation is needed throughout the therapy (pp. 100–101).

Masterson (1981) gave this example of a confrontation: "Since these interactions disappoint you or are painful to you, why do you seek your mother out at these times? Why do you let your mother treat you this way?" (p. 32). This confrontation, he observed, calls attention to how destructive the behavior is and invites the patient to investigate why. An interpretation, on the other hand, suggests why the patient behaves in a certain way. In a confrontation, the answer comes from the patient—not the therapist—thus avoiding the possibility that the patient will use the therapist's interpretation for resistance and transference acting out instead of for insight.

But Masterson (1976) also stated that confrontation has dangers of its own and suggested the following guidelines:

1. The therapist must be really there, empathic and tuned in to the patients' feeling state.
2. The confrontation must pertain to the content of the patients' association and feeling state.
3. The confrontation must clearly be in the patients' best interest; otherwise, it becomes a manipulation through the use of authoritarian power.
4. The therapist must confront quietly, firmly, and consistently without being angry or contentious. "He must be able to disagree without being disagreeable." (p. 101)

Masterson and Kernberg firmly believe that the therapeutic alliance will not solidify unless the negative transference is confronted. They differ from Hedges and Blanck and Blanck, who frequently but not always view hostility as a differentiating behavior and verbally support it. Hedges and the Blancks may reward what would appear to Masterson as the withdrawing SORU, but Masterson would probably confront it.

Other psychoanalytic theorists also use confrontations combined with explanations instead of interpretations. For example, Kernberg (1982f, p. 192) pointed out that in supportive psychotherapy he focuses consistently on the contradiction between beliefs and behavior or between competing beliefs. In addition, he expresses his opinion directly if it appears that the patient needs it. For example, Kernberg said to a male patient, "If you make even mildly angry comments to your boss and he is as revengeful as you say, won't you be threatening the job you so want to keep?" The patient then verbally attacked Kernberg for siding with his authoritarian boss. In response, Kernberg reminded the patient how badly he had felt when he had lost other jobs because of making critical remarks to his boss and commented that he himself was reacting to the patient's concerns. Kernberg clarified the reality aspects of his remarks, ultimately trusting the patient to make his own decision.

Chessick (1979) reported that sometimes he uses a simple confrontation combined with explanation, whereas Kernberg might use a sophisticated interpretation. When patients over a period of time experience either a negative or an eroticized transference, Chessick uses a

technique which consists essentially of confronting the patient as tactfully and as calmly as possible with the common-sense reality of the therapeutic situation . . . pointing out the discrepancy between the kinds of affect . . . or even the kinds of cognitive distortions the patient is experiencing—and the reality of the therapy and the relationship. (p. 540)

An example would be a patient who demands unlimited access to the therapist, acting as though the therapist were indeed a mother who was deliberately withholding contact. In this situation, the therapist needs to reaffirm the therapist–patient role and the nature of the therapeutic contact, by explaining that it is not possible to be available constantly to the patient. Everyday language rather than obscure metapsychological terms should always be used for such an explanation.

More heroic confrontations are sometimes necessary because of the patients' persistent resistance, the seriousness of their acting out, or suicidal or homicidal threats (even against the therapist). In the case of persistent resistance, Masterson suggests one major exception to his rule that confrontation be carried out without much affect: When resistance continues to impede progress despite a major confrontation, a certain amount of "therapeutic astonishment" is necessary in order to alert the patients to the dangers of their resistance. In other words, although the confrontation should not be aggressive or angry, it can be effectively stated.

Giovacchini (1979a) asserted that therapists make many interventions in order to retain personal or professional boundaries, identity, and integration. Sometimes therapists confront and set limits simply to maintain their own integrity as human beings (e.g., when the patient's hostility is so excessive that the therapist becomes angry or when the patient intrudes so much into the therapist's life that the therapist cannot maintain personal privacy). Kernberg (1975a) believes that therapists should first interpret acting out or patient demands (e.g., often telephoning at night), and if this is unsuccessful, then they will be forced to set limits to protect their own integrity.

Epstein (1979, pp. 392–393) noted that in an extremely vicious cycle of psychotic proportions, patients may need to be confronted with the therapist's counteraggression. The patients may be pouring out hate or trying to induce feelings of badness in the therapist. The therapist expresses counter-aggression (under good ego control, it is hoped) because the patients often need such a strong, openly aggressive response. This response helps re-establish the patients' self-other boundaries, which tend to become obliter-ated by such attacks, and it also reassures the patients about the therapist's survival. Epstein reported that usually the patients become angry in return, which enables them to see the feelings and thoughts that they had been concealing behind their negative behavior. Epstein does not give an example of a "counteraggressive response," but it is clear that he does not mean that the therapist goes out of control, throws a temper tantrum, or says hateful things. Instead, for example, the therapist with a chronically silent patient might show controlled irritation by saying, "I refuse to keep trying to get you to talk. When you are ready, I will respond." Epstein says that direct counteraggression showing real feelings is often less lethal than is the hate-infested interpretation that such patients recognize but cannot directly address. An example of this approach will be shown in Mary Markham's clinical case in Chapter 12.

Interpretation Skills

One of the ways that psychodynamic psychotherapy proceeds is by making the unconscious conscious. The better that patients understand the uncon-scious underpinnings of their behavior, the more self-awareness they have. In turn, with greater self-awareness, these underlying needs, wishes, and fantasies can be more easily controlled (Weiner 1975, p. 38). The basic element in interpretation is linking the present with the past.

Interpretation generally refers to statements that imply unconscious motivation: "Your fears of succeeding at your own business may well be related to your fears of surpassing your father, who failed at all his business ventures" is a typical interpretation. (Of course, this would not be stated early in the therapy.)

The essence of interpretation is that the patients must know the thera-pist is on their side, even if he or she disapproves of certain behavior. Ilan

(1977) points out it is the mode of communication, not only the content, that makes an interpretation worthwhile. For example, Ilan would try to convey to the patient, "I can understand your longings, your fantasies, your aggression. I don't always agree with your behavior but I don't blame you and I'm with you." This message would be communicated on both a verbal and a nonverbal level.

How successful is this interpretative approach with borderline adults? Opinion among the experts is mixed. Masterson believes that interpretation does not work; only Kernberg supports early interpretations of the contradictory introjects and their defensive and conflictual functions. He states that interpretations ultimately strengthen the ego and reality testing, by dissolving primitive and pathological structures that support the "weak ego." This aids the therapeutic alliance by helping the patients develop an observing ego. It has holding aspects, in that the therapist has tolerated and integrated through interpretation what the patients found too painful to experience (Kernberg 1980b, p. 198). All experts believe, however, that the use, timing, dosage, and form of interpretation must be tailored to each patient's developmental level. They agree that the areas that should be interpreted (as well as confronted and clarified) are (1) the negative transference, (2) the continued reliance on primitive defenses, and (3) the patients' affectomotor storms. The areas that should not be interpreted, particularly in the early phase of treatment are early genetic-dynamic material and dreams or fantasies (except by relating them in a simple way to here-and-now issues).

Searles (1978, p. 59) has argued against interpreting too early the patients' most basic self, and I concur. Searles has elaborated on the suicidal-despair-engendering effect of premature interpretation:

> That much of what the patient has felt to be the core of his self consists, instead, in large part, in an unconscious identification (introject) derived from experience with a parent. . . . [This] is especially injurious if the analyst [psychotherapist] gives the interpretation in a spirit of disavowing implicitly that he himself possesses, in his own personality functioning, any appreciative element of the particular personality trait in question. An interpretation so given tends to foster the patient's feeling isolated from (a) his usual sense of identity, (b) his parent from whom the introject had been largely derived, and (c) the analyst [psychotherapist]. (p. 59)

Modell (1976) and Searles (1978) both have reported that premature interpretations may be misunderstood, dismissed, ignored, or resented by the patients as an intrusion. Modell (1976) concluded that in the early phases of treatment, patients rarely distinguish interpretations from the therapist's general empathic responses unless the interpretations are unusually intrusive. And if the patients do notice them, it is usually because they want to ascertain the therapist's emotional attitude toward them (Rycroft 1956). This is one reason that Masterson recommends confrontation.

Just because the therapist finds a pattern worthy of interpretation does not mean that it should be immediately shared with the patients. Strachey (1934) wrote that the interpretation must be emotionally immediate, that the patients must experience the interpretation as something actual and relevant. He added that the interpretation must be directed to the point of urgency—the patients must be affectively ready for it. Only then does interpretation bring about structural change, which requires innumerable small steps. The therapist, in other words, must be empathically in tune in order to recognize this moment; otherwise, a good interpretation will just be wasted.

I believe that interpretation should be used sparingly in the beginning of therapy. It should be directed toward elucidating and labeling here-and-now problems such as "When you get angry it scares you. You should push those feelings away and start sleeping instead." Later in the therapy, a correctly timed and tactfully worded interpretation can be a potent tool.

Rinsley (1982a, pp. 130–132) noted a phenomenon similar to the dilemma of premature interpretation: a stumbling block to effective therapy may be the propensity to view all the patients' primitive thoughts and feelings toward the therapist exclusively as projections and displacement. If the therapist ignores the realistic or accurate aspect of those perceptions, the patients will feel attacked. In response, these patients reactivate the bad self-representation, continuing the cycle of derogation-idealization that typifies the borderline transference. The implication here is that some acknowledgment of the patients' accurate perceptions should take place. Kernberg (1984) has suggested acknowledging those aspects that are clearly visible without elaborating further ("I can see that you've noticed that I am distracted—what does that mean to you?").

When an interpretation appears warranted, Searles (1978) advises the therapist "to acknowledge the patient's conscious view, using his own phraseology, but then adding a bit of elaboration to this, which is intendedly interpretive in effect" (p. 53). Searles (1978, p. 57) also pointed out that the therapist's use of silence is problematic at such times and should be used judiciously. This is because the connotation of silence can range from dispassionate to withholding and hostile.

Another debate centers on whether the patients' destructive hate and envy should be interpreted (Kernberg 1975a) or dealt with more directly (Epstein 1979). Epstein argues that a good interpretation of envy may make the patients even more envious of the therapist and can lead to treatment stalemates. I agree that if the therapist reduces interpretations when the patients demonstrate envy by belittling remarks and/or acting out and, instead, concentrates on confrontations and clarifications, the envy will diminish. It has been my experience that the material will reemerge when it is safe.

See Table 11-2 for a summary of the techniques discussed above.

Table 11-2   Techniques of the Mixed-Model Approach

Techniques for Bonding and Deficits

1. Providing a good-enough holding environment and listening carefully to the patients' material.
2. Providing supportive interpretation of the patients' affectomotor storms, particularly when these storms confuse, overwhelm, and terrify the patients.
3. Providing limits and parameters of support (e.g., hospitalization) to rescue the patients from their self-destructive behavior, taking full responsibility for these limits (e.g., not blaming the patients—"You forced me to put you in the hospital"), and exploring the meaning of such acts with the patients.
4. Supplying empathic interpretations or explanations of the patients' emerging inner world experiences.
5. Reinforcing (by means of the above techniques) the patients' positive transference to the therapist, in order to promote identification.

Techniques for Weaning and Conflicts

1. Titrating the confrontation of acting-out behavior (e.g., rewarding and withdrawing SORUs).
2. Exploring, confronting, and interpreting the negative transference and at times highly unrealistic positive transference.
3. Using insight or interpretations of unconscious motivation and analysis of the transference when the patients can tolerate them.
4. Not interpreting to patients who are temporarily regressed, but also not engaging in suppressive, supportive measures when the patients can work.
5. Not denying the patients' accurate "early warning system" perceptions of the therapist's thoughts and feelings, anticipating the patients' paranoid reaction, and expecting them to work eventually with their part of the projections and to reclaim them.

THE SPECIAL CONTRIBUTION OF TRANSFERENCE AND COUNTERTRANSFERENCE TO THERAPY

Transference and countertransference are common terms in the literature that imply that the therapist and the patient react to each other in ways that may influence the quality and outcome of the psychotherapy. An understanding of both phenomena is important because in many ways the bulk of the psychotherapy of borderline adults revolves around the therapeutic relationship and the reactions of the patient and the therapist to each other.

In its traditional meaning, as discussed in Chapter 10, *transference* refers to the patient's unrealistic transfer of problems from past relationships to present ones (e.g., that with the therapist), with the patient's acting as though the therapist were indeed the figure in the past relationship. In addition, transference can include the projection of superego, ego ideal, id, or ego aspects onto the present person. Finally, Gill (1982) goes beyond the traditional definition in stating that transference reactions are usually organized around significant contributions from the therapist in the here and now and that the best transference interpretations usually include references to these contributions as construed by the patients (e.g., a patient with control problems may construe the therapist's silence as a way of controlling the patient and thus may talk about struggles with other people when he or she is really reacting to the therapist's behavior and construing it rightly or wrongly as controlling).

In its narrow meaning, *countertransference* refers to the therapist's conscious or unconscious reaction to the patient's transference. In its broad meaning it refers to all of the therapist's conscious or unconscious reactions to the patient.

Because borderline conditions comprise a spectrum falling between the psychoses and the better-functioning narcissistic personality (Rinsley 1981b, 1984a), it should come as no surprise to the reader that the intensity of these patients' transference and the therapist's countertransference reactions varies. Reactions extend from highly intense to subtle and mild, with an entire range of manifestations (e.g., idealizing, devaluing, aggressive, suspicious to the point of paranoid, erotic, victimizing) (Meissner 1982–1983a). The transference reactions of higher-level borderline patients may be more subtle or take much longer to emerge and are more manageable in the therapy. Therapists may often learn of their countertransference problems through stalemates or feelings of confusion in the therapy. With lower-level borderline patients, the transference and countertransference are usually intense and graphic (e.g., the patients accuse the therapist of trying to hurt them, believe the threat is real, and experience terror toward the therapist). The therapist may come to believe that he or she is indeed sadistic toward such a patient, may become paralyzed, or may gradually begin to treat the patient sadistically.

Some borderline patients enjoy defeating the therapist in a repetition of a life-and-death struggle with an important person from their past. This time, however, patients take an active role, whereas previously they were passive, helpless, and vulnerable victims. This state of affairs often elicits intense feelings in the therapist and produces a detrimental transference-countertransference aggressive spiral that can stall the therapy.

Therapists may use their reactive feelings to assess the internalized object relations that patients are reliving with them and thus respond in a fashion that does not repeat the assaultiveness or the abandonment of the patients' early environment. Patients repeat, but therapists should not participate very long in that repetition, according to most experts.

Both transference and countertransference have several aspects. The following list may not be accepted by all experts, but many do accept these conclusions:

1. All patients and therapists have transference and countertransference reactions.
2. Patients' transference reactions may be solely related to genetic material (be independent of the therapist's behavior) but are more frequently related to some amalgam of genetic material and reactions to the therapist's behavior. There is usually some kernel of truth in the patients' transference reactions. Whatever therapists do and say will be the core around which the transference is woven (Gill 1982, p. 2).
3. The patients' transference reactions and the therapists' countertransference operate similarly to the mechanism of projective identification. Each party reacts to the other's projection by consciously or unconsciously processing the projection and then engaging in some behavior that the other responds to; even silence has interpersonal meaning for the patient (Sandler 1976, Gill 1982).
4. Therapists inevitably enact, more or less, the role that their patients assign to them, often without realizing it. Therapists should recognize the role they are playing and use it for interpretative work. They should always consider the role that their behavior played in setting off a transference reaction and possibly make some reference to it in the interpretation (Gill and Hoffman 1982).
5. Therapists often find that their interpretation of the patients' view of the therapeutic relationship in fact confirms the patients' perceptions of it (e.g., the therapist has been talking a lot in session; the patient complains of intrusive people; the therapist interprets that the patient may experience the therapist as intrusive, and indeed the patient finds the

interpretation intrusive; and thus, the patient's experience of the interpretation must also be clarified and worked through) (Gill 1982).

6. The patients' transference reactions and the therapists' countertransference reactions give valuable and essential information about the patients' and the therapist's internalized object relations.

The experts disagree as to whether or not the therapist must, before interpreting, emotionally partake of the transference projections for some period of time or whether cognitive recognition is sufficient.

Representatives of various schools of thought on this topic are DeWald (1964), Freud (1913), Greenacre (1971), Little (1981), Sandler and colleagues (1969) on transference; and Heiman (1950, 1960), Little (1951), Racker (1968), Kernberg (1965, 1975b), and Sandler (1976) on countertransference. Meissner (1982–1983a) has written on transference and countertransference in the therapy of borderline adults. Chrzanowski (1979), Gill (1982), Gill and Hoffman (1982) and Langs (1973, 1975, 1980, 1982) all have written on the transactional aspects of transference and countertransference.

Transference Problems

Most theorists agree that borderline patients exhibit one of three types of transferences, with many subtle variations and fluctuations. These can be broadly categorized as the (1) idealizing transference, (2) devaluing transference, and (3) transference psychosis. Rinsley (1982a) has referred to the first two types as the two d's—deification and devaluation. In working with transference, the therapist can work on its manifestations in relationships outside the therapy (extratransference work), its manifestations in the here-and-now relationship with the patient, and in terms of the past (genetic transference work). The material in this chapter is mainly oriented toward transference manifestations in the therapeutic relationship. Although the other two forms of transference work are legitimate, I believe the first priority is to the therapeutic relationship.

Idealizing Transference

In a clinging, idealizing transference, patients view the therapist as perfect, with unblemished health and endless knowledge. This perception is a projection from the patients' psyche, with the therapist's qualities and role distorted by the patients' fantasies. The patients are responding in many ways to a projection of their own idealized self. Kernberg believes that beneath the idealization are envy and paranoid fantasies. Basically, the patients do not treat the therapist as though he or she has a self. They simply, deliberately, and selectively ignore the human aspect and instead regard the therapist as a transitional object. While idealizing the therapist, these patients often present themselves as less worthy or good, and the therapist must be alert to this victim posture.

Devaluing Transference

Adler (1970) noted that the patients' devaluation of the therapist can have many overlapping motivations: (1) an expression of rage (against fantasied rejection or the therapist's inability to meet unrealistic expectations), (2) a protection against wishes for nurturance (a defensive refusal to take in what the patients long for), (3) a protection against envy (if the patients regard the therapist as worthless, they will have no one to envy, (4) a protection against projected anger (if the therapist is seen as a potential enemy who will attack and hurt the patients, a worthless therapist will not be threatening, (5) a projection of low self-esteem (the patients transfer to the therapist their own feelings of low self-esteem) and (6) a transference manifestation (the patients relive real or fantasied devaluation by a parent). Afterward, the patients feel compelled to maintain contact with the therapist, who now carries the projected impulses. As a result of this transference, the patients fear retaliation and thus feel a great need to control the therapist.

Transference Psychosis

Properly used in reference to borderline patients, transference psychosis applies to patients who lose their reality orientation during the psychotherapy. But although borderline patients may experience hallucinations and delusions in the sessions, they are able to leave the session and function in their outside life. Thus, they differ from psychotic patients, whose transference psychosis permeates their entire life.

We should emphasize the intensity of these transference reactions and the fact that patients may vacillate rapidly between them. Chessick (1977) found that transferences stir up intense feelings of panic, impotence, the desire to be rescued, and the desire to escape the psychotherapy. One can often identify transference reactions as those that are inappropriately intense, tenacious, capricious, and highly ambivalent (Greenson 1967).

Techniques for Dealing with Transference

The therapist should not stifle emerging transference responses. The patients' disruptive introjects (SORUs) must, in a sense, be thawed from the mental blocks of ice in which they have been preserved over the years. As the ice melts and the introjects emerge, the patients for the first time have a safe arena with appropriate limits (the therapeutic environment) for discussing and exploring the introjects. As the therapist comes to understand the introjects, make appropriate interpretations, and interact with the patients, the patients should take in new internalizations that will replace their disruptive introjects.

Often the patients' associations or discussion of some external event (extratransference material) will hint strongly at a parallel experience in the therapeutic relationship, but the therapist cannot see what in the situation serves as a realistic basis for this reaction. If confused, the therapist can ask for the patient's help in this matter, remarking (Gill 1982):

> "The theme of this hour is that you feel criticized by someone and I suspect you feel criticized by me, but I do not see what I have said or done that you might have taken as a criticism. Are you feeling criticized by me? And if so, what do you think has led you to feel that way?" (p. 111)

Gill (1982) continued that it is not necessary for the therapist to take any position on how much the patient's reaction is psychodynamic-genetic in nature and how much it is determined by the actual interpersonal transaction between the therapist and the patient. All that is necessary is a continuing clarification of the patients' view of the therapeutic situation. Gill noted that patients frequently have a difficult time sharing their perceptions or reactions to the therapist and that the therapist should help them.

Epstein (1979) has taken a rather strong stand against a typical analytic interpretation made during a phase of negative transference: "I think you must be so intolerant of your own deficiencies that you are putting them into me and attacking them" (p. 383). He reported that when the analyst is perceived as a bad object, such interpretations will either be rejected or invalidate the patients' need to project their badness. Adler (1982) stated that in the midst of an intense transference reaction, it is easy for the therapist to justify using confrontation and interpretation as being good for the patients or as helping them see something important, when really it comes from the therapist's sadistic hate. How does one tell the difference? The therapist needs considerable personal therapy to make such a distinction.

This contrasts with Kernberg's (1975a) major technical recommendation for dealing with negative transference: "Confrontation with and the interpretation of those pathological defensive operations which characterize borderline patients, as they enter the negative transference" (p. 72). Epstein (1979) recommended a somewhat different approach from the above traditional interpretation, which he calls "containing, reflecting, and investigating the projections" (p. 391). He stated that a safe course for therapists who become the depository of projection is first to contain the projections and then to direct comments and questions toward how the patient perceives them. If the patients find fault with the therapist, the patients' perceptions and ideas should not be challenged; instead, they should either be reflected by the therapist—"I am such-and-such a kind of person" or "I am really out to get you"—or be objectively investigated. The patients can be asked, for example, to describe the therapist's faults more fully and to suggest how they should be corrected. The patients can be encouraged to elaborate on their ideas concerning the therapist's motives, especially whether they think the motives are conscious or unconscious. In addition, the patients can be asked in a nonchallenging way whether or not they can describe any of the evidence on which they are basing their conclusions. I believe that if the therapist is uncertain about how to make a transference interpretation, it is probably far better to study it in the manner described by Epstein, Gill, or Chessick or to confront in the manner of Masterson—"Why are you so angry with me when I am just doing my job?"—than it is to let the matter pass unacknowledged.

Epstein (1979) has pointed out that some therapists' insistence on immediately dealing with transferences actually represents their own anxiety and need to make the patients take back their projections.

Countertransference Problems

Kernberg (1980b, 1984) stated that countertransference in its broad sense comprises the following:

1. Strict countertransference in the narrow sense defined earlier.
2. Realistic reactions to the patients' transference (e.g., the therapist becomes annoyed when the patients become intensely dependent and make numerous demands).
3. Realistic reactions to the patients' life situation (e.g., the therapist feels anxious when the patients attempt suicide).
4. Realistic reactions to the therapist's situation (e.g., the therapist worries about money when the patients drop therapy without paying their bill).

Over time, the therapist will probably develop countertransference reactions in response to the patients' profound transference problems as well as to their behavior. The patients' problems may well reactivate the therapist's own early conflictual part-object-relations, and the therapist may start to have a transference reaction to the patients. As a result, the therapist may begin to lose his or her clinical objectivity. He or she may immediately recognize the problem or may not become aware of it until after a particularly difficult session or after talking with a colleague. The therapist may even become aware of having what Kernberg (1975a) has called *micro-paranoid reactions* to real or fantasized remarks that the patients are making about him or her to others in the community or even to colleagues.

Countertransference reactions have been categorized in several different ways. Chessick (1974), quoting Singer (1970), has identified the following three types: (1) reactions of an irrational "kindness" and "concern"; (2) reactions of irrational hostility toward the patients; and (3) anxiety reactions by the therapist to the patient (p. 156). A therapist may have a brief acute episode and at other times may become aware of a chronic or permanent countertransference reaction. Kernberg has noted that chronic counter-transference difficulties can be difficult to detect while they are in progress, that often they can be diagnosed only after they have been resolved.

Racker (1957) reported that the therapist may develop either of two types of countertransference—*complementary* or *concordant* identification. In concordant identification, the therapist identifies with the patients and what they are feeling, and the patients often identify with the sadistic object image. In complementary identification, the therapist identifies with the patients' object image, and the patients experience themselves as the child-self interacting with the parent image. For example, if the patients project a maternal rescuing figure onto the therapist, the therapist will then act in a rescuing manner, and the patients will feel nurtured, although they may feel that the nurturance was undeserved. On the other hand, the patients may project a stern, angry father image. Then the psychotherapist may identify with a superego function connected with a stern, angry father. The therapist may feel critical and may be tempted to control the patients in some way, whereas the patients may feel fear, submission, and rebellion connected with their relation with their father. Racker (1968) commented that therapists often fluctuate between the two forms of identification. More specifically, the therapist can react to the patients' devaluation and angry attacks in a number of ways (Adler 1970): (1) by withdrawing, feeling bored or angry, or wishing that the patients would leave treatment; (2) by self-defense, making the patients feel that the therapist cannot "take it"; (3) by proving om-nipotence and love by active demonstrations, which may help temporarily but eventually infringe on the patients' autonomy; (4) by retaliating, often as an angry counterattack, and masking envy of the patients' feelings of entitlement; and (5) by interpreting the anger as masking love, which may be true but does not allow exploration of the patients' potential true rage.

Chessick (1977) noted that countertransference problems can be mani-fested in several other ways: (1) by seducing dependency while urging growth; (2) by ignoring the patients' personal growth timetable and trying to force improvement unrealistically; (3) by dealing poorly with personal anxiety because of the material that the patients are revealing; or (4) by becoming anxious, overprotective, or too controlling from fear that the patients will commit suicide. Other countertransference reactions may occur in response to suicide threats, manipulation of prescribed medication, and missed sessions. Finally, certain countertransference problems can be narcissistic in nature—involving a mutual admiration and endearment between the patients and the therapist that stalls the therapeutic process because the therapist unconsciously avoids certain conflictual areas. The following is a list of 20 common ways in which countertransference appears.

1. The inability to understand certain kinds of material that touch on the therapist's personal problems.
2. Depressed and uneasy feelings during or after sessions with certain patients.
3. Carelessness with regard to certain arrangements for the patient's appointment, being late for it, letting the patient's hour run overtime for no special reason, and so on.
4. Persistent drowsiness of the therapist during the session or even falling asleep.
5. Over- or underassiduousness in financial arrangements with the patient or the same over- or underassiduousness regarding time arrangements and changes in appointment.
6. Repeated experiences of neurotic or unreasonable affectionate feelings toward the patient.
7. Permitting or encouraging acting out or acting in.
8. Trying to impress the patient or a colleague with the importance of the patient.
9. An overwhelming urge to publish, or give a lecture, about the patient.
10. Cultivation of the patient's dependency, praise, or affection.
11. Sadistic or unnecessary sharpness toward the patient in his behavior or the reverse of this.
12. Feeling that the patient must get well for the sake of the therapist's reputation or prestige, being too afraid of losing the patient.
13. Arguing with the patient or becoming too disturbed by the patient's reproaches or arguments.
14. Finding oneself unable to gauge the point of optimum anxiety level for smooth operation of the therapeutic process, thus, alternation of therapy from one extreme of great patient anxiety to the other extreme where the patient is bored, disinterested, and shows no motivation.
15. Trying to help the patient in matters outside the session.
16. Getting involved in financial deals and arrangements with the patient on a personal or social level, recurring impulses to ask favors of the patient, with all kinds of rationalizations as to why one is asking the favor from that particular patient.
17. Sudden feelings of increased or decreased interest in certain cases.

18. Dreaming about the patient.
19. Much preoccupation with the patient or his problems during one's leisure time.
20. Finally, a compulsive tendency to hammer away at certain points. (Chessick 1974, pp. 160–161)

It is crucial for the therapist to recognize that countertransference is taking place, because unresolved countertransference is most likely to be acted out and to obstruct understanding and interpretation. Conversely, identifying the causes of countertransference offers valuable insight into the patients' psyche.

Just how much countertransference should be shared with borderline patients? Some theorists say that it should be resolved personally by the therapist and not shared at all. Others contend that the selective sharing of countertransference, after it has been studied and resolved by the therapist, can be a useful therapeutic technique. It can be reassuring to the patients because it confirms their perception of reality and helps consolidate the discrimination between fantasy and reality. Meissner (1982–1983a) gives a clinical example of selective sharing of countertransference:

> The patient, a quite primitive borderline woman ... [had been seen] for about a year in twice-weekly psychotherapy, it happened that a holiday came along and [the therapist] neglected to remind her that they would not be meeting on that particular day. As it turned out, the patient came to the therapist's office door and found it locked.
>
> The patient went away in a rage ... [she] was able to call the therapist the following day ... he replied with some concern.
>
> When she subsequently came to his office, the episode was still obviously on her mind. ... The therapist asked her about her feelings ... she felt bitterly disappointed and hurt, and then was overwhelmed by a wave of anger.... She was afraid that her anger would destroy him somehow. ... She felt that this oversight had been deliberate ... derived from his anger at her.... The result of his own wish to get rid of her. ...
>
> The therapist told her that he was not really aware of the sorts of feelings that she ascribed to him, but that, in looking at the behavior, both she and he had reason to be suspicious. ... Her perception might in some way be accurate, namely in that his forgetting might have been motivated by some anger at her and some wish to retaliate in ways that he might otherwise not even consider.
>
> The effect of this admission was quite striking. She seemed to be relieved. ... The discussion led on to a consideration of the patient's fear of the therapist's anger ... from there to an extremely useful discussion of her fear of her father's explosive and somewhat paranoid anger. (pp. 98–99)

The therapist should carefully weigh the advantages and disadvantages of selective sharing of countertransference. An argument for sharing such feelings is that denying the accurate feelings that patients attribute to the therapist is not very persuasive. Then the therapist is in the untenable position of denying that he or she may be influenced by unconscious motivation (Gill 1982). An argument against sharing such feelings is that it implies a warding off of criticism and thereby puts the burden back on the patient. Gill (1982) suggests a compromise between these two positions, concluding that a good interpretation may validate both a perception and the plausibility of an inference but takes no position on its "truth" (p. 113). However, in cases of significant countertransference that has stalled the therapy, the therapist may want to acknowledge his or her countertransference contribution. I agree with this compromise position, and in the cases that follow the reader will see instances of sharing of countertransference.

Interactional Paradigms

I have noted several common interactional patterns between the therapist and borderline patients. These paradigms are based both on demands or unconscious cuing by the patients and on the therapist's own object relations.

The Rescuing Interaction

The rescuing interaction arises from the patients' demand for merger, in this case a symbiotic relationship in which the therapist takes care of them without complaint or acknowledgment. Often the therapist initially enjoys the merger but eventually overdirects the patients as if they were helpless children. To bring the therapist to this point, the patients often engage in such inept and incompetent behavior that the therapist feels compelled to rescue them for fear that they will not survive. The patients relax and derive comfort as long as the therapist conforms properly. While on this course, the patients may ignore any interpretation or confrontation until the therapist conforms to their desired control pattern. It is important that the therapist confront and interpret this to the patients, providing supportive parameters in case of emergency.

The Depleted-Helpless Interaction

The depleted-helpless interaction is also related to separation-individuation or an earlier stage of development. In this situation, the patients behave as if they were small children, depending completely on the therapist for all types of maternal functions and making implicit demands for total parenting and caretaking. Their endless needs, however, can never be truly satisfied. In this case, I disagree with the Kohutian belief that the problem will go away if the therapist is empathic. This is because the patients long for a state of total, never-ending caretaking which, of course, they can never attain.

In response, some therapists initially struggle to perform some of these functions and then start to feel devoured. Often, the therapist either feels paralyzed or gives up and wants to transfer the patient. The therapist may even alternate between these feelings. The slightest provocation, such as the patients' being late or missing a session, is used by the therapist to announce that psychotherapy is not working and that the patients need to be terminated. Or the therapist may angrily reject the patients, reprimanding them for being overly dependent and needy. An obsessional therapist may make too many premature and intellectual interpretations in an attempt to reduce and control anger and anxiety. The therapist may counter-project and blame the patients or try to reason with them about the problem. When feeling guilty, the therapist may simply try to do more and more until reaching the breaking point.

The Push-Pull Interaction

The push-pull interaction could also be described as "come close versus go away." It is often induced by the patients' need to differentiate, even angrily, out of symbiosis. The patients often set the therapist up to give advice, to help solve problems, to come closer. This entices the therapist to talk too much, to tell the patients what to do, and to take them over. Then the patients, who feel engulfed, try to distance themselves by disobeying or ridiculing the therapist. The therapist then feels angry, bored, disinterested, and, depending on personal style and problems, may want to terminate the patients.

Walking-the-Tightrope Interaction

Patients who use the walking-the-tightrope interaction often have problems from the practicing subphase. They usually either demand that the therapist support them in their omnipotent, grandiose, and magical thinking or act in such a way that they hardly notice the therapist, whom they tend to treat somewhat as a "thing." This leads the therapist alternately to suffer the abuse in silence, feeling boredom and helplessness (masochistic position) or lash out in anger (sadistic position). Guilt about "being mean" restarts the cycle. Some therapists tend to operate more in one part of the cycle, depending on their own problems.

Teetering-on-the-Pedestal Interaction

The teetering-on-a-pedestal interaction, which may have occasional aspects of rescuing and depletion, is most common with borderline adults. Here, the patients project onto the therapist some godlike, adored, wonderful qualities (deification). Often, the therapist is lulled into a therapeutic quietude and indulges the patients. Eventually, the therapist fails the patients in some way and falls from grace (devaluation). Feeling the inevitable disappointment, the therapist reacts angrily and defensively, often blaming the patients. Some therapists so love the deification that they create a mutual admiration society with the patients, tending to overlook their acting out, and rarely experience devaluation.

I cannot stress enough the emotional intensity of many of these interactions. The therapist must be alert to these common reactions and must use them to understand both the patients' inner world and interpersonal style in order to start "healing the splitting" that they represent.

MEASURING THERAPEUTIC SUCCESS

Chessick (1977) pointed out that no one has fully documented why therapists fail in some cases and succeed in others. Various theorists feel that the patients' degree of sadism and consequent need for talionic punishment may prove to be a determinant. Modell (1968, cited in Chessick 1977) observed that patients whose sadism is intense and overwhelming and who do not possess some capacity for love or tender regard for others seem to remain permanently unable to take in something good from the environment: "to learn from others and the capacity to love others are at the bottom similar; both are based on the capacity to identify. Without this capacity there is no possibility of psychic growth" (p. 227). In other words, these patients are unable to identify with the therapist's healthier ego and thus are unable to form new identifications. Such patients are unable to profit from experience.

Indicators of Positive Change

In a time-limited supportive therapy, the therapist expects only to control the patients' impulsivity. In intensive therapy, one expects to resolve the splitting (SORUs) and work through abandonment depression and other problems discussed earlier.

Chessick (1977) reported that the most characteristic sign of positive change is an increase of ego span—the patients begin to tolerate a frustrating event, such as waiting for an important letter without exhibiting explosive behavior. But they are usually unable to explain why this improvement has come about; they know only that in therapy they have found someone whose consistency, honesty, determination, and reliability give them what Chessick has called an "almost animal faith in the therapist."

The patients' ability to control some acting out also indicates initial improvement (Masterson 1981), which may result from the therapist's confrontation and the patients' willingness to talk about rather than act out their thoughts, feelings, wishes, and impulses.

An improvement in the patients' relationships with people outside the psychotherapy is an indication of positive change, cited by DeWald (1972). The patients begin to manifest more realistic expectations and responses to others and are increasingly capable of tolerating and adapting to realistic stress and frustration in relationships.

The patients' modulated reaction to previously traumatic and anxiety-provoking material is another benchmark mentioned by DeWald. Improved patients now can remember, accept, and understand experiences without being unduly traumatized. In addition, they can remember childhood and infantile fantasies and memories, which are imbued with a conviction of reality and can aid them in understanding themselves and their feelings.

Once some of the basic conflicts have been resolved, other, more subsidiary problems will change spontaneously, sometimes even without conscious effort by the patients or therapist. Patients often experience this with a great delight and sense that for the first time their mind, particularly the unconscious, is allowing them to modify their feelings in positive directions.

Another indication is the patients' growing dissatisfaction with previously gratifying infantile relationships. They wish to replace these relationships with more age-appropriate and realistic friends and ambitions. The therapist can see withdrawn or affectively limited patients become more spontaneous and vivacious, expressing their feelings more fully. The patients often learn to empathize with others even in the midst of conflict with them. Such patients show the ability to form friendships and have love relationships, which was impossible at the start of therapy.

I have observed that toward the end of the change process, patients often realize with surprise that early in psychotherapy certain things upset or traumatized them strongly enough to trigger various degrees of aberrant behavior. Basically, genuine improvement in borderline patients can begin only when primitive defenses and internalized pathological object relations have been uncovered and discarded. The patients must recognize that they can get on in the world without this pathology, because they now have moved forward in psychological development. But to get to this point sometimes requires a very long period of intensive psychotherapy.

Measuring Structural Change

Chessick (1977) and DeWald (1972) suggested two ways that structural change can be studied. The first method uses patients as their own control, comparing their current behavior symptoms and structural conflicts with their status before the beginning of treatment. The second determines how closely patients' various intrapsychic dynamics approach a theoretical ideal or composite image of psychic structure.

Why Patients Fear Change

Despite the pain that patients are feeling, they also dread and fear change. Why is this so? First, great anxiety about the risk of change is an obstacle to the patients with a weak ego structure. Although they may not like their present behavior, it is all they have; it is how they know themselves. Patients often experience change as total annihilation of the self without any assurance that the new self will be better.

A second reason that change is difficult pertains to the great paradox in therapy: "If the therapist likes me as a person, why should I have to change at all?" At an even more primitive level, the patients may wonder why they should change because they consider themselves to be perfect. Although they may express low self-esteem on the surface, an omnipotent grandiose self underneath may simply feel that it should be loved the way it is. This belief often causes psychotherapeutic stalemates.

Fear of separation is yet another reason that change may be difficult. The patients recognize that as they change, they become truly separate from their internal objects and others and from the therapist. They fear the unleashing of abandonment depression, which underlies the fantasy of merger, aggression, or envy, and they are afraid that they will not be able to survive without merger with a powerful other. This may be very difficult to accept.

Finally, therapists must realize that not all patients can get better. We must accept that at times the damage is so great that only limited progress—or no progress at all—is possible. Before they can fully appreciate this, therapists must first accept its implications for their own narcissism.

Table 11-3 (on pp. 422–424) summarizes some of the important points in this chapter. The reader will note that this table parallels and completes the table at the end of Chapter 6.

Table 11-3 Developmental Phases as Related to Therapy

Phase	Patient's Inner Fears (Conscious or Not)	Therapist's Tasks	Common Therapist's Countertransference (Patient's transference message is in parentheses)
Normal autism (birth to 4 weeks)	Pseudoserenity: "I am omnipotent; nothing else exists; I will feel intense rage if encroached upon"	Soothe	Not applicable
Symbiosis (4 weeks to 5 months)	Schizoid depersonalization: "If I give up on human relationships I will lose myself in the void and become totally disoriented" (retreat to autism)	Help patient attach in therapy, which provides interpersonal relatedness within which ego development can proceed	Rescuing: ("Merge with me, take care of me")—doing too much and over-directing, as though patient is helpless child
	Annihilation through overstimulation: "I will become so excited/anxious/rageful that I will explode"	Soothe patient through empathic interpretations, especially during patient's "internal storms"	Depleted and Helpless: ("You can never give me enough")—struggles to avoid being "devoured"; immobilization (giving up) versus angry rejection
	Dangerous permeability: "People can pierce me with their eyes, (personality, anger, and I'll shatter into a thousand pieces"	Provide stable, consistent, honest relationship	
	Being torn limb from limb: "If I am angry at you, you will retaliate and rip me to shreds"	Explore full range of feelings—gradually help patient "own" all feelings (heal "splitting")	
	Claustrophobic suffocation: "If I like you and get close, I will be absorbed into your personality and be obliterated"	Start process of clarification of patient confusion over self versus other, fantasy versus reality, thought versus action, past versus present	
	Merger wish/Engulfment fear: "I must be like you, or you'll go away; but if I am like you, I'll disappear"	Protect patient from overwhelming impulses/eruptions—use of drugs	
		Protect from fragmentation arising from real or fantasized object loss—use of hospitalization	

Table 11-3 (*Continued*)

Phase	Patient's Inner Fears (Conscious or Not)	Therapist's Tasks	Common Therapist's Countertransference (Patient's Transference message is in parentheses)
Separation-Individuation			
Differentiation (5 to 10 months)	Oppositionalism: "I won't do what you want, but I won't let you leave, either"	**Continue above with particular attention to attitude of nonintrusiveness**	**Push-Pull Paradigm:** ("Come close but go away")—Talks too much, tells patient what to do, takes over for patient, then becomes angry, disinterested, bored (wants to terminate patient)
		Be a "container" for patient's rage so that normal self-assertion can emerge	
		Continue to explore feelings and self and object representations so that true self can emerge, including psychotic elements	
		Gradually and empathetically confront "defensive detachment" and thereby help patient relinquish it	
Practicing (10 to 16 months)	Narcissistic control/Narcissistic vulnerability: "If you don't cater to my every wish perfectly, I will destroy and/or reject you; but underneath I feel empty, inferior, and envious"	**Maintain consistent attitude of concern in face of demands for specialness, entitlement and ensuing rage**	**"Walking the Tightrope" Paradigm:** ("Only I exist; you are just a convenience")—suffering abuse in silence or boredom (masochistic position), alternating with angrily withholding support or lashing out in anger (sadistic position). Guilt about "being mean" restarts the cycle
		Interpret defensive/protective aspects of omnipotence and magical thinking	
		Interpret/confront defeating aspects of grandiosity and corrupt superego so that mature goals/superego can develop	
		Work with depression and separation anxiety that underlies grandiose self	

(continued on next page)

Table 11-3 (*Continued*)

Phase	Patient's Inner Fears (Conscious or Not)	Therapist's Tasks	Common Therapist's Countertransference (Patient's Transference message is in parentheses)
Separation-Individuation			
Rapprochement (16 to 25 months)	**Abandonment depression:** "If I lose you, I will fall apart and go crazy" **Oppressive guilt:** "My bad feelings can destroy you, and I will be crushed by the burden of guilt" **Compliance-defiance bind:** "I will do anything you want to keep you from rejecting me," and "I must refuse to do what you want to feel separate and Ok," and "Thus I have to control you to feel OK"	**Maintain consistent concern in face of rage, depression, and binds:** Expect adult behavior while tolerating some dependency Confront "wish for reunion" as defeating the development of an adult, healthy life Clarify/interpret good and bad aspects of the self and object units (reality test) Set appropriate limits and interpret rage, acting out, and lying as defeating growth	**"Teetering on the Pedestal" Paradigm:** ("I will deify you until you fail me, then I will devalue you")— Feels adored, lulled into a "therapeutic indulgence" of patient; after the inevitable "fall from grace" reacts with anger and defensiveness
On-the-way-to-object-constancy (25 months to 3 years)	**Ambivalence toward maternal function:** "I will hate myself if I am like my mother because I can't stand her" **Changing passive to active** (to avoid abandonment): "I must leave as soon as I feel essential to a partner" "I am cracking under other's demands, but I can't stop giving" "If I am always good, I will be loved, and no one will ever leave me"	**Minor aspects of above:** Confront any remnants of past transferences intruding into present relationships (differentiation of past from present which is final aspect of good reality testing) Interpret loss of self-cohesion occuring in intimate relationships Help develop a sense of a personal future ("destiny") with appropriate reality testing around goals	**Minor aspects of above:** Therapy feels more smooth and less intense There is a danger of being lulled into premature complacency

CHAPTER 12

Three Individual Psychotherapies

Models and paradigms—even those discussed in the last several chapters—can provide no more than a guide to relevant therapeutic issues. They do not tell the therapist how to handle moment-to-moment dilemmas, such as understanding the meaning of what patients are saying, or how to keep the total process in mind while coping with immediate crises. Nor does theory tell the therapist how to deal with resistant, clinging, or suicidal patients or how to handle the difficult transference and countertransference of acting-out patients.

Only experience can teach a therapist these necessary skills. But experience must be supplemented by an examination of one's own work, supervision, consultation with colleagues, and exposure to the cases of others that contain enough raw data to encourage debate and speculation.

This chapter offers examples of therapy with both low- and high-functioning borderline adults to make it easier for the reader to understand what the patients are saying and to acquaint the reader with the roles of transference and countertransference in shaping the treatment. Enough raw data will be provided so that the reader can compare these techniques with his or her own experience and speculate about what other strategies could have been used.

To capture the spirit of the sessions with Mary, John, and Sarah, I decided to be as frank and honest as possible, including sharing the interpersonal difficulties and countertransference binds that sometimes occurred. In these cases, both effective and ineffective interventions are given equal time. Thus, I am not saying that every intervention in these cases was successful. In fact, few experts even agree as to the "best" technique at a given moment, and so labeling an intervention as excellent is itself a subjective matter. Remember that all of these theories and techniques are only guideposts. Although we often speak of them as though they were divine injunctions, they are not. And there always are, of course, alternative approaches.

It should be stressed that a therapist cannot change patients, mend the splitting, or heal the sense of basic fault. Nor is it possible to force them to identify with the therapeutic function or to give up infantile ways of responding or acting out. Only the patients themselves can do these difficult tasks. But ultimately, they will want the therapist to do these magical acts for them. The therapist who understands in advance that he or she cannot do this is better prepared to maintain perspective; in a sense, such an understanding helps control the therapist's feelings of omnipotence. Once the therapist accepts this outlook, the therapy will take on a less urgent quality.

GUIDELINES OF THE THERAPIES

The therapy for Mary and John evolved from supportive to intensive psychotherapy. John needed only a brief period of supportive psychotherapy before he changed to intensive psychotherapy twice a week. Mary needed much more. She was originally seen once a week for 18 months, twice a week during the middle phase, and three times a week when hospitalized. Sarah received confrontive psychotherapy during weekly visits because she lacked both motivation and money. I used Masterson's confrontive approach because I wanted to try a technique that held so much potential for change. The sessions for all three cases were 50 minutes long and face to face.

Mary and John had complete psychiatric workups before being placed into treatment. All three patients underwent initial history-taking and assessment sessions. The therapist may require several sessions with a patient in order to decide exactly which type of psychotherapy is best (based on severity of pathology, ability to introspect, motivation, time, and money). But this does not mean that the first few sessions do not constitute the practice of psychotherapy, because they definitely do. It is during these early sessions that the patient sizes up the therapist, and the therapist sets the tone for what will follow. For example, during the early assessment sessions, the therapist may frequently ask questions and direct the conversation. Because the patient may come to expect such a directive format throughout the treatment, the therapist should clarify how the therapy will differ from the evaluation phase.

Finally, I was well into the middle phase of therapy with both Mary and John before reading the work of either Masterson or Rinsley. How this new knowledge would have changed the therapy cannot be predicted. Sarah's case, which used a confrontive approach modeled more or less on Masterson and Rinsley, was shorter than the other cases because it was limited as to time.

Lacking a social work support team, I provided most of the supportive interventions (e.g., writing reports, arranging for hospitalization, and intervening with the family). Consequently, these interventions shifted the therapy more into the supportive approach. Because I was often operating with interpretations, this may have complicated the therapy. However, in many ways, such deviations, if not too pervasive, can simply be seen as "grist for the mill." After all, desperate patients should not be deprived of an essential social intervention just to keep the therapy clean. When these interventions do occur, the therapist should always explore them with the patients in order to assess the patients' fantasies about such assistance.

Thus, the approach in this chapter would be seen by Kernberg as mixing supportive and expressive approaches, and several of the patients may not have met Kernberg's criteria for expressive therapy. Interestingly, despite some deviations from pure psychoanalytically oriented technique, all the patients got much better, and John showed signs of a true structural character change. I believe that these results bode well for the general clinician who has never been trained to make sophisticated interpretations, does not have an adjunctive support staff, and hence cannot keep the therapy totally pure.

Organization of the Clinical Cases

Because the material in the following cases has been organized to highlight certain themes, it may appear from this vantage point that I was able to identify the patterns in each case from the start of treatment, though that was not the situation. It usually takes many months, if not years, for certain patterns to emerge from the wealth of clinical material, and the therapist needs to work at finding the pattern. The primitive split-object-relations units do not always leap out of the therapy in bold relief; sometimes they have to be painstakingly teased out.

In these cases, I tried to strike a balance between painting the big picture and merely giving "critical incidents" that illustrate specific intrapsychic conflicts or therapeutic techniques. Consequently, Mary's case will be given in some depth, whereas the other two cases show only specific critical occurrences.

Certain incidents and themes had to be eliminated to keep the cases within manageable proportions. Whenever possible, I tried in specific sessions to convey some of the complexity and confusion that always overwhelm even the most experienced clinicians at some point. Many rich psychodynamics have been ignored in order to focus on a few selected themes related to the emergence of split-object-relations units or introjects, as well as the development of a holding environment in the therapy. The reader will see, for example, interesting competitive incestuous themes, but I did not elaborate on them if they were not directly relevant to the central theme.

For the sake of readability, all the "speech disturbances" of the conversational mode (e.g., sentence fragments, pauses, "ahs," and other speech characteristics) have been eliminated.

Mary Markham's case material came primarily from detailed process notes made immediately after the session. Although process notes have the benefit of being a nonintrusive approach to data collection, this method has the usual disadvantages caused by problems with accurate recall of what was said by both parties and with distortion of the material. Mary was audiotaped several times during the second year of her therapy, before her decision to terminate, and several times during the period immediately following her discharge from her second hospitalization, 3½ years after starting therapy. John Elliott's case material came primarily from process notes made immediately after the session; he was audiotaped regularly during the final year of his therapy. Sarah Gardner's therapy was audiotaped from start to finish. She and I agreed that when the tape recorder was not available or not working, I would take notes during the session. This happened on four or five occasions.

For the sake of brevity, these extratherapeutic influences on the therapy will not be discussed in the case unless they became a definite problem or assumed some clear significance. Of course, these patients had feelings and fantasies about the note taking or audio recording, but none of the fantasies or affects pertaining to the fantasies was particularly intense or suspicious, even in regard to John Elliott's early problems regarding privacy.

However, because what therapists do is often as important as what they say, all extratherapeutic interventions were closely monitored and explored with each patient as they occurred. The fact that these discussions were not included in the cases should not be taken as evidence that I consider extrainterventions unimportant. It is only that other events at the time assumed more prominence in the therapy, and thus the discussions concerning data collection were eliminated from the cases.

Division of the Cases

For the sake of readability, the traditional pattern of dividing the cases into phases—early, middle, and final—was followed, although these divisions are always a bit arbitrary. The early phase usually includes the major acting out and testing by the patients, often over and over again, before a true therapeutic alliance can emerge. This phase can last several years.

The middle phase represents the period when the therapeutic alliance is established. By this point, the patients often are committed to controlling their acting out because they realize that it is self-destructive. And they usually are working through the split-units (Kernberg) or the abandonment depression (Masterson, Rinsley). The patients now turn more to their own inner world of dreams, fantasies, and other private processes and pay less attention to everyday events.

The final phase involves termination issues. The therapist often sees a resurgence of some of the patients' old problems pertaining to the loss of significant objects, although they are less intense. In addition, the patients have one last opportunity to work on problems of separation-individuation when they must give up the therapist.

Conceptualization

I followed Chessick's (1977) recommendation that each clinical case be scanned with an eye toward selecting the most appropriate conceptual framework. Although the basic approach to each case is an object-relations strategy, many clinicians have provided important clinical insight into the treatment of specific personality subtypes or problems. Therefore, I included conceptual frameworks that helped me understand each case more completely.

MARY MARKHAM: SUPPORTIVE PSYCHOTHERAPY LEADING TO INTENSIVE PSYCHOTHERAPY

Review of Mary's Problems

Mary started her therapy stating she was unhappy and depressed and wanted to change. What Mary did not realize was that despite her words, she was not ready to change. What she really wanted was a parent–child relationship, modeled on her relationship with her mother. Yet she could not admit this desire until years later.

Mary met the borderline diagnosis according to all the theorists reviewed in this book. She also fulfilled the *DSM-III*'s criteria for both borderline and schizotypal personality disorders. According to Masterson's and Rinsley's criteria, she used distancing defenses to mask her intense symbiotic longings, which both frightened and confused her. She represented a lower-level borderline adult. Under Kernberg's criteria, Mary functioned on the overt borderline level but could episodically lose reality testing in close relationships with her family and therapist. She also was capable of having a transference psychosis (both in its narrow and broad meanings).

In terms of personality subtype, Mary was an example of a schizoid patient with mixed features, particularly narcissistic. Most pressing for her immediate survival in psychotherapy, however, was her long history of self-mutilation and serious suicide attempts, acts that she talked about with pride.

Kernberg (1980a) has noted that a patient such as Mary, who appeared to be fixated at the differentiation phase rather than the later rapprochement subphase, is struggling with the possible refusion of self-object images. This contrasts with the psychotic patient, who has fused images, and the typical borderline adult, who fantasizes only about wishes for merger. Patients such as Mary constantly struggle with issues of autonomy versus merger and true self versus false self. Such patients develop several pathological devices for insulating themselves from these difficulties, including denial, avoiding, and occasionally acting them out.

These patients are considered difficult to treat, particularly on an out-patient basis. When Mary was accepted into treatment, I did not have the accumulated wisdom of the many clinicians who urge caution in taking such patients.

What were Mary's negative and positive prognostic signs? The negative signs included her willingness to engage in life-threatening behavior in order to punish herself and the therapist, at times to destroy anything good that the therapist had given and to triumph over her fear of death. She had a very limited social life, had had no sexual experiences, and wanted to play out her life via her therapy and her relationship with her therapist. She lied in therapy about hoarding pills and having suicidal fantasies, primarily to show her previous therapists what fools they were, and she had almost no guilt about doing so. Finally, she entered altered states of consciousness in which her reality testing was greatly impaired.

Among Mary's more positive prognostic signs was the fact that she had maintained some interpersonal relatedness, albeit limited, with her parents and coworkers. She was able to maintain some dependence on her former therapist until terminated from individual psychotherapy and could tolerate therapy under some moderate conditions of negative affect. Overall, she had a good, reliable superego in areas other than pill hoarding and suicide attempts.

It is difficult for me to convey the intensity of the first three years of therapy with Mary, who more than any other patient challenged my skills and patience. I did not always have "perfect" timing or "perfect" empathy, or make "perfect" interpretations, and Mary often reacted with an onslaught of self-mutilation or planned suicide attempts. Both the treatment facility staff and I had countertransference reactions and made mistakes. But over the years Mary showed a certain ability to forgive my human errors and to make progress in spite of them. It might be said that with time Mary came to accept her own imperfections more realistically, as she had previously come to accept mine.

Had I known as much about such borderline patients as I know now, I would have been far more reluctant to accept Mary into outpatient treatment. However, given Mary's slow but continuing growth, turning her away would have been a loss. Perhaps inexperience sometimes does pay off! Doing everything the experts advise is not always the best way to help a patient, because the therapist is relying on old truths. Rather, it is only through making mistakes that new truths can be found.

The Early Phase

Task 1: Creating the Holding and Limiting Environments

Mary had just made a major suicide attempt and had been transferred to my facility when I first saw her. Several weeks into her hospitalization, Mary's psychiatrist and I met with her on the ward to discuss her future treatment. We talked with her about what she wanted (individual psychotherapy with me and antidepressant medication) and what we were willing to offer (individual psychotherapy and a brief trial on a new antidepressant). We informed Mary of the clinic's policy on a maximum 1½-year time limit for individual psychotherapy. After two years, she would have to have her financial resources sufficiently in hand to afford to go into the private sector for treatment, which she could do with me if she chose. Mary accepted these conditions stoically and made little comment except, "It's a sensible plan." I saw her two days later for her fifth individual session.

Mary arrived early for her fifth appointment, a habit she kept throughout her therapy. She sat in the waiting area, looking withdrawn and morose. When I went to meet her, she followed me to the office without comment or eye contact, sat down, and looked at me expectantly.

I silently waited until Mary finally asked, "Should I start?" I nodded my head. From this session onward, she began without asking for assistance.

"I don't know quite how to express what I am feeling, but my ward therapist says I should discuss it with you," she said. (This was the second meeting at which she brought up what she thought someone else wanted her to talk about. She seemed compliant and somewhat intellectualized.) She explained that she now greatly distrusted all therapists because of her experience with Mrs. Jensen. She said she was uncertain whether she could be honest and share her true thoughts and feelings with me.

After a long pause, Mary announced in a highly restrained but menacing tone that she expected to "test" me to see whether I listened carefully to and understood her. She continued by stating she intended to test whether I would pick up the hints she planned to drop about her frame of mind, mood, or suicide potential. She would wait to see whether I "blew it" by bossing her around or being too passive and nice. She implied that if I did not do the right thing, she would start to hurt herself or plan another suicide attempt. (Apparently she had begun this suicide strategy in her mid-20s and saw then what a strong impact it could have on others.)

There was another long pause that gave me time to think. I was startled by her sudden menacing tone. Wondering whether she was angry over the limits set by her psychiatrist and myself and was acting out, I asked her whether she was trying to tell me that such a disruptive process was starting between us. She replied, "No, not that I know of." Because Mary was unable to explore her feelings, I decided to attack the problem from another angle and I asked her to clarify how such a process got started. She launched into a scenario of how it would happen in our therapy—either she would react negatively to my comments or behavior or the urge would just start for no apparent reason.

Mary: I'll start to plan to kill myself . . . I won't even know why. I'll set a date several months ahead. Then I'll stop taking my prescription medications and won't tell the psychiatrist.

       I may drop a little hint and see if you or he pick up on it [magic gesture, analogous to infancy]. A part of me wants one of you to read me the riot act and terminate me. If you're smart you'll do that, because I'll never leave on my own [said emphatically and firmly] . . . only by dying can I leave. [She becomes tearful]

       [Wiping away tears as though they are an embarrassment] The nicer and more understanding you are, the more I'll feel compelled to trick you. I know this is going to happen between us sooner or later.

I thought to myself, "She is probably right." I felt somewhat angry at her threatening behavior. Rather than react immediately, I examined my feelings and tried to figure out why she was threatening me. I developed several hypotheses. The meeting with the psychiatrist may have angered her and she was unable to separate her anger toward me from her anger against herself. That is, when someone disappointed her, she hurt herself, indicating perhaps an inability to keep separate her self- and other images. Also, hurting herself could be her way of punishing me for failing her in some way.

But it would have been premature to share those hypotheses. Instead, I decided to clarify the scenario. Because she had alluded to it several times before, I asked her to explain the test. She could not elaborate, and when I asked her why she could not leave a relationship, she replied, "I don't know; I just can't." I decided to confront her reality testing while trying to help her recognize this destructive behavior as something she needed to examine. Therapeutically, I was already beginning to deal with her undifferentiated bad self-object—maternal—introject:

Therapist: [Firmly, but with concern] Let me see if I understand this. You intend to trick me and thereby in some way test me. You fully expect me to fail the test, and my failure will lead you to cut on yourself or make a suicide attempt. Whatever is this process all about? Why would you waste your time coming to therapy if you are going to trick me rather than talk about your unpleasant feelings?

Mary: [Looking startled] I don't know. I've never thought about it before.

Therapist: That is what we must understand together.

Mary sat silently for a few minutes and then offered to try to explain further. She now appeared more emotionally involved and reported that she wished she could stop the destructive process but that the longer it went on the less control she had.

I asked what she meant by "less control." She described having another part that took over in these situations. I asked her to describe the part, and in the process of doing so she named it the Megalomaniac. The Megalomaniac appeared to be a presence with a will and life of its own. When it spoke to her in her head she knew it belonged to her, but she still felt it as somewhat independent of her. Once the Megalomaniac appeared on the scene, Mary felt she had lost all control of herself. At those times, she experienced no emotion, not even her usual anger.

At this point I was feeling that I must go slowly because of Mary's regressive potential, although at the same time I had to set some real limits on her attempts at suicide. She looked at me in despair.

Therapist: You're feeling hopeless about ever changing this destructive pattern.

Mary: [Nods her head and starts to cry quietly]

Therapist: I sense that part of you desperately wants to stop this cycle, and another part (the Megalomaniac) even likes it and eggs it on.

Mary: That's exactly it. I feel whole when the part doing the "testing" takes over. It's the only time I feel all together, but then I start to get crazy. I know that.

Therapist: Which part is talking to me right now?

Mary: [Thinking for a moment, then responding somberly] The part that doesn't want it to happen any more.

Therapist: Then I want to talk with that part about how we can deal with the "testing situations" when they arise. Clearly, the other part [Megalomaniac] steps in to save you from some painful feelings and helps you feel whole and even punish the person who has hurt you. Perhaps we can all work together to find a more creative solution.

I was somewhat more active than usual because I felt that this problem had to be addressed early and decisively. Mary seemed intrigued, and we talked about options. But she doubted that the Megalomaniac would let her try anything different. I commented that she was actually predicting that the therapy, herself, or I would fail. (In some ways she was predicting a negative therapeutic reaction.) She had little to say and changed the subject to the details of her suicide attempt.

We then explored her fantasies of how her former therapist and family felt upon learning of her suicide attempt. "I suppose they felt concerned," she volunteered. But she could not elaborate, explaining that she really did not think much about others when she got to the stage of what she called "serenity."

After a pause, I shared my reactions to her self-reported testing and tricking of her former therapists and told her the following: I wanted to help her understand this process better, but it was her responsibility to convey her feelings honestly in therapy. I presumed some part of her wanted to do this, too, or she would not have alerted me to the process. I believed she was clever enough to trick me and, indeed, could die from her own cleverness. I would feel sad if that happened, and it would also represent a failure of the therapy. However, under such deceitful circumstances, I refused to take responsibility for her death because it would have been caused by her cleverness, not my inadequacy.

The astonished look on her face told me I had struck a responsive chord, but she said nothing. Continuing, I explained that I would try to help her when she was in the middle of such a terrifying battle within herself, even when she distrusted me. If she told me that this process was under way, I could be available to see her more frequently, take her phone calls, or even hospitalize her if she needed a protective environment in order to work with me.

There was a 5-minute silence, and then I asked her what she was thinking about. Mary replied, "I don't think I like hearing this," laughing nervously. She mused for a few minutes and then added, "However, a part of me feels relieved—now I just have to see if you keep your word."

It was now just a few minutes until the end of the session. After sitting silently, Mary looked startled and then said slowly and tensely, "You haven't said what you're going to do if I start to hoard pills. Are you going to tell my psychiatrist? Because if you do, I'll probably never trust you again. I have to have my antidepressants! And I need to know what you are going to do."

Because she was still on the inpatient ward, I was not particularly concerned about whether she was hoarding pills (although patients can hoard pills on psychiatric units). But I did consider this as another move to try to control, provoke, or test me. I responded:

Therapist: You're putting yourself, and me also, in a no-win situation again. If I treat you as an adult and let you make these important decisions alone, you've already told me you'll hoard pills. If I withhold information from your psychiatrist, I will be colluding with you to let you die, which will mean to you that I don't care. If I set limits for you and communicate with your psychiatrist, you will believe I'm treating you as a helpless child and am violating your confidentiality. You will feel betrayed and probably will terminate with me. Can you see the dilemma you're creating?

Mary: I know it doesn't make sense—I have to do it my way. Everything always ends up in a mess and gets destroyed [said with restrained savagery in her voice].

I acknowledged that I understood her need for autonomy but that she seemed to regard freedom to act as she pleased as being equivalent to hurting herself or others. She nodded her head in agreement. I calmly repeated that I expected her to talk about her urges to hoard medication, and if she started hoarding (e.g., acted out instead of talking about the urge), I did expect *her* to talk with her psychiatrist about it. If she did not do so, then I would consider that a plea for help and would talk with him myself. He and I would have to consider hospitalizing her. I explained that because he and I worked with her together, I would not withhold important information from him or lie about her pill usage. In other words, I would neither lie for her nor collude with her so that she could harm herself.

Mary seemed relieved to hear this but hinted that perhaps she would not tell me if she hoarded medication. "Why be in therapy, then?" I asked. (I noted to myself that perhaps she was trying to get me to collude with her against her male psychiatrist, just as her mother had tried to turn her against her father. It was simply too early to talk of such major problems.) Mary looked and seemed relieved with this safety net under the therapy.

I also told her that her therapy would not be discussed with anyone else, except the matter of medication with her psychiatrist. She responded indifferently, "I'll have to see how I feel about this." (Even though my hospital limited her medication fairly quickly after her discharge, over the next six months, Mary continued to collect prescriptions from private sources and flaunt them to me endlessly, and I, in turn, confronted her endlessly.)

Therapist's Observations   It has often been said that the first moves in therapy reveal the major psychodynamic that will be played out throughout the treatment. Let me recapitulate what transpired between Mary and myself:

1. Her psychiatrist and I met. We set limits on medications and length of treatment.
2. Mary met with me alone. She started off mildly but after a silence became threatening.
3. I confronted her about her threats and stated that I would not be responsible for her death.
4. She looked astonished but reported feeling relieved.
5. She escalated, making a second threat that was even harder for me to deal with: if I talked with her psychiatrist, she would hurt herself.
6. I set limits again, at the same time trying not to limit her autonomy and confidentiality or enter into a collusive agreement against another team member.

How can this material be understood? From the Masterson perspective we could say that her RORU behavior had been labeled and confronted and that she responded, not surprisingly, by acting out the WORU. From the Kernberg perspective she had shifted from being the compliant self interacting with the loved other to enacting the sadistic object image and projecting the helpless child image onto me. She had become aggressive.

What caused the shift? There are a number of ways to explain it. She could simply have been testing me to see how I would act. Could she control me with her threatening behavior? However, given her enmeshment in the twin themes of engulfment and abandonment, so common to the borderline patient, there is another way to view this scenario.

A review of Mary's background was helpful to me when I tried to understand the implications of this sequence of events. Mary did not believe it was safe for her mother and herself to separate. Her mother did not allow Mary to have friends, nor did her mother have friends. Mother vilified the father, and so Mary could not be close to him without defying her mother. In short, her mother indicated in effect that only if Mary were close to her and supported her would she care for Mary; additionally, whenever Mary was not "sick," her mother left to go live with one of her more "needy" siblings. Thus, Mary grew up believing separation was not possible, was dangerous, happened only as a punishment, and should never be discussed. She had been traumatized by this belief. Utilizing this information, I expected Mary unconsciously to test me to see whether I could handle separation and control these problems without being traumatized. In other words, she would become the torturing maternal introject and force me to be in her predicament, that is, to feel scared and suspicious. I would be responsible for her condition, just as she had felt responsible for her mother's. Mary would test me to see whether she could learn new ways of mastering her painful belief, by reintrojecting how I handled my own feelings when in her predicament.

How exactly did this scenario occur in these first sessions? In retrospect Mary may have interpreted the meeting with the psychiatrist as my trying to control her by making all information go through me—making her be totally loyal to me—and denying her a relationship with a man. She entered her next session feeling distant and distrustful. When I failed to pick up on her distress and link it to the meeting with the psychiatrist, she may have assumed that indeed I intended to control her life. I had failed the test and thus was no different from her mother. She then raised the ante and threatened to hurt herself if I did not discover how to behave correctly. Although I had missed an opportunity to explore her fears about being controlled, I did respond by confronting her about the meaning of her threats. The fact that I did not abandon her and was not helpless in the face of her sadistic behavior may well have given her some hope that I was not traumatized by her sadistic, suspicious maternal introject. In effect I said, "If you are deceitful, I will not feel inadequate. If you die, I will not be responsible for your death." In other words, I treated her like an adult. She now looked surprised and started to speak more convincingly of her despair about her feelings. The surprised look could have meant Mary was aware I had understood the meaning of her test. She may have been relieved because at some level she had always felt such guilt and responsibility for her mother, who could not tolerate separation, while being so scared of her mother's potential for abandonment. Perhaps now she could start to reintroject my less frightened attitude. We could say that our interaction, which she termed "reading her the riot act," was the first step in the taming or mastering of the maternal introject. I was not scared, but I was also not going to let Mary wander off (as her mother had when Mary got better).

But when I showed her I was not as terrified as she had always been, she decided to give me an even harder test. She demanded to know how I would interfere with her medication and her relationship with her psychiatrist. Here again she was checking to see what limits and boundaries I would impose. Also, could I be scared into compliant behavior? Her mother could be. (In this model, we would expect Mary either to show new, improved behavior or escalate her acting-out behavior to see whether I really could handle the conflict and whether I could be trusted (personal communication, L. Beall, September 5, 1983). I saw many such moves from Mary throughout the next sessions.

Because Mary was unconscious of her covert symbiotic relatedness, how should this dynamic be addressed in the therapy? Ogden (1979, 1981) warned against premature interpretation of projective identification. Searles also warned against premature interpretation of dependency. Too early an interpretation of such deep issues could actually drive Mary to attempt suicide and could represent my countertransference wish to "cure" her too quickly in order to be rid of her.

Thus, I chose to limit and confront the destructive behavior while clarifying it as fully as possible. In addition, I included myself in the process by asking how "we" would deal with this situation. Although some experts may criticize this approach, it was important to show Mary that I was willing to treat her suicidal-homicidal feelings as a mutual task. I did not contest her implicit demand that I relate symbiotically by understanding her totally, although I differentiated myself by refusing to collude in her suicide attempts. Finally, I fully explored her feelings and the degree to which she understood her own motivations. I cannot stress enough that the very act of exploring and listening to a patient's reactions is a differentiating function.

After Mary's discharge from the hospital, about six weeks after our sessions had begun, she returned to her job and her own apartment in a neighboring state. Her parents, in a panic after her suicide attempt, moved back into her apartment to look after her. She protested angrily about their presence, describing them as hovering over her like protective mother hens. She complained that she could not even go to the bathroom without one of them knocking on the door to see if she was all right. Yet it was clear to me that Mary was privately proud of the attention and that she doth protest too much about how annoyed she really was. She seemed totally unaware of the contradiction between her underlying feelings and her words, but I let this pass in order to build the therapeutic relationship.

During her weekly visit, she reported that she often felt empty (which she called "depressed"). Only once in a while did she feel good. She talked about her work, her relationship with her parents, and her limited affection for her cats. Yet she acted as if none of them really mattered to her. I listened, asked a clarifying question or two, and made several interpretations in each session. This soothed and helped clarify her thoughts and feelings. She experienced my empathic comments as forms of emotional feeding, and so I restricted my confrontations in order to allow the therapeutic symbiosis to flower (Rinsley 1980b).

Task 2: Understanding the Narcissistic Defense against the Emergence of Dependency Feelings

During the first three months, I directed most of my energy toward understanding her inner-world experiences. She reported few feelings and rarely gave me very much information about her thoughts. At times she hardly seemed to notice me, unless I changed the way I dressed or wore my hair.

Most of the time she talked about her moods and their changes and seemed to bask in the warm ambience of the session. Sometimes I detected a vaguely threatening quality in her verbalizations, as if the mood to die could strike her at any moment if I missed any nuance. She obliquely let me know that she found me helpful and subtly hinted that she thought I was a good therapist (no doubt the start of the idealizing transference). There were moderate periods of silence in many of her sessions, but they seemed to soothe her. Because she remained so distant, I felt that I must be especially attentive in order to stay in touch with her feelings.

She was beginning to talk more about the Megalomaniac. She reported that this part of her was haughty, condescending, hostile, a show-off that felt like an alien being. It collected grievances against others and demanded that she reject those people. It also demanded that she kill herself if she made a mistake at work so that it/she could be at peace. It put her down for being less than perfect, and caused her to feel intense self-hatred. The Megalomaniac seemed both to gratify and transcend Mary's symbiotic needs, helping her rise to a state of sublime indifference. At these times she experienced it as powerful and even exhilarating.

Each time the Megalomaniac intervened in a situation, we discussed its role and the feelings associated with it. I made it clear to her that I did not want the Megalomaniac to be eliminated; this part carried some very positive attributes (e.g., healthy aggression, as seen in self-assertion, self-esteem, ambition) that needed to be integrated into her conscious behavior. But that part also got her into self-destructive situations. She appeared reassured and showed an interest and willingness to explore her inner experiences. *well put*

Around the sixth month of therapy, I was sick for a week and missed one session. Mary arrived at our next meeting looking distant and acting haughtily cool. She had little to say and mentioned a few trivial things. Her tone, facial expression, and tense body posture radiated hostility. I anticipated a reaction to my illness, but she did not mention my absence. I let her go on for 15 or 20 minutes before saying, "You are talking indifferently about very minor events and acting quite distant. I wonder why."

She admitted that she had become depressed and angry over the missed appointment, and then she stopped talking. We sat in silence, and I eventually asked whether she was willing to share what she was feeling. She said she was feeling overwhelmed and told me that she became so depressed after the missed appointment that she slept whenever she was not working and started mutilating herself again. At times she felt as though parts of her body were disconnecting from her torso. During the same period, the Megalomaniac told her she was worthless and should die. She reaffirmed that she knew the Megalomaniac was a part of her but felt a loss of willpower in its presence.

I listened carefully and explored her reaction to both my illness and my absence. Apparently, Mary had developed a severe panic because she thought I might be dead. There could be many reasons for this fear, one of which was probably the intense rage she directed toward her internal image of me for abandoning her. This destroyed her evocative memory of me and left her feeling totally empty of any good images (introjects). In addition, the undermining of Mary's idealized union with me might have precipitated a subjective sense of worthlessness that was unbearable. Under such conditions the patient may have severe suicidal fantasies as a way of gaining relief or punishing whoever is considered responsible (Buie and Adler 1982–1983). I did not interpret either of these possibilities to her.

I acknowledged how frightening all of this must have been and pointed out I was still alive and here in the room. I asked what feeling she had when my secretary called to say I was sick. "Angry," she replied, "but it went away." She still appeared quite hostile, and I strongly suspected that she had set a suicide date. We sat in silence for a few minutes, and then I remarked, "I notice you've not said anything about hoarding pills or setting suicide dates." Mary grinned tauntingly and replied that she had filled all her old prescriptions, slyly adding that she now had 500 tablets of assorted drugs from former physicians and planned to use them in the near future.

Gently I confronted her: "I wonder why you have the need to dangle the threat of suicide in front of me. Your purpose here is to talk about your feelings, including your feelings toward me, to understand them, and with time to work them out, not to act on them."

"I don't know if I can give the pills up—they are my security blanket," she answered. Her tone and manner implied that the medication was her only weapon against me and that she intended to use it. She added that the Megalomaniac had told her that I was the enemy and should not be trusted.

I then pointed out to her that the pill hoarding had come after a missed session. Because she had already told me that she was disappointed and angry, I presumed that the session meant a lot to her. I observed that her suicidal feelings seemed to be very much related to her rage at me—perhaps she wanted to punish me for failing her by missing the session. I could understand her anger, but that did not have to make me an enemy.

Mary surprised me by conceding "What you say may be true" and seemed less distant and hostile. She talked with more affect about her reaction and her relationship with her mother. Then I asked how she felt. "Still like taking the pills," she replied. I responded firmly that I took her suicidal feelings seriously. Furthermore, I felt that she needed to decide whether she was going to talk about those feelings or act them out by taking the pills. After mulling over my statement, Mary inquired, "Are you asking me to destroy the pills?" "That is certainly one possibility, but I am asking you even more about your commitment to work on your problems," I responded. Mary decided she would take a chance and put the hoarded pills down the drain. I said nothing in order not to infringe on her autonomous decision.

At the next session, Mary reported feeling much better. She had even started dieting. She volunteered that part of her wanted me to think she still had the drugs, although she really had put them down the drain. She was not sure why she wanted me to think that. I was uncertain whether she felt better because I second-guessed her pill hoarding or because I was consistent in my confrontation. Either way, I decided to continue monitoring her reactions to my interventions as a way of correcting my approach to her therapy.

At the next session, Mary immediately reported feeling depressed again. She was in an intensely emotional state and sobbed throughout the session. She had reacted with rage when her boss gave her a compliment at work. She felt that the compliment put her into a crisis, and she now blamed him for making her feel bad. Most of the session was devoted to clarifying Mary's reaction to this event.

Mary's boss had complimented her by suggesting that she was management material and might want to take some courses to prepare herself for a promotion. After considerable exploration, Mary reported feeling insulted that he did not think she was good enough the way she was. She wondered whether she had to be a success in order for him to like her, and she questioned whether she really wanted to be a success. But at the same time, she was terrified of success—"people expect things of you"—but could not elaborate.

She expressed rage at her boss for putting her in the middle of this dilemma. "I am scared of all my anger. It makes me feel like I am coming apart and flying into a million pieces. I can drown in the anger and die. Anger is my most overwhelming feeling." She had thought about mutilating herself again when she started to lose touch with her body but did not actually cut herself.

She then stated that people almost never knew when she was angry; she never let it show. She was afraid that she would act so irrationally that others could not tolerate her. "I wouldn't want to act in front of them as I have acted in the session," she said, not looking at me. I waited a few minutes and then replied, "You're wondering how I reacted to you in this session?" She nodded her head affirmatively. I explained that the role of therapy was to allow all these unpleasant, frightening, and embarrassing feelings to surface and be understood and that I did not feel negatively toward her for talking about her true feelings. (I gave Mary a form of reassurance, understanding that it might be easier for her to ask how I feel about her, than vice versa.)

Mary seemed much calmer now. She started to acknowledge her own ambivalent feelings about success, about being an authority figure, and how being a "failure" had saved her from having to handle the pain of dealing with people. She oscillated between talking about her inner feelings and debating whether or not she should have confronted her boss about his remarks. On her own, she decided she should not have confronted him because her reaction was so out of line. I agreed that in this case it probably was better to bring the matter to therapy than to deal with it on the spot. I added that at other times, however, the price she paid for not asserting herself was her feeling of helplessness. She seemed intrigued by this comment.

Mary speculated about whether or not she wanted to work for a promotion. It was clear from the way she maneuvered several of her statements that she wanted my opinion. However, I was conscious of her compliant false self and did not want to support it at the cost of suppressing the emergence of her true self. I stated that what was really important was whether she thought she should try for the promotion. "I don't know how comfortable I am with doing that, but I'll have to think about it," she said, stating that she felt much better.

Therapist's Observations The missed appointment incident brought Mary's dependency needs to her conscious attention. These needs were not for a healthy dependency expressed in the therapeutic alliance, with mutual goals directed toward change, but rather the immediate gratification of her infantile hunger for an incorporative, soothing mode of interaction. Her narcissistic defense was activated when her infantile desires were not satisfied. Mary distanced herself haughtily in the session and plotted revenge against me and herself (aggression turned against the fused self-object).

Several concepts shed light on what this behavior might mean. For example, when Mary's boss complimented her, he unwittingly suggested an individuation move. Mary had two reactions: (1) a narcissistic injury (the boss's suggestion of self-improvement implied that she was not already totally worthy) and (2) fear of the abandonment depression that would be released if she made a separation move. Both processes stirred up intrapsychic conflicts. They also pointed up the ease with which Mary confused the locus of control for her feelings (e.g., "He made me feel I was bad"). Interestingly, the terror of success (= growing up) that typifies borderline and psychotic persons was noted by Freud (1916) in his classic paper on the "exceptions."

The following is another interesting possible explanation of this rather strange reaction to a compliment. Two sessions earlier, when Mary had reported destroying her hoarded pills, we had explored her reaction to doing so. Although it seemed like a positive move, she wondered whether she had done it for herself or to please me. At some level, it may have felt like a real submission to me. It is possible that her fear of individuation (as well as fear of submission to me through doing something positive for herself) was displaced onto the compliment from her boss rather than where it belonged—onto the success of therapy with me or of doing something positive for herself. Although I briefly explored this possibility with her, she was unable to verify it.

During the next year Mary alternated between wanting to assert herself and fearing assertion. She started to feel better, assert herself with others, and make plans for the future. Then she became depressed, experienced altered subjective states, slept, overate, and dwelt on committing suicide. She had terrifying nightmares or persistent fantasies of being mutilated and abandoned. Session after session, Mary came in depressed, hopeless, and helpless, only to make some positive move for herself (e.g., fix her hair, ask a coworker to lunch, assert herself) and then to feel depressed and helpless again a few hours later.

Task 3: Reality Testing Regarding Mary's Mother and Therapist

From the fifth to the eighth month of therapy, Mary periodically tested me with tentative suicide dates and threats of self-mutilation. Neither Mary nor I could figure out why this was happening. I remained concerned but not overly preoccupied by these manifestations, and they passed quickly. I admit that she created a certain suspense in the therapy: I was never quite sure whether she would be alive for the next session. It was not always clear what set off these episodes, and so I remained alert to them. At this point the threats did not seem very serious.

Mary sought out a new general physician, who gave her antidepressants and pain medication (thus meeting her oral needs far better than I could). I was careful to distinguish between pointing out the destructive aspects of gathering medication and exploring its meaning, and preserving her autonomy, thus letting her decide how to handle the matter.

Therapist's Observations   Once again with Mary I found myself feeling uneasy, even paranoid and suspicious. What medication was this physician prescribing? How much medication was Mary hoarding? It seemed that once again Mary presented me with another situation or relationship designed to make me fearful. It was as though she were trying to provoke me into taking control or ordering her around. Together we explored her need to make me concerned and suspicious, but she was unable to clarify her motivations. Once again Mary appeared to be enacting the sadistic object image and projecting the helpless child image onto me, but this projection was not accessible enough to consciousness to explore with Mary. Although I kept an eye on the medication issue, ultimately the important aspect of our interaction regarding this physician may have turned out to be the preservation of her autonomy, letting her have a relationship with someone other than me. Later after the session, it also occurred to me that Mary was seeking out a new general physician so that she did not have to confront her fears of being engulfed by our relationship. The idealized male was one escape from the stifling maternal orbit or its substitute. From Mary's perspective, her mother demanded an exclusive relationship with a needy daughter or else she lost interest in the relationship and turned to another sibling. Once again Mary turned from passive into active and watched to see how I handled with her what she could not handle with her mother.

Mary spontaneously talked more and more about her mother. She started with her usual litany of complaints but then began to attribute her intense dependency to her mother. Perhaps this consciousness was emerging because of our gradual and tentative work on her convoluted messages about her growing dependence on me, which I allowed to take place without interpretation. Mary alternated between complaining about her mother and speaking glowingly of her ability to meet Mary's every need, to sense her innermost concerns, and to fill her up by just being there. Mary was starting to experience some guilt because she felt split loyalty between her mother and me. She reported that her mother had disliked me ever since (a month ago) I refused to report over the phone about how Mary was doing in therapy. Mary considered my protection of her confidentiality a turning point in the therapy in terms of trust, and this no doubt represented a test that I had passed, one that was quite important to Mary, with her fears of intrusion into relationships. Mary also felt that if I met her mother, she would turn me against Mary. But she was unable to explain this intriguing fear (perhaps a projection of Mary's wish to turn me against her mother).

At one session, Mary recited a variety of complaints about her mother:

Mary: I've been really upset with my mother. I've been hiding in my room. The only good thing is that I haven't been cutting on myself. But I'm lying in bed fantasizing all the time. I'm having fantasies that I'm a man, and I'm married and have children. Then a terrible disability strikes me. I lose my legs and my arms. I am totally bedridden, and other people have to look after me. And eventually they start leaving me, one by one, and I am totally abandoned. [She pauses, and I sit quietly waiting for her to continue.] Mother probably doesn't even know I'm upset with her. I just clam up and refuse to talk.

Therapist: Hmm.

Mary: Mother's been running up the long-distance phone bill again. I've explicitly told her not to use the phone for long-distance calls (an unrealistic demand, because her mother lives in the house now and pays many of the expenses). She says she'll pay the bill. I don't know why I don't trust her. She has always paid it, but she has run out on bills with other people. But basically she just refuses to do what *I* tell her to. (She begins to cry and is silent for about five minutes.)

We sat in silence, and Mary finally remarked, "I never have an impact on her—that's what really upsets me." I wondered whether she was also talking about how she experienced me, but I continued to pursue the extratransference material at this point. We then talked about how powerless she felt:

Therapist: You have a fear that holds you back from dealing with this situation. What is that fear?

Mary: That they'll ignore me ... it will be as if I don't even exist. That will make me furious, but I'll never say anything about how angry I am.

Therapist: You'll never say anything about your anger?

Mary: I guess I think if they don't do what I want, I'll get so mad I'll kick them out and then be totally alone. [Starts to cry silently]

For the first time, Mary and I examined her fears of being alone. She said she hated herself for needing others, including her mother. The phone calls were not really the issue, Mary added, but rather that she felt out of control with her mother, needing her too much, feeling totally empty when she was not around, and hence needing to control her. But, she sighed, her mother sometimes refused to go along with her wishes. I commented that she counted on her mother a lot and that her mother probably counted on her. Mary responded tentatively that she was probably dependent (her word) on her mother.

Therapist's Observations   Mary's long silence gave me a chance to reflect on her report. It could have been that Mary was simply worried about her mother's keeping her agreement about money, but I doubted it. There was a more significant possibility. Mary may have had unconscious wishes and fears about rejecting me by hiring a new physician in order to decrease her dependency on me. Because the conflict felt intolerable, she projected it onto her mother, accusing her of rejecting her (a projection frequently contains at least a kernel of truth). As I listened to her, I became more and more aware of my increasing anxiety and strong urge to undo the anxiety by supporting Mary in her stand that her mother had acted badly. I examined my reaction with some curiosity. Were my own problems with abandonment being stirred up? Was I identifying with Mary and Mary's fear of her mother's independence?

I decided that my identification with Mary was not the only dynamic at work here. There was one, or possibly two, more. The first was her "abandoning" me for the new physician. The second was her displacement onto her mother of Mary's abandoning me. The third and most important problem, linking the other two, was that it seemed easier for Mary to talk about her mother's abandoning her than it was for Mary to confront her fears about how I would retaliate if she "abandoned" or tried to separate from me. But Mary was unable consciously to talk of this fear. When I missed this important dynamic and focused instead on why she would not assert herself, she talked of how she could never "impact" her mother. It was quite late in the session when I realized Mary was criticizing me for missing the chief problem. For reasons of my own, I had counterphobically focused on her mother to avoid dealing with Mary's fears concerning me.

Mary entered the next session icily furious. Our session exploring her relationship with her mother had greatly upset her. Afterward, she had started mutilating her upper arms, had been having severe headaches, and found sleeping difficult. She felt that somehow I was an enemy trying to make her feel bad about herself and destroy her. She seemed verbally disorganized and talked about voices (the Megalomaniac) telling her to die and another part of her just "crying and crying." This was the first time she had mentioned another part of her self. She felt she was losing her mind, literally going crazy.

I suggested that we explore what was happening to her and that we could consider hospitalization if needed. I encouraged her to tell me frankly how she thought I was destroying her. She talked about all the symptoms she had been having and how wrenched apart she felt—how stirred up she was by our recent work. As I listened carefully and calmly, she responded, "I can't talk about this subject; it will destroy me."

I then asked how she had interpreted my comment about how she counted on her mother so heavily. "You implied I was a bad person for being so dependent," she replied, highly distorting my remark. When I clarified it, she retorted, "I just don't like to think of myself as needing my mother. But I guess if I look at my own behavior, I do need her—just like I am beginning to need you. I'd rather not need anyone, though. I'd rather be dead."

After a pause, Mary said, "I am willing to talk about it a little." We started to clarify her various feelings related to dependency and, specifically, her dependency on me. We also explored her fears that if she separated from me at all, I would retaliate and abandon her in a rage. She was picking up the theme from the earlier session that I had missed. We explored and clarified her fantasies about separating from others and her fears about how others would react, including me. This took us briefly into some past history, her perceptions of her mother's reactions, as well as her own. At the end of the session, Mary appeared relieved, and we decided against hospitalization.

During the next year and a half, Mary and I clarified an interaction or interpretation in countless other incidents during this period, and she continued to maintain a somewhat threatening posture whenever I deviated from saying or doing what she wanted.

An example of Mary's threatening behavior occurred in the eighth month of therapy, when I was ten minutes late. At the following session, her posture, behavior, and vocal tone signaled that she was obviously annoyed, enacting her feelings rather than talking about them. She mentioned that her latest physician had given her a new antidepressant and asked casually how dangerous it was. I thought to myself that she was trying to make me angry at the physician so as to avoid her angry feelings toward me. "What are you really telling me?" I asked. She looked indifferent and responded nastily, "What do you think?" Our eyes met; she laughed at her maneuver; and then we smiled at each other.

I then asked, "What is your reaction to my being late—what do you make of it?" She thoughtfully replied, "I don't know." After a long pause, I commented that I thought she was understandably annoyed at me for being late. I would be, too, under the circumstances. Perhaps she feared that I took her therapy cavalierly and would like me to be punctual. I said I thought she was uncomfortable verbalizing her annoyance and was going to take revenge instead of talking about her feelings. She then relaxed noticeably and spent the rest of the session talking about her loving and hateful feelings toward me. Clearly, Mary wanted a blissful relationship, and so any interruption in the relationship induced rage. I listened carefully and said very little.

In the next session, Mary felt good about having spoken her mind. She believed that I did not hate her and she did not hate me. This was a first for her. She was still uncomfortable about being angry to my face but felt that the session went well. Such an assertive act was met in the next sessions with further resistance, as Mary threatened a new suicide date in the distant future.

During this period Mary brought in various life events (e.g., making her first friend, taking a night class, starting a small private business outside her regular job) which allowed us to work on her intrapsychic problems in terms of how they were manifested in her real life. At times I used educative efforts, in the Blanck and Blanck manner. I worked on Mary's understanding of the everyday implications of symbiosis and individuation (terms I did not actually use with her) vis-à-vis her mother. I pointed out her splitting each time it happened (e.g., "Last week you spoke well of your boss, and this week he had no redeeming qualities") and helped her understand the meaning of her rapid mood changes. Her depressions lessened, and in small doses the educative work proved helpful. However, I remained ever cognizant that Mary's deeply buried rage and neediness would not just go away because she could function better.

She began to have greater self-control and to talk of a career move. She was able to set some modest limits on her parents and had some social activity. But she talked very little about making friends, her impulsive eating and spending, or her problems with sexuality. During this period we clearly identified and clarified the Megalomaniac and the Baby. Both parts felt to her as though they had lives of their own. The Megalomaniac was sadistic and punitive. The Baby bawled and threw tantrums but could never be satisfied. The Megalomaniac stepped in to stop the Baby from crying, both to shut it up and to rescue it.

These parts felt more real to Mary than did her compliant false self, but she did not know what to do with them because they were so extreme. We talked about how neither had been allowed to grow and how it would take time to help them grow up. At this point, Mary did not want the two parts to communicate; she wanted to keep them separate within herself because she feared them (a classic example of splitting). Grotstein (1981) has described the role of such introjects in blocking or allowing linking behavior to take place, resulting in constant fragmentation of the patient.

Around the end of the first year of therapy, Mary was offered an outstanding position in another state. She discussed the job with me and felt able to cope with it, and so we set a date to terminate the therapy. Mary was by now aware that the clinic's policy on long-term therapy was in force and that she would need to transfer anyway within six months, but she seemed unconcerned about it because she was leaving. Within two months, however, her new job unexpectedly fell through because of corporate financial problems. When Mary learned about it, she telephoned me in crisis for the first time in her therapy. I spoke with her briefly and commiserated with her.

In the next session, she told me that it felt very good to feel my concern without being "bossed around" and given advice. She asked what would happen now with the therapy. I reiterated that the clinic's policy limited long-term therapy—she would not be able to continue at my clinic for longer than another six or seven months. She was disappointed but agreed to terminate in about six months. I gave her several other options, including seeing me in my private practice. But she decided that she wanted to see a therapist nearer her home. Because she had been driving 1½ hours each way to come to therapy, this decision did not seem unreasonable, although I saw it also as a rejection of me for rejecting her. She was also told that if she and the new therapist felt that they could not work together, the clinic would review the situation—in other words, she would not be abandoned.

Over the last month, she valiantly worked on overcoming her dependency on me and prepared to separate from me. At one point, she said that she had lied to me the month before and had hoarded pills until she decided on her own to put them down the drain. She attended all the sessions until the last one (which she warned me she might do), when she wrote me a note saying she could not face saying goodbye. In the note she told me that she had made an appointment with the psychiatrist near her home whom I recommended and intended to keep it.

Several years later Mary admitted how terrified she had become about her dependence on me and how much she counted on just being in my presence to be soothed and calmed. She felt good only around me and came to the sessions to drink in my words. Being terminated was just like her mother's abandoning her.

Therapist's Observations   Mary's termination went far better than I had anticipated, because during the process she was constantly threatening to drop out. Believing that she might do so, I had discussed it with her early. Even if she did drop out, which was her choice, we had done considerable positive work regarding termination, and I would remember her with good memories. She found this difficult to believe because she expected to forget me immediately (her evocative memory problem again). We studied from a number of angles her feeling that I would be forgotten, including her anger at me for abandoning her. I accepted this, and we were able to work on what that would mean. In addition, we worked extensively on the fact that she would be seeing a male therapist.

I realized how very fragile Mary's gains were, linked as they were by the symbiotic bond she felt with me. But her new psychiatrist was very competent, and I was hopeful that the relationship would last. I told Mary that she could call me to talk about other options if she encountered any problems. So far, she had been in once-a-week psychotherapy with me for 1½ years.

Task 4: Managing and Interpreting Projective Identification Regarding Dependency

Soon after Mary's termination, I got a telephone call from her new therapist. She had seen him several times and promptly made a mild suicide attempt. He decided that her terror of seeing a male therapist was probably too overwhelming for her. Would my facility consider taking Mary back? He would like to convey such an option to her. He reminded me that the area in which she lived had a limited selection of therapists, and few, if any, would be sophisticated enough to handle her.

After an extensive review, the clinic administrator decided that a few long-term cases would be permitted. Accordingly, my supervisor suggested that we notify Mary of her option to return and said that I could give her an open-ended therapy contract if I wished; we all agreed that toying with the contract was antitherapeutic.

The psychiatrist reported that he had not seen Mary since his telephone call to me, adding that she said she had been told that we would contact her. I then telephoned Mary with the news. She told me that she had started seeing an older female therapist (in her 70s) who was particularly interested in a holistic approach to treatment (e.g., vitamins, acupuncture). Mary was uncertain whether or not she wanted to continue with that therapist or return to me. I suggested that she think about the clinic's new offer and also that it was quite acceptable to turn it down. I said that the decision was hers and that she should discuss it with her current therapist. Then I mentioned that I was getting ready to go on a three-week vacation. When I returned, Mary called me immediately for an appointment.

Mary was withdrawn and somewhat haughty at our first session since her termination. She talked in an intellectualized manner about her life since I last saw her, dropping only oblique hints about the termination and my telephone call. She seemed disappointed in me but did not say so directly. Instead, she made low-keyed, off-handed remarks such as "When you telephoned, I felt pressed." She also discussed other recent events in which people had pressed her and she hated it. Eventually I commented that she seemed upset about my call but did not put this disappointment into words, perhaps for fear of criticizing me.

Mary remained silent for a few minutes. She then launched a barrage of accusations: I did the most terrible thing—I changed my mind about letting her continue in therapy with me. Worse yet, I chased after her, something I said I would never do. (She accurately remembered this promise from our first month of therapy.) Now she doubted my character and my competence. On the other hand, she felt that she had to come back because of her attachment to me. She also believed that I had the skill to help her, despite my temporary fall from grace. In addition, she realized that there were few, if any, other therapists she could afford to see.

She spent this session ruminating about whether returning was good or bad, whether I was any good or so fatally flawed that she had better escape from me, and what disaster would befall the therapy because she had returned. After all, look what happened when she returned to Mrs. Jensen— Mary almost died in a suicide attempt. She insinuated that the same thing would happen with us.

As I listened, I began to feel a sense of unease and then guilt. She was quite right. I did "chase after her," probably unnecessarily because she knew she could call me, and I capitulated to a bureacratic regulation that I should have disregarded, limiting her therapy and thereby conveying to her my impotence and submissiveness. I sat with these feelings for a while to get them under control.

After Mary finished, I responded thoughtfully, "I can see you experienced my telephone call as emotionally seductive. You are perhaps concerned about how I can help you with your issues of dependency, given your perception that I cannot control mine." She seemed surprised that I was not arguing with her about the telephone call and answered, "That's it exactly." She then conceded, "I guess you're not perfect; you can make mistakes." I asked her how she felt about that, and she replied, "Uncomfortable." We studied her reactions, including her many fears about the therapy becoming "messy" and "tortured." At the end of the session we discussed the frequency of future sessions and agreed to meet twice a week.

During the next few sessions (the 20th month of treatment), Mary continued to be distant and to debate whether she should leave or stay. She increasingly condemned my telephoning her and was still enraged by that action. But I noted to myself that she had shown up promptly for every appointment. She seemed to be getting enormous gratification from telling me how destructive my attachment needs were and how hopelessly I had enmeshed the two of us in the web of my symbiosis. She was not certain she could work with someone as "imperfect" as I was.

I started to believe that my behavior was inexcusable and destructive. And I began to feel paralyzed in our sessions, a sensation I had never felt before with Mary. I almost wished that she would leave therapy because the situation felt so sticky and convoluted. However, I realized her leaving the therapy was not the problem and was careful never to suggest that to her.

After about five sessions of angry accusations and ruminations, I began to feel less stunned and finally regained my perspective. I had been operating as though what I had done was bad (e.g., I had *acted out* my rescuing fantasies as though this were a mortal sin). Now I found myself being curious and intrigued not only about why I made that phone call but also about why I found it such a bad thing. In privately examining my reactions, I found Racker's notion of concordant countertransference to be a useful tool in highlighting this process.

Mary disowned her dependency feelings, which deeply frightened her, and experienced hostility instead, which she frequently projected onto me. In regard to the phone call, Mary was able to point out accurately that I, not she, was the dependent one and that she was enraged over my intrusiveness as well as trapped by it. I began to identify with Mary's partial self-image as helpless, needy, and engulfing, and she was able to identify with her superior, sadistic, condemning object image (also superego identification). She was the poweful one, and I was the needy child deserving to be condemned, although she was not so powerful that she could free herself from me because she felt stuck in the therapy.

After silently owning my part in the interaction, I decided that allowing her hostility to continue would simply create a resistance to future work. I felt ready to venture into an interpretation of Mary's projective identification. But this became unnecessary when she reported at the next session that she felt she could trust me again. She started to work on issues of her dependency and her terror of feeling dependent on her mother and me.

Mary now admitted how desperately I mattered to her. She said she never started therapy to change herself; she came because she needed a friend, a person who would listen to her (as she now realized her mother never listened). Despite her original goal, she was changing anyway—and hated it. She came to understand how dependent she was on her mother, but she also saw how dependent her mother was on her. Mary, quite on her own, realized how little her mother gave her (e.g., she now saw her mother's flaws and lack of true empathy), although, of course, her mother was not as bad as Mary was now seeing her. All of these feelings were intensely overwhelming:

Mary: How am I going to survive now?

Therapist: What leads you to believe you can't survive?

Mary: I don't know. I feel so overwhelmed by feelings—I try to avoid having feelings. I'm really scared!

Therapist: I can appreciate how frightened you must feel, and yet the only way to get better is to experience and explore all these scary feelings.

Mary: I don't know if I want to do that. The fantasy was better than real life. [Turning to me somberly] I'm not sure I can fully trust your strength since you "blew it" by being weak enough to pursue me.

Therapist: Perhaps time will answer that question for you. In the meantime, by returning constantly to the subject of me, you're avoiding having to deal with your fears, anxieties, and anger around feeling dependent.

Mary: [Laughing] Well, you're right on that one.

It was close to the end of the session, and Mary twisted and turned in her chair. She confessed that before restarting therapy with me she had set a suicide date that was now one month away. She said that she no longer felt a need to keep the date, although she might, of course, change her mind. But for the first time she reported that she did not feel ashamed about giving up a date.

Therapist's Observations   What happened in these five sessions? Whereas earlier Mary had accused me of letting her go, now she was accusing me of a worse sin, luring her back. Hence, I was damned both for letting go and hanging on, not surprisingly the twin themes of separation-individuation.

But there was a new element in Mary's rage. Because it was reality based (I had indeed chased after her), Mary felt less ambivalent about her anger. In other words, my behavior caused her to believe I was intensely attached to her. But this allowed her to disown her own attachment needs by projecting them all onto me. Because of that kernel of truth, she could now dump all her anger on me and feel good about it, without having to feel responsible for her own part of the projections.

From Mary's perspective, she had once again embroiled herself in a stifling relationship, one she hated but could not leave because she needed it. I had, again, become the bad object, destructive but necessary.

I experienced the projection and began to fear that my own action would destroy Mary. As I recognized what was happening and processed my own guilt and anxiety, I was able to recognize both her part and my own in the projective identification. I acknowledged my part without excessive apology, thus showing her that attachment need not be lethal and hostility need not destroy.

At this point Mary's attitude changed, and she felt ready to work on her dependency problems. I was not sure what contributed to this change. Perhaps it was the fact that I had tolerated her rages. Perhaps I had communicated nonverbally my comfort with dependency. For whatever reasons, Mary was now ready to accept her own attachment as well as her mother's. With time, she even came to admit that her greatest fear was that her mother was really not attached to Mary as herself but only to Mary as a need-satisfying object, and indeed Mary operated likewise with other people. In other words, Mary manifested aspects of her both loved and hated mother. Mary had an interesting layering of dynamics. On the surface she used denial of dependency while claiming her mother met her needs perfectly (hardly confirmed by reality). The next layer was an unconscious desire for engulfment that she enacted by an incorporative mode of behaving. Beneath that was the awareness that she was totally alone and that her mother narcissistically used her without any real sense of Mary's true needs. This entire process was transferred onto me and was being worked out with me. During these sessions I continually clarified the reality of our termination and restarting of therapy. I emphasized that what happened with us need not be a repeat of what happened in her former therapy.

Although well into her second year of therapy, Mary was still moderately shaky, although she seemed to have reestablished trust in me. Her fantasies oscillated between being growth producing and highly regressive. In one fantasy she was married and living happily for the first time; in the other she was dying or abandoned. It is as though birth and death fantasies were being activated simultaneously.

She discussed the Baby part of her more frequently now and thought that it was the part that drove her to suicide attempts. The Baby could not be soothed or quieted, and Mary felt tortured by its needs. She did not know what it wanted or how to satisfy it. We talked some about how she could look after herself and how she could care for the Baby part-self in nondestructive ways. This helped temporarily, but she continued to be overwhelmed and tortured. She spent many sleepless, nightmare-filled nights and looked haggard and enormously depressed.

Sometimes she icily defended herself, charging, "You have done this to me—you've made me see how needy I am. I want to hurt you, but I can't bear to be without you." I continued to clarify, confront, and interpret during this period, with an eye to maintaining a stable therapeutic environment. She seemed to do better one session and worse the next. The therapy was beginning to have a dangerously unstable and unpredictable quality, which I pointed out to her, but she replied, "I know too much now, and I can't stop changing." She reported fearing that she would lose me if she told me all her true feelings. Then she predicted that a disaster was about to befall both of us. Choked with emotion, Mary announced that there was an enormous pool of anger inside her. Even more importantly, she reported that there was also an enormous pool of neediness. Over the rest of the second year, Mary struggled with her intense feelings but made no suicide attempts. She did make several suicide threats, which were dealt with in the usual way and passed without incident.

Task 5: Managing the Transference Psychosis

We were now beginning the third year of therapy, and Mary continued to be seen twice a week. She casually reported that her mother and father were moving from the area. When I asked what she was feeling about that, she replied, "Nothing much. I doubt that they'll do it. They are always threatening to leave." I asked her to explain that remark to me. She said she had noticed that whenever she appeared to do a little better or was barely holding her own, her mother got a great urge to live with Mary's brother or sister and their families. We studied her reactions, and she offered, "I guess when I get well, she leaves. Then I have to make a suicide attempt to get her back." I asked her what else came to mind. She replied, "I guess you'll leave me, too—drop me from therapy and I'll be totally alone." She started to cry. I asked her what evidence she had that I would do that. "None," she answered. However, I understood that the therapeutic relationship would hardly supply her oral neediness. A few minutes later she reported feeling better.

The first six months of the third year represented the deepest point of Mary's therapy because the transference psychosis emerged during this period. Mary increasingly lost control and became totally preoccupied with my every move. Each session was a crisis in which she dropped a new bomb.

Near the end of one session, she demanded antidepressant medication from our facility. (She had not been on medication for about a year.) She threatened that if I did not obtain medication for her that day, she would stop therapy, get the medication elsewhere, and probably would kill herself. The clinic psychiatrist refused to give Mary an antidepressant because of her history and offered her an antipsychotic instead. Mary stormed out of the room in a fury. I realistically debated whether I should have her followed or committed to the state hospital, but some sixth sense told me she would be all right. In fact, several hours later she telephoned me to say she was fine.

In another session, she announced menacingly that she was going crazy because of her feelings toward me—she could not leave me, but she would die if she stayed. She seemed exhausted and acted increasingly paranoid and chaotic. She said she had made an appointment with a therapist at her former clinic. I asked her what she meant by this. She replied that she wanted to see another therapist while she was also seeing me, or perhaps even transfer to that therapist.

I told her that she had the right to see someone else but that she would, of course, have to work out the same problems with another therapist that she faced now with me. She wearily replied, "But not for the first year or so, and that buys me some time." I did not try to stop her but emphasized that I would not continue to see her if she decided to see another therapist regularly.

Mary saw the other therapist for three visits while also keeping her appointments with me. I asked her if she wanted to discuss these visits, and she said no, "not yet." I honored this. With Mary's permission, the other therapist, who was male, called me to brief me and commiserate because Mary was well known to that clinic. She soon decided on her own to return to me and to stop therapy with him.

Mary kept her next appointment, when she informed me that she intended to torture me the way I tortured her. (It was unclear what she meant by this and what prompted this outburst.) I tried to clarify, but she could not or would not answer. I thus decided to interpret the emerging process as I saw it.

Therapist: I think you want me to feel what you've felt all these years with your mother. You want me to know what it is like to try to rescue your mother from her depression and chaos but never be able to do it and to feel totally helpless.

Mary sobbed helplessly for a prolonged period. After she recovered her composure, she agreed with this interpretation and spontaneously talked about her many attempts to save her mother. She reported that she experienced her mother as "toying" with her (e.g., moving away just as Mary got better or was vulnerable, as though she were aware that such a move would precipitate a crisis). We explored this perception further, and then I asked Mary if she ever felt like torturing others as she experienced her mother doing to her, and Mary said yes.

I then pointed out that Mary had shifted roles. Many times she had played the victim to someone else's aggressor. But now, having found the victim's position too painful, she tried to become the controller by seeing me as a weak, helpless child who deserved to be tortured and punished. This interpretation opened Mary up, and for the first time she discussed her identification with her mother's sadistic side and its relationship with the Megalomaniac.

Mary did much better for the next several months and continued to work productively on the material from the interpretation. In addition, her parents decided to delay their move because of financial difficulties, which certainly took the emotional heat off Mary. I started to feel that therapy was back under control.

Then, for no apparent reason, there was a sudden turnabout. Mary reported in a session that she was feeling frightened of her closeness to me. She would not or could not elaborate, and I silently speculated about a homosexual panic. Mary asked if she could see the male therapist on the inpatient unit who had been her ward therapist during her previous hospitalization. She felt that she needed to see him to get some distance from me. Once again, she was unwilling to clarify this wish. Although I felt uneasy about the request, the other therapist and I conferred, and we agreed to a limited number of sessions.

Therapist's Observations Mary could have interpreted my allowing her to see another therapist, particularly a male, in one of two ways. I could have been responding to her need to individuate. I could also have been allowing her to drift away from me at a key point in the therapy, just as her parents had always drifted away when she needed them most. She always felt that she had to let them move away without protesting—so as "to be reasonable." I explored both of these conflicting needs with Mary, but she was unable to clarify her feelings.

I then made the following interpretation: "Right now, you seem to need distance from me and to see a male therapist, but on the other hand, you could be trying to escape from working on your own problems by wandering off to a new therapist. If I try to stop you, you probably will experience me as controlling you; if I don't try to stop you, you may experience me as not caring." Once I had put this conflict into words, Mary explored both possibilities before finally stating that her most pressing need was to get away from me. Letting Mary make the decision seemed to soothe her, although as usual I felt uneasy and a little unnerved by her decision.

After several weeks of calm, Mary came to a session in a panic and announced that her parents were definitely moving away within the next five weeks. She acted suspicious and hostile toward me, and in the next session she appeared to be disorganized cognitively. She was threatening suicide and appeared out of control. I convinced her to be hospitalized (she was hospitalized for four days); however, she recompensated quickly and asked to be discharged so as not to lose her job. But within a week she was once again suspicious, agitated, and making wild threats. Now I insisted on hospitalization, and she agreed. Once on the ward, Mary argued with the charge nurse over a regulation, started crying, and ran down to the woman's bathroom on the first floor. The nursing staff followed her and brought her back to the ward, and she immediately left the hospital against medical advice. As soon as Mary returned to her apartment, she telephoned the ward to reassure them that she was all right and that she intended to keep her therapy appointment with me.

Now a new complication arose. The ward administrator declared that Mary was not an appropriate candidate for this particular ward and that she could not be readmitted. The only other local facility that Mary could use was the state hospital, which was crowded and would discharge her almost immediately. I realized that my options for providing a safe environment were dwindling.

Over the next three weeks, session after session, Mary claimed that the therapy was destroying her. I asked her to clarify that fear for me, but she was either unable or unwilling to do so. I said little but pointed out that it seemed likely to me that her parents' upcoming move was really disturbing her. But she replied, "It doesn't matter. It's all the same thing." I now became concerned that Mary was in a transference psychosis, if not a full psychotic episode. I considered committing her to the state hospital but did not have grounds for committal because Mary was still functioning at work and had not made a suicide threat.

As her parents' moving date drew nearer, Mary presented as increasingly confused and overwhelmed. She said that she was definitely going to kill herself—not now, but in three months. I interpreted her suicidal feelings as rage directed toward me for not rescuing her from this situation. This interpretation seemed to calm her, and she reported feeling more in control and no longer intended to make an attempt on her life. I asked what she had told her parents of her reactions to their leaving. "Nothing," she said, "because I don't want them to know how much power they have over me." She mentioned she was overeating and spending too much. I said nothing, as these seemed to me to be relatively minor problems.

In the middle of this period, on her own, Mary took control of her financial affairs and even opened a savings account. Afterward, predictably, she came to a session visibly upset over her actions. She felt that she was a bad, evil person and was going to lose me because she had exerted control over her life. The Masterson-Rinsley notion of an individuation move → abandonment depression → defense appeared applicable here. She said she did not want to hear my opinion about her savings account because it would contaminate what she had done. So I said nothing.

She was angry with me at the next session, and I once again clarified what had precipitated her feelings. She was furious that I did not order her to stop overeating and to control her spending, as her mother would have done. She felt that I did not care and that I was not listening because I did not order her about. She was beginning to feel that she would have to do something drastic to get my attention. Only if I screamed or took over would she know that I cared. She was now clearly confusing me with her mother, and I stressed that observation.

Therapist's Observations   Mary's overeating and overspending were undoubtedly not the true problem. On an unconscious level, Mary may have been upset with me because I did not take a firmer stand. This indicated to her that my boundaries were as flimsy as hers. She could not control her own behavior or that of her parents, and her parents could not control their behavior. Everything was out of control, and so Mary was looking to me to provide some structure and limits. However I was not doing so. She identified with the maternal introject and I was proving it could not be controlled. Regardless of the limits I provided, Mary might well have continued to confuse me psychotically with her parents.

In the next session, I stressed that she must come to grips with the fact that her mother was leaving. Mary agreed but admitted that she was overwhelmed and totally confused by all of this. I suggested a longer hospitalization, and she agreed to think about it for a few days. We discussed hospitalizing her in a state facility nearer her home.

Before the next session, Mary sent me a note saying that she was stopping therapy for a while. I decided that she was waiting to see whether I would treat her like a child by calling to rescue her. I also realized that she both did and did not want me to do so. I decided against calling her.

Later that afternoon, Mary came to the clinic and angrily demanded her medical records. She looked haggard and angry. She had been sleeping in her car and had decided to go to another state to get help. I spoke with her briefly, reminding her that wherever she went, she would take herself along. She calmed down and left without her medical chart, but it was unclear whether she intended to continue her therapy.

Mary called to reinstitute the therapy, and I saw her for a session at her usual time. She admitted that she had been feeling powerful in "an evil sort of way" and that I was inadequate as her therapist. This was the Megalomaniac's influence again, and it feared that I would try to destroy it. I observed that the Megalomaniac, as Mary well knew, came around to protect her from her dependency feelings. We explored this, and it was clear that she demanded that her primitive needs be met.

Finally, Mr. and Mrs. Markham left despite knowing about Mary's instability, and Mary became unhinged. She was totally preoccupied by the nuance of my every word in the sessions. Over a two-week period she set and ignored several suicide dates. The ward agreed to take her back, and so Mary was hospitalized twice again; she recouped quickly each time and soon left the ward.

During this time, she mutilated herself with razor blades. In addition, she fired me by mail four times within a six-day period. She telephoned me after making a mild suicide attempt that she had been able to sleep off. I insisted that she be hospitalized, but she refused. So I telephoned the highway patrol in her state and asked them to go to her apartment. When they reached her apartment, however, Mary was not there. She finally turned up at a local emergency room, where the staff released her because they decided she was not committable.

Until this point, I had felt consistent and fairly nonanxious. But now I was exhausted by the therapy, with its dangerous oscillations and threats—for this was the first time Mary had actually attempted suicide while in therapy with me. Confused by the turn of events in the treatment, I reviewed all the possibilities. I understood that suicide attempts could represent the patient's containment of the therapist's murderous fantasies, and I felt the need for assistance in looking at this possibility. Perhaps my immobility in this situation was caused by my fear of my aggressive fantasies. Overwhelmed by the chaos, I requested a consultation with an expert in another state.

Therapist's Observations   Mary let me know that she desperately needed time and space to work this out on her own. On the other hand, I saw her tottering on the brink of disaster. The immediate clinical problem was to determine when I should step in and insist on a long-term protective environment, even if it meant hospitalization out of state and the loss of her job and her therapy with me. In the past, she had refused to be hospitalized for longer than her regular days off from work for fear of losing her job, which would force her into bankruptcy and total financial dependence on her parents. However, now that she was flailing around so dangerously, changing therapists, firing me, taking me back, and making but not keeping suicide dates, I believed that she was unable to work this through without a hospital environment for her own protection.

Until now, I was confused about whether or not taking over for her and controlling her behavior would be unwise because of the symbiotic implications. Now I felt I must do so, but there really were no rules to guide me on timing in this matter. When Mary demanded that I order her around, I became even more confused. Should I do that, or would it be counterproductive? Was she testing to see if I would take over? Could she really control herself if told she must? What did she really need now? As Rosenfeld (1978) noted, the therapist often does feel totally confused about what to do and what to avoid during this phase. I shared Mary's confusion over limits versus autonomy. But Mary did not know what she needed, and she felt as though she were out of control—and I did not know what she needed, either.

I scheduled an appointment on a Friday for my consultation. I examined all my own feelings with my consultant, and I realized that I had become immobilized by Mary's threats. She was telling me that she would die if she stayed in therapy but that she also would die if she left. She could not stay, but she could not leave; and I was somehow to solve her ambivalence. However, it was a complete and unsolvable double bind. I dreaded seeing her and almost hoped she would go to another therapist so that when she died I would not be left with guilt.

At long last I had bought into her "script" and felt paralyzed by her transference hatred of me. I could not make interpretations during this period because she took them to mean that she was all bad. She projected, and I took in (for my own countertransference reason), her totally confused and ambivalent self. I, in fact, no longer knew what was going on. I again felt like a battered child, with Mary the tormenting, cruel mother. I had, in fact, regressed in terms of my ability to cope with this situation. But the consultation proved useful, and I came back ready to deal with the situation.

When I returned to my office the following Monday, I learned that Mary's mother, who now lived 500 miles away, had telephoned my secretary to tell her that Mary had been missing since Saturday. Her father, who had returned to the area for the weekend, had dinner with Mary on Friday night and reported that she was fine. When he did not see her on Saturday, he assumed that she had gone away on a brief trip to California because she had mentioned that she was planning to do so, and so he left for a visit with his parents. When her father returned to the apartment Sunday night, he received a call from Mary's employer reporting that she had missed two days of work.

Hysterical with worry, the mother called me and a number of other people in an unsuccessful effort to locate Mary. Finally, at my request, she called the police, who broke into Mary's apartment and found her semiconscious on the floor, apparently having returned and taken the pills several hours earlier because her father had been in the apartment all morning. (She might well have been watching for him to leave so she could reenter the apartment.) Mary was comatose in intensive care for 24 hours but was well enough to be released from the hospital three days later. Interestingly, during this episode Mary's mother told me that she and Mary had always had a very close relationship and that she felt that she knew Mary better than she knew herself!

When Mary called to make a therapy appointment and again when she arrived, she acted as though nothing had happened. I commented on her ignoring her most recent suicide attempt. "It cleaned me out. I have no feelings from the past. I can make a fresh start now," she said. However, she casually mentioned that she had an old prescription refill for 150 tablets of Elavil, which she could use when she felt the need. She also reported that her parents were moving back to the area and intended to live with her! No longer caught up in this dynamic, I told Mary my observation of our process (e.g., that I had been standing around helplessly in the face of her behavior, just as she had stood around helplessly in the face of her mother's behavior, who either smothered her or unpredictably moved out of state). I also told her I could no longer permit either of us to continue this way. I gave her an ultimatum: she could have an intensive hospitalization in which we would work on this process in a protective environment, or we would terminate.

Surprisingly, Mary accepted the offer after months of refusing a long-term hospitalization. She seemed relieved and to need and want this limit. I also insisted that she give up the prescription refill, and she telephoned the physician in my presence to have him recall it. She elected to do that because she said that she wanted to work on her problems (and perhaps to regress in the hospital). What I had done was once again "read the riot act" to her, as I did in the fifth session.

I realized that I had been overlooking the fact that Mary could tell that her mother cared for her only by her displays of anger or insistence on moving back in with her daughter. Apparently, Mary needed me to set limits so that she would know I cared. Interpreting this dynamic was not adequate, though at one point, I did make an interpretation of it. I had to prove in action that Mary's machinations would bring attention from me. However, I had been unable to find a way to do that without totally playing into the controlling scenario, which I resisted doing. Hence, I had missed my creative opportunity to deal with the situation the first time around.

After 3½ years of treatment, Mary moved into the hospital for four months. She quit her job and declared bankruptcy, having refused to consider any other options. After a month she began making demands of the ward staff, though at first her demands were reasonable and easily satisfied. Then she demanded a room change because her roommate snored. But because they were the only two women on the ward and because no other beds were available, her demand was refused. Mary then dramatically threatened to kill her roommate. She severely bruised her own hand by angrily smashing it through a partition and that night insisted on sleeping in the bathroom. The next night she insisted on sleeping in the day room, which prevented the janitor from cleaning the room. The staff ignored her acting out.

She attended her psychotherapy session with me and screamed at me for not helping her get a new room. She ranted about how inadequate I was and how much she hated me and stormed from my office. During this session I said very little, listening empathically to her anger, acknowledging her needs, and trying to explain the reality of the situation. She remained angry, returned to the ward, and bruised her other hand by suddenly slamming it on a table. The staff were stunned and overwhelmed because nothing anyone said seemed to help. A replay of the incident before the hospitalization was occurring. Would she get her way? Would we take over and prove our caretaking?

The ward administrator gave Mary several choices—stop the behavior, be discharged, or go to the state hospital for protective care. She decided to go to the state hospital (probably for its regressive opportunities) and was transferred there.

The next day, Mary telephoned me in a panic, voice trembling, medicated with Mellaril (a new drug to her), and barely coherent. She needed to know that I was all right. I asked her why I would not be all right. She replied, "I don't know. I am afraid you don't exist anymore, or if you do exist that you won't want to see me." I reassured her that I was still alive, that her rage had not destroyed me, and that the staff and I did not hate her. In reality, however, she had created quite an uproar on the ward, and I did feel worried and annoyed. She calmed down and asked to return to our facility soon; she was transferred back within two days. I saw Mary three times a week during the rest of her four-month hospitalization. She worked productively on her problems for the rest of her stay. She remained on a low dose of Mellaril, which seemed to help with her thinking during rage attacks.

Therapist's Observations   During this period, Mary increasingly used projective identification, which was a concept that clarified some of the confusion of the previous several months. Along with her self-object confusion, she alternated between desperately wanting me to fulfill her most primitive dependency needs and pushing me away. She ignored my interpretations of this behavior, that only physical action on my part, or magical understanding, could possibly meet her intensely infantile needs. On the other hand, she still feared my taking her over, although this fear was less predominant than the demand that I meet her needs. As she became more psychotic in her relationship with me, the Megalomaniac once again predominated, and Mary plotted revenge on both me and her mother for not meeting her needs. In turn, I became confused and enraged about what was happening in the therapy and could not determine what to do, believing that my only choices were to kick her out of therapy or order her around.

What allows us to label Mary's condition as a transference psychosis? First, her attention was totally on me and my every move as they pertained to her. I had become more important than her mother, and in some ways, I received the rage that Mary directed toward her mother. We could also say that Mary sacrificed herself to return the caretaking role to mother. Yet, allowing her mother to resume this caretaking role had benefits for Mary. She could allow herself to be taken care of and still rescue her mother at the same time. It was apparent to me that Mary had begun to be unable to judge realistically our interactions; she seemed to view our relationship as a life-and-death matter. Sometimes, she lost reality testing and attributed non-existent motives and statements to me, confusing me with her mother. Yet she continued to function outside therapy, to go to work, and to maintain her basic routine.

Middle Phase

Task 6: Experiencing Merger Longings and Struggling with Differentiation

After being discharged from her four-month stay in the hospital, Mary moved to the city where my clinic is located and got a job and an apartment of her own. She had lost 50 pounds and now dressed more colorfully and stylishly. In addition, she started to make friends for the first time. She began to maintain eye contact and now showed a greater range of affect. This phase started toward the end of the third year. She became much more committed to controlling all forms of her acting out. A partial and tentative therapeutic alliance committed to change and growth seemed to be in effect, although it could be lost under stress.

Mary immediately wanted to know if she would be given antidepressants to help her mood "just in case I get depressed." She was told that she would be given Mellaril for a limited time but would not be given antidepressants. She looked annoyed and said menacingly, "You know I can get them if I want to." I responded, "Yes, I know, and we need to talk about that." I then told her that I would no longer be willing to work with her if she made any more suicide attempts. I stressed that she needed to come to therapy to discuss suicidal feelings, but any action taken on these feelings would lead to immediate termination. If she called me after ingesting pills, I would assist her with emergency help and hospitalization, but there would be no future individual sessions. Mary listened quietly and then said, "I think that is fair. I don't think you will see me risk losing my therapy to test you out." After that time, Mary made no suicide attempt and cut herself only one time that I know of.

This did not mean that the therapy was easy now. Mary was aware of the tremendous mutual dependence she and her mother had now, and she still visited her mother three to four times a month. She looked at the dependency with less self-hatred and struggled with it more realistically.

Perhaps a brief review of several sessions from this phase will show some of the change in Mary and some of the problems with which she still struggled.

Mary had been in therapy for 4½ years. She went home on a weekend to visit her family just before this session, the first time in months that she had stayed overnight. The visit was disconcerting because she found that she really did not enjoy her mother's company. Mrs. Markham chattered incessantly and never asked Mary anything about herself. During the visit, Mary made some tentative moves to engage her father in private conversations, but he was so inept that she felt hopeless about getting to know him. In addition, she still worried that her mother would consider her as disloyal if she spent time with her father.

She reported that she was particularly uneasy at home and started to experience many of the old feelings (e.g., fear of displeasing her parents, drinking in their presence, blanking out during their fighting). That night at her parents' apartment, she dreamed that she was an alcoholic who had been dry for months but went on a binge while everyone watched helplessly. The dream then flashed to the city where I work—it had been destroyed by a bomb, even the facility where I work was gone. She wondered whether I was alive and awoke in a panic, not remembering what I looked like. The dream seemed quite clear in one of its meanings. Mary was controlling her addictive dependency but could not and did not want to maintain it. She regressed, and the therapy and I ceased to exist, perhaps destroyed by her rage over her oral neediness. She had few associations to the dream, and I did not interpret it, instead letting the real-life events that followed do the clarifying.

Therapist's Observations   In addition, on a more positive note, the dream could be seen as a recapitulation of what had happened in the previous months of therapy. Mary had been out of control and believed that her acting out had destroyed me. She was relieved that I had set limits and that she found me still alive. However, given the current therapeutic context, my sense of the dream was that it represented a loss of evocative or even recognition memory following a particularly regressive visit home.

At the next session, Mary reported that her mother had telephoned and asked her to ask me how much longer she was going to be in therapy so that they could plan to move away together. Mary was clearly expecting that life would go on as always after therapy stopped, thus discounting the real meaning of treatment. Mary told her mother that it would be at least another year. She then reported conversationally that her mother did not recognize how much stronger she had grown in therapy. Mrs. Markham liked Mary's new assertiveness with others but did not want her to be assertive at home. Since her recent overnight trip home, Mary had canceled plans to go out with friends in order to stay home to sleep and daydream. Also, she had been spending all her time fantasizing. She added that she would let her mother think the two of them would move away together but doubted that she really would do it:

Mary: I won't tell her for another year; that buys me some time.

Therapist: What do you mean, "buys you some time"?

Mary: I can have a relationship with her the way it has always been.

When I asked her to clarify this further, she said she would pretend to be her mother's little girl and let her mother think Mary believed everything she said. Thus, Mary would remain taken care of, including financially.

Therapist: By letting your mother believe the old relationship is intact—you and she will always live together—you also continue to believe in that myth. The consequences of continuing to think that way are readily apparent: you give up your friends and social life in order to settle for a fantasy life. That's the price you pay.

Mary looked somber and depressed, and then started working on her rage and depression over her inability to give up the fantasy relationship she had with her mother (because she actually saw little of her mother these days).

At the next session, Mary was both depressed and distant. She complained that the therapy was not helping and that she did not want to come today, which was highly unusual for her. She said she did not know what she felt, and then she said nothing. I silently reviewed the session and hypothesized that either my confrontation had elicited some depression or that she had suffered a narcissistic injury from my strong confrontation. I mentioned her depression regarding her mother and my remarks at the end of the last session and asked whether her feelings last session might be related to her "blankness" now. She responded that she thought the depression was related to my comments. Mary told me the Megalomaniac had come back, telling her to deceive and punish me for my remarks—she could too have it all. What was so bad about living one's life in fantasy? Reality was not so great after all!

We sat silently for a few minutes before she remarked, "I don't really want to live the rest of my life alone in a dream world." She began to cry. She reported that the Megalomaniac was not exerting as much power over her these days. After the last session, she made herself keep a date with friends and actually felt better, but part of her was still grieving for the loss of fantasy about her mother and their so-called perfect relationship, which she now knew was false. We explored this fully in the next session.

Not unexpectedly, in the next several weeks Mary started to overeat massively (after all, she no longer had any credit cards to act out with since her bankruptcy). She regained 16 pounds and felt helpless to control her appetite. I confronted this by saying that a pattern was developing here. Each time she got control of herself and experienced independence, she became anxious of what that meant and then overate or engaged in some other destructive behavior.

She started to talk openly about her fear of growing up (e.g., having to take responsibility for herself, being alone at times). She feared losing everyone. I looked at her, and she responded, "Yes, I am afraid you'll stop seeing me if I get better." I pointed out that eventually she would feel strong enough that she would want to stop seeing me. "That will be novel," she laughed.

Over the next sessions she struggled with her overeating. I continued to confront it and also point out that getting control of her appetite did not mean that she had to diet at this point. In the next session, she reported that she had controlled her overeating and that it felt exciting. Furthermore, she had started seeing her friends again and had started some social activities. Now she began to express poignantly the recognition that friendship did not always match her old fantasies, including those regarding her mother. Talking extensively of her fantasies, how powerful and mesmerizing they were, she said, "Going to a movie with friends or out to dinner just seems like such a letdown in comparison to staying at home and daydreaming." We studied this, and Mary finally said, "The fantasies are always under my control, even when I am hurt in fantasy—real life isn't that way." We talked about what "real life" could offer that might be better than fantasy, but she was not convinced.

For the next six or seven months Mary worked productively on various issues in therapy. Once or twice she brought up her worries about her lack of sexual desire, but these were fleeting moments.

At the end of this period, in the fifth year of psychotherapy, I took a three-week professional trip. It was my first long time away from therapy in 1½ years. I told Mary about my plans a month in advance; we explored her feelings, and she asked to see a colleague in my absence if she needed to, and I concurred. Upon my return, Mary had some difficulty reconnecting to her therapy. She and I examined all the possibilities, and she was able to express how angry she was that I left.

Another crisis arose about a month after my return. Mary started the session by mentioning that she was no longer having a difficult time relating to me. She repeated that she hardly remembered me while I was gone. She let me know once again how wonderful she found my colleague to be and that until this week she had not even been sure she wanted to reconnect with me. I listened to her carefully and remained silent. After a brief pause, she stated that there was something she must tell me. She now appeared agitated and nervous, commenting that the entire matter did not make any sense to her. She said in puzzlement that if she did not really miss me when I was gone, why did she do it? I was, of course, uncertain as to what she meant, but I waited for her to continue. She took a breath and said that before I left for my trip, she overheard my home address in the clinic office. While I was gone, she started driving by my house. She did not know why she did it, but somehow it was soothing.

After I returned, she stopped driving by my house until last week, when she started doing it again. This need to drive by my house was making her anxious, particularly because it seemed to be increasing. In the last few days she had driven by my home or place of employment a number of times each day. "I can't stand it any longer. I'm afraid I'll get to the place where I won't be able to do anything else," she said.

I listened in amazement. Initially, I had felt quite concerned about her. As the session progressed and she became calmer, she conveyed another subtle message. She assumed that she could drive by my house and watch my comings and goings. I started to feel angry; I resented her intrusion and aggressiveness. But I did not feel so angry that I could not explore her feelings and reactions. I asked several questions about what she felt during these forays, what her fantasies were, and what she gained from the experience. She was unable to say much except "I keep feeling that you're not alive unless I see your house. I keep worrying that something has happened to you."

My mind flashed to her dream of being an alcoholic who went on a binge and her fear that I was probably destroyed. I speculated to myself that our symbiosis had been ruptured by my trip and that Mary was trying to reestablish it by these extra contacts. Perhaps she felt unconscious rage at the rupture and was having stimulated oral urges in which she felt like devouring me and then feared rage over her own cannibalistic urges and worries that I was dead. I asked her why she thought I would not be alive, and she was unable to answer. I suggested that perhaps my being gone had stirred up some feelings in her and that she feared that those feelings would destroy me. But she had no associations to this tentative hypothesis.

Over the next few sessions we continued to examine the meanings of these trips by my house, which she labeled as "spying." I was also debating how I would handle these trips if she were unable to bring them under control. As we explored these issues, I was invited to give a talk in another state. Again, I told Mary that in a month I would be gone on one of her therapy days and offered to reschedule it. She became extremely quiet, looked angry, and acted distant in the session. I suggested that the change of appointment was no doubt upsetting her, particularly in regard to the problems we had been dealing with. Nodding affirmatively, she commented that she would check out my house on the day I was gone, just to make certain that I was not there. "Whatever is that about?" I asked. Mary told me her fantasy: that I could not stand her and wanted to hurt her by withholding each session that was rightfully hers. She never really believed that I went away for three weeks. She checked my house because she believed that I had taken time off from work just to torture her. When she did not see me for those three weeks, she then believed her fantasy was not true. "You know I can't stand for anything to change. Even when I have to change an appointment, it is upsetting to me. I can't stand it when you do it. I don't think you want me, nobody could want me," she said. She cried, and I sat with her.

She then admitted that she had driven by my house that very morning and saw my car when she thought that I should have been at work. She was positive that my secretary was then going to call, say I was sick, and cancel our appointment. She let me know that if I had canceled the appointment, she would have watched me all day long to see if I left the house, went to my private practice, or did anything else that a "sick" person would not do. She would then have had proof that I did not really care about her and wanted to torture her.

Once again I felt stunned by the intrusion into my personal life. As I examined my feelings and fantasies, I also found myself feeling paranoid (e.g., what "bad" behavior would she catch me in? I had better be careful). As I noticed these feelings, I was struck by a similar theme regarding Mary and her mother that had emerged earlier in the therapy. Mary had felt stuck with her mother; to keep her mother's love she had to forgo friends and social activity, stay home all the time, remain quiet, and not make trouble. Although Mary was saying that she was the desperate one (the victim), it was again as though she had unconsciously changed roles and now was the controlling, intrusive mother and I the guilty, bad child. I was to be at certain places at certain times—and nowhere else. Mary could not tolerate any tampering with my symbiotic fantasies because tampering led to rage, feelings of desperation, and abandonment.

I had two reactions at this point. I felt some empathy for the little Mary, who had to watch every step she took so that her mother would be placated and would not abandon her. I also felt angry at Mary's attempt to control me through such intrusive measures. However, I wanted to avoid playing out any complementary transference role (e.g., be the critical superego telling her that she indeed had reasons to fear exposing her dependency because it was bad). I shared my observation with Mary: "The safe rhythm of our twice-weekly sessions has been tampered with, and this is very unnerving and disruptive to you." She appeared quite moved by this comment, and we used the rest of the session to study her need to control me in order to obscure all types of dangerous feelings (e.g., romantic longings, anger, dependency).

I waited for the next session to see how Mary had integrated this work, but she had not been successful. Over the next several weeks she continued to report driving by my house and now seemed to regard such actions as accepted behavior. She said casually, "Oh, I drove by several times yesterday, and I probably will today, too."

At this point I felt comfortable offering her both an option and a limit. I wanted her to stop this behavior and instead talk about her urges, including any feelings related to them. If she needed more sessions in order to contain her behavior, we could arrange them. Surprisingly, she became enraged, stating, "I have a right to go by your house if I want to—it's not against the law to drive on a public street. If you don't like it or try to stop me, I will just lie to you."

I realized that Mary had me over a barrel because there was no way I could verify her honesty. I announced to her calmly but firmly that she and I had a professional relationship. I was uncomfortable with her spying (her word) on me. I could not make her stop, but I would like her to honor my request. If she did not comply (and I suspected she would not), it would affect her therapy. I continued that I would have to discuss my suspicions with her because otherwise I would not feel emotionally free to do my best for her. She got angry over this statement but eventually agreed to control her behavior and freely admitted that part of her wanted to torture me and part of her wanted me to put limits on her. We explored the options to help her during this period (e.g., increased visits, even hospitalization). She decided that her two visits per week plus one brief scheduled phone call would be adequate, and this was the schedule we maintained.

Although there were several more brief schedule changes over the next six months, Mary was able to continue working on her problems. During this entire period she made no suicide attempts, engaged in no self-mutilation, and even participated sporadically in a number of positive, self-enhancing activities (e.g., dieting, moving into a more comfortable apartment, visiting with friends, planning a job change).

Therapist's Observations   Many other issues came up in the therapy during the following months. However, the "spying" issue provided a forum for looking at Mary's behavior through several theoretical lenses. According to the Kohut perspective, my trip ruptured the symbiotic selfobject relationship, which Mary was trying to reestablish by learning more about me personally. Some therapists might even ignore the forays by their houses. According to the Masterson-Rinsley perspective, she was acting out her wish for reunion. According to the Kernberg perspective, she was also acting out, particularly in regard to problems of sadistic control. According to the Gill perspective, my limit setting, offering her more time, albeit a healthier option, was my controlling her—a matter she and I explored. The proponents of each perspective might have handled the incident differently, of course.

I chose to acknowledge the longings (in the Rinsley manner) but also to set limits on those longings. My basic premise was that I had accepted a selfobject relationship for a considerable period, with the inevitable failures that Mary and I then discussed. Each failure and occasional limit that was set when needed had helped Mary move closer to differentiation, which was certainly one of my goals.

Some Kohutian clinicians may consider my position one of "developmental moralizing." My response is that in order to actualize herself, Mary would eventually have to give up her particularly distorted form of selfobject relating and progress to a more adaptative and socially rewarding form of relating. Second, I had a right to protect my privacy, which I did by setting the limit.

Summary

Mary's borderline problems were especially graphic and intense. Over almost six years, Mary moved out of a schizoid-narcissistic cocoon and began to experience her full dependency longings, which heretofore she had defended against. As this occurred, her perceptually fused self-object images, so typical of the lower-level borderline patient, were revealed and understood, and she had to start the process of differentiation.

It seemed to me that Mary's therapy had several layers. The first layer was her detachment that masked convoluted, intense merger longings, and her poor self-other differentiation that could be seen in her confusion over aggression directed toward herself and others. Beneath that was a second layer comprising an inner world of warring feudal lords and helpless subjects—the Megalomaniac and the Baby. The Megalomaniac appeared to be both an aspect of the grandiose self and a primitive, punitive, sadistic conscience. As this second layer was worked through, albeit partially, Mary started to feel less false and disingenuous and more authentic. Then she experienced dependency in its real unworked-through form, feeling overwhelmed and desperate. She once again alternated between her self- and object roles and acted toward me as her mother acted toward her (e.g., controlling and coercive).

The reader may wonder exactly how each part of the puzzle fell into place, at least up to this point. That is impossible to say. By the end of the fifth year it was clear the Megalomaniac part, which had been modified, was now less punitive and sadistic. Mary was able to do some self-soothing as well as to allow a few friends to soothe her. But her split-object-relations units were still not integrated, and her abandonment depression was not yet worked through (as shown in her angry, clinging behavior and coercive demands). However, given Mary's serious problems and the fact that she was a very high-risk patient, she had done surprisingly well.

Main Themes of Mary's Therapy

The following themes proved helpful in understanding Mary's behavior:

1. A persistent, unconscious search for replication of the symbiotic experience with the primary maternal object (e.g., real love is subjugation; one dies when one's primary object dies, and vice versa).
2. The conscious use of distancing as a protective maneuver against both her fear of merger and her unacknowledged longings for merger (symbiosis) (Rey 1979).
3. The use of revengeful and self-destructive behavior whenever the symbiosis was perceived to be ruptured. When Mary perceived that the symbiosis was working, she saw herself as a quiet, compliant, nondemanding child and the therapist as a totally loving, appropriately matched, nonintrusive mother. Then Mary experienced bliss, if only temporarily. When the symbiosis was broken, she felt both desperately alone (borderline problem) and worthless (narcissistic problem).
4. A constant attempt to deal in therapy through the false self, with great fears about the split, undeveloped, psychotic aspects of the hidden true self (e.g., particularly the Baby and, to a lesser extent, the Megalomaniac).
5. The ever-present reality that quiet acting out would take place (often not reported for weeks), through overspending, overeating, self-mutilating, and planning suicide attempts.
6. A Masterson-Rinsley sequence that every move toward separation-individuation (the individuation drive) led Mary to feel intensely empty, angry, and depressed, which she fended off with resistance, acting out, and occasionally with psychoticlike states of pseudoserenity.
7. Mary continually denied her dependency needs; to her, dependency was a state of affairs that could not be acknowledged to exist.
8. A heavy reliance on projective identification or turning passive into active, in which Mary assumed the parental role and treated the therapist as she had been treated in order to both test the therapist and to reintroject a new, better way of handling her traumas so her development could resume.

A Model for Understanding Mary's Psychotherapy

Mary's behavior and psychodynamics (e.g., suicide attempts and denial of her covert demands for caretaking) could be perplexing without the assistance of a developmental framework. My approach to understanding Mary was drawn from the conceptual models of Searles (1951, 1955) on incorporation as a model of relating and the problem of dependency; Masterson (1981); Kernberg (1982b); Rinsley (1982b) on revenge and the talion principle; and Rosenfeld (1978, 1979) on transference psychosis.

For Mary, dependency of any sort was malevolently transformed into a hateful experience that should have been denied. But this left her alone in her neediness and forced her to seek covert ways of manipulating significant others into providing caretaking. Symbiosis, of course, was operative here. It manifested itself when Mary attempted to train me to provide a soothing atmosphere, which she then absorbed like oxygen from the air. More active therapeutic interventions (e.g., giving advice or dealing with reality issues) led to rageful feelings and acting-out behavior and occasionally to compliant false-self behavior. The purpose of her acting out was, in part, to punish and then train me to behave in an appropriate unspoken symbiotic way and partly as a form of outlet and relief.

Incorporation

Searles (1951) has explained that incorporation is the earliest mode of relating. The infant in the mother's arms globally senses her mood from scanning her face, feeling her body tension, and interpreting her tone and manner. If the mother is warm, responsive and cues appropriately, the infant will feel safe and incorporated within her nurturing orbit. When she is cold and forbidding, the infant will feel irritable and agitated. This mode of relating continues in some adult patients, including Mary. Sometimes she was unaware of any degree of separation between her own personality and that of the other. As best as could be determined at the start of therapy, this had been Mary's primary mode of relating to both her mother and her various therapists. For example, Mary's beliefs that she and her mother shared ESP and that her mother understood everything she thought and did formed an unspoken link between them. But when her mother was bossy or intrusive (e.g., "out of sync"), Mary became enraged at her for destroying the blissful symbiotic state. Yet Mary rarely could express this rage and instead hurt herself.

Searles (1951) noted that such a mode of relatedness has several defensive functions. First, it preserves the omnipotence of infantile symbiosis by enabling the patient to avoid dealing with the inherent disappointments and compromises of relationships in the real world. Second, it is also a mode of defense to repress feelings of hostility and rejection toward significant objects.

Dependency

In regard to the intertwined parent–child processes that lead to such a dilemma, Searles (1955) commented that (1) the normal dependency needs of infancy were frustrated and had to be repressed, and omnipotence continued past its age-appropriate stage as a defense against the awareness of such needs; (2) the mothering figure, who had never relinquished her own in-fantile omnipotence, felt that she should be able to satisfy all of the child's needs and felt guilty when she could not. The mother conveyed her omnip-otence to the child and also that the child, as an extension of the mother, was potentially omnipotent as well.

In Mary's case, the Megalomaniac was a good example of omnipotence defending against her awareness of repressed dependency needs. The de-scription of the mothering figure fit Eleanor Markham surprisingly well. She convinced Mary that she would always be there to take care of her. She also taught her daughter that the world was bad and should be avoided. Finally, Mrs. Markham became jealous when anyone else met Mary's de-pendency needs (e.g., she was usually jealous of Mary's current therapist). Naturally, this caused great conflict for Mary whenever she began to like or depend on anyone other than her mother.

Eleanor Markham had also given her daughter a contradictory message. She had praised Mary for her adult behavior at a young age, while at the same time subtly and negatively reinforced any overt signs of dependency by complaining that the dependency of her oldest child, Alan, had drained her. Thus, Mary experienced her mother's response to dependency as basi-cally hostile and did everything she could to avoid being actively dependent. Although the mother and daughter still maintained the fantasy that they were very close and understood each other completely, Mary's real de-pendency needs were never met.

Thus, Mary was protected from two realities—her mother's belief that she had met all of Mary's needs and Mary's recognition that a part of herself was identified with her mother as the hated object (e.g., Mary sometimes acted sadistic, controlling, and unconcerned about others' true needs).

The reader is encouraged to review a comprehensive article by Searles (1955) on the dependency process in schizophrenia, as it pertains equally well to the lower-level borderline patient. Searles (pp. 115–126) has compiled the following six reasons why dependency feelings induce such anxiety in severely disturbed patients:

Patients may experience their needs in a hopelessly conflictual combination of dependency needs plus various defenses. These defenses (e.g., hostility, grandiosity, competitiveness, scorn, and guilt) have developed as a means of coping with the anxiety attendant upon having dependency needs. Dependency needs themselves, in turn, evoke anxiety. (Note: Other experts might not call these defenses but, rather, manifestations of defenses.) In addition, the combination of needs plus defenses plus anxiety often leads patients to be unable to have their needs met realistically. At times, patients are unaware of their pure dependency needs and regain their sense of such needs only late in the therapy.

Patients find their dependency needs unacceptable. First, these needs often involve desires related to infantile or small-child needs (e.g., sucking at the breast, total caretaking) that are not acceptable among adults. Second, they involve feeling "the other person [particularly the psychotherapist] is frighteningly *important*, absolutely indispensable to the patient's survival" (Searles 1955, p. 117).

Patients worry lest their dependency needs lead them to take in harmful things or to lose their identity. These patients cannot tolerate the frustration of dependency needs so that they can subject them to mature judgment once these needs emerge into consciousness. The patients fear that in their vulnerability, they will take in "bad" (symbolic) milk, perhaps in the form of bad advice or bad feelings. In addition, the paranoid position in which they see the world as rejecting and persecutory embodies the avoidance of acknowledging the cannibalistic, devouring quality of their dependency needs. This urge to devour has two associated fears: (1) that they will destroy others and (2) that they will take in too much and not be themselves, thereby obliterating their own identity. Patients who have learned in their families that being dependent means total conformity to the parent avoid dependency because it is hateful to them.

Patients perceive (correctly or incorrectly) that the person on whom they depend is hostile and rejecting. Among the reasons for this fantasy are

1. the patients' dependency needs were met with hostility by the parents, and so they believe others will react accordingly.
2. the patients project their own hostility regarding their hated dependency feelings onto the other person. (Initially, in therapy both dependency and hostility may be repressed, and the patients may feel indifferent toward the therapist.) By projecting this hostility, they protect themselves from becoming dependent and also preserve the hostile side of their ambivalent feelings, which they feel will be destroyed by the positive side. Because their healthy self-assertiveness is bound up in the hostile feelings, that fear is understandable.

3. the patients project their hostility because they fear that the therapist is as unreliable in relationships as they are.
4. the patients believe that there are only enough limited resources to meet their own needs and no one else's, including the therapist's. Rinsley (D. B. Rinsley, personal communication, October 16, 1984) has added that projection also threatens to empty out the patients, thereby impoverishing the ego of both its good and bad objects because these objects are fused.

The patients' repressed dependency needs are closely associated with the repressed feeling of loneliness. Recognition of dependency needs (lifting of repression) leads to an awareness of how alone these patients really are.

Patients fear relinquishing the fantasied omnipotence that defends them against anxieties and gives them gratification. The effect of relinquishing this omnipotence should never be underestimated because it involves intense feelings of loss (even to psychotic proportion).

Mary's hostility toward her own dependency needs and toward her therapist was manifested in several ways. She played out her hostility toward me through sadistic control and dishonesty in the therapeutic relationship (e.g., lying about pill hoarding and suicide attempts). Because I did not know that this was going on, Mary proved how impotent I was to meet her needs. This process fulfilled several contradictory needs simultaneously —she defeated her therapist, thereby becoming the aggressor not the victim, while simultaneously disowning her own dependency needs.

Mary punished both herself and me (therapist) by hurting herself. At these moments she indeed acted as though she and the other were merged and that to harm herself would cause harm to the other. Mary tried to induce in me feelings of hopelessness and helplessness. How can we understand this?

The Talion Principle

Masterson's (1981) description of the talion principle in therapy is particularly apt in Mary's case:

> The borderline child experiences the parent's exploitation of his dependency and helplessness as the grossest form of cruelty and torture. . . . Unable to express his hurt and rage because of his need . . . fear . . . of his parents. . . . He discharges the rage by attacking himself, fantasizing revenge on his parents . . . [and] by destroying their possession [himself] . . . this is . . . [both] a defense against homicidal urges . . . [and] a compensatory . . . fantasy . . . that, if he dramatizes his sorrowful state sufficiently, the parents will provide the wished-for response. (pp. 187–188)

See also Rinsley (1980a) for a discussion of the talion principle.

Kernberg (1982b) reported that chronic self-destructiveness and suicidal tendencies can have several important meanings. With a patient such as Mary, these behaviors represent an unconscious triumph over the therapist. Under conditions of regression, Mary identified with her own position as the victim, but through projective identification and reintrojection of the projection, she also identified with the aggressor. (This was usually the therapist, so that Mary could preserve her mother as a good object.) The self-mutilations and suicide attempts represented both a triumph over dependency on the therapist and a release from fear by identifying with the aggressor (with resultant feelings of closeness and belonging).

Late in her therapy, Mary was able to verbalize this exact process. She spoke of her fantasy that after her death I would grieve for her, that I would feel that I had been very, very bad and would punish myself for my sins against her as she watched from afar. I would spend my entire life punishing myself for her death. I might even kill myself in penance, and we would hence be together in death. This corroborates Searles's (1956) formulation that vengefulness often represents a defense against separation anxiety and repressed grief. Mary and I would be joined forever. She would die, but she and I would also never be really apart—either through my supposed death or my guilt, she would remain forever in my thoughts.

Transference Psychosis

The reader can now understand how a transference psychosis can take place with a patient such as Mary. Once her intense longings for dependency and the concomitant hostility were revealed, several processes were released. Her projective-reintrojective mechanism operated so rapidly that she was easily confused over what was hers and what was the therapist's. In addition, the intensity of her hostility could be overwhelming, which, combined with her self-other confusion, contributed to her massive loss of reality testing. The therapy became filled with primitive, rapidly alternating self-other projections, and she felt totally crazy, stunned, and out of control.

Rosenfeld (1978, 1979) noted that as the therapist desperately tries to interpret this situation, a patient such as Mary hears only that somehow she is all-bad. Mary felt that the therapist did not understand her and was trying to inject something bad into her. To defend herself, she counterprojected and said that the therapist was all-bad and was trying to destroy her. Trying to clear up such a situation, the therapist may feel increasingly confused, battered, and crushed by guilt for being so bad. The therapist starts to feel that what the patient has said is accurate. Rosenfeld suggested that the therapist work with the patient to demonstrate an understanding of the patient's reactions to the interpretations.

How, then, is psychotherapy carried out with such a patient? According to Kernberg (1980a, p. 28), the best approach for the schizoid borderline patient is holding in the Winnicott (1965) meaning of the term—being empathized with and yet permitted autonomy vis-à-vis the therapist.

But there were other major management problems with Mary: (1) her sadistic control via suicidal attacks, (2) her activation of massive narcissistic defenses, and (3) her fear of dependency. These made it difficult to provide the holding environment, as her psychotherapy illustrated. The following theorists have offered some help with each of these management problems.

Kernberg (1982b, p. 17) observed that interpretation of the patients' suicidal wishes as an attack on the therapist often lessens the suicidal pressure and unmasks the patients' hostility toward the therapist. Kernberg points out that often the therapist may have to prove his or her power of survival in the face of rageful aggression before the patients will trust that reliability and concern.

Both Modell (1976) and Volkan (1979) have commented on the early stages of work with patients with major narcissistic components, stating that the idealization and the patients' inability to absorb interpretation should be respected and held—but not interpreted—by the therapist. Volkan refers to this as the *cocoon* phase.

Finally, Searles (1955, p. 139) has said that the major task of such a therapy is to help the patients arrive at a full and guilt-free awareness of their "pure" dependency needs. During this process, the therapist helps them recognize a variety of feelings about past deprivations. But the road to such a destination is fraught with many perils. These patients have "lost in antiquity" the ability to experience pure dependency needs. Therefore, before they can experience these needs, many defenses have to be relinquished, including the ultimate defense that the therapist can meet all their needs and that they and the therapist are omnipotent. The therapist must not fulfill the patients' unmet needs because this will prevent the emergence of hostility that needs to be worked out. Rather, the therapist should bring concern and curiosity to the process of helping the patients experience their dilemma and work it through.

JOHN ELLIOTT: INTENSIVE PSYCHOTHERAPY

John Elliott represented the typical borderline adult so often seen in mental health clinics and acute inpatient units. He was impulsive and had poor anxiety tolerance. In addition, he had problems with anger and dependency. He also abused street drugs to medicate himself.

John's symptoms met both Kernberg's descriptive and structural criteria and the *DSM-III*'s criteria for borderline personality disorder. In addition, he partially met the criteria for a schizotypal personality disorder. John fit the profile of an infantile personality with major masochistic elements.

John sought treatment because of an acute panic state caused by the breakup of a love relationship. But as the panic subsided, he finally realized that he had many problems that would not go away by themselves, so he and I agreed on intensive psychotherapy. During the early phases of his treatment, his drug usage severely complicated the treatment, and not until he drastically reduced it was I really able to ascertain that he could maintain reality testing.

I saw John twice a week for most of his treatment. Although his therapy was rich and complicated, it will be reduced here to several themes and major critical incidents to illustrate how three critical processes emerged and were resolved. These themes were (1) John's original lack of a holding introject (Buie and Adler 1982–1983) and how he subsequently developed one; (2) his split-object-relations units, how they emerged and how integration began; and (3) the modification of his primitive and sadistic superego.

The Early Phase

John started the therapy in a state of chaos. In addition to abusing street drugs, he was paranoid, convinced that his long-absent father was having him followed; he fell in and out of love with various women; and he had erratic and dangerous homosexual experiences. He seemed unable to calm himself or guide his life, indiscriminately turning instead to people or substances to provide what he could not provide for himself.

Task 1: Establishing the Holding and Limiting Environment

Within the first several sessions, I informed John that I would not see him if he used drugs before a session. I gave him several reasons, including the fact that learning in drug-induced states does not carry over to nondrug states. He listened to my rationale and seemingly accepted it. He stated that he could meet this condition but doubted whether he could give up the "benefits" of regular drug usage on nontherapy days. He argued that the "recreational" use of drugs was accepted by our generation and asked where I stood on this issue. I reported that I accepted as an adult that he could make up his own mind; however, I believed that his reliance on drugs went far beyond recreational usage and had caused him major life difficulties.

John: I know you're concerned about me and how crazy I get on drugs— suicidal and all—but I need them, and I don't want to give them up.

Therapist: I am concerned about you. I am also concerned for your therapy. When you use drugs to avoid experiencing difficult feelings, you limit your chances to eventually feel good about yourself. You sell yourself out for short-term relief.

John: [Thoughtfully, but ignoring the deeper issue] Well, what's the bottom line?

Therapist: The bottom line is that I won't do therapy if you've used drugs prior to the session. Beyond that, all I ask is that we can explore what leads you to use drugs on a given occasion.

John: [Nods his head in agreement]

Therapist: And if it appears that your drug usage is interfering with your work in therapy or is causing you harm, I will point that out to you.

John: [Nodding his head again, says quietly] That's fair enough.

We discussed hospitalization in a drug rehabilitation program, which would mean a move to another state, but he decided to stay in this area and try to control his excessive usage by himself. By the second or third month of therapy, John had reduced his marijuana consumption from one joint every hour to several per day, and he had almost completely stopped using other drugs. His gains in control were always, of course, subject to losses under stress. This problem arose again and again. Sometimes I did confront John on the destructiveness of his drug usage, and he eventually brought his habits under control.

Was John just complying with me (e.g., playing a false self) by controlling his drug habits? That was, of course, a difficult question to answer. But given that John finally realized how much he had been avoiding by keeping himself doped up (and because he never completely gave up marijuana usage), it seemed that if he had complied just to please me, it was because he had worked out a system that gave him the best of both worlds.

John entered the session and, as had become his style, threw himself into the chair, slouching until his head almost rested on his chest. He ran his hand through his hair in agitation and said, "Everything is wrong. I can't stand what's happening. I'm so depressed I can't stand it." I waited for him to elaborate, but he became even more agitated. Finally I asked, "What's been happening?" He responded testily, "I don't know. I don't know," and started to cry. I sat quietly, and within a moment he calmed down. Then I said, "Let's just take this a step at a time. What has happened to you since our last session?"

John gulped, visibly slowed himself down by breathing deeply, and said, "I don't know. Nothing, really. [Long pause] I've been upset since last night,

I guess." He became agitated again and added, "Nothing that should make me this upset." I suggested that perhaps together we could figure out what had happened to set off his anxiety. John calmed down and then spontaneously started talking about the activities of the previous day. Among other things, he had felt a little "paranoid" at work and did not know why. Upon exploration, it became clear that several customers at the casino were rude to him. He seemed surprised to learn that he had experienced a number of feelings about their behavior.

Then, as he continued his list of activities, he offhandedly mentioned that a new woman he was dating told him that she wanted to date another man, too. John then fell silent. After a long pause, I asked, "How did you feel about that?" John thought for a minute and then answered, "Fairly upset." As we studied his reaction to this request, John spontaneously remarked, "Maybe I was really upset because right after she left, I got stoned, ended up paranoid, and was so scared that I huddled in the corner of my bedroom thinking someone was out to hurt me." As we explored these events, it became clear that John was unable at this point to make even modest connections between his behavior and the events occurring in his life.

It became increasingly clear to me that John had no idea about what set off his moods. Consequently, he frequently gave me important information wedged in among inconsequential-appearing material. Only after much clarification was John able to start to link his moods and real-life events. This problem became apparent time and time again (e.g., John became paranoid in a restaurant because he thought his father was having him followed), and we then examined and clarified until the precipitants became clear.

Over the next three to four months, John formed a clinging dependence on me. His dependence was not particularly pronounced, except for the following interaction that seemed to take place at each session. John came to the session in a fairly good humor. At first, he reported that he felt comforted by coming to therapy: "We seem to make sense of what is going on with me, and I feel less overwhelmed." Then he talked about his latest girlfriend and her "troubled" behavior. He speculated that the relationship would go nowhere and that he should end it, but he did not feel that he could. Then he wailed, "Oh, God, I don't know what to do," running his hands anxiously through his hair, and looking hopefully at me. I had noticed in several previous sessions that he had a distinctive way of letting his sentence trail off whenever trying to resolve a problem and then turning expectantly to me.

Initially I responded by turning the question back to him, but he rarely came up with any solutions. Eventually I gently responded in this way:

Therapist: From everything you've told me about yourself, I do understand that making decisions makes you intensely anxious. You can certainly use this session with me to strategize on ways to handle difficult situations, but I wonder why you feel so helpless in these matters and want me to instruct you?

John: [Sitting quietly] I don't know.

He soon announced that he had always distrusted his own abilities, fearing that if he made a mistake, he would be harshly punished. Because he also feared punishment from me, he had decided that it was always better to defer to my superior knowledge. However, he concluded with a smile, "I guess you're not going to let me play that script."

At this point John spontaneously started to talk about his relationship with his father, who in many ways supplied the maternal caretaking of John during his mother's physical and emotional absence. John claimed that he never wanted to see his father again, that he despised him and blamed him for all of his own problems.

John then brought up his massive problems with asserting himself in angry and annoying situations. He reported often letting grievances build up inside until innocuous situations caused him to explode irrationally and immaturely. He gave numerous examples in which he had allowed people to use or abuse him. For example, he told me that he did nothing when his former wife brought a lover to their summer cabin and had a two-week affair with him in John's presence. John said he took long walks on the beach just to avoid them. He finally moved away, leaving most of his belongings behind in order to avoid dealing with his wife on this matter. John clearly would go to any length to avoid asserting himself.

It seemed premature to work much with John's anger or to try to get him to express it, given his fear of identifying with the way his father had acted. I noted from a number of incidents he reported that any attempt to control him, criticize him, or frustrate his needs would precipitate intense depression and/or rage leading to feelings of fragmentation. He stated in one session, "I really have problems with anger—it overwhelms me to talk about it." So I simply said, "I understand that's how you experience it. Anger does seem to be a major problem for you, and we can try to understand it each time it arises." My rationale here was to tag anger as a problem and to alert John to the fact that together we would try to understand it. I saw this as simultaneously a holding and a differentiating maneuver.

Therapist's Observations   John's problems with experiencing anger were noteworthy. One hypothesis I considered was that his reluctance to be assertive was related to an unconscious fear of activating his sadistic father introject. John's greatest fear was that he would be like his father, and being assertive activated this fear, which he immediately tried to undo by being compliant and masochistically submissive.

The following sessions from John's fifth month of psychotherapy demonstrate how a brief therapeutic misalliance facilitated a projective identification of the bad father image onto me. John, as the helpless victim, influenced a countertransference reaction in me that helped me understand this primitive transference paradigm. This incident also shows not only how I corrected this situation but also how the experience both provided a more stable, soothing introject for John and stimulated a rudimentary internalization of my holding and limiting function.

John developed a severe dermatitis and had to be medically hospitalized at my facility for several days. During his second day on the inpatient medical ward, I received a tense, frazzled call from the head nurse. She said that although John seemed to be a likable guy, he was arguing, crying, complaining, and threatening to hit the physician or kill himself. She asked me to try to calm him down. It was standard procedure for the psychotherapists in the clinic to respond to medical requests for consultation, and so I scheduled a time to see John.

John and I met briefly to discuss his perception and feelings. He reported that his physician was young, contemptuous and arrogant, refused to give John information about his medical condition, and generally treated him as though he were acting like a baby (which he undoubtedly was). John observed that this kind of treatment, which resembled interactions with his father, threw him into an overwhelmed state, which I inferred to mean a diffuse rage and a panic. After talking for a while, he felt soothed and understood. I asked whether he thought he could manage his tension and anger while on the inpatient ward. He volunteered several ideas (e.g., thought-stopping exercises regarding his ruminations, appropriate assertiveness with the physician) that seemed manageable, and we agreed that he would try them. Afterward, I entered our meeting on the ward chart along with some suggestions for the nursing staff.

Early the next morning, I received a second call from the ward. The nurse reported that John had done much better after I left, but then for some reason early this morning started hitting the wall with his hand, which by now was black and blue. He had wrapped himself in blankets and was lying on his bed in a fetal position, sobbing. Could I come immediately? I had another patient to see, and so I advised the nurse how to talk with him and promised to be up in an hour.

When I arrived, John was in his room looking exhausted and staring at the wall. I sat down next to him and asked gently what had happened to set off this episode. He answered dully that he had become "paranoid" about what everyone was writing about him in his chart. There was a long pause, and then he admitted shamefacedly that he had "liberated" his chart from the chart rack, taken it into the bathroom, and read it from cover to cover. He said he found the notes of the physician and nursing staff to be humiliating. He conceded that overall, my notes were acceptable because they were brief, vague, and nonjudgmental. But he was offended by my original hospital treatment plan, which set out, among other things, the goal of reducing his dangerous homosexual acting-out behavior. He began to sob and asked how I could have put that in his chart. Because several staff had referred to him in their notes as homosexual, what would the nursing staff and physicians think of him now?

As a young professional, only recently employed in a hospital setting where the chart (with all types of notes) traveled from clinic to clinic, I felt totally responsible for his reaction. I wondered whether I had done something terribly wrong in my compulsively accurate record keeping, and I was shocked that he had read the chart. I also wondered whether allowing John to get the chart was an unconscious attempt by the disgruntled nursing staff to punish him. But I realized that he was quite right—many others in the hospital could also read those notes in the chart. I felt torn between problems of confidentiality and those of required accurate record keeping. For a moment I wondered whether my charting had indeed influenced the staff's attitude toward him, and I felt both guilty and a little angry that he was making such an issue out of this.

I managed my guilt and anger internally and asked John to talk some more about his feelings after reading his chart. He acknowledged that he had never accepted his episodic homosexual behavior (it went against his heterosexual self-image), and he presumed that others would disapprove of his acts as strongly as he did. He viewed the physician (who was about his age) as a superior authority figure who treated him as though he were trash. He thought that the nursing staff probably looked down upon him, too, now that they knew of his homosexuality.

I listened thoughtfully to his fears and concerns, and he gradually calmed down. I pointed out that he was assuming that others would judge him as harshly as he judged himself. I asked him what evidence he had of the nursing staff's attitude toward him. He pondered this and then acknowledged that the nursing staff seemed to like him. He volunteered that his interaction with the physician did not generally reflect how other people on the ward felt about or treated him. He sheepishly speculated that his suspiciousness (paranoid fears) might have contaminated all his ward relationships. However, he hinted that he really did not want his sexual peculiarities put on the chart. We then discussed the clinic's requirements for charting, and I thanked him for drawing my attention to the realistic aspects of the breach of confidentiality in this setting. I told him I wanted to think about what he had said and would get back to him.

At that point John became anxious and said, "I am not asking you to do anything that will get you in trouble; I can really live with this" (perhaps feeling guilty because I implied that the clinic policy and I were in the wrong, and he believed that I was warding off criticism by capitulating). I responded that I appreciated his concern on my behalf but that I would not get in trouble and did want to consider his point. After discussing this problem with the clinic director and staff, we all decided that greater discretion was required with this new type of charting.

I simply reported to John that such material would be deleted from his chart, and he seemed pleased. The rest of his hospitalization passed quietly, and he was discharged after the successful treatment of his dermatitis.

At our first session after John's discharge from the hospital, I was 15 minutes late because of a dental emergency. When I arrived, John was chatting animatedly with the secretary. I apologized and offered him another appointment if he preferred. He passed it off casually, saying the delay gave him an enjoyable opportunity to visit with the secretary. It was like John to be compliant and agreeable in such matters. He talked mainly about his "overreaction" (his words) on the medical ward.

John spent the next session telling me about his new girlfriend but mentioned nothing about my being late or the charting incident. Then, at the end of the session, he told me that his girlfriend was worried because he was in therapy. She wondered what it meant—was there something really wrong with him? He laughed off her worries with a self-deprecating joke but added that perhaps it would be useful if I met with her and explained why he needed treatment. Would I do that? He asked me this as he was standing at the door, ready to leave. I was taken aback by his request.

I responded that I was unclear about the purpose of such a visit and suggested that we talk about it next time, leaving my position on the matter undefined. Afterward, I was perplexed about his request. Just a few days ago John was hysterical when other people read his chart, and now he was asking that I meet with his girlfriend privately and talk about him. I was concerned that some type of menage-à-trois replication was being set up among the three of us (replicating the relationship among his father, stepmother, and John)!

Although there were several possible reasons for John's request (including a magic wish for me to rescue him from his girlfriend), I speculated that he might need to sacrifice himself in some way as punishment for asserting himself earlier and for his guilt over his power in getting his chart changed. Stated differently, he needed to subjugate himself to me by sacrificing his privacy in order to keep my caretaking and approval as well as denying his anger by being compliant. I simply took note of that process.

At the next session four days later, John did not mention his request. However, he appeared tense and slouched in the chair, reporting with agitation that he could not think of anything to say. I sat quietly and waited for him to continue. After a few minutes of fits and starts, he began to talk about a coworker who upset him by implying that he was not doing a very good job. I asked a clarifying question regarding what he meant by "upset" but said little else. John then mentioned a small disagreement with his girlfriend, who in his view had treated him in a somewhat cavalier way. She had turned up late last evening for a date, and she never called when she promised that she would. I wondered to myself whether he was talking in part about how he saw me (e.g., I did not keep my promises or appointments). He offhandedly mentioned that he and his girlfriend had recently gone to a party where he had a bizarre sensation that she might talk about him behind his back (possibly a projection of his own wish to tell his secrets to others). He had kept this feeling under control, but it haunted him all evening, as she spent the night talking with other people, and he found himself wondering whether she really cared for him. "What did you fear she would say about you behind your back?" I asked. "Just something negative or hurtful," he replied. Just like the charting incident, I thought to myself.

John then casually remarked, not looking at me, that he had been feeling distrustful of everyone. He quickly added that during the last several days he had started using drugs again, despite his resolve. Then he passed off the suspiciousness with "Maybe the drugs are doing this to me," therefore blaming his paranoid feelings on himself and his drug usage rather than on his interpersonal experiences with me.

Several thoughts occurred to me. First, John's tentative, indirect confrontation of me in the hospital regarding my charting was an assertive act. Was the activation of the paranoid feelings (the withdrawing SORU) a reaction to that? Would I abandon him? Or perhaps his girlfriend's indifferent acts stimulated his paranoid feeling. But it was equally possible that the breach of confidentiality combined with my lateness at the next appointment had prompted some regressive replication scripts, particularly because the therapeutic frame was not exactly stable.

So I asked John what other feelings his suspiciousness and the resumption of drugs had uncovered. He eventually associated to the times he had made love to his young stepmother, believing that she returned his affection. He described how shocked and hurt he was to learn that she was merely giving him sexual lessons at his father's bidding and how mortified he felt when he realized his father was watching. He seemed to be stating, in part, that he was not sure of others' honesty. I ignored the Oedipal, incestuous, competitive aspects of this interaction.

John associated that he was worried that his girlfriend might not care for him. He feared that she had some surreptitious reason for being involved, perhaps because he took good care of her, and that she would drop him as soon as it was convenient. I wondered whether the charting incident had reactivated all types of voyeuristic concerns as well as problems of loyalty and betrayal. Perhaps he believed that he was taking care of me by not complaining about my lateness; after all, I had been "sick."

He reported a dream from the previous night: "I am driving a car, someone runs into me and I scream at him. Then I am at my father's house, and he tells me it's all my fault—I can't even drive right—I am so undisciplined—didn't the military teach me anything?" Then he said, somewhat spontaneously, "God, it was really hard to come here today. I just didn't want to come. I just wanted to stay home and sleep." I pointed out that he said he was suspicious about everyone and did not want to come to therapy today, but he had not mentioned whether he was feeling suspicious of therapy or of me, and I thought that that might be a possibility. He admitted, with embarrassment, that he had been feeling distant and suspicious of me since the last session but did not know why.

Although these brief associations had many rich possibilities, one particularly important aspect was that John was processing in his associations the charting incident, my being late, and his need for me both to break his confidentiality and to take care of him (as his father did) by meeting with his girlfriend (I had not dealt with this yet).

Let me summarize what John had said. He reported that although he took good care of the girlfriend, he felt that he was being rejected and would be talked about behind his back. In the dream, he was struck by another car and then screamed in anger, but when he arrived at his father's house, all the blame was put back on him. In real life, John had not screamed when I was late. He was congenial and agreeable. He had, in fact, "taken good care" of me. In addition, the "insult" of my being late seemed to have restimulated his need to submit to sadistic others. This, in turn, related to his father's watching John's sexual activity with his stepmother, a problem that he had not dealt with in terms of either his feelings about the loss of his stepmother as a friend or his feelings of competition and anger. Now his request that I talk with his girlfriend seemed to be setting me up to resemble his father and to share his life for the voyeuristic pleasure of others.

Although I wanted John to associate more to these problems before I made any comment, it seemed appropriate to say something in a way that showed both acceptance and acknowledgment of the complexity of his reactions. And because he was feeling suspicious of and paranoid toward me, this might help consolidate the therapeutic relationship. After a pause, I told John that his associations and dreams seemed to contain the clues of what he was experiencing and trying to tell me. John looked pleased and amazed and answered that he could not imagine what it was. I suggested that we look at the material together and see whether my hunches made sense, and he agreed. I started sequentially working through the elements:

Therapist: My first thought is that the dream, the incident with your girlfriend, the charting incident, and my being late are all related.

John: [Looking amazed] How so?

Therapist: Let's start with the dream because it is the most recent event. In the dream you are hit by another car, and you scream.

John: That's right.

Therapist: In real life, when I was inadvertently late, you didn't scream or get angry, as you did in the dream when you were hit by the other driver. Why was that?

John: I don't know.

Therapist: Perhaps you were afraid I would turn the blame back on you, as your father did in the dream.

John: [Perks up and becomes more active] It is interesting you say that, because after the session I went home and I did feel angry for a few minutes. I remember feeling paranoid that you were deliberately late because I made such an ass out of myself over the hospital chart. I guess I also feel that I need therapy so much that 15 minutes seemed like a lot of time to lose [Begins to cry].

Therapist: I can appreciate that [said empathically; I wait for John to compose himself, and we sit quietly for a moment. I decide to respond to his fear of retaliation.] I cannot say for certain that I was not retaliating for the brouhaha on the ward. If I was, I am unaware of it; but given my painful tooth, I don't think so. . . .

John: [Nods his head in acceptance]

Therapist: . . . You, yourself, just brought up my second point, the link between the charting incident and these other events.

John: [Looks startled but pleased]

Therapist: In the charting incident you felt anger, but then you worried that your anger would alienate me, so perhaps you felt a need to accept my lateness without protest. But because you suppressed your thoughts and feelings, you had an experience with your girlfriend that seemed to be a complete replay of the charting incident. . . .

John: [As though having an insight] Yeah! [Long silence]

Therapist: . . . Yes, this time you asked me to violate your confidentiality by talking with your girlfriend. I wonder if you felt you needed to appease me for

> experiencing anger toward me? To sacrifice yourself? To victimize your-
> self?

John: [Sits quietly for a minute] I think you're right. [He starts to explore the interpretation]

In summary, what I said to John was that I imagined that my inad-vertent lateness had probably seemed like indifference to him. It appeared from the dream that he had been angry but could not give himself permis-sion to express it in real life (as he had in the dream), for fear of being criticized and abandoned. I speculated that perhaps my being late reac-tivated the anger from the charting incident (when he had been angry and felt put down) and stirred up some new anger. This made him afraid and led him to appease me for his unexpressed anger by sacrificing himself by having me reveal his secrets to his girlfriend, thus replicating an early childhood scenario.

John started to talk about many aspects of his here-and-now interpreta-tion. He was beginning to count on me. Would I hurt him? He feared that he had to be compliant or else I would not like him or would hurt him (e.g., take away his therapy). Through this exploration John and I were able to see how he victimized himself, how this replicated an aspect of his childhood that he still needed to hold on to, and how he had been enacting this with me (albeit around a real series of interactions). This interpretation gave John considerable grist for his mill, and he reflected on parts of the interpretation for some time to come.

I had inadvertently fallen into the replication script. I had felt the shock and guilt of being "caught" doing something unknowingly hurtful to some-one else—probably what John had experienced as a child and adolescent. He felt too powerful in this incident and had a need to undo it by putting himself in the exact position he said he hated (turning passive into active). But this enabled me to understand the script much better and also to help John understand it. By tacitly acknowledging my part of the interaction and by helping him understand what he had been feeling, our therapeutic alliance was reaffirmed by our mutual commitment to understand this dynamic and to stop enacting it endlessly.

I also told him that I trusted him to talk about his problems with his girlfriend, but I did not want to breach his confidentiality by talking with her and replicating an undesirable aspect of his childhood. He was greatly relieved and said that it had never occurred to him that he had a right to privacy. He speculated that this must be what the charting incident had been all about.

There were many other intricate meanings to this interaction. One could even say that expressing feelings in psychotherapy replicated for John his submission to his father, including sharing feelings and thoughts for his therapist's (father's) voyeuristic interest. But in regard just to his separation-individuation problem, his reaction to me permitted us to label several of his chief problems—compliance, fear of his own anger, and voyeurism. All of these were tied together as part of John's replication of a significant relationship in the past and his symbiotic ties to his father.

Therapist's Observations   I learned the following from this incident:

1. As John started to feel close to me, he needed to ascertain whether or not I would hurt him by violating the privacy of our therapeutic relationship or by writing hurtful comments about him in the chart, just as his father had talked to John's friends about him and said hurtful things. This replicated the parental relationship, with John as the victim and the therapist (parent) as the sadist.
2. At the same time, John showed his hidden identification with his father, by, for example, voyeuristically peeking into his medical records, thereby experiencing disappointment in me just as he had felt his father's disappointment in the way that John and his stepmother were having sex. Although John acted out the victim role (SORU), he was also revealing an aspect of his identification with the aggressor SORU.
3. John then apparently felt guilt over either being the aggressor or being assertive (perhaps both) and suggested that I violate his confidentiality as a way of maintaining the therapeutic symbiosis (perhaps insisting on the sadomasochistic pattern because I had tried to stop it).
4. Because I refused to continue the pattern and insisted on protecting the integrity of his therapy, I gave him a new experience: (a) I listened to his anger without retaliating, and (b) I refused to continue to violate the privacy of the therapeutic relationship.
5. John began to control himself (the rudimentary process of internalizing my function) by realizing that he was allowed to have privacy (boundaries), that anger did not lead to retaliation or abandonment, and that my healthier ego supported his not acting out.

There were many ways that I as the therapist could conceptualize John's dilemma, but it should be noted that John himself was unable to conceptualize his problems or to provide possible hypotheses and reported mainly chaos, confusion, and panic. When asked what he thought was wrong, he replied, "I am just a hopeless mess." However, in retrospect, an important part of his early treatment was the new object-relations experience he had with me over the charting incident, my being late, and his request to me to talk with his girlfriend. He spoke many times over the next few months about his right to have privacy, to say "no," and to protect himself in realistic ways.

Task 2: Experiencing Tolerable Disappointment in His "Holding Introjects"

Over the next four months, John increasingly relied on psychotherapy as a safe place to talk and to experience his feelings and fantasies. During this period he felt the inevitable small disappointments in me. For example, at one point he needed to change his regular appointment time because his new job conflicted with his therapy schedule. I was unable to accommodate him immediately and could see him only once a week, for several weeks, until other appointment times opened up. John panicked when I told him, and admitted that he was angry because I could not immediately cater to him because he needed the therapy so badly. We explored this reaction together, and I patiently explained the reality of the situation. Little by little, his capacity to tolerate these disappointments increased.

In regard to his relationship with women, John reported more and more that his girlfriend turned to him for caretaking, though she dated other men. She let him pay her bills (promising to pay him back but not doing so) and broke dates with him. In general, she "used" him, and he did nothing to stop her. For several months I listened, clarified, and explored his reactions to her. Finally, I started confronting his willingness to be treated badly.

Initially, John reported only hurt feelings over her behavior, and no feelings of anger toward her. When I asked, "Why do you let her treat you that way?" he seemed startled but still could not summon any feelings of anger. I did not press him but did tell him that I was astonished that he continued to put up with her behavior, that he deserved better treatment. He became increasingly depressed about his girlfriend but put no limits on her behavior. After my confrontation, I mainly listened and clarified. Perhaps my confrontation (to get him to assert himself with women and to take better care of himself) led to John's experiencing abandonment fears, which he deflected by acting out in a variety of ways.

During the seventh and eighth months of therapy, John reported thoughts and fantasies that if enacted would (and did) put him in legal and physical danger. This was shown especially in one session in the seventh month of treatment.

John entered the session and sat on the floor of my office in a heap, with his face hidden in his arm. I asked him what was wrong. He responded that he could not bear to face me. I sat quietly, and eventually he said that he had been having "terrible" thoughts, thoughts that he had had off and on since Vietnam. He repeated that he could not face me while he told me these thoughts. I told him that it was all right for him to continue to talk from his position on the floor but that he might be more comfortable in the chair. After all, I reminded him, therapy is the place to talk about these forbidden thoughts and fantasies.

He slid into the chair with his face turned away from me and said rapidly, "I am having continual thoughts of picking up a young girl in my car, taking her somewhere, and making love to her." Before I could say anything, he quickly added, "I can't imagine, as a woman, how you could stand to hear me talk about this. I feel repulsed by it myself." He started sobbing uncontrollably. I sat with him until the sobbing subsided. I shared my appreciation of how difficult it was for him to tell me such painful and self-revealing material. I asked him how close he was to doing this. He responded, sobbing, "Very close." I emphasized how important it was for him to explore these fantasies and understand them and that we would have to talk about the potential dangers and legal ramifications if he should act on these fantasies. He appeared soothed and asked which aspect we should discuss first. I responded that I would like to understand these urges better before we talked about the legal implications.

John said that he had intensely "obsessional" (his word) thoughts of picking up girls, usually ten years old or older. These thoughts haunted him night and day, and he had begun to plot ways of carrying them out. He had no idea what set off these fantasies. He did not see himself as hurting these girls but, rather, gently and affectionately making love to them.

John told me that the day before this session he actually had gone to a school and waited on a corner, where he talked with a young girl but could not bring himself to entice her into his car. "I came damned close," he said with agony. He reported feeling deeply shamed and mortified by these urges, but he also felt terrified about being so close to acting on them. Despite various attempts on my part to obtain further associations or information, John was unable to say any more.

I confronted him by pointing out matter of factly that such an act constituted several prosecutable offenses, including statutory rape, child endangerment, contributing to the delinquency of a minor, and possibly also kidnapping, all of which could get him into serious legal trouble that would follow him for the rest of his life. John appeared quite sobered by this possibility, as well as my statements that such acts could negatively affect the young girl for the rest of her life. John admitted that he had never thought of the consequences of such an act and wanted very much to establish control over that fantasy. He brought his urges into therapy each time he felt them and reached the place where he felt he would not act them out.

In another session, John reported being compelled to seek out physically dangerous homosexual encounters in which he ran the risk of being hurt. I confronted him about why he was not taking care of himself and why he subjected himself to potential harm, but he said he could not stop these actions.

In yet another session, he reported with embarrassment that he went into a bar, suffered an insult, and ended up picking a fight with several men (winning), something he had never done before. He was amazed at himself because he tended to see himself as a gentle soul, not "macho."

John was unable to suggest any reasons for this sudden rash of dangerous behavior. I silently reviewed the situation and wondered whether his acting out pertained to his inability to set limits on his girlfriend, fears of abandonment, and expressing in behavior his feelings toward her or a reaction to some interactions in treatment. But John was unable to link his thoughts and fantasies to his behavior. When exploring each incident, though, John reported a particular feeling associated with each one as well as a certian way he saw himself and the other person involved. John and I pieced together the following. With the teenaged girl, he saw himself as a powerful but gentle adult seeking unconditional love from an immature, accepting, and less complex person than his girlfriend. In the homosexual incidents, he felt like a bad, evil child who needed to be punished by a cruel, harsh other (John did not mention his father at this point or his incestuous, homosexual feelings toward his father). In the fight, John was the powerful one who could take care of himself and hurt anyone who crossed him; the other men were weak and puny in comparison.

During several sessions, John examined each of these states, images, and their associated feelings in some detail. He was amazed that he had such a variety of roles for himself and such a range of feelings. While carrying out this exploration in therapy, he spontaneously confronted his girlfriend for the first time, and they ended their relationship.

In the following session, he said that immediately after the breakup, he seriously thought about going on the street and buying all kinds of mind-altering drugs, but he controlled that urge (it seemed to me that he now had some alliance with my reality ego). But later that night he ragefully rammed his head through a wall in his house. Then he went to a homosexual hangout and had sex in the bathroom, even though he knew he was risking arrest because the police were actively patrolling the area. I interpreted that to mean whenever John asserted himself positively, it seemed to set off a cycle in which he would have to victimize himself. He found this a useful hypothesis, and we studied in some depth both his victim posture and his repressed but emerging aggressor posture (e.g., picking a fight).

Eventually, these acts ceased as John began to recognize and identify his own feelings and to obtain some relief by discussing them in therapy. He started to explore in more depth his relationships with women and to experience a range of feelings, including anger.

During the same period, John examined his reactions to several small incidents between us that had made him feel paranoid, victimized, and distant (e.g., my vacation, a change of appointment, a hurtful remark I made). John also considered himself and his interactions with others and his affective responses in greater depth.

In the next session, I observed to John that when he could not obliterate his feelings with drugs, he acted out violently and then played a passive sexual role in which he risked being hurt (e.g., punished). He said he did not know what to do with his feelings; he only knew how to enact them. He admitted that he felt a desperate need to be punished and that his homosexual behavior allowed him to play a passive, female role and get the punishment he deserved. He was beginning to be aware of these feelings, but he still did not believe that he had much control over them. Yet he was able for the first time to see the connection among self-assertion, being alone, feeling desperate, acting out, and then seeking punishment.

John was starting to explore his choice of women. He recognized that he regarded his women as flawless and irreplaceable, and he conceded that he was usually especially needy and dependent when he began a new relationship. He said that he always took care of the women in his life so well that they felt smothered and eventually left him—usually after he had helped them out financially as well as given them his time. Then he admitted that he had started to feel "a little" anger at being dumped.

He tried to intellectualize, but I kept commenting on his feelings and the price he paid for not experiencing and working them through. In addition, I brought him back to his part in the relationship, and he started to explore his hidden motivation for such altruistic behavior: if he gave to his girlfriend, she should love him and be totally devoted to him. There was a hidden contract for John—if he loved a woman, she should repay him with total oneness.

Therapist's Observations   John was beginning to see other parts of himself in addition to the victim as he examined incidents both inside and outside the therapy. He realized that he presented himself in therapy as a compliant little boy who wanted love interacting with a powerful controlling authoritarian other (me) to whom he had to submit. If he submitted, he received warmth and caretaking, and he would not comment on my flaws or even allow himself to note them.

But John had negative feelings underlying this SORU, and eventually his defiance, anger, and hostility toward the sadistic, controlling other leaked out. This moved him to violence, thereby activating the John-as-sadist SORU, which made him feel both guilty and sexually aroused (probably in part due to incestuous implications). Then he subjected himself to a dangerous situation in which he felt humiliated and punished (and received temporary relief). He was beginning to realize that the homosexual acting out, with its dangerous quality, occurred when he felt guilty about having expressed anger. He debased himself as a way of self-punishment while simultaneously maintaining the object tie.

The Middle Phase

The middle phase lasted through the second year and part of the third year. John and I now had a solid therapeutic alliance, and he greatly reduced his acting out except for brief, transient episodes.

John was working more calmly in therapy. As Masterson (1976) has pointed out, the therapeutic alliance is formed when the patient internalizes the therapist (as a positive external object) who can intervene when the regressive tendencies emerge. John now recognized the personal cost of selling out his own needs for dubious caretaking. On his own, he decided to limit his relationships with women until he could understand himself better and could choose a healthier woman. In addition, he was now talking more introspectively of his memories, dreams, and fantasies.

Task 3: Revealing the Malevolent Introjects and Modifying the Primitive Superego Forerunners

At the start of the second year, John felt ready to get a better job and landed a promising position in the scientific field. He expressed to me some negative feelings about his new coworkers: they were older than he was and had long-standing friendships among themselves. Feeling excluded socially upset him and stimulated his old conflicts with his father. Lately he had been feeling somewhat shaky and had urges to use drugs, which he had so far avoided.

He was now able to admit that these situations made him feel angry, but he still had difficulties asserting himself appropriately with his coworkers, particularly with what appeared to be some legitimate complaints. It was still difficult to tell how many of his grievances were warranted and how much "entitlement" was present. I avoided blaming the others and instead tried to help John examine his part in the difficulties. I also encouraged him to devise a strategy for managing the situation.

In one session John looked tense and said that he had had a terrible couple of days since our last meeting. He described a recurring fantasy that he had disregarded until recently, when he finally realized how persistent it had become. The most recent episode occurred when he had been feeling badly treated by the secretary in his office. He then had an intensely obsessional, repetitive fantasy of brutally ravishing a woman. This fantasy was extremely upsetting because he considered himself to be nonviolent (e.g., "I didn't think I wanted to hurt women"). Another facet emerged as we explored this experience. While having this fantasy, John sometimes became a woman being ravished by an unidentified man. Weeks later, John realized that the man symbolized his father.

John's feelings regarding his fantasy, particularly the role changes, were so intense that they caused episodes of depersonalization. That very morning, while taking a long, warm shower to relax, he had the sensation that his body was changing into a woman's and that he was actually developing breasts and wider hips. He found this fantasy, which had occurred many times before but which he had never fully noted until now, to be rather soothing.

In the next session he recalled his persistent fantasy of gently making love to a teenaged girl. The girl was always naive and totally adoring. Again, it was clear that each fantasy represented an ego state. Each ego state had a self-image of John interacting with another person, with a linking affect. The fantasy of making love to a teenaged girl was safe because she was so innocent of the ways of the world; the affect was warm, loving, and blissfully symbiotic; and he was powerful in a kind way (an identification with his father's choice of a young second wife). In the fantasy of a young woman or girl (or himself) being raped by a man (often his father), he felt either helpless and cruelly abused (victim posture) or that he was being justifiably punished for his passivity and weakness; the object image was cruel, powerful, and sadistic. In the fantasy in which he roughed up and raped a woman, John felt powerful, self-righteous, and furious (aggressive posture) because the woman had treated him badly and deserved her punishment.

As we explored the feelings and images of each fantasy, John got in touch with how terrified he was of being a man raping a woman, which he felt would duplicate his father's behavior, with his father's perceived love of sex and violence. We then examined all the interpersonal and intrapsychic meanings of these ego states, touching a little on the Oedipal, competitive issues. For John, being angry and assertive meant that he was being like his father—identifying with an evil, aggressive person, being the totally bad object, and hurting others as he had been hurt. John's alternation between being the victim SORU and the aggressor SORU overwhelmed him, causing massive depersonalization and even a loss of body boundaries. However, this was John's inner world, and his developmental history represented his need to preserve some firm relationship with the loved but hated object in order to protect against abandonment and loss.

As Rinsley (1982a) has pointed out, borderline patients generally are unable to use fantasy in constructive ways. Here, for the first time, John was bringing in a fantasy that revealed the disparate parts of himself. Early in psychotherapy he had always seen himself as a victim. Now he was starting to experience his identification with his wishes to be aggressive as well as his experiencing primitive fears that assertion equaled violence. Self-assertion also initiated abandonment, followed by intense depression and panic. He began to own his various images of himself and felt more accepting of the affect that accompanied them.

As we explored and clarified his fears, John began to become more realistic about these ego states and less fearful of them and asserted himself more appropriately. After he had been particularly hard on himself, I remarked, "You don't take very good care of yourself, and you are terribly cruel to yourself at times." John started to internalize this holding function, saying to himself at stressful times, "I need to take good care of myself and be nicer to myself." He began to recall what I said to him and the tone in which I said it and use it between sessions. He reported having internal dialogues with me in order to resolve problems between sessions.

Over the next few months John made a number of decisions. He had a good job with considerable responsibility. His employers were encouraging him to go to college, and for the first time he felt that he could manage a college career. He used street drugs very seldom now and had engaged in no homosexual activity in the last six months. And after the work on his fantasies, two other processes spontaneously started to occur.

John mentioned his mother very seldom in the first year and a half in therapy, a fact that I called to his attention when he casually mentioned her now. Because some of his preoccupation with his father had lifted, John could attend to his relationship with his mother, and his thoughts and feelings about her emerged for the first time.

Originally he had had a highly idealized view of his mother, but now he saw her as a somewhat passive, ungiving woman. Although she did "all the proper things" such as washing his clothes and feeding him, she was never emotionally connected to him. He remembered frequently being left alone to entertain himself. He started to experience some intense sadness over his relationship with his mother.

Around this time, John received a letter from his father, who wrote that he had undergone numerous treatments for cancer and had only a few months more to live. He seemed to be trying desperately to make amends before his death. As John debated whether or not to respond, he began dealing with a new problem. For the first time, he felt like taking revenge on his father. John was torn between taking pleasure in torturing his father by not responding and yet wanting to reach out to him.

Kernberg, Masterson, and Rinsley have discussed issues of talionic revenge, as manifested in John's behavior. He had to face the fact that this was his last chance to see his father. John now realized that his attachment to his father had prevailed through all these years in both good and bad ways. His father, in fact, tried harder to have a relationship with John than did his mother, and John came to acknowledge that.

During this time, John struggled with some homosexual acting out, his first in a year. He allowed himself to be picked up at a homosexual hangout by an extremely violent and dangerous man. They drove into the country and had sex, and John had to escape to avoid being harmed.

John arrived at the next session desperate and helpless:

John: Please, please, tell me what to do and what to talk about. I'm just so overwhelmed.

Therapist: You're feeling so anxious you're falling into an old pattern of inviting me to take over for you and to tell you what to do. If I do that, it will help out temporarily. I trust that you can work on your feelings in here.

John agreed and started to work on his mixed feelings toward his father.

In the next few sessions John worked actively on his revengeful feelings toward his father. He came to realize that beneath the revenge was a part of him that was still deeply attached to his father, although John was highly ambivalent toward him. He felt stronger and decided that he wanted to see his father. Their visit went well.

For the first time, John realized that his father was a basically good but highly limited man who was extremely ineffectual in dealing with his feelings. Undoubtedly, Mr. Elliott had dealt poorly with his teenaged son. John saw his father as very powerful in a certain sense but also weak and inadequate. Yet he was pleased to find some traits in his father that he really liked.

John was able to initiate a discussion of how they both felt about his father's impending death, and this interaction generated a warm bond between them. But John never mentioned the past because his father clearly was not psychologically adept enough to handle it. John could accept his indirect admission of poor parenting. When his father died two months later, John was able to grieve and to recount both bad and good times with his father. As this mourning process was taking place, John started to act increasingly competent in his dealings with others and to assert himself more appropriately.

Therapist's Observations   During the second and third years, John was able to unfreeze his hidden, fragmented identifications when he felt sufficiently safe in the therapy. As he revealed these introjects and they were clarified and interpreted from an object-relations perspective, he underwent the process of modifying his punitive superego forerunners. This allowed him to untie his normal self-assertive behavior from primitive fears regarding assertion, sexual violence, and aggression.

John began working through the abandonment depression associated with his mother's limited nurturing. In the middle of this process, he came to grips with his own talionic response to his father. His mourning for his father freed him to be like his father in positive ways (e.g., assertive and authoritative). In all of these experiences John started introjecting my attitude toward him—that he was worthy of good treatment, that he should take good care of himself, and that he needed to provide good treatment for himself when others did not.

At this point I found Masterson's and Rinsley's concept of the drive toward individuation and the borderline adults' abandonment depression to be an approach that made sense of John's behavior. John now seemed to be dealing actively with two problems associated with the abandonment depression. First, he realized that he had never developed a sense of self and instead had a series of fragmented selves that were manifested in various ways. For example, his angry, belligerent self got into altercations at the slightest provocation, and his compliant self tried to please the others at all costs. Put differently, they represented victim-aggressor introjects (Meissner) for John.

John was dealing with the profound depression and anger that lay at his core. (He was beginning to feel that he would never obtain the love he missed). At the same time, he dealt with the various self-destructive ways in which he still tried to obtain that love, although he recognized that returning to that state was not possible. Underneath the compliant self-image was a demanding one that felt profound problems of entitlement—"I deserve to be taken care of." He could now acknowledge a need to take care of himself, drawing on his newly emerging self-esteem and positive memories.

Final Phase

John's final phase of therapy lasted from the middle of his third year to almost the end of his fourth year, when he decided to terminate the treatment.

He had been promoted to a professional level at work, where he was an authority figure dealing with other people. In his new position he struggled with some of his own authoritarian attitudes and some narcissistic problems, but overall he began to work out these problems. He was able to give constructive feedback to others and to hear criticism of his performance. All in all, he coped well and received excellent performance ratings. He now valued himself and felt realistically competent.

He was dating a young woman who appeared to be far less disturbed than his previous girlfriends had been, and he was pleased with the relationship. In addition, he had enrolled at the university and had achieved a 4.0 grade point average at the end of his first semester. He was pleased by his ability to assert himself and to control all aspects of his acting out.

At termination, old conflicts reemerged to be worked through one more time. Predictably, John expressed considerable fears about giving up therapy, although he very much wanted to try.

He had a number of termination dreams and at one point asked me whether we could be friends after the therapy ended. I worked through with him one more time that having me as a friend would be a way of not having to deal with the reality of giving up the therapeutic relationship. In other words, if he and I became friends, he would not be able to return to me if he needed therapy later, and he would not work through losing the relationship.

We worked with his fantasies, and he finally conceded that he had fantasized a perpetual relationship with me to avoid dealing with another abandonment depression such as the one he had had to deal with early in therapy regarding his mother. But he worked through his feelings regarding losing me and ended the therapy.

How much had John worked out in this therapy? He had fairly well controlled his acting out, both drug related and sexual. He had a more cohesive and differentiated sense of self with both good and bad aspects. He had more realistic interpersonal relationships. But had he really worked everything out? I would say no, but he had come a long way in four years.

Epilogue

Several years later, John came back for a few sessions to work on difficulties at work and on a relationship problem. I saw him again several years after that, when he was applying to graduate school.

Five years after his termination, it was clear that John had maintained many of his gains. He saw himself and others more realistically. He was able to tolerate his good and bad aspects. He regulated his tension and soothed himself. His job performance was outstanding. Neither his drug nor sexual acting out had recurred, and he was generally performing in a highly creative manner. He had friends and a good social life.

John still has some problems in intimate relationships and has not been able to maintain a long-term relationship. He finds it difficult to get involved without giving too much of himself away and feeling appropriated in the relationship, although he believes he chooses better partners now. We might have been able to work this out more fully had he remained in therapy because intimacy is often the last stronghold of separation-individuation issues; however, it is an issue he is struggling with on his own.

Main Themes of John's Therapy

The following themes dominated John's therapy:

1. Heavy reliance on various forms of acting out (e.g., drug usage to numb or exacerbate feelings, episodic physically dangerous homosexual activity, and urges for sexual contact with adolescent girls). The purpose of his acting out was to relieve tension and enact his psychodynamics through motor behavior rather than through verbalization in psychotherapy.
2. A conscious search for a loving symbiosis with an unconscious search for replication of sadomasochistic situations.
3. Extreme sensitivity to the moods and attitudes of others toward himself, giving a paranoid flavor to some interactions (Carter and Rinsley 1977).
4. Multiple, unintegrated identifications (including sexual) that gave a chaotic cast to his identity. John unconsciously feared that by experiencing the emotion of anger, he would become identical with his hated father. Thus, underlying his fears and obvious ego weakness were both an identification and a hatred of that identification with his sadistic father. This appeared to be what Kernberg meant by saying that primitive object-relations units were beneath simple ego weaknesses. Some of John's fantasies did show a partial identification with his father (e.g., rape fantasies).
5. A pattern in which each separation-individuation act led to fears of abandonment with its depression, which led to defense.

A Model for Understanding John's Psychotherapy

The mutually compatible approaches of Dorpat (1982), and Buie and Adler (1982–1983) contribute ways of viewing John's therapy. Dorpat (1982) made the following points regarding the object-relations basis of masochism, both as self-sabotaging behavior and as seeking sexual pleasure through pain. Masochism is learned from the mother (or father) who both understimulated and overstimulated the child, who had to submit passively to this behavior. Now, as adults, such patients can recreate and control this infantile situation. Thus, the repetition compulsion gives them the opportunity to achieve active mastery over a traumatic situation in which they were formerly helpless and passive.

For such patients there is often an eroticized master–slave relationship with others. Interpersonally, these patients are often most aware of playing the submissive, deferential roles. But hidden within the interpersonal relationship are often ways that they play the complementary role of dominating tyrant (making the others submit to them), even though they are not aware of this. Thus, masochism is a way of maintaining a tie to the primary love object with an unconscious identification with the aggressive object. This tie was played out in John's drug-induced delusion that his father was having him followed by private detectives (e.g., that his father had not abandoned him and would continue to punish him). John's identification with his father was also apparent in his rape fantasies and other angry, violent fantasies projected onto others. John's punishing relationship with his father was unconsciously repeated in dangerous homosexual activity, his interpersonal relations, and his attitudes toward himself. He would often be highly critical of himself or push himself hard at work by visualizing his father scolding him.

Dorpat has stated clearly that a patient such as John will play out and project his victim-aggressor images onto the therapist, often alternating between seeing himself first as a victim and then as a sadist, with the therapist playing the complementary role.

The following generalizations incorporate many of Dorpat's (1982) helpful ideas:

1. In adult life, masochistic relationships are repetitive reenactments of traumatic childhood object relations. They give patients the illusion of actively controlling situations that they once endured passively.
2. Masochism is an adaptive and defensive ego function that is used to maintain a vitally needed love relationship with a primary object.
3. In masochistic patients, "the central dynamic involves introjection of the parents' sadism. It is not the patient's sadism that is turned against the self, but rather, the sadism of the introjected love object" (p. 506).
4. In John's case, his punishing relationship with his father was unconsciously repeated in masochistic homosexual behavior that John sought out whenever he felt guilty or bad about himself.
5. John felt guilty whenever he had feelings that he believed were displeasing to his introjected father.
6. Because John dreaded identifying with his father in any way, he refused to acknowledge any similarity between them. The affective bridge to his father (e.g., by feeling angry or assertive) had to be suppressed. John's deepest fear was that at his core he was like the hated part of his father (see Searles 1951, for a discussion of this fear in patients).
7. An important part of therapy is the recognition and interpretation of the rules that governed childhood object relations and how they have been unconsciously transferred onto the therapist. This process is an important aspect of dealing with resistance and transference work in the therapy (Dorpat 1982, p. 503). One of John's family rules amounted to the belief that symbiosis would be perpetuated if John masochistically submitted to his father, who would take care of him (often inadequately and

immaturely), and John would not comment on that in order to take care of his father.

8. John's symbiotic bond with his mother had been displaced to his father, further confounding his gender identity.

Buie and Adler (1982–1983) believe that the core defect of borderline personality psychopathology is the failure to develop adequate internal resources for the holding-soothing needs of adult life. Thus, borderline adults have a terrifying sense of aloneness because they lack "holding introjects." Buie's and Adler's definitive treatment of the borderline adult is similar, if not fully analogous, to Rinsley's (1980a, 1980b) and Masterson's (1976) triphasic concepts of treatment and the problem of the inability to self-soothe, although the types of interventions differ among them. The concept of developing a "holding" introject was central to John's therapy.

SARAH GARDNER: SUPPORTIVE-CONFRONTIVE PSYCHOTHERAPY

Sarah was a transitional case between borderline and neurotic, perhaps even a narcissistic personality in the Rinsley sense of a higher-level borderline. On the surface, her profile appeared neuroticlike, though her symptoms met the *DSM-III*'s criteria for a borderline personality. And with some probing, she also met Kernberg's criteria for a borderline personality.

Sarah's childhood history (e.g., adolescent death anxiety), her current symptoms (e.g., depression when alone or without a partner), and her behavior in psychotherapy (e.g., wanting me to take care of her) all indicated that she was still struggling with issues of separation-individuation. She was highly dependent and could not maintain a good self-image without others' support, and it appeared that her self-image was very much perceptually tied to the object image. These deficiencies were manifested, for example, when she felt good about herself only if others approved of her and when she felt bad and rejected if criticized (mainly because she feared losing the support of others).

Sarah's borderline issues tended to show up mainly in intimate relationships. She kept her acting out within socially acceptable norms or hid it from others (e.g., her extramarital affairs). She generally functioned well in school, on jobs, and with her new business.

Masterson's and Rinsley's object-relations point of view helped make sense of Sarah's behavior, and their concepts were used throughout this case. Sarah's chief dynamic seemed to be a constant search for gratifying her wish for "reunion." She expressed her symbiotic longings by clinging to the object; however, she also distanced herself from the object because of her competitive feelings. She had not yet reached a point that she could support her own good self-image unless it was perceptually fused, at least at a fantasy level, with an approving object image, particularly one that offered regression by taking care of her.

Sarah and I agreed on a time-limited psychotherapy because of financial limitations as well as her anticipated move to another metropolitan location. We met once a week and focused on her recent severe depression, her relationships with men, and her parenting of her daughter, Tracey.

When reviewing this case, it is important to note that Sarah demanded that her symbiotic fantasies be met; she did not want to give them up. Efforts to confront her with this were met with resistance in order to protect against the deep anguish that underlay her fun-loving facade.

(I used the confrontational approach of Masterson and Rinsley as I understood it from their writings at the time of this therapy. Had I been aware at that time of some of their newer information, I might have said different things or performed some of the confrontations differently.)

The Early Phase

Task 1: Securing the Frame of Therapy, Getting Clarity, and Confronting Acting Out

After our first two crisis sessions, Sarah's mood improved. She began to pay more attention to her business and to work artistically again. She cheerfully announced, "I am feeling much better since seeing you last week. My life feels great now. You've been really helpful." I smiled encouragingly. After a long pause, Sarah turned to me and asked engagingly, "Well, what do you think we should talk about today?" She had been trying to establish a style of asking me to initiate a topic, give her advice, or share my personal ways of dealing with life events. I usually turned the question back to her, but this time I responded:

Therapist: I wonder why you are turning to me to decide on a topic.

Sarah: [Laughingly] Oh, I don't know. Why not have you choose it?

Therapist: [Lightly] Have you noticed that when I put the question back on you, since this is, after all, your therapy, you turn around and try to get me to direct you? What's that about?

Sarah: [After sitting silently] I really don't feel like I need to be here today. However, I promised myself and you to follow through this time. But I really can't think of anything to say or talk about.

We sat in silence again while Sarah pondered, and eventually she talked superficially about water skiing with friends over the past weekend and coming up with a new design for the business. I asked whether she was telling me about these happenings because they were related to her feeling better, but she had no answer. This was an attempt both to label a potential cause-effect relationship and indirectly to confront her avoidance of feelings.

After another pause, Sarah casually mentioned that after our last session she had telephoned Mike (her former husband) to let him know how she was doing. She concocted an excuse about how she needed to talk to him about Tracey, but she really just wanted to hear his voice. Mike was pleasant and concerned and said he still cared for her as a friend and wanted her to be happy. Then he broke the news about his upcoming marriage to Connie. "I didn't tell him that I'd be happy if he would leave that bitch and come back to me," Sarah confessed. (I suspected that she really believed this still might happen.) Now Sarah looked and sounded mildly depressed, but she launched into an enthusiastic and slightly desperate catalogue of events at work, recent social activities, and gossip about members of the business community. She was entertaining and amusing. This went on for ten minutes or so as I listened carefully. Finally, she wound down and sighed.

Therapist: [With concern] Could it be that you're talking about all these events to try to manage your depression, but it isn't working?

Sarah: Perhaps. [Shrugs, and changes the subject]

Therapist: [After Sarah completes her verbalizations] Did you notice what just happened?

Sarah: No. [Looks surprised, then changes her mind and says laughingly] Oh, yes, I changed the subject.

Therapist: What's that about?

Sarah: I guess I don't want to feel depressed. [Falls thoughtfully silent for a moment] . . . I just want Mike.

It appeared that Sarah had been denying the existence of an unpleasant reality. She and Mike were incompatible in many ways, although the abrupt way she left the marriage certainly did not give them a chance to try to resolve their problems. But Sarah now saw Mike as the only man for her, the perfect caretaker, while cognitively denying his chronic impotence and depressions, smothering caretaking, and impending marriage.

Sarah had telephoned Mike after a previous session in which she had acknowledged her depression about being alone. Operating in this model, I viewed the telephone call as a resistance or flight into defense against the abandonment depression that had been revealed in the session. Now I felt the need to make an intervention because Sarah was defending so heavily against that realization; but as Rinsley (1982a) has noted, early confrontations of the rewarding SORU must be made very tactfully. Nevertheless, I decided to intervene at this point:

Therapist: [Empathically but firmly] I can appreciate the relief you get from knowing Mike still cares. Unfortunately, however, it also keeps you from acknowledging that he is about to marry another woman. The cost of such avoidance is that you're setting yourself up for a later emotional crash.

Sarah: [Looking somber] I wonder why I keep avoiding reality when it comes to men. I doubt that Mike will leave Connie for me, but I know that I pretend that he will, particularly after we have a good conversation.

Therapist: How did you feel just before you phoned Mike?

Sarah: I'm not really sure, but I think I was depressed after leaving the session with you [Starting to cry].

Sarah spontaneously talked more about the good aspects of her relationship with Mike, particularly his loving caretaking when she was anxious about starting her own business. I acknowledged his positive contributions, but I pointed out that although he took care of her then, the price she paid was bad sex and never having much fun. She laughed bitterly and said, "Well, I guess I am willing to sell myself out for your basic male mother-substitute." Sarah then began to express some guilt for using Mike, calling him "an adoring little puppy dog that I hurt deeply." Then she mentioned Connie, Mike's future wife. If Connie were not in the picture, Sarah observed, she and Mike might have another chance to make it as a couple—after all, Mike did wait several months for her while she was running around with her industrialist friend. Sarah then related some amusing stories about how "gauche" Connie could be, always qualifying her competitive statements with "She is really a nice person, and I am really only joking." As usual, Sarah was inventive, witty, and amusing as she shared her perceptions.

I decided not to touch the material regarding Connie except to point out once again how Sarah had just avoided her unpleasant feelings. "Your storytelling is so witty and engaging that it is easy to miss what has just happened. Did you notice what you just did?" I asked. Sarah looked surprised and answered, "No." I then explained, "You shifted away from your feelings of loneliness, depression, and guilt to talking about Connie, just as you shifted from starting the session yourself to asking me to begin."

Sarah spent the rest of the session talking about how difficult it was for her to let herself feel depressed, guilty, or angry. She said her family was "turned off" by unpleasant feelings, and she had learned to never mention them. We talked about how she suppressed her feelings, and I concluded the session with "Perhaps you can share those feelings here as a way of working through your avoidance and ultimately as a way of feeling better about yourself."

Therapist's Observations   As in chess, Sarah made her first move: "Let me avoid; let me externalize; let me get you to take care of me." My counter-moves then confronted her: "You're avoiding and denying—this is your therapy."

The SORU is often first detected by noting two processes in the therapy: (1) the verbal or nonverbal demands made by the patient for caretaking and (2) the appearance of depression, anger, anxiety, and emptiness whenever caretaking is not provided. It is only with time and effort that the self- and object images associated with the patient's good and bad affect states can be teased out from the material.

Sarah felt like "an adorable child" or at times like a "swinger" when the rewarding SORU was in force, the object image was "an idealized, highly competent other," and the affect was bliss. When the withdrawing SORU was in force, she felt like a "defective child-woman, vaguely evil and incompetent"; the object image was "punishing and cruel"; and the affect was depression. She oscillated between projecting the self- and object images of both SORUs onto Mike. However, at this moment, Sarah projected the rewarding part-object image onto Mike; she believed that if he just took her back, she would feel good about herself. All of Sarah's positive feelings were tied up in the part-object component of the rewarding SORU ("the powerful other is what makes me feel good and be good"). In Masterson's and Rinsley's terminology, Sarah had a pathologic alliance between the pleasure ego and the rewarding part-unit.

I devoted much of Sarah's therapy to prying loose her affect (both good and bad) from the associated object part-units and helping her attach them to her own self-image so that she could experience separation, individuation, and, eventually, good feelings regarding her autonomy (Masterson 1983a). Interestingly, as I confronted her various avoidances of feeling, she spontaneously turned to talking about her family.

Sarah felt stronger during the next several sessions. She did not phone Mike, preoccupying herself instead with her business. Now she was thinking of hiring a business manager so that Mike's and her life would be less enmeshed in her business (he did her books, a matter she had not mentioned before). I commented, "You can really take good care of yourself when you put your mind to it." She was also paying more attention to Tracey, who had been wetting her bed for the last several months (something else Sarah had not mentioned until now). Finally, Sarah negotiated a large, lucrative contract that would help her live more comfortably and achieve her goal of moving her company to a larger metropolitan area. She seemed more mature and competent as she talked about her business, particularly her artistic pursuits. However, she had doubts about a full-time career and was still unsure what she really wanted out of life. Nonetheless, she was taking care of her business now.

During this period, I spent a great deal of time listening to her and clarifying the sequence of events regarding her feelings, cognition, and actions. I periodically asked for details, clarified her feelings and thoughts, established sequences, and helped her to label her feelings. Overall, however, I was not very active during these sessions.

Task 2: Dealing with the Return of Resistance and Acting Out

At the end of the second month, Sarah threw herself dramatically onto my couch and announced, "I have nothing to say. I am just totally depressed." Then she commanded, "Well, talk to me. Tell me something useful. Don't just sit there like a stick." I replied by asking, "Why are you turning to me?" She responded that she did not know and that she was not having any feelings about me. There was a long silence. I asked her, "What happened to what we talked about last session [her fears of competence]?" She replied, "I can't remember what we talked about."

Now Sarah seemed more genuinely involved in the therapy and responded that she was feeling depressed again. She told me she still got the urge to phone Mike but had resisted the temptation. She blamed me and charged that if it were not for therapy, she would feel it was all right to phone him. Then she quickly added that she realized it was not my fault—her own inadequacy was at stake here. (This observation might or might not have been accurate, but it was interesting how quickly she moved in to protect me.)

She thought she should stop therapy because it was making her feel worse. She said soberly, "I don't really mean that. Why am I feeling so terrible?" I responded, "All the devices you've used to stay away from your feelings aren't working, and you feel more depressed." She then changed the subject. I said that once again she was running away rather than facing her unpleasant feelings. In other words, it was important to work through these bad feelings if she were ever going to improve.

After a long pause, Sarah said, "I just can't get clear what I am feeling about Mike. I keep remembering what you said, that I have positive feelings toward Mike but I also have all these things I don't like about him. So why do I feel he is the only man for me and that I will die without him?" "Why do you feel so helpless?" I inquired after another long silence. Sarah answered that she had always felt helpless. When her parents were alive, she felt she could depend on them. She then talked glowingly about her parents. She had previously told me details of negative interactions with them, and the examples she was giving now clearly also had negative implications, which Sarah had not yet acknowledged or recognized.

Then she described such a negative process with her father. When Sarah was 17, her father took her to an expensive French restaurant in New York City. There they saw one of her father's business associates dining alone and invited him to join them. The two men joked throughout dinner about how no one would believe that Sarah was really the daughter because, being so beautiful and nubile, she looked more like a mistress. Based on her previous experience with her father, Sarah felt she was expected to flirt with the other man, who was behaving in a mildly lecherous manner toward her. (Her father seemed to enjoy the incident fully!) Sarah fleetingly thought that he wanted her to sleep with the other man, but she pushed the idea out of her head. After dinner, she felt "dirty" and wished she had never gone along with the coquettish game. Yet she had felt compelled to play along to get her father's approval, as her father always presented her as the "southern belle" of the family, whereas he regarded her sister Margaret as the "intellectual."

Sarah recalled that frequently she went along with both her mother's and father's agendas instead of her own wishes in order to please them. She remembered feeling guilty when her mother commented casually about her father's attachment to Sarah; she felt that she was somehow a bad person for taking her mother's place in his affections. (Sarah said nothing about the incestuous implications or the competitive elements in all of this.)

I interpreted that her inability to work through her feelings toward her father, in particular, might have had a great deal to do with how she related to men now. I observed that although she clearly had many good memories of her family, she also had some unpleasant ones. "Yes, I seem to have inherited more than just money from my parents," she said, and started to weep.

Therapist's Observations   As with so many other borderline adults, when Sarah performed an individuated act, such as starting to control her acting out, she became anxious about abandonment and felt she was bad. This simultaneously activated the withdrawing self- and object images, which were still perceptually fused. For example, Sarah felt bad about herself and then projected the withdrawing part-object image onto me (e.g., projecting that I would dislike and reject her as she felt that her mother and father did whenever she was independent). Then she blamed the therapy, thereby projecting the withdrawing SORU onto me and the therapy. It was as though she was saying, "When I start to get control, I have bad feelings, just as I did with my father whenever I tried to be independent. You are like him, and I end up feeling bad in therapy. The problem is you, not me." Under the influence of strong affect, she could not bring herself to recognize that this was contrary to reality—that I really was not the parent and really did support her individuation. She thought that the therapy and I caused the bad feelings, and the bad feelings caused her to act out in the hope of regaining the good feelings associated with symbiotic fantasies.

If I had fallen into the trap of "feeding" Sarah at this point, she would have felt better. But that would also have reinforced her primal belief that the parent (and therapist) could not tolerate individuation, that abandonment depression was to be avoided at all costs, and that her symbiotic fantasies would continue to prevail.

It was the third month, and Sarah was now functioning well at work, although she still refused to control her attachment to Mike. Several days after a session with me, she met Mike at his office to discuss her business. She told him how guilty she felt about leaving him and hurting him the way she did. He put his arm around her in consolation when she started to cry, and they ended up making love in his office. Mike regretted it afterwards and told Sarah he did not know how he let it happen! He was just feeling so worried about her and so guilty. He told her that it was too late to patch up their relationship and that they just were not very good for each other. He loved Connie, he said, and now both Sarah and he should move on with their lives.

Sarah telephoned me in crisis three times before our next session. In the first call, she hysterically told me what had happened in Mike's office. She said that for the first time in her life she did not feel like living. She was so exhausted that she could not function and had not been going to the office for the last four or five days. She asked when the therapy was going to help. I pointed out that as difficult as it was for couples to give up a relationship, continuing to see Mike and to sleep with him when he had told her over and over again that reconciliation was hopeless just defeated her work in therapy. She was trying to bring about change in her dependency without coming to grips with the fact that she really could not have Mike—and she needed to deal with her feelings about that.

During the second call, I asked her how she was feeling before phoning me, and she answered, "Lonely." "A few words with me will give you only temporary relief. We need to work on your loneliness and its impact on your life during the session," I told her.

At the beginning of the third call, Sarah said, "I don't really feel like I need to talk—I can wait until the session." "Fine," I responded.

But Sarah had little to say at the next session. She was quite depressed and complained again that the therapy was not helping her much. I tactfully and supportively once again asked why she felt so helpless and hopeless. She responded that she could not give up Mike or anyone else she was dependent on. I pointed out that although she felt she could not live without a supportive partner, there was no evidence to prove that she could not make it without Mike; instead, it appeared that she simply would not do so. She agreed and told me that all of her life she had wanted other people to make decisions for her because she did not dare to do the wrong thing. Then she reflected more about her relationship with her mother and how she sold herself out in order to please her. I asked her whether she was acting that way with me. "Yes and no," she replied, and we explored her reactions to my confrontations.

Toward the end of this period, Sarah started to take care of her business in a more mature and thorough way. She could talk more realistically about some of Mike's personality faults and the couple's incompatibilities, while remembering some of his good traits.

Therapist's Observations   As the reader can see, a rhythm was being established in the therapy. Each act of self-control (separation-individuation) led to abandonment depression, which was defended against by acting-out behavior and projecting the withdrawing SORU onto the therapy ("therapy is useless") as a way to avoid dealing with the abandonment depression. When this process was confronted, Sarah internalized the new reality ego and started to work again—or else defended against working through the abandonment depression.

Task 3: Managing the Refusal to Work in Therapy

We were now in the fourth month of therapy. Sarah came to the next five sessions with little to talk about. She speculated about stopping the therapy because she had made some achievements; she was back at work and was less depressed. Sarah did not believe that therapy was really going to help any more, as she was not sure there was anything more to work on. She had given up Mike now and was dating, although not seriously. I pointed out several times that she was indeed functioning better and could stop therapy if she wished but that she was still avoiding working through her depressive feelings, this time by leaving therapy. She eventually acknowledged this interpretation and started to work again in therapy.

Task 4: Experiencing the Beginnings of Abandonment Depression and the Consequent Return of Acting Out

Sarah admitted now that she became attached to women as well as men. She reported several long-term friendships with women: overall, the friendships appeared to be reciprocal and fairly healthy, based on give and take. But one friendship, with an old college friend that Sarah had recently hired, had become difficult. Sarah reported that this friend was turning out to be a leech and constantly demanded special favors and loans against her salary, which Sarah had reluctantly granted in order to maintain the friendship. There also seemed to be competition between the two over their artistic talents. Eventually, Sarah decided that she had had enough with her friend but had avoided dealing with the problem. Instead, she tried not to be at work when the other woman was there and refused to return her phone calls. As we talked about her friend, Sarah changed the subject to some delightful behavior of Tracey's. I asked, "Why is it that when we attempt to look at this, you cut it off?" Sarah responded, "I just feel overwhelmed—I don't want her to get mad at me because I'll feel guilty."

We explored Sarah's unjustified guilt feelings toward this woman. Eventually I pointed out, "This is, after all, your business. You need to find a way of dealing with her so you are not hiding out." Finally Sarah appropriately confronted the woman, who was greatly offended and quit on the spot. Sarah was proud of her self-assertion and felt better about herself, although she was hurt by the lost friendship. "It does hurt to lose a friend—but it is also important to take care of yourself," I told her. Afterward, she started again to feel some depression. She also remembered more childhood events in which she was never supported for making her own decisions.

In the sixth month, Sarah spent one session dealing with her relationship with her parents and sister. She was beginning to realize how little they really saw her as an individual or recognized what she really needed. She was also beginning to see that she had tried to use Mike as a parent figure instead of a husband. She now admitted to feeling real sadness about the parental nurturing she had never received; she could see now that she avoided certain realities to protect herself against this painful knowledge. She cried genuinely, without dramatics, for the first time. She also recognized and acknowledged on her own the sexualization of her relationship with her father, the unfortunate competition with her mother, and her dependency on both parents. Sarah reported feeling less evil now, as she was beginning to understand how her problem evolved.

Over the next six sessions, Sarah engaged in a flurry of acting out. Looking particularly sheepish, she confessed with great embarrassment that she had recently seen her industrialist friend again. Over dinner, he told her about his sexual fantasies, including that she had come to his hotel room wearing only a trench coat. Then he graphically described how he envisioned them engaging in bondage activities, taking turns tying each other up. She told me that she drank more than usual that night, and extremely aroused by all this, she went back with him to his hotel and enacted the fantasy. She said that she came close to having her first sexual orgasm that night (shades of prostitution fantasies) and felt fantastic for a few hours because she was able to please this man. But after thinking about the things he said to her, she began to feel degraded. I listened quietly, asking very few questions. At the end, she asked, "How weird am I? Am I crazy?" I did not answer her question, but instead I started to explore the elements of the interaction—older man, sexuality, feeling degraded. I traced this interaction back to our earlier discussion about her parents, especially how bad she felt about successfully competing with her mother. (I ignored any transferential references to me.) I asked how those feelings might be linked to this event. "I don't know," she replied. I once again pointed out that not knowing was a way to avoid confronting unpleasant feelings, just as she used to telephone Mike to avoid depression. She then started to talk about how she felt sexual only when she had been naughty and how sexually exciting it was to be with an older man. She said she had found her father to be very attractive but experienced considerable guilt over this feeling.

Sarah engaged in other acting out between the next few sessions. On one occasion, she picked up a totally inappropriate man at a singles bar. I supportively confronted her after each episode, and we discussed her behavior.

Task 5: Control of Acting Out

By the end of the seventh month, Sarah finally was able to control her acting out. In addition, she was much more aware of the various ways that she elicited caretaking, including allowing herself to be degraded, and started to control these impulses. She made a new female friend, with whom she was especially compatible. She also dealt more effectively with Tracey, using techniques she learned in her therapy.

During the last three months of therapy, Sarah worked more on her fundamental problems of depression. Whenever she started to act out, she stopped herself by saying, "That isn't really going to help." She was beginning to label her feelings—"I am depressed" or "I am angry"—and analyze the reasons for them. She decided to not date for a while. She took up jogging, which she found helpful in controlling her mood.

Therapist's Observations The initial confrontation of Sarah's various forms of acting out the wish for reunion led to greater perception of her neediness and conflicts with both her ex-husband and her parents. This, in turn, led to depression and anger (the withdrawing SORU), which she then (1) projected onto the therapy, believing that it had caused her pain and thus was useless, and (2) combined with sexual acting out in the hope of having her dependency needs and symbiotic longings met elsewhere. As she controlled the acting out, the deep depression and anger associated with her parents, sister, and men in general started to emerge but was not worked through because of time constraints.

Task 6: Termination

By the tenth month, Sarah was financially ready to relocate her business. She started the process of termination and dealt with giving me up. During her last session she said, "I know that I have just started growing up, but at least I am not a victim of my feelings as much as I used to be."

Epilogue

Approximately a year later, Sarah telephoned me long-distance. She said that her business was doing well and that this had greatly enhanced her self-esteem. However, her problems in selecting men and being dependent on them had continued. Although she could recognize her pattern, she still felt unable to control it. She wanted to reenter therapy, which she now could afford to do intensively, and she asked me to recommend a therapist in the metropolitan area where she now lived. She told me how helpful the therapy with me had been and said that Tracey was doing well: "In fact, she's more mature than I am, in some ways."

Six months later, Sarah sent me a brief note thanking me for the referral. She was being seen three times a week in psychoanalysis, and the treatment was working out well. "Given what I am learning, I'll probably be here for years!" she wrote.

We simply did not have the time and financial resources to work through Sarah's abandonment depression. But she did develop some skills to help control her depression, including the use of work in her life. In Kernberg's terms, Sarah's primitive object relations, as activated in the transference, were only partly identified and certainly were not resolved. But she was functioning at a far higher level now, had not lost ground, and was pursuing intensive psychotherapy.

Main Themes of Sarah's Therapy

The following themes predominated during Sarah's 10 months (45 sessions) of psychotherapy:

1. A global and diffuse cognitive style that made it difficult to establish a causal relationship between events and feelings, cognitions and affects.
2. The use of clinging defenses with her ex-husband, child, boyfriend, and therapist to defend against the depression associated with individuation.
3. The use of splitting with men—reliance on one man to provide caretaking and another to provide excitement and sexuality.
4. Reliance on various forms of acting out, including transference acting out to avoid dealing with unpleasant affect.
5. The borderline triad: separation-individuation → abandonment depression → defense.

A Model for Understanding Sarah's Psychotherapy

Sarah was a hysterical personality functioning at the high end of the borderline spectrum. Sarah tended to perceive events vaguely and impressionistically and had little sense of their context or order. She tended to not translate conflicted material into words but rather presented it through body language or fantasies. She was dominated by the pleasure principle (e.g., if she fantasized winning back her ex-husband, she felt they really would be reconciled).

M. Horowitz (1977) has summarized the typical cognitive style of such a patient as (1) an impressionistic distortion of incoming perceptual stimuli, (2) a rapid and short-circuited appraisal of meanings, (3) limited and stereotyped self and object categories, and (4) a limited memory to assist in problem solving. In addition, M. Horowitz (1977) stated that these patients require a therapeutic strategy that embodies repetition and clarification and a relationship that avoids the pitfalls of excessive coldness or excessive rescue (p. 395). He suggested the following techniques: (1) repeated interpretation of cause-and-effect relationships, (2) provision of verbal labels for feelings, (3) construction of sequences of events, and (4) requests for details.

Allen (1977) is one of several theorists who have written about the treatment of hysterical patients (see also Marmor 1953, Halleck 1967, Lazare 1971, M. Horowitz 1977, and Sugarman 1979). Allen (1977) reported that historically the major task of therapy had been to "teach the hysteric to think and the obsessive to feel" (p. 317). He added that in both cases, however, the patients' choice of mental mechanisms and styles defends against their feelings. Allen believes that the therapist needs to point out that the hysterical patients really do not feel as much as they seem to feel. Thus, the therapist teaches the patients to think more thoroughly about certain situations and to feel more authentically. Allen argues that patients who dramatize their plight by role-playing their feelings actually avoid experiencing the threatening feelings and that these pseudofeelings actually serve as a screen against the true threatening feelings.

Allen's and M. Horowitz's guidelines are basically compatible with the second approach for dealing with Sarah—an adaptation of the supportive psychotherapy approach of Kernberg (1982c, 1982f) and the confrontive approach of Masterson (1976, 1983b) and Rinsley (1982a). Although this case did not follow precisely either M. Horowitz's or Allen's conceptual framework, their framework provides two important elements: (1) it explains Sarah's cognitive style and the fact that her dramatics masked her true feelings, and (2) it identifies that vagueness must be confronted and labeled.

Masterson's and Rinsley's approach offers a rationale for understanding a key issue underlining Sarah's cognitive diffusion: the SORU and her fear of separation-individuation. This approach is particularly useful in a time-limited or once-a-week therapy to bring the pathologic pleasure ego-rewarding SORU alliance under control. It follows the following principles:

1. The majority of the work is done in the here and now of the patients' life and relationship with the therapist.
2. The chief task is to help the patients get control of their primitive defenses and self-destructiveness (as expressed in regard to the withdrawing and rewarding SORUs).
3. Clarification and confrontation are emphasized, whereas interpretation is used very little (especially until acting out is under control).
4. The patients are treated as autonomous adults; therefore, the therapist does not "rescue" them or even ask many questions.
5. The therapist remains silent when the patients are working productively and confronts them when they are defending.
6. Environmental intervention may be necessary for the more disturbed patients.

This supportive-confrontive therapy is my own adaptation of the approaches of Kernberg, Masterson, and Rinsley for Sarah's situation. It was not sanctioned by Kernberg or Masterson. After reviewing this therapy, Rinsley (D. B. Rinsley, personal communication, October 26, 1983) found that it followed the general confrontive model as he outlined it. The reader who is interested in precise methods should refer to each theorist's books on the subject.

CHAPTER 13

Alternative Treatment Modalities

Although individual psychotherapy remains the treatment of choice for borderline adults, these patients often can benefit from concurrent treatment in another modality. For example, borderline patients may require a structured environment (e.g., inpatient unit or day-treatment program) in addition to the therapy. They may have disruptive marriages or a family life that can be improved by another modality (e.g., marital or family therapy), or they may have poor interpersonal skills that should receive attention (e.g., group psychotherapy). Borderline patients and their therapists must determine whether immediate help can be obtained for more specific problems while the long-term psychotherapy is taking place (e.g., relaxation for severe anxiety, anger control, weight control, control of alcohol or drugs).

This chapter will review what the experts have said about the efficacy of various treatment modalities for borderline adults. The discussion of hospitalization will be the longest section. Many of the issues that are grouped under hospitalization also pertain to the other modalities (e.g., day treatment) that many lower-level borderline patients may require during their treatment.

PSYCHIATRIC HOSPITALIZATION

Once the decision to hospitalize is made, the next question is whether it will be short term or long term, reality oriented or structural change oriented.

Gordon and Beresin (1983) report that the assumption behind selecting the type of hospitalization is whether inpatient treatment can help borderline patients achieve basic structural personality change or can bring about only superficial but important adaptation in the world. The first approach tends to be long term, and the second short term. These two different approaches sharply disagree over the issue of treatment.

Gordon and Beresin (1983) conclude that inpatient treatment designed to effect structural change tends to be intensive, have greater tolerance for regression, and require a longer stay. Examples of those advocating the long-term approach are Kernberg (1980d), Adler (1977, 1980), and Lewis (1982). Therapies designed to maximize adaptation tend to have limited goals, discourage regression (which is viewed as beyond the patients' capacity), and shorter hospitalization stays (Friedman 1969, Zetzel 1971, Nurnberg and Suh 1978).

As Gordon and Beresin pointed out, even *within* these approaches there are important theoretical differences. For example, Masterson (1976, 1981) advocated long-term intensive individual psychotherapy and the potential for structural change, but he did not recommend anything but a short-term hospitalization for the typical borderline patient. Kernberg (1984) has stated that most borderline patients require brief hospitalization, and that only a few require long-term stays.

Although a variety of approaches can be effective with borderline patients—there is no single right approach—Gordon and Beresin (1983) have identified a fundamental problem that occurs when different approaches are mixed with the same patient:

> Serious problems arise for many borderline patients when the distinction is blurred between the two fundamentally different treatment paradigms of structural change and adaptational adjustment. Unless they are clearly delineated, aspects of both models may be inadvertently mixed, yielding a hybrid that is faithful to neither point of view, or both models may be brought to bear on the treatment of a single patient. Therapeutic inconsistency, the bane of all borderline patients, then often ensues. (p. 979)

As they found, such patients often regress seriously and are blamed for their regression when the treatment system, in fact, is conflicted and inconsistent.

Based on my own experience, I agree that mixing modalities can work only with some borderline patients who can survive staff inconsistency over the milieu's model; however, many patients do become the inadvertent victims of a system that is confused about its own goals and strategies. The best that the clinician can do is to be aware of the problems associated with paradigm mixing and to place the patients in a system that has a clear model and is compatible with what the therapist is doing in individual psychotherapy.

Indications for Hospitalization

Nurnberg and Suh (1978) have noted that patients with a diagnosis of borderline personality organization represent a significant proportion of all inpatient hospital admissions. Yet only a certain proportion of the borderline patient population will ever need hospitalization (e.g., patients in the middle-to-lower end of the borderline spectrum). Many high-level borderline patients seen in outpatient therapy will never require hospitalization. According to Nurnberg and Suh (1978, p. 422), borderline patients are initially hospitalized for one or more of the following reasons:

1. *Minipsychoses.* Minipsychoses may last from minutes to weeks. They may include affective lability, sharply circumscribed thought disorder, marked depersonalization and/or derealization, or unstable paranoid-type delusions and/or hallucinations. The sudden onset of minipsychoses is usually related to a precipitant (e.g., separation experiences).
2. *Suicidal or assaultive threats, attempts, or other dangerous behavior.* In addition to suicidal and homicidal threats, these behaviors can include severe antisocial acts that severely limit the effectiveness of outpatient treatment.
3. *Diagnostic evaluation or consultation.* It may be impossible to make an accurate diagnosis in the patients' chaotic family situation, or the patients may have such a persistent negative reaction to psychotherapy that they must be removed to a more structured environment before the diagnosis can be more carefully assessed.
4. *Crisis intervention.* The patients' social situation may be severely deteriorating, or there may be a collapse of environment support (e.g., a spouse leaves or dies).
5. *Malingering and other manipulation of the environment.* Social agencies often can be manipulated by patients or their family into arranging hospitalization so that the patients can receive various disability benefits. Although such actions do not constitute a psychiatric reason for admission, the treatment team still must carefully assess these situations.

Kernberg (1984) noted three broad reasons for hospitalization: psychosocial, symptomatic, and psychotherapeutic. He also listed many of the above criteria (Nurnberg and Suh 1978) and added severe emotional breakdown with drug and alcohol abuse as well as severe regression in individual psychotherapy. Sometimes a therapist may select a longer hospitalization simply to provide environmental structure while the patients attend individual psychotherapy, particularly if other options do not appear viable (e.g., a combination of day treatment and a board-and-care home).

Selecting a Hospital

Selecting the best hospital for the patient may be simple or very difficult, depending on the facilities available. If the therapist has several suitable hospitals from which to choose, the following variables should be considered: (1) Does the patient need short- or long-term hospitalization? (2) Does the hospital's treatment model mesh with the therapist's approach? (3) If it is an intermediate- or long-term facility, can the therapist continue to work with the patient? (4) Does the hospital emphasize family involvement if it is indicated by the patient's situation? (Adler 1977).

What happens if there is only one nearby hospital or no convenient hospital at all? And what if the patient lacks funds and must be hospitalized at a state facility? In these cases, the therapist may be forced to select from a limited number of nearby facilities or may even have to resort to distant hospitals. Under the circumstances, the therapist often needs to make do.

Short-Term Hospitalization

Short-term hospitalization is increasingly becoming the preferred approach of many hospital units, because of the economics of funding, insurance reductions on the payment for extended hospitalization, and theoretical reasons. For better or worse, short-term hospitalization is what most borderline patients will receive.

Length of Stay

The meaning of *short term* is, of course, somewhat ambiguous. Masterson (1983a) recommended a few days to a week, and Friedman (1969) advised a maximum of three months, preferably less. Others have stated from a few weeks to a month. A month or less would be a reasonable time frame in this approach.

The Short-Term Adaptational Approach

The basic tenet of the short-term adaptational approach is that regressive behavior must be reversed as quickly as possible so that patients can return to "normal" functioning in the community. Advocates of this approach believe that prolonged stays in the hospital actually promote regression by borderline patients, who see themselves having a large pool of staff who magically gratify their needs. Gordon and Beresin (1983) termed this approach the *sobering environment* (as opposed to the *holding environment*) of the structural change model. To "sober" the patients, the following general guidelines culled from Nurnberg and Suh (1978) as well as other experts are recommended. Experts recommending the sobering environment may not accept every point but they accept the majority.

Time-Limited Hospitalization   Nurnberg and Suh (1978) have recommended that patients be told that a certain number of hours will be devoted to history taking and formulation, after which a specific plan will be agreed upon and a discharge date set. It should be clearly stated that if the patients are unable to leave the hospital at the discharge date, they will be transferred to a state facility. This is because research has shown that certain borderline patients' unmanageable regression, acting out, and suicidal gestures are perpetuated by an intensive supportive milieu. Research has also indicated that these behaviors rapidly remit in the more structured state-hospital setting, which offers less staff contact.

Nurnberg and Suh (1978) stress that this transfer policy should be stated clearly and emphatically at the beginning of treatment so that the patients will not view a transfer as a punitive gesture. This, of course, does not prevent all patients from treating the transfer as confirmation that they are bad (e.g., projecting rage onto the staff and then experiencing the transfer as an angry rejection from the staff) or as an opportunity for a sado-masochistic struggle with the staff. Although not all theorists would agree with such a rigid timetable for discharge, there is a great danger that patients will drift or settle into the treatment milieu if care is not taken to limit the hospitalization.

Structure, Limit Setting, and Confrontation   In the limit-setting approach, patients are told that they, not the unit, are to control their behavior (Gordon and Beresin 1983). Other writers have suggested that the staff must strongly limit the patients' disruptive behavior, regardless of the extent of rationalizations and entitlements that they present (Nurnberg and Suh 1978). A unified, clear, and firm response in an atmosphere of non-punitive concern is recommended. Contracts concerning behavior between the ward and the patients are frequently used, and breaking these contracts or acting out often leads to a quick discharge or transfer to a more secure facility (Friedman 1969). Nurnberg and Suh (1978) state that disruptive behaviors within the therapy sessions, premature ending or overtime extensions of the sessions, and nontherapeutic contact in hallway discussions between patient and therapist are to be avoided; all of these should be dealt with through limit setting. Proponents of this approach believe that these patients require firm but concerned confrontation of specific behaviors in order to stop a regressive spiral (Friedman 1969). Nurnberg and Suh (1978) have commented that the staff frequently have difficulty setting limits because of their antiauthoritarian concerns and unconscious masochistic conflicts.

Reality Oriented, Limited, Individual Psychotherapy Individual psychotherapy on the short-term unit is limited. The inpatient unit usually provides only some psychotherapy, working only on reality concerns (e.g., finances, job, repairing ruptured environmental support) and supporting positive aspects of the patients' defensive structure in order to promote their rapid recovery. The outpatient psychotherapist is often asked not to do any therapy until the patients have been discharged (Gordon and Beresin 1983).

Nurnberg and Suh (1978) recommend a more intensive dynamically-oriented psychotherapy than described above, however it should be time-limited and should focus on current problems, not genetic reconstruction. The patients should focus on the problems that brought them there. In addition, therapy should focus on the patients' problems on the ward and their eventual separation from the inpatient therapist.

The emergence of major transference and countertransference problems indicates the need for more structure (Nurnberg and Suh 1978). The inpatient therapist should not focus on the transference relationship with the patients, except to clarify the therapist's limited role in the patients' life, to guard against sadomasochistic interactions, and to provide boundaries for their relationship (Friedman 1969, Nurnberg and Suh 1978).

Multidisciplinary Staff Meetings Nurnberg and Suh (1978) have recommended frequent multidisciplinary staff meetings directed toward the elimination of splitting by focusing on the covert aspects of the patients' behavior. The staff must be aware of the problems addressed in longer-term hospitalization (e.g., splitting, projective identification), although they may not work on them directly with the patients except in practical ways.

Infrequent or No Milieu Meetings Because of the short hospital stay, rapid turnover, and focus on individual patients' reality concerns, the therapeutic community, milieu meetings, and group psychotherapy are not offered because they are believed to be inappropriate and even regressive for such patients (Gordon and Beresin 1983). Active problem-solving groups and adult education classes are considered more appropriate.

Environmental Intervention The treatment team must define the basic support structure that can be achieved in the patients' environment. This includes talking with patients about their life situation in relation to their strengths and weaknesses (Nurnberg and Suh 1978). It may include bringing the relatives into family sessions, but only in a limited fashion directed toward resolving a specific problem. Like individual therapy, family therapy is considered to be able to produce regression (Gordon and Beresin 1983). Nurnberg and Suh (1978) recommend that the multidisciplinary team must consider whether or not the patients need the support of a halfway house, day hospital, job rehabilitation program, or other social services.

Medications Most psychopharmacological experts agree that there is no medication for borderline personality organization, though some medications do relieve specific target symptoms (e.g., depression, mood shifts, panic, depersonalization). Because borderline adults frequently manipulate their medication for suicide attempts, any medication should be given cautiously. It should not be used to help patients avoid working through their problems (Nurnberg and Suh 1978).

Supervision Nurnberg and Suh (1978) feel that various issues, including the staff's reactions to the patients, must constantly be discussed at open treatment-team meetings. In addition, any inexperienced or untrained therapist assigned to an inpatient borderline adult should be closely supervised.

Expression of Affective Material How much should patients be allowed to cry, scream, and rage? There is a fine line between using emotion for acting out and resistance and for working through important psychodynamics. Sometimes it is only with some sophistication by the clinician that the difference can be understood and limits drawn. Therefore, patients are expected to bring "excessive" emotion under control, with the help of increased structure, if necessary (Masterson 1981).

Problems Between the Short-Term Unit and Structural Change–Oriented Outpatient Therapist

Gordon and Beresin (1983) pointed out that serious problems can emerge when a short-term adaptational unit and a structural change therapist do not understand or accept each other's assumptions. They note the following problems. Patients who have been in structural change therapy often view the strict limit setting and restricted time frame of a short-term adaptational unit as punitive, angry, and frustrating. They see the outpatient therapist as betraying them. Not being used to such structure and strictness, these patients may panic and fall back on primitive defense mechanisms and acting out. They may also see the limits and structure as confirming their own sense of being bad and evil. Finally, they may envy the attention given to more psychotic patients and may act out to obtain the necessary holding, which is no longer provided as it was in outpatient treatment.

The outpatient therapist may be shocked by the adaptational unit's demand for contracts, sudden discharges, and lack of psychotherapy, concluding that the unit does not want to treat disturbed patients. Thus, covert as well as overt conflicts can develop in regard to treatment issues; some solutions to this conflict will be presented later.

Long-Term Hospitalization

Certain borderline patients may require a long-term hospitalization because of their poor motivation for treatment, inability to control anxiety or tolerate frustration, intense impulsivity, chronic serious acting out, and history of many hospitalizations for acute psychotic episodes (Hartocollis 1980b). Kernberg (1984) noted that these patients have severe problems (e.g., severe negative therapeutic reactions with chronic self-mutilation) that preclude working with them on an outpatient basis. They may feel misunderstood and abandoned in a setting that expects them to accomplish something beyond their capacity (e.g., a period of hospitalization that is unrealistically short). Therefore, when patients start regressing during a short-term hospitalization, the staff must determine whether supportive limit setting can help the patients regain control or whether they are truly displaying an inability to maintain in anything other than a long-term hospitalization.

Long-term hospitalizations in some areas of the country may be required simply because of a paucity of intermediate-care facilities such as day treatment, halfway houses, and other environments in which the more seriously disturbed borderline patient can maintain while undergoing out-patient psychotherapy. For some seriously disturbed borderline patients, long-term hospitalization provides the required protection during the initial resolution of the life-and-death problems that emerge in the transference.

Length of Stay

Kernberg (1980d) has reported that hospitals directed toward structural change (1) should be organized as therapeutic communities, (2) should accommodate stays of longer than six months, (3) should not treat acutely psychotic patients, and (4) should have an administration commitment to this form of treatment. Patients needing structural change may require one to two years of hospitalization.

Adler (1977) has not recognized the need for special units for borderline patients, believing instead that structural change can be achieved on an unmodified, open psychiatric ward as long as the staff are united in their approach and can tolerate a certain amount of regression.

The structural change approach, except for the exceptions noted earlier, accepts that important and enduring personality changes can be effected in borderline adults through long-term hospitalization. As in individual psycho-therapy, ego defects can be reversed by using the negative transference to clarify the patients' view of themselves and the world, thereby increasing their reality testing and reducing their reliance on pathological defenses. This requires an inpatient unit that can tolerate and work with regressive behavior. The staff must perceive such behaviors as rage, criticism, provocation of other patients to aggression, escape or defiance of rules, altercations, and many other acts as a reactivation of primitive object relations that need to be understood as well as modified. Long-term hospitalization for adult borderline patients consists, as Hartocollis (1980b) has termed it, of a tripartite approach involving therapeutic milieu, individual psychotherapy, and family involvement.

The Therapeutic Milieu

The therapeutic milieu is based on the premise that the staff and the patients work together and openly share responsibilities. In addition, the influence of the staff's interactions on the patients' behavior is crucial, including any detrimental influences of hidden staff differences, tensions, and alliances on individual patients and the milieu in general.

Bion (1961), Kernberg (1973), Rice (1965, 1969) and Rinsley (1980a) have noted that the best milieu for intensive work is one with firm boundaries and specific tasks. Open-ended wards that provide little task structure offer an unproductive regressive structure for borderline patients. Leadership of the ward is important, as Adler (1977) has noted:

> The ability of the hospital or unit director to maintain equanimity in the face of the regressive propensities of staff and patients may be a crucial ingredient in successful hospital treatment. The administrator who respects staff and patients, can tolerate their anger without retaliating, and yet be firm when necessary, and who can delegate power unambivalently can provide the mature "holding environment" and a model for identification for the staff that facilitates a similar experience for the patients. (pp. 321–322)

Lewis (1982) found that the treatment team's organizational structure is essential to the establishment of a good holding milieu. This includes a good working relationship between the administrative psychiatrist and the head nurse; treatment teams characterized by firm but shared leadership, reliance on negotiation, clear individual boundaries, high levels of closeness, and flexible responses to stress; and one person on the ward who has the final responsibility and accountability for the patients. Overall, Lewis (1982) recommends that the team plans should decide (1) how to prevent the patients from injuring themselves, (2) how to develop a therapeutic alliance, and (3) how to deal with the staff's feelings about the patients, including the staff's confusion. The treatment plans should use information gathered from interviews with the patients as well as from the staff's affective reactions to the patients.

Caltrider and Robinson (1983) list 19 danger signals in staff–patient relationships that should alert the nursing staff to problem areas.

1. A disproportionate amount of time spent is with a patient.
2. Off-duty time is spent with a patient.
3. The patient stays up to see the nurse when he or she is on the night shift.
4. The patient dresses in a particular fashion prior to the nurse's arrival on duty.
5. The nurse feels that he or she is the only one who understands the patient, that other staff are too critical of the patient or jealous of the nurse's relationship with the patient, that their criticism of the nurse's relationship is "their own problem" or simply "acting out."
6. Nurse and patient keep secrets.
7. The nurse tends to report and communicate only negative or positive aspects of the patient's behavior.
8. The nurse "swaps" patient assignments.
9. The nurse is guarded and defensive when someone questions his or her interaction or relationship with the patient.
10. The patient talks freely and spontaneously with the nurse, especially in light, superficial conversation, and perhaps even with sexual overtones, but remains silent and defensive with other staff, or may avoid them altogether.
11. The nurse's style of dress for work has changed since working with this patient.
12. The nurse receives visits, gifts, cards, letters, or telephone calls from the patient after the patient's discharge.
13. The nurse does not accept the fact that the patient is a patient.
14. The nurse views the patient possessively as "his" or "her" patient.
15. The nurse allies with the patient against the patient's spouse or children.
16. The nurse answers the patient's personal questions in a vague manner or gives the patient "double messages" that subtly encourage a social relationship between the two.
17. The nurse responds to requests for medications, passes and the like differently for different patients.
18. The patient continually turns to the nurse because "other staff members are all busy."
19. The nurse disregards the danger of fostering a nontherapeutic relationship. (p. 376)

Caltrider's and Robinson's (1983) nursing treatment interventions for patients who feel angry, depressed, and helpless are shown in Table 13-1. These danger signals and interventions are useful also for personnel other than nurses.

Many theorists have noted that patients often experience peer feedback as less destructive than confrontation from the staff. Therefore, helping patients give an appropriate blend of support and feedback to one another is an important treatment goal.

Finally, there is an interactive effect between the patients and the staff. Gunderson (1980) has commented that patients' current pathological behavior may be directly related to either the treatment team's structure or a relationship to a primary object. Lewis (1982) pointed out that when the structure is warm, supportive, and flexible, the patients may experience themselves as sad, depressed, and lonely, and they may want connections to other people. But when the structure is perceived as overcontrolling, conflicted, or frustrating, the patients may view the ward as dangerous, rageful, and primitive. When the ward is perceived as disorganized, some patients panic and then have dissociated reactions or psychotic episodes (Lewis 1982, p. 133). Finally, Ogden (1981) found that the phenomenon of projective identification on an inpatient unit graphically shows how the intrapsychic and interpersonal relate and gives valuable information about both the patient and the status of the milieu.

Individual Psychotherapy

The optimal approach is a psychoanalytic psychotherapy that offers a less-structured experience that is designed to fulfill the needs of each patient within the more structured milieu. In many psychiatric facilities, the outpatient therapist may continue to see patients for individual sessions and may consult with the team about treatment planning. A primary care staff person or inpatient therapist usually will oversee the patients' total treatment program while they are in the hospital. In some facilities, the patients are assigned an inpatient therapist, and the outpatient therapist assumes a peripheral role or no role at all during their hospitalization. Both systems have their inherent problems. Whenever possible, however, it is useful to have the outpatient therapist continue some contact with the patients. In addition, attempts by the patients to divide the staff and therapist or the normal course of disagreements between inpatient and outpatient therapists should be worked out in staff meetings.

Adler (1977) reported that the individual psychotherapist should continue the therapy, pointing to the intense rage and panic of the abandoned-child theme that will emerge if the therapist does not do so. Adler believes

Table 13-1 Nursing Strategies for Target Areas in the Treatment of Borderline Patients

Nursing Diagnosis	Intervention	Short-term Goals	Long-term Goals
The patient is angry.	Reality testing. Set limits to self-destructive behavior. Set limits to force verbalization rather than acting out. Confrontation if negative transference occurs.	Patient will not act out. Patient will become aware of his/her unreal expectations of significant other. Patient will become aware of his/her idealization of others.	Patient will verbalize anger to therapist. Patient will not form unreal expectations of significant other. Patient will respond to therapist in "here and now" context.
The patient is depressed.	Clarification of precipitating event. Interpretation of underlying feeling (devaluation of self, rage, etc.). Affirmation of patient's worth.	Patient will recognize underlying problem through awareness of precipitating event. Patient will stabilize.	Patient will not measure self-worth by competing with others.
The patient feels helpless.	Clarification of thought. Clarification of underlying fear.	Patient will identify actual issue in which he/she experiences helplessness. Patient will join therapist in exploring options for problem-solving around the issue.	Patient will relinquish wish for total dependency and give up strategies to maintain passivity.

Source: Caltrider, J., and Robinson, L. (1983). The borderline personality. In L. Robinson (ed.), *Psychiatric Nursing as a Human Experience* (3rd ed.), p. 373. Copyright 1983 by W. B. Saunders. Reprinted by permission.

that a hospital that encourages therapists to continue with these patients can offer a forum for this rage to be safely experienced and analyzed. The therapist's willingness to continue with the patients also presents an opportunity for a corrective emotional experience that will convince them that their dangerous and provocative behavior will not cause them to be abandoned.

Fromm-Reichmann (1947) has noted that the psychoanalytically oriented therapist must remain flexible in technique, occasionally letting the patients remain silent in the session and on rare occasions even permitting them to cancel a session because they feel too overwhelmed. In addition, the therapist should not be too reassuring about the progress of treatment, which thereby convinces the patients that the therapist cannot tolerate their whole personality. Finally, the therapist should also realize that family visits may cause temporary setbacks.

Adler (1977) pointed out that a major aspect of the patients' hospital evaluation consists of clarification of the patients' relationship with their outpatient therapist, including the transference-countertransference issues. There may be times when the therapist will begin to realize that countertransference problems have played a role in precipitating the patients' decompensation or acting out.

An important task for the hospital staff is developing a safe environment in which the patients can experience and express their tumultuous feelings toward the outpatient therapist (Adler 1977). While exploring their feelings toward their outpatient therapist, inpatients may engage in splitting between themselves and the outpatient therapist, seeing the therapist as the bad object and themselves as the good object. On the other hand, sometimes the outpatient therapist's countertransference problems have interfered with treatment. But when confronted by the staff, he or she denies the countertransference and blames the staff for engaging in splitting (e.g., colluding with the patient). Difficult as it may be, outpatient therapists need to maintain an open mind so that they can examine their own problems regarding their patients, and the inpatient staff must guard against splitting the patients and their outpatient therapist.

I have observed that some therapists, because of the intensity of their countertransference problems, probably need to use the hospitalization as a way of looking at these problems and perhaps even terminate the patients. Adler (1977) stated that the goals in this situation include (1) protecting and supporting the patients while helping them understand the existence of an impasse that was not caused by their own badness or failure and (2) helping the therapist maintain self-esteem in the termination process and at the same time learn from the experience (p. 319). This, of course, is a very delicate problem and requires the utmost tact and sophistication by the hospital staff.

Family Involvement

Patients usually receive family assessments, and their families are invited to attend special sessions in order to work on family problems and psychodynamics. Families of borderline patients should be involved early in their treatment. When not included, families may become increasingly isolated from the patients, leading to a loss of support for the patients. Families may come to believe the staff are blaming them for the patients' problems. They may become alienated and sabotage the treatment in a variety of ways, including removing the patients from the hospital. Finally, the staff should remember that patients' regressions may be caused as much by recent family interactions as by ward processes. Family therapy allows all of these issues to be addressed. Feedback from the family therapist to the ward also may help the staff maintain a realistic attitude toward the family and not align with the patients against their families.

Phases of Hospital Treatment

Various theorists (Masterson 1972, Rinsley 1968, Brown 1981) have divided the hospital treatment of borderline patients into three stages, each with its own problems. Summarizing Lewis (1982, pp. 131–132), these stages are described below.

In Phase 1, described as *testing* (Masterson), *resistance* (Rinsley), and *confusion and containment* (Brown), a repetitive pattern of defensive behavior protects the patients from the emergence of disruptive introjects, abandonment depression, fears of engulfment, and rage. Sarcasm or argumentativeness, threats, manipulations, extreme rage, and persecutory anxiety are typical manifestations in this phase, although the combination of symptoms varies with each patient. During this phase, borderline patients use a variety of projective mechanisms to rid themselves of the bad introjects by projecting them onto others, with attempts to control the others. Patients' rapid oscillations from anger to depression often confuse the staff, who may respond by behaving as though they are bad or impotent.

During Phase 2, patients gradually relinquish their fantasies of reunion, decrease their rage and projection, and experience a period of sadness and hopelessness. The staff may wonder whether the patients will ever recover. This phase has been referred to as *working through* (Masterson), *introject work* (Rinsley), or *helplessness and replacement* (Brown). The integration of contradictory ego states does begin, however, as the patients continue to work in psychotherapy and on the unit.

Phase 3, described as *separation* (Masterson), *resolution* (Rinsley), or *gratitude and concern* (Brown), comprises the patients' separation from and mourning of important objects in the hospital.

Using Limit Setting, Confrontation, and Interpretation

Limit setting involves the use of seclusion or loss of privileges, which is intended to supplement and buttress the patient's ego functioning (Gordon and Beresin 1983). Early in the process, the milieu must protect the patients from self-destructive or other dangerous behavior, and there must be clear guidelines for managing physical assault. The staff must always ask themselves, however, "Given how we understand the disruptive behavior, what interventions will help the patients modify and control their behavior while encouraging the early development of a therapeutic alliance?"

Limit setting that is too firm and is used too rapidly and readily may seriously impede the unfolding of the patients' psychopathology, both non-verbally and verbally. Among the consequences of such an approach, the therapist may miss an opportunity to understand the patients' fears because they will not be permitted to emerge. Thus, the unit must serve to some degree as a holding environment for the projections of such behavior. If the limit setting really masks the staff's angry aggressive feelings, the patients will see it as an attempt to punish them and are not likely to forget the staff's aggressive behavior.

On the other hand, when the limit setting is so lax that patients can act out their problems to a frightening degree, their individual chaos can spread throughout the ward structure, involving other patients and staff. Adler (1977) reported that

> a major aspect of a successful limit setting depends upon whether it is utilized as part of a caring, concerned, protective, and collaborative intervention with a patient . . . or as a rejecting response and manifestation of countertrans-ference hate. (p. 314)

Lewis (1982) stated that although both confrontation and interpretation are valuable techniques, they should be used very little in Phase 1. He observed that premature use of these techniques in the first weeks of hospitalization is painful for patients, who will remember these experiences in follow-up interviews years later as hostile, counterproductive assaults. Thus, considerable preliminary work must be done to minimize the damaging effects of confrontation and interpretation. Lewis has recommended developing (1) respectful interventions, (2) interventions that are circumscribed and directed toward specific behaviors rather than the patients' entire personality structure, and (3) interventions that are delivered in a matter-of-fact manner. Other possible interventions designed to minimize unnecessary hurt are having the patients daily monitor their own behavior and moods and discuss their moods with ward personnel and the use of patient-oriented feedback. On the other hand, other theorists such as Kernberg (1980d) have recommended earlier interpretation of contradictory ego states as manifested in negative transference, and Masterson has advised the earlier use of confrontation.

Importance of Transference and Countertransference Reactions

As in individual psychotherapy, transference and countertransference reactions are considered important sources of information about the patients' internalized object relations as well as the current structure of the milieu. Common transference reactions include projecting the aggressor or victim role onto the staff or a particular staff member while playing out the opposite role, or projecting devaluing or idealizing images onto the staff or a particular staff member while playing a complementary role. Common countertransference reactions include those stemming from the projection of a staff conflict onto the patients as a group as well as onto a particular patient (e.g., using a patient as a scapegoat) or emotions elicited by the staff's internalization of the patients' projections.

Many theorists, including Main (1957) and Burnham (1966), have noted the effects that borderline patients have on staff and the psychotherapeutic milieu. Naturally, these patients bring with them the mechanisms that they use in their life and their individual therapy. For example, in the hospital setting, patients have the unique advantage of a large, 24-hour pool of helping people. The presence of this pool arouses immense expectations, and patients experience rage, depression, and behavioral regression when those expectations are not met.

Although many staff members may have achieved much higher levels of maturity and personality integration than their patients have, repressed primitive aspects can become readily reactivated. When selecting a staff member onto whom to project aspects of themselves, borderline patients almost always intuitively choose someone whose repressed aspects reverberate with theirs. As a result of this projective identification, the patients need to control that staff member. The staff's countertransference need to control the patients compounds the chaos of the splitting phenomenon.

When the patients are viewed as negative manipulators, the staff often feels entitled to make unrealistic demands, punish them, or threaten them with discharge. As Adler has noted (1977, p. 320), an impartial observer may assume that the staff has almost no empathy for the patients' distress. At such times, the staff may be unable to see any positive attributes in overly manipulative patients. Yet it is important that the staff not overlook the pain and distress that underlies the patients' manipulation. As a number of theorists have found, the staff's countertransference hate is potentially lethal for these patients. Countertransference can be categorized as follows:

All members of the treatment team develop much the same countertrans-ference response to the patient. Lewis (1982) noted that each staff member experiences a similar feeling toward the patients. There is no evidence of splitting; the staff appears to react uniformly to the patients. However, Lewis (1982) discovered that changes in "the patient's ego state, with consequent change in the content of the patient's projections, may lead to a clear shift in the nature of the shared staff countertransference response" (p. 134). An example of this might be the hospitalization of Mary Markham, which took place in the third year of her individual psychotherapy with me. Upon entering the inpatient ward, Mary was genuinely liked and perceived as cooperative by the staff. However, as she worked with her deeper prob-lems of longing for engulfment and rage at that longing, she began to blame all of the staff members for not meeting her needs and not being available. At one point, Mary complained that her roommate's behavior was annoying and said that she would probably have to kill her if the staff did not move her to another room. The entire staff became annoyed with Mary. They felt they had been extremely supportive and could not understand why she was so angry, condemning, and demanding of perfection from them.

Team divides because of splitting. As Lewis (1982) observed, members of the treatment team divide into two camps that correspond to the patients' projection of contradictory ego states. One group, for example, may see the patients as helpless, in pain, and requiring more attention, but the other group may view the patients as manipulative and mean, requiring more structure or punishment (Hartocollis 1980b). Lewis (1982) noted that the two ego states rarely occur simultaneously but usually are experienced consecutively. Certain staff tend to tune in and relate to the one set, whereas the remaining staff relate to the other.

Main (1957) referred to the splitting of the staff into good and bad groups as the formation of the *in and out-groups.* The in-group becomes the "good mother ideal," and the out-group becomes the "bad, frustrating mother" as perceived by the patients. The formation of the in-group begins with the "sentimental appeal" from the patients and the "arousal of omnipotence" in some of the staff. The staff have an overwhelming desire to rescue the patients who have been deprived of nurturance. These staff members feel they are the only people who can save the patients—they have been "chosen." This group becomes the patients' "special people," and they often collude against the out-group. As Main and others have shown, membership in the in-group and out-group can change, and the patients can exchange the staff in the groups in order to ensure that the conflict remains external. As many theorists have noted, the in-group members often become drained and depleted by the demands and needs placed on them by the "special patient." These demands are endless and most often unrealistic. The patients' frustration tolerance is very low when these needs are not met, provoking anger and resentment from the staff trying to fulfill their demands.

Mistrust usually develops between the two groups, and in the extreme case, the staff angrily refuse to talk to one another. The in-group people feel justly praised, chosen, and accurately assessed, and the out-group people feel unjustly appraised and inaccurately assessed.

Burnham (1966) recognized the patients' ability to perceive and exploit incipient splits within a staff. Patients who unconsciously identify and capitalize on staff schisms can become a powerful force within the inpatient ward. Burnham discovered that the staff divides according to their own abilities to accept frustration and conform to the reality principle. The out-group is often more reality oriented and more comfortable with frustration, though some may be unable to allow any dependency needs and may harshly conform to the reality principle. The in-group usually rebels against the idea that frustration is a fact of life in the real world, but they may also rebel against the out-group's inability to accept some caretaking.

Carser (1979) observed that staff splitting can also be symptomatic of covert conflict among the staff over previously latent disagreements about policies or rules. Carser has recommended leadership and group cohesion as a requisite for dealing with this problem.

The in-group identifies more with the deprived child and wants to provide an attachment that is pleasurable and tension reducing. The out-group may feel that the patients must be weaned from dependency and often give short shrift to the patients' dependency needs because of their own problems. However, both orientations have validity, and it is only because of inadequate discussion and staff resolution that the problems exist. Once both groups start to talk and understand their individual conceptual differences as well as personal countertransference, both approaches often can be used with the patients. As the staff begins to set personal limits regarding not being drawn into discussing one another, belittling one another, or undermining the approach of other staff, the patients start to feel better. In other words, after testing the staff to reassure themselves that they are cohesive and consistent, the patients may begin to work productively.

Case Example   An illustration of this occurred during my training, when a particularly attractive and bright young borderline woman gave up her own name and substituted a highly unusual one. She told her male individual therapist (a resident) why she had taken this new name but swore him to secrecy, saying that he was the only person who could possibly understand her reasons—he was the only person who treated her as a respected individual. He then refused to share the meaning of the name with other staff, and this resulted in an enormous power struggle between the therapist and the staff.

But over the months it developed that this young woman had also told other staff members the reason for her new name. One day during a staff process group, all the people she had confided in confessed that they, too, had been told that they were special and were the only people who treated her individually. This led to a staff discussion between the in-group and the out-group about how they felt. This discussion created greater understanding of what exactly the patient was projecting onto each group and how this projection represented internal object relations problems for the young woman.

Book, Sadavoy, and Silver (1978) reported the most common countertransference reactions to be treating patients pejoratively, viewing their prospects either overly optimistically or too hopelessly, staff disagreements leading to contradictory behavior toward patients or fragmentation of the team, and having difficulties (either too lax or too sadistic) in limit setting (p. 531). Main and Burnham would add to that list the special problem patients who receive extreme privileges either because they are the favorite of the treatment team or because they instill more fear or have more psychosocial prestige than the other patients do.

Management of countertransference refers to two interlocking processes: nurturing of attitudes among staff that minimize the countertransference reactions, and the honesty by which countertransference responses are understood and identified when they do occur (Book et al. 1978, pp. 529–530). Using a psychoanalytic framework to examine the patients' behavior in terms of fragmented object relations and the staff's reactions as a way of internalizing differing aspects of the fragmented selves and objects is one means of accomplishing the first task. Such a perspective helps the staff see the behavior as primitive and disturbed, and it frequently helps bind both the staff's rage and their urges to rescue.

Problems When Long-Term Unit and Adaptation-Oriented, Outpatient Therapist Clash

Gordon and Beresin (1983) discovered that ventilation of an inpatient unit organized as a therapeutic community pursuing structural change encourages regression, which the patients used to an adaptive psychotherapy may find unnerving. They found the following problems. These patients act out more and more in an effort to stimulate limit setting, only to be met with more regressive holding. The staff's rapport with the outpatient therapist may be damaged because the holding environment may make the outpatient therapist appear cool and uncaring. Dangerous conflict may arise between the unit and the outpatient therapist, in which the therapist sees the staff as encouraging regression and the staff sees the therapist as denying the patients the chance to change.

Resolving the Hospitalization Dilemma

According to Gordon and Beresin (1983), one of the first steps in hospitalizing patients is to be clear about one's own orientation and the orientation of the admitting facility. Whenever possible, an outpatient therapist should seek a facility that is compatible with his or her own approach to therapy. When this is not feasible (e.g., there are few facilities available, or the therapist wants a different approach or only short-term hospitalization), then the admitting therapist and the staff should discuss the differences in approach. The patients should be helped to realize that there will be a difference from their usual individual psychotherapy while they are on the ward.

GROUP PSYCHOTHERAPY

Although there is much literature on group psychotherapy, relatively little of it is devoted to group psychotherapy and the borderline personality. L. Horowitz (1977) commented that "this state of affairs is particularly surprising inasmuch as group therapists have long recognized the special contributions groups make to patients with significant ego weakness" (p. 399). He noted that very few articles, if any, have dealt with homogeneous groups of borderline patients.

Group therapy can be an excellent setting for highlighting difficulties in relationships. Consequently, despite the ego weaknesses that often prevent optimal functioning by borderline patients in a group, a group may be the ideal medium in which to resolve or attenuate these handicaps. Groups are also suitable for dealing with such problems as competition and the need for emotional feeding. They enable borderline adults to listen to and explore other patients' problems and to wait for their own turn. L. Horowitz (1977, 1980) also argues that the group can be used to work with the deep-seated pathological object-relations units described by Masterson, Rinsley, and Kernberg.

The type of group psychotherapy discussed in this section is psychoanalytically oriented, often modified to the point of being a psychoanalytically informed supportive therapy. Although not stressed by L. Horowitz, the clinician must decide whether mainly supportive or intensive treatment is to be provided, because too much support certainly changes the modality from intensive work via interpretation to supportive maintenance.

Contraindications for Group Psychotherapy

There are no hard-and-fast rules for choosing borderline patients for group psychotherapy. L. Horowitz (1980) noted that the very characteristics that make treatment so necessary for borderline individuals are the same that lead to treatment failure (p. 195). He identified two major factors that determine overall success: (1) the patient's ability to tolerate the frustration and pressures of a group and (2) the group's ability to tolerate the demands of the patient. L. Horowitz recommends placing no more than two borderline patients into a group composed mainly of neurotics. These borderline patients should be able to (1) tolerate some frustration without always getting angry or seriously acting out, (2) maintain cognitive organization under some frustration (e.g., not become psychotic), and (3) be in tune with the group's norms (e.g., not stand out as too deviant, such as too paranoid or living too isolated an existence). Although borderline patients can get into difficulties in the group over their abrasive characteristics, they may also help loosen up group norms because of their ability to perceive unconscious motivation and to act unconventionally (Hulse 1956, 1958; L. Horowitz 1980).

There is no literature on groups completely made up of borderline patients. I have run several such supportive groups and found that they can work if there is a balance between the *clingers* and the *distancers* and if the group leaders provide considerable nurturance, direction, and modeling of appropriate group behavior. This is particularly true in the group's early stages.

The Leaders' Roles

Various theorists generally agree on the necessity for special measures with borderline patients, whether in homogeneous or mixed groups. L. Horowitz (1977) stresses the importance of supportive measures such as increased therapist transparency (e.g., sharing feelings, giving feedback) and activity, encouragement of socialization among members, and symbolic as well as actual feeding of patients. He recommends such special measures include the therapist's active friendliness in order to provide the kind of emotional support that the patients need to maintain their group membership and participation. Wolman (1960) recommended that the therapist assume a warm, caring, and nondemanding attitude. Much support should also come from fellow group members, and the group leaders should encourage it.

The literature points out that borderline patients in group therapy at some point also require individual treatment. Most, but not all, theorists agree that the individual therapy should be with someone other than the group therapist. L. Horowitz (1980) stated that failure in group therapy can usually be attributed to the patient's not being in individual psychotherapy. Thus, it is probably best to start patients in groups simultaneously with starting individual therapy and perhaps even to make individual therapy contingent upon attending the group sessions, as many borderline patients prefer dyadic relationships and will avoid group sessions. The following special features of group psychotherapy, summarized according to the schema and findings offered by L. Horowitz (1977, 1980), are useful with borderline patients:

Dilution of Transference

Freedman and Sweet (1954) and Stein (1963) pointed out that patients with ego weakness do especially well in group therapy because the transference dilution reduces regression. Spotnitz (1957) explained that the group's multiple targets permit borderline patients to diffuse transference reactions (negative feelings toward parental introjects) against one or more peers instead of the therapist. L. Horowitz (1980) stated that dilution occurs because of (1) multiple targets, (2) opportunities for emotional and social distance, and (3) the greater stress on reality and socially appropriate behavior. However, transference can also be intensified in groups, and this must be noted and balanced against the treatment goals. Individual psychotherapy for patients can often help dilute the transference in the group.

Activation

For passive and withdrawn patients who have difficulty communicating during individual therapy, some type of group interaction appears to be the only way to free them from their passivity. Group treatment offers these patients both stimulation and a supportive setting that allows them to participate at their own pace. Although inclined to focus on the problems of others rather than disclose their own, these patients may experience within the group their first substantial emotional participation with others. Spotnitz (1957) also identified a greater reality orientation in group, as opposed to individual, psychotherapy. Hulse (1958) noted the group also approximates an ordinary social interaction and hence stimulates appropriate social responses.

Emotional Gratification

Although groups have built-in frustrations, one of the advantages of group treatment is an increase in self-esteem, as the effects of sharing and positive reinforcement flow from member to member within the group. These gratifications often contribute to long-term personality change. And for lonely, isolated people, group therapy may provide their only real social experience (Scheidlinger and Pyrke 1961).

Expressions of Hostility

Patients unable to deal with hostility and aggression undergo within group therapy an "unfreezing experience" (Horowitz 1977, p. 407) in which they identify vicariously with both aggressor and victim roles during group exchanges. Such patients, blocked by their own passivity and inhibition, witness and learn from other patients' ways of handling these problems. Witnessing confrontation between peers within the group is often more effective than discussions of confrontation with an individual therapist.

Multiple Identifications

Because of the variety of patients within a group, this form of psycho-therapy allows patients to identify with more people than just the therapist. Shaskan (1957) has pointed out the interesting group phenomenon of "borrowing courage" from others within the group: members either support one another's progressive moves or offer examples from their own lives illustrating adaptive responses to interpersonal conflicts.

Modification of Character Armor

The group milieu provides on-going and varied stimuli and reactions that serve as a repertoire from which patients may draw. This is particularly helpful for patients with maladaptive defenses. The group also provides a setting in which patients with severe character disorders may be able to handle confrontation from group members more readily than from the therapist alone, because the therapist frequently is either excessively idealized or devalued (Glatzer 1972).

Dilution of Countertransference

Borderline patients are especially difficult to treat because of the strong affective or countertransference responses they evoke. L. Horowitz (1977) noted that the dilution and intensification of transference also apply to the phenomenon of countertransference. Group psychotherapists have noted somewhat milder countertransference responses in a group than occur in a one-to-one situation. However, the group's countertransference toward a particular patient must be monitored and modified, if necessary. Borderline patients in a primarily neurotic group must be carefully watched for scape-goating and alienation.

Techniques of Treatment

Most theorists agree that supportive measures must be used in group therapy in order to facilitate cohesiveness and a sense of belonging and to reduce feelings of alienation (Feldberg 1958). The leader may protect members from being scapegoated, acknowledge their efforts in the group, and stress the similarities rather than the differences among group members, all of which help reduce splitting.

In regard to confrontation, all theorists agree that one must "go beyond mere friendliness and encouragement in order to be therapeutic" (L. Horowitz 1977, p. 413). Confrontation should be carried out tactfully and with concern, and the patients' response to the confrontation must be noted and used. There is also general agreement that uncovering and interpretation should be minimized in such a group.

DAY TREATMENT

Day treatment is the treatment of choice for many lower-level borderline patients who need to structure their lives because they cannot function at work or school. Many of the problems discussed in the sections on hospitalization and group psychotherapy are pertinent here. The day treatment program should have a task-oriented and firm but flexible structure. It should be supportive. The staff must process their affective responses to the patients in order to understand both the patients' and staff's projections and in order to provide good clinical interventions of the types discussed by Kernberg in supportive individual psychotherapy.

But day treatment has a unique focus in its very structure. Crafoord (1977) noted that the day program's mode of operation—having the patients arrive in the morning and leave in the afternoon—is in itself a daily experience of fusion and separation (p. 395). He commented that this experience contributes to the modification of the patients' internalized object relations:

> The staff members of the day hospital or even the physical structure itself become a transitional object for the patient—a mother image without the threatening characteristics of a real mother, an object the patient may love, introject, toss around, spit out, and take in again. It offers the possibility of re-enacting the experience of separation over and over, enabling self- and object images to become integrated and ego boundaries to acquire stability. (p. 395)

When patients attend both individual therapy and day treatment, the therapist must maintain close contact with the treatment facility staff. The therapist, in particular, needs to clarify what information can be shared with the day treatment program so that the patients do not perceive a breach of confidentiality.

CRISIS COUNSELING

Crisis counseling, which is frequently needed with borderline patients, can be helpful. As a treatment modality, it uses a number of supportive techniques, including giving advice, confrontation, direct support, and mobilization of environmental supports. Two primary considerations are involved in this treatment modality. First, if the patients are in an intensive psychotherapy, the crisis intervention should be done by someone other than the ongoing therapist (e.g., emergency room, crisis center, or other team member). Second, the person doing the crisis counseling should be careful that it does not drag on and become institutionalized as an ongoing intensive therapy, because the very techniques that are so helpful in the short run may be problematic if used on a long-term basis (Kernberg 1984).

MARITAL AND FAMILY PSYCHOTHERAPY

There is little literature on the marital or family psychotherapy of borderline patients, though various writers have discussed an object-relations perspective for marital and family treatment (Dicks 1963; Mallouk 1982; Mandelbaum 1977, 1980; Stewart, Peters, Marsh, and Peters, 1975; E. R. Shapiro et al. 1975; Sharpe 1981; Zinner and R. Shapiro 1972), and several have written specifically on the family dynamics and treatment of borderline adults. I assume that many of the strategic, communication-oriented, and structural family therapists do work with borderline patients and their families but that when writing up their case experiences, they do not usually use diagnostic labels.

In reviewing the family constellations of many hospitalized borderline patients, two major patterns emerge. The first is the overinvolved or enmeshed family, and the second is the underinvolved family. The first pattern is most frequently discussed in the literature because these families are quite visible during the patients' hospitalization. Most of the material in this section pertains to that group. The second type of family, the underinvolved, requires considerable wooing and often education before they will even become involved in the patient's treatment.

The general consensus from psychodynamic clinicians working with families and couples is that the treatment goals must be focused and limited. For families with adolescents, the goal is establishing appropriate boundaries among generations, identifying projective identification among family members, and helping the adolescent with the process of emancipation.

There is some controversy about whether the family therapist should also be the individual family member's therapist or the adolescent's therapist, and to date this controversy has not been resolved. Some experts recommend that family therapy be conducted by a team made up of the adolescent's individual therapist and the couples' therapist. There is agreement, however, in family therapy a major goal is to create a boundary around the parental subsystem (they are the parents and work as a team) and to extrude the symptomatic children to the sibling subsystem (they are the children). In working with couples (as with families), the goal is to identify the various projective identification processes and collusive behavior between partners.

Clinical Example A couple seeks treatment. The husband is cool, distant, and angry, and the wife is kind but helpless and dependent. The therapist points out that each carries a disowned part for the other. The goal is for husband and wife to re-own and reexperience the projected bad part carried by the other partner (Stewart et al. 1975, p. 163).

As with individual psychotherapy, clarification, confrontation (particularly of acting out), and interpretation remain major techniques. Thus far, no major family or marital therapist has claimed that borderline character structure can be remade in this treatment modality. The goal is to control acting out, to reduce projective identification, and to enhance each member's separation-individuation process so that the couple's relationship is improved and a higher or more healthy level of homeostasis is achieved.

MEDICATION

I believe that the psychotherapist first should decide whether the patients must have medication in order to function in their daily life and to attend therapy. Once this has been decided, the therapist can turn to the growing literature on nosology and choice of medication.

Gutheil (1982) observed that the taking of pills has great symbolic meaning to many patients. It may be a way of receiving nurturing and caretaking, and it may represent a magical expectation that the medicine rather than the patients themselves will bring about change.

Many important physician–patient conflicts are fought out through the patients' drug regimen, as happened with Mary Markham and her various suicide attempts with prescribed medication. That is why it is so important to determine whether the patients can manage their therapy without medication; if they do require medication, the therapist should monitor its psychological meaning to the patient.

D. Klein (1977) and Cole and Sunderland (1982) have extensively reviewed the drug treatment of borderline patients and agree that there is no one medication for the borderline personality. The general consensus is that the patients' cluster of symptoms should be identified and that medication should be prescribed to address those specific symptoms. As a review of Klein, Cole, and Sunderland will reveal, finding the right drug out of the hundreds on the market has become a sophisticated and complicated task. For example, a patient who is depressed might be considered for an antidepressant; a patient with rapid cycling moods might be considered for an MAO inhibitor; a patient with intense impulsive anger or psychotic episodes might be given an antipsychotic drug; a patient with panic or anxiety attacks might receive a minor tranquilizer for two or three weeks; or a patient with minimal brain dysfunction might be considered carefully for a stimulant (Kernberg 1984). Medication seems to be indicated if the patients' psychotic episodes are frequent and debilitating, or if the depression, anxiety, or phobias are so severe that they interfere with self-care, the ability to engage in work or recreational activities, including therapy.

Once the decision has been made to have medication prescribed, two factors must be considered: (1) the patients' symptoms (e.g., if an antidepressant does not cause improvement, the patient should be taken off the drug, and the condition should be studied again) and (2) the psychological meaning to the patient of taking medication (e.g., the magical misinterpretation that the medication rather than the patient will bring about change). The therapist must remember that medication should help, not hinder, the deeper work in treatment. After all, a certain level of anxiety is useful to treatment. In addition, medication should not be given indefinitely, if possible.

OTHER MODALITIES

Although few theorists who have written about the modalities mentioned in this section have specifically referred to borderline patients, their case material reveals patients who seem to meet the borderline diagnosis. Thus, these approaches may well be helpful, if only in part, to many borderline patients. The following problem-focused cognitive and behavioral approaches (either in group or individual format) can be helpful: anxiety reduction (Bernstein and Borkovec 1973), anger management (Novaco 1976), improving mood (Lewinsohn, Muñoz, Youngren, and Zeiss 1978), assertive training (Jakubowski and Lange 1978), phobia reduction (many theorists), and such other approaches as smoking reduction.

The literature on hypnosis and hypnotherapy is vast. A review of the prolific writings of M. Erickson (1980) reveals cases that seem to meet borderline diagnosis, although the diagnosis is rarely if ever mentioned in his writings. The little written on hypnosis and the borderline patient usually deals only with multiple personalities (which Masterson and Kernberg consider to be a subtype of borderline patient). It seems that hypnosis could be helpful in working on issues of resistance, as well as on an affect bridge to parts of the self and internal objects. But this technique should be used only by a hypnotherapist who has had experience with severe character disorders.

Many borderline patients cannot deal with substance abuse and addictions without the assistance of organizations such as Alcoholics Anonymous (AA) or Narcotics Anonymous. Many clinicians will not even begin psychotherapy with alcoholic borderline patients unless they also attend AA. Although one of the goals of AA and therapy are at odds (e.g., turning everything over to a "higher power" versus taking responsibility for oneself), in the early to middle phases of treatment this conflict is rarely important. Psychodrama is another treatment that can prove useful in illuminating conflicts. Vocational training or rehabilitation may be another important option. Each of these treatment modalities requires clinicians who have had experience working with severely disturbed patients. Many modalities can be helpful to borderline patients at certain points in their treatment. However, I believe that because the rupture in the patient's growth occurred during a preverbal period in a dyadic relationship, only the context of an individual psychotherapy can fully replicate the original situation and permit its full repair.

Credits for Excerpts

The author gratefully acknowledges permission to reprint excerpts from the following sources:

Blanck, G., and Blanck, R. *Ego Psychology II: Psychoanalytic Developmental Psychology.* Copyright © 1979 by Columbia University Press.

Caltrider, J., and Robinson, L. The borderline personality. In L. Robinson (ed.), *Psychiatric Nursing as a Human Experience*, 3rd ed. Copyright © 1983 by W. B. Saunders.

Chessick, R. D. A practical approach to the psychotherapy of the borderline patient, *American Journal of Psychotherapy, 33*(4):531-546. Copyright © 1979 by the Association for the Advancement of Psychotherapy.

Greenberg, J. R., and Mitchell, S. A. *Object Relations in Psychoanalytic Theory.* Copyright © 1983 by Harvard University Press.

Horowitz, L. Group psychotherapy of the borderline patient. In P. Hartocollis (ed.), *Borderline Personality Disorders: The Concept, the Syndrome, the Patient*, pp. 399-422. Copyright © 1977 by International Universities Press.

Kernberg, O. F. Technical considerations in the treatment of borderline personality organization, *Journal of the American Psychoanalytic Association, 24*(4): pp. 795-829. Copyright © 1976 by International Universities Press.

Kernberg, O. F. The structural diagnosis of borderline personality organization. In P. Hartocollis (ed.), *Borderline Personality Disorders: The Concept, the Syndrome, the Patient,* pp. 87-121. Copyright © 1977 by International Universities Press.

Kernberg, O. F. Structural interviewing, *Psychiatric Clinics of North America,* 4(1):169-195. Copyright © 1981 by W. B. Saunders.

Kernberg, O. F. Supportive psychotherapy with borderline conditions. In J. O. Cavenar, Jr., and H. K. H. Brodie (eds.), *Critical Problems in Psychiatry,* pp. 180–202. Copyright © 1982 by Lippincott.

Masterson, J. F. *Psychotherapy of the Borderline Adult: A Developmental Approach.* Copyright © 1976 by Brunner/Mazel.

Masterson, J. F. *Narcissistic and Borderline Disorders: An Integrated Developmental Approach.* Copyright © 1981 by Brunner/Mazel.

Masterson, J. F. The borderline and narcissistic disorders: An integrated developmental approach. 1982, unpublished paper.

Nurnberg, H. G., and Suh, R. Time-limited treatment of hospitalized borderline patients: Considerations, *Comprehensive Psychiatry, 19*(5):419–431. Copyright © 1978 by Grune and Stratton.

Peterfreund, E. How does the analyst listen? On models and strategies in the psychoanalytic process, *Psychoanalysis and Contemporary Science, 6*:59–101. Copyright © 1975 by International Universities Press.

Searles, H. F. *Collected Papers on Schizophrenia and Related Subjects.* Copyright © 1965 by International Universities Press.

Shapiro, E. R. The psychodynamics and developmental psychology of the borderline patient: A review of the literature, *American Journal of Psychiatry, 135*(11): 1305–1315. Copyright © 1978 by the American Psychiatric Association.

Stone, M. H. *The Borderline Syndromes: Constitution, Adaptation and Personality.* Copyright © 1980 by McGraw-Hill.

Stone, M. H. Borderline syndromes: A consideration of subtypes and an overview. Directions for research, *Psychiatric Clinics of North America, 4*(1):3–24. Copyright © 1981 by W. B. Saunders.

Bibliography

Adler, G. (1970). Valuing and devaluing in the psychotherapeutic process. *Archives of General Psychiatry, 22,* 454–461.

Adler, G. (1977). Hospital management of borderline patients and its relation to psychotherapy. In P. Hartocollis (ed.), *The Borderline Personality Disorders: The Concept, the Syndrome, the Patient* (pp. 307–323). New York: International Universities Press.

Adler, G. (1979). The myth of the alliance with borderline patients. *American Journal of Psychiatry, 136*(5), 642–645.

Adler, G. (1980). A treatment framework for adult patients with borderline and narcissistic personality disorders. *Bulletin of the Menninger Clinic, 44*(2), 171–180.

Adler, G. (1981). The borderline-narcissistic personality disorder continuum. *American Journal of Psychiatry, 138*(1), 46–50.

Adler, G. (1982). Helplessness in the helpers. In P. L. Giovacchini and L. B. Boyer (eds.), *Technical Factors in the Treatment of the Severely Disturbed Patient* (pp. 385–408). New York: Jason Aronson.

Adler, G., and Buie, D. H. (1972). The misuses of confrontation with borderline patients. *International Journal of Psychoanalytic Psychotherapy, 1*(3), 109–120.

Adler, G., and Buie, D. H. (1979a). Aloneness and borderline psychopathology: The possible relevance of child development issues. *International Journal of Psycho-Analysis, 60*(1), 83–96.

Adler, G., and Buie, D. H. (1979b). The psychotherapeutic approach to aloneness in borderline patients. In J. LeBoit and A. Capponi (eds.), *Advances in Psychotherapy of the Borderline Patient* (pp. 433–448). New York: Jason Aronson.

Adler, G., and Shapiro, L. N. (1969). Psychotherapy with prisoners. In J. H. Masserman (ed.), *Current Psychiatric Therapies* (vol. 9, pp. 99–105). New York: Grune Stratton.

Adler, G., and Shapiro, L. N. (1973). Some difficulties in the treatment of the aggressive acting-out patient. *American Journal of Psychotherapy, 27,* 548–556.

Akhtar, S., and Byrne, J. P. (1983). The concept of splitting and its clinical reliance. *American Journal of Psychiatry, 140*(8), 1013–1016.

Akhtar, S., and Thomson, J. A., Jr. (1982). Overview: Narcissistic personality disorder. *American Journal of Psychiatry, 139*(1), 12–20.

Akiskal, H. S. (1981). Subaffective disorders: Dysthymic, cyclothymic and bipolar II disorders in the "borderline" realm. *Psychiatric Clinics of North America, 4*(1), 25–46.

Alexander, F. G., and French, T. M. (1946). *Psychoanalytic Therapy, Principles and Application.* In collaboration with C. L. Bacon et al. New York: Ronald Press.

Allen, D. W. (1977). Basic treatment issues. In M. J. Horowitz (ed.), *Hysterical Personality* (pp. 283–328). New York: Jason Aronson.

American Psychiatric Association. (1980). *Diagnostic and Statistical Manual of Mental Disorders* (3rd ed.) (*DSM-III*). Washington, D.C.: American Psychiatric Association.

Andrulonis, P. A., Glueck, B. C., Stroebel, C. F., and Vogel, N. G. (1982). Borderline personality subcategories. *Journal of Nervous and Mental Disease, 170*(11), 670–679.

Balint, M. (1968). *The Basic Fault: Therapeutic Aspects of Regression.* London: Tavistock.

Basch, M. F. (1981). Psychoanalytic interpretation and cognitive transformation. *International Journal of Psycho-Analysis, 62*(2), 151–175.

Basch, M. F. (1983). Empathic understanding: A review of the concept and some theoretical considerations. *Journal of the American Psychoanalytic Association, 31*(1), 101–126.

Bellak, L., Hurvich, M., and Gediman, H. K. (1973). *Ego Functions in Schizophrenics, Neurotics and Normals: A Systematic Study of Conceptual, Diagnostic, and Therapeutic Aspects.* New York: John Wiley (Wiley-Interscience).

Bemporad, J. R. (1980). Review of object relations theory in the light of cognitive development. *Journal of the American Academy of Psychoanalysis, 8*(1), 57–75.

Bernstein, D. A., and Borkovec, T. D. (1973). *Progressive Relaxation Training: A Manual for the Helping Profession.* Champaign, Ill.: Research Press.

Bernstein, S. B. (1982). Some psychoanalytic contributions to the understanding and treatment of patients with primitive personalities. In A. M. Jacobson and D. X. Parmelee (eds.), *Psychoanalysis: Critical Explorations in Contemporary Theory and Practice* (pp. 74–117). New York: Brunner/Mazel.

Bion, W. R. (1957). Differentiation of the psychotic from the non-psychotic personalities. *International Journal of Psycho-Analysis, 38*(3-4), 266–275.

Bion, W. R. (1961). *Experiences in Groups: And Other Papers.* London: Tavistock.

Bion, W. R. (1963). *Elements of Psycho-Analysis.* New York: Basic Books.

Blacker, K. H., and Tupin, J. P. (1977). Hysteria and hysterical structures: Developmental and social theories. In M. J. Horowitz (ed.), *Hysterical Personality* (pp. 95–141). New York: Jason Aronson.

Blanck, G., and Blanck, R. (1979). *Ego Psychology II: Psychoanalytic Developmental Psychology.* New York: Columbia University Press.

Blanck, R., and Blanck, G. (1974). *Ego Psychology: Theory and Practice.* New York: Columbia University Press.

Blasi, A. (1976). Issues in defining stages and types. In J. Loevinger with the assistance of A. Blasi, *Ego Development: Conceptions and Theories* (pp. 182-202). San Francisco: Jossey-Bass.

Blumenthal, R., Carr, A. C., and Goldstein, E. G. (1982). DSM-III and structural diagnosis of borderline patients. *The Psychiatric Hospital*, *13*(4), 142-148.

Book, H. E., Sadavoy, J., and Silver, D. (1978). Staff countertransference to borderline patients on an inpatient unit. *American Journal of Psychotherapy*, *32*(4), 521-532.

Bowlby, J. (1969). *Attachment and Loss: Vol. I. Attachment.* New York: Basic Books.

Boyer, L. B., and Giovacchini, P. L. (1967). *Psychoanalytic Treatment of Schizophrenic and Characterological Disorders.* With a contribution by E. D. Holdemaker. New York: Science House.

Breger, L. (1974). *From Instinct to Identity: The Development of Personality.* Englewood Cliffs, N.J.: Prentice-Hall.

Brende, J. O., and Rinsley, D. B. (1981). A case of multiple personality with psychological automatisms. *Journal of American Academy of Psychoanalysis*, *9*(1), 129-151.

Brown, L. J. (1981). The therapeutic milieu in the treatment of patients with borderline personality disorders. *Bulletin of the Menninger Clinic*, *45*(5), 377-394.

Buie, D. H., and Adler, G. (1972). The uses of confrontation with borderline patients. *International Journal of Psychoanalytic Psychotherapy*, *1*(3), 90-108.

Buie, D. H., and Adler, G. (1982-1983). Definitive treatment of the borderline personality. *International Journal of Psychoanalytic Psychotherapy*, *9*, 51-87.

Burnham, D. L. (1966). The special-problem patient: Victim or agent of splitting? *Psychiatry*, *29*(2), 105-122.

Bursten, B. (1973). Some narcissistic personality types. *International Journal of Psycho-Analysis*, *54*, 287-300.

Bursten, B. (1978). A diagnostic framework. *International Review of Psycho-Analysis*, *5*, 15-31.

Bursten, B. (1982). Narcissistic personalities in DSM-III. *Comprehensive Psychiatry*, *23*(5), 409-420.

Caltrider, J., and Robinson, L. (1983). The borderline personality. In L. Robinson (ed.), *Psychiatric Nursing as a Human Experience* (3rd ed., pp. 364-377). Philadelphia: Saunders.

Capponi, A. (1979). Origin and evolution of the borderline concept. In J. LeBoit and A. Capponi (eds.), *Advances in Psychotherapy of the Borderline Patient* (pp. 63-147). New York: Jason Aronson.

Carser, D. (1979). The defense mechanism of splitting: Developmental origins, effects on staff, recommendations for nursing care. *Journal of Psychiatric Nursing and Mental Health Services*, *17*(3), 21-28.

Carter, L., and Rinsley, D. B. (1977). Vicissitudes of "empathy" in a borderline adolescent. *International Review of Psycho-Analysis*, *4*(3), 317-326.

Chessick, R. D. (1974). *The Technique and Practice of Intensive Psychotherapy.* New York: Jason Aronson.

Chessick, R. D. (1977). *Intensive Psychotherapy of the Borderline Patient.* New York: Jason Aronson.

Chessick, R. D. (1979). A practical approach to the psychotherapy of the borderline patient. *American Journal of Psychotherapy, 33*(4), 531–546.

Chessick, R. D. (1982a). Current issues in intensive psychotherapy. *American Journal of Psychotherapy, 36*(4), 438–449.

Chessick, R. D. (1982b). Intensive psychotherapy of a borderline patient. *Archives of General Psychiatry, 39*(4), 413–419.

Chrzanowski, G. (1979). The transference-countertransference transaction. *Contemporary Psychoanalysis, 15*(3), 458–471.

Clarkin, J. F., Widiger, T. A., Frances, A., Hurt, S. W., and Gilmore, M. (1983). Prototypic typology and the borderline personality disorder. *Journal of Abnormal Psychology, 92*(3), 263–275.

Cole, J. O., and Sunderland, III, P. (1982). The drug treatment of borderline patients. In L. Grinspoon (ed.), *Psychiatry 1982: The American Psychiatric Association Annual Review* (pp. 456–470). Washington, D.C.: American Psychiatric Press.

Crafoord, C. (1977). Day hospital treatment for borderline patients: The institution as transitional object. In P. Hartocollis (ed.), *Borderline Personality Disorders: The Concept, the Syndrome, the Patient* (pp. 385–397). New York: International Universities Press.

Deutsch, H. (1942). Some forms of emotional disturbance and their relationship to schizophrenia. In *Neurosis and Character Types: Clinical Psychoanalytic Studies* (pp. 262–281). New York: International Universities Press, 1965.

DeWald, P. A. (1964). *Psychotherapy: A Dynamic Approach.* New York: Basic Books.

DeWald, P. A. (1972). The clinical assessment of structural change. *Journal of the American Psychoanalytic Association, 20,* 302–324.

Dickes, R. (1974). The concepts of borderline states: An alternative proposal. *International Journal of Psychoanalytic Psychotherapy, 3,* 1–27.

Dicks, H. V. (1963). Object relations theory and marital studies. *British Journal of Medical Psychology, 36,* 125–129.

Dorpat, T. L. (1982). An object relations perspective on masochism. In P. L. Giovacchini and L. B. Boyer (eds.), *Technical Factors in the Treatment of the Severely Disturbed Patient* (pp. 487–513). New York: Jason Aronson.

Edward, J., Ruskin, N., and Turrini, P. (1981). *Separation-Individuation: Theory and Application.* New York: Gardner Press.

Eissler, K. R. (1953). The effects of the structure of the ego on psychoanalytic technique. *Journal of the American Psychoanalytic Association, 1,* 104–143.

Eissler, K. R. (1958). Remarks on some variations in psycho-analytical technique. *International Journal of Psycho-Analysis, 39*(2–4), 222–229.

Epstein, L. (1979). Countertransference with borderline patients. In L. Epstein and A. H. Feiner (eds.), *Countertransference* (pp. 375–405). New York: Jason Aronson.

Erikson, E. H. (1950). Growth and crises of the healthy personality. In *Identity and the Life Cycle* (pp. 51–107). New York: Norton, 1980.

———— (1956). The problem of ego identity. *Journal of the American Psychoanalytic Association, 4,* 56–121.

Erickson, M. H. (1980). In E. L. Rossi (ed.), *The Collected Papers of Milton H. Erickson on Hypnosis* (4 vols.). New York: Irvington.

Fairbairn, W. R. D. (1952). *Psychoanalytic Studies of Personality* (American title: *An Object-Relations Theory of the Personality*). London: Tavistock; New York: Basic Books, 1954.

Fairbairn, W. R. D. (1963). Synopsis of an object-relations theory of the personality. *International Journal of Psycho-Analysis, 44*(2), 224–225.

Feldberg, T. M. (1958). Treatment of "borderline" psychotics in groups of neurotic patients. *International Journal of Group Psychotherapy, 8,* 76–84.

Fourcher, B. I. (1979). The relevance of Mahler's research to psychoanalytic clinical theory. *Bulletin of the Menninger Clinic, 43*(3), 201–216.

Frank, J. D. (1976). Restoration of morale and behavior change. In A. Burton (ed.), *What Makes Behavior Change Possible?* (pp. 73–95). New York: Brunner/Mazel.

Freedman, M. B., and Sweet, B. S. (1954). Some specific features of group psychotherapy and their implications for the selection of patients. *International Journal of Group Psychotherapy, 4,* 355–368.

Freud, A. (1936). *The Ego and the Mechanisms of Defense.* New York: International Universities Press.

Freud, A. (1965). *Normality and Pathology in Childhood: Assessment of Development.* New York: International Universities Press.

Freud, S. (1913). On beginning the treatment. In J. Strachey (ed. and trans.), *The Standard Edition of the Complete Psychological Works of Sigmund Freud* (Vol. 12, pp. 121–144). London: Hogarth Press, 1958.

Freud, S. (1916). Some character types met with in psycho-analytic work. In J. Strachey (ed. and trans.), *The Standard Edition of the Complete Psychological Works of Sigmund Freud* (Vol. 14, pp. 311–333). London, Hogarth Press, 1957.

Freud, S. (1923). The ego and the id. In J. Strachey (ed. and trans.), *The Standard Edition of the Complete Psychological Works of Sigmund Freud* (Vol. 19, pp. 12–66). London: Hogarth Press, 1961.

Friedman, H. J. (1969). Some problems of inpatient management with borderline patients. *American Journal of Psychiatry, 126*(3), 299–304.

Fromm-Reichmann, F. (1947). Problems of therapeutic management in a psychoanalytic hospital. In *Psychoanalysis and Psychotherapy: Selected Papers of Frieda Fromm-Reichmann* (pp. 137–159). Chicago: University of Chicago Press, 1959.

Frosch, J. P. (1964). The psychotic character: Clinical psychiatric considerations. *Psychiatric Quarterly, 38,* 81–96.

Frosch, J. P. (1970). Psychoanalytic considerations of the psychotic character. *Journal of the American Psychoanalytic Association, 18,* 24–50.

Frosch, J. P. (1983). The treatment of antisocial and borderline personality disorders. *Hospital and Community Psychiatry, 34*(3), 243–248.

Gedo, J. E., and Goldberg, A. (1973). *Models of the Mind: A Psychoanalytic Theory.* Chicago: University of Chicago Press.

Gill, M. M. (1982). *Analysis of Transference: Vol. 1. Theory and Technique* (Psychological Issues, Monograph 23). New York: International Universities Press.

Gill, M. M., and Hoffman, I. Z. (1982). *Analysis of Transference: Vol. II. Studies of Nine Audio-Recorded Psychoanalytic Sessions* (Psychological Issues, Monograph 24). New York: International Universities Press.

Giovacchini, P. L. (1979a). Countertransference with primitive mental states. In

L. Epstein and A. H. Feiner (eds.), *Countertransference* (pp. 235–265). New York: Jason Aronson.

Giovacchini, P. L. (1979b). *Treatment of Primitive Mental States.* New York: Jason Aronson.

Gitelson, M. (1951). Psychoanalysis and dynamic psychiatry. *AMA Archives of Neurology and Psychiatry, 66,* 280–288.

Glatzer, H. T. (1972). Treatment of oral character neurosis in group psychotherapy. In C. J. Sager and H. S. Kaplan (eds.), *Progress in Group and Family Therapy* (pp. 54–65). New York: Brunner/Mazel.

Glenn, J. (1979). The developmental point of view in adult analysis: A survey and a critique. *Journal of the Philadelphia Association of Psychoanalysis, 6,* 21–38.

Goldberg, A. (ed.). (1978). *The Psychology of the Self: A Casebook.* New York: International Universities Press.

Goldstein, W. N. (1981a). The borderline personality. *Psychiatric Annals, 11*(8), 22–26.

Goldstein, W. N. (1981b). Understanding Kernberg on the borderline patient. *Journal—National Association of Private Psychiatric Hospitals, 13*(1), 21–26.

Gordon, C., and Beresin, E. (1983). Conflicting treatment models for the inpatient management of borderline patients. *American Journal of Psychiatry, 140*(8), 979–983.

Greenacre, P. (1971). Notes on the influence and contribution of ego psychology to the practice of psychoanalysis. In J. B. McDevitt and C. F. Settlage (eds.), *Separation-Individuation: Essays in Honor of Margaret S. Mahler* (pp. 171–200). New York: International Universities Press.

Greenberg, J. R., and Mitchell, S. A. (1983). *Object Relations in Psychoanalytic Theory.* Cambridge, Mass.: Harvard University Press.

Greene, M. A. (1984). The self psychology of Heinz Kohut: A synopsis and critique. *Bulletin of the Menninger Clinic, 48*(1), 37–53.

Greenson, R. R. (1965). The working alliance and the transference neurosis. *Psychoanalytic Quarterly, 34,* 155–181.

Greenson, R. R. (1967). *The Technique and Practice of Psychoanalysis* (Vol. 1). New York: International Universities Press.

Greenson, R. R. (1971). The "real" relationship between the patient and the psychoanalyst. In M. Kanzer (ed.), *The Unconscious Today* (pp. 213–232). New York: International Universities Press.

Grinker, R. R., Sr., and Werble, B. (1977). *The Borderline Patient.* New York: Jason Aronson.

Grinker, R. R., Sr., Werble, B., and Drye, R. (1968). *The Borderline Syndrome: A Behavioral Study of Ego Functions.* New York: Basic Books.

Grotstein, J. S. (1981). *Splitting and Projective Identification.* New York: Jason Aronson.

Grotstein, J. S. (1982, October). Some newer perspectives on the borderline. Paper presented at the University of California extension symposium, Narcissistic and Borderline Disorders: Current Perspectives, Los Angeles.

Gunderson, J. G. (1980). Psychotic regressions in borderline patients. Paper presented at the annual meeting of the American Psychiatric Association, San Francisco.

Gunderson, J. G. (1981). Self-destructiveness in borderline patients. Paper presented at the annual meeting of the American Psychiatric Association, New Orleans.

Gunderson, J. G. (1982). Empirical studies of the borderline diagnosis. In L. Grinspoon (ed.), *Psychiatry 1982: The American Psychiatric Association Annual Review* (pp. 415-437). Washington, D.C.: American Psychiatric Press.

Gunderson, J. G., and Kolb, J. E. (1978). Discriminating features of borderline patients. *American Journal of Psychiatry, 135*, 792-796.

Gunderson, J. G., and Singer, M. T. (1975). Defining borderline patients: An overview. *American Journal of Psychiatry, 132*(1), 1-10.

Guntrip, H. (1960). Ego-weakness and the hard core of the problem of psychotherapy. *British Journal of Medical Psychology, 33*, 163-184.

Guntrip, H. (1961). *Personality Structure and Human Interaction: The Developing Synthesis of Psycho-Dynamic Theory.* New York: International Universities Press.

Guntrip, H. (1962). The schizoid compromise and psychotherapeutic stalemate. *British Journal of Medical Psychology, 35*, 273-287.

Guntrip, H. (1969). *Schizoid Phenomena, Object-Relations and the Self.* New York: International Universities Press.

Gutheil, T. G., (1982). The psychology of psychopharmacology. *Bulletin of the Menninger Clinic, 46*(4), 321-330.

Gutheil, T. G., and Havens, L. L. (1979). The therapeutic alliance: Contemporary meanings and confusions. *International Review of Psycho-Analysis, 6*(4), 467-481.

Halleck, S. L. (1967). Hysterical personality traits: Psychological, social, and iatrogenic determinants. *Archives of General Psychiatry, 16*, 750-757.

Hartmann, H. (1939). *Ego Psychology and the Problem of Adaptation.* New York: International Universities Press, 1958.

Hartmann, H. (1950). Comments on the psychoanalytic theory of the ego. *Psychoanalytic Study of the Child, 5*, 74-96.

Hartmann, H., Kris, E., and Loewenstein, R. M. (1946). Comments on the formation of psychic structure. *Psychoanalytic Study of the Child, 2*, 11-38.

Hartocollis, P. (1980a). Affective disturbance in borderline and narcissistic patients. *Bulletin of the Menninger Clinic, 44*(2), 135-146.

Hartocollis, P. (1980b). Long-term hospital treatment for adult patients with borderline and narcissistic disorders. *Bulletin of the Menninger Clinic, 44*(2), 212-226.

Hedges, L. (1983). *Listening Perspectives in Psychotherapy.* New York: Jason Aronson.

Heimann, P. (1950). On counter-transference. *International Journal of Psycho-Analysis, 31*, 81-84.

Heimann, P. (1960). Counter-transference. *British Journal of Medical Psychology, 33*, 9-15.

Hoch, P. H., and Polatin, P. (1949). Pseudoneurotic forms of schizophrenia. *Psychiatric Quarterly, 23*, 248-276.

Horner, A. J. (1975). Stages and processes in the development of early object relations and their associated pathologies. *International Review of Psycho-Analysis, 2*(1), 95-105.

Horner, A. J. (1976). Oscillatory patterns of object relations and the borderline patient. *International Review of Psycho-Analysis, 3*, 479-482.

Horner, A. J. (1979). *Object Relations and the Developing Ego in Therapy.* New York: Jason Aronson.

Horowitz, L. (1977). Group psychotherapy of the borderline patient. In P. Hartocollis (ed.), *Borderline Personality Disorders: The Concept, the Syndrome, the Patient* (pp. 399-422). New York: International Universities Press.

Horowitz, L. (1980). Group psychotherapy for borderline and narcissistic patients. *Bulletin of the Menninger Clinic, 44*(2), 181-200.

Horowitz, M. J. (1975). Psychodynamics: An information-processing approach. Unpublished manuscript, University of California, San Francisco.

Horowitz, M. J. (1977). Structure and the processes of change. In M. J. Horowitz (ed.), *Hysterical Personality* (pp. 329-399). New York: Jason Aronson.

Horowitz, M. J. (1979). *States of Mind: Analysis of Change in Psychotherapy.* New York: Plenum Press.

Hulse, W. C. (1956). Private practice. In S. R. Slavson (ed.), *The Fields of Group Psychotherapy* (pp. 260-272). New York: International Universities Press.

Hulse, W. C. (1958). Psychotherapy with ambulatory schizophrenic patients in mixed analytic groups. *AMA Archives of Neurology and Psychiatry, 79*, 681-687.

Ilan, E. (1977). The effect of interpretation in psychoanalytic treatment in the light of an integrated model of internal objects. *International Journal of Psycho-Analysis, 58*, 183-194.

Jacobson, E. (1954). The self and the object world: Vicissitudes of their infantile cathexes and their influence on ideational and affective development. *Psychoanalytic Study of the Child, 9*, 75-127.

Jacobson, E. (1964). *The Self and the Object World.* New York: International Universities Press.

Jakubowski, P., and Lange, A. J. (1978). *The Assertive Option: Your Rights and Responsibilities.* Champaign, Ill.: Research Press.

Kasanin, J. (1933). The acute schizoaffective psychoses. *American Journal of Psychiatry, 13*, 97-126.

Kernberg, O. F. (1965). Notes on countertransference. *Journal of the American Psychoanalytic Association, 13*(1), 38-56.

Kernberg, O. F. (1970). A psychoanalytic classification of character pathology. *Journal of the American Psychoanalytic Association, 18*(4), 800-822.

Kernberg, O. F. (1973). New developments in psychoanalytic object-relations theory: Part II. Instincts, affects, and object relations. Paper presented at the Royden Astley Memorial Symposium on Narcissism, Pittsburgh.

Kernberg, O. F. (1975a). *Borderline Condition and Pathological Narcissism.* New York: Jason Aronson.

Kernberg, O. F. (1975b). Transference and countertransference in the treatment of borderline patients. *Journal—National Association of Private Psychiatric Hospitals, 7*, 14-24.

Kernberg, O. F. (1976a). *Object-Relations Theory and Clinical Psychoanalysis.* New York: Jason Aronson.

Kernberg, O. F. (1976b). Technical considerations in the treatment of borderline personality organization. *Journal of the American Psychoanalytic Association, 24*(4), 795-829.

Kernberg, O. F. (1977a). Structural change and its impediments. In P. Hartocollis (ed.), *Borderline Personality Disorders: The Concept, the Syndrome, the Patient* (pp. 275-306). New York: International Universities Press.

Kernberg, O. F. (1977b). The structural diagnosis of borderline personality organization. In P. Hartocollis (ed.), *Borderline Personality Disorders: The Concept, the Syndrome, the Patient* (pp. 87-121). New York: International Universities Press.

Kernberg, O. F. (1978a). Contrasting approaches to the psychotherapy of borderline conditions. In J. F. Masterson (ed.), *New Perspectives on Psychotherapy of the Borderline Adult* (pp. 75-104). New York: Brunner/Mazel.

Kernberg, O. F. (1978b). Discussion of J. F. Masterson's The borderline adult: Transference acting-out and working-through. In J. F. Masterson (ed.), *New Perspectives on Psychotherapy of the Borderline Adult* (pp. 153-155). New York: Brunner/Mazel.

Kernberg, O. F. (1979). Technical considerations in the treatment of borderline personality organization. In J. LeBoit and A. Capponi (eds.), *Advances in Psychotherapy of the Borderline Patient* (pp. 269-305). New York: Jason Aronson.

Kernberg, O. F. (1980a). Developmental theory, structural organization and psychoanalytic technique. In R. F. Lax (ed.), *Rapprochement: The Critical Subphase of Separation-Individuation* (pp. 23-38). New York: Jason Aronson.

Kernberg, O. F. (1980b). *Internal World and External Reality: Object-Relations Theory Applied.* New York: Jason Aronson.

Kernberg, O. F. (1980c). Neurosis, psychosis and the borderline states. In H. I. Kaplan, A. M. Freedman and B. J. Sadock (eds.), *Comprehensive Textbook of Psychiatry* III (Vol. 1, 3rd. ed., pp. 1079-1092). Baltimore: Williams and Wilkins.

Kernberg, O. F. (1980d). The therapeutic community: A re-evaluation. *Journal— National Association of Private Psychiatric Hospitals, 12*(2), 46-55.

Kernberg, O. F. (1981). Structural interviewing. *Psychiatric Clinics of North America,* 4(1), 169-195.

Kernberg, O. F. (1982a). An ego psychology and object relations approach to the narcissistic personality. In L. Grinspoon (ed.), *Psychiatry 1982: The American Psychiatric Association Annual Review* (pp. 510-523). Washington, D.C.: American Psychiatric Press.

Kernberg, O. F. (1982b, October). Paranoid regression, sadistic control and dishonesty in the transference. Paper presented at the University of California extension symposium, Narcissistic and Borderline Disorders: Current Perspectives, Los Angeles.

Kernberg, O. F. (1982c). The psychotherapeutic treatment of borderline personalities. In L. Grinspoon (ed.), *Psychiatry 1982: The American Psychiatric Association Annual Review* (pp. 470-487). Washington, D.C.: American Psychiatric Press.

Kernberg, O. F. (1982d). Self, ego, affects, and drives. *Journal of the American Psychoanalytic Association, 30*(4), 893-917.

Kernberg, O. F. (1982e). Summarizing comments at University of California extension symposium, Narcissistic and Borderline Disorders: Current Perspectives, Los Angeles.

Kernberg, O. F. (1982f). Supportive psychotherapy with borderline conditions. In J. O. Cavenar, Jr. and H. K. H. Brodie (eds.), *Critical Problems in Psychiatry* (pp. 180-202). Philadelphia: Lippincott.

Kernberg, O. F. (1984, April). Lecture material from University of California conference, The Cutting Edge: The Psychotherapy of Borderline and Narcissistic Disorders, San Diego.

Kernberg, O. F. (in press). *Severe Personality Disorders: Psychotherapeutic Strategies.* New Haven, Conn.: Yale University Press.

Kernberg, O. F., Burstein, E. D., Coyne, L., Appelbaum, A., Horowitz, L., and Voth, H. (1972). Psychotherapy and psychoanalysis. Final report of the Menninger Foundation's Psychotherapy Research Project. *Bulletin of the Menninger Clinic, 36*(1-2), 1-275.

Kernberg, O. F., Goldstein, E. G., Carr, A. C., Hunt, H. F., Bauer, S. F., and Blumenthal, R. (1981). Diagnosing borderline personality. A pilot study using multiple diagnostic methods. *Journal of Nervous and Mental Disease, 169*(4), 225-231.

Kety, S. S., Rosenthal, D., Wender, P. H., and Schulsinger, F. (1968). The types and prevalence of mental illness in the biological and adoptive families of adopted schizophrenics. In D. Rosenthal and S. S. Kety (eds.), *The Transmission of Schizophrenia: Proceedings of the Second Research Conference of the Foundation's Fund for Research in Psychiatry* (pp. 345-362). New York: Pergamon Press.

Klein, D. F. (1967). Importance of psychiatric diagnosis in prediction of clinical drug effects. *Archives of General Psychiatry, 16,* 118-126.

Klein, D. F. (1973). Drug therapy as a means of syndromal identification and nosological revision. In J. O. Cole, A. M. Freedman, and A. J. Friedhoff (eds.), *Psychopathology and Psychopharmacology: The Proceedings of the Sixty-Second Annual Meeting of the American Psychopathological Association* (pp. 143-160). Baltimore: Johns Hopkins University Press.

Klein, D. F. (1975). Psychopharmacology and the borderline patient. In J. E. Mack (ed.), *Borderline States in Psychiatry* (pp. 75-91). New York: Grune Stratton.

Klein, D. F. (1977). Psychopharmacological treatment and delineation of borderline disorders. In P. Hartocollis (ed.), *Borderline Personality Disorders: The Concept, the Syndrome, the Patient* (pp. 365-383). New York: International Universities Press.

Klein, G. S. (1976). *Psychoanalytic Theory: An Exploration of Essentials.* New York: International Universities Press.

Klein, M. (1935). A contribution to the psychogenesis of manic-depressive states. *Melanie Klein: Love, Guilt, and Reparation and Other Works, 1921-1945* (pp. 262-289). New York: Delacorte Press/Seymour Lawrence, 1975.

Klein, M. (1940). Mourning and its relation to manic-depressive states. In *Melanie Klein: Love, Guilt, and Reparation and Other Works, 1921-1945* (pp. 344-369). New York: Delacorte Press/Seymour Lawrence, 1975.

Klein, M. (1946). Notes on some schizoid mechanisms. In *Melanie Klein: Envy and Gratitude and Other Works, 1946-1963* (pp. 1-24). New York: Delacorte Press/Seymour Lawrence, 1975.

Knight, R. P. (1953a). Borderline states. *Bulletin of the Menninger Clinic, 17,* 1-12.

Knight, R. P. (1953b). Management and psychotherapy of the borderline schizophrenic patient. In R. P. Knight and C. R. Friedman (eds.), *Psychoanalytic Psychiatry and Psychology: Clinical and Theoretical Papers* (Vol. 1, pp. 110-122). New York: International Universities Press.

Kohut, H. (1971). *The Analysis of Self: A Systematic Approach to the Psychoanalytic Treatment of Narcissistic Personality Disorders.* New York: International Universities Press.

Kohut, H. (1975). The psychoanalyst in the community of scholars. *Annual of Psychoanalysis, 3*, 341–370.

Kohut, H. (1977). *The Restoration of Self.* New York: International Universities Press.

Kohut, H., and Wolf, E. S. (1978). The disorders of the self and their treatment: An outline. *International Journal of Psycho-Analysis, 59*, 413–425.

Kroll, J., Pyle, R., Zander, J., Martin, K., Lari, S., and Sines, L. (1981). Borderline personality disorder: Interrater reliability of the diagnostic interview for borderlines. *Schizophrenia Bulletin, 7*(2), 269–272.

Kwawer, J. S. (1979). Borderline phenomena, interpersonal relations and the Rorschach test. *Bulletin of the Menninger Clinic, 43*(6), 515–524.

Langs, R. J. (1973). *The Technique of Psychoanalytic Psychotherapy* (2 vols.). New York: Jason Aronson.

Langs, R. J. (1975). Therapeutic misalliances. *International Journal of Psychoanalytic Psychotherapy, 4*, 77–105.

Langs, R. J. (1976). *The Bipersonal Field.* New York: Jason Aronson.

Langs, R. J. (1978). *The Listening Process.* New York: Jason Aronson.

Langs, R. J. (1978–1979). Some communicative properties of the bipersonal field. *International Journal of Psychoanalytic Psychotherapy, 7*, 87–135.

Langs, R. J. (1980). *Interactions: The Realm of Transference and Countertransference.* New York: Jason Aronson.

Langs, R. J. (1981). *Resistances and Interventions: The Nature of Therapeutic Work.* New York: Jason Aronson.

Langs, R. J. (1982). *Psychotherapy: A Basic Text.* New York: Jason Aronson.

Lazare, A. (1971). The hysterical character in psychoanalytic theory: Evolution and confusion. *Archives of General Psychiatry, 25*, 131–137.

Lewinsohn, P. M., Muñoz, R. F., Youngren, M. A., and Zeiss, A. M. (1978). *Control Your Depression.* Englewood Cliffs, N.J.: Prentice-Hall.

Lewis, J. M. (1982). Early treatment planning for hospitalized severe borderline patients. *The Psychiatric Hospital, 13*(4), 130–136.

Lion, J. R. (1972). The role of depression in the treatment of aggressive personality disorders. *American Journal of Psychiatry, 129*, 347–349.

Lion, J. R. (1978). Outpatient treatment of psychopaths. In W. H. Reid (ed.), *The Psychopath: A Comprehensive Study of Antisocial Disorders and Behaviors* (pp. 286–300). New York: Brunner/Mazel.

Lion, J. R., and Leaff, L. A. (1973). On the hazards of assessing character pathology in an outpatient setting: A brief clinical note. *Psychiatric Quarterly, 47*, 104–109.

Little, M. (1951). Counter-transference and the patient's response to it. *International Journal of Psycho-Analysis, 32*, 32–40.

Little, M. (1981). *Transference Neurosis and Transference Psychosis: Toward Basic Unity.* New York: Jason Aronson.

Loevinger, J. (1976). *Ego Development: Conceptions and Theories.* With the assistance of A. Blasi. San Francisco: Jossey-Bass.

Loewald, H. W. (1960). On the therapeutic action of psycho-analysis. *International Journal of Psycho-Analysis, 41*, 16–33.

Luborsky, L., and Spence, D. P. (1971). Quantitative research on psychoanalytic therapy. In A. E. Bergin and S. L. Garfield (eds.), *Handbook of Psychotherapy and Behavior Change: An Empirical Analysis* (pp. 408–438). New York: John Wiley.

Mack, J. E. (ed.). (1975). *Borderline States in Psychiatry.* New York: Grune & Stratton.

Mahler, M. S. (1968). *On Human Symbiosis and the Vicissitudes of Individuation: Vol. 1. Infantile Psychosis.* In collaboration with M. Furer. New York: International Universities Press.

Mahler, M. S. (1971). A study of the separation-individuation process and its possible application to borderline phenomena in the psychoanalytic situation. *Psychoanalytic Study of the Child, 26,* 403–424.

Mahler, M. S., and Gosliner, B. J. (1955). On symbiotic child psychosis: Genetic, dynamic and restitutive aspects. *Psychoanalytic Study of the Child, 10,* 195–212.

Mahler, M. S., and Kaplan, L. (1977). Developmental aspects in the assessment of narcissistic and so-called borderline personalities. In P. Hartocollis (ed.), *Borderline and Personality Disorders: The Concept, the Syndromes, the Patient* (pp. 71–85). New York: International Universities Press.

Mahler, M. S., and McDevitt, J. (1982). Thoughts on the emergence of the sense of self, with particular emphasis on the body self. *Journal of the American Psychoanalytic Association, 30*(4), 827–848.

Mahler, M. S., Pine, F., and Bergman, A. (1975). *The Psychological Birth of the Human Infant: Symbiosis and Individuation.* New York: Basic Books.

Main, T. F. (1957). The ailment. *British Journal of Medical Psychology, 30*(3), 129–145.

Malin, A., and Grotstein, J. S. (1966). Projective identification in the therapeutic process. *International Journal of Psycho-Analysis, 47,* 26–31.

Mallouk, T. (1982). The interpersonal context of object relations: Implications for family therapy. *Journal of Marital and Family Therapy, 8*(4), 429–441.

Mandelbaum, A. (1977). The family treatment of the borderline patient. In P. Hartocollis (ed.), *Borderline Personality Disorders: The Concept, the Syndrome, the Patient* (pp. 423–438). New York: International Universities Press.

Mandelbaum, A. (1980). Family characteristics of patients with borderline and narcissistic disorders. *Bulletin of the Menninger Clinic, 44*(2), 201–211.

Mark, B. (1980). Hospital treatment of borderline patients: Toward a better understanding of problematic issues. *Journal of Psychiatric Nursing and Mental Health Services, 18*(8), 25–31.

Marmor, J. (1953). Orality in the hysterical personality. *Journal of the American Psychoanalytic Association, 1,* 656–671.

Masterson, J. F. (1972). *Treatment of the Borderline Adolescent: A Developmental Approach.* New York: John Wiley (Wiley-Interscience).

Masterson, J. F. (1976). *Psychotherapy of the Borderline Adult: A Developmental Approach.* New York: Brunner/Mazel.

Masterson, J. F. (1978). The borderline adult: Transference acting-out and working-through. In J. F. Masterson (ed.), *New Perspectives on Psychotherapy of the Borderline Adult* (pp. 121–147, 157–162). New York: Brunner/Mazel.

Masterson, J. F. (1980). *From Borderline Adolescent to Functioning Adult: The Test of Time.* In collaboration with J. Costello. New York: Brunner/Mazel.

Masterson, J. F. (1981). *Narcissistic and Borderline Disorders: An Integrated Developmental Approach.* New York: Brunner/Mazel.

Masterson, J. F. (1982, October). The borderline and narcissistic disorders: An integrated developmental approach. Paper presented at the University of California extension symposium, Narcissistic and Borderline Disorders: Current Perspectives, Los Angeles.

Masterson, J. F. (1983a, March). Lecture series and supervised case presentations at conference, Borderline and Narcissistic Disorders in the Adult: Diagnosis and Treatment, Differential Diagnosis, San Francisco.

Masterson, J. F. (1983b). *Countertransference and Psychotherapeutic Technique: Teaching Seminars on Psychotherapy of the Borderline Adult.* New York: Brunner/Mazel.

Masterson, J. F., and Rinsley, D. B. (1975). The borderline syndrome: The role of the mother in the genesis and psychic structure of the borderline personality. *International Journal of Psycho-Analysis, 56*(2), 163–177.

Meissner, W. W. (1978a). Notes on some conceptual aspects of borderline personality organizations. *International Review of Psycho-Analysis, 5,* 297–311.

Meissner, W. W. (1978b). Theoretical assumptions of concepts of the borderline personality. *Journal of the American Psychoanalytic Association, 26*(3), 559–598.

Meissner, W. W. (1979). Narcissistic personalities and borderline conditions: A differential diagnosis. *Annual of Psychoanalysis, 7,* 171–202.

Meissner, W. W. (1982). Psychotherapy of the paranoid patient. In P. L. Giovacchini and L. B. Boyer (eds.), *Technical Factors in the Treatment of the Severely Disturbed Patient* (pp. 349–384). New York: Jason Aronson.

Meissner, W. W. (1982–1983a). Notes on countertransference in borderline conditions. *International Journal of Psychoanalytic Psychotherapy, 9,* 89–124.

Meissner, W. W. (1982–1983b). Notes on the potential differentiation of borderline conditions. *International Journal of Psychoanalytic Psychotherapy, 9,* 3–49.

Meissner, W. W. (1984). *The Borderline Spectrum: Differential Diagnosis and Developmental Issues.* New York: Jason Aronson.

Menninger, K. A. (1958). *Theory of Psychoanalytic Technique.* New York: Basic Books.

Menninger, K. A., Mayman, M., and Pruyser, P. (1963). *The Vital Balance: The Life Process in Mental Health and Illness.* New York: Viking Press.

Mitchell, S. A. (1981). The origin and nature of the "object" in the theories of Klein and Fairbairn. *Contemporary Psychoanalysis, 17*(3), 374–398.

Modell, A. H. (1961). Denial and the sense of separateness. *Journal of the American Psychoanalytic Association, 9,* 533–547.

Modell, A. H. (1963). Primitive object relationships and the predisposition to schizophrenia. *International Journal of Psycho-Analysis, 44,* 282–292.

Modell, A. H. (1968). *Object Love and Reality: An Introduction to a Psychoanalytic Theory of Object Relations.* New York: International Universities Press.

Modell, A. H. (1976). "The holding environment" and the therapeutic action of psychoanalysis. *Journal of the American Psychoanalytic Association, 24*(2), 285–307.

Murray, M. (1979). Minimal brain dysfunction and borderline personality adjustment. *American Journal of Psychotherapy, 33*(3), 391–403.

Novaco, R. W. (1976). The functions and regulation of the arousal of anger. *American Journal of Psychiatry, 133*(10), 1124–1128.

Novick, J., and Kelly, K. (1970). Projection and externalization. *Psychoanalytic Study of the Child, 25,* 69–95.

Nurnberg, H. G., and Suh, R. (1978). Time-limited treatment of hospitalized border-line patients: Considerations. *Comprehensive Psychiatry, 19*(5), 419-431.

Ogden, T. H. (1979). On projective identification. *International Journal of Psycho-Analysis, 60*, 357-373.

Ogden, T. H. (1981). Projective identification in psychiatric hospital treatment. *Bulletin of the Menninger Clinic, 45*(4), 317-333.

Ornstein, P. H. (1974). On narcissism: Beyond the introduction. Highlights of Heinz Kohut's contributions to the psychoanalytic treatment of narcissistic personality disorders. *Annual of Psychoanalysis, 2*, 127-149.

Ornstein, P. H. (1982). On the psychoanalytic psychotherapy of primary self pathology. In L. Grinspoon (ed.), *Psychiatry 1982: The American Psychiatric Association Annual Review* (pp. 498-510). Washington, D.C.: American Psychiatric Press.

Paolino, Jr., T. J. (1981). *Psychoanalytic Psychotherapy: Theory, Technique, Therapeutic Relationship and Treatability.* New York: Brunner/Mazel.

Patton, M. J., and Sullivan, J. J. (1980). Heinz Kohut and the classical psychoanalytic tradition: An analysis in terms of levels of explanation. *Psychoanalytic Review, 67*(3), 365-388.

Perry, J. C., and Klerman, G. L. (1978). The borderline patient: A comparative analysis of four sets of diagnostic criteria. *Archives of General Psychiatry, 35*, 141-150.

Peterfreund, E. (1975). How does the analyst listen? On models and strategies in the psychoanalytic process. *Psychoanalysis and Contemporary Science, 6*, 59-101.

Peterfreund, E. (1978). Some critical comments on psychoanalytic conceptualizations of infancy. *International Journal of Psycho-Analysis, 59*, 427-441.

Peters, C. P. (1983). An historical review of the borderline concept. *Occupational Therapy in Mental Health, 3*(3), 1-18.

Piaget, J., and Inhelder, B. (1969). *The Psychology of the Child.* New York: Basic Books.

Pruyser, P. W. (1975). What splits in "splitting"? A scrutiny of the concept of splitting in psychoanalysis and psychiatry. *Bulletin of the Menninger Clinic, 39*(1), 1-46.

Pulaski, M. (1971). *Understanding Piaget.* New York: Harper & Row.

Racker, H. (1957). The meanings and uses of countertransference. *Psychoanalytic Quarterly, 26*, 303-357.

Racker, H. (1968). *Transference and Countertransference.* New York: International Universities Press.

Rey, J. H. (1979). Schizoid phenomena in the borderline. In J. LeBoit and A. Capponi (eds.), *Advances in Psychotherapy of the Borderline Patient* (pp. 449-484). New York: Jason Aronson.

Rice, A. K. (1965). *Learning for Leadership: Interpersonal and Intergroup Relations.* London: Tavistock.

Rice, A. K. (1969). Individual, group and intergroup processes. *Human Relations, 22*(6), 565-584.

Rinsley, D. B. (1968). Theory and practice of intensive residential treatment of adolescents. *Psychiatric Quarterly, 42*, 611-638.

Rinsley, D. B. (1977). An object-relations view of borderline personality. In P. Hartocollis (ed.), *Borderline Personality Disorders: The Concept, the Syndrome, the Patient* (pp. 47-70). New York: International Universities Press.

Rinsley, D. B. (1978). Borderline psychopathology: A review of aetiology, dynamics and treatment. *International Review of Psycho-Analysis*, *5*(1), 45-54.

Rinsley, D. B. (1980a). Commentary on James F. Masterson's paper: The role of the talionic impulse in the development of morality. *Bulletin of the Menninger Clinic*, *44*(5), 493-497.

Rinsley, D. B. (1980b). The developmental etiology of borderline and narcissistic disorders. *Bulletin of the Menninger Clinic*, *44*(2), 127-134.

Rinsley, D. B. (1980c). *Treatment of the Severely Disturbed Adolescent*. New York: Jason Aronson.

Rinsley, D. B. (1981a). Borderline psychopathology: The concepts of Masterson and Rinsley and beyond. *Adolescent Psychiatry*, *9*, 259-274.

Rinsley, D. B. (1981b). Dynamic and developmental issues in borderline and related "spectrum" disorders. *Psychiatric Clinics of North America*, *4*(1), 117-132.

Rinsley, D. B. (1982a). *Borderline and Other Self Disorders: A Developmental and Object-Relations Perspective*. New York: Jason Aronson.

Rinsley, D. B. (1982b). Object relations theory and psychotherapy with particular reference to the self-disordered patient. In P. L. Giovacchini and L. B. Boyer (eds.), *Technical Factors in the Treatment of the Severely Disturbed Patient* (pp. 187-213). New York: Jason Aronson.

Rinsley, D. B. (1984a). A comparison of borderline and narcissistic personality disorders. *Bulletin of the Menninger Clinic*, *48*(1), 1-9.

Rinsley, D. B. (1984b). Notes on the pathogenesis and nosology of borderline and narcissistic personality disorders. Manuscript submitted for publication.

Rinsley, D. B. (in press). The development of self and object constancy. In R. F. Lax, S. Bach, and J. A. Burland (eds.), *Self-Constancy and Object-Constancy*. New York: Guilford Press.

Rinsley, D. B., and Bergmann, E. (1983). Enchantment and alchemy: The story of Rumpelstiltskin. *Bulletin of the Menninger Clinic*, *47*(1), 1-14.

Robbins, M. (1980). Current controversy in object relations theory as outgrowth of a schism between Klein and Fairbairn. *International Journal of Psycho-Analysis*, *61*(4), 477-492.

Robbins, M. (1982). Narcissistic personality as a symbiotic character disorder. *International Journal of Psycho-Analysis*, *63*(4), 457-473.

Rochlin, G. (1973). *Man's Aggression: The Defense of the Self*. Boston: Gambit.

Rosenfeld, H. (1978). Notes on the psychopathology and psychoanalytic treatment of some borderline patients. *International Journal of Psycho-Analysis*, *59*(2-3), 215-221.

Rosenfeld, H. (1979). Transference psychosis in the borderline patient. In J. LeBoit and A. Capponi (eds.), *Advances in Psychotherapy of the Borderline Patient* (pp. 485-510). New York: Jason Aronson.

Rycroft, C. (1956). The nature and function of the analyst's communication to the patient. *International Journal of Psycho-Analysis*, *37*, 469-472.

Sandler, J. (1960a). The background of safety. *International Journal of Psycho-Analysis*, *41*, 352-356.

Sandler, J. (1960b). On the concept of the superego. *Psychoanalytic Study of the Child, 15,* 128–162.

Sandler, J. (1976). Countertransference and role-responsiveness. *International Review of Psycho-Analysis, 3,* 43–47.

Sandler, J., Holder, A., Kawenoka, M., Kennedy, H. E., and Neurath, L. (1969). Notes on some theoretical and clinical aspects of transference. *Internationl Journal of Psycho-Analysis, 50,* 633–645.

Sandler, J., Holder, A., and Meers, D. (1963). The ego ideal and the ideal self. *Psychoanalytic Study of the Child, 18,* 139–158.

Sandler, J., and Rosenblatt, B. (1962). The concept of the representational world. *Psychoanalytic Study of the Child, 17,* 128–145.

Schafer, R. (1968). *Aspects of Internalization.* New York: International Universities Press.

Scheidlinger, S., and Pyrke, M. (1961). Group therapy of women with severe dependency problems. *American Journal of Orthopsychiatry, 31*(4), 776–785.

Searles, H. F. (1951). Data concerning certain manifestations of incorporation. In *Collected Papers on Schizophrenia and Related Subjects* (pp. 39–69). New York: International Universities Press, 1965.

Searles, H. F. (1955). Dependency processes in the psychotherapy of schizophrenia. In *Collected Papers on Schizophrenia and Related Subjects* (pp. 114–156). New York: International Universities Press, 1965.

Searles, H. F. (1956). The psychodynamics of vengefulness. In *Collected Papers on Schizophrenia and Related Subjects* (pp. 177–191). New York: International Universities Press, 1965.

Searles, H. F. (1960). The Nonhuman Environment in Normal Development and in Schizophrenia. New York: International Universities Press.

Searles, H. F. (1965). *Collected Papers on Schizophrenia and Related Subjects.* New York: International Universities Press.

Searles, H. F. (1976). Transitional phenomena and therapeutic symbiosis. *International Journal of Psychoanalytic Psychotherapy, 5,* 145–204.

Searles, H. F. (1978). Psychoanalytic therapy with the borderline adult: Some principles concerning technique. In J. F. Masterson (ed.), *New Perspectives on Psychotherapy of the Borderline Adult* (pp. 41–65). New York: Brunner/Mazel.

Searles, H. F. (1979). The countertransference with the borderline patient. In J. LeBoit and A. Capponi (eds.), *Advances in Psychotherapy of the Borderline Patient* (pp. 309–346). New York: Jason Aronson.

Shane, M. (1977). A rationale for teaching analytic technique based on a developmental orientation and approach. *International Journal of Psycho-Analysis, 58*(1), 95–108.

Shapiro, E. R. (1978). The psychodynamics and developmental psychology of the borderline patient: A review of the literature. *American Journal of Psychiatry, 135*(11), 1305–1315.

Shapiro, E. R., Zinner, J., Shapiro, R. L., and Berkowitz, D. A. (1975). The influence of family experience on borderline personality development. *International Review of Psycho-Analysis, 2,* 399–411.

Sharpe, S. A. (1981). The symbiotic marriage: A diagnostic profile. *Bulletin of the Menninger Clinic, 45*(2), 89–114.

Shaskan, D. A. (1957). Treatment of a borderline case with group analytically oriented psychotherapy. *Journal of Forensic Sciences, 2*(2), 195-202.

Singer, E. (1970). *Key Concepts in Psychotherapy.* New York: Basic Books.

Singer, M. T. (1977). The borderline diagnosis and psychological tests: Review and research. In P. Hartocollis (ed.), *Borderline Personality Disorders: The Concept, the Syndrome, the Patient* (pp. 193-212). New York: International Universities Press.

Singer, M. T., and Wynne, L. C. (1965). Thought disorder and family relations of schizophrenics: IV. Results and implications. *Archives of General Psychiatry, 12*(2), 201-212.

Spitz, R. A. (1957). *No and Yes: On the Genesis of Human Communication.* New York: International Universities Press.

Spitz, R. A. (1965). *The First Year of Life.* New York: International Universities Press.

Spitzer, R. L., Endicott, J., and Gibbon, M. (1979). Crossing the border into borderline personality and borderline schizophrenia. The development of criteria. *Archives of General Psychiatry, 36*(1), 17-24.

Spotnitz, H. (1957). The borderline schizophrenic in group psychotherapy: The importance of individuation. *International Journal of Group Psychotherapy, 7*(2), 155-174.

Spotnitz, H. (1969). *Modern Psychoanalysis of the Schizophrenic Patient.* New York: Grune & Stratton.

Stein, A. (1963). Indications for group psychotherapy and the selection of patients. *Journal of Hillside Hospital, 12*(3-4), 145-155.

Stern, A. (1938). Psychoanalytic investigation of and therapy in the border line group of neuroses. *Psychoanalytic Quarterly, 7,* 467-489.

Stewart, R. H., Peters, T. C., Marsh, S., and Peters, M. J. (1975). An object-relations approach to psychotherapy with marital couples, families, and children. *Family Process, 14*(2), 161-178.

Stierlin, H. (1970). The functions of 'inner objects.' *International Journal of Psycho-Analysis, 51,* 321-329.

Stolorow, R. D., and Lachmann, F. M. (1978). The developmental prestages of defenses: Diagnostic and therapeutic implications. *Psychoanalytic Quarterly, 47*(1), 73-102.

Stolorow, R. D., and Lachmann, F. M. (1980). *Psychoanalysis of Developmental Arrests: Theory and Treatment.* New York: International Universities Press.

Stone, M. H. (1979a). Contemporary shift of the borderline concept from a subschizophrenic disorder to a subaffective disorder. *Psychiatric Clinics of North America, 2*(3), 577-594.

Stone, M. H. (1979b). Psychodiagnosis and psychoanalytic psychotherapy. *Journal of the American Academy of Psychoanalysis, 7*(1), 79-100.

Stone, M. H. (1980). *The Borderline Syndromes: Constitution, Adaptation and Personality.* New York: McGraw-Hill.

Stone, M. H. (1981). Borderline Syndromes: A consideration of subtypes and an overview. Directions for research. *Psychiatric Clinics of North America, 4*(1), 3-24.

Stone, M. H. (1983). Conflict resolution in schizotypal vs affective borderlines. *Journal of the American Academy of Psychoanalysis, 11*(3), 377-389.

Strachey, J. (1934). The nature of the therapeutic action of psychoanalysis. Reprinted in *International Journal of Psycho-Analysis, 50*, 275–292, 1969.

Strupp, H. H. (1982). The outcome of psychotherapy: A critical assessment of issues and trends. In J. O. Cavenar, Jr. and H. K. H. Brodie (eds.), *Critical Problems in Psychiatry* (pp. 399–421). Philadelphia: Lippincott.

Sugarman, A. (1979). The infantile personality: Orality in the hysteric revisited. *International Journal of Psycho-Analysis, 60*, 501–513.

Sullivan, H. S. (1953). *The Interpersonal Theory of Psychiatry.* New York: Norton.

Tolpin, M. (1971). On the beginnings of a cohesive self: An application of the concept of transmuting internalization to the study of the transitional object and signal anxiety. *Psychoanalytic Study of the Child, 26*, 316–352.

Tolpin, M. (1982, October). Injured Self-cohesion: Developmental, clinical and theoretical perspectives: A contribution to understanding narcissistic and borderline disorders. Paper presented at University of California extension symposium, Narcissistic and Borderline Disorders: Current Perspectives, Los Angeles.

Tolpin, P. (1980). The borderline personality: Its makeup and analyzability. In A. Goldberg (ed.), *Advances in Self Psychology* (pp. 299–316). New York: International Universities Press.

Vaillant, G. E. (1975). Sociopathy as a human process: A viewpoint. *Archives of General Psychiatry, 32*(2), 178–183.

Vaillant, G. E., and Perry, J. C. (1980). Personality disorders. In H. I. Kaplan, A. M. Freedman, and B. J. Saddock (eds.), *Comprehensive Textbook of Psychiatry* III (Vol. 2, 3rd ed., pp. 1562–1590). Baltimore: Williams and Wilkins.

Volkan, V. D. (1976). *Primitive Internalized Object Relations: A Clinical Study of Schizophrenic, Borderline and Narcissistic Patients.* New York: International Universities Press.

Volkan, V. D. (1979). The "glass bubble" of a narcissistic patient. In J. LeBoit and A. Capponi (eds.), *Advances in Psychotherapy of the Borderline Patient* (pp. 405–431). New York: Jason Aronson.

Volkan, V. D. (1982). Narcissistic personality disorder. In J. O. Cavenar, Jr. and H. K. H. Brodie (eds.), *Critical Problems in Psychiatry* (pp. 332–350). Philadelphia: Lippincott.

Weiner, I. B. (1975). *Principles of Psychotherapy.* New York: John Wiley (Wiley-Interscience).

Weiss, J., and Sampson, H. (1982). Psychotherapy Research: Theory and Findings, Bulletin 5, Psychotherapy Research Group, Department of Psychiatry, Mount Zion Hospital and Medical Center, San Francisco.

Wender, P. H., Rosenthal, D., and Kety, S. S. (1968). A psychiatric assessment of the adoptive parents of schizophrenics. In D. Rosenthal and S. S. Kety (eds.), *The Transmission of Schizophrenia: Proceedings of the Second Research Conference of the Foundation's Fund for Research in Psychiatry* (pp. 235–250). New York: Pergamon Press.

Werble, B. (1970). Second follow-up study of borderline patients. *Archives of General Psychiatry, 23*, 3–7.

Winnicott, D. W. (1953). Transitional objects and transitional phenomena: A study of the first not-me possession. *International Journal of Psycho-Analysis, 34*(2), 89–97.

Winnicott, D. W. (1960). Ego distortion in terms of true and false self. In *The Maturational Processes and the Facilitating Environment: Studies in the Theory of Emotional Development* (pp. 140-152). New York: International Universities Press, 1965.

Winnicott, D. W. (1963). Psychiatric disorder in terms of infantile maturational processes. In *The Maturational Processes and the Facilitating Environment: Studies in the Theory of Emotional Development* (pp. 230-241). New York: International Universities Press, 1965.

Winnicott, D. W. (1965). *The Maturational Processes and the Facilitating Environment: Studies in the Theory of Emotional Development.* New York: International Universities Press.

Wolberg, L. R. (1967). *The Technique of Psychotherapy* (2 vols., 2nd ed.). New York: Grune & Stratton.

Wolf, E. S. (1980). On the developmental line of selfobject relations. In A. Goldberg (ed.), *Advances in Self Psychology* (pp. 117-130). New York: International Universities Press.

Wolff, H. H. (1971). The therapeutic and developmental functions of psychotherapy. *British Journal of Medical Psychology, 44*, 117-130.

Wolman, B. B. (1960). Group psychotherapy with latent schizophrenics. *International Journal of Group Psychotherapy, 10*, 301-312.

Yerevanian, B. I., and Akiskal, H. S. (1979). "Neurotic," characteriological and dysthymic depressions. *Psychiatric Clinics of North America, 2*(3), 595-617.

Yochelson, S., and Samenow, S. E. (1976). *The Criminal Personality: Vol. 1. A Profile for Change.* New York: Jason Aronson.

Zetzel, E. R. (1971). A developmental approach to the borderline patient. *American Journal of Psychiatry, 127*, 867-871.

Zilboorg, G. (1941). Ambulatory schizophrenias. *Psychiatry, 4*, 149-155.

Zinner, J., and Shapiro, R. (1972). Projective identification as a mode of perception and behaviour in families of adolescents. *International Journal of Psycho-Analysis, 53*, 523-530.

Subject Index

Author Index